AF685806

Learn Design with Flash MX

Linda Goin
Kris Besley

Learn Design with Flash MX

© 2002 friends of ED

All rights reserved. No part of this book may be reproduced, stored in a retrieval system or transmitted in any form or by any means, without the prior written permission of the publisher, except in the case of brief quotations embodied in critical articles or reviews.

The authors and publisher have made every effort in the preparation of this book to ensure the accuracy of the information. However, the information contained in this book is sold without warranty, either express or implied. Neither the authors, friends of ED nor its dealers or distributors will be held liable for any damages caused or alleged to be caused either directly or indirectly by this book.

First Printed October 2002

Trademark Acknowledgements

friends of ED has endeavored to provide trademark information about all the companies and products mentioned in this book by the appropriate use of capitals. However, friends of ED cannot guarantee the accuracy of this information.

Published by friends of ED

30-32 Lincoln Road, Olton, Birmingham.
B27 6PA. UK.
Printed in USA

ISBN 1-904344-00-3

Learn Design with Flash MX

Credits

Authors
Linda Goin
Kris Besley

Editors
Steve Rycroft
Phill Jackson

Commissioning Editor
Andy Corsham

Graphic Editors
Ty Bhogal
Matthew Clark
Chantal Hepworth

Reviewers
Kay Aubrey
Guylaine Couture
Steve McCormick
Elizabeth Scott
Al Wasco

Indexer
Fiona Murray

Project Manager
Vicky Idiens

Author Agent
Laura Jones

Managing Editor
Sonia Mullineux

Cover Design
Katy Freer

Proof Reader
Mel Orgee

Special Thanks
Chris Matterface for the anime illustrations in Chapter 2

Linda Goin

Linda Goin's art career began when she won a Betsey-Wetsey doll with her crayon skills. Since then, she's been into print, pastels, pixels, poetry, real-unreal-surreal life, her daughter Cora, Gilgamesh, mycology, and mid-1800s Appomattox tobacco farmers.

Despite her unwillingness to stay in one place for too long, Linda's managed to win 13 Colorado Press Association Awards, numerous art and design awards, and receives mentions in various publications for online content development. Her degrees are in graphic design, fashion design, and visual communications, and her interests lie in research and writing.

Hats off to the patience of Bob, Joanne, and Hugh.

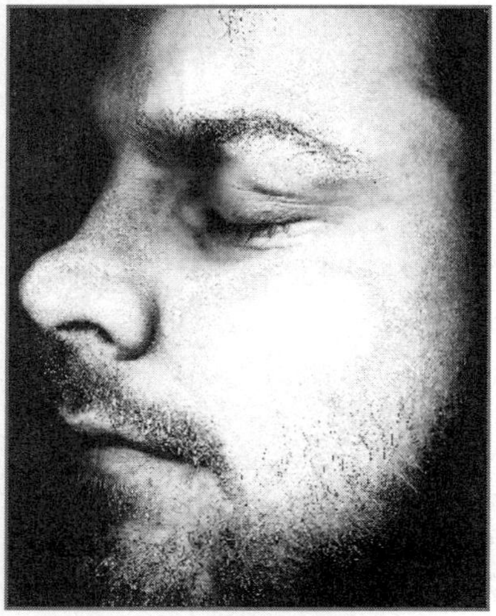

Kristian Besley

Kristian would like to thank Laura, Vicky, and Andy, and especially Linda, Steve, and Phill for their patience and support on this book.

Thanks also to Pete for helping out on the 3D stuff.

Introduction 1

Chapter 1

Welcome to the Class! 7

Chapter 2

Dissecting the Elements of Design 53

Chapter 9

Select and Implement 363

Chapter 10

Unifying the Design Concepts 405

Chapter 11

Creativity Unleashed 441

Introduction

This book is different from any other design book that you've ever seen.

The truth about this book

Most books that teach you how to use software tools for web design make some pretty big assumptions; principally, that you already know how to design!

This book challenges that assumption head on, recognising that most people who want to design for the web, and often those that already do, don't have formal design training. We aim to fill that training gap for web design novices and professionals alike:

- If you're an absolute **beginner** and you want to get it right from the start,
- If you're a **self taught** designer who wants to add academic structure to experience, or
- If you're an **expert** with the software but need another angle to get an edge on your competitors...

If you design for the web, this is the book for you.

Flash is arguably the most exciting and essential web technology of the moment. We've chosen it for this course, not only because of its importance, but because it's also **a great tool to teach design with**. If you've never used Flash before, then don't worry; every thorough example is taught assuming no prior knowledge, and a **free trial version** is even included on the CD.

Even if Flash isn't your field, or if you design in other formats, you'll find all the design skills taught here just as relevant and transferable – ***Flash is the tool, design is the skill***.

Learn Design with Flash MX takes the unusual, but highly effective (not to mention entertaining!) path of shadowing a class of six very different students. People who – maybe like you – are right at the start of the *formal* design learning curve.

You'll sit in the classroom beside them as they're taught the basic phases and skills of the design process, learning at a pace that allows you to fully understand and absorb each concept. However, this is no passive learning environment: each student has their own needs and attitudes, and they'll be asking the tutor questions – the kind of questions that design students are dying to ask, but are sometimes afraid to voice.

In this classroom there's no fear or barriers... and best of all ***you're not alone***. This means that every assumption is questioned, allowing the students, and you, to get right to the heart of the subject. This will let you learn design right from the ground up, and give you a solid, intuitive understanding of the issues, ultimately providing you with the framework to explore the world of design with confidence.

This book demystifies design and liberates you to go forward into the design world on your own. You'll come away from this book with:

- A rich, solid understanding of the core **principles** and **elements** of design.
- Insight into **universally applicable design processes** and techniques.
- **Practical tips and advice** relating specifically to the **designer/client relationship**.
- A **firm base of Flash knowledge** from which to build upon.
- The **skills to implement the principles and elements of design in Flash MX**.

Learn Design with Flash MX *bridges the gap between creativity and technology.*

What's on the CD?

The accompanying CD makes this book a complete learning package. Everything you need to follow the classes and join in with the fun is supplied:

- A free trial version of Macromedia Flash MX for both Mac and PC operating systems.
- All the relevant Flash files used in each lesson, including the finished class projects – three fully functional example websites designed with Flash MX.

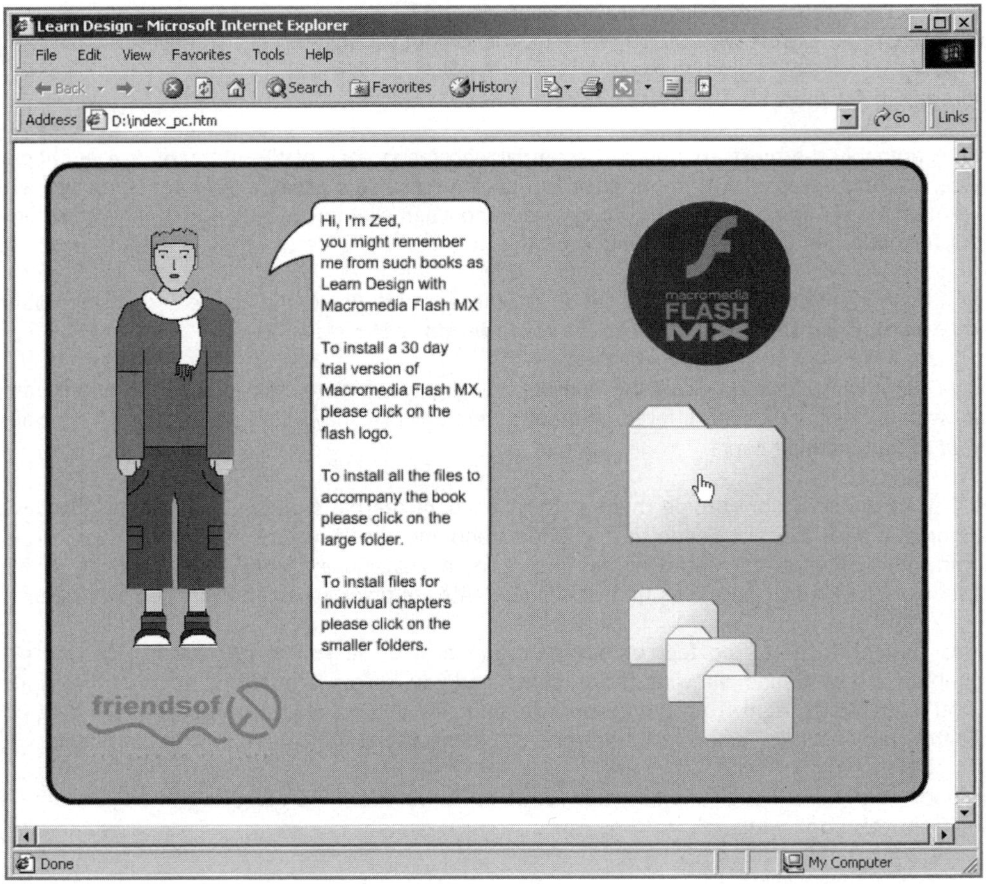

Meet your classmates

Throughout this book you'll be studying with six other students who each have very different personalities and perspectives to bring to the learning experience:

- **Bonnie** – in her early thirties, has had a couple marriages before getting into web design. Bonnie taught herself HTML so she could design websites for a living, and she now prides herself on her awareness of usability and accessibility issues. She's taking the course to find out why her clients keep asking her to design Flash sites.

- **Deb** – a highly independent and extremely logical computer programmer, forced to take the *Learn Design* course by her boss. At first, she's determined not to enjoy the class...

- **Lisa** – rather timid and shy, she's taking the course to improve her communication skills and, hopefully, her self-confidence. Lisa admits that she can't draw very well, but she's already got a good grasp of some of the design basics through her experience as a lighting tech at the local theater.

- **Steve** – a rather sensible and mature student who has worked as a graphic designer and printer for newspapers and magazines for many years. Steve has taken this class to catch up with the latest design tools and software, and to expand his design skills beyond the print industry.

- **Wes** – artist, sculptor, and a bit of a scholar. Wes is very fond of art history, and loves to talk about what he knows. He's used many different materials for his artwork in the past, and is always looking for new formats. Wes has enrolled on this course to learn how to create art with Flash MX.

- **Zed** – an enthusiastic and energetic high school kid who wants to learn Flash "*because it's cool!*"

Styles used in this book

We use some simple layout conventions to make things clearer throughout the book:

- We'll use **this style** to introduce **new terms**, and to stress **important things** in the text.

- URLs will be shown in this style: www.friendsofed.com.

- Menu path descriptions will appear like this: File > Open > Monkey > Banana.

- Keyboard stroke sequences will be displayed in this style: F4 *and* CTRL+ALT+DEL, and wherever relevant we'll give you both Windows PC and Apple Macintosh shortcut keys.

- Although code is not heavily featured in this book, if we do mention it we'll indicate it with `this style`. We'll use the same style to represent the names of files from the CD that we discuss in the text, for example: `babyMonkey.fla`.

> *When we want to draw your attention to something really important, we'll put it in a bubble like this.*

Support at friends of ED

This friends of ED book is fully supported at www.friendsofed.com, and you can also visit our support forums for help, inspiration, or just to chat: www.friendsofed.com/forums/.

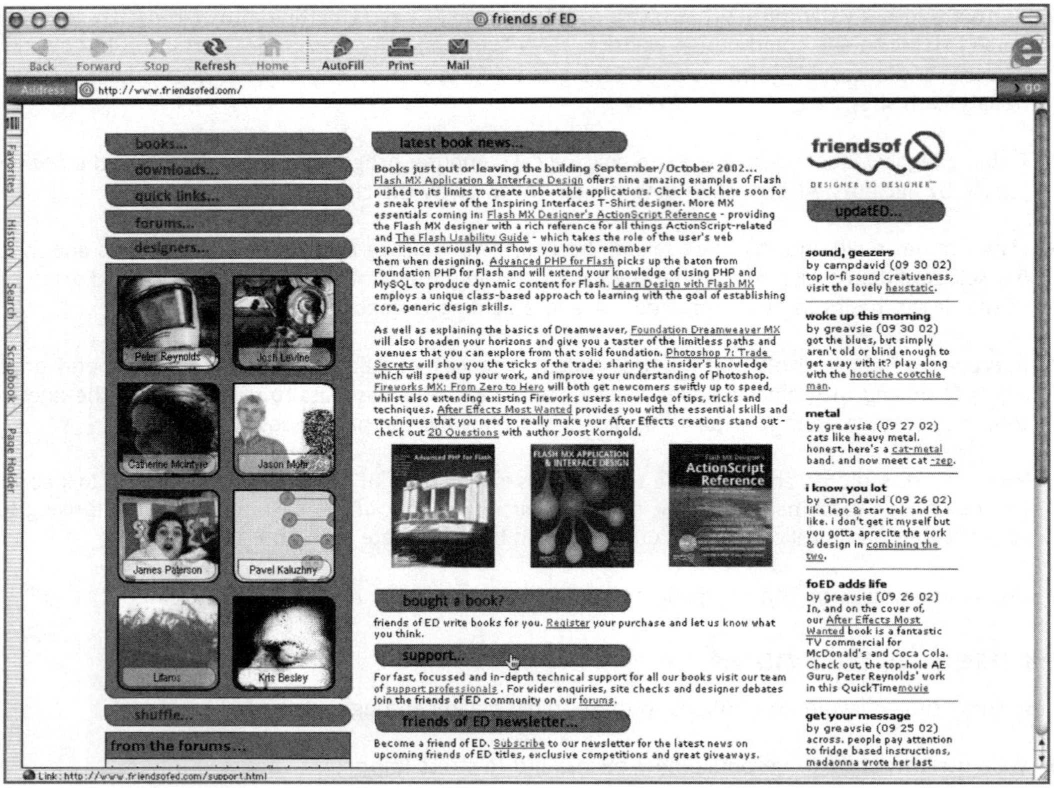

If you do run into any trouble maybe you have a problem with a certain file or tutorial, or if you just get plain confused by something, we're right here for you. Leave a message on the forum, use the online feedback form in the back of this book, or drop an e-mail to support@friendsofed.com – we'll get you sorted and back on track in no time. Even if you don't have problems, let us know what you think by e-mailing feedback@friendsofed.com, or filling out the reply card – we'd love to hear from you!

Chapter 1

Welcome to the Class!

Objectives

In today's class you will learn about:

- The importance of design and the creative process
- The motives behind your desire to learn design with Flash
- Understanding the creative problem-solving process
- Establishing design as a creative solution to a visual problem
- The difference between two- and three-dimensional design
- The fundamental elements of design, and how to recognize them in everyday objects

Introduction

"I hope this class is worth my time!" A feminine voice edged with an air of exasperation met me as I entered the classroom. I plunked my briefcase and laptop on the desk and turned to face six students seated around their computers. A few of them appeared slightly uncomfortable with the coincidental timing of that remark and my entrance.

"Hello, and welcome to *Learn Design with Flash MX*," I ignored the tense feeling in the room and welcomed the students. "Today a door will open for some of you. One or two of you might struggle with that door, because the hinges will be a little rusty. For others, this door will fly open so quickly it might swing back and hit you in the face."

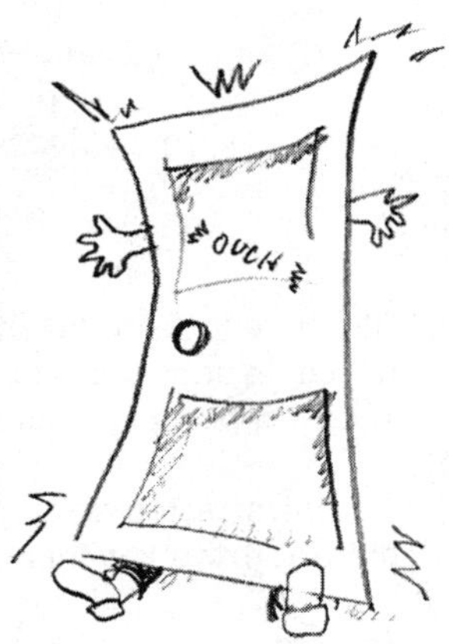

A few students chuckled at that last remark. I smiled, "Hopefully, I can help you open the door to the world of design without too much pain."

I clicked open my briefcase and selected a marker. With my back to the class, I scribbled my name on the whiteboard lining the wall. "My name is Linda. My design experience began with fine art instruction, but I soon realized that I couldn't pay the rent with my paintings, so I went back to school and studied graphic design."

I turned to the class. "After many years working both solo and with teams at advertising agencies, I realized I couldn't pay my rent with graphic design either!" This statement produced a few raised eyebrows.

"To be more specific, I couldn't pay the rent with my design skills unless I learned a new tool..." I pointed to the bank of computers where the students had settled. "However, the computer wasn't built with designers in mind," I stated. "It was mainly a tool for processing information. For instance, web designs produced for early browsers had some variety in size and color, but the design was highly sterile, with little or no capacity for creativity, sound, and moving images.

"To make a short story even shorter," I said, "It wasn't long before the creative community demanded more from these new tools. They wanted the ability to add pictures, more color, and basically more variety to their design compositions. They wanted more efficient machines and programs, and they wanted it all to be standard across the board.

"However," I added, "Before most of these creative individuals could define and analyze this new landscape, an avalanche of design software almost buried us alive.

"The bright side," I emphasized, "Is that we now have numerous formats for visual communication with the help of computer imagery. Most of us managed to dig through these drifts of software to find the ideal tool for our purposes, and we learned to work with it, combined with our various skills."

A man seated on my right grinned, and nodded his head in agreement. I continued...

"Some of you are here to learn more about design and the creative problem-solving process. This process applies to all arts, whether they're paintings or Flash movies. Some of you want to learn more about the capabilities of Flash MX - we'll cover both issues in this course."

"I'm here to learn how to use the software!" a man in the back of the room interrupted with a laugh. He waved his arms dramatically and announced, "As an artist, my mission is to beautify the computerized image. There's a painful amount of bad design floating around cyberspace."

A woman seated across from him retorted, "But there's another side to that story – the fact is, it's rather difficult to work within the limited capabilities of browsers and their color palettes."

She crossed her arms and added, "Besides, great information isn't always beautiful. The purpose of the computer is to make information accessible to as many people as possible. I believe this eliminates a lot of debate about design issues in this medium."

I wasn't surprised to find resistance, defiance, and a little drama in the first session. Some people believe design is a mystery solved only by those born with talent, while other folks nurse panic attacks at the thought of learning yet another piece of software. Both reactions require attention to maintain a comfortable classroom environment. A description of what to expect on the course always helps...

What to expect

Before the discussion about the form and function of computers could go any further, I diverted their attention with an overview of what to expect during this course. I sat on the edge of the desk and addressed the class.

"Before we tackle the issues of design and the limitations and capabilities of hardware and software," I said, "Let me outline what's in store for you over the next few weeks.

"This course aims to provide you with a solid foundation in design skills, using Macromedia Flash MX as our tool.

"First, we'll discover our motives for learning design, and why design is important. We'll define the concept of design and familiarize ourselves with some design lingo. We'll use every tool available to help you become good designers. Some of the tools are going to be in your head." I pointed at my forehead. "Other tools are tangible, like the Flash MX.

"We'll cover the creative problem-solving process and apply this process to your work during the entire course.

"Over the next several weeks I'll also teach you the elements and principles of design. You'll learn why these structures are important in visual communication, and how you can implement them with Flash MX."

I retrieved the *Learn Design with Flash MX* book from the briefcase, and held it up to the class. "We'll cover everything in this book during this course...

> *"Each chapter represents one scheduled session, including project assignments to tackle between each class. We'll discuss each week's project before you leave that day, so you know exactly what's expected from you the following week."*

Someone groaned as I continued, "Your participation in these classes and assignments will propel you into the next week's topic of focus, and it will help you visualize and utilize the function of a design team." I laid the book on the desk. "Each assignment is an element in the progression of a larger project that will span the length of this course."

"What's the project?" a young man asked. Several people leafed through their books, absorbed in the contents.

"The project takes the form of a real-time design assignment utilizing Flash MX," I answered. "We'll face issues inherent to a designer-client relationship. You'll discover how to solve a client's problem with a visual solution, and you'll learn how to present these ideas to your client with professional conviction.

"Each class will begin with a review of the assignments," I continued. "Then we'll learn new concepts through the creative problem-solving process with lectures, discussion, and hands-on practice. We'll implement our designs in Flash along the way."

"What's Flash actually used for?" one student quizzed.

"It's a graphic environment used to make interfaces, animations, and games for the Web," I answered.

Before I had a chance to continue, one young man could hardly contain his excitement. "Games? Animations?" he leapt up from his chair and scrambled to a computer at the other side of the room. "Wow! When do we start?"

"Hold on a minute!" a woman intervened. The man froze like a stone statue, hardly breathing, much to the humor of class. "You'll have to learn to crawl before you can run. Making games requires a considerable degree of programming knowledge."

After he unfroze, one of the other classmates helped him back to his seat and consoled him with a friendly pat on the back.

"You'll be surprised how quickly you can make your first animation in Flash though," I said. "In fact, before its functionality was enhanced, enabling it to be used for website design, among other things, Flash was used exclusively for animation.

"And I'm sure you'll be glad to know that we'll be covering some animation in Flash MX later on in the course."

"Excellent!" the young man said, bouncing back to life again, and almost out of his seat.

"Flash MX is used for all manner of things on the Web and off it," I said. "But before we explore these avenues, we've got a few other things to cover."

I asked everyone to move to the front of the room, away from their books and computers. "Everyone, bring your chairs up here so we can meet each other," I said. "We have a lot of ground to cover today, so let's get the show on the road."

Meet your classmates

I was eager for the students to feel comfortable, since I knew at least one person had already expressed doubts about this class. From experience, I knew that each person in the class would bring a wide variety of opinions and skills to the design process.

I began, "The entry level requirement for this class is simply a basic computer knowledge, which might include familiarity with image manipulation software like Adobe Photoshop and some hands-on experience with a text editor program like Microsoft Word. Some of you may also have experience in the world of design or with Flash itself. Let's begin with some introductions." I nodded to the sensible looking man seated at my right. "Let's begin with you and work our way around the room."

He straightened up and looked everyone in the eye as he waved. "Hi everyone, my name is **Steve**. I'm obviously a bit older than the rest of you. I have a degree in graphic design, which I received before computers were even used in this field." He smiled at me, "In fact, I was probably working in graphic design before most of you were born!

"My initial experience was in print publication layout. I used waxers, linotype, and other camerawork pasted on grids. I also have experience in design programs on the computer, but I'm self-taught. I had to learn computers and design software or I'd be out of a job.

"In fact, I've been so busy staying abreast of new software and upgrades as I worked, that I've lost touch with my original goals – those of becoming a competent designer. I hope I can gain skills and confidence with this course." he said. "Ultimately, I want to become more comfortable with the software so I can free myself up to be more creative. I want to break out of the incompetent box, so to speak. Plus," he added, "with some practical Flash experience under my belt, I'll be able to offer my clients another outlet for their communications."

"Thanks, Steve," I said. "Does anyone else have graphic design experience?"

Bonnie looked at Steve with a puzzled smile. "I don't know what you just said about grids and waxing, because I don't know anything about print design. My name is **Bonnie** and I have my own business designing websites; I've been concentrating on this for two years now." She shrugged, "I don't have a degree, but I've managed pretty well on my own. I've learned how to build sites using resources on the Internet and in books. I always check my code to make sure that it resolves within every browser possible – I validate every page so it's accessible to as many people as possible.

"My clients are fairly happy, but I'm losing some of them to other designers. They want more action in their pages, including stuff that probably can't be validated. I'm not sure I buy into this, because it's not accessible to everyone. I keep telling my clients they're losing possible markets by using Flash and other programs, but they don't seem to care. I'm here to find out if I can learn to use this program and still be compliant with all the rules."

The young man next to Bonnie grinned and jumped into the introductions. "Hey everyone!" He waved. "This is awesome! I'm **Zed**, and you guys are going to teach me a lot, I can tell. I'm on the Internet all the time, since I was a kid in school. My friends tell me I have a lot of great ideas, and I want to stick them up on the Web for everyone to see. I like cartoons, especially Manga – I draw anime all the time. I have my own home page, but it doesn't work half the time. All the stuff I use on the Internet is free, because I don't have a job yet. I really want to find work with Flash MX so I asked for this class as a birthday present. So here I am!"

Zed settled back in his seat with a grin.

Everyone laughed at Zed's enthusiasm, except for the woman seated next to him. She spoke up. "My name is **Deb**, and I'm a computer programmer. I have several programming certifications, and I've worked in this field for almost four years. My boss sent me to this class because he wants me to learn about design. I'm not very happy about this, because while I'm here, the guys at work are probably planning ways to get rid of me. I'm the only woman at work, and it's pretty competitive."

Bonnie watched Deb with interest. Deb continued, "Plus, I don't understand why I need to learn design when my boss can hire someone to do this. As far as I'm concerned, design and programming are two different issues, and I'm happy with programming. On top of this, I'm fairly proficient with Flash MX. I hope I won't be bored, but I don't have a choice. I either take this class or lose my job."

The man next to Deb nodded his head and spoke next. "Hey Deb. Hi everyone. My name is **Wes**. Deb, I can relate to how you feel. I'm on the other end of the spectrum, because I'm an artist with a degree in fine art. I'm a little afraid that I'll want to control the creative aspect of this class. I have years of experience in fine art, including shows, awards, and publications. But, frankly, I'm bored with watercolor, pastels, and found-art sculpture. I want to reach beyond my present skills and develop digital artwork with computers. The possibilities are enormous!"

Wes looked up and put his hands together in mock prayer. "I hope to quickly move beyond the frustration of the software basics so I can rapidly develop my skills in Flash MX. I want to combine this skill with my other ideas to produce some cutting edge artwork in order to stay ahead of the pack – my field is very competitive and I don't want to be seen as a dinosaur. Amen!"

Steve laughed, "I think your prayers might be answered here, Wes."

I nodded at the last student, a woman who seemed shyer than the rest of the class. "What about you?" I asked.

She ducked her head as she spoke softly. "My name is **Lisa**. You are all so experienced and talented, but I'm afraid I'm not very skilled in web design or with computer programs. I'm taking this course for several reasons. I hope I can learn to design, and I hope I'm smart enough to learn this software. I do have basic computer skills, and I've surfed the Internet, so I know some of what you're talking about. I just hope I don't slow the class down."

"Lisa, we're all here to learn," I responded. "I learn from my students every time I teach a class. Hopefully, we'll all help each other overcome any perceived or real hurdles as we learn the design process with Flash MX."

What's your motivation?

After each one of the students identified their levels of experience, I helped them define and analyze their motivations for this class. I stood and said, "It's clear we have a wide variety of experiences and hopes for success in this class," I said. "Steve, you bring years of print design experience to the class. Your perspective on 'coming of age' in the computer era will be invaluable."

I addressed the class on Steve's strengths. "His point of view can help you all appreciate the access and ease of today's design tools. His insight in dealing with the designer's work environment will be important."

"Oh, I can tell some stories about working in a design environment," Steve laughed. "I'll be glad to share that part. My goal is to feel competent. I hope I've taught myself well. If I have, then the validation will be priceless."

"Validation of success is important," I answered. "Especially when it's in a learned skill that seems so overwhelming and competitive."

Everyone nodded in agreement, except Zed. He seemed ready to fall out of his chair as he craned his neck to watch everyone. I said, "Zed, you'll add some excitement to this class, I'm sure. What are your goals?"

"Man, I'm into feedback. I want to hear what everyone thinks of my work. I'm afraid I don't have much to say about anyone else's work, though. I wouldn't know where to start, except that I know what works for me." He leaned back and stuffed his hands in his pockets. "I'm not sure if what I know is enough, though. I mean, I think I know what works in design, because it's probably the artwork that turns me on."

"That's how a lot of people feel about artwork and design, Zed." I answered. "Before computers, critics basically only had the fields of art, literature, and architecture to praise or tear apart. Now, there's a whole new world of computerized art and design to critique."

"Amen again!" Wes jumped in with his viewpoint. "I know where you're headed here. No offense, Zed, but it seems everyone and their mother knows what they like and don't like. In my opinion, only educated critics and artists understand there's a whole value system that comes into play here. They're the only ones who deserve to be critical of another person's designs."

"Wes, you have one of the keys to the problem of critical assessment of design," I responded, "Education helps us understand the design process." I turned to speak to the rest of the class. "You'll be pleasantly surprised to learn that this 'value system' Wes mentioned is fairly simple to learn. The guidelines and rules you'll learn in this course can be memorized. But, it's the way we use these tools and guidelines that defines our roles as serious designers."

"The whole process helps define our styles, too." Wes added. "I want to know if I can replicate my style with Flash."

"I don't know if creative design has a role with building websites." Bonnie stated as she glanced at Wes, "Other than working with basic formats like tables and the addition of some visual elements, there's very little room to be creative and still be user-friendly to everyone."

"Bonnie's experience will be vital to us, also." I responded. "She's defined her experience with rules, so she's halfway into the design process. Her design discipline is actually part of the graphic design field, but she deals with more extreme limitations than Steve does in print production."

"I know what you mean," Wes grinned and added, "These limitations lead to what is known as obsessive-compulsive behavior. These attributes aren't always healthy for our creative side. Rules are great for defining our boundaries, but evolution has a way of helping us bend or even break those rules."

Bonnie smiled and sighed, "I'll admit it's a real headache to validate every page in a client's site. I limit the sizes of most sites just because I can't handle the tedious work. I want to know if I can be creative and still manage to work across all browser platforms. Accessibility issues are a problem, too. If the site isn't available to the hearing or sight impaired, then it's not useful at all."

"Bonnie, design isn't just about building websites. It's the structure for a creative person's life." Wes opened a can of worms with this statement. Deb jumped in, and her anger about having to attend this course was apparent.

"I live my life just fine, thank you. Life isn't by design, in my opinion, it's much more logical than that!" Deb continued, "I understand the rest of you might have all the time in the world to expand your horizons, but I'm ready to go back to work. Plus," she added, "I can critique just fine. Either you know the software or you don't!"

"Yeah, Deb, you bet!" Zed interrupted. "I remember writing the first ever code for my website. Man, that was a rush! It's so cool to watch my thoughts turn into code and then turn into words presented exactly how you want, with all those different colors, fonts, and backgrounds!"

Deb sighed, and rubbed her forehead. "Gee, that's great, Zed. My point is that there's a great deal of competition at my job. I don't understand why I need to learn design, because it's not my goal."

"Deb, hang in there with us," Steve said. "I don't understand your side of this process any more than you want to understand my side. But, I have a gut feeling we're going to need each other to get ahead here."

Steve had Deb's attention. "I understand competition. In this business, it helps to know every possible angle. Even if we're not experts, at least we can learn enough to not get ripped off."

Bonnie agreed. "I'll vouch for that! One reason I took this course is because I tried to hire a Flash designer for a client, against my better judgment. The prices were outrageous! I figured I'd at least try to understand why the cost was so high, even if I never use the program for my clients."

"The price is high, because it must take a lot of skill to use the program," Wes stated. "The problem is there's a lot of really lousy design on all formats, not just the Internet. It would be cool to see everyone understand the artistic side of life in addition to the software skills. You know, because we're not taught the basics of visual literacy in our standard education, most people never have the chance to learn how to express themselves visually."

"Whoa, dude," Zed replied. "Not all of us are award-winning artists, man. But, that's why I'm here. I'm your new competition!"

"And," Deb added, "I'm positive everyone here has the faculties to learn Flash MX. That's partly why I worry about my job!"

Lisa remained quiet and watchful. "Lisa," I asked, "How do you see your role in this class?"

"Well," she paused. "I'm not sure I'm going to be any help at all. I don't even know how to draw a straight line. Plus, I've never used software to design, except maybe to play around with holiday snaps in Photoshop."

"Hey Lisa!" Wes got her attention. "I learned how to draw a straight line using a ruler and a pencil." He shrugged and held out his hands, "It's not that hard."

"This course might seem difficult now, Lisa," I added. "The process of design takes discipline, perseverance, and practice. When we learn to walk, it takes time and a lot of arms and sofas and chairs to lean on to get from one side of the room to the other. I'll give you the information and the parameters. Hopefully, we'll help each other with our own unique perspectives."

I felt it would be wise to simplify everyone's motives for clarity. "I would like to define what everyone's hopes are for this class," I said. I turned to the whiteboard and began to write. "What I heard from each of you were the following reasons to take this class." I wrote this list on the board:

* Bonnie – Reach a variety of people with visual information
* Deb – A better job or advance in current job
* Lisa – Learn new ways to communicate
* Steve – Feel confident with Flash MX software
* Wes – New vehicle to express creativity
* Zed – Understand the concepts of good design

"Wow! You got all that from what we just said?" Zed seemed amazed.

"Do you all agree with this assessment?" I asked.

Deb said, "I didn't realize I had a motive." She glanced at her watch, "If that's my goal, I'm ready to begin. What's next?"

"Lisa? Everyone? Are you ready to begin?" I asked.

"I think I'll be ready if Deb removes her watch," Lisa replied with a small smile. "Maybe I'll be able to relax."

"Hey! Great idea!" Wes unbuckled his watchstrap. "Let's all get into the spirit of art, where there's no time, and no relevance to the world of business!"

I wasn't going to refute that remark, not at this point. Everyone bared their wrists, and we were ready to begin.

The creative process

I asked everyone to bring their books and notepads to the table on the left side of the room. Papers were shuffled and chairs scraped along the floor. I erased the motivation list from the whiteboard and replaced it with the following list:

1. Define
2. Analyze
3. Ideate
4. Select
5. Implement
6. Evaluate

"Now that we've broken the ice and defined our goals," I said, "Let's get down to the business of creativity.

"These are the steps in the creative problem-solving process. This process isn't complicated. But," I added, "The individual components can be difficult to clarify at first. The process is vital to your course. We'll use this tool throughout the course and in various projects to help keep our goals focused."

Define

Steve spoke up, "This process is a lot like the scientific method."

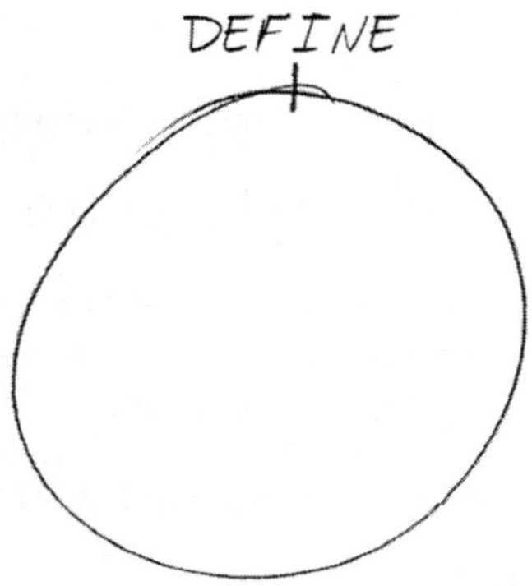

"The scientific method of what?" Zed asked. Deb rolled her eyes and began to chew on the end of her pencil.

"Steve's right," I responded. "You didn't realize you'd learn science here, did you, Zed?" I turned and drew a circle on the whiteboard. At the top of the circle, I wrote the word *define*.

"Steve," I turned to him and asked, "How is this term used in the scientific method?"

Steve answered, "It's the observation phase, where scientists look at a problem and begin to define parameters."

"So what's the relevance to this class?" Deb asked.

"The first step helps us define the client's problem, doesn't it?" Bonnie asked in response to Deb's question. "My clients have so many issues, it's hard to find the real problem sometimes."

Wes spoke up. "Bonnie, I think you're almost right. I think the definition phase is when the designer decides which format to use for a visual problem."

"Wes, you and Bonnie are both correct," I said. "In a design situation, we'll probably have a client who needs to have a problem resolved." I continued, "Once the problem is *identified*, the designer needs to decide which *format* to use to help the client communicate to his customers."

Deb doodled on her notepad as I continued, "Through research, a graphic designer will decide whether the format will be print, television, radio, multimedia, or indeed a website on the Internet. Sometimes, it's a combination of all these formats."

Analyze

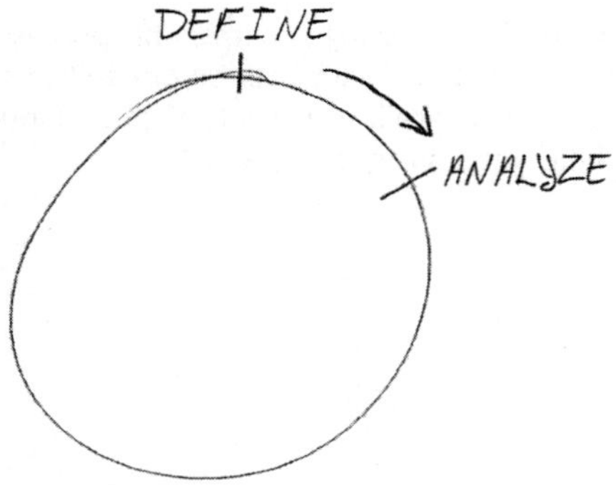

Time to introduce the next stage of the creative process, I thought. "For this class, the ***define*** stage begins with isolating the client's problem. The final format has already been decided for you by the fact that we're going to be using Flash MX." I turned and wrote the word *analyze* along the right side of the circle. Then I drew an arrow from *define* to ***analyze***.

"Steve," I asked, "What does the scientist do in this next step?"

Steve answered, "This is where the scientist pulls in his knowledge to set parameters for the problem. He begins to decide how to put the next step into words."

"When designers analyze a problem," I added, "They employ the elements of design to the chosen format."

Zed looked puzzled. "Is this something we're going to learn?"

"We certainly are! We'll cover the elements of design before we're through today," I said. I turned back to the rest of the class. "During this course, we'll **analyze** the problem with information gathering and fact-finding. The only facts we need are the ones that are relevant to the client's problem and the possible solution." I turned back to the whiteboard. "As we work through the problem, we may find we need more information. We can always backtrack in this process to fill in the gaps."

Ideate

I wrote the word *ideate* on the board, and drew an arrow from *analyze* to *ideate*.

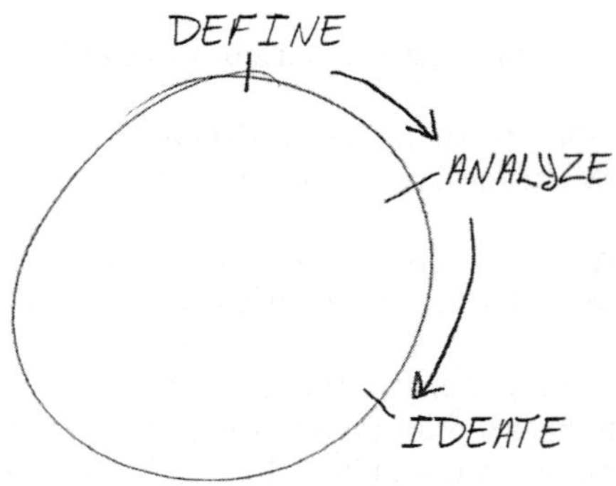

"I know what that is!" Zed said. "It's like when you idolize someone."

Deb laughed. "I think we need to buy you a dictionary for your next birthday, Zed."

Zed blushed. "So I'm wrong. What's ideate mean, teach?"

"Actually, Zed isn't too far off the mark," I said. "We can ideate a person in our mind, and make them appear to be more ideal than they are in real life. Basically, **ideation** is the formation of *creative ideas*."

Steve added, "This is where the scientist begins to generalize and propose the hypothesis for his problem. A physicist will write the hypothesis in numbers. Numbers are the language of physics."

Deb perked up at the mention of numbers. "It's just like creating code for a program," she said. "We test every possibility before we find the code that works best for a given problem."

"You're all catching on quickly," I smiled. It was good to see Deb become involved in the process. "For this class," I explained, "Ideation is the **brainstorming** process, where we'll generate possible solutions for a visual problem."

Wes rubbed his hands together. "Ah! The benefit of numbers! I'm so accustomed to working alone; the addition of other ideas will be a luxury."

Steve laughed, and Bonnie asked, "What exactly do you mean by *brainstorming*?"

"It's when brains storm! They collide!" Wes slapped his hands together for dramatic effect. "It's when designers play with ideas until they find solutions for a specific visual problem!"

Bonnie grimaced. "I'm not sure that my ideas are all that hot. I'm not so creative."

"Bonnie," I replied, "You'll soon realize that no one's brainstorming ideas are right or wrong. We should never judge an idea during the process – this is what many people have a problem with. In fact, we could go as far as to say that, for once, it's not the quality but the *quantity* of ideas that's important. I hope you'll soon discover the same enthusiasm Wes has about this process. We'll practice this tool when it comes time to brainstorm our client's project."

Zed asked, "Who's our client?"

"Shh!" Deb shot a dangerous look at Zed. "I want to know what's next."

Select

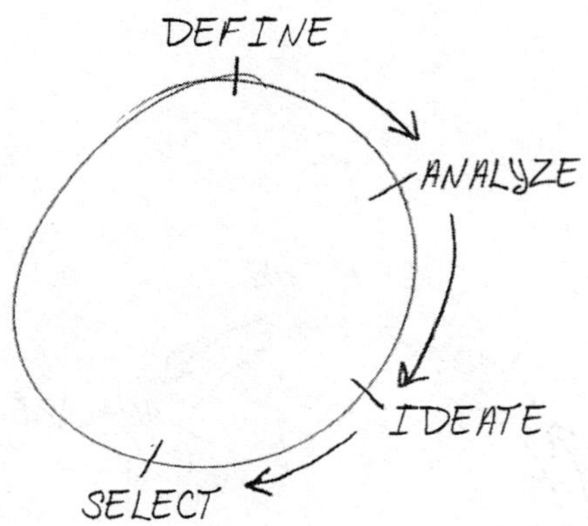

Zed raised his eyebrows, and looked at me. "I guess it's time for *selection*...," he added, "...of the fittest, I'm sure."

I wrote the word on the whiteboard, and drew an arrow from *ideate* to *select*.

Steve said, "This is where the scientist experiments to see if his hypothesis works."

"Right, Steve." I added, "Selection is also where the designer aligns the elements of design with the chosen format."

Everyone looked at me with expectant faces. "Yes," I answered, "We'll learn the principles of design soon."

Implement

"For this class," I said, "**Selection** is a three-pronged process. You'll use selection to visualize your solutions in the Flash MX format. You will also select the three best ideas to show the client, who will then select the best idea to..."

"...*implement*!" Deb finished my sentence.

I wrote that word on the circle, and drew an arrow from *select* to *implement*. "Steve, what's the scientific analogy to this process?" I asked.

"This is when scientists publish their theories, like Einstein did with his theory of $E=mc^2$." Steve said. "The publication would

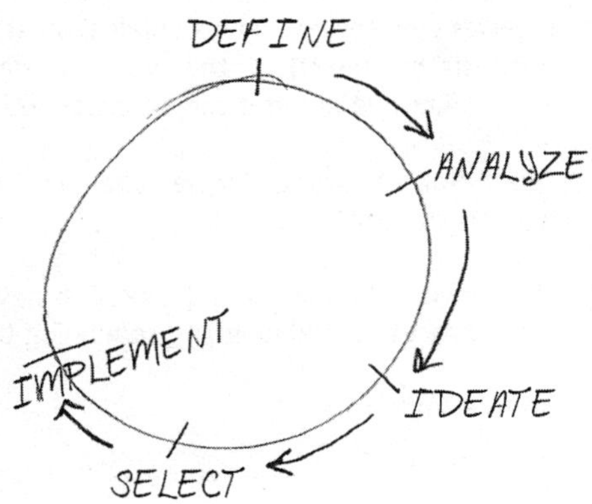

include the hypothesis, experiments, theories, and a conclusion." He added, "They might even publish experiments that failed, too."

"I don't think our client would publish projects that don't work, would they?" Bonnie asked.

"Bonnie just asked a good question," I replied. "When we don't have the benefit of testing the client's market with professional research, we might publish what the client chooses, rather than what works for his bottom line."

"That isn't very professional, is it?" Wes asked.

Steve answered, "We don't have the advantage of a market research department at work, and we can't afford a high-end research team outside of the studio. We find solutions from the client's perspective, and we do a little research on our own."

I added, "That's about all we can do without a professional research team on board. We won't have that advantage in this class, either. We'll learn what to look for when we work on the class project."

"That's back in the analyzing stage, isn't it?" Zed asked.

Bonnie interrupted, "Oh, I thought you meant that we would publish something that didn't work, like a website that had poor code, or a site that wasn't validated."

Deb laughed. "Bonnie, you're very focused."

"Thanks!" Bonnie replied.

Evaluate

I held my hand toward Zed. "As Zed just mentioned, target markets will be covered when we analyze our information." I wrote the word *evaluate* on the whiteboard, connected with an arrow from *implement*.

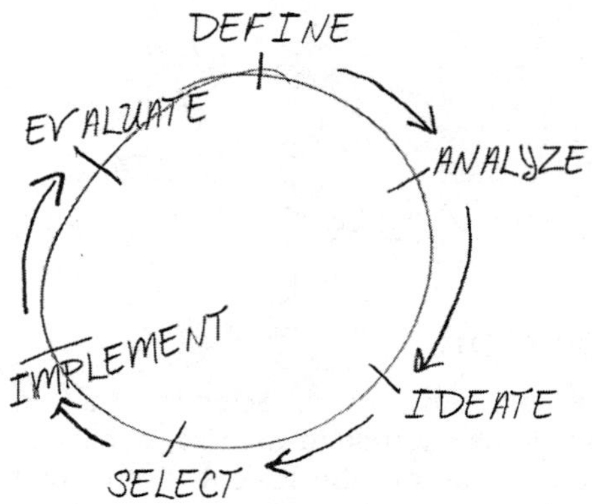

"Can any of you guess what this word means?" I asked.

"I guess that's when you discover if the design works," Bonnie answered.

Steve added, "In the scientific method, it's where the scientist receives peer reviews on his publication. It's also where other scientists double-check the work, or decide whether the work is finished and if it can be expanded upon."

"Oh!" Bonnie jumped in her chair and raised her hand for attention. "It's the same as an upgrade on a website design!"

"I think you all understand this process never ends," I replied as I pointed at the circle on the board. "**Evaluation** is the process of defining and redefining the goal of the design, *just like an upgrade to a website design*."

Bonnie smiled smugly.

"If you noticed, I drew an arrow from *evaluate* back to *define*. We can use this circle to continue upgrading our work, or we can use it to move on to other projects. You'll find," I added, "That sometimes the arrows double back on themselves as we go back and forth between stages."

I sat at the table with the students. "Do any of you have questions about the overall creative problem-solving process?"

"I do," Zed said. "Are you saying this process works for anything?"

"I think I can answer that," Steve said. "This is the logical process to use to solve any problem. In this situation," he added, "We'll meet the client and **define** the problem. Then, we'll **analyze** the situation and its parameters or boundaries."

He leaned back and folded his arms across his chest. "Then," he said, "We'll **ideate**, or brainstorm, and **select** the three best ideas to present to our client. We'll **implement** the chosen idea, and we'll send that baby out to see how the rest of the world **evaluates** our work."

"Crikey! I think he's got it!" Wes applauded.

Lisa had been attentive through the discussion, but remained quiet. I looked at her and asked, "Do you understand this process, Lisa?"

"Yes," she replied. She twirled her pencil as she talked. "I've just learned how scientists, physicists, mathematicians, and designers resolve problems." She paused and smiled. "I think I've also just learned how to handle my teenage daughter!"

"Bravo!" Wes bellowed. Even Deb laughed at this response.

"This is a good time for a break," I said. "When we come back, we'll study the definition of design, format, and layout."

Formats: the designer's landscape

In contrast to the formal thought process that we just encountered, I wanted to introduce physical attributes to the creative problem-solving process. The students should then begin to define the creative problem-solving process for themselves as they discover the definitions of design and the concept of format.

As everyone returned from break, I asked them to sit at the table again. "OK everyone," I began, "What's the definition of design? Zed, do you know?"

Zed seemed caught off-guard. He stuttered, "Well, I think it's drawing. Umm... and thinking too."

"You're very close to the definition, Zed. We do draw, and we think along the lines of the creative problem-solving process." I looked at Deb. "What about you, Deb? What does design mean to you?"

Deb seemed self-assured as she answered. "It's ideas and the creation of those ideas."

"Don't ask Bonnie what design is," Wes blurted. "She'll say it's a website."

Bonnie laughed. I turned to Deb and responded to her answer. "We do create a visual solution to a problem using our ideas, Deb. You're close, but no banana just yet." I looked at Lisa. "What's design mean to you, Lisa?"

Lisa looked up and said, "A design is a plan."

Everyone looked at Lisa, as she bent her head and continued taking notes.

I smiled at Lisa's to-the-point explanation. "Lisa's got it. In essence, a **design** is simply a **plan**. When we design a house, we plan how that house will be built within the format of a landscape. Similarly, when we design a website, we plan to use certain elements for that particular format."

"If a design is a plan," Zed said, "Then a designer is a planner, right?"

"That's right," I said. "In our case, we'll learn to plan a visual solution to our client's problem using Flash MX."

"Oh!" Deb leaned forward. "So a house designer is an architect. A designer for computer code is a programmer, right?"

"And as we all know, a designer for websites is called a web designer!" Bonnie laughed. "I wanted to beat Wes to that definition," she winked at Wes.

Wes said, "I'll play this game. Designers for solutions to visual problems are named according to their specialized formats. For instance," he explained, "Steve would be a graphic or print designer."

Steve nodded, "And you, Wes, would be an artist, because you design within the format of a canvas."

"Don't forget I'm a sculptor, too," Wes said. "I design beyond the flat surface of a canvas."

"Would I be considered a designer of anime?" Zed asked. "Or would I be a cartoonist?"

I answered, "Zed, you're actually a writer, an artist, an illustrator, and a graphic designer. You wear a lot of design hats." Zed seemed thrilled with my response.

I turned to Lisa. "Do you have any experience with design?"

Lisa smiled shyly, "I used to manage the lights for the theater down the road. I guess you could say I have the skills of a light designer for the format of a stage."

"Wow, Lisa. How exciting!" Wes said. "All that color and so much space!"

"Our designs do take up space," I added. "And this space is called a **format**. A format is a tangible thing with physical properties. For Wes it's a canvas or a block of stone maybe. For Lisa it's a stage, and for Steve it's the format of a magazine or newspaper page. Format can consist of a huge variety of materials.

"Although it sounds obvious, we should also note that formats have dimensions," I said. "The format has height and width, and often it has depth. For instance," I explained, "This room has all three dimensions. The architect laid out the rooms with a specific problem, and he designed a visual solution."

I continued, "By the time you finish this course, you'll all be Flash MX designers, and you'll work within the format of the computer web browser."

Zed grinned. "Cool!"

Bonnie looked around the room and asked, "Why are the computers on one side of the room, and this table on the other side?"

I answered Bonnie's question, being sure to maintain the context of the topic so as to emphasize the idea of formats, "The physical structure, or format, of this classroom is designed – planned – for two methods of learning," I replied. "The computer side is where you'll learn to apply design with our chosen implementation tool – Flash MX. You each have a computer with the appropriate software already installed." I pointed at the computers, "As you can see, there's very little room for anything else other than your book, notes, and sketches."

Bonnie muttered, "Sketches?"

"This side of the room, with a larger table with room to move is where we'll brainstorm and sketch out our concepts. Don't worry if you don't know how to draw." I looked at Bonnie. "You'll learn how to look at things from a different perspective with this course, and you'll learn how to portray your ideas many different ways.

"It's also a good idea to incorporate this kind of setup at home, or at your office or studio," I added. "Many design firms today are returning to the model of ideation with the tools of thumbnails and roughs before the designer even touches the computer."

"We're designing rough thumbnails?" Zed asked as he looked at his hands.

Steve laughed, "I can explain thumbnails. I remember using them years ago, before computers arrived on the scene."

"Go ahead, Steve," I said. Everyone looked at Steve, and he began his explanation.

Thumbnails and roughs: the designer's blueprints

"**Thumbnails** are small layouts or sketches of an idea, usually no larger than the size of a stamp," Steve explained. "Mainly, they were used to help sort through ideas so the best idea can be further developed."

I stood and turned to a drawing pad clipped to an easel by the table. I drew six rectangles on the paper with a pencil.

"Thumbnails are typically quite small," I said, "But I'll make these larger so you can see them from where you're sitting. These little sketches are an important part of the design process," I added. "Thumbnails help you work through design problems. These tools will help you remember your thought processes."

Wes grinned, "I'm familiar with this process, but I've never called them thumbnails before. I always draw my sketches on napkins and scraps of paper, whatever's available when I'm inspired to draw, and add them to my idea file. This is where I keep all my spur-of-the-moment thoughts and ideas for future paintings and sculptures."

"Wes," I said, "We're on the same wavelength. That's exactly what we'll do in this class." I turned to draw a few loose lines within the top left rectangle. "You don't have to be a Michelangelo to convey an idea, or to work through ideas for a design. You could equate this process to drawing the blueprints for your new house."

"Great," Bonnie said. "First we're scientists and mathematicians. Now we're architects."

"That's the idea," I remarked as I turned back to the sketchpad. "At this stage, we're taking everything we know about the client, and we're thinking with our pencils. We'll sketch these ideas, and then we'll develop the best ones further."

"For instance, if I needed to design a page for a website, I could indicate a headline with a few lines." I drew in another box, and shaded it lightly. "This could indicate a body of copy, and this," I drew a vague shape, "Is a photograph."

I continued to draw rough concepts in the rest of the squares. "I may want to move the headline down here, and the photograph over here," I said as I drew new sketches. "Or, I may try this idea for a change."

"Why can't we do this on the computer?" Bonnie asked.

Wes leaned back and answered, "Bonnie, the computer screen is a limited format in size and shape. Sometimes our best ideas come when we move beyond these restrictions and try new formats and new textures for our work."

"Exactly, Wes. Remember," I explained, "The design process incorporates ideation. Our ideas are often fleeting and fragile, and the first idea isn't always the best.

"As you work through your thumbnails, you'll have these ideas in your hands. These ideas have elements you might miss or delete if you work on the computer.

"In addition," I said, "When you work on the computer, your roughs often appear to be finished, when they're far from complete. You might accept this design, when you could have gone further by doing these sketches.

"We should also keep *time* in mind, too", I continued, on a roll, "Often, if you've got a strict deadline for a particular design project, it's much easier and quicker to mess around sketching all your immediate thoughts by hand, especially when a significant proportion of the raw ideas will go no further than a 10 second drawing."

"You drew the boxes in the format of a computer screen," Steve noted. "It's wider and shorter than the format for a magazine or newspaper page."

"Thanks, Steve – well spotted." I looked at the rest of the class. "You don't need to use boxes for your thumbnails. The idea is to let your thoughts flow freely. However," I added, "It helps to give yourself a format so you can begin to see how the elements will fit in a page."

"But," Bonnie argued, "You just said we need to break away from the format of the computer screen!"

"Designers often need to set parameters in the analyzing stage and apply them to the ideation stage to save time." I replied, "However, we tend to gravitate to familiar ideas. For instance," I added, pointing to the second thumbnail down on the right side of my pad, "This sketch looks a little like a postcard, doesn't it?"

Everyone agreed. "The ideation process helps us move beyond familiar ground into unknown territory. If you look at the thumbnail right below the postcard image, you can see I've loosened up a bit, and I've moved beyond boxes. We can break out of these familiar boxes as we think with our pencils."

I spoke to the rest of the class. "Most great designs only come to fruition after many thumbnails and roughs. After a few exhausting design jobs, we'd have a difficult time tracking all these images in our hard drives."

"I'll add my two cents," Steve said. "I don't know how much time I've wasted searching for an idea I thought I saved on my hard drive. I began to print out my computer roughs, because I was too embarrassed to use my old design skills at the office," he added. "No one uses pencils to sketch ideas anymore."

"Steve," I said. "The execution of thumbnails and roughs is a very professional and logical way to develop a design. You can go back to the office with that reasoning for sketching your ideas. You'll also save on printer ink."

"Wait a minute!" Zed held up his hands in surrender, "What are roughs?"

"**Roughs**," I explained, "are larger versions of your thumbnails. When the sketches are larger, you begin to see things you might not have seen with a smaller sketch."

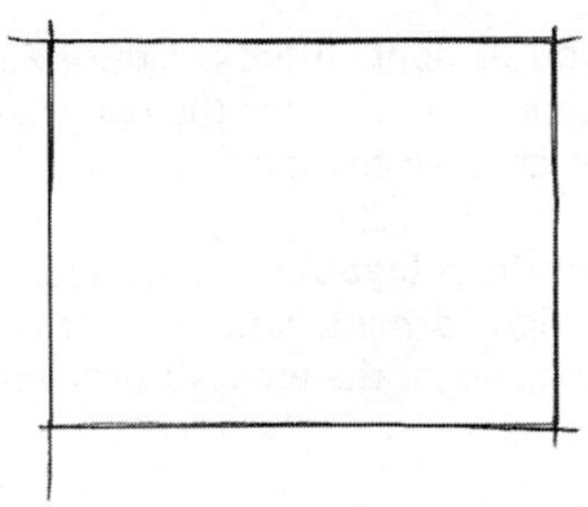

I turned a new sheet over on the drawing pad, and set the pad on the easel horizontally. I drew a large rectangle on the page. "This rectangle is larger than roughs need to be," I explained. "But, if I wanted to expand on the third thumbnail, I would sketch it in here with a bit more detail, adding some finer features to the rough."

Lisa said, "I notice you're using a ruler."

Amid chuckles from the class, I replied, "That's right, Lisa. I want the rough to be a little more finished, so I can take elements from the thumbnail I've chosen, and begin to see them within a more structured format." I continued, "Although I use a ruler to visualize the boundaries of the box for composition, I'm still going to be a little loose with the visual elements within this box.

"First, I'll add a headline. This is just an indication of where I want the type," I added. "This is a rough, which is different to a working rough."

"So the rough gets a job, eh?" Wes asked. "What's the difference between the two?"

"The **working rough** indicates type as closely as possible to the type you've chosen after working through this ideation phase. Plus, you'll add color, and the layout will be fairly close to what you'll execute in the final product." I added another element to the page as I spoke. "This," I waved at the drawing pad, "Is the stage between thumbnails and working roughs."

"Can't we use the computer for any of these stages?" Bonnie seemed distressed.

"Yes, Bonnie. The working roughs can be done on the computer," I answered. "At that stage, you're ready to add the actual visual elements to the design, so it's best to begin working within the software environment at this point.

"But remember," I added with a smile, "You can do this as long as you don't invest your hopes in the working rough phase as a finished product."

"Now," I continued, "I've added an area for the text. Notice I've indicated text with wavy lines."

"Why did you do that?" Deb asked.

"This adds gray tone to the area," I said, "And I can begin to see what I need to do to balance the elements on the page. If I feel there's too much white space on the left, I can add an element." I continued to draw. "I can add a photo for interest, or a list of items the reader can refer to as he or she reads the page."

The rough was finished for the moment, and I turned back to the class. "Can you see how I expanded on the rough, to include more definition to the smaller sketch?"

Bonnie answered, "I can see what you've done. It looks like one of my web templates, with a slot for a menu, a place for the copy, and spaces for images. It's not really that creative though."

I nodded. "That's right, Bonnie. This is a simple and familiar **layout** for a website. A **layout**," I explained, "Is the placement of text and images within a format. In the use of web design formats, you also include navigation. As we learn more about the tools in the ideation, or brainstorming part of the creative problem-solving circle, we'll learn to expand on this format to be more creative."

"Well, that's simple enough," Bonnie stated. "I think we're through with this stage." She pointed her pencil to each item in her notepad as she spoke. "Now I know everything I need to know about design, formats, thumbnails, roughs, and layout."

Wes groaned, and Steve grinned. Deb looked at Bonnie with surprise and said, "Bonnie, this is just the definition stage of the creative problem-solving process." She looked in my direction and asked, "I imagine the next stage is analyzing the problem of becoming Flash MX designers, right?"

"Deb, you've almost got the plan," I answered. "Our problem is learning design utilizing the Flash MX format. Through the creative problem-solving process that we discussed, we've discovered the essential definition of a designer. We also defined some of the formats we'll use for the ideation process."

I looked at Zed as I asked, "Now, can anyone else tell me what we're missing in the definition phase?"

Zed raised his arm, "Oh! Oh! I know! We've gotta get into Flash MX!"

I didn't have time to respond to Zed's correct answer. He flew out of his seat and made himself comfortable at the first available computer. Everyone else looked at me with raised eyebrows. "I guess you all need to follow Zed's example," I laughed as I waved my arm in his direction.

Everyone headed toward the bank of computers. I followed, towing the drawing pad and easel with me.

Introducing Macromedia Flash MX

Once they were all seated at the computers, all of them looked settled except for Bonnie, who was fidgeting and looking around.

"Bonnie, is something wrong?" I asked.

"Uh... well..." she replied, her voice quickly faded to nothing.

"I think I know what it is." Steve said, observing Bonnie. "I don't think Bonnie is used to only having one mouse button to play with!"

Steve grinned. Bonnie nodded and replied, "I'm not too familiar with using Apple Macintosh computers. I only ever use them when I have to test my web pages on them."

"How about you Steve?" I asked, "Are you OK using a Macintosh?"

"Sure," Steve replied, "I'm the opposite to Bonnie, I just can't seem to understand PCs! Because I've worked in the print industry for a while, the first computers I ever used were Macs, so I've used them ever since. Bonnie, why don't you see if someone will swap with you?"

Wes stood up without hesitation, "I'll swap with you."

"Thanks Wes!" Bonnie exclaimed.

"Go Wes!" Zed chanted, pumping his fist, "Go Wes!"

Steve laughed and the two of them swapped seats. Wes sat down and adjusted to his new surroundings, "What's the difference anyway?"

"That's a whole can of worms!" Steve shook his head.

"Well Wes," I said, "When it comes to working in Flash MX, there aren't really any differences. The software works the same on PC and Mac. When we come to open it up in a second, you'll see what I mean."

"What about when you come to publish your work on the web?" Bonnie asked. "PCs and Macs always tend to show things differently. I often to have to try and work around this."

"I think you might have found a medium that works for you then Bonnie," I said, "As long as your web browser has the Flash Player, or plug-in as it's also known, the files that Flash MX produces will display in exactly the same way on both PC and Mac.

"That's why Flash is so popular, because everyone can see the same thing and get excited about it!"

At this point Zed looked a little puzzled, "What do you mean by *plug-in*? I've heard that used before, and it's always confused me. Will I have to buy one for the next lesson?"

Deb chuckled and came to his rescue, "Zed, a plug-in is just a piece of software that extends the capabilities of your web browser."

Zed remained puzzled, "Like what?"

"Well," Deb said, "Have you ever watched a video on the web?"

"Yeah, I've got some awesome Get Up Kids MPG files!" Zed replied, "They rock!"

"Well, your browser uses a plug-in to show the MPG video files, usually Windows Media Player or QuickTime." Deb replied, "The Flash Player is a plug-in to show another file type – Flash files."

"Spot on Deb!" I said. I then wrote some file types down on the whiteboard:

.MPG – Video file
.MP3 – Sound file
.SWF – Flash file

"As Deb pointed out," I started, "the Flash plug-in enables us to play Flash files. Note how I pronounce them as *swiff* files rather than abbreviating letters, like with MP3. Are you all familiar with MPG or MP3 files?"

Everyone in the class nodded except Wes, "I'm sure I've heard about MP3s, but I've never seen one."

"I don't think you can see them Wes", Steve grinned, "They're music files!"

"What does SWF stand for anyway?" Zed asked, "Computer jargon is way too full of nasty abbreviations!"

"SWF stands for **Shockwave Flash**," I replied, "But the name isn't as important as the file type. When you come to test or publish your designs in Flash MX, you'll be creating your FLA Flash movies and turning them in to SWF files for publication.

"Hmm... is this the right time to ask what might be a really stupid question?" Lisa nervously asked.

"Lisa, in this class, no questions too stupid to ask!" I smiled back.

"OK, well I was just wondering why we're actually using Flash? I mean, I know we all signed up for this class knowing we'd be learning Flash MX, but what are its advantages over other design and web technologies?"

"Actually, that's a pretty important question – and I was hoping some bright spark would ask it! In fact, I've already prepared a few *Flash facts* for you all to check out." I reached into my briefcase and pulled out a few photocopied handouts, and began to pass them round the class.

Reasons to use Macromedia Flash

- **Easy to learn** – getting started with Flash and creating your first website is probably a lot easier than any other web technology. It consists of a single *WYSIWYG* visual environment, with no real need for any other applications, which is highly user-friendly.
- **Accessible to all** – Flash allows cross-platform and cross-browser compatibility. A Flash movie will always render exactly the same, wherever you view it.
- **Small downloads** – Flash uses vector graphics, and output SWF files are efficiently compressed, leading to websites with very small file size.
- **Enables interactivity** – Flash allows the creation of truly interactive designs and sites through a number of elements, and we can easily embed sounds and video in our movies.

After some quiet studying of my list of Flash highlights, I asked the students if they were all happy with these benefits.

Zed was first to ask a question, "Yeah, it all sounds awesome... but what's *WYSIWYG*?"

"*What you see is what you get!*" I answered, "By this I'm talking about how straightforward the Flash user interface is to work with – I'll talk about this next."

Wes was next, "And what are vector graphics? I know about digital photography and bitmaps, but I'm not so sure about these vectors."

"Don't worry too much, Wes, all will be revealed about vectors and bitmaps very shortly! OK, if that list has given you all a few more reasons to stick around, let's take a step closer towards creating our first Flash movie by studying the design environment. Turn to your computers and double-click on the Flash icon on your desktop. This will launch the Macromedia Flash MX application."

The Flash MX user interface

Everyone then turned to their computers, both Apple Macs and Windows-based PCs, to launch the Flash application. Following the frenzy of mouse-clicking, everyone's monitors were filled with the Flash MX interface. Zed began to show his excitement.

"Cool!" he said. "How do I make an anime animation?"

"He's obsessed!" Wes exclaimed.

"You've got to admire the enthusiasm though!" Steve added.

"Well Zed, making an animation – like design – takes a lot of planning and work before you even get to sit down at the computer." I said. "For now, we'll concentrate on getting to grips with the various elements within Flash MX, but you should feel free to start sketching out and planning your animation outside the class...."

"I for one would love to see it!" Wes injected.

"OK, I'll start working on it." Zed maintained his enthusiasm, "I already have some cool ideas that I could work on. I think we're gonna have to get some popcorn ready for the premiere!"

"Sure thing." I said, "Now, the first thing to point out is the similarity between the Mac and PC versions of Flash MX. Wes and Steve, take a look at any of the PC monitors and compare them to your own. The rest of you might like to look at either of the Macs to see how similar they are to your screens."

The whole class then leaned, stretched, pointed, and stared, making a lot of noise as they did so. First they studied the layout of Flash MX on a Mac:

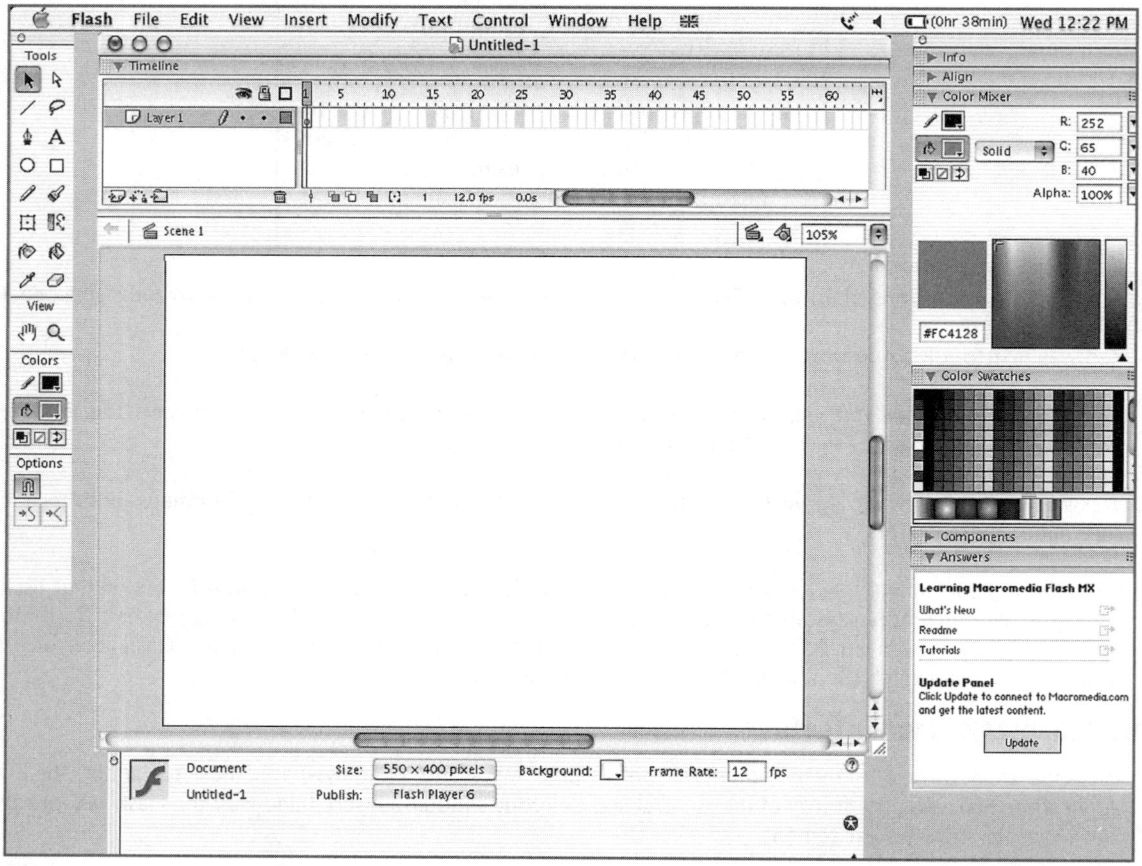

And then they turned to look at the PC version:

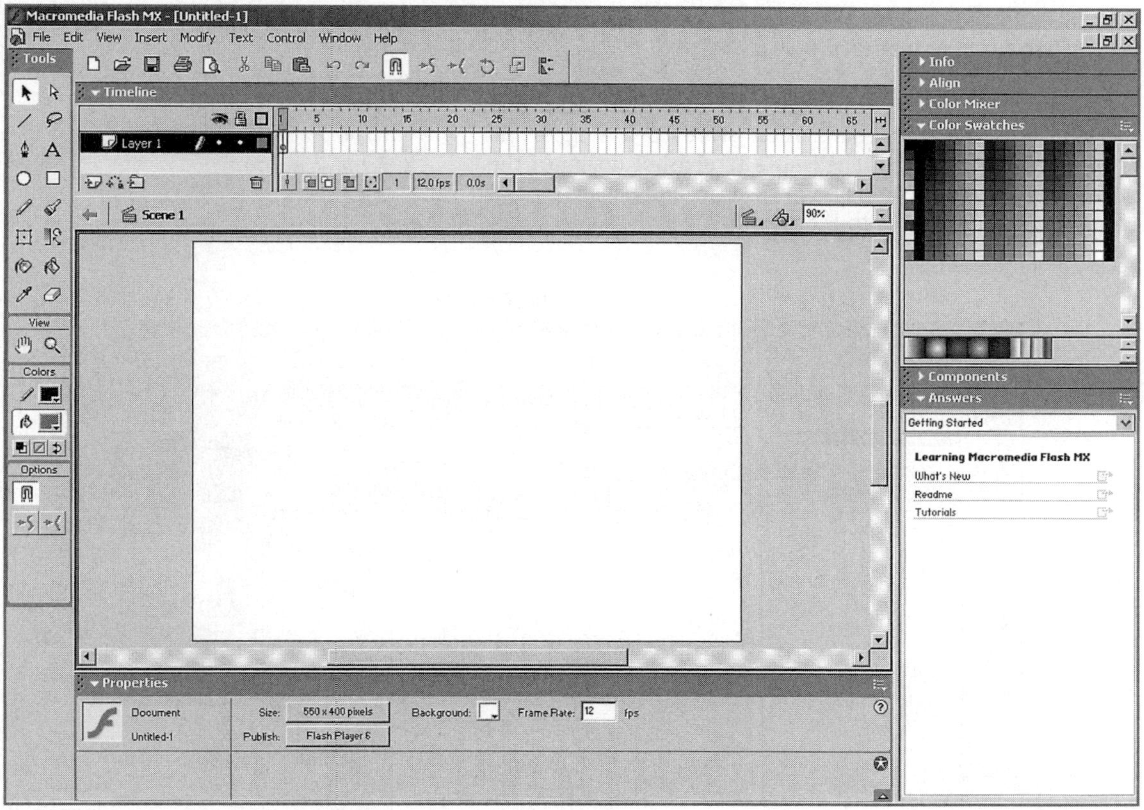

Bonnie was the first to break the ice, "They're not so different after all."

"That's right Bonnie." I said. "And because there aren't many differences, I can just give you all the same instructions, regardless of whether you using a Mac or PC."

The class then settled back down, so I decided it was time to begin.

"The Flash MX environment that you see on your screens is called the **user interface**, often abbreviated as UI. The Flash UI is where you will do many things, from testing compositions to creating the final website for the client.

"As you can see, the interface has many elements, some of which might be familiar to you from using other applications. Can anyone see any familiar elements? How about you Lisa?"

"The toolbar on the left is like the one in Adobe Photoshop." Lisa replied.

"That's right – Photoshop and many other graphics packages. The **toolbar** is where we select the right tool for a particular job. It's the Flash MX equivalent of an artist's tools palette."

"The central area must be the artist's canvas then." Wes said.

"That's right Wes. In Flash MX this canvas is referred to as the **stage**."

I turned to the drawing pad to list the primary elements of the Flash MX user interface:

THE FLASH MX INTERFACE

1. The Stage
2. The Timeline
3. The Toolbar
4. The Property inspector
5. Various panels

Next, I connected my own laptop PC to the projector and aimed it at the whiteboard. After swiftly browsing to the appropriate folder, I opened up a screenshot image of the Flash MX UI that I'd prepared in advance, and began to point out the main elements to the class:

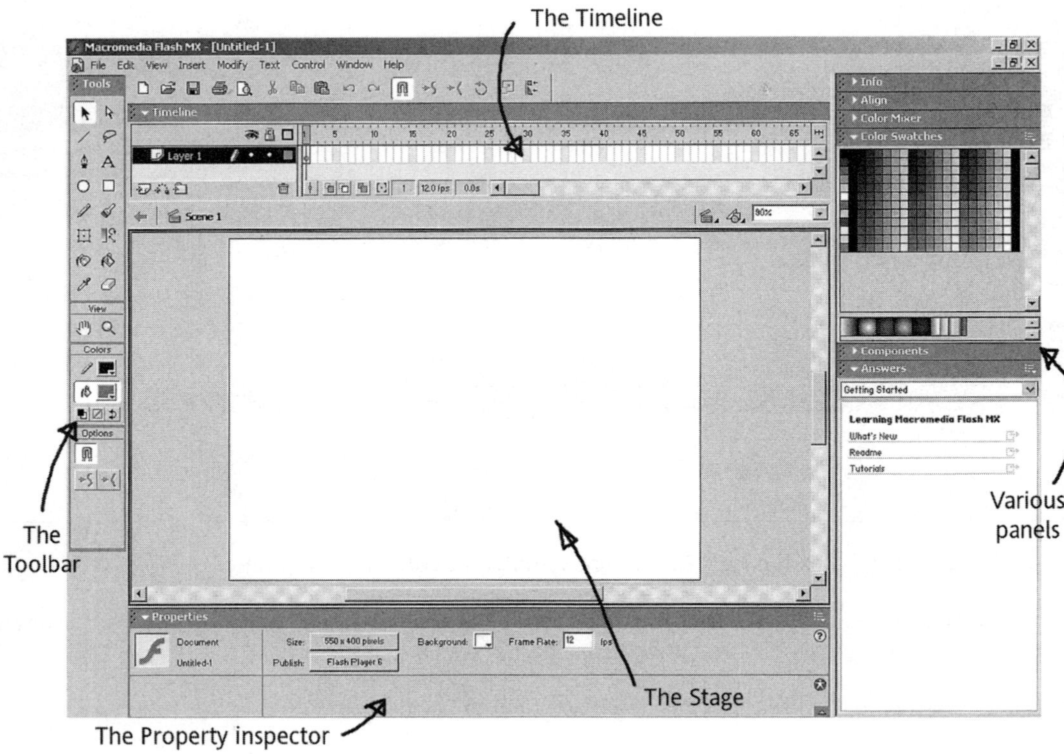

After highlighting these five elements and their positions within the Flash environment, I said to the class, "Let's now run through all of these interface elements in a little more detail, starting with one of the most important, the stage."

The Stage

"The stage, as Wes pointed out, is the Flash canvas. It is where we put things that we want to be seen in our published work. It's the viewable area for the audience."

"This is what will be seen in the browser then?" Bonnie asked.

"Yes, that's right Bonnie." I replied, "There is also an area that isn't seen too. I clicked open another image which was projected onto the whiteboard – this time, a close up of the stage area:

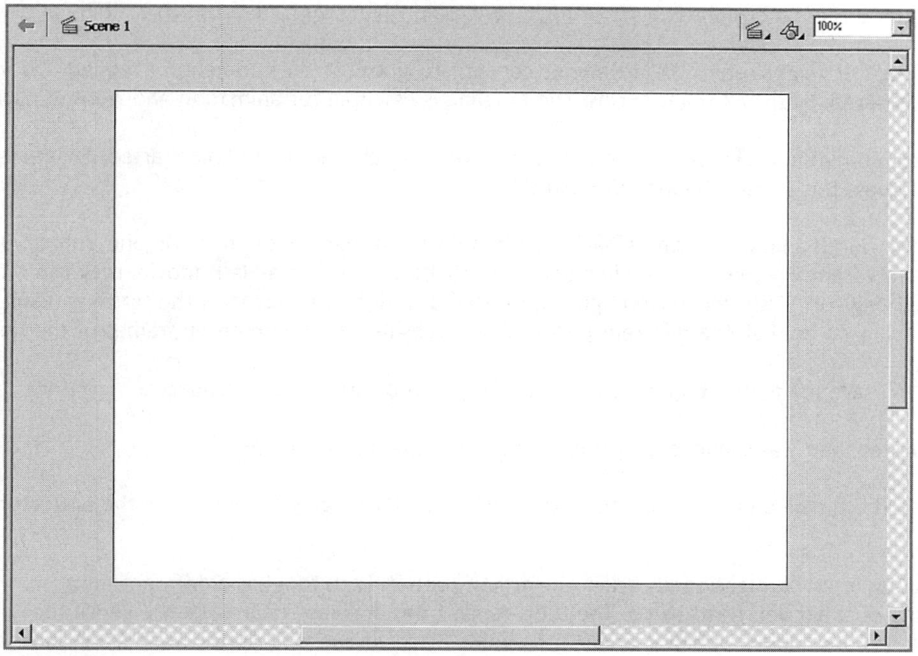

"Notice the gray area around the stage?" Lisa nodded. "This is known as the **work area**. If you imagine that the stage is like a theatre stage, then the work area is everything that the audience is unable to see from their seats – such as the backstage costume changes or the actors waiting to take stage. So, while the actors are on-stage are performing, there is a great deal of activity happening off-stage too."

"So, things can be waiting off-stage in the work area before coming onto the stage?" Wes asked.

"Sure," I replied, "You might use this tactic when you want to reveal something on the stage later in your movie. We'll explore this a little more in the next lesson.

The Timeline

"The next element is essential if our movie is to play smoothly." I changed the projector image to reveal the next element:

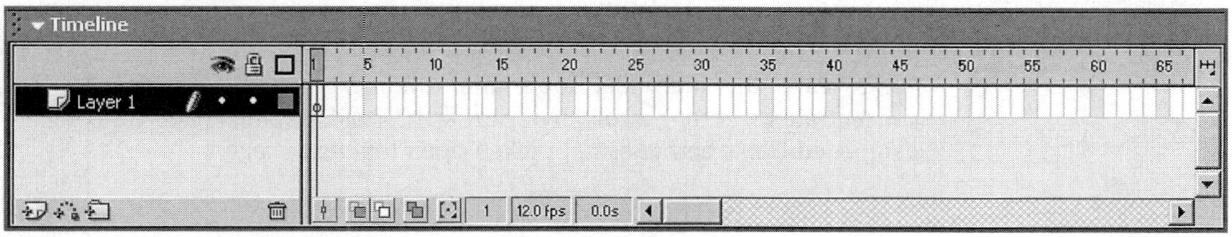

"The timeline in Flash MX relates to the elusive fourth dimension, time. If we use the theatre metaphor again, we know that certain things take place at different points in a play, such as actors coming on stage, the curtain being raised or dropped, and so on. The same thing happens in Flash, only we are in the driving seat and determine where things start and end."

"That makes us all directors of our Flash movies!" Zed said with the enthusiasm showing again.

"Working in three dimensions is hard enough," Wes said, "Now we have a fourth to think about."

"Even though it might seem like a difficult concept to grasp at the moment," I replied, "Working with a timeline is where Flash MX really excels. The timeline is essential for animation and website navigation."

"But when someone clicks on a hyperlink in one of my web pages," Bonnie started, "A new web page is loaded. I guess this doesn't happen in Flash SWFs."

"Under the hood, a Flash website is navigated in a different manner to an HTML one Bonnie. But what the user sees is essentially the same – when someone clicks on a link in a Flash movie, they can be sent to the requested page. In Flash, this page might be located at a different **frame** in the timeline. One Flash movie has the ability to hold all the different pages of our website via the numbered frames of the timeline."

"It sure will save me a little time when I validate my web pages!" Bonnie replied.

Wes chuckled, and was silenced by a friendly punch in the arm from Steve.

"We'll see the timeline in action in the next lesson." I said, changing the image on the projector.

The Toolbar

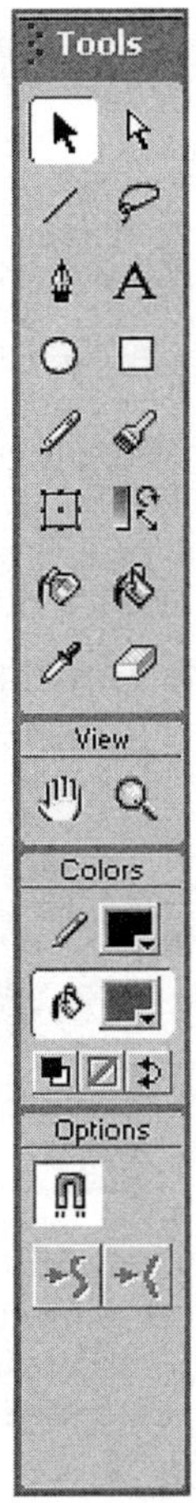

"The toolbar is, as we mentioned earlier, the artist's toolset. Each tool has a different purpose, depending on what you need to do. The tools range from drawing tools – like the Pencil tool – to text, editing, and graphics manipulation tools. Each of these is useful for making and changing content that you have created."

"How do we know which is which?" Bonnie asked.

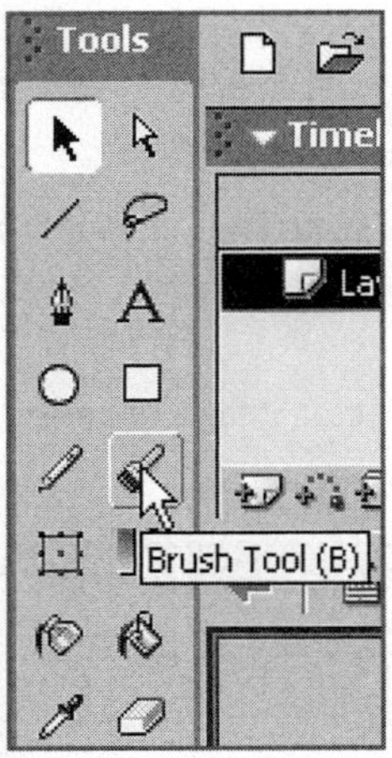

"We won't cover them in this lesson, but if you want to take a peek, hold your mouse cursor over any of them for a little while and a little textual hint will tell you."

After trying this for a little while, Bonnie said, "Oh yes, that's really useful!"

"Great, that means I won't have to write them down!" Zed said, putting down his pencil in revolt.

"Hmm, so what does the Free Transform tool do?" asked Deb, following a brief search.

"Let's leave the individual tools until the next lesson – we'll concentrate on getting a solid overview first." I said. Hoping I hadn't dampened Deb's enthusiasm, I clicked open the next image.

The Property inspector

"The next element is perhaps the most useful panel in Flash MX," I stated, pausing for dramatic effect and wishing I had a drum roll, "The Property inspector. "

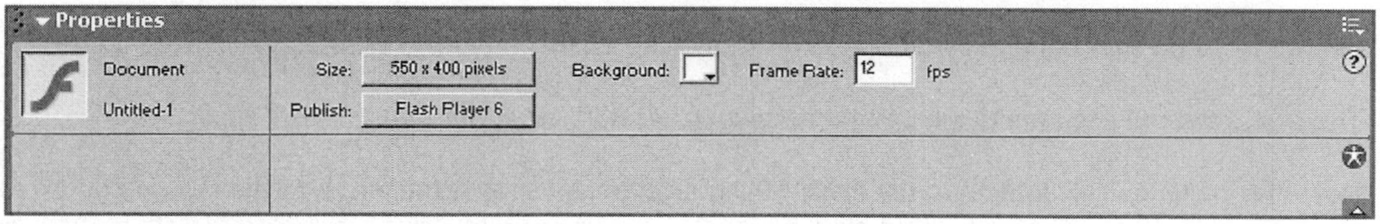

"Why is the Property inspector so special?" asked Wes.

"Simply put, the Property inspector is a central location showing information relating to the tools, objects on the stage, and anything else you can throw at it. It makes using Flash MX a lot easier because you always know you can look there for the information you need."

"What is it telling us now?" asked Zed, staring hard at the screen.

"It's showing information on the Flash movie that you have open Zed. When you come to draw or create something, it'll show you information regarding whatever object or tool you have selected – it is **context sensitive** and will change to give options for that particular item."

"Aha! It's the oracle of Flash MX!" Steve added.

"If you want to call it that, Steve, you can! The Property inspector certainly acts like a wise friend to the Flash designer!"

Various panels

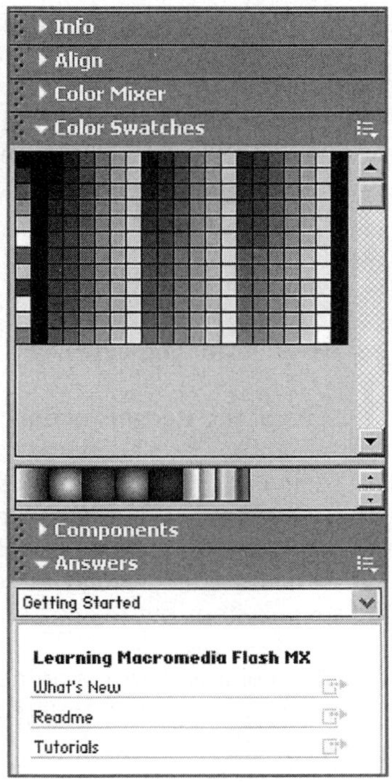

I opened up another screenshot to demonstrate the final elements of the Flash MX interface that we'd consider, "Note that there are numerous panels on the right-hand side of your Flash interface – these can provide many different services. In fact, there's a panel for almost everything you can imagine! The ones that you can currently see are just the default set, but there are many more."

"So what can the panels do?" Wes asked.

"They do anything from allowing you resize things on the stage to mixing colors."

"Why would you need to mix any more colors?" asked Bonnie, "The web-safe palette in the Color Swatches panel has all you need. If you use any other colors, it'll look different on other platforms."

"Bonnie has a point, but we shouldn't let this be a restriction on our designs. At this stage we want to keep our options open.

"The web-safe colors palette is adhered to make sure that colors used in a website are rendered the same on every possible browser and platform. Flash MX has this palette as a default, but you are not restricted to using it. You might be making content for a Macintosh CD, or for a specific web audience, and in both cases you should keep your options open."

"I still might need to test my web pages though." Bonnie responded.

"I know you'll do that Bonnie! I wouldn't expect anything else from you." I said. Bonnie smiled a little.

"The true power of the panels will be revealed when we start using the tools in next lesson.

"Now that we've quickly looked at the Flash MX application, let's resist the allure of the mouse and explore one of the dilemmas of being a world-class designer – the use of dimensions to create realistic designs and the concept of faux depth."

The class reluctantly got up from the computers and slid back into their chairs, shifting around until comfortable.

Frames and keyframes

Before I rounded off the introduction to the Flash interface I wanted the class to learn a little about a very important asset of the Flash timeline – frames.

"The timeline we just looked at is the heart of Flash – it controls motion and illustrates the passing of time. A single timeline frame represents a single segment of time, and a number of frames make a second of motion. The Flash default is 12 frames-per-second, or 12 **fps**.

"This is the same idea as film or animation. Hollywood films are shot at about 30 frames-per-second, meaning that 30 frames or images pass through the projector and onto the screen every second, providing the illusion of motion.

"Animation is very similar, but usually relies on better planning and a little cheating to make the motion look fluid and for the viewer to be convinced. If the animation is poorly executed, or the number of frames shown every second is too low, then the audience will notice."

"In film and animation it’s all about suspending the audience's disbelief," said Wes. "If the camerawork or motion is unconvincing, then the audience is aware that it's watching celluloid, and is unable to get pulled into the fantasy."

"It also helps that the audience is in a dark room," said Lisa. "And that the sound is in stereo! This allows even the most cynical viewer to give in to escapism and suspend their disbelief."

"Have any of you ever heard of Cine or Super 8 cameras?" I asked.

Most of the students nodded.

"Cine or Super 8 film runs at 8 frames-per-second. The fluidity of the motion is noticeably different, and it is a lot less convincing to the eye. The feel of Cine film has quickly become a part of filmic nostalgia, with many motion pictures like Butch Cassidy and the Sundance Kid, and Natural Born Killers using it for a particular effect. Many desktop editing applications provide a Cine film filter – a filter that simply plays at 8 fps and strips out the rest of the recorded frames.

"The point is that motion needs to be convincing and needs to fool the brain into seeing fluidity. If your motion is choppy or stuttered, then it will not only look unprofessional, but will also not convince the viewer.

"Flash allows you to work with any frame rate from 1 up to 120 fps. You'll normally find that the default of 12 is enough for most tasks and websites, but when it comes to specialized animation, you might like to hike this up."

Zed made some frantic scribbles in his pad.

With my PC still projecting onto the whiteboard, I opened a blank movie. "At the top of this empty movie, you can see the timeline."

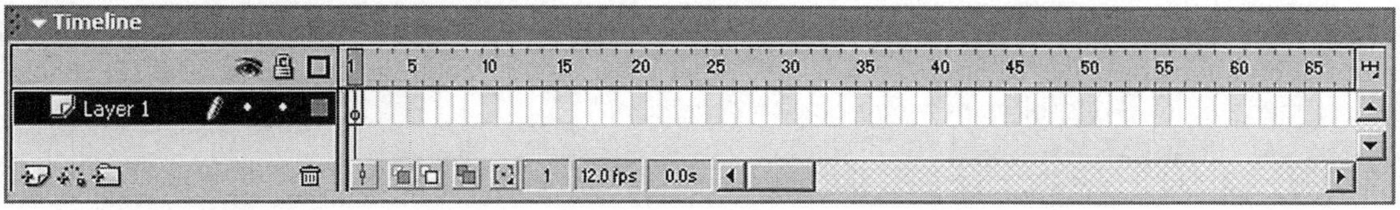

I pointed to the top of the timeline. "This part allows you to count the number of frames."

"The red box on frame 1 is the **playhead**. This shows you the current frame position in the animation. When your movie has a number of frames, you can drag the playhead along this bar, to preview or test your motion."

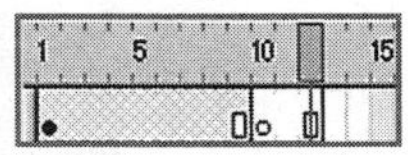

I opened a new Flash movie with some basic content. "This timeline has twelve frames, or a second's worth at the standard Flash frame rate. It's important here to distinguish between the different types of frames available. Frames in Flash come in two main flavors – **keyframes** and **frames**.

"A keyframe *with content* is displayed by a black filled circle in the timeline, as you can see in frame 1. A keyframe is where something significant happens in the Flash timeline, and normal frames are used to prolong the content of any keyframe. If you look at the timeline on the screen, the black circle on frame 1 shows that frame 1 has content, and the following frames, up to frame 9, are gray to show that they have inherited the content of that keyframe.

"An *empty* keyframe, like the one on frame 10, is displayed by an unfilled circle. It is important to know that you can only create or edit content on keyframes. When you open a fresh Flash movie, you'll notice that you are given a blank keyframe to work from. Normal frames are simply used to extend the content of keyframes, and therefore cannot be edited.

"Normal frames don't have any signifying icons, but a straight sequence of them will appear as a gray or white mass, with the end of the sequence being signified by a square, as at frames 9 and 12.

"Frames 2 to 9 are shaded gray to represent the fact that they replicate the content of the keyframe at frame 1. Frames 11 and 12 of the timeline are shown as white because the keyframe before them, at 10, is empty, so they too have no content to replicate.

"If any of you are a bit confused by what I've just said, don't worry, as we'll be covering it all again in greater detail later in the course. I just wanted to give you an awareness of these important Flash features."

Vectors and bitmaps

"Another very important feature of Flash is that it is a **vector-based** graphics application." I said. "Vector graphics are rendered from a set of mathematical instructions, storing information about lines, shapes, and colors. These instructions are then interpreted by Flash and are displayed as graphics. Other vector applications you may have heard of are Adobe Illustrator and Macromedia Freehand.

"Vectors are very different to bitmap images, such as JPGs, GIFs, and all files created in Photoshop, for example."

I went on to explain, "Bitmap images are made up of a grid with units called **pixels**. These pixels store color information and, when they're arranged on a grid, they make up the complete image that we see. Because they're made up of pixels, bitmaps are *resolution dependent*."

I opened a bitmap image file on my PC and projected it on the whiteboard.

"You can see this by looking at the inset in the photo, where I've zoomed-in on St. Paul's cathedral in this photo from a recent trip to London.

"At normal magnification, this bitmap image looks fine, but where I've zoomed in, you can see the limitations as it goes blocky.

"Vector graphics, on the other hand, are composed of points and color information that precisely describe lines and fills. They are therefore *resolution independent* because they will be rendered with the same clarity at any size through some pretty clever math."

I opened a similar image, but in vector format, and could see the class looking hard at the new image.

"Vectors are especially powerful," I continued, "Because they can be scaled to any size and the quality of the image never changes. As you saw, the bitmap image scales poorly because the individual pixels simply grow in size, but in this vector image, the magnified inset has exactly the same detail and quality as the unmagnified part.

"Vectors are also lean in file size because of how the information about each vector shape is stored. For example, a single line might be stored as six pieces of information: the x and y position of the start point, the x and y position of the end point, the color, and the thickness of the line.

"A bitmap equivalent would need sufficient information to draw a grid of pixels, and color each of them, storing lots of extra information. This means that a standard vector image will be made of far fewer instructions than a bitmap equivalent, and so will be a lot smaller in file size."

"Why use bitmaps at all then?" Zed asked, looking confused

"There are some advantages to bitmap images, though," I replied. "They should be used when photo-realistic renderings are a must, such as product photos or pictures of people, as for very complex images they look much better, and can even save file size over vector format.

"Generally speaking vector images are more suited to icons and illustrations, or technical diagrams, and bitmaps are better for photographs.

"Flash can handle both formats for images, but one of its great advantages is that anything you draw or type in Flash can zoomed in on..."

"...without losing quality!" burst Bonnie excitedly, "This will be great for accessibility on my websites, if users have poor eyesight. They'll be able to zoom in on the text without it going all blurry!"

"You've got it Bonnie," I smiled at her enthusiasm.

Dimensions in design

"Right, it's time to get away from Flash and the computer for a bit, and get back to thinking about design. We've seen the four dimensions of Flash – the three spatial dimensions and time; so now I'm going to re-introduce you to two- and three-dimensional space." I began, sensing the confusion arising in some of the students judging by their furrowed brows. "This should enable you to understand the concept of depth, and how we can render realistic images within a flat format. So, it's back to the drawing pad!"

"Wes," I continued, "You're an artist, and you work on two-dimensional surfaces, but you also build three-dimensional work, don't you?"

"I do," Wes answered. "But I can also create the illusion of three-dimensional objects and space on a two-dimensional format."

"What are you guys talking about?" Zed asked. "It sounds like a plot for a bad sci-fi movie – Dirk Dodgers' Adventures in the Tenth Dimension!!"

"Wes basically said he has the ability to portray a box that appears to be real on a flat surface." I drew a square on the paper. "OK, although this isn't a realistic box, it'll demonstrate the idea."

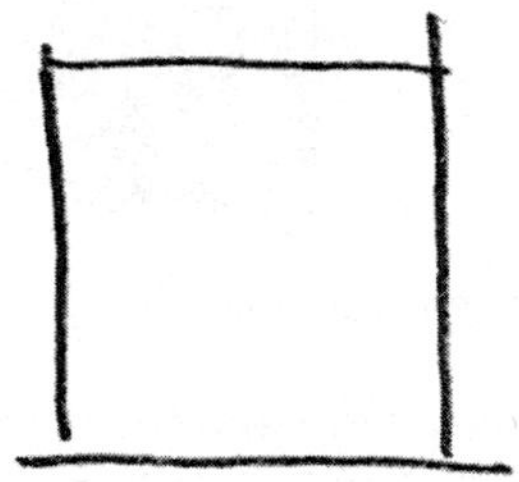

"Remember," I said, "A format is an actual product composed of various materials. This particular format is this paper drawing pad, and it happens to be **two-dimensional**, or **2-D**. Note that such 2-D formats are obviously flat, and they're also called *picture spaces* or *planes*." I looked at Bonnie. "A computer screen is another 2-D format that you use for your web designs.

"So, as you've just seen, you'll be designing your Flash MX work on a 2-D space. When Wes paints, he probably uses a canvas. This is his 2-D format, made from..."

"Layers and layers of paint from rejected paintings, mostly." Wes laughed. "I reuse my formats a lot!"

I noticed Lisa was quiet, but attentive. "Lisa, can you tell us what you think a **three-dimensional** format is?"

Lisa paused and looked around the room before she spoke. "I think a 3-D format would be something like this room," she said. "If a format is an actual product, then it's our physical environment, including everything within that environment."

"Lisa's right, everyone." I began to add lines and shading to the square on the drawing pad. "If we had a box in this room, it would be a 3-D object within a 3-D space."

I finished drawing the box. "This is a rough drawing of a three-dimensional object on a two-dimensional format."

"Add a shadow below the box," said Bonnie, "And you have a floating box!" Everyone laughed.

I added a rough shadow to emphasize Bonnie's observation, and mentioned that this technique is referred to as adding a **drop shadow.** "This is the problem many designers face," I said. "Some designers, like architects, begin plotting their 3-D designs on a 2-D format. "However," I added, "They have the luxury of eventually seeing their design created into a *real-life* 3-D object.

"You don't have this advantage," I swept my arm around to include all the students, "You'll design many three-dimensional objects that will remain framed within two-dimensional formats.

"Your problem," I added, "Is that you need to convince your viewers that these elements are 3-D within this 2-D format."

"I get it," Zed said. "We're faced with a problem, and we've defined it. Now we need to analyze how we can manage to deal with this problem. Anyone ready to brainstorm?"

"Slow down there, Zed," I said. "You'll have to be patient a bit. First, we need tools for future brainstorming sessions. You now understand the definition of design, and the formats that we'll be using in this class. What you need next are the building blocks of design."

"Is this where we learn about the elements of design?" he asked.

"Yes," I answered. "And as we do, we'll discuss this week's project."

Elements of design

I asked the students to take notes on our discussion of the elements of design, because it would be highly relevant to this week's project. Accordingly, I wanted to identify the project before I introduced the elements of design because these elements can take on complex identities. The assignment is fairly simple, and would help introduce the discussion on the depth of these tools next week. This would give students the luxury of time to observe the elements of design around them.

"Next week," I began, "I want you all to gather at least three examples of every element of design. There are eight crucial elements, and we'll discuss them in just a few minutes. I'll also explain how I want you to present the information for next week's class.

"I know all of you are familiar with the Internet," I continued. "So for this assignment, I want examples from any medium *except* the Internet."

"Oh, man," Zed complained. "This means I'll have to buy magazines and newspapers, doesn't it?"

I didn't want budgets to be blown on these projects. "No, Zed, not necessarily. I want you to look around you, and find everyday examples that will represent these elements."

"Can they be three-dimensional objects, or do they need to be flat?" Steve asked.

"Flat?" Wes turned and stared at Steve, "You mean two-dimensional, don't you?"

Steve laughed. "I'm not a full-fledged Flash designer yet, Wes."

"Practice, practice, practice," Wes intoned. "Say the words, and you will become the words."

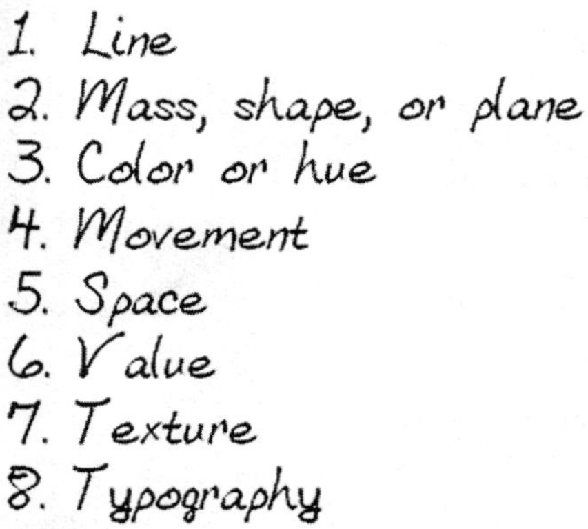

"That's a little deep for me, Wes," Deb said. She turned to me and asked, "So we can use any objects – photographs, packaging, and... maybe even things like leaves if we don't have access to anything else, right?

"That's the creative spirit, Deb," I said. "Yes, you can use anything to portray each of these elements, but the objects will need to fit on the format of a drawing pad like this." I pointed to the pad on the easel. "Let's talk about the elements, so you'll have a better idea of what you might choose to portray them."

Turning to the whiteboard, I began to list the elements of design. After noting down each element, the plan was to cover the basic description of each one individually.

Line

"The first element of design is **line**," I said as I turned to face the class. I looked at Deb. "You may know this already, Deb. In geometry, a line is a point in motion, with only one dimension – length."

Deb nodded and I continued, "In design, however, this isn't a practical concept. If a line only contained the dimension of length, would we be able to see it?"

"No sirree!" Wes answered with mock urgency. "When we draw lines, they automatically contain **length** and **width**. Even the thinnest line contains a tiny amount of width. Otherwise," he added, "We wouldn't be able to see the line at all."

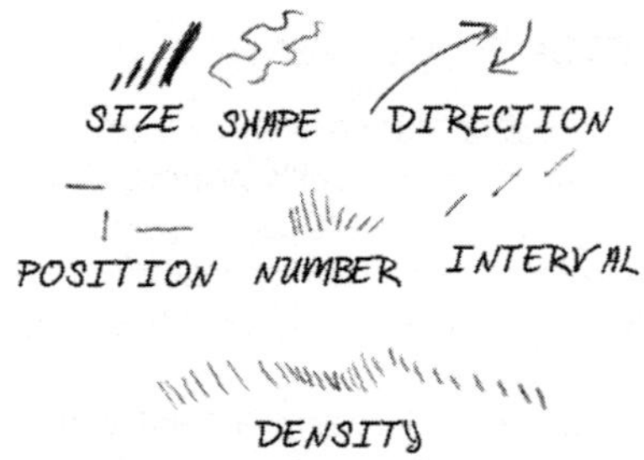

"Wes is right," I said. "In addition, line has both a position and a direction in space. The attributes of a line, or variables if you prefer," I added, with a quick glance at Deb, "Are the **size**, **shape**, **direction**, **position**, **number**, **interval**, and **density**." I drew a number of lines on the drawing pad with their descriptions.

"In case you're wondering how lines are created, many artists and designers understand they're made by creating a series of dots, or points." I drew a series of dots in a wavy line. "In fact, this is especially true with digital artwork, where the image is made up from a large number of picture elements, or **pixels**. For example, a number of similar points can create a dotted line with the same attributes of position and direction as we've just mentioned."

Mass, shape, or plane

"Now, if a point becomes large enough, it's not part of a line anymore," I explained. "It becomes a **mass**, otherwise known as a **shape** or **plane**."

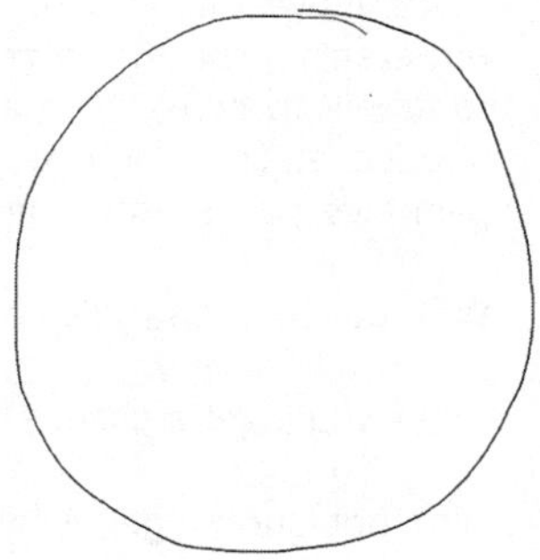

I drew a large circle. "Here's a basic shape – a circle." I said. Next I drew a square. "And here's a simple square created with four lines," I added. "Remember, a shape that's two-dimensional contains height and width. A shape that's three-dimensional contains height, width, and depth, right?"

"Just like that box you drew earlier," Zed answered.

I flicked back through the flip pad to the box again, to enforce the difference between the two- and three-dimensional shapes. "This mass is composed of planes, built up from lines, that give the illusion of volume."

"Shapes can also be created with **color**, **value**, **texture**, and other elements," I explained.

"OK," Bonnie said. "I get that one. But with a simple HTML website design, I can create colored boxes without borders in tables. So, I'm creating a two-dimensional shape *without* lines."

"That's a good point," I said. "Wes, do you ever create shapes without lines?"

Wes answered immediately, "Oh, sure. I create a lot of shapes without lines. Having obvious lines in a painting, for instance, would make the images appear too flat."

Zed looked like he was in serious thought. "Zed," I asked, "Do you have a question?"

"Not really," he answered. "I was just thinking about how lines are used to show different things in anime. They're mainly used to outline the characters, but can also be used to show action scenes."

"Great observation, Zed. We'll discuss how we can use lines to suggest motion in just a minute," I said. "Zed, be sure to bring some anime with you for the next class, OK? That way we can see exactly what you're talking about."

Color or hue

"Let's move on," I said. "The next element is **color**, often known more specifically as **hue**. This word represents a specific color or wavelength of light found in the color spectrum, ranging from red, to yellow, to green, to blue. There are two special focuses in color, one being *additive*, which is found in lighting," I nodded at Lisa, "and in television and computer screens. The other area is *subtractive* color, found in paintings, prints, and other tangible objects colored with pigments or paints."

Wes looked at Lisa. "I've always wanted to experiment with additive color in my work," he said.

"Now you'll get a chance," Lisa replied. "This is the kind of color we work with on the computer."

"I'm not sure I get what you mean by *additive* and *subtractive* color?" Bonnie seemed puzzled and embarrassed. "I feel left out, and I make a living working with computer colors."

"We'll get more into color theory over the next few weeks," I answered. "In the meantime, just remember that **additive color** means that we can mix up various colors to create brand new hues."

I continued, "The term **subtractive color** is appropriate because an object will subtract every color except the color that you see." I pointed at a plant on the window ledge. "Those leaves appear green to you all, don't they?"

Everyone nodded in agreement. "In fact, the leaves are conceptually every color except green," I stated. "When light hits a leaf, every color is absorbed, except the green light which bounces off, and so this is what your eyes comprehend the color to be."

Deb interrupted, sarcastically, "This getting a little too metaphysical!"

"Woah duuude, I think you've blown my mind!!" Zed drawled, mimicking the hippy stereotype.

"Can't you combine additive and subtractive colors for different effects?" Wes asked, not letting the others affect his obvious genuine interest.

"Yes," I replied. "As I mentioned, all color emanates from light sources. If you paint with a fluorescent bulb as your only light source, your painting will appear very different in daylight than if you paint using white light as your source of illumination.

"You can also use light sources to make things appear to be different colors."

"You can play lots of visual tricks with light." We all turned to look as Lisa spoke up, and her face took on a pink hue, "And I promise to share those with you when it's appropriate."

"Lisa, I'm sure you'll probably teach me a thing or two," I responded. "Stage lighting is a wonderful way to understand the properties of additive color, and an art form in itself."

"Maybe I can get us into the theater to show you how it works," she replied.

"Great!" everyone seemed excited about this prospect.

"Consider it a field trip, then," I said, "If it's no problem to arrange."

Movement

I pointed to the next word on the board. "**Movement** portrays the act or process of an object that appears to change place or direction, orientation, and position on a plane." I explained.

"Like animation?" Zed asked.

"At the moment, no." I answered. "This list is basic. We'll talk about the animation of objects later. For now, the kind of movement that we're talking about is the visual tricks you see to portray the *illusion* of movement. These are shown through starting and stopping points, blurring of an image, or a repetition of an element that makes this object appear to be moving across a page."

I drew a baseball on the whiteboard, with lines showing the direction of the ball's movement.

"Oh!" Zed replied. "I know what you mean now. It's like those lines in the anime I mentioned before. The lines that show action."

"You catch on fast, Zed." Wes was seated close enough to pat him on the back. Zed grinned. "This is going to be a piece of cake for you," Wes added.

"The use of line, color, texture, and space can all add to the illusion of motion," I said. "Movement in a two-dimensional format is difficult to find at first. However, if you felt you just saw an object go from one place to another in the format, shake your head and look closely to see how this illusion was created."

Space

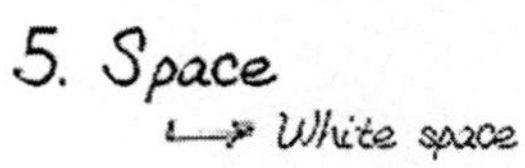

"The next element," Again I pointed towards the word on the whiteboard, "Is **space**. This is a two- or three-dimensional element defined by the structure of the other elements of design." I wrote another word on the board under the word space. "**White space** is a term used to define space that contains nothing but space, possibly color, and certainly value."

"Trippy!" Zed said. "There's a value placed on nothingness."

Steve and Wes laughed. "You have a great way of incorporating information," Steve said. "You said at the beginning of class that you're going to learn a lot from us. I think I'm going to learn from you!" Zed grinned and sat straighter.

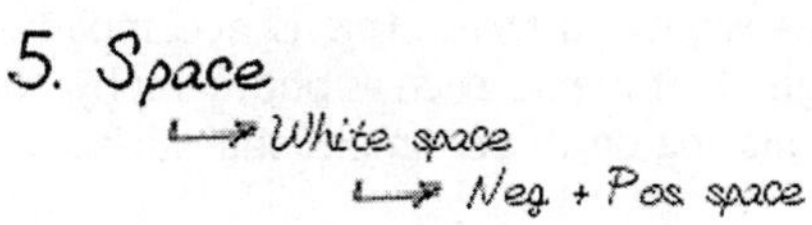

"You're right, Zed," I said. "This *value on nothingness* is the importance placed on positive and negative space, which I'll explain in a moment. In this case, white space is the space surrounding an object or a block of type."

I wrote more words on the whiteboard as they talked. I turned and said, "Zed, you'll have more fun with these two terms. **Negative space** and **positive space** are defined by the placement of elements, and the importance placed on each element with line, texture, color, value, and shape. If the object is noticeable, it's positive. The background that supports the positive image is the negative space."

Zed scratched his head. "I'm not sure if I have anything positive or negative to add right now," he said. "I just want to know about this value thing. Is it something like the worth of an object?"

Value

Highlighting the word *Value* on the board, I looked at Wes and asked, "Can you tell us about value, Wes?"

Wes replied, "That's a piece of cake. **Value** is just another word for the lightness or darkness of an area. It's brightness measured in relationship to a graded scale from light to dark. Of course," he added as he glanced at Lisa, "It has a lot to do with light."

I pulled a visual aid out from under the desk and placed it on the easel. The board showed a value scale that went from white to black. "Wes is right," I said. I pointed to the board. "You can see how this value scale works. This is a value scale for white and black, also known as the **gray scale**."

Bonnie seemed to understand this concept. "Oh! Now I feel I'm on more solid ground," she said. She confirmed her understanding, "That's similar to the value scale of grays in the hexadecimal color coding system. Only," she added, "The web-safe gray scale isn't as varied as this one."

"Well, Bonnie," I said. "You've got it! Why don't you draw a gray scale for web-safe colors next week as part of this project?"

Bonnie gasped. "Uh, I'll try. I've never done anything like that before."

Lisa looked at her and stated, "I would suggest using a ruler."

Everyone laughed, including Bonnie. "OK," she said. "I'll give it a try."

"We can draw our examples?" This came from Wes.

"Sure, Wes," I said. "But, only one of each element. Remember, I want three different examples of each element."

"Let's move on to texture," I said, as I wrote the word on the whiteboard.

Texture

"**Texture** is used in two-dimensional design to replicate three-dimensional surfaces. This is accomplished through various drawing techniques. Texture can also be shown through other media, such as photography. This tool can show you the visual texture of an object as light is captured playing on three-dimensional surfaces."

"I love texture," Wes said. "That's why I love the concept of drawing thumbnails and roughs. Paper has a wonderful texture. So has canvas. Come to think of it," Wes spread his arms, "Everything is worth touching, because it all feels so great!"

Deb rolled her eyes. "Wes, you're too much."

"Actually, Wes just described how we discover texture in three-dimensional objects," I said. "We touch the object to learn the texture. With two-dimensional objects, all we can do is imagine the rendered texture, based on our memory."

"That's another reason why I like to touch things," Wes laughed. "I want to have lots of memories."

"OK Wes," Steve choked. "I'm even having a hard time with that one."

Typography

I laughed. "I think it's time for this class to end," I said. "But we have one more element to take home with us." I motioned to the word *Typography* on the whiteboard. " **Typography**," I said, "Is an element that is made of line, shape, color, value, space, texture, and movement. It contains every element of design, and it is an element of design itself."

"I didn't realize *type* would be considered an element of design," Bonnie said. "I thought it was...well, just type."

Steve responded, "Bonnie, when you place type in your web designs, doesn't it add something to the page?"

"Sure," Bonnie said, "It adds content."

"No, that's not what I mean," Steve said.

Zed said, "It adds value, for sure." A few chuckles interrupted him, but Zed held his arms out for silence. "I'm getting this," he whispered. "Type adds value to a space in a format. It's a positive shape against the negative shape of the background.

"Plus," he added, "It adds color, if it's anything other than transparent. Even if it's transparent, it would show the color behind it...that would incorporate line, too, and it also adds movement, if the type is slanted..."

"*Italic*," Bonnie said. "Italic type is slanted."

Bonnie seemed to break Zed's spell with the element of typography. "I think you see how important this element is in design," I grinned. "I'm looking forward to seeing the examples you'll find over the next week, Zed."

"Yeah, I think I'm really into it now," Zed confirmed with a glazed look in his eyes.

"Let's go over the elements of design again," I said, once more gesturing to the list of elements on the whiteboard, and then turning back to the class:

1. Line
2. Mass, shape, or plane
3. Color or hue
4. Movement
5. Space → White space
6. Value → Neg. + Pos space
7. Texture
8. Typography

"These are your elements of design," I repeated the list out loud. "Remember, I want three examples of each one, so you should each have twenty-four examples to bring with you to class next week."

"You were going to tell us about the format," Wes reminded me.

"Yes," I said. "We'll get to that now."

Deb interrupted me. "I did learn one thing today."

"What's that?" I asked.

"I didn't realize math would be involved in design. That's great."

"Then you'll be happy to know you'll have more math to look forward to," I said.

Some of the students moaned.

"I won't overtax you today," I promised. "It's about time to talk about what you'll need to complete this week's project."

The basic tools for graphic design

"So, what tools do we need to bring to class next week?" Wes asked. "Are all the materials included, or are we all playing art students?"

Bonnie looked puzzled again, "What does Wes mean?" she asked, looking around the room.

Steve answered, "Wes means that most art students have to pay for their art supplies. It's not included in tuition. On the other hand," he added, "When a student studies software design, they usually get the book and software included in the cost of their class."

"Oh," Bonnie said softly. "Will this cost much?"

"They're all inexpensive tools." I assured her. "Wes, maybe you can guess what we'll need?"

Wes nodded, "Sure! I'm positive you want us to have pencils, and not just regular school pencils with the eraser on the end." He looked at the other students. "I use different brands, but there are four grades of graphite that I use most often."

"That's a great start, Wes. Which grades do you use?"

"I use an H for clean, light lines, and an HB for lines that are a bit darker and softer. This is what's known as a **medium grade**. For sketching, I use B and 2B for darker, softer lines. But," Wes added, "There are many other grades to choose from. I just find these four provide enough variety for me in what you referred to as the thumbnail stage."

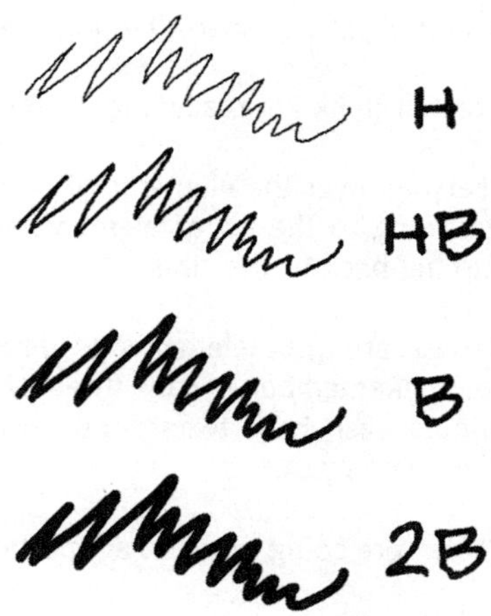

"Wes has a handle on your first items to purchase," I said. "The pencils are important to convey your thoughts. They will become an extension of your ideas, and you'll put those ideas in words or in sketches on a newsprint pad."

"I suppose you want Lisa to bring the rulers?" Zed asked, smiling at Lisa.

"Lisa, do you think we need rulers?" I asked.

"Sure, and I'll bet they aren't plastic rulers, are they?"

"No," I replied. "If you're going to buy something, buy a product that will last a while. A metal ruler with cork backing will be best."

"I'll bet Wes sharpens his pencils with a pocket knife like a real artist, don't you Wes?" Deb smirked.

Wes laughed, "I think a plain old pencil sharpener will do."

Deb stated, "I don't see any reason for all this extra work in a software class. You said we're learning to design with Flash MX, not with pencils and paper."

Steve spoke up, "Deb, you already know where we're going with this. Computing uses one side of the brain, and drawing uses another side of the brain. Sometimes creative ideas happen when we use a different method to convey our thoughts."

"Steve's hit the nail on the head." Wes looked at Deb. "Deb, give this a chance. I'm just as scared of learning to design with software as you are of learning to design at all."

Deb shrugged her shoulders; "Well you all talked me out of my watch. I guess you can talk me into using a pencil instead of a keyboard."

I handed them a list detailing all the tools they'd need for the next class, with quick sketches depicting each tool, just to get into the spirit of things:

Tools of the Trade

- One or two **pencils** of each of the following grades: **H**, **HB**, **B**, and **2B**: each pencil will give you a different *feel* and *use* in the design process. Also, a **pencil sharpener** will obviously be useful.

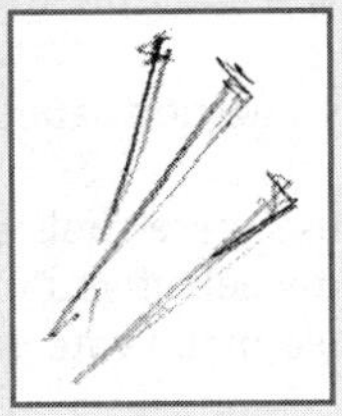

- **Kneaded eraser** – much easier on paper than a regular hard eraser as it is soft and pliable.

- **Newsprint tablet**, no smaller than 11" x 17" – white, recycled, acid-free paper is ideal, but newsprint is less expensive, and fine for beginning projects. As your skills progress and evolve, you may want to upgrade the paper quality. One hint: never use newsprint to present an idea to a client – this gives a poor first impression.

- **Rubber cement**, a glue stick, or spray-on adhesive - don't use a water-based glue, as it will warp paper. If you like the ease of rubber cement, you can go one step further and buy some rubber cement remover. This will help remove the extra cement from your projects, and will give you something to play with as you sit and think through the creative process. Glue sticks are a little messier, but with experience you can become quite skillful.

Tools of the Trade cont.

- A **sharp knife or scalpel** with extra blades for fast and easy cutting of paper and other items. There's a proper way to use this tool, and that's by cutting away from your body, at an angle. You also need to remove your fingers from its path, or it will remove them for you!

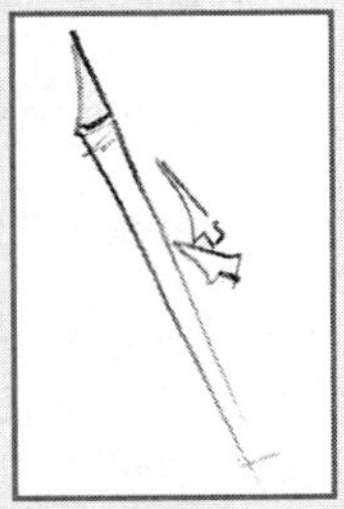

- A pair of **scissors**.

- 24" **metal ruler** with cork backing – the cork helps to prevent the ruler from sliding around. The metal is stronger than plastic, and will also keep the scalpel from cutting your ruler in half. Don't soak your ruler in water to clean it, as the cork will come away from the metal.

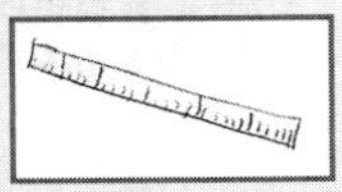

After studying the list, Wes said, "But this isn't everything we need for the whole course, is it?"

"No, Wes, but it's all we need for the moment," I replied. Everyone seemed immersed in the list, so I took the opportunity to ask if there were any questions.

"I don't know what some of this stuff is," Bonnie complained. "How do I know I'm getting the right thing?"

"If you take the list to an art supply store," Wes answered, "The employees will know exactly what you need. They'll get the right things for you." He kept looking at the list.

"Do you have everything on this list?" Steve asked Wes. "I think I have everything at the studio."

"Actually, no, I don't," Wes replied. "These are the essential tools of a designer, rather than an artist or sculptor."

"That's true to a certain extent Wes, but remember that every designer has different tools," I explained. "These are the tools of a graphic designer. A Flash designer is a graphic designer who specializes with Flash and a web browser as their format."

Zed said. "I'm eager to get to the brainstorming phase, so I'll get my tools."

"I'm keen to see all your ideas, Zed." I asked again, "Any questions about the assignment or the materials?"

When no one spoke, I said, "If you don't know how to use these tools effectively, just do the best you can. I'll answer any doubts and questions about their use next week, if you have problems. We'll also learn some basic drawing skills over the next few weeks so you can communicate your ideas to your satisfaction."

"This isn't like learning to walk," Bonnie said, insightfully. "It's more like learning to talk in a new language."

Wes turned to Bonnie. "I'm sure we'll all help each other learn this new language, Bonnie."

Zed nodded, "I've always wanted to be multi-linguini." And everyone laughed.

"Now, how to present your project," I continued. "Use one page of your drawing tablet for each element of design." I turned to the whiteboard, erased all the notes, and then drew a rectangle on the board. "This is how I want you to lay your page out," I said.

"You'll have eight pages, and each one will look like this." I drew a line down the side of the page. "This line is three inches from the edge of the page," I said. "This is a visible line that you should draw with your pencil and ruler."

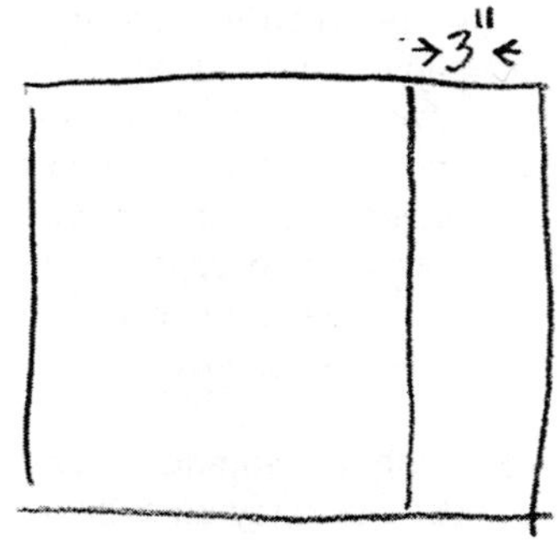

"Which grade pencil do you want us to use?" Wes asked.

"Use any grade you like for this project," I answered. "In fact, I'd prefer you used different grades to get used to the way they feel."

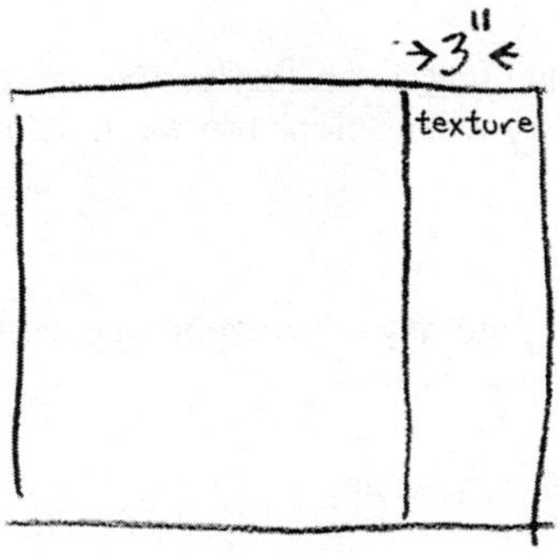

I wrote *texture* at the top of the three-inch margin. "You'll then need to name the page with the element you're going to portray on that page."

I drew some shapes on the page. "Then you can use your glue stick or rubber cement to attach the objects you find for each element on that page. Remember, don't use a water-based glue, or your pages will warp."

"Do you want the elements in any particular order?" Deb asked.

"No," I answered. "That's entirely up to you."

"I want to see how Lisa's going to paste additive light on her color page," Wes said. "And I'm curious as to how I'm going to attach tree bark to my texture page."

Lisa actually laughed. "Tree bark is a great idea, Wes."

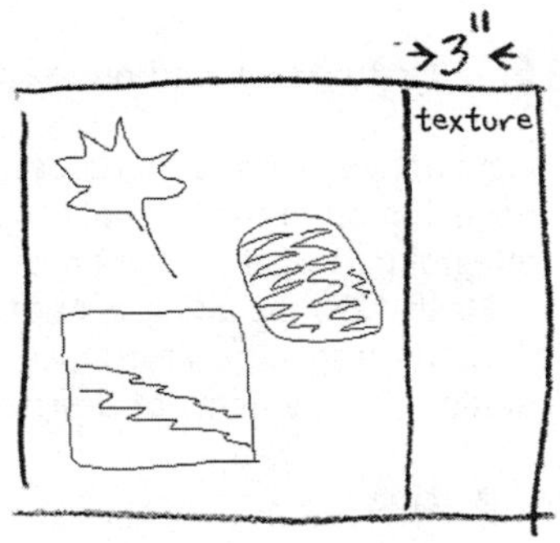

"If you can't paste or attach your item to the page," I suggested, "You can use the right-hand column to talk about the other items you find, or to make notes about how you feel about the items you have on the page." I drew some lines to indicate text.

"This is almost like a journal, isn't it?" Bonnie asked.

"It is," I confirmed. "It's a journal for designers.

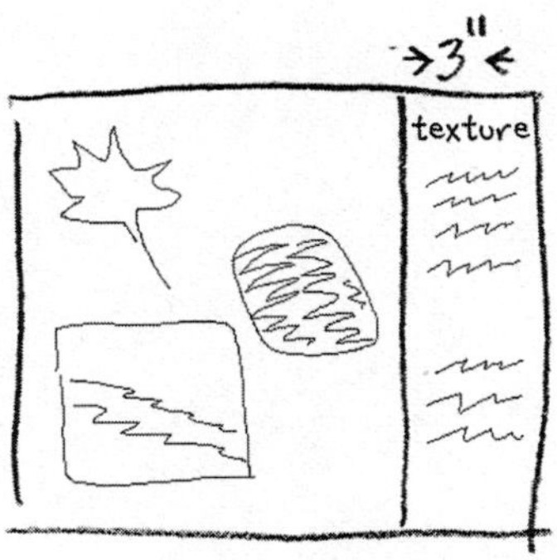

"We'll discuss this project next week at the beginning of class," I stated. "Bring in all your tools, projects, books, and notepads with you. We'll go into the elements of design in more detail, and then we'll introduce these elements to Flash MX."

I sent the class on their separate ways with my email address in case they ran into insurmountable obstacles. I was really looking forward to seeing what this group discovers for their projects next week. With such a diverse mix of characters and talent I was sure that there'd be some very creative ideas.

"Hey, great class, teach!" Zed waved as he left. As I waved back, I noticed Deb's arm as she walked out the door. She hadn't bothered to put her watch back on...

Summary

We've covered a lot of ground in this first lesson of the course. First of all, using an analogy to the rigorous procedure of scientific research, we outlined the various stages of the creative problem-solving process as follows:

1. **Define** - identifying the design problem and selecting a format.
2. **Analyze** - research into potential visual solutions, including research into any information needed for the site.
3. **Ideate** - the brainstorming process that generates as many solutions as possible.
4. **Select** - choosing one or more optimum design solutions.
5. **Implement** - apply and finalize the selected design in the chosen format.
6. **Evaluate** - based on reactions and feedback to the finished and published design.

Next up, we learned that a designer is a planner, and the developed design is a plan. Then we explained the need for different **formats** in design, and then learned about producing **thumbnails** and **roughs** as an integral part of the ideation of our designs. Then, after an introduction to the chosen format of this course – **Flash MX**, including a brief discussion of its major elements: the stage, the timeline, the toolbar, the Property inspector, keyframes, and its use of vectors – we turned our attention to the building blocks of design. The elements of design are summarized as follows:

- **Line**
- **Shape**
- **Color**
- **Movement**
- **Space**
- **Value**
- **Texture**
- **Typography**

In the next lesson we're going to study visual tools in design and how to utilize the fundamental elements of design.

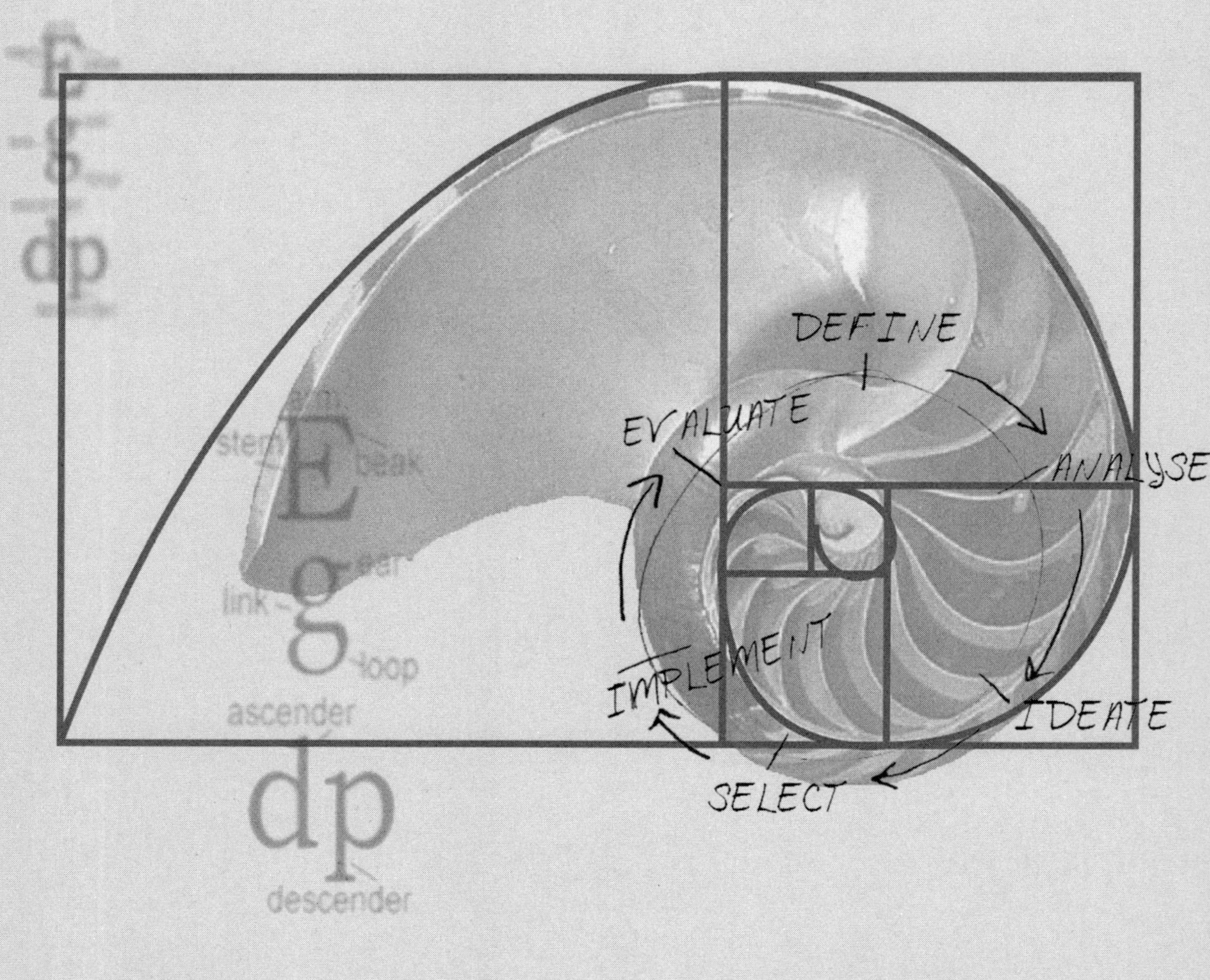
DEFINE
ANALYSE
IDEATE
SELECT
IMPLEMENT
EVALUATE
stem
beak
ear
link
loop
ascender
descender

Chapter 2

Dissecting the Elements of Design

Objectives

In today's class you will learn about:

- Basic design elements:
    - Lines and shapes in design
    - How the elements communicate an idea and create mood, shape, and organization
- Value systems:
    - Color basics
    - The emotional value of texture
    - Hidden meanings of typography

Introduction

The sound of my footsteps seemed to emphasize the room's emptiness as I arranged my tools for class, but remembering last week's session forced a smile to my lips. Fortunately, this group of design students created a real dynamic energy with their diversity of skills and experiences. As I studied the space around me, I thought, "This blank format needs their varied personalities to brighten it up!"

Within minutes, my wish was answered. Zed bounced into the room with his drawing pad and half-closed backpack – the end of a metal ruler waved from the top of his pack.

"Morning, teach!" Zed said. I had little time to respond. Steve, Wes, Bonnie, Deb, and Lisa arrived on the echo of his greeting.

Salutations out of the way, we all settled at the table. Before we began to expand upon the elements of design that I'd introduced in the previous class – more specifically, studying examples of their uses – I reviewed what we'd covered in last week's lesson. "If you remember," I began, "last week we discussed the definition of design and the role of the designer."

> *"In simple terms, a design is a plan, and a designer is therefore a planner. The plan is conveyed through visual communications, and the planner – the designer – needs to accomplish this feat with the tools we'll learn over the next few classes."*

"We also discussed the creative problem-solving process, and the issues associated with whatever format we may use, two- and three-dimensional space. Here, we introduced our chosen format for this course – Macromedia Flash MX – and we highlighted its essential elements. Finally, we covered the basic definitions of the elements of design."

Deb added, "You also convinced me that design is important! I realized design is part of everything we do in life. All of us design something every day, even if it's just what we eat for dinner".

Wes clapped his hands together and laughed, "Trust me, Linda," he said. "I didn't coach her on that remark!"

"Brilliant, Deb," I responded. "I'm happy you've been convinced." I looked around at the rest of the class. "Did anyone have problems finding three examples of each element of design for this week's project?"

Wes answered, "The newsprint didn't hold up very well for me, so I used different paper. I hope that's alright."

I nodded, "Wes, that's fine. Whatever works best for you."

"You probably tried to glue a whole tree into that drawing pad of yours," Steve laughed. "I'm not surprised newsprint didn't work!"

Bonnie wasn't smiling. "I tried to draw some of my elements, but I wasn't very successful."

"You made the effort, Bonnie, and that's important," I replied. "We'll learn some drawing techniques as we brainstorm the client's project in a few weeks."

"Yes!" Wes rubbed his hands together in anticipation. "I smell brainstorming just around the corner."

"I think we have to meet the client first, don't we?" Deb asked.

"You will meet the client in a couple of classes time," I answered. "So we're a few weeks away from the brainstorming process."

"If we were all in Steve's shoes," I explained, "With many years of experience in the tools of design, you would have met your client last week.

"Instead," I added, "We need to analyze the elements of design to understand why we use them in visual solutions to our client's problem. Between this class and next week's class, you'll utilize the various drawing tools and color options in Flash to create several practice projects."

I looked around at the piles of books, bags, and drawing pads on the table. "It seems you all brought your design tools with you," I said.

"Were we supposed to carry our tools in something special?" Zed seemed worried.

"No," I answered. "As you can see, everyone has their own creative ideas for carrying their design tools. I waved my arm around at the variety. There were backpacks, fishing tackle boxes, and even a paper bag. "You need to take care of your tools if you want them to last a long time," I said, as I looked at Wes.

Wes dumped everything from his paper bag onto the table. The rubber cement jar rolled towards Steve, and he caught it before it fell to the floor. "I know," Wes shrugged, "You've just seen the worst side of me. I'm terrible with organization."

Steve laughed. "Wes, I'll bet you have half-filled paint tubes and dried-up brushes all over your studio."

Wes agreed. "I need to take care of my materials. They're expensive to replace."

"Did anyone have trouble finding these tools?" I asked the class.

Zed answered, "Not at all! In fact, I found a bunch of really cool stuff! I wish I had another birthday this month, because I'd ask for half the supplies in that store."

Bonnie agreed. "I thought I would have a hard time finding the supplies, but I had no trouble at all. The only problem I had was my own skill at drawing."

Steve nodded. "I remember the first time I used design tools. No one showed me what to do, but I found my instincts carried me through half the time."

"What did you do the other half of the time?" Bonnie asked.

"I asked for help." Steve grinned. "I found that most folks like to share what they know. All I did was give them their chance to take center stage."

"Speaking of stages," I said, grateful for the obvious link, "I think it's time for me to open the curtain on this week's performance."

Basic elements of design

I wiped down the whiteboard, ready for this lesson's demonstrations, "Today, we'll study some of the basic design elements, and how their everyday use can relate to design. We'll cover points, lines, and planes first, which will lead nicely to a discussion of shapes. When we get to value and color, we'll move over to the computers, so you can see how these elements will be utilized in Flash."

Points, lines, and planes

We began with the element of line, its origin as a point in space, and the function of line in the formation of a plane. I reminded the students of the origin of lines in design and their importance. "The line is the most significant element since nothing can be formed on or within a two- or three-dimensional format without its actual or suggested use. If you remember our definition of the line element from last week, you'll know that lines begin with a point in space."

I drew a dot on the whiteboard with my marker pen. "Deb," I asked, "Would you tell us more about the geometry of points, lines, and planes?"

•

Deb answered straight away, "A point has no dimension. The only attribute of a point is to define a location or position in space."

"A line is a point in motion within space, with the dimension of length." I drew a line to show the progression of her thoughts. "Practically speaking, lines also have thickness."

"A plane," she explained, "Is a flat surface created by lines. This flat surface has height and width, but no depth."

"I remember this problem from last week," Zed said. "If you put planes together, you can form the illusion of three-dimensional mass with the appearance of volume."

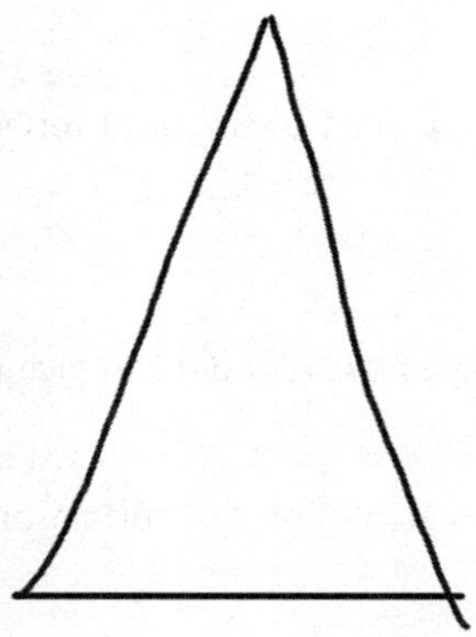

"Right," I said. I finished the drawing of the triangular plane. "We've just defined, analyzed, and selected the solution to our problem. We had to take these geometrical concepts of point, line, and plane, and represent them visually."

"And simply by drawing the triangle on the board, you're visually representing a number of elements." Wes added.

"Correct, Wes." I said. "Deb explained an abstract theoretical concept, and I've displayed the visual representation of these concepts for clarification."

"This is how architects design buildings," I continued. "They visualize a point in space where they will construct their building. This building will have width, height, and depth. The space is confined to a plot of land, which is effectively their format.

"As they visualize this building, they can see the view from the bedroom window, the fireplace in the living room, and the table and chairs in the kitchen. Somehow, the architect needs to communicate to others how the building appears to them.

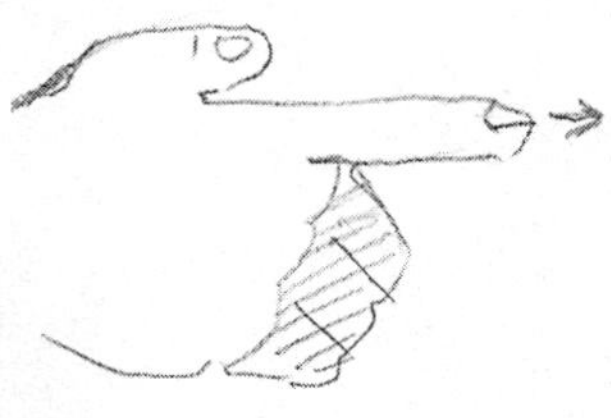

"The architect can stand on this format of land and point to the window, or point to the door that opens to the patio. As he does this, the viewer will follow his finger, and try to imagine the scene. I drew a hand pointing off into space with an arrow to indicate the direction of the line of sight.

"The architect is using a **psychic line**, as the viewer follows the direction of his finger," I said. "This form of line is very powerful, but it's sometimes too subtle for the viewer to follow."

Zed laughed, "So sometimes you need a crystal ball to visualize the image!"

"Maybe, Zed..." I answered, "But the best way for the architect to explain his vision of how this building will look is to draw an image – a representation of his ideas. He'll start with a point, and begin indicating the layout of the house." I drew lines to show a foundation. "These are **actual lines**. They can't be mistaken for anything else. However," I added, "This line *represents* more than just a line; it now represents the actual wall for this house."

I drew some more lines. "As the architect draws more lines, he begins to form planes, which in turn represent walls that create the space within the house."

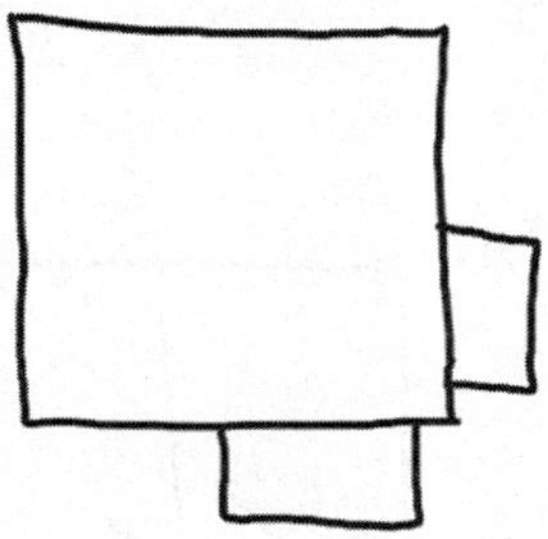

I added some dotted lines to indicate a room off to the side of the house. "These lines are called **implied lines**. They indicate a room that the architect might want to add, if the budget and space allows for it.

"In fact," I added, "The architect often doesn't know if his ideas will work until he puts his concept on paper. The creation of these images helps the designer decide what can be used and what will be discarded in the actual building of the house."

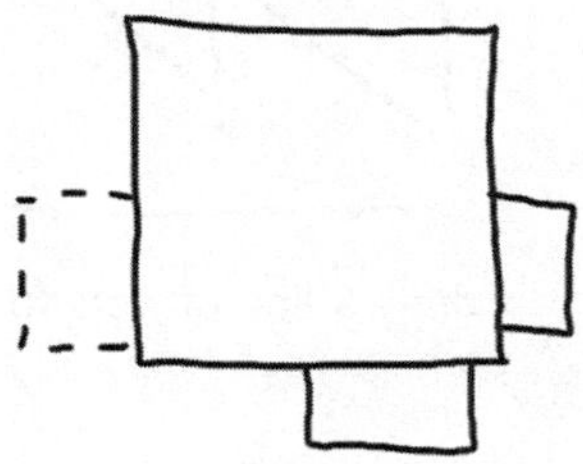

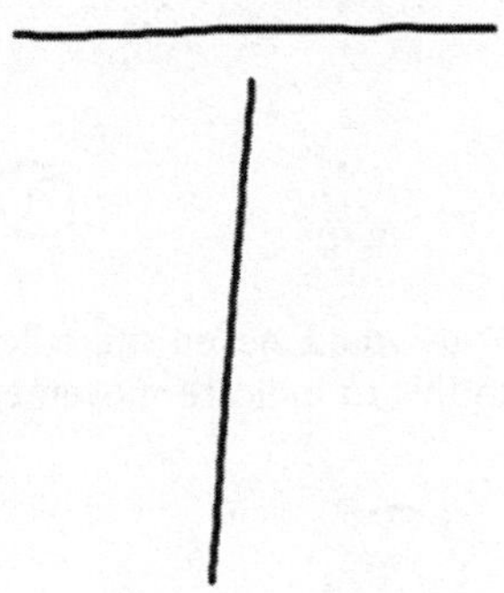

On a fresh part of the whiteboard, I drew two new lines. One was horizontal, and one was vertical. "Line also has **direction**," I said. "Historically, western culture has interpreted horizontal lines in art and design as implying peace and quiet, similar to a body lying at rest.

"Along the same reasoning, the vertical line implies power and strength," I added. "Similar to the structure of a house."

I drew more vertical lines in a row. "Vertical and horizontal lines add structure and boundaries to the space within a format. If you notice," I said, "The vertical and horizontal lines imitate the edges of the format. These lines will stabilize and reduce any feeling of movement within the lines."

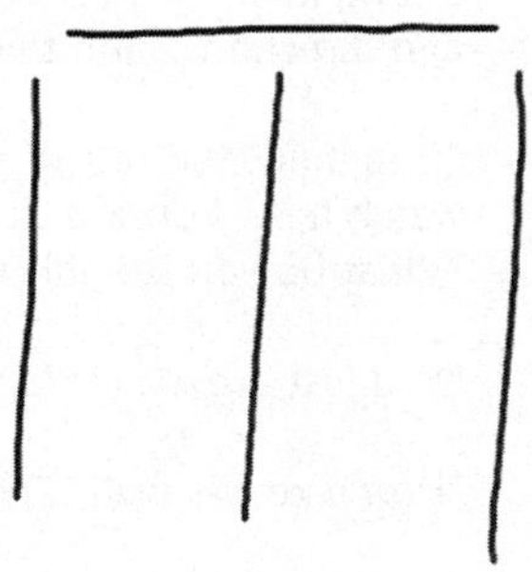

"Just like the structure and walls within a house restrict the movement of the people inside," Zed responded. "Or just like a cartoon panel restricts the movements of the characters in that panel."

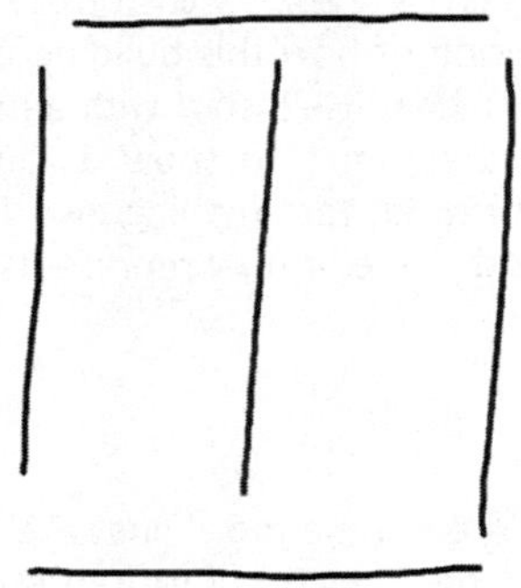

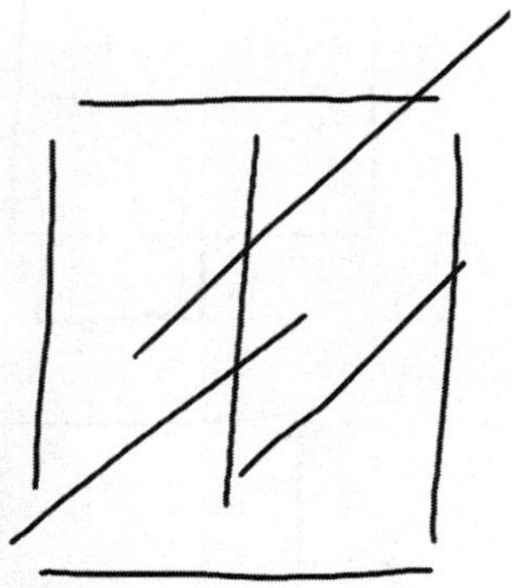

"How do lines indicate movement, then?" Bonnie asked. "I can follow the lines you drew up and down and around the format, but there's no real action that I can see."

I drew some lines at an angle. "That's a good question, Bonnie. Lines drawn at an angle represent movement more than any other line. When a runner is sprinting down a track," I added, "his body isn't straight up and down, and it isn't flying horizontally through space like a bullet. The runner's body is actually slanted toward his goal of the finish line."

Bonnie spoke up, "I don't get the part about points forming lines. Are you saying that all lines are formed from little dots?"

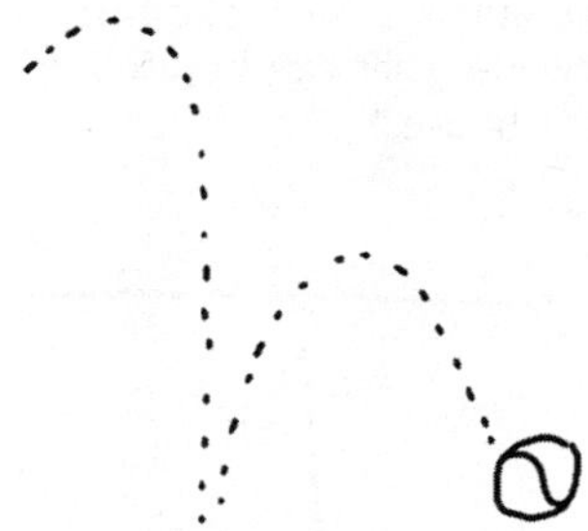

I drew a line of dots following the drawing of a bouncing ball. "Bonnie, perhaps I can help you simplify this concept. Do you see a line here?"

"Well, yes," Bonnie replied. "It's a line formed with dots."

"Our minds are tuned to see complete images." I said. "Bonnie, you see a line formed from the dots, because your mind has closed the distances between these points to form a line for you."

"But, the line isn't real," Bonnie insisted.

"This is an implied line indicating movement and direction," I explained. "You would never see a line following a ball like this in real life. However, an illustrator might use a line like this to indicate movement and direction of the ball."

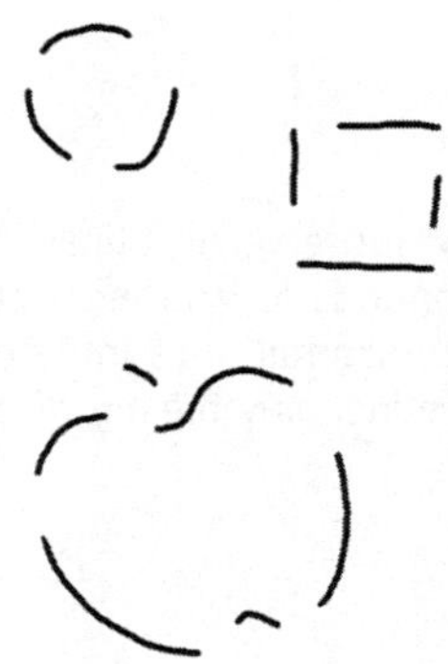

I continued, "It helps to have an indicator to show the ball's movement and direction – and this implied line serves our purpose."

"Hopefully, the rest of you see the action of this ball," I continued. "Now, watch this." I drew a circle, a square, and an apple with unconnected lines. "What do you see this time, Bonnie?"

"You just drew a circle, a square, and an apple," she answered.

"How hard was that?" Zed said. "You just drew those images with implied lines."

"That's right, Zed." I explained, "When you can visualize a complete form or figure from an incomplete representation, you've tuned in to the **law of closure**."

Steve chuckled, "I didn't realize there was a *law* for the idea of visual continuity. A lot of printed images are developed with dots that vary in size and value. These dots are used to create printed images and text."

"Oh, please slow down," Bonnie moaned. "I don't understand any of this."

I was glad Steve had raised this important issue that other elements can be created by points. As I pulled a newspaper and magnifying glass from my briefcase, I explained the concept of forming texture, tone, and dimension with points.

"Pass this newspaper around the room," I handed the paper to Zed. "Look closely at the images in the paper. You'll see they're created by a series of dots."

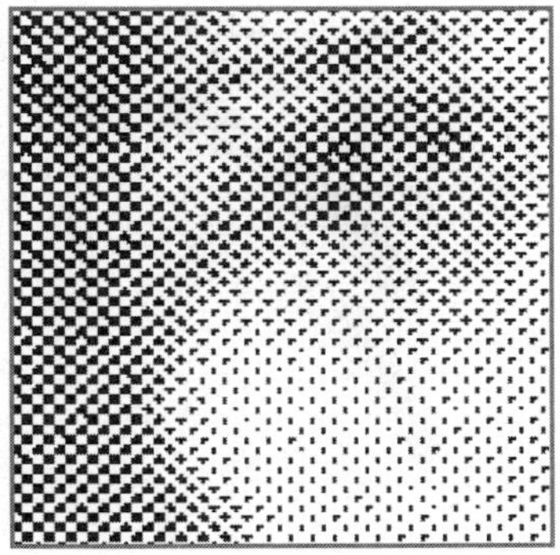

"When you create distance between yourself and that image," I added, "The dots become less apparent as individual marks. They blend together to form an image. You can imply distance with smaller and softer dots. You can also create texture and shapes with dots and lines."

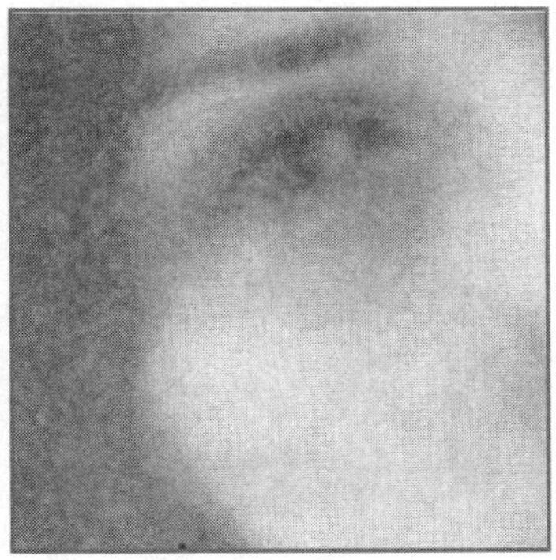

I sat with the students as they passed the newspaper around. "This is a good time to take a look at your line examples," I said. Everyone opened their drawing pads, and we began to look at the items they used to portray this element of design.

Zed took out a couple of anime images that he'd been working on, and we discussed the movement and actions created by the lines in the drawing.

"This is great Zed! You see – can create **mood** with line, just like you can create movement, texture, and value," I said. This image is a perfect example – notice how the lines of the exaggerated eyes and mouth convey information about the mood of the character?"

"She's obviously very happy!" said Bonnie

"That right Bonnie, and you might say that you can almost sense the emotion through her eyes."

"In this next drawing, the character is still happy, but you can also say that she now has an aura of innocence about her – the lines that make up her body posture give this additional information..."

Zed suddenly came to life, "Yeah, but you should see her in the next scene when she pulls out a big gun to take on the bad guys!"

I was laughing as I answered, "OK Zed, perhaps the rest of the class can look at some more of your work after the lesson, but for the moment I'd like to continue with looking at these basic design elements."

"Sure thing!" said Zed.

Next, I drew two thick lines on a piece of paper. "Zed's anime artwork serves as a great introduction to the idea that lines can create mood and emotion in your designs. Thick lines can represent strength, while thin or light lines can symbolize delicate and fragile objects." I finished by contrasting the thick lines with a flower drawn with light lines.

I asked Lisa what she found as an example for the element of line. She had a map, a line drawing of a leaf, and a piece of string. "As you can see with Lisa's choices," I explained, "Line can show direction, it can form a shape, and it can be formed by an actual object."

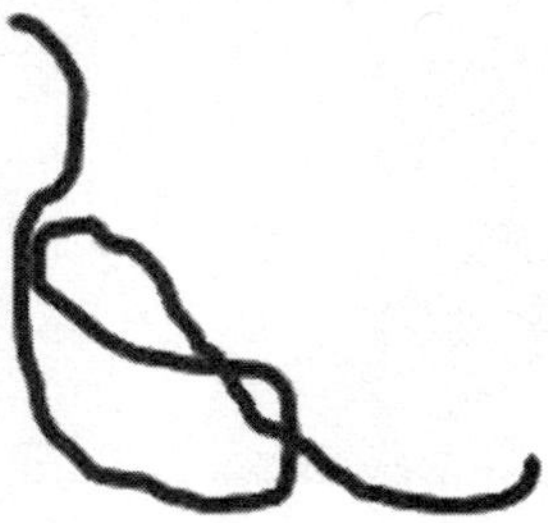

Lisa looked closely at her string. "I didn't realize it before," she said, "But there are lines within this piece of string."

I asked her to pass her drawing pad around so everyone could see the string, as well as her other examples of line. "This is a great example of just about every element of design," I stated. "These lines of fiber create an object that has texture, color, shape, and value."

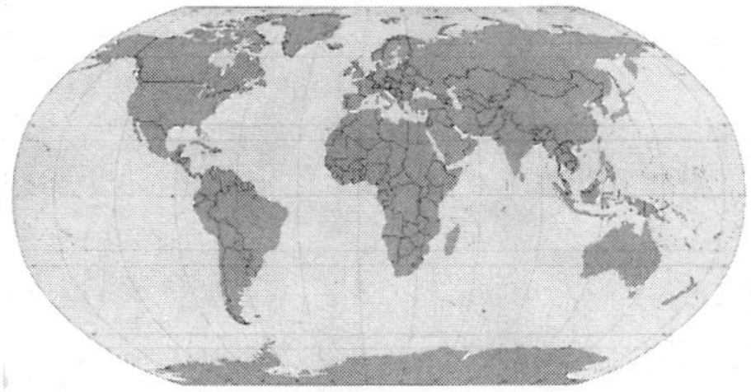

Steve pointed at a map pasted in his drawing pad. "I think you forgot one thing," he said. "Lines can also be used to organize information. I use them all the time to organize and separate text and images in magazines and newspapers." He pointed at the lines of latitude and longitude. "The lines indicate a separation of information."

"Steve brings up an important point," I said. "Lines can be used to form grids and guidelines. We'll learn about these tools when we begin to create our compositions next week."

I asked Wes for his drawing pad, and leafed through his pages. "A line can be active and visible like the ones you saw in Zed's cartoon image," I said. "Or line can also be passively created between contrasts of color or value, as you can see here." I pointed at the edge of cloud in a picture Wes had drawn. "Wes didn't draw a line to indicate the edge of the cloud," I said. "The line is implied by the change in value between the light cloud and the darker sky behind it.

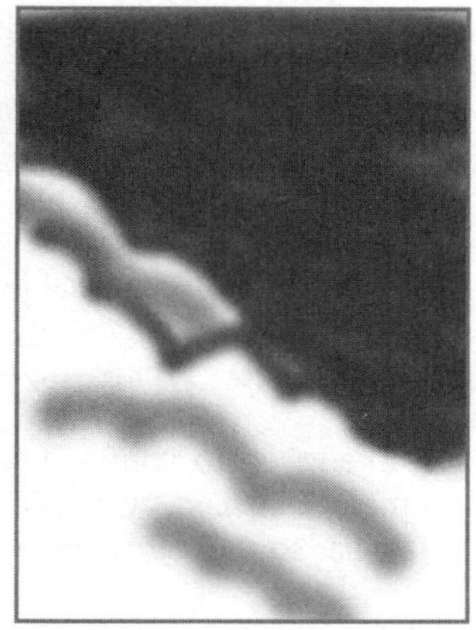

"Perhaps the simplest thing to remember about line," I added, "Is that it is either straight or curved. From these two line types, you can create any number of rhythms, moods, and perspectives."

I stood and wrote the following list on the whiteboard:

1. size
2. shape
3. position
4. direction
5. number
6. interval
7. density

I pointed at the list. "These," I said, "Are the **variables of line**. As we progress today and start looking at more shapes, keep these variables in mind to see how we can deconstruct images to their raw elements, which in turn are controlled by these variables. We'll use this list as we begin to design the project for our client."

"Wow," Zed sighed. "I can see how important line is to design. It's almost as if nothing can exist without lines! " He pointed at everyone's drawing pads, "It seems that all the examples we've looked at demonstrate how every other element of design is made up from lines."

"You're right, Zed," I said. "Lines are especially useful for defining shapes. Let's talk about these shapes now." I asked everyone to hand their examples to me so I could use them to define more complex shapes.

Shapes

We've learned that planes define the transition between line and shape. As we moved into this topic, we began to define the concept of shape and identify the many varieties. I used the images the students had collected during the past week as examples to define and analyze this element of design.

Geometric shapes

"**Planes** are two-dimensional surfaces," I began. "They're geometric expressions of finite or infinite height and width. Any line that we've just discussed could be used to define the interior space of these planes. Most often," I added, "The plane is represented by actual or passive lines on a two-dimensional surface."

I showed the class a simple image of a circle in Bonnie's drawing pad.

"This plane forms a familiar shape," I explained. "This is a circle, one of the most primal shapes known to man. This two-dimensional shape could represent a number of objects in our daily life. It's a useful shape for designers, because it can help convey many meanings in visual communications."

I continued to find examples of shapes as I looked through the student's images. "There are a number of categories for shapes. One of them is the **geometric shape**. These shapes are defined within mathematical parameters, like circles, ovals, spirals, squares, rectangles, and triangles." I pointed to various shapes within the drawing pads.

"Let me get this straight," Bonnie said. "Planes create geometric shapes, and these geometric shapes are defined by mathematical borders."

Deb laughed. "I think you're beginning to understand, Bonnie. Math can be very abstract *and* very precise."

I asked Deb to continue with her explanation. "Geometry has been considered an art form since ancient times," Deb said. "What is known as **plane geometry** was used to create polygons; these polygons became familiar to us as they were used to create shapes.

"For example," Deb continued, "An equilateral triangle – a triangle with all three sides the same length – was used as the basis to build the pyramids.

"So," she concluded, "You're correct in the assumption that planes are geometric shapes, and that they are also shapes defined by mathematical borders."

Bonnie looked dazed. "I didn't realize there was so much behind the simple triangle."

"Don't feel alone," Zed responded. "I'm amazed."

I said. "We'll be seeing more examples before the course is over, and most of the concepts will be simple. The important thing to remember here is that geometric shapes are defined by mathematical borders."

Organic vs man-made shapes

I pointed at a leaf pasted on the same page as the circle. "This," I explained, "Is an **organic shape**. These shapes are formed in nature, and many of them are undefined. Organisms like algae and some cells have shapes that aren't necessarily defined by name, since they can change shape or they appear in different shapes at different times.

"We can name a leaf by with definitions like maple, oak, or birch," I continued, "But the shape is called organic, since it was formed by nature. Man-made shapes that resemble natural shapes are also referred to as organic shapes."

"Let's now talk about **man-made shapes**." I showed everyone the gear that was falling off one of Wes's pages. "Man-made shapes are found anywhere from buildings to clothing, computers to artwork."

Steve laughed. "Wes, you found a great shape. Was that gear hanging around the studio, or did you pick it up off the street?"

Wes grinned. "I used to make man-made sculptures from found objects," he said. "This is a leftover from one of those projects."

Found shapes

"Wes, that's a great point," I said. "When we create shapes, we often borrow our ideas and actual forms in math and nature. You've also helped me introduce the next category of shape. This is the **found shape**."

"Oh, that's a hot topic," Steve interrupted. "Some people argue that there's no shape outside of the categories you just mentioned. Other people say there's a world of shapes beyond geometric, organic, and man-made."

I agreed. "I mention this category, because if I didn't, then Wes would argue with me to include it!"

Wes laughed. "I can explain how I feel about this," he added. I nodded for him to continue with his train of thought.

"We can break out of the box," he explained, "With our powers of observation, imagination, and inventiveness to form shapes.

He looked around at the class. "Have any of you ever found shapes in clouds?" he asked.

"Oh, I played that game all the time when I was a kid" Lisa said.

Wes was delighted. " Well, that's an example of found shape. When we say a cloud looks like a fish or a bird, we've found a shape."

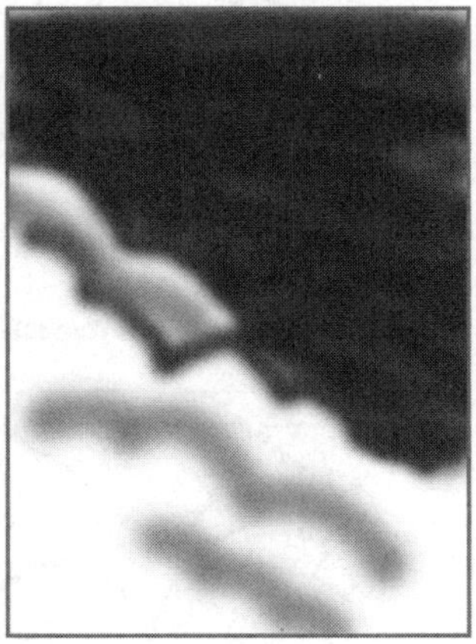

"That example is a shape that's fleeting and fragile. Although," he admitted, "It's a shape based on an organic object."

I showed the class the picture of Wes's cloud again. Lisa smiled and said, "I see a face!"

Zed leaned over to view the picture. "Where? Oh, wait – I see it, too!"

"So there, Wes," Steve laughed. "You've *found* a shape within that picture of a cloud."

"Well, it may be found, but I still haven't discovered it yet," Wes laughed.

Deb seemed perplexed. "Steve, I see what you mean about the category of found shapes. It seems pretty confusing and controversial."

Bonnie asked, "Is found shape the same as abstraction?"

Abstract and nonobjective shapes

I answered, "No Bonnie, **abstraction** is developed from shapes that have been simplified. We can take a picture of a landscape and pull different shapes from that picture to create an abstract landscape," I said. I looked through Wes's drawing pad and found an image of a pile of cut wood. "May I draw in your pad, Wes?" I asked.

Wes shrugged and grinned, "Sure, it's only a photocopy. But autograph the drawing, too, if you don't mind!"

I smiled and held up his photograph, "This is a form of abstraction. We know, instinctively, this pile of wood came from trees. This wood represents a tree, or several trees." I drew a square around a section of the picture, and the students focused on this area. "Let's consider this small portion of the photo, and we'll expound on abstraction."

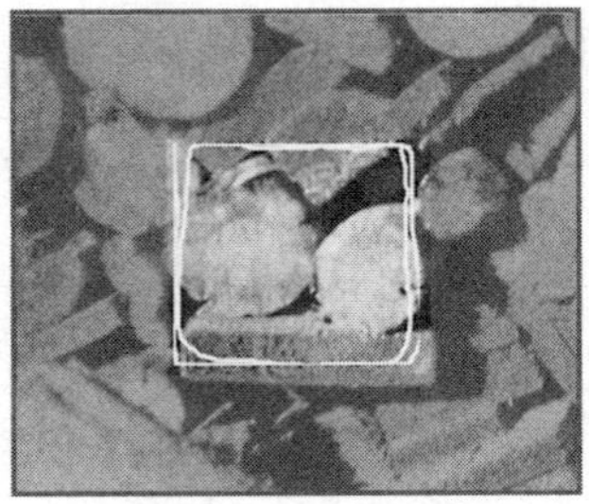

Bonnie interrupted as I began to draw. "Do abstractions involve just landscapes, or can they be made from man-made images, too?"

Wes answered for me as I finalized the image. "Abstractions can be developed from anything we see, Bonnie. Basically, an abstraction is the opposite of something tangible. By this, I mean that the artist or designer is pulling the *essence* of an object out and creating shapes from the original image."

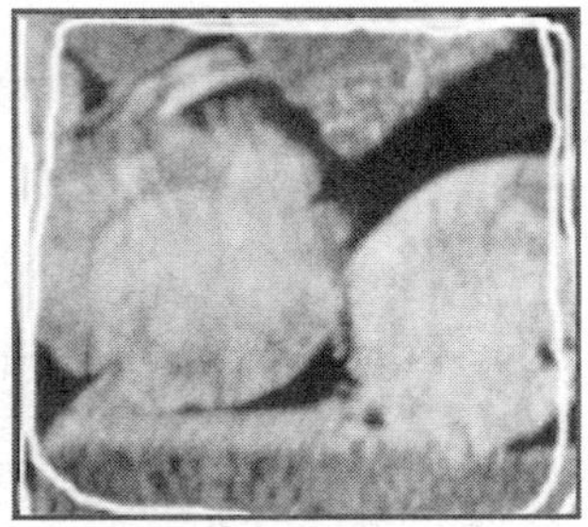

Bonnie shook her head. "That's very abstract."

"Exactly," I responded. I showed them the image I created from Wes's photograph. "Abstracts can be objective or nonobjective. *Objective* means that the viewer will recognize the shape; the photograph is objective. This," I pointed at the drawing, "Is *nonobjective abstraction*. If you looked at this without knowing it came from the photograph, you'd never know it was from a pile of wood, let alone a tree."

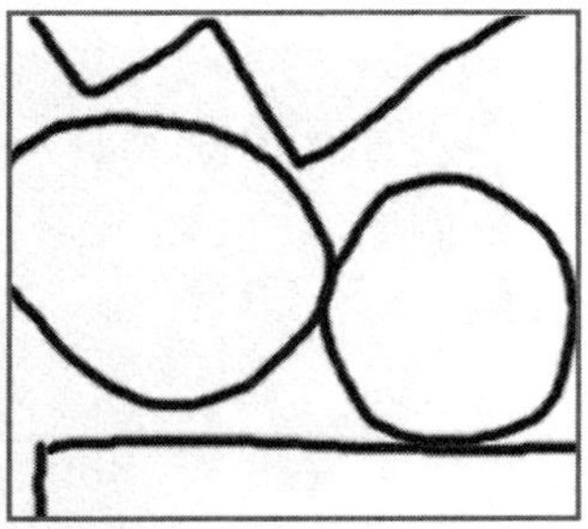

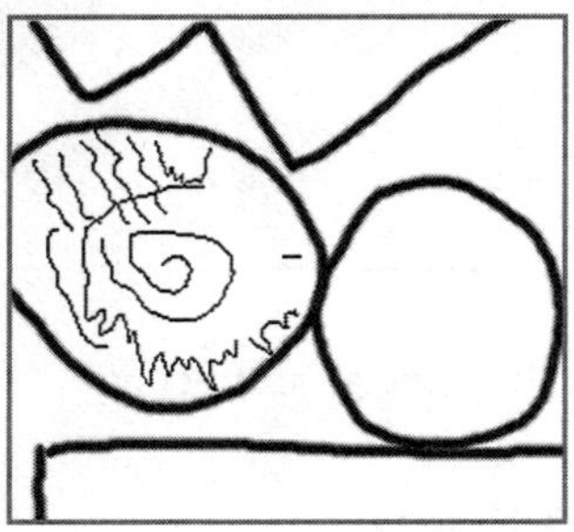

"OK," Bonnie stated. "I know what objective is now. What is nonobjective?"

"**Nonobjective shapes** are another category, and although these are different from abstract or found shapes, the word can be used to define other shapes" I said. "Nonobjective shapes are those that have no objective reference, and don't suggest subject matter," I pointed at the drawing I made again. "This is nonobjective abstraction, but if I include lines to suggest the texture of wood, this shape would change and be somewhat objective, since the wood texture is familiar. You might, at this point, be able to recognize this shape as part of a tree." I drew in some light lines.

"Oh!" Bonnie said. "I get it now!"

"Abstraction is simplification, but nonobjective abstraction is beyond simplification. It's another world altogether, and it leaves the viewer questioning what the shapes really mean."

Wes laughed, "I think you're stepping into an abstract world, Bonnie."

I showed everyone a picture of one of Wes's sculptures.

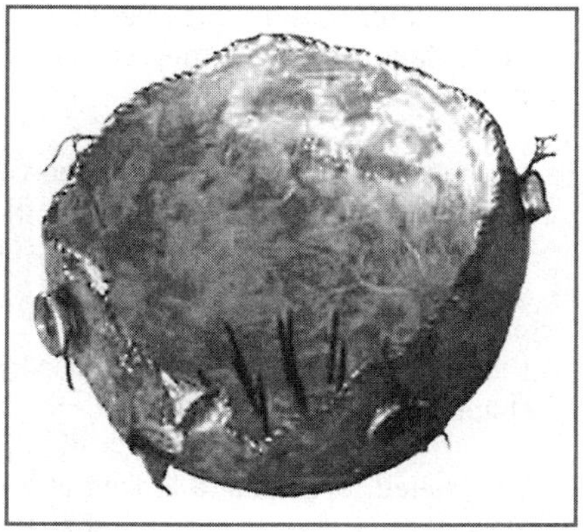

Wes laughed. "I used found objects to create a bowl. It's not nonobjective, because it represents an actual bowl, which is a recognizable object. It's not objective, either. It *is* a bowl, even though it can't be used."

"So what is it?" Bonnie asked, perplexed.

Steve grinned, "It's art!"

Everyone laughed.

"I would call it objective abstract," I said. Wes nodded in agreement.

"Back to nonobjective shapes," I looked at Bonnie. "Some backgrounds for web pages are nonobjective. They're often created from patterns that introduce various elements of design without distracting, hopefully, from the content within the format of the page.

"For this class," I explained, "We need to know the difference among these categories for general design purposes.

"Each category represents a mood and an image for your client," I explained. "You wouldn't use a man-made shape to represent an organic grocery store, unless you wanted to use the image for contrast. Abstracts and nonobjective shapes would only be used for pattern or backgrounds, since these mean nothing to the client's audience, unless you define what they mean somewhere in the site.

"It's important to remember these categories, as they define the format of your design, and they set the mood for the viewer. The moods you create could also help you choose which line, color, texture, and type you choose for your site.

Volume and mass

"We'll define these categories as we study the client's case during this course," I added. "Now, let's talk about volume and mass."

"**Mass** is a term that is usually applied to three-dimensional shapes." I pointed to a photograph of a basketball in Zed's drawing pad "This is also a bit complex," I looked up at the class.

"This is a mass, as it's a three-dimensional shape. It has volume, but we can't touch or feel the mass or the volume.

"However," I added, "We know it has volume and mass because we're familiar with the shape, feel, and use of a basketball." Wes was shaking with glee. "I know what's going through your mind, Wes..." So I asked him to explain the difference between mass and shape from an artist's point of view.

"Artists can be very picky about the difference between mass and shape," Wes chuckled. "A painting is a shape, and a sculpture is a mass. A painting can be viewed only from a limited number of angles. A sculpture can be viewed from many different angles, and that's the main issue."

Bonnie leaned forward, listening with interest, and Wes continued, "When we view a sculpture, we're in a constant changing relationship with the form. It's *fluid*, like water, since the view changes from every angle."

Bonnie interrupted, "But what about three-dimensional objects that we see on the Internet or in multimedia presentations? Aren't they considered fluid, especially when they're animated, and they present several different sides?"

"Ah!" Wes exclaimed. "There's the catch – these images are *represented* as masses, but because they exist within a two-dimensional format, they are actually just shapes. The disciplines of painting and sculpture overlap here, with a multitude of issues to be tackled." He gripped his hair in mock anguish, suggesting he'd given this topic a lot of thought.

I looked at Lisa with amusement. She was grinning. "Lisa, what about theater? Is that format conducive to shape or mass?"

She leaned forward and looked at Wes. "I can see the dilemma Wes outlined from the fine artist's point of view. Within theater, we use shapes painted on two-dimensional surfaces to represent three-dimensional forms. We also place three-dimensional objects in front of the backdrops. Theater is a mish-mash of shape and mass."

Zed shook his head. "Does it really matter what we call these... things?"

"I hate to say it, Zed, but yes," I replied. "We can simplify this process a lot by calling a box a box, instead of that *three-dimensional square shape* or *that square mass you can keep your junk in*. Part of becoming a graphic designer is understanding the definition of dilemmas that all designers are faced with," I added.

"Can we define mass by the same categories as shape?" Bonnie seemed absorbed in this subject.

"Yes, and thanks for bringing that up, Bonnie." I answered. "We can, in fact, define mass as man-made, organic, found, abstract, or nonobjective. Mass is also similar to shape in that both are formed by straight or curved angles."

"I want to know about positive and negative shapes," Zed said. "I just couldn't wrap my head around that one."

Positive and negative shapes

I was glad that Zed had been honest enough to let everyone know what was confusing him. Most students find it pretty easy relating to everyday visuals – once they grasp the concept of living within a space, surrounded by shapes, then the principles of design come easier for them. This is one of the reasons that we were spending this time observing the objects around us, and those that the students had collected, before starting to concentrate on computers. I leafed through the drawing pads to find a simple example, "OK, here's a good example to explain positive and negative shape," I stated.

They all looked at a picture of a person's shadow. "In this photograph, the shadow is a positive shape, and the surrounding lighter values are the negative spaces," I said "The positive shape actually defines the negative space here, the area surrounding the shadow forms a negative shape."

"I thought negative shapes had to be flat like that photograph," Zed said. "Can people be positive shapes, too?"

"We are positive masses," Wes answered. "And we define a negative shape. A three-dimensional negative shape is also negative space," Wes stated. "Are you dizzy again, Zed?"

Bonnie threw her arms up and laughed. "I'm probably more dizzy than Zed right now." She pointed at each one of us. "Do you mean we're all positive shapes... I mean masses... sitting in a negative shape? Or is it a negative mass?" She continued to laugh. "Maybe it's a negative space!"

Steve grinned, "Don't get hysterical on us, Bonnie." He looked at the rest of the group. "I think I can help simplify this topic. **Positive shapes** are areas that stand out from their surroundings. These areas can be either two- or three-dimensional. **Negative shapes**, on the other hand, are defined by the positive shapes, and they are non-dominant areas that help define the positive area. They can also be two- or three-dimensional." He looked at me and grinned. "Did I handle that OK?"

I laughed, "Steve, you did fine. As we go along, you will find that all these terms are relative. A point can become a plane, and a plane can be a shape. A shape can become space, and a space can become your format.

"Let's keep it simple and stay with two-dimensional formats for the moment." I showed them a picture that Wes had drawn "This is a very interesting example of positive and negative shapes interacting. In this picture we can also see positive and negative spaces," I said. "If you see the flower, it becomes the positive shape, and the black area becomes the negative space this flower occupies. If you see the profiles of two faces, those are the positive shapes, and the white becomes the negative space separating the two shapes."

Everyone looked closely at the picture. "I can see that the profiles of the woman and the child are positive shapes and the space around them is negative." Zed said.

"What profiles?" Bonnie asked. "I see a flower. That flower is the positive shape, and the black background is the negative space, right?"

Lisa grinned. "What's on your mind, Lisa?" I asked.

"That's a visual trick," she said.

Wes was puffed up with obvious pride. "I thought I came up with a great image," he boasted. "It's two profiles, *and* it's a flower."

Everyone leaned in to look closer. "Wow!" Zed was the first to respond. "I see it now! Trippy!"

"This is an **ambiguous** figure," I explained. "**Ambiguous figures** are images that usually represent two entirely different subjects. As you can see, each shape is in competition for your attention. I pointed to the line that separated one profile from the flower. "This passive line functions as the line that defines both shapes. That's why your mind is confused as to which shape is positive and which is negative.

They all leaned back, and a few of them shook their heads. Wes was still flying high on his effort to confuse the class with this image. "Let's throw in another term for this topic," he said. "Let's talk about figure-ground relationships."

Bonnie looked at Wes like he was a fly in her soup. "I can almost guess the figure is the positive shape, and the ground is the negative shape," she muttered.

"I think you've got it, Bonnie," I said. She looked sincerely surprised. "A **figure** is an outline or contour of a shape, and the **ground** is that which is behind the dominant figure. The ground can consist of shapes or space. The **figure-ground relationship** is the dynamic created between the figure and the ground.

"We'll cover all this information in much more depth as we brainstorm and work out our design solutions. Let's move on to value."

"I wonder how much that subject is worth?" Zed quipped, as he shook his head. With that remark, I decided it was time for a break.

Value systems

As we learned last week, **value systems** are defined by the lightness or darkness of a color or hue. To explain this element of design, I usually begin with the gray scale for clarification and simplicity. Bonnie's example of the web-safe hexadecimal gray values will help the class understand the use of color within the Flash format.

As the class returned from break, I asked them to sit at the computers. I wanted them to begin understanding the toolbar and color tools within Flash. I asked Bonnie to bring along her example of the hex value scale to show the class.

"Don't turn your computers on just yet," I asked. "We have a few examples of value to experience before we actually practice with the Flash tools."

"Bonnie's example of the value scale in hexadecimal grays will help us understand two important points," I said. "It will clarify the definition of value as a design element, and it will also help explain some limitations of color within our computer browsers.

"The **hexadecimal**, or **hex,** system is based on a numerical system, and it's represented with numbers and letters. Each set of numbers represents the value of the color shown on the monitor." I looked at Wes, "Now we're entering Bonnie's territory," I said. "So maybe she'd like to introduce some of the alien concepts? "

Wes nodded, "I'm ready to confront alien concepts! Bring it on, Bonnie."

Bonnie held up her example, and began to explain the grayscale system. "The gray scale you see here is based on the computer hexadecimal system." She waved her hand up the scale, showing the equations:

- Black = #000000
- Dark Gray = #333333
- Midtone Gray = #666666
- Light Midtone Gray = #999999
- Light Gray = #CCCCCC
- White = #FFFFFF

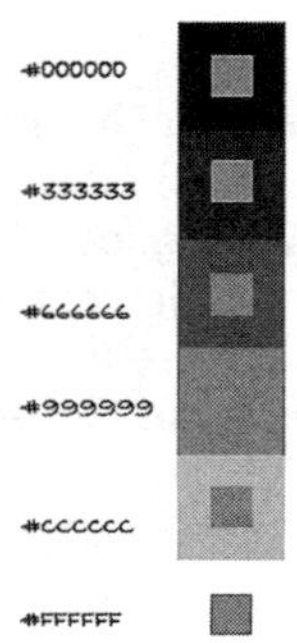

"The smaller square within each grayscale square is #999999. I included this color in each square to show contrast, or lack of contrast. This is an example of a value scale for web-safe grays," she said. "The bottom square is white, written in hex as #FFFFFF. Moving up the scale, the next gray is #CCCCCC – note how the hex values are represented by the # symbol followed by the letters...

"From this point," she continued, "The letters change to numbers."

Wes raised his hand. "Why are there six letters or numbers for each value?"

Bonnie explained, "I think Deb could probably explain more about how these numbers work, but I'll try. What I know is that this color system is based on additive colors. Three colors are used in the system, and numbers and letters represent the colors.

"These colors," Bonnie continued, "Are red, green, and blue, and this system is therefore known as **RGB**." She pointed at the next gray value. "Although this gray, also known as #999999, has six numbers, it's actually made up of three sets of two numbers.

"The hexadecimal numbering system starts at 0 through to 9, and then continues with A, B, C, D, E, and F, where A represents 10, B is 11, and so on until F which takes the place of 15. The series 0 to F forms a sequence of 16 digits that we can add just like binary numbers – for instance, decimal 15 equates to 0F in hex, and decimal 16 is hex 10. So the digit 1 in hex 10 represents the number 16..."

Deb couldn't wait to help with the technical explanation, "That's right! Whereas decimal numbering is a base-10 system, hexadecimal is what we call a base-16 system. So, in the RGB gray that we've just looked at, 99 in hex is the same as 153 in decimal – nine times sixteen, plus nine – 153!"

Grateful for the help, but eager to continue her story, Bonnie continued, "The units of light for web-safe colors are expressed using the two hex numbers and letters, and as we've seen the grays are easy," Bonnie added, "They have the same numbers and letters across the board."

She looked at Wes. "This particular gray is a combination of equal amounts of red, green, and blue light. So," she explained, "The gray is expressed in the same numbers – there's hex 99 red, 99 green, and 99 blue in this gray. This number actually refers to the intensity of the color, and in the decimal numbering system the intensity can range from 0 to 255. This gray is made up from the three colors all with intensity of 153."

Bonnie was almost finished, but added an afterthought. "By the way, it's useful to remember that the hex numbers of web-safe colors are divisible by three."

Deb was the first to applaud. "Great job, Bonnie," she said. Bonnie bowed to the class, and glided dramatically back to her chair.

Lisa grinned, "You did a great job with that gray scale – the addition of the light gray square in each block for contrast was really clever."

I agreed. "Bonnie did an excellent job of simplifying the hex system for us. Notice how dark the little block of #999999 appears within the lighter grays, and how light it appears in the dark end of this value scale.

"This leads us to analyze the properties of value," I said.

"Is gray a color?" Zed asked.

"We often refer to grays, white, and black as colors," I answered, "But these are considered neutral or achromatic values. **Achromatic** means a value without color, hue, or chroma. In turn, **chroma** refers to pure color, without a tint of white, gray, or black. It can also refer to the intensity of a color. As you see, gray isn't very intense by itself. However, when you place grays within color formats, you can create some very interesting contrasts and the illusion of intensity.

"Wait a minute, gray, black, and white aren't colors?" Zed asked. "Then why are they used like color? Why do we call them colors?"

I laughed, "One question at a time, Zed, please!" I pointed at Bonnie's gray scale. We'll learn more about the RGB system later in this course; we'll devote a whole class to color. For now, the simplest answer for all your questions is that black absorbs all colors, and white reflects all colors. They're more like a format for the entire spectrum of the rainbow.

"Grays are just values of black and white, so they fall into the same category of achromatic values," I continued. "Unless, of course, you make a gray from mixing a few colors, like we do in the RGB system. These grays are chromatic grays if you don't add any achromatic white, black, or gray.

"What I'd like you to remember is that value and color are related. Color offers a wider variety of experience and visual difference than achromatic values. Color also has value, but we'll stick to grays for the moment."

I asked Lisa to turn down the lights again. As we sat in the dark, I continued to explain value. "As Wes said last week, value is just another word for the lightness and darkness of an area. **Value** is how we perceive forms, and it is defined by the amount of light we have to define our surroundings.

"If we walked around in this room right now, we might bump into chairs and tables, because until our eyes become adjusted to the limited amount of light available to help us define shapes, we'd be at a loss for visual clues. We would be hard pressed to see where we were or to visualize other objects in the room with us."

"This value gradation or difference between light and dark areas, no matter how limited, is also known as **chiaroscuro**. This is an Italian word for the combination of light and dark. This word also suggests depth, or space, within the areas of values.

"Clever use of chiaroscuro can be a great way to draw attention to your designs – by exposing your viewers to highly contrasting areas."

Steve remarked, "I've never thought about creating that kind of reaction with viewers. That's interesting."

Wes added. "If I know I'm going to display my work with artists who specialize in pastels or other low value work, I bring my high contrast paintings. They get noticed, and I usually make more sales."

"That's a wonderful example to explain of how we can use value systems to our advantage," I said. "When you place different values together in the same environment, the attention will be drawn to the areas of high contrast."

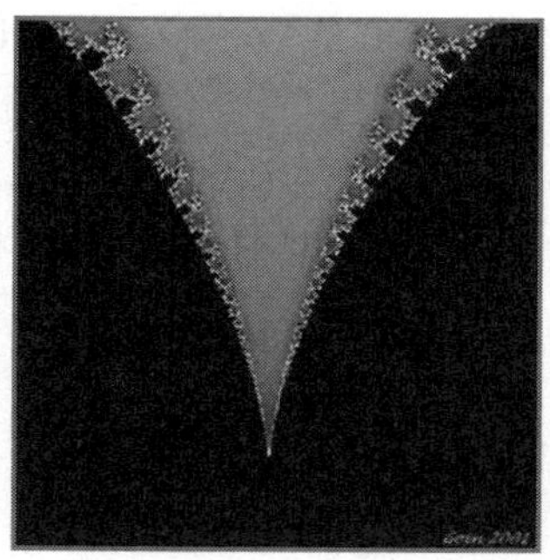

I showed them a low contrast nonobjective painting. "You can begin to see a value pattern in this photograph. **Value patterns** are formed by the arrangement and amount of variation in light and dark values, independent of any color used. When contrast is minimal, you see a limited range of values. The effect can be very subtle and soft."

"Does contrast mean the same thing as opposites?" Zed asked. "Like hard and soft, or light and heavy?"

"It does, Zed." I answered. "In relation to value, **contrast** deals with the amount of light within a visual field. The illusion of light can be dramatic." I displayed a high contrast painting. "With **high contrast**, the light areas here seem to come forward," I explained. "The darker areas recede to the background.

"This stark contrast can lead to visual disorientation," I added, "Especially when the dark areas are in the foreground, and the light areas are in the background."

"Oh, just like Wes's ambiguous figure, right?" Bonnie asked. "Did the high contrast of black and white have anything to do with our confusion over the shapes?"

Wes smiled, "That's exactly why I used black and white. I wanted to add to the visual confusion with high value contrast."

"That was a smart choice for that particular piece," I asked them to turn on their computers so we could begin to see the use of value in the format of a monitor.

I addressed the use of white type on black backgrounds. "Bonnie, you probably know that white type on dark backgrounds is discouraged in most instances."

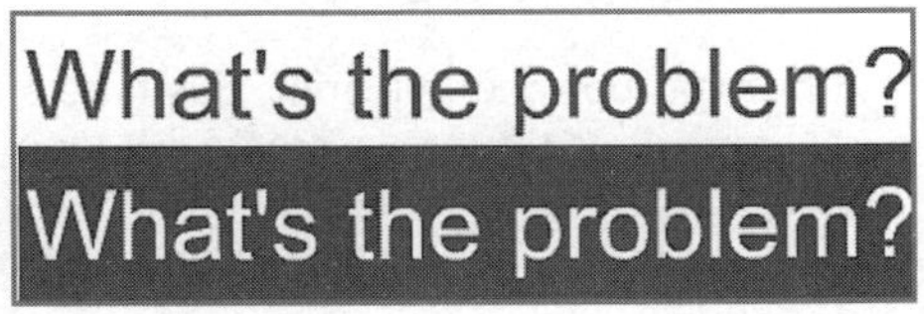

Bonnie said, "I know, but I use it occasionally, for small blocks of type. Why is that a problem?"

Zed answered, "I guess it would give the viewers the same experience we had with Wes's ambiguous shapes. It would sort of vibrate with all that black for a background." Zed thought a minute and added, "Unless, of course, the type was larger?" he asked.

The problem of white type on a black background, especially within additive color formats," I explained. "Is based on the concept of irradiation." I could hear a few chuckles. "No, this doesn't have anything to do with nuclear waste in this context. **Irradiation** is the amount of light or luminance within your format. The problem with irradiation is the after effect imposed on viewers after looking at blocks of high contrast. If you expose them to this effect for long periods of time, their vision becomes disoriented.

"White text on a black or dark background seems to vibrate or sparkle. This high contrast distracts the viewer, even if they may not consciously notice what's happening. They will have a more difficult time remembering your message."

"But, I see white type on dark backgrounds a lot," Bonnie insisted. "Are there times when it's OK to use this style?"

"The contrast can be used to develop a mood of disquiet, or one of almost theatrical drama and excitement." I answered. "It can be used in headlines, or in small portions of copy for emphasis. You might notice that pages with dark backgrounds will often have a lighter block set aside for body copy, so they can render the typefaces darker.

"The major problem within the monitor format," I added, "Is that you're working with a canvas that is backlit. This adds to the problem of irradiation."

Steve added, "It's a real temptation to use light type on dark backgrounds in print, too. I've seen advertisements where it works well, but they've used only a few words of type.

"We definitely shouldn't use white type on dark backgrounds for large blocks of body copy," Steve added. "It just doesn't work for the readers. I guess you just explained why."

"Thanks for your input, Steve," I said. "Dark backgrounds can be very classy, and it's difficult for many folks to avoid them. There are ways to resolve this problem, and one way is to back off from high contrast in the area of the body copy."

I showed them a painting using low value patterns. "An image that uses a value pattern of dark color or values throughout the image is called **low key**. This gives the image a mysterious quality, one that creates a mood of mystique or tranquility."

I brought out another print, this time a painting of a baby playing in bed. "A **high key** piece can create a mood of lightness." I said. "Most likely appealing to a wide audience, high key designs are often interpreted as offering the viewer a sense of lightness and happiness.

"One way to deal with a point of focus or contrast is to create an area of high or low value in a piece, and to surround that area with a contrasting area of low key or high key ranges of value."

"Another perspective to consider is how the tools you use will render value. If you use black ink, your range of values will be wide. If you are using an H grade pencil, your value range will be rather limited."

I continued, "Yet another way to check the focal point against your contrasting areas, especially in color, is to reproduce that image in achromatic gray. When you design an image on the computer, you can change that image to grayscale, or reduce the saturation of color, and you can see how the image works."

Wes nodded, "It was years before I could see my values when I worked in color. Working within achromatic grays can be a blessing, because the values are a lot easier to see."

I agreed, "Luckily for you, the tools in Flash are flexible enough to allow you to work and test your value levels in a fluid manner. The Pencil and Line tools allow you to work with a variety of pen or brush thicknesses. In graphics programs like Flash, these are called **stroke widths**.

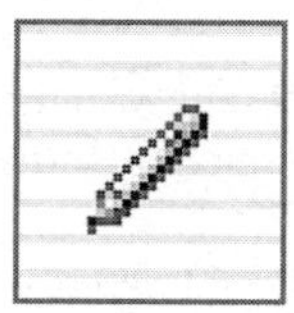

"In Flash, a stroke width can be changed at any time via the Property inspector – remember, you'll find this near the bottom of the screen in the Flash authoring environment." I reached over to the Mac computer that Wes was sitting in front of and demonstrated the simplicity of using the Property inspector:

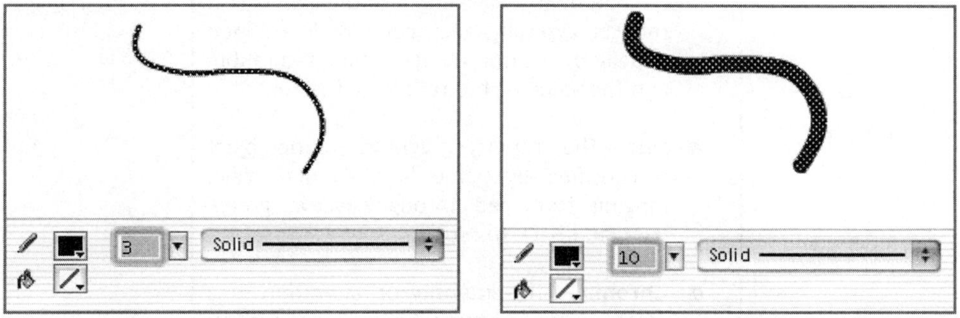

"I knew that the Property inspector would be a useful panel!" Steve proclaimed.

"Changing the stroke width allows us great flexibility in getting the right balance for our designs. Play with it a little to see the value that different stroke widths can add to your overall value and contrast."

"When do we get to work in full color? Why all the dull grays?" asked Zed.

"Zed, remember that chromatic grays in fact contain color. So since we're in the neighborhood of color," I added, "Let's knock on that door."

Wes laughed, "Actually, color has a huge house!"

I agreed. "Today, we'll just view one room. We'll take the house tour later in the course."

Color basics

Color is an immense topic, and one that's vital for designers to understand. As we introduce and analyze this design element, we'll only cover the tip of the iceberg of the topic. The focus here will be on additive color and its properties, and on color schemes.

"So far we've barely touched on the terms color, hue, and chroma," I began. "This handout briefly explains the various terms we'll use in this class." I passed a handout around the students.

Color

- **Color** – A quality of an object or substance defined by the wavelength of the light that it reflects. Typically, each color is determined visually by measurements of hue, saturation, and the value of the reflected light.

- **Hue** – The property of light where the object is classified by name in a circular scale, ranging from red through yellow, green, blue, and back to red.

- **Chroma** – The intensity or saturation of a color or hue. Chroma ranges from neutral colors to the brightest, most intense color provided by pigment or light. This also refers to a color's *purity*, free from white, black, or achromatic grays.

- **EValue** – A property of color or hue referring to the lightness or darkness of a color, also known as *tint* or *shade*. Tints are lighter in value, and shades are darker in value.

As the class scanned through the definitions, I started to address the topic of color. "We all deal with color every day. We make decisions about which colors to wear. Our habits are defined by color, too. When you encounter a red light on the road, you know this color indicates the requirement by law to stop your vehicle.

"Colors can be used to manipulate people." I added. "We saw how value can be used to elicit a mood. Color is even more powerful."

Steve nodded, "I've had my experiences with color," he said. "I didn't realize some colors mean one thing in one culture, and might mean something entirely different in another culture."

Bonnie added, "I hope we address the issues of accessibility to the colorblind and to the blind."

I raised my hands and stated, "As you all see, the element of color is already complex, and it can be overwhelming.

"The word implies so many aspects that any given person could give you their own definition. To an artist or a designer, color is either their worst nightmare or their best friend. If you use watercolor, your idea of red is quite different to that of the artist who uses pastels. If you design websites, your palette is limited but not any less problematic than that of an artist with hundreds of oil paints at their disposal. And as graphic messages begin to go global, color takes on a special burden in psychological and social contexts.

"Let's tackle this topic with definitions before we go further. These," I added as I pointed at their handouts, "Are the definitions of color, and their three characteristics, or properties."

"So there's a fine line between the terms color and hue," Steve murmured. "Wes, did you know this?" He glanced at Wes.

Wes shook his head, "I've always used the terms hue and color as if they were synonymous with each other," he said. "Obviously, I've been wrong!"

"Not really, Wes," I assured him. "But hue is slightly different to color when we become specific about the descriptions. For instance, if you use the colors blue, purple, and aqua, these are all different colors, but the hue in each case could be blue. The same hue or color could have many different commercial names, with paints for instance, all aimed at enticing you into buying them.

"However," I added, "They might be just a different name for the same hue or color.

"Different color systems will also have different names for the same color or hue. One color system might name purple as violet, or blue-green as cyan or aquamarine.

"An essential fact of color theory is that color is a property of light. It is not an object in itself. The object itself also has no color. An apple is not red or green or yellow. The apple merely has the ability to reflect certain rays of white light, which contains all the colors (hues) of the rainbow. A yellow apple is reflecting the yellow portion of the white light.

"The significance of this is that as light changes, so do the reflective properties of the object. The object shows the changes by reflecting back this light, modified by the light involved. This is especially important to remember for painters and printers.

"When you mix the primary colors of red, yellow, and blue with light, you end up with a white light. As we mentioned last week, this is called the **additive model**. The additive model can be used to its best advantage by photographers, stage light directors, and creators of computer graphics viewed on monitors – that's us!

"When mixing colors with paint and ink, you are mixing colors with the objects of paint or ink. The paint is not color – it is an object that reflects the light of that color. If you combine the primary colors of red, blue, and yellow using paint or ink, you get a dark brown or black. This is called the **subtractive model**.

Bonnie shuddered. "I'm so happy I have a limited color palette to work with!"

It was Wes's turn to grimace. "I hope I'm not too limited in my color choices," he replied.

"You will be slightly limited in some respects, Wes," I replied. "But, you'll still be able to apply various color concepts to your work."

"Bonnie mentioned earlier that there are three primary colors used in the additive color system. These colors are different to the ones used in the subtractive color system. These colors are also affected greatly when we begin to mix colors."

Wes folded his hands on the table and said, "The primary colors used in subtractive color mixing are red, blue, and yellow. I heard Bonnie say the primary colors used in additive color mixing are red, green, and blue."

Deb added, "You said it correctly, Wes, and it's important to remember the additive colors in that order, since that's how they're recognized by the computer software."

I opened up a couple of Flash files in my laptop that showed examples of the additive and subtractive color mixes.

"Wes is right," I said. "The problem with our color monitors is they display a limited number of additive colors within some formats."

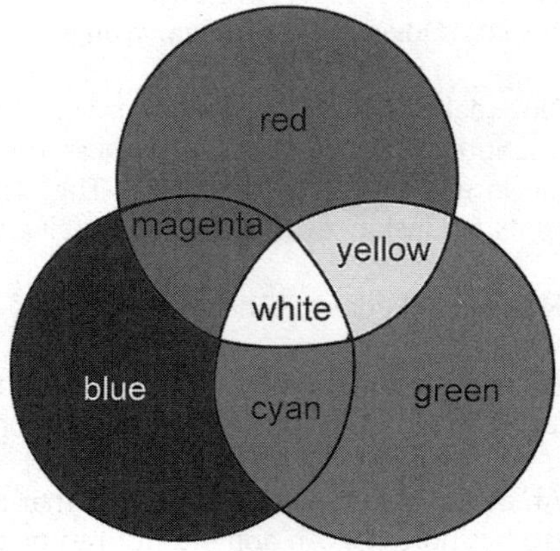

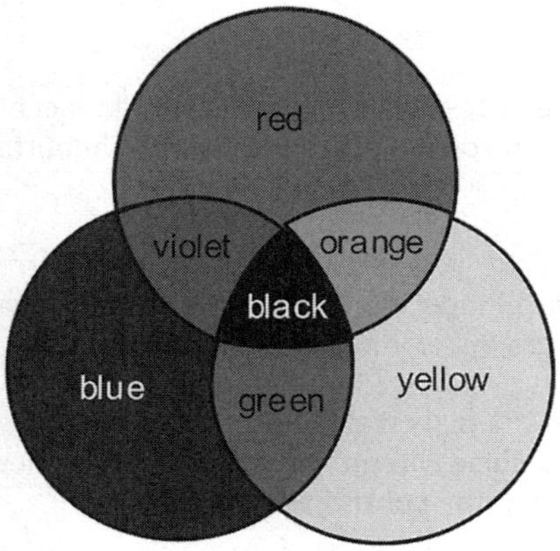

"This leads to the use of color schemes," I said. "These schemes are based on subtractive color mixing, but we can apply the same concepts to additive color systems. In fact," I added, "Most fine artists rely on instinctive color schemes for their paintings, since they have more colors to choose from in their palettes.

"Graphic artists benefit most from these color schemes, as they use limited color for the most impact on the viewer."

Next, I opened up a Flash file containing picture of a trichromatic color wheel, and projected it for all the students to see. "There are many different theories on color, and just as many different color wheels," I stated.

"We're going to stick with this simple color wheel for today, and tackle some of the more technical issues relating to color later in the course.

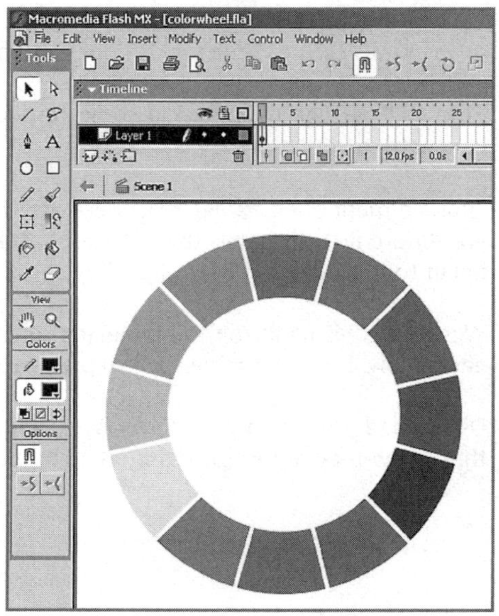

"The color wheel is a by-product of Isaac Newton's theory that when light is bent, it produces a spectral range of seven colors in a circle. Since then, artists have agreed the trichromatic color wheel shown here is the most useful in determining color combinations. **Trichromatic** means the primary colors are separated by three colors. These three colors are developed from even mixing of the primary hues at either end."

Pointing at the color wheel, I continued with my description, "We see the primary colors on the color wheel as follows: red is at 12 o'clock, blue is at 4 o'clock and yellow is at 8 o'clock. The secondary colors are mixed from the primaries, and the tertiary colors are formed by combining a secondary and a primary color. Take a look at this handout to see how we can create the various colors..."

I produced some more handouts from my briefcase and passed them around the students.

The Color Wheel

- **Primary + Primary = Secondary**

  Red + Blue = Violet
  (located at 2 o'clock on color wheel)

  Blue + Yellow = Green (6 o'clock)

  Red + Yellow = Orange (10 o'clock)

- **Primary + Secondary = Tertiary**

  Red + Violet = Red-violet (1 o'clock)

  Blue + Violet = Blue-violet (3 o'clock)

  Blue + Green = Blue-green (5 o'clock)

  Yellow + Green = Yellow-green (7 o'clock)

  Yellow + Orange = Yellow-orange
  (9 o'clock)

  Red + Orange = Red-orange (11 o'clock)

As the students digested the information in the handouts, I continued, "Notice that the tertiary colors lie between the primary and secondary colors that are mixed to form them. Be aware that any combination of primary or secondary combinations in subtractive or additive color mixing will probably not produce the colors you see on any particular color wheel."

"Why is that?" Bonnie asked.

Wes answered, "Because color wheels are printed with ink, and the ink is mixed from any number of inks provided at that particular printer's business. You could spend half a lifetime trying to match their colors with your colors."

"Wes is right," I said. "When we use color, it's helpful to have these tools around. But, don't bang your head on the table just because you can't match the colors to the wheel exactly."

"When you choose colors, your first dilemma is to decide if you want to choose warm or cool colors," I noticed I had Zed's interest.

"You mean colors have a temperature?" he asked.

"Not exactly, Zed," I smiled. "These colors can appear to be what we perceive as warm or cold, though." I held up the color wheel marked with warm colors. "**Warm colors** range from 8 o'clock to 1 o'clock on the wheel, between yellow and red-violet. These colors are used to portray warmth, warm objects, heat, and fire. They're also used to emphasize something to the viewer – these colors will stand out over **cool colors**."

Wes turned to Zed, "If you painted a huge blue elephant, and gave that elephant a red eye," Wes explained, "The viewer would notice that red eye before they'd notice the whole blue elephant."

"Wes raises an important point," I said. "Warm colors appear to come forward, cool colors appear to recede, but it depends on the colors you use. Some warm colors appear cooler when placed on a cool background, and visa-versa. We'll experiment with this during your project this next week."

Zed turned to Wes, "Then it's a good idea to wear sunglasses to hide bloodshot eyes, right?"

"Not if you're a blue elephant," Steve laughed. "People would notice you even if your eyes were normal." He looked at the warm color chart. "So the remaining colors are the cool ones?"

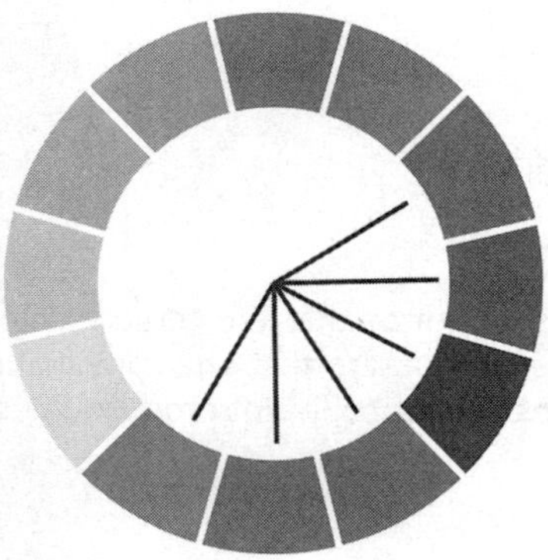

"That's correct, Steve. The cool colors range through violet, or purple, to yellow-green. You can remember them as the colors from 2 o'clock through 7 o'clock.

"These colors will help you add emphasis to the warm colors. They can be used liberally in contrast to warm colors. They also help you define depth in your work, as they appear to recede when used your formats.

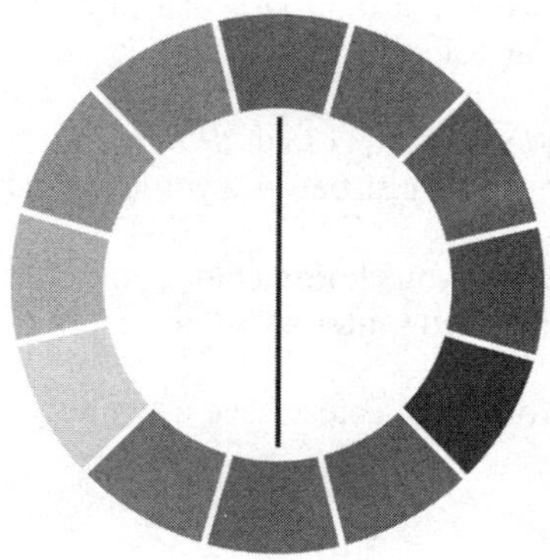

"Let's move on." I said. "The next form of our color wheel to consider is the **complementary color scheme**. This is a simplistic color tool, and it means exactly what it says. You choose one color on the color wheel and pick the color directly opposite for a complement to the first color. This combination will give you a warm color and a cool color. The colors connected here are red and green."

"Those are Christmas colors," Bonnie said.

"They sure are," Steve replied, "And, that's good to remember when designing holiday advertisements for clients. But," he added, "As we become more global in our communications, we'll find these two colors typically represent the Christian winter holiday.

Other religions also observe their separate holidays during that time, and red and green are not used in the representation of their celebrations."

"Steve's spot on," Wes agreed. "Solstice celebrations are often represented with earth colors. Cool colors would do more justice to winter solstice, like low values of blue."

I nodded, "These are important points to remember with global clients. Another point is that not everyone experiences snow and ice at that time of year. When the northern hemisphere experiences winter, the folks in South America, Southern Africa, and Australia are sweating through their summer weather."

"Wes brought up another point," I added. "Colors also have value, and you'll find that many colors on your monitors are very high key and appear to have a great deal of contrast. This is due to the backlighting on your monitor."

"The use of complementary colors is handy for those clients who have a limited print budget," I added. "This is the easiest color scheme for most people to use for two-color printing. For our uses in Flash, this tool can help us simplify our palette, so the important message will be seen.

"However," I warned, "Using complementary colors can have the same effect as using white type on a black background. Can anyone tell me why?"

Bonnie answered, "Well, you showed us how irradiation affects the viewer. Black and white are opposites, so I assume they're complements. I guess this means that any complement would have that affect on a viewer."

"Bonnie's right," I said. "Be aware of the irradiation effect on your viewers if you stick to two complementary colors. When both complimentary colors are the same value, you'll get a sort of vibrating effect when you place those two colors together or on top of each other," I explained "Also, when you mix complimentary colors, you can achieve your chromatic grays."

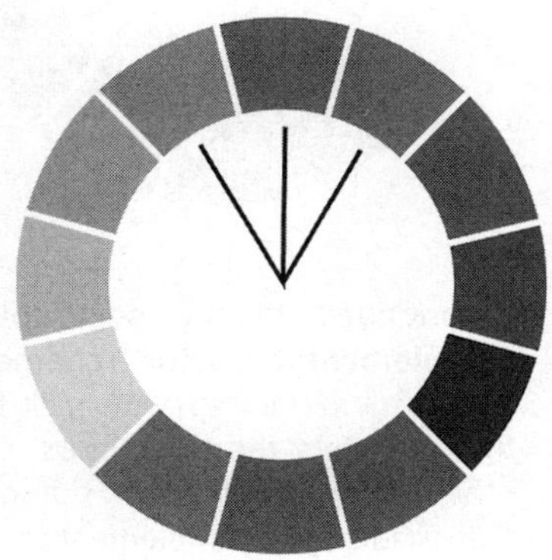

"This next color wheel highlights neighbors on the color wheel. The **analogous color scheme** consists of three colors next to each other. In the example, you see red-orange, red, and red-violet grouped together. Use this color scheme to produce work that is either totally *warm* or totally *cool*. When you pick three colors that overlap into either the warm or cool color range, you can use the warm or cool color for contrast."

I explained how many of the colors seem to change when placed in close proximity or on top of each other. "The analogous color wheel was used by many impressionists to create lights and darks without muddying up their pictures with complementary colors. When you place the analogous colors on top of each other, they vibrate, but they don't seem to jump around like the complementary colors in the same situation."

"Isn't that a monochromatic color scheme?" Bonnie asked.

Wes shook his head, "No, Bonnie. Monochromatic is just one color produced with a range of values."

"Wes is right," I stated. "A **monochromatic color scheme** consists of one color with black or white added to it to produce a range of values. The most simplistic rendering of this idea is to use three variations of that color, as you see with the blue range here. Work produced with this color scheme can be very easy on the eyes, even with red hues. However, it's a bit more difficult to place emphasis within this color scheme, unless you use white for the contrast.

"Once again, let's tackle color value," I said. "Blue is lower in value than red, for example. But either color can have the same intensity."

"Using a monochromatic color scheme would produce work that's low key value, right?" Zed asked.

"Not exactly, Zed," I answered. "You can produce a range of values, so any value system is possible with monochromatic colors. A low key illustration would use the darker values of a particular color, and a high key value illustration would use lighter values of that same color."

"Got it!" he nodded.

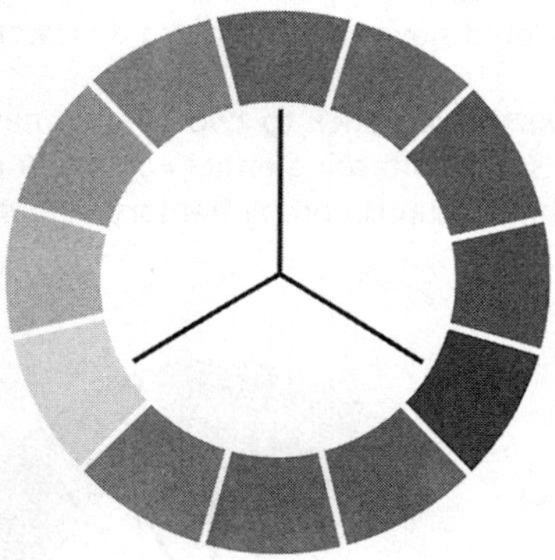

"The **triadic color scheme** consists of three colors that are placed at thirds on the color wheel. For instance, using a triadic color scheme of red, yellow, and blue – the primary colors in the subtractive color system – will produce vibrant work, giving plenty of room to utilize warm and cool colors both in contrast and emphasis. Triadic schemes also give you flexibility for a range of balance."

I pointed at the lines that connected the colors. "In most of these color schemes, it might help you remember that they can be connected with simple geometric shapes. While you can use a ruler or any straight edge to pick out your complementary colors, triadic color schemes can be chosen with the use of a regular or isosceles triangle."

I continued to the next color scheme. "The **triadic split complementary color scheme** is just like the complementary color scheme, except you pick two colors at one end of the line that connects the two colors. One is the original color, and the other colors are on either side of the original color's complement. This triadic split complementary uses three colors."

"For example, we might first choose red, and then the two other colors would be yellow-green and blue-green. This scheme will give you an emphasis color, in this case red, and two other colors which will complement as well as contrast the original color. This also gives you a great balance for warm and cool colors.

"The **tetrad complementary color scheme** consists of two pairs of complementary colors. Red and green, paired with the complements of yellow-green and blue-violet would form a tetrad complementary scheme."

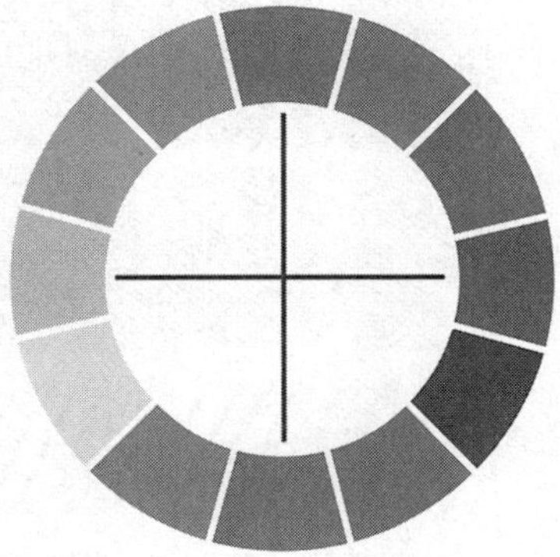

I commented, "This color scheme is really effective to use in graphic presentations, but just like the complimentary color scheme, you need to be careful with the values. If you use all the same values with the colors in this scheme, the images could vibrate right off the page.

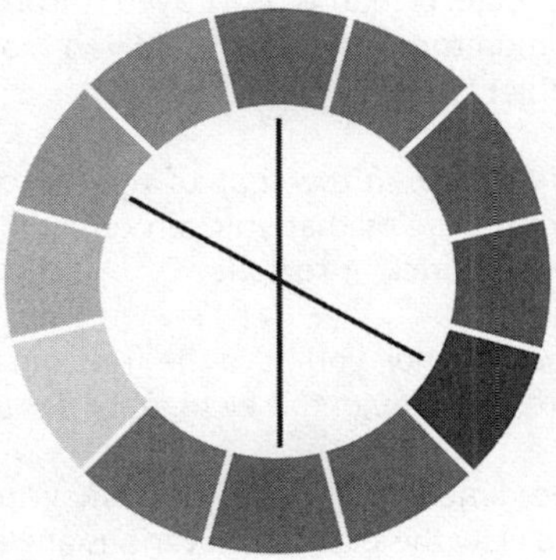

"Let's look at one final scheme – the **tetrad split complementary color scheme** consists of four colors: two pairs that are complements, spaced with one color between each pair. This example shows the complements of red and green, and the complements of orange and blue. This is an interesting color scheme to use in rendering abstracts for vibrant contrasts." I added, "But these colors are not so vibrant that you would worry as much about your values."

"Wow," Zed looked exhausted. "That's a lot of schemes to remember."

"I guess it would be a good idea to keep our notes and these schemes handy when designing for clients," Bonnie added. "In fact, I think I need to redesign a few of my sites, now that I see how color works."

Wes laughed, "Bonnie, there's a lot more to learn about color yet. We could spend many years studying the mixes and affects of colors on viewers."

"What if we want to just mix it up, and ignore the rules?" Zed asked.

"Oh, there's a name for that scheme, too," I answered. "The **incongruous color scheme** is completely liberal – just utilize any colors that don't fit into the schemes above."

Wes laughed. "I didn't realize there was a scheme behind my color style!"

"The point of color schemes is to help develop a formula to break away from artistic intuition," I replied with a smile. "You might have trouble here, Wes. For the rest of us, these schemes will save time in the development of our graphic messages."

Wes threw up his hands and shrugged, "My life needs simplifying; I'm game!"

"Good," I replied. "Let's move on to texture."

The value of texture

Designers use **texture** for viewers to visually grasp the *feel* of our work. Texture defines the surface of objects and can enhance our surroundings. My plan for this part of the class was to teach the concepts of texture in design to the students and get to grips with the various tools in Flash MX that can be used to add the illusion of texture to their work.

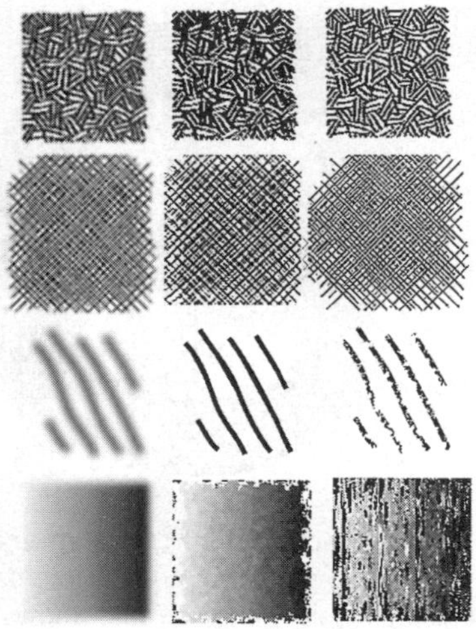

"If you all remember from our introductory class last week," I began, "Texture is a complex problem for two-dimensional work. I'm going to talk to you about texture, and then we'll discuss the problems and see how we can create illusions of texture for our viewers in Flash.

"You remember we can create various lines with various drawing tools. These lines can be used to create texture. We can also use shape to depict texture." I held up a sample of various textures rendered with pencil. "We'll learn to depict texture with our drawing tools when we brainstorm about our client," I said. "For now, I want to explain how texture can affect our viewers.

"We can touch three-dimensional objects and grasp the feel of them, but we can't touch an object that is portrayed through photography or through the monitor. We have to rely on our memories to tell us what this object feels like.

"This can be accomplished successfully in most cases, since our memory can *fill in the gaps* of the sensory information that we receive. For instance, if you look at a sketch of a brick, it helps that you can remember the feel of the brick. Of course, this can happen only if you've ever touched brick in real life.

"All objects have texture, even if it's the slick gloss of a photograph. As the designer, you have the freedom to revel in developing contrast, depth, and direction for the viewer's visual interest through this element of design.

"Earlier, Wes mentioned the relationship we have between two- and three-dimensional pieces of work. When we view architecture, collage, or sculpture, we have a chance to touch and view the piece from various angles.

"I remember visiting one of Frank Lloyd Wright's homes as a student. The house, Falling Waters, was an amazing example of contrasting textures. Now, when I see a photograph of Falling Waters, I can remember how that house felt. I can even remember the sounds of water as I walked through the house.

"However, if you haven't visited this house, your experience will be totally different than my experience when we both look at the same photograph.

"When we talk about texture within a two-dimensional field, this is called **visual texture**. The texture in a three-dimensional field is **tactile texture**. You can use the term tactile texture to also refer to a painting or illustration that has been developed with uneven paint surfaces. A surface that has been prepared with thick pigments or on a format that is textured gives more depth to an illustration or painting. Even when this work is photographed or scanned for printing, this texture carries over into the flat image, giving the image a visual depth that has more impact.

"The illustrator or painter adds texture to their work by creating the illusion of texture. When a painting or illustration is rendered with lush reproduction of texture, this alone can catch our eye and imagination. Fantasy artists use computer tools to imitate life, lending realistic form to their imaginary landscapes.

"This realism in texture development is most prominent in what is known as **trompe l'oeil**, French for *to fool the eye*. The next time you visit the library, take a look through the section on interior design. You'll find books dedicated to this subject, showing how a painted window, door, or plant on a wall adds the illusion of space and focus. These paintings, when rendered with care, are true optical illusions.

"When you create the illusion of wood, stone or other textures, you add contrast, depth, and direction of interest. Repetition of a pattern within a two-dimensional piece often adds texture." I held up a pattern that could be used in wallpaper or fabric.

"This use of pattern is not to be confused with the regularity of pattern found in the design of gift wrap or textiles. The difference is whether or not the pattern arouses our sense of touch, or if it is displayed as a tool for an appealing design."

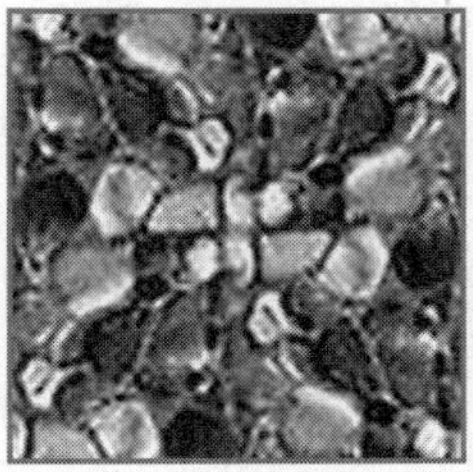

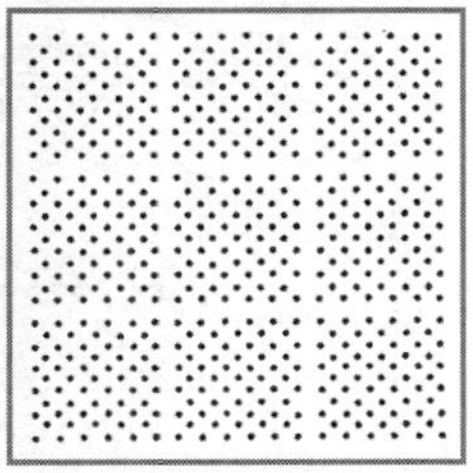

I held up two more pictures. "You can see the difference in this pattern of stones compared to the recurring pattern of dots. The stones appear tactile; while the dots are a graphic pattern that lends little to texture our memories on texture.

"As artists and designers, there is one clue about texture we need to remember: visual distance is a factor in how we deliver the goods. From a distance, everything appears much smoother than when we're in close proximity to an object. In a painting or illustration, the artist renders distant objects with less detail than the object they want to appear closer to the viewer's eye. On the other hand, you can create optical illusions by creating detail in distant objects and less detail in foreground objects."

I set the visual examples aside and asked if there were any questions.

"I don't have a question," Wes began. "I have a complaint." We all looked at him expectantly. He turned to Bonnie and said, "Why do web designers feel they need to use so much pattern and texture in their site designs?"

Bonnie laughed. "That's a fair accusation – I know I've been guilty of this in the past, when I've been so inspired by all the bells and whistles that came with various software programs."

"Since then, I've learned three things." She continued, "First, I learnt that all these little fun items I used to portray motion, texture, and pattern all take time to download. Most people aren't patient enough to sit there for the length of time it takes for all these elements to display on their screens."

"Then," she added, "I discovered that some people even turn their images off for that very reason. They just want information, not all the visual effects. In fact, I remember reading a story about the inventor of the World Wide Web, Tim Berners-Lee, and the fact that he originally preferred web pages to be image-free, simply plain text, never mind any fancy textures, because it "*forced people to be literate*". His original vision was that of a serious medium for sharing and publishing scientific information. A noble aim indeed – of course, this was way back in the early '90s, long before Flash came along!"

It was encouraging to see that Bonnie was already starting to see the advantages of Flash. She went on, "Anyway, accessibility should be the key issue here. Although my sites may not be color-coordinated, they are pretty simple and highly accessible to anyone."

She concluded, "In fact, I doubt I have the illusion of texture rendered in any of my clients' sites."

"Bonnie's raised a number of good reasons why we need to be careful about visuals rendered for the Internet," I responded. "Texture is one element that can be used, but we often need to use images to portray textural surfaces.

"Another point to remember about texture," I added, "Is that a little texture can go a long way. There's no need to overwhelm your viewer with a glut of visual texture. Small uses of texture with the intent of contrast is appropriate for any tool of visual communication."

Wes tapped his pencil on his drawing pad, concentrating on drawing dots on his page. "Here, Bonnie." He held up an image. "Pretend the lines are values, and it portrays water. Do you see the dots at the bottom?"

"You mean the sand?" she asked.

"Exactly," Wes answered. "I only needed a few dots to communicate the sand to you. The context helped, though. You don't have to draw in every little dot of sand."

Bonnie laughed, "I probably would, to be honest."

"How can you create texture in Flash then?" Zed asked.

"Actually, you might find it easier to use Photoshop or a similar bitmap application and import your image into Flash MX. Remember, Flash is a vector graphics program so it produces solid shapes with little or no texture.

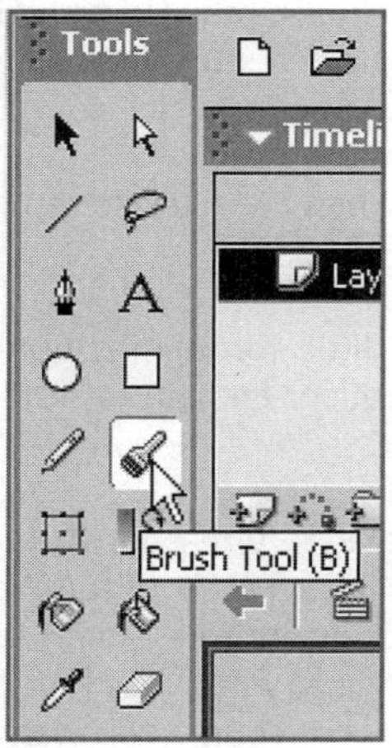

"But if you want to create texture in Flash, you can manage it with some of the standard tools, like the Brush tool..."

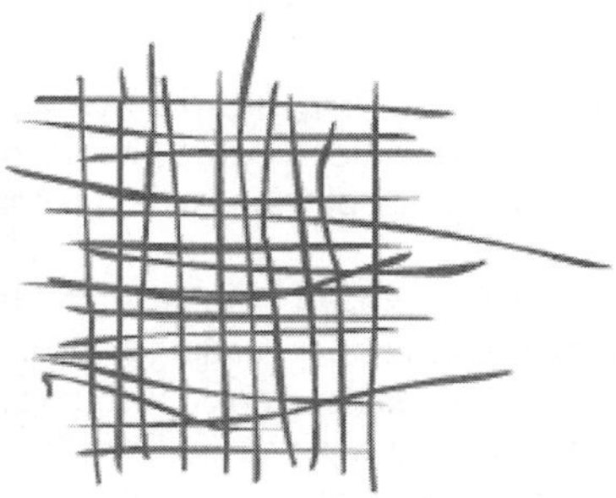

"Also, it's worth taking a look at the different stroke styles available via the Property inspector..."

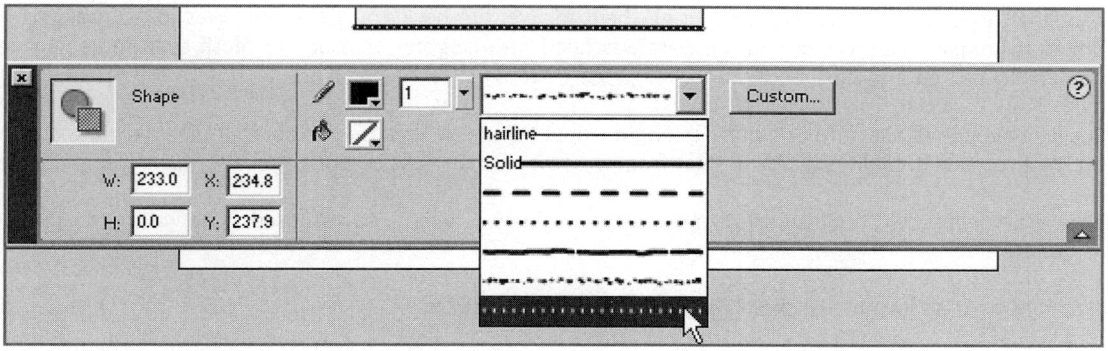

"These styles give a textural feel immediately, but we should note that vectors graphics are anti-aliased and..."

As I expected, Zed was first to interrupt and announce his confusion, "You kind of lost me there on that anti-alienating thingy?!"

"**Anti-aliasing** is where pixels are smoothed out on the screen, so the viewer can't see any harsh edges. If you examine a zoomed bitmap image of a curved line in Photoshop and compared it to a zoomed anti-aliased vector shape created in Flash, you'd see a clear difference between the two – the Flash vector line would be appear nice and smooth."

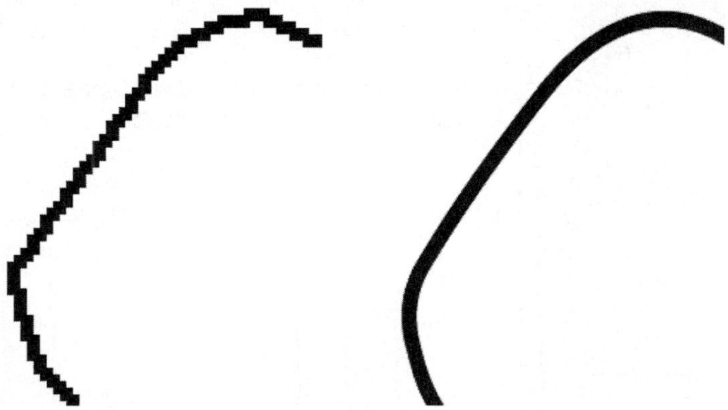

Wes was quick to try this out on his computer, "You're right, one of the shapes is really blocky and ugly." Said. "Other than that, they look like the same curve."

"Correct Wes." I replied. "They are the same shape, only that the Flash one is anti-aliased and the pixels are smoothed, and the other one is jagged."

"Sometimes, the edges of my transparent GIF images look like that," said Bonnie, "Even when they are unzoomed!"

"Although it is rough," Steve started, "It has a bit of texture, whereas the Flash curve doesn't. So it seems obvious that we'd need to use bitmap images in Flash for any real texture. We learned about the difference between vector and bitmap graphics in last week's class, but how does Flash actually work with bitmap images?"

"Flash MX allows you to use bitmap images in virtually any way," I said, "From making a texture with them, to resizing or recoloring them."

"But that doesn't mean you can start using them for website backgrounds again!" Wes joked, wagging his finger at Bonnie. She blushed and the class was filled with laughter, making her blush even more. Her red face finally retired into her hands.

"Using an image as a texture or pattern is alright – depending on the pattern!" I said. "If the image is too heavy on the eye, then it could not only detract from the rest of your website, but could also make it unreadable."

"I have a few images I took on my digital camera on the way here," Zed enthused. "Can we try to use them as textures?"

"I'm sure we'd all love to see them Zed. Load them in," I replied.

After Zed had uploaded his pictures, the class gathered around and witnessed a slideshow of his wanderings that morning, with highlights of graffiti and a shiny red fire truck. When a photo of a road tunnel came on the screen, Zed stopped clicking, "This one is my favorite!" he said.

"OK, let's use this one." I said.

I pointed out the Color Mixer panel to Zed, and asked him to focus on the drop-down menu therein. After selecting Bitmap from the drop-down, he was prompted to browse for an image to import into Flash. Zed browsed for the tunnel image file, confirmed the import, and then the image appeared in the Color Mixer palette.

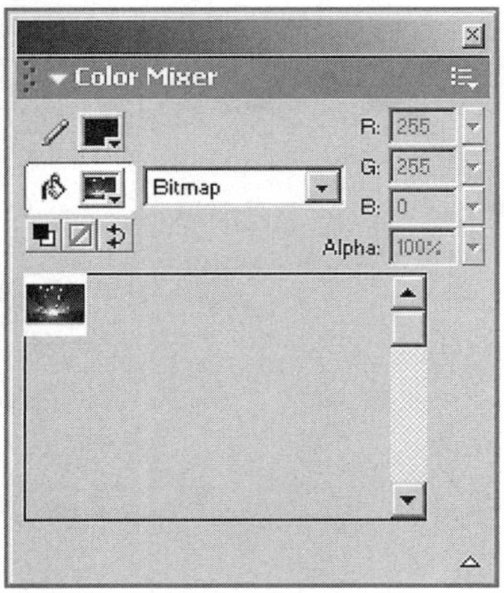

I then instructed Zed on the next few things to do, "Select the image, as you would any color, and use the Circle or Square tool to draw a shape."

Zed pulled out a circle and was amazed, "Wow! That's so cool!" He went on to draw a rectangle too.

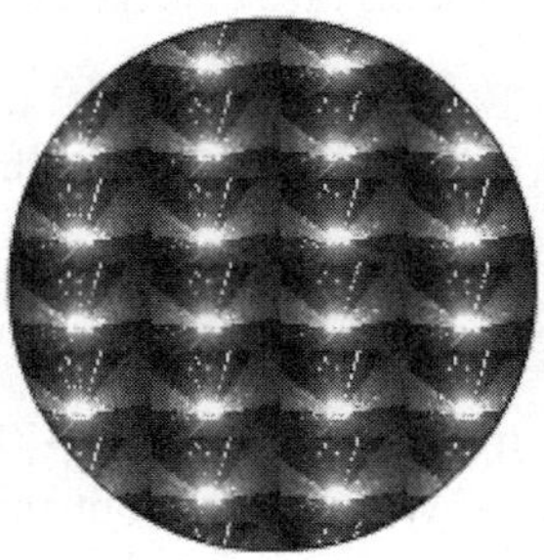

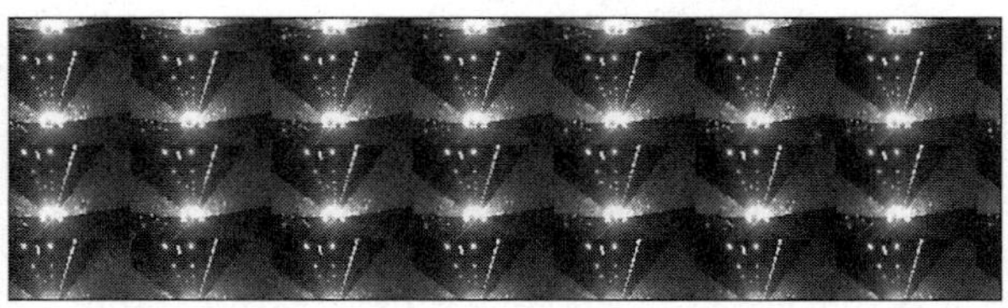

"Eek, that's ugly." Remarked Wes.

"I have a load of photos I can do that to that will look amazing." Zed said.

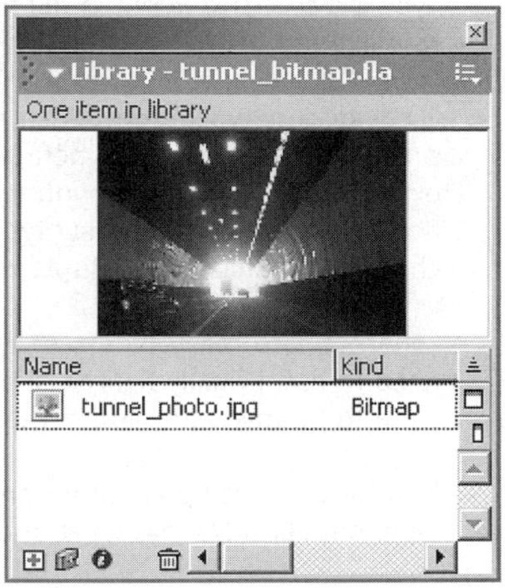

"Remember not to lose focus of your design goals though," I started, "And don't be blinded by the abilities of the application. Just because a particular tool is available in Flash MX, it doesn't mean you have to use it. You should always rely on both your design ability *and* the appropriate tool for the job."

"I don't think I'll fall for that one again." said Bonnie.

"Flash MX can use bitmaps for more than just textures though. Zed, if you open the Library from the Window menu, you'll see your photo in there too."

Zed opened the Library. "Oh yeah, that's my tunnel image that I used in the bitmap palette."

"That's right. Now you can just drag it onto the stage and it'll be shown at its real scale."

"That's much better!" Wes said.

On that note, I moved the class on to the next subject.

Typography essentials

Type is a crucial element in the field of graphic design, so in this part of the class I wanted to get the students to make use of the Text tool in Flash. Firstly, we'd talk about the use of typeface as an element of design.

"Let's discuss typography as an element to your designs," I began. "Type can create mood in your work. A single character of any typeface can be whimsical, serious, heavy, light, and a thousand other styles. For example, the flowing type you see in wedding announcements and invitations denotes elegance, whereas the heavy hand of some display type could give the feeling that ***you must buy the product!*** Type should be chosen strategically and displayed depending on how overt or subtle you want a message to be seen as."

"There are so many typefaces out there," Bonnie complained. "I often have trouble deciding which one I need to use. I finally figured out that most browsers only identify a limited number of typefaces. The others need to be made into images so they display the same across all browsers."

"You've brought up an important point, Bonnie." I continued, "Browsers have limited capabilities to render type, but Flash MX has ways of easily getting around that limitation."

I looked at Steve. "To begin, maybe Steve could help by highlighting the difference between serif and sans-serif typefaces before we go further?"

"Sure," Steve said. "Basically, **serif** type has *beaks* and *ears* attached to the figure of each letter, whereas **sans-serif**, or *without* serif, doesn't. These additions to the type are said to help the reader's eye move smoothly from word to word in body copy."

Serif

Sans-serif

I showed the class a visual describing the anatomy of several letters. "Here we see the arms, stems, ascenders, and descenders of a few characters. You can see that the letters are formed from several other pieces of anatomy. Each letter is composed of line, and these lines create planes. Other elements are utilized in type, and they all contribute to the feelings we're trying to convey to the reader."

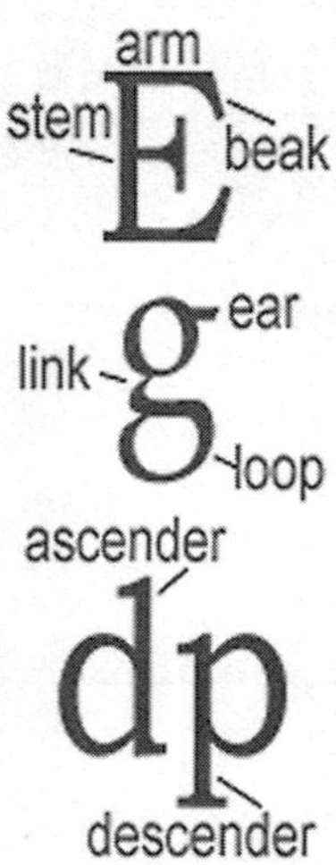

Zed peered at the letters. "Wow, they're like living beings. I've never thought about letters in terms of ears or beaks before!"

Wes laughed. "I've used letters in my artwork before," he said, "But I never knew they had beaks either!"

"They are like living objects," I said. "When you use words in graphic design, think about the feeling or mood you want to convey. Do you want to evoke comedy or tragedy? Are you going after a deconstructive look? Is your typeface harmonizing with the color and artwork in your design?

"Along with this emotional aspect, we also need to consider the readability of our type. Steve just mentioned that serif typefaces are often easier to read in large bodies of type. The next time you pick up a book, take a good look at the type in the headlines compared to the type in the body copy. If the book has no illustrations or images, you'll more than likely see serif typefaces." I pointed at our *Learn Design with Flash MX* book, "On the other hand, a book that has many images, tables, bulleted lists, and other visual tools may use a sans-serif type for easy scanning.

"As a general rule, you should never mix these two type categories, **serif** and **sans-serif**, unless you want to achieve a mood of confusion! Typefaces can also age on you. In the 1960s, Blippo was a very popular typestyle. It's not used much anymore, unless you see it in a retro look. Many of the faces have been around for years, and you are probably very familiar with them.

"Take some time to learn the stories of different fonts. You might find some fascinating history, full of business deals, artistry, and politics. You will learn how to develop your own style with type, which will likely change over the years as you learn more, and as you change in your own tastes.

"I'm a history buff, so I'm digressing," I laughed. "Back to the issue at hand – **readability**. Recent studies have shown that the format of the computer monitor brings with it a new problem with type altogether."

"On-screen readability tests have shown that people are able to read **Verdana** just as well as some common serif typefaces." I looked at Wes, who seemed slightly puzzled. "**Verdana**, Wes, is a popular san-serif typeface. The other sans-serif typefaces often used for screen text are **Arial** and **Helvetica**. Common serif typefaces are **Times** and **Georgia**."

"Newspapers often use sans-serif in headlines, because this type can easily be read from a distance. The serif type is reserved for body copy in newspapers, some magazines, and in novels that don't use heavy visuals, because it's easier to lead your eye from word to word," I emphasized, "Just as Steve mentioned. If you are creating a page with several blocks of type, you will need to be careful how many different typefaces you use. You can indent the first lines in each paragraph to help lead the eye into the text, but if you have other elements on the page you may consider just using a space between paragraphs.

"If you use one technique to separate paragraphs, please remember to use that technique throughout your project. Consistency is important.

"Until you become familiar with the different names and types of fonts, you'll find the standard sans-serif and serif fonts available in Flash MX useful.

"You can find these by selecting the Text tool and choosing from the drop-down menu of fonts in the Property inspector."

At this point, I set the class working with the Text tool in Flash. This would benefit them by familiarizing them with this important tool and getting them actively working with the rules of type.

"Select the Text tool, and click where you wish to type on the stage. You can change the font and font size in the Property inspector. If you need to reposition your text boxes, use the Arrow tool."

"How are there so many other fonts on the list?" Bonnie asked, "Doesn't Flash have to follow the same rules as HTML web pages?"

"Flash has a number of ways to get around the standard web-font list, from embedding fonts in the Flash SWF file, to enabling you to break the font apart into a graphic. In both cases, it allows you to use any font installed on your system in one way or another."

"How about using all of them?" asked Zed.

"I think that's what they call *punk* Zed." Replied Steve. "You might only want to do this if you are creating some form of chaos or anarchy."

"Cool!" replied Zed.

"Steve is right, unless you are going for a particular effect, stick to a set number of fonts, such as three. This'll allow you enough styles for headings and body text." Glancing over at the students' screens, I noticed Deb's work.

"Deb, what can you tell me about your effort?" I asked.

"Well, I stuck to the rules that you gave us, using the Flash sans-serif and serif fonts," she said.

"What else has Deb used?" I asked the class.

"Isn't that bold text in the header?" asked Bonnie, staring hard at the screen.

"Yes it is, I used it for a little emphasis, where I thought it was required," replied Deb.

"Good work Deb." I said. "You've also created a shape with your text.

"When you lay out type on a two-dimensional piece of work, you create a line with the type. This line may flow to connect together, forming intriguing shapes. When you place a lot of type on a page with small words and letters, the value will create a shape. The paragraphs on a web page, for example, are basically square or rectangular shapes."

I had them step back from their screens so they could see the shapes created with bodies of type. "Another consideration of this element is size. Do you want to overwhelm your viewer with a huge heading? On a poster, where people will be viewing from a distance, this might be totally appropriate. On a printed page or a book or on a greeting card, you don't have to go that large. The format will often dictate type size.

"You can use type as texture for a background or to fill in a shape. Visualize an image of a dentist peering into a child's mouth. With a plain background, somehow the image has no impact. With the word *Ah* screened into the background you suddenly bring humor and *sound* to the viewer." I held up a visual of text used to create shape. "This poem about the moon was creatively shaped into a moon crescent," I said. "Let's learn how to create some of these shapes with the Flash tools."

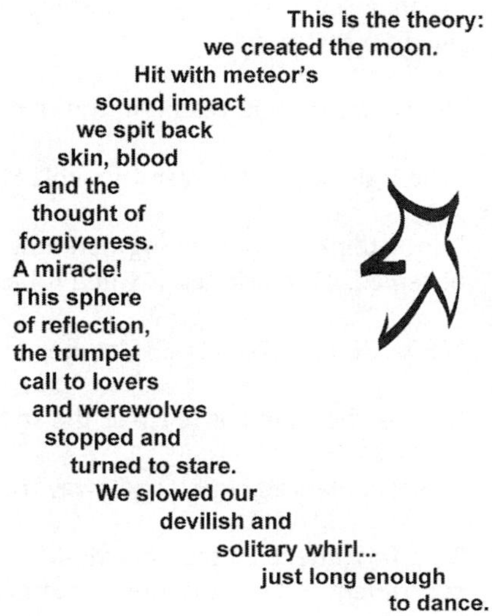

"Flash MX gives you the ability to manipulate type in a myriad of ways. Not only can you work with the style and color, but you can also rotate, reshape, and mirror text boxes."

"I can hear the cogs of Zed's scheming brain beginning to go into overdrive!" Steve joked.

"Where do we find all these magic abilities?" asked Bonnie. "They sound like a lot of fun. Using text on the web is usually so limited."

I quickly ran through the different options available to manipulate text or any other object within Flash. I showed them:

- The flip options – Modify > Transform > Flip Horizontal/Vertical
- The Transform panel – Window > Transform
- The option to turn text into a graphic – Modify > Break Apart - and then use the Free Transform tool on the toolbar

I let the class run loose for a while, instructing them to work with the elements that we'd covered into today's class, while I went to fetch a coffee.

When I returned to the class, all of the monitors were filled with diverse typographics.

"Is everyone finished?" I asked. After a few frantic mouse clicks, they all agreed. "Who'd like to show their work to the rest of the class?"

Zed leapt out of his seat, "I'll go first!" he enthused.

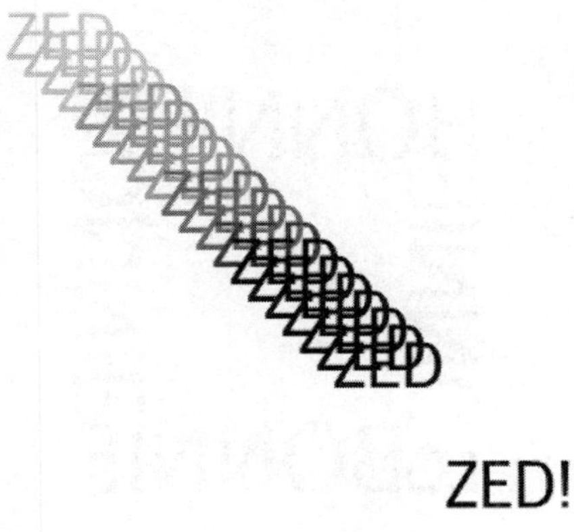

Zed came to the front of the class, away from his computer and began his show and tell animating with his hands. "My piece is called *The Exclamation*," he said, "I think it says a lot about me."

Zed then turned up his nose and bowed theatrically. The class filled with rapturous applause.

"Bravo! Bravo!" a few of them shouted.

"Good work Zed." I said. "I think it is pretty true to your personality."

"I think it should be bigger though," Wes added, "How about printing it on a billboard?!"

"Thanks Zed. This is a great display, demonstrating the use of text to form a shape, and using gradation to build up the message."

"It also makes you read it in the rhythm of a moving train." Deb added.

"The train seems to crash though!" Steve added.

"No, I think the increasing darkness of the text suggests that the train is speeding up from a halt." Wes observed. "The last Zed is when it has reached full speed."

"ZED... ZED... ZED... ZED..." Zed began in rhythmical fashion, until Deb touched his shoulder to silence him.

"I think the train has reached the station Zed." I said, "Time to get off. Who's next?"

Wes volunteered, and stood away from his computer giving the others the chance to take a look.

"For this effect I used the Modify > Break Apart option twice – first, to break the phrase down to its constituent letters, and then once more to break the letters down to basic graphics. Next, I selected all of the letters and used to Envelope option of the Free Transform tool to make some animated waves." Wes announced. "The frequency of the waves gets larger as they go along."

"Very mathematical Wes." Deb observed.

"That's cool!" exclaimed Zed, "Why didn't I do something like that!?"

"Excellent work Wes." I said, "You've managed to combine motion and drama here, without any other devices like color or lines. "OK, who's next? How about you Lisa?"

"Alright." Lisa said, standing up. "I've used a little contrast and flipping to make my top word stand out.

"Good work Lisa. Very theatrical – that's a really effective technique. Anyone else?"

"I guess that'll be me." Said Bonnie, standing up. "I've made a rather obvious shape with my text."

"Bonnie's text is more like lines than text, because there is no emphasis on any one element of text. This makes a pretty rigid square.

"Excellent work class! You've all used type to convey all sorts of design elements brilliantly. Let's learn more about making use of them now."

Utilizing the elements of design

Analyzing the elements of design takes more than one lesson. In fact, it can take years of instruction, observation, and practice to gain a complete design education. With this in mind, it's clear that the students will learn more about the elements of design through their own practical experience. It was time to set this week's class project, and start to work with the tools in Flash MX.

"We've covered a lot of ground today," I said. "So I think it's time to wrap it up until next week."

"We didn't cover space!" Bonnie said.

"I'm all spaced out," Zed replied. "My brain feels like it's just eaten a huge meal. I'm stuffed!"

Wes laughed. "You're going to hit us with space next week, aren't you?" he said. "I know it's a complicated element, and it can be developed through all the other elements of design."

"You're right, Wes," I replied. "You'll learn about space next week. We'll also cover the element of movement as we get more involved in using Flash."

I hadn't heard much from Lisa all day. I looked at her and asked if she had any questions.

"No, I think you've explained everything pretty clearly," Lisa replied. "I do have an announcement, though." Everyone perked up and looked at her. "We have permission to go to the theater, but it won't be for a few weeks. They're practicing for a new play, but when the play begins, the theater will be free during the day to play with lighting."

"Great!" I almost laughed out loud at Wes's reaction. He was beside himself with obvious delight. "That will help us understand more about the properties of additive lighting," I said.

"Yeah," Zed said. "We can pretend we're standing inside a huge monitor."

Bonnie laughed. "That's all I need. I'll begin thinking like you and Wes. If I get too creative, I might even get a grip on the difference between negative shape and negative space!"

"You're doing great, Bonnie," I assured her. I looked at Deb's wrist. "And, Deb's doing great as well. I notice you left your watch off again today."

Deb laughed. "I figured I may as well relax and enjoy this process," she said. "The guys at work are actually a bit jealous about my time off for this class. Plus," she added, "I finally realized the boss has some plans for me. Otherwise he wouldn't have sent me here in the first place."

"That's the spirit, Deb!" Wes stood and applauded.

Steve stood and stretched, too. "What's the plan for next week, Linda?" he asked.

"No groans this week," I warned. "Otherwise I'll add more work to your project." Wes put his hand over his mouth, and I laughed, "You're probably not going to enjoy this, Wes, so I want you to keep that hand in place for a moment.

"This week, I want you all to create the color schemes that we've looked at today using the standard tools that you find in graphics software like Photoshop," I began. I noticed Wes tightening the grip on his mouth. "You can use any graphics program you have access to on your computers to create these images, and we'll import them into Flash to help us learn about composition." I turned to write on the board.

"First, you will create a color wheel, using only the 216 web color palette."

1. Create a color wheel using the 216 web color palette.
2. Create images using the following color schemes:
   - 3 warm colors
   - 3 cool colors
   - complementary
   - analogous
   - monochromatic
   - triadic
   - split complementary
   - tetrad comp
   - tetrad split comp

I continued to write a list of the different color schemes. "Then, you'll create images using the different color schemes. You'll use three warm colors and three cool colors to create two images."

"Then use the seven other schemes to create seven more images. These images don't have to be complicated. You can create a square with another square in the middle for the complementary color scheme. Keep it simple, so you can begin to see how the colors affect each other together."

"These can be saved as JPG or as GIF," I continued. "That's ten images altogether. Any questions?"

"What if we can't find the right color?" Bonnie asked.

Wes berated her, "Bonnie, remember what we learned earlier? We can't possibly match the colors exactly, especially with the limits of the 216 color web-safe palette. Just go for the best you can."

Bonnie looked surprised. "Oh, right. I forgot we don't have to be perfect!"

We all laughed. "I have one more assignment for you," I added. Zed almost moaned, but Wes poked him before the sound could escape.

"Play around with the tools in the Flash MX toolbar," I said. "Especially the Pen tool, if you're not already comfortable with it. I would like to see some of you take an initiative and begin to create textures and shapes with value with the Flash tools. We'll cover these tools later in the course, but there's no harm in getting a head start!

"Now, go on, get outta here!" I laughed. "See you all next week." And with that, everyone packed up their tools and headed off, hopefully to have some fun exploring the wonders of the Flash tools...

Summary

In this class we focused on some of the core elements of design – points, lines, planes, shapes, color, texture, and typography – and studied the relevance of these concepts to everyday life, and their importance in the context of graphic design.

First we highlighted the variables of line, which are also applicable to the other design elements:

- **Size**
- **Shape**
- **Position**
- **Direction**
- **Number**
- **Interval**
- **Density**

Then we looked at the various types of shapes and analyzed their subtle meanings:

- **Geometric** shapes
- **Organics** versus **man-made** shapes
- **Found** shapes
- **Abstract** and **nonobjective** shapes
- **Positive** and **negative** shapes

Next up, we turned our attention to the various value systems in design, starting with the fundamentals of color. After defining additive and subtractive color models, and warm and cool color schemes, we used the color wheel to study some of the important color schemes:

- **Complementary**
- **Analogous**
- **Monochromatic**
- **Triadic**
- **Split complementary**
- **Tetrad complementary**

Finally, we outlined the value and use of texture and typography in web design, and started getting to grips with some of the tools in Flash MX.

In the next class we'll start to get our hands dirty by outlining and following the fundamental the principles of design to learn how to create the illusions of space and depth. These *design blueprints* will form the core methodology for any design projects that we undertake.

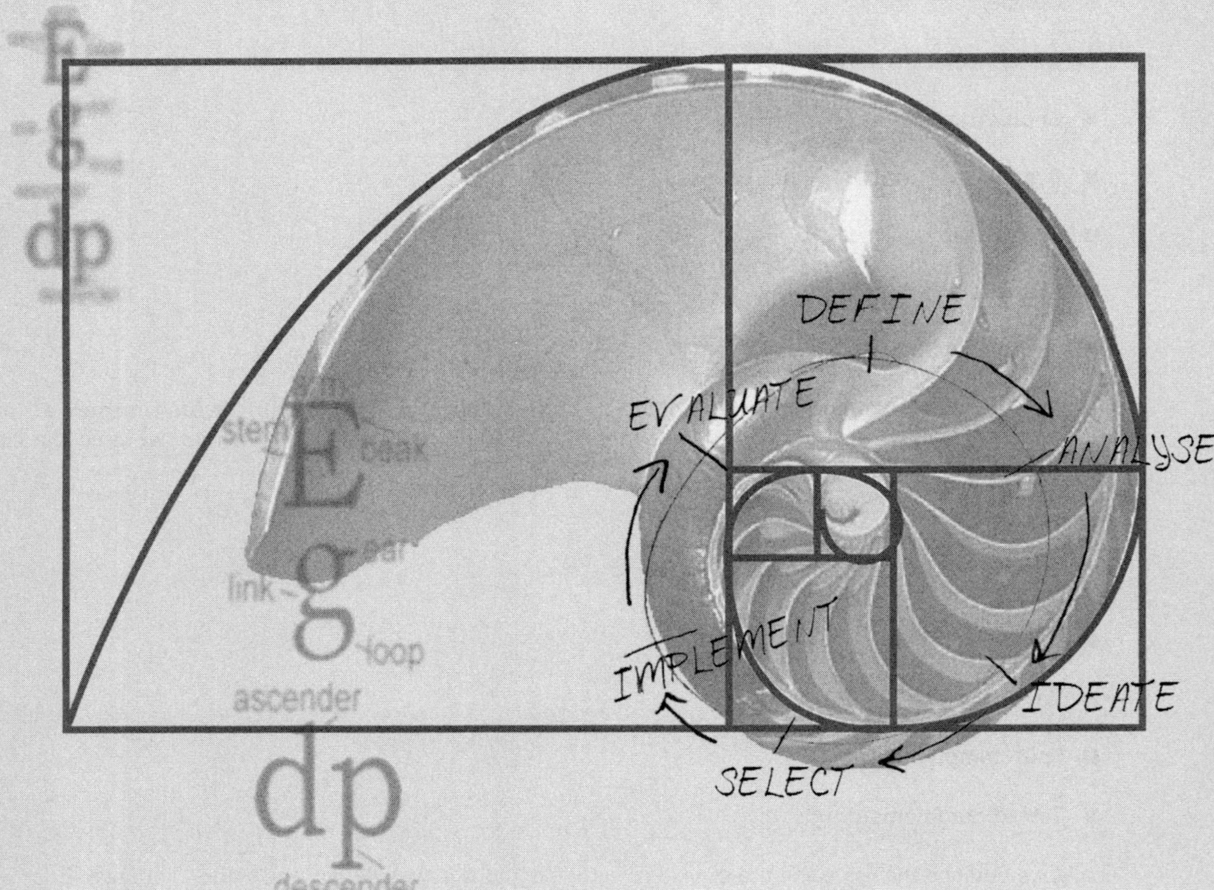
DEFINE
ANALYSE
IDEATE
SELECT
IMPLEMENT
EVALUATE
stem
peak
link
ear
loop
ascender
descender

Chapter 3
The Principles of Design

Objectives

In this class, you will learn:

- How to use the elements of design to create spatial relations and the illusions of depth and perspective
- Basic animation with the timeline in Flash MX
- The fundamental principles of design:
    - Contrast
    - Direction
    - Emphasis
    - Economy
    - Proportion
    - Balance
    - Rhythm
    - Unity

Introduction

I shuffled into the classroom, weighed down with visual aids and tools for today's class. I was surprised to find half the students already seated at the table, discussing elements of design.

"I'm seeing elements everywhere!" Zed shook his head. "I even feel like a different person. I'm not sure I like it, but I sure don't have any control over how I see things now."

Wes laughed and slapped Zed on the back, "How would you like to help me in the studio?"

Zed looked up with excitement, "Would I ever!" As he exclaimed his enthusiasm, he saw me enter the room and looked over excitedly, "Did you hear that?!"

"Sure did Zed," I looked at Wes and winked. "Are you sure you want to take this kid on?"

Lisa laughed, "He's really remarkable," she boasted. "A few of us met to work on our projects this past week, and Zed already had his work done. It was really useful because he approached the project from a totally different angle than we would have thought of," she explained, pointing at herself and Wes, and then nodding at Zed. "He definitely understands color problems inherent when using the computer screen as the format."

Zed shrugged, as his face turned a light shade of red. "I just subscribe to a lot of email discussion lists. During the last two weeks, I changed some of my subscriptions to include lists on design, where the subscribers talked about various problems when designing for the Internet."

Deb walked in, and Steve and Bonnie followed. They sat at the table and joined the conversation. "Good morning!" Steve nodded at everyone. "What's up?"

"Wes and Lisa were just bragging on Zed's new-found talents," I explained. "It seems we have a very intuitive designer on our hands."

Steve looked at Zed, "It's about time you found focus in your life." Everyone laughed.

"Zed explained that he was tapping in on resources on the Internet to help him solidify the material from this class." I looked at Bonnie. "Just like you've done in the past."

Bonnie responded, "I have learned a lot from folks on the Internet," she said. "I've also learned that a lot of design information is opinion, not fact."

Wes looked at her with a raised eyebrow, "Bonnie, opinion is good. Especially within the field of design." He leaned back in his chair. "The important thing is to make sure that the source of the information understands the elements and principles of design – if they have something to teach me, I'm all ears. We're learning the basics here. There are a lot of influences on these basics, and it would take a lifetime to learn them all."

Zed laughed. "Well, there's my advantage over you old design students."

Deb growled and leaned in, ready to pounce. "Old design students eat new design students alive!"

Everyone was still chuckling as I sat at the table and began my review of last week's class. "So, I've heard that Zed, Lisa, and Wes worked on their projects this week. Did the rest of you have any problems with last's week's project? I know from experience that replicating color wheels and color schemes using web-safe colors can be a task."

"Well," Bonnie glanced up at the rest of the class, "I had problems in the beginning, because I was trying to precisely match web colors to the color wheel." Wes groaned, and Bonnie interrupted, "I eventually loosened up, Wes. After an hour or two of fretting over it, I realized I just couldn't do anything about what I had to work with, and I got over it. I just used blobs of color to display the different schemes, though, rather than any intricate designs."

I asked Bonnie if I could see her work and looked around at the rest of the class. "Blobs are no problem," I smiled. "The real aim of the exercise was to become familiar with the various color schemes this past week. If you did this, then the project was a success." I leafed through Bonnie's images in her drawing pad and nodded. "Keep this work, because we'll refer to it later in the course."

At this point, Deb spoke up, "By the way, I found a great resource at www.visibone.com/colorlab/big.html – here you'll find an interactive color palette containing the set of web-safe colors. I found this really useful!"

"Ah yes, that is a good resource Deb – I've got it bookmarked myself. Thanks for letting the class know." I replied.

"I just want to know for my own edification," Steve asked the class, "Did you all pick #FF0000 for red, #FFFF00 for yellow, and #0000FF for blue?"

Many of them nodded positively. "I had trouble with orange," Deb said. She looked at me, "Is there a correct answer?"

"You all had a very limited palette to work with," I stated. "If you came close, then you did well. We'll get more involved with the properties of additive color, the color model used for web design, when we tackle the class project.

"You all did great," I commended them. "Special kudos to those of you who took the initiative to find more information on the Internet." I nodded toward Zed and Deb. "But, I also want you all to take your heads away from the monitor when you're searching for resources – take a trip to the library, for instance.

"Books are a great resource, and they've been through rigorous peer review and editing; the information within a book presents us with a tangible and reliable reference." I said. "You could even start collecting books and building up your own libraries on design topics. You'll find books that go into great depth on each element of design. You'll also find designers you like, and others you don't like. Part of becoming a designer is looking at what other designers create, and understand why they create them with their own particular styles."

I was ready to change the course of this conversation to focus on today's subjects. "Last week, we covered six out of eight elements of design. We analyzed the elements of **line**, **shape**, **texture**, **type**, **value**, and **color** on the surface level. We also utilized the Flash tools to help us bring these elements to life within your projects.

"This week," I continued, "We'll continue with our tour of the building blocks of design by looking at the concept of **space** and how all the elements of design can create space. We'll also practice with perspective, and we'll learn a few different established layout techniques and see how they fit in with our particular format – the web. Then," I added, "We'll cover the various layout concepts and highlight the principles of design.

"We'll also cover the element of **movement** today, before wrapping everything up by outlining the *blueprints*, or fundamental principles, of design." I said.

"One thing I've noticed," Deb added slowly, "Is that all the elements seem to intertwine with each other. Lines make up planes, planes produce shapes, and shapes," she continued, "Form the elements of space."

"Ah!" Zed sat up, "So we did cover space last week!"

Deb glanced at Zed. "Ahem," she cleared her throat for attention, "And space often defines our format. Line also forms the different letters in our language, and these letters can be the shapes we use as an element in graphic design.

"All of these elements provide pattern and texture to our design," she concluded.

Wes began clapping slowly, and the rest of the class joined him in congratulating Deb. Wes said, "Now, all we need to do is deconstruct what you just said."

Steve bent down and banged his forehead on the table. "I think I'll go back to standard layout formats," he moaned

Bonnie patted Steve on the back, "I know what you mean, Steve. It seems I missed out on a lot of design while I was busy designing. I'm a little overwhelmed and embarrassed."

"It's OK to feel embarrassed," I assured Bonnie. "We all feel this way when we learn new ways to construct our lives and our work."

"Amen!" Wes interrupted. "When I look at my first art work, I shudder. I thought I knew it all back then. The point is that we should keep ourselves open to learning more," he continued, "To add to what we already know."

Zed shrugged. "I don't know much, so I guess you could say I'm a blank canvas. I don't even know what Steve meant by a standard layout."

"You're a primed space, ready to soak up the elements, Zed." I said. I looked around at the other students, "Everyone ready to talk about that blank canvas?"

They all nodded, and I continued, "Let's go to the computers, because we'll be doing some hands-on learning now to get to grips with the illusion of depth and perspective."

They all settled at the bank of computers, and we dived into a discussion of the element of space.

Creating illusions of space and depth

My plan was to begin this portion of this class by defining the concept of space, and how elements create spaces within our format. This short lecture should then lead naturally into the topic of perspective, in both static and dynamic images. These topics would be addressed as students worked at their computers within our chosen format – Macromedia Flash MX.

"I'm going to talk to you briefly about the element of space," I began. "And then we'll begin working within Flash, getting some practical experience so that we truly understand this concept.

"**Space** is an element that indicates open areas and depth in two- and three-dimensional design. A two-dimensional space is a picture plane, or format, and includes height and width. A three-dimensional space consists of open areas bound by frames or points of reference, and includes height, width, and depth. A 3-D space would be the open area in this room. Some space," I added, "is boundless or unlimited by boundaries in all directions – many scientists think this is the case for the universe, that it is an infinite expanse.

"It should be obvious by now that space has dimension, even if it's just height and width. As designers, we have these dimensions available to help us display depth in our work. This chore can be accomplished in a variety of ways, with a number of elements.

"In the last class we talked about how the architect shows the space within his design. He can point to the view and provide a ***psychic line*** for our eyes to follow, but a better way to communicate would be through a blueprint, or plan, of the house. Some people," I added, "Can't envision the house, even with a detailed blueprint."

I looked at the class. "What would the architect do in this case?"

Wes answered, "I guess the architect would revert back to the psychic line. He would have to describe the space by using a point of reference that would be familiar to the both himself and the client."

"Very good, Wes! The architect would try to help his client *see* his house with visual clues. These clues are based on familiar frames of reference, and would help the client with space perception."

"So," Deb said, "The architect would wave his arm around the room and state that a particular room would be this size?" She waved her arm around the room.

"Exactly," I answered. When an architect and his client stand together in a space, they have a familiar frame of reference. This reference is based on the visual distance between these two people and the objects around them.

"If a client can't get his head wrapped around what the architect is saying, the architect would have to build a model, right?" Zed asked. "And the architect probably uses models of human figures or cars to show size with comparisons. The humans and cars are more familiar than the building, so they have a frame of reference."

"You're right, Zed." I answered. "The architect would also use the elements of design to explain the problem within a visual format. He would use value, color, line, texture, and motion to portray the space around them. If he used three-dimensional clues, he would include scale models to portray height, width, and depth. If he used two-dimensional formats, he would use tools to display the illusion of depth within that space.

"We'll begin with the visual clues for depth perception within a two-dimensional space," I said, and then turned to Lisa. "Lisa, can you tell me how color helps us perceive depth?" I asked. I stood and began to write on the whiteboard behind me.

Color:
* Cool colors most often recede (blues, greens, cool chromatic grays)
* Warm intense colors most often pop out and appear to come toward the viewer (reds, yellows, oranges, warm chromatic grays)

Lisa closed her eyes and answered, "I think it would be in the use of value and intensity of color. It would also include the use of various hues. Warm colors come forward, so the architect would use cool colors to show depth and distance against the warm colors."

I started to make some notes on the whiteboard relating to what Lisa what correctly saying, and she continued, "Darker colors would also stay in the background, while lighter colors come forward." Lisa opened her eyes.

Value:
* Lighter values appear to come forward
* Darker values appear to recede
** Exception? - with aerial perspective, light values appear to recede and dark values are used for foreground.

"That would make sense, Lisa," Bonnie said. "You always put the spotlight on the star in the theater, right?"

Lisa laughed. "That's what I was thinking."

"Lisa's right," I responded, "Except in the case of **aerial** or **atmospheric perspective**."

"I was wondering if you'd bring that up," Wes stated. "But, this perspective also allows for overlapping, texture modification, detail, and size. It's the natural perspective of the effects of the atmosphere."

"Uh-oh, Mr. Art is getting excited!" Zed laughed. Wes looked smug.

To put this discussion back into context, I showed them an image of hills fading into the horizon. "Wes is right," I said. "If you've ever seen mountains, you'll understand how this works." I pointed at the first mountain. "The darker mountain appears to be closer. The lighter mountains appear to be further away, even though they appear to be larger than the first mountain. The mountains in the foreground overlap the mountains in the distance, and this gives us the impression that the first mountain is closer. Of course, in real life," I added, "There would be more detail and texture in the darkest mountain.

Perspective in Flash

I drew everyone's attention back to their computers, instructing them to open up Flash MX. "Flash has an easy way of working and organizing different levels of depths.

"Like Photoshop and a number of other graphics programs, Flash can store content at different *depths,* using what are known as **layers**. Not only do they make organizing and working easier, but they can easily enhance the illusion of depth in your designs."

"I guess making the mountains in Flash would be easy then?" Bonnie asked.

"More specifically, Bonnie," I replied, "It *will* be easy... we're going to do exactly that!"

"Is that a challenge?" asked Zed, flexing up. "I'm gonna ace this!"

"Well Zed, now is your chance to learn some Flash skills to add to your design knowledge." I stood up to get their attention. "We're going to make the mountains in Flash using the Oval tool, some simple distortion effects, and most importantly of all, we'll be storing the different depths on individual layers."

I began the tutorial by opening up Macromedia Flash MX on my laptop PC, which I then connected up to the projector so I could demonstrate to the students how to create layers. "Make sure you have a new Flash movie opened – this is the blank canvas for our landscape. If not, choose New from the File menu.

"Now we need to add the required number of layers for our landscape scene. The layers are shown in the timeline, and you'll notice that Flash creates an initial layer by default."

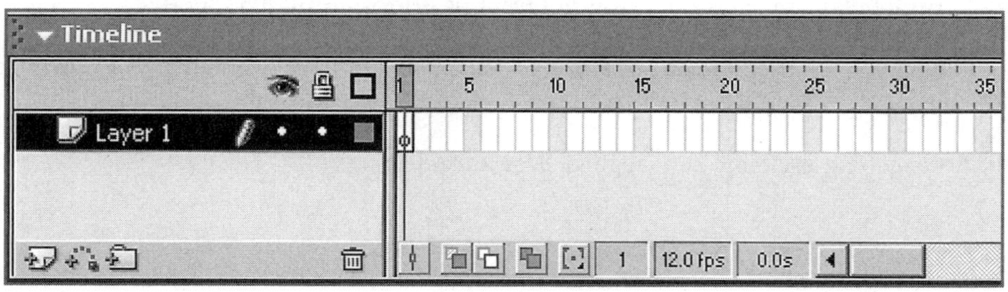

"Inventively called Layer 1!" Wes added. "I assume these can be renamed?"

"Sure Wes. Renaming your layers may sound like a trivial and pointless task, but it can make a significant difference when you are working on a more complex Flash file and you need to be able to distinguish between different elements of the design."

"I always name my Photoshop layers," said Bonnie. "Otherwise the simple task of manipulation becomes a living nightmare. I learned this the hard way, but I always name them as a rule now."

"I guess this is one thing that I might have to learn to do," sighed Wes. "Sometimes I have to squeeze out paint from a tube before I even know what color it is!"

"A degree of organization in your designs can really help to improve your work flow." I said. "Once you've worked on a few Flash movies, you'll quickly come to realize that naming layers is an efficient way to work, especially if you're working in a team and want your files and work methods to be perfectly clear to everyone else involved. "OK, let's add some layers to our file, to set us up ready for the mountains.

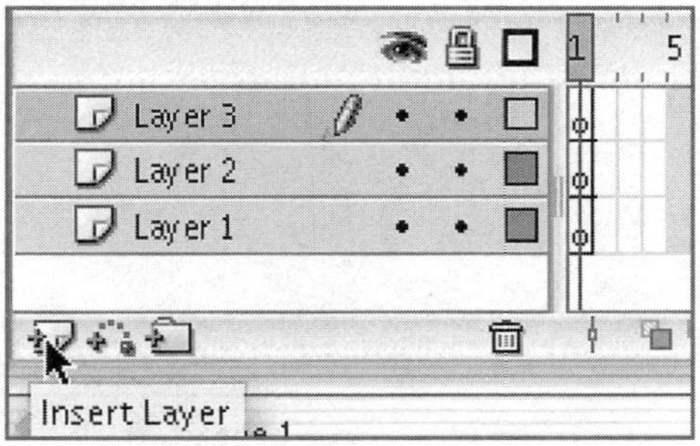

"Click on the Insert Layer button on the far left just below the timeline." I went around the room checking until everyone could find it. "Now click on it again, so that you have three layers. Your new timeline should now look something like this..." I pointed to the file that Steve was working with on his Apple Mac.

"The first thing to point out here is precisely how depth works in Flash. The uppermost layer is at the highest depth level, and the depth order goes down from there."

"So Layer 3 is the highest layer?" Steve asked.

"That's right Steve, visually this makes perfect sense: the top layer in the list is the top layer of your design, and the bottom layer in the list is at the bottom of the pile."

"Can we name the layers now? I think I might find it easier then." Steve said.

"That's the next thing we're going to do Steve." I replied. "Just double click on the name Layer 3 and enter front. In fact, you can also just double click on the layer icon to the left of the layer name to open up the Layer Properties window – here you can rename your layers. So, rename the next two layers middle and back."

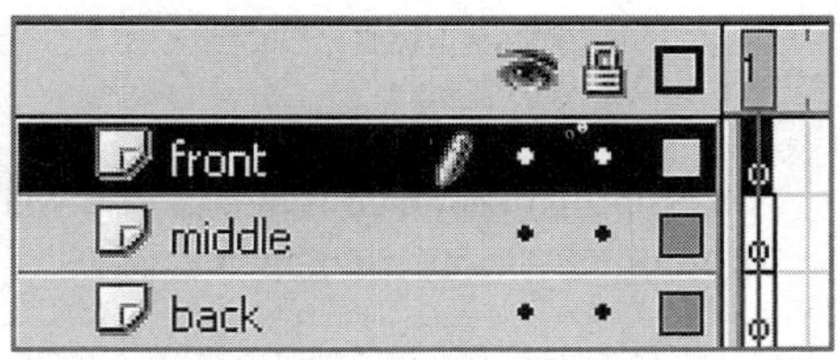

"I think I can guess where we go from here." Zed said. "We draw the different depths on these different layers, right?"

"Correct Zed, Now we'll make the landscape. Select the back layer, choose a light gray fill, and draw a shape with the Oval tool. As you draw, you'll notice that the keyframe on frame 1 of the back layer changes to become filled. This is because it has content."

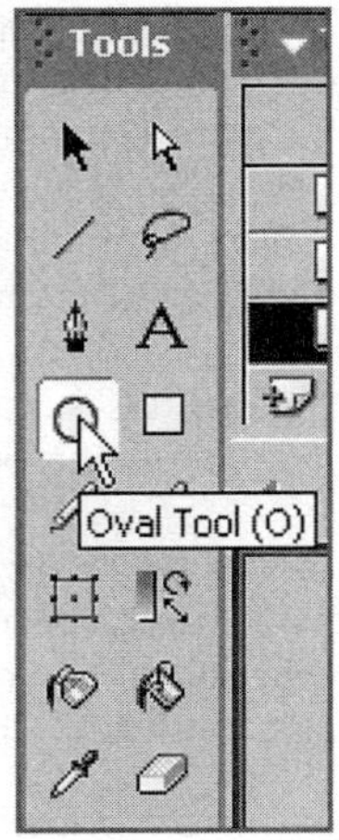

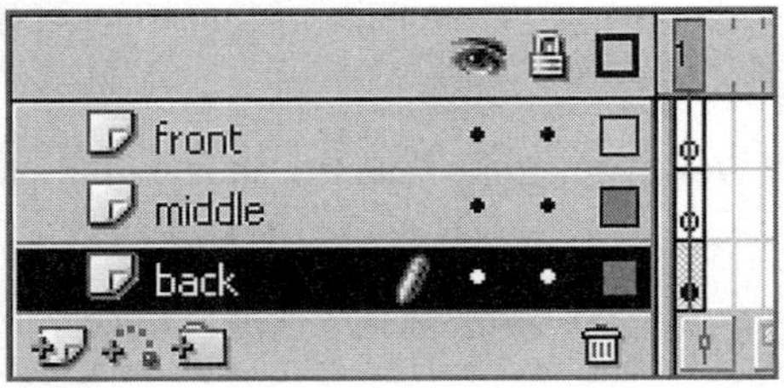

"Note that you can select all of the content in a keyframe by simply clicking on this solid keyframe."

The class then went silent as they began to render some simple shapes. Bonnie then broke the silence, "Um... my shape doesn't look much like a mountain."

"Well Bonnie, that's because you need to manipulate the circle or oval that you've just drawn. Do this by selecting the Arrow tool and placing the cursor over the edge of the unselected circle.

"When the cursor shows a little curve icon, click and drag to distort the circle." I went over to Bonnie's machine to observe. She quickly caught on.

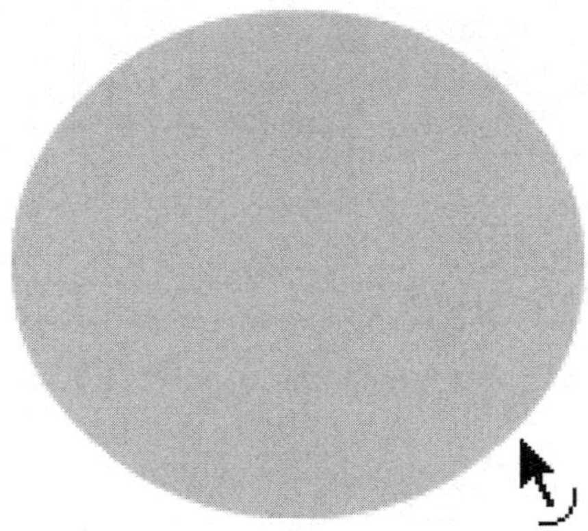

"Yeah, I get it now." Bonnie said. "I just need to keep manipulating it until I have a suitable shape. Easy once you know how."

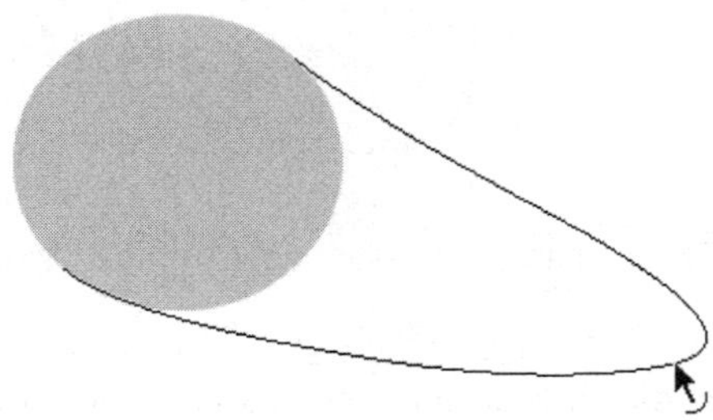

"It helps to know that Flash has an undo option to do this!" added Deb.

"Psst..." said Wes loudly, "Where is it Deb?"

"Try Edit > Undo." Deb replied. "This will remove the last action that you performed. The keyboard shortcut for undo comes in really handy – CTRL+Z on a PC or APPLE+Z on a Mac."

I thanked Deb for her input, and continued, "Flash allows you to set the number of levels of undo actions available. This is changed via the Flash Preferences... option. Although it is best to have a large number of undo levels, this demands more memory."

Pointing at Bonnie's developing mountain, I added, "Don't worry if the shape extends into the work area. When we come to render the Flash file, we'll only see the contents of the stage."

Bonnie's shape was now almost worthy of being called a mountain:

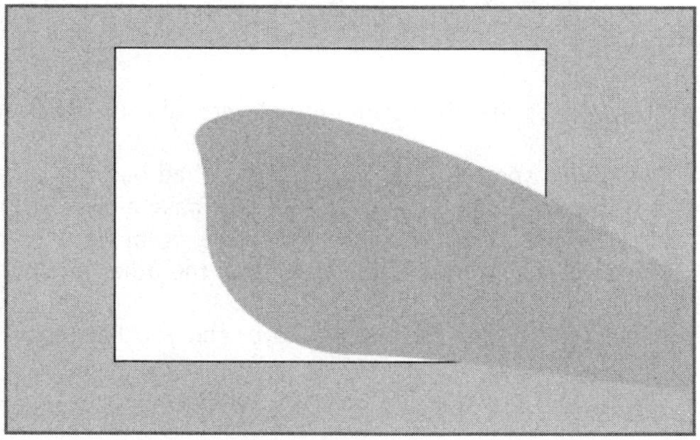

"Once you all have something like Bonnie, we'll move on to the next mountain."

"Bonnie's mountain doesn't look finished at all," said Deb.

"Taken out of context, you may be right Deb – but I think Bonnie has already considered that this is the back layer and, therefore, much of this won't be seen, and, therefore, she doesn't need any more detail."

"That's right," said Bonnie, grinning smugly. "I'm already aware of the depth of the image and the illusion that I'm about to create."

"Smarty pants!" said Deb, smiling.

The class returned to their mountains and after a bustle of activity, they were ready to move on. "Now that our furthest mountain is complete, we need to add the middle distance mountain.

"We could go ahead and draw it straight onto the middle layer, but you might accidentally affect the content of the back layer. Flash MX has a few tricks to help you get around this, allowing you to lock a layer to prevent you from changing it, or hiding a layer to hide it away from view."

I showed the class the **Lock** and **Hide** layer buttons alongside the layer names

"The lock option disables you from editing or writing to the a locked layer. This is useful when you are working with content that overlaps, and you don't wish to accidentally edit the alternate layer.

"The Hide option, signified by the eye icon, conceals a layer from view. This also locks the content from being edited.

"Both options are toggled by clicking on the dots below the relevant columns.

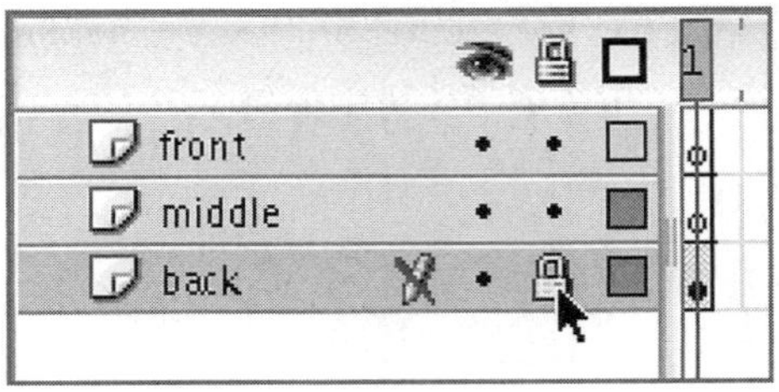

Zed let out a mock scream, "Argh! My mountain has disappeared!"

"Maybe David Copperfield had something to do with it!" joked Wes.

"You two make a good double act. Where can I catch your next show?" Steve asked.

"Don't you worry, I'm sure they'll be here next week." I said, winking at Steve. "Now, let's create our second mountain.

"Lock the back layer, and select the middle layer. Draw your second mountain, with a slightly darker shade of gray."

"Hey, what's that third icon in the layers list – the black square?" asked Zed.

"Aha! Well spotted Zed." I said. Zed pushed back his shoulders and swelled up with pride. "The last option is **Show Outlines**. This enables you to make a layer virtually transparent, except for its outline. If we were drawing the mountain range in reverse, from front to back, then we'd probably use this option to give ourselves a little idea of the space that the other mountains occupy.

"Select this option for the back layer and you'll see that it disappears, all except for a colored outline."

"That looks pretty useful actually," said Bonnie.

"It sure is Bonnie!" I replied, "If you have to maintain the perspective between layers then be sure to use this. OK, finish off your mountain range with the front layer and stand back to admire them!" The class then proceeded to finish off the detail."

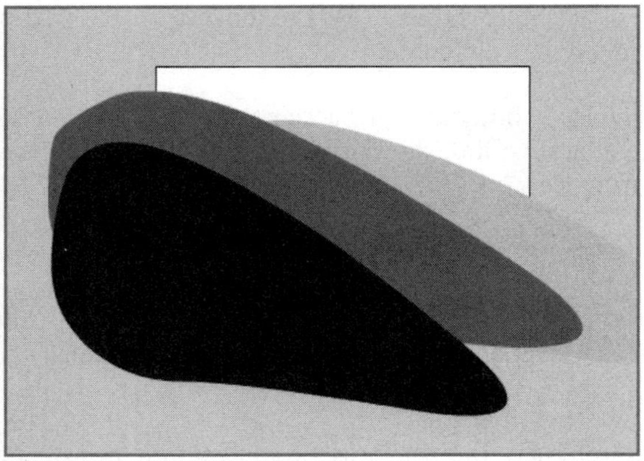

"Mine's hardly the Rockies is it?" asked Steve.

"Never mind if it isn't Steve, the main principle of depth in Flash MX is all that we're really interested in here – you can all start working on your masterpieces in your own time.

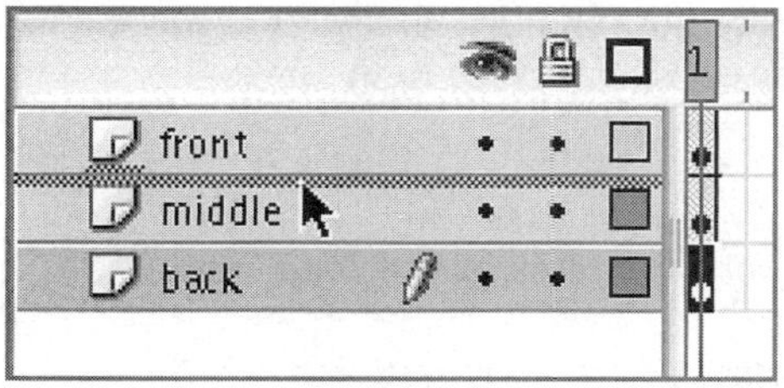

"Now, let's take a look at the importance of the ordering of these layers. For instance, if you wanted to ruin the basic illusion of depth, you could shift the order of the layers around. Layers are moved by clicking and dragging them up or down in the order.

"It's pretty obvious how this can affect your finished design!" I said.

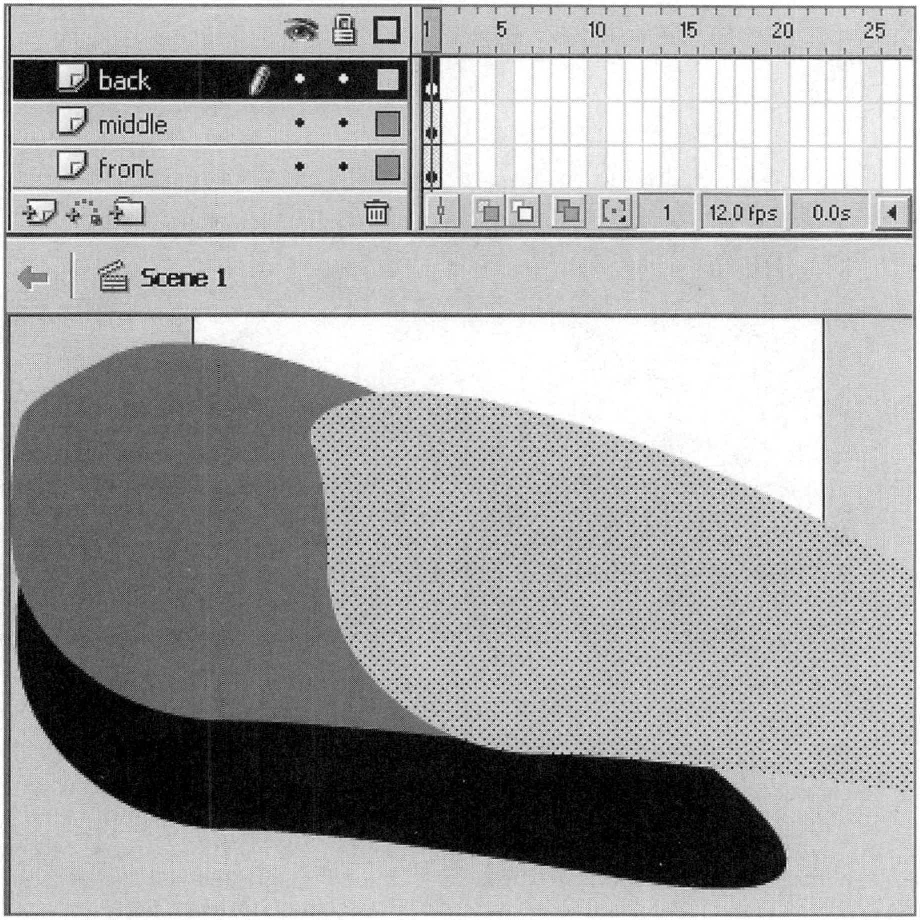

"OK, place the mountains back in their correct order and select Test Movie from the Control menu – this will publish a SWF file, which will be stored in the same directory that you've saved your FLA file in."

Once they had all done this, the SWFs were greeted with a few moans and groans from some of the class members, and obvious satisfaction from Wes and Steve.

"How come we get to see the work area on a PC, and Wes and Steve don't?" asked Zed.

"This is one of the few differences between the Mac and PC versions of Flash MX, but it isn't anything to get disgruntled about." I said, "The Mac version simply opens a preview window sized to the stage size, and the PC version usually opens a full screen window.

"If you just want to just see the stage area, click on the Minimize icon and the window will be reduced to stage size. Wes and Steve, alternatively, if you want to see the work area, click on the Zoom button."

Bonnie was the first to act. "That's better. Now they look like a mountain range, as opposed to just a bunch of shapes!"

"Excellent!" exclaimed Zed.

"Quite!" I said. "Now that you've all had a play with the depth tools in Flash, you can see how convincing depth can be illustrated by color and light. If you select the different layers and change their color, you'll notice that it doesn't look quite right. It loses its depth and becomes somewhat *flat*."

"But size has something to do with distance, right?" Zed asked as he peered at the image. "That would make sense. If something is smaller, it's further away. So if I want to make something look far away, I would draw it as I would actually see it in real life – small and fuzzy!"

Bonnie laughed. "Either you're right, or you need an eye exam."

I showed them a computer-generated fractal image to further demonstrate depth in design. "This picture shows distance by using the technique of increasing the size and overlapping the image elements. There's no blurring of image, and there's no change in value. Yet," I added, "You can perceive depth in this image. The upper left images appear to be closer than the images in the lower right.

"Of course, your images don't need to be this complicated," I added. "Let's try using the layers with one image. We'll reduce that image and layer it under the first one so you can see how size affects our perception of depth.

"We're going to draw two circles, one big and one small to show how size can influence depth.

"Start with a fresh file and add a layer. Rename the layers big circle and small circle. On the big circle layer, draw a large circle and place it on the left side of the stage.

"Now select the circle and copy it. Paste the circle into the small circle layer and place it on the right hand side of the stage."

"Now we need to scale the second circle right? What tool do we use for this?" asked Bonnie.

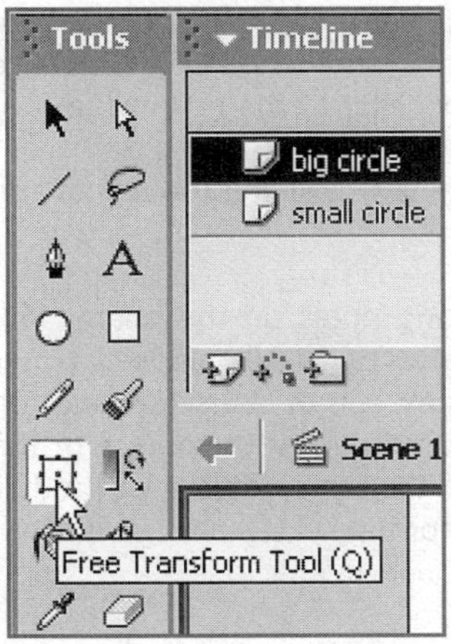

"Well, you have a choice here. You can either use the Free Transform tool or the Transform panel, which you can open from the Window menu."

"What's the difference?" asked Wes.

"Well Wes, the Transform panel is far more precise than the Free Transform tool, but the latter has more flexibility. For this task, I'd recommend using the Transform panel."

"It sounds like the Transform panel is for the meticulous and mathematical, while the Free Transform tool is for those who like to play it by ear and judge things for themselves," said Deb.

"I think I can guess which methods Bonnie and I will use, and I doubt it'll be the same," said Wes. "Not sure about the rest of you!"

"For now, let's go with the Transform panel, which you can open up by selecting Window > Transform." I said. "Select the second circle and with the Transform panel, type in 50% in one of the top two boxes. These boxes represent width and height scales, so make sure that Constrain is ticked, as this'll keep them even. Once you've done this press ENTER and the circle will be resized."

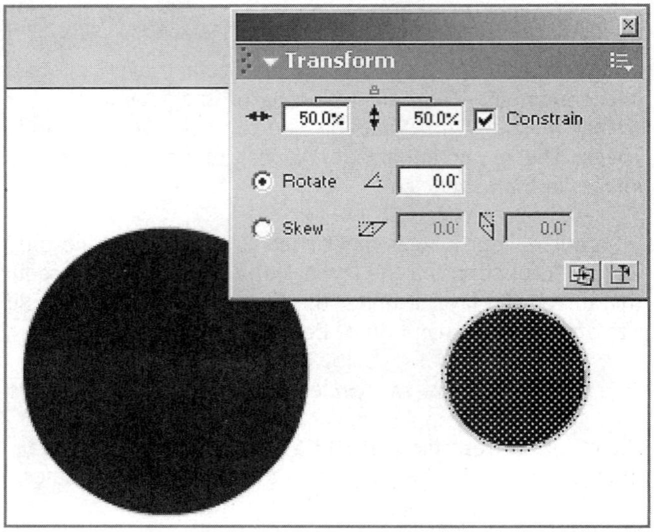

"I see a universe forming," said Zed, "Or at least a couple of planets!"

"Let me translate: I think Zed is saying that he can see the illusion of depth," said Steve.

"Even though we see exactly the same shapes," I started, "And their appearance is not enhanced with color, we are still fooled into seeing depth."

"If you stand in the middle of a railroad track," I continued, "The tracks in the distance appear to be smaller, but we know from experience that the tracks under our feet and the tracks in the distance are really the same size. Without changing the color or focus, you can't make the images the same size and still manage the appearance of depth, so each distant image needs to be proportionately smaller to the first image.

"We'll learn how to do this with linear perspective," I added. "For now, let's finish outlining the use of size and overlapping as tools to define depth in a two-dimensional format."

* Size - larger images usually appear closer than smaller images, depending on their value, texture, and color.
* Overlapping - an object behind another object will appear further away.

I continued using notes on the board. "So, larger sized objects usually appear closer than smaller ones. This of course depends on the value, texture, color of the object, or the relationship of the larger object with other objects in the format."

I drew a quick sketch of vase with an apple and some grapes, and continued, "There are times when a larger image is a *foil* for the smaller image, like the grapes, compared to the apple, compared to the vase. Just be aware of your values and colors. If the larger image is too bright or colorful, you may create visual distortion," I said. "Overlapping is a great tool to display which object comes first in the hierarchy of viewing the images. There might be other visual clues that will throw this size concept out of whack, too."

"What do you mean?" Bonnie asked.

Zed jumped in his seat, "Wait! It's like that red eye in that blue elephant you mentioned last week. The red eye was small, but that color is an intense hue, and it was against a large cool background. All those signals made that small red eye stand out."

Wes rifled through his work. "Wait a minute," he said. "I have something for you, Zed." Wes pulled an image of a blue elephant with a red eye from his pile of papers. "Now you can see the small red eye in action!"

"Awesome!" Zed took a closer look at the image. "This is for me?"

Wes nodded. "This way, you won't forget the power of red!"

I looked at the image as Zed passed it around for everyone to see. I pointed at the blue elephant profile, and demonstrated how it defined the red eye. "In many instances, negative space is more important than positive space, because it defines the edges of the positive space and the frame, or border. The designer can use just the negative space to balance the composition. You might say a composition *works* when a balance is struck between positive and negative space within the framework of the piece."

"So the blue elephant filled the format, and it was important because it defined the elephant's red eye." Zed commented. "I get that part. But," he asked, "What's the frame in this context? Are we going to frame our Flash designs?"

I almost forgot this important piece to the puzzle of space. I answered, "The frame is the edge of a canvas, the edge of a print, the edge of a folded brochure – which will change as the brochure is opened. The frame is the zoning and property boundaries for a skyscraper, or a room for a piece of installation art, the size of a browser screen for a web page. For Flash ..."

"It will be the work area around the stage," Deb finished my sentence.

"That's just about right, Deb." I replied. "You actually have two frames in Flash MX, and they surround two different spaces. One is your work area, and the other is the actual stage. The difference between these two frames can be described as the *design space* versus the *display space*.

"Your computer monitor, and the work area are your **design spaces**. The **display space** is the stage in Flash, and it's also the environment used to show your published work – typically a web browser for us. So," I added, "The display space is the frame that we should always consider before publishing our Flash designs – the stage is essentially the window through which our designs will *sell* themselves."

Wes shook his head. "This is a lot more difficult than designing and painting on a single canvas."

"Don't let it throw you, Wes," Zed replied. "I'll help you when you get confused."

Everyone laughed. "I don't want you taking over my job, Zed," I laughed. "Wes, use every resource you can to learn more about the display space. Zed will be able to help a lot, I'm sure.

"The difference between the design and display spaces is similar to shooting a home movie," I explained to the class. "When you become more aware of the negative space surrounding your object, you become aware of any other objects vying for your viewer's attention.

"When you shoot a movie of your family, you often aren't aware of the telephone pole sticking out of your dad's head until you display the movie on a screen. Eventually, you become aware of the delicate balance between negative and positive spaces and shapes. You also become more aware of how you can eliminate these distractions so your subject becomes the main object of interest to your viewer.

"Let's remember that negative space in any design is not only a tool to show distance, size, and depth of the positive shapes. It's also the surrounding that gives your subject effective emotional impact. Be it dramatic or subtle, the viewer should note the negative space in your design only as a support for the subject itself. If your negative space isn't executed satisfactorily, the viewer will remember the negative space more than the subject – or even worse – they won't remember your work at all."

"You said last week that texture can help us perceive distance, too," Deb stated. "It's natural, then, that we'd see more texture in objects up close, and less texture in objects further away."

* Texture - more details give the visual clue that the object is closer; fewer details or blurring places the object further away

"That's right, Deb," I answered, as I wrote this element's use on the board. "You can use various tools in most graphics programs, like Photoshop, to render texture and blur that texture to imply depth."

"All of this seems to be common sense," Steve added. "But I never think about it when I'm working. I'm going to make myself some lists." He turned to Wes, "Do you think about these kind of things when you're painting?"

"All the time," Wes answered. "It surprises me to hear that you don't think of these tools – you use different sizes of text to show headlines, subheads, and body copy. The type size lets a reader know what's most important, and what's next in line. This is a form of depth perception, because the larger typeface in a headline places emphasis on it – it clearly becomes more important."

"I guess so," Steve admitted.

"It is, Steve!" Bonnie insisted.

"Whoa, you guys are all getting way ahead of me," I laughed. "Let's satisfy Zed's intrigue now by talking about movement in our designs, and how this can define space."

Movement in static design

"Before we tackle animation," I said, "Let's clarify how we can portray the illusion of movement in static design. Can anyone give me some examples of how we would accomplish this?"

Wes promptly answered, "We can show the illusion of movement with **repetition**, with **blurring**, and with **multiple images** showing the process of movement."

I asked Wes if he would come to the board and show some of these images in action. He agreed, and proceeded with the illusion of multiple images. "One artist who was a master of showing movement with repetition was Marcel Duchamp," Wes said. "In his *Nude Descending a Staircase*, he showed an abstract figure repeated and overlapped to show motion." Wes drew a similar image. "Duchamp made the images in the back very vague and slightly blurred and lighter than the front image. He overlapped the multiple images, and it gave the illusion of an object descending a staircase."

The students asked if they could retrieve their drawing pads before Wes went any further. "I want to copy this information down, just like he's doing," Zed said. "That way I won't forget how to use static space to show motion."

Wes waited for them to get their materials, and then moved on to blurring an image. "Now I'm going to draw four butterflies, and I'll show you the difference between motion blurring and blurring to show distance," he said. Wes scribbled away on the board, and the students followed his example in their drawing pads.

"This first butterfly is pretty much static. But, we instinctively know this butterfly is either flying or landing on an object, because this is when we are used to seeing butterflies in this position. This is an example of showing motion with the process of movement. We know from our observations when something is about ready to move," he said.

He then smudged over the butterflies to make it more faded. "This is an example of a butterfly in the distance," he grinned. It's the same size as the original one, but it appears to be further away because the details aren't as clear and the image is lighter."

He drew another butterfly on top of the original, and smudged it even more around the edges. "This is how I would portray a butterfly in motion. It's similar to the blurred, distant butterfly, but I've added another dimension by keeping the details. This way, you have an idea that the butterfly is still close, but it's also moving its wings."

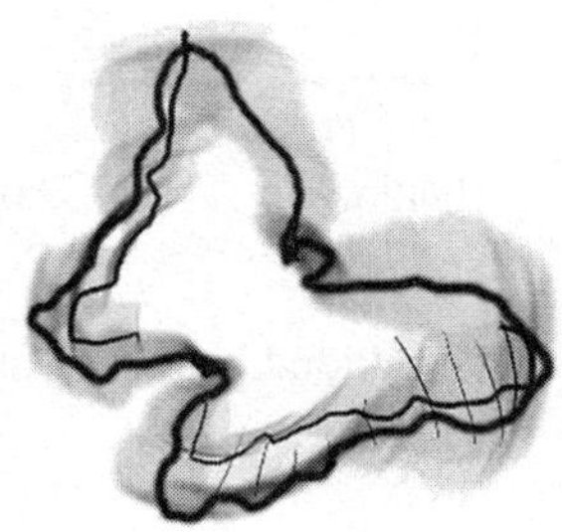

He turned to the last butterfly and drew in some squiggly lines. "Another way to show motion is to use Duchamp's technique with the repetition of lines or multiple images." He shrugged, "It's not as pretty as the blurred motion image, but you get the idea."

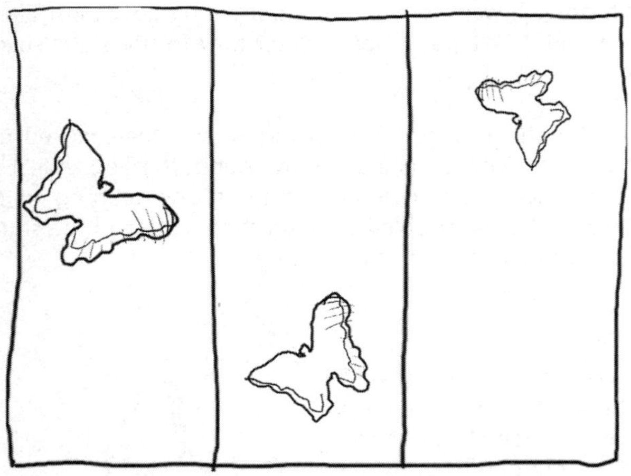

Wes continued, "Sometimes artists use panels or multiple images to show movement in static design." He drew a panel with three different sections, and drew three different butterflies in different positions and sizes. "From this panel, you either know this is one butterfly moving, or three different butterflies are in motion together. The context, or surroundings would help you decide whether this is one butterfly or three different ones."

He drew a tree in the background. "This tree is staying in one place, so it might help you to realize it's one butterfly moving in relation to the tree."

"Since you drew the tree lighter, we also know that tree is in the background, right?" Zed asked. "I think I'm getting the hang of this!"

"That's right, Zed," I answered. "You're right about the tree, and you're right about getting the hang of this. You're doing great!"

Wes handed the marker back to me and returned to his computer.

"Thanks, Wes," I said. "You did a great job showing us how we can portray motion in a static format." I looked at Zed. "I guess a few of us are ready to move on to showing movement in a timeline in Flash."

Zed nodded, and everyone else put aside their drawing pads to begin working with Flash MX.

Depth in basic animation

We began this topic with my question, "How does motion define space?"

Zed looked up from his monitor. "I know how motion defines space," he said. "Anytime an animated object moves, it implies space with its rate of speed and with the distance it travels."

"Wow," I grinned. "You really did do some studying this week, didn't you?" I turned to the class. "Zed's right again! Earlier, when Deb waved her hand to show the expanse of this room, she defined the space of this room. She also defined the size of her body and her arm in relation to the size of this room."

"How did I do that?" Deb asked.

"Deb," I explained, "Your arm movement indicated math on a visual level. Your arm moved in a radius from the center of the arm's socket. We were able to tell from the visual length and span of your reach how much space you filled with the sweep of your arm."

"Oh, I see," Deb smiled. "And you were able to tell the approximate space of the room by the psychic line drawn by my hand."

"Right." I asked the rest of the class, "Did you all understand this?"

Steve nodded, "It's like watching a car go by on a television screen. The car comes from the right side of the screen, and exits on the left side. From this movement, I know that there's more space on either side of the screen. It's not visible, but the motion of the car just told me it's there."

Bonnie said. "I get it. But how does speed tell me anything?"

"Use a point of reference, Bonnie," Zed replied. "If you sit in a moving car and look out the window, everything closer to you will move faster than things located farther from you."

"OK," Bonnie scratched her head. "Like if you pass a house with mountains in the background, the house will go by faster than the mountains. When the house seems to go past faster, it's because it's closer. The mountains move slower because they're further away."

Wes laughed, "Except the house and the mountains aren't moving. You are!"

"I think this might be the time to let Zed loose with a little animation." I said. This was greeted with a swift cheer from Zed.

"Let's create an animation where we look out the window of the car. For this you'll need to create a tree, a house, and some mountains. Go ahead and draw these, but don't be too precise about them. Remember to draw each element on a different layer to make them easier to work with later."

The class was filled with deep concentration at first and followed by the occasional chuckle at unsuccessful drawing attempts.

"Don't be too concerned about scale when you are drawing the items, remember that Flash MX is vector-based and everything is scalable without any loss of detail or distortion."

When the class was done, they each had a tree, a house, and a pretty rugged mountain range:

"So how's is this going to work?" asked Zed. "What is the tree for?"

"The journey in the car takes us along a long boulevard, and trees line the roadside. The houses on this boulevard have long driveways, and the neighborhood has mountain views."

"Sounds like a nice town," said Steve.

"OK, you all have your graphic elements, all of which are going to be animated, but before we can do this, you'll need to learn a few crucial things about Flash MX.

"Firstly, as we saw briefly in the previous class, Flash MX has a neat storing place for graphic elements, called the **Library**. The Library is useful because once something is in there, you can just drag as many copies as you like from there onto the stage."

"No more cutting and pasting then!" said Steve.

"Sure Steve," I replied, "And there is no limit to the number of copies that you can pull out of it. Now onto the second and one of the most important facts about Flash. For an item to get into the Library, it has to be one of two things, either an imported file, like one of Zed's digital photos, or what's known as a **symbol**."

"A symbol?" Bonnie asked, looking a little confused. "What's a symbol? It's not a rock star with personality issues is it?"

"A symbol is simply an item that Flash can clone time and time again. Symbols are stored in the Library, and when copies of it are needed they can be pulled out of the Library onto the stage."

I opened up a Flash MX file called `bricks.fla` that demonstrated the concept of cloning symbols quite nicely:

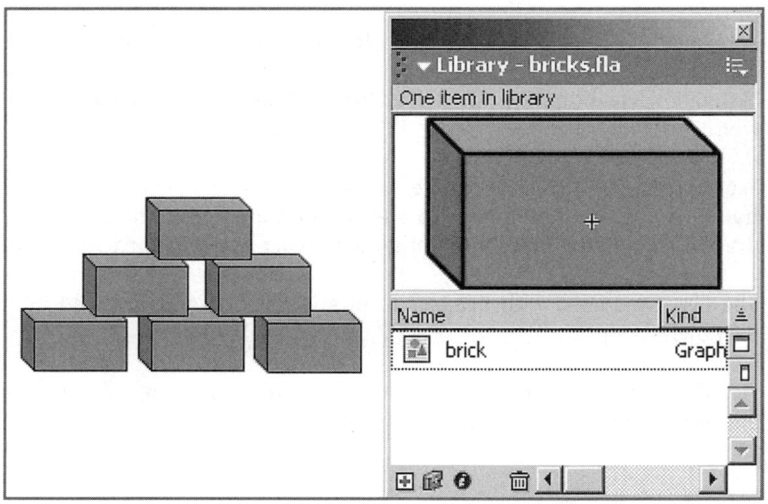

"In this Flash movie, the Library contains a symbol called `brick`. A number of clones of this symbol have been placed on the stage, making a wall."

"That's not a wall," said Wes, somewhat pedantically, "It's a pile of bricks!"

"The clones of a symbol are called **symbol instances**. Each symbol instance has a special link with the original symbol, so if the original is changed, every instance is updated with the same change."

"It's like fashion then," said Deb. "As soon as a leading figure changes their look, all of the people that idolize them also change their look to reflect it."

"I'm sure it is Deb." I said. "Later in the course we'll learn how symbol instances can break away from their parent symbol and seek their own independence.

"Symbols are also what makes Flash produce such small file sizes. Once something is made into a symbol, it only needs to be loaded once for the entire SWF, no matter how many times it is used. This means that a SWF with a hundred instances of a symbol on the stage will produce the same file size as one with a single use of the symbol, because that symbol is reused so efficiently."

"Why is this important now?" asked Zed.

"Learning about symbols is not only important for producing small file sizes, but is also important for animation. Returning to our first example, for the particular type of animation we want to do, it helps to turn the graphics into symbols.

"You do this by selecting the graphic and then selecting Insert > Convert to Symbol. Do this with your house figure first. If you have problems selecting only the house, lock the other two layers. You only need to select the house layer, which will then highlight its contents."

I went through the steps again with the class, reminding them to select the whole graphic and to choose the Convert to Symbol option. "Another tip when converting graphics to symbols is the shortcut key F8 – after selecting the image that you want to change to a symbol, just hit F8 to bring up the Convert to Symbol dialog box."

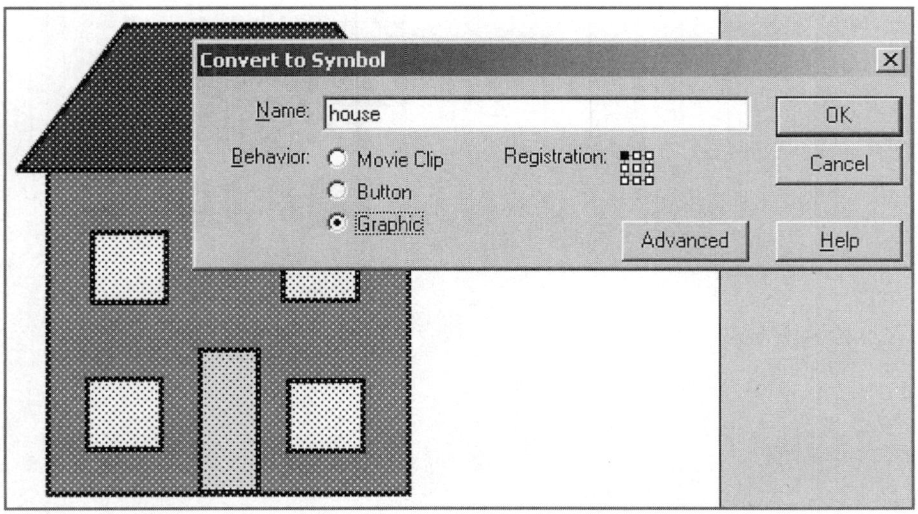

"In this window, give your symbol a relevant name, like house, and check the Graphic radio button on the bottom left. Don't worry about any of the other options for now, just click OK."

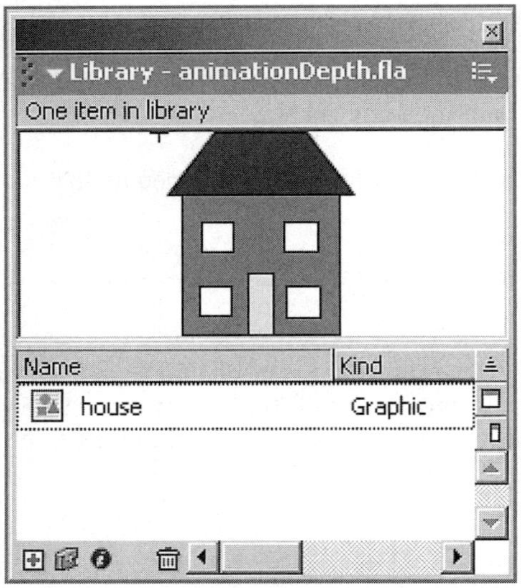

"Now open the Library from the Window menu and if you look in it, you'll have a symbol named house. This symbol is now perfect for our first Flash animation, and ready to use in a **motion tween**."

"What's a motion tween?" asked Bonnie.

"We're getting to that Bonnie. Firstly, be aware that a motion tween is defined by two points, or two keyframes – hopefully you all remember from our first class that keyframes are essential for creating animations in Flash MX.

"Zed, do you know why it is called a tween?"

"Should I?" Zed said, scrunching up his face as he scanned his brain. "I don't think I know."

"Tweens are named as such because Flash creates the animation *in between* the two keyframes that you define. In traditional animation, a lead animator would draw the first frame of a shot, and the last frame of a shot, and a person called an in-betweener would have to draw in all the missing frames.

"Because Flash is doing the in-betweener's job for us, they are called *tweens*. Let's make our first motion tween so that you can see what I mean."

The next step was going to be a pretty big leap for the class – their first motion tween in Flash. "OK. Seeing as we'll be tweening the house, lock and hide the other two layers. Now position the house at the top right of the stage – this will be the place where the house starts its tween. This is the first keyframe.

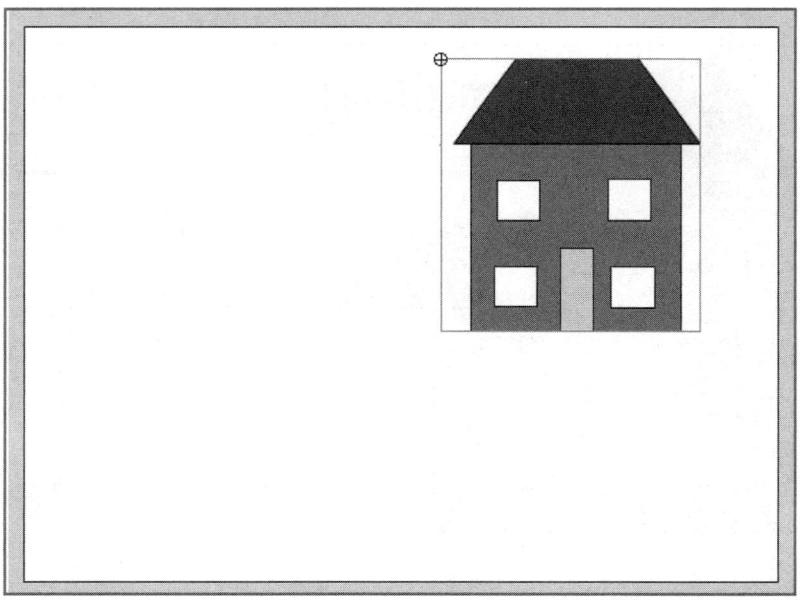

"The next thing a tween needs is a second keyframe. Select a later frame in the timeline on the house layer, frame 60 say, and select Keyframe from the Insert menu. This will insert an identical copy of our initial keyframe."

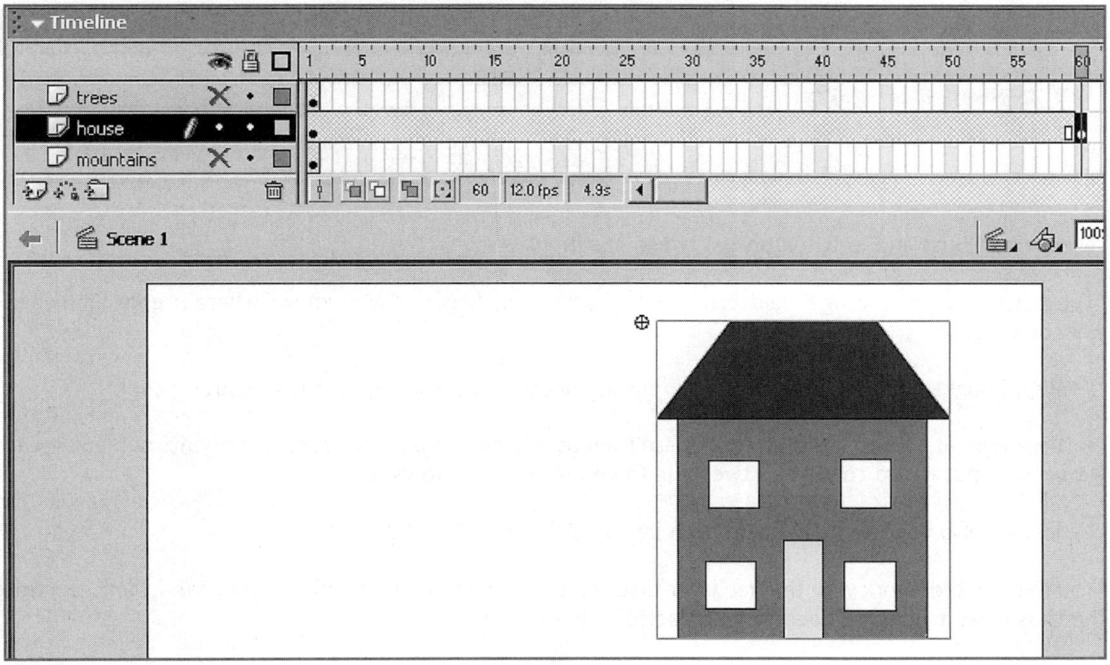

"Why do we need to do this?" asked Wes.

"This is done to define our second keyframe. The frames *in between* these two keyframes will contain the tweening that Flash does for us. Now we need to reposition the house on the second keyframe, so Flash has some work to do.

"On frame 60, select the house symbol on the stage and move it to the left half of the stage. A handy tip here is to hold down the SHIFT key as you drag to keep the vertical position the same.

"Once you've done this, you just need to tell Flash that we want to create a motion tween. Click on any frame in between either of the two keyframes, and then select Motion from the Tween drop-down menu in the Property inspector." As I instructed the students, I pointed this out on Steve's Mac:

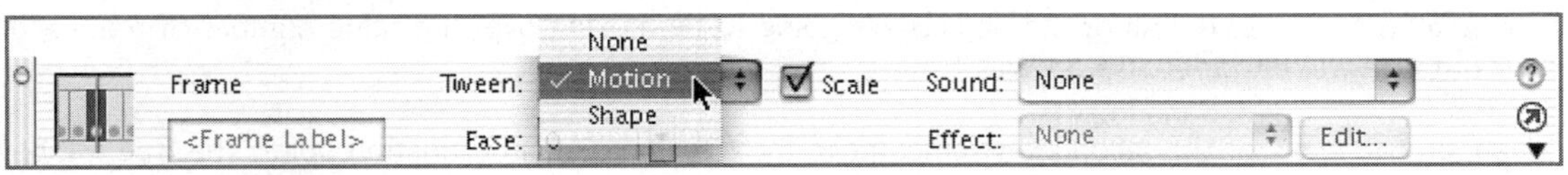

"The frames in the timeline will now turn blue, and you'll see an arrow from one keyframe to the next. This is how Flash MX indicates that a tween has been defined.

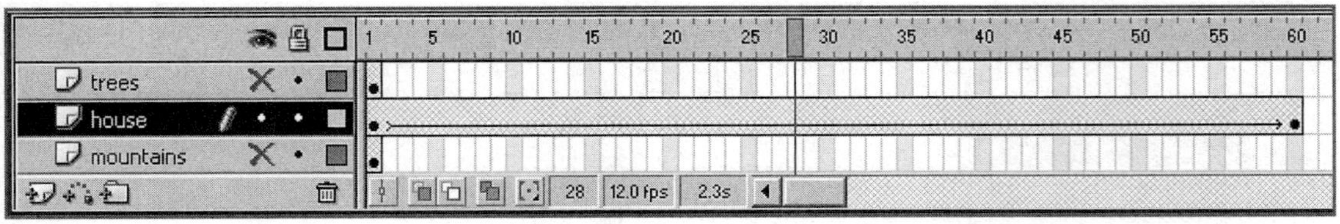

"Now, press ENTER and watch your first tween in action!"

"The house is floating away!" said Zed spookily waving his fingers. "Who knows where it goes and when it will come back?!"

"I never thought I'd say it about a ghostly moving house," said Bonnie, "But that is pretty cool!"

"At the moment," I said, "The motion doesn't tell us anything about the space of the environment because we need to put it into context by tweening the mountains and trees too."

"I guess we also need to make them both into symbols then?" said Zed.

"You're right Zed. Work with the tree layer first, remembering to hide the other layers. Who wants to remind the class what actions we need to do to perform the tween?"

"I think I can," said Lisa. I nodded to encourage her. "The first thing to do is to make the tree into a symbol so we can use it for the motion tween – F8 is the shortcut key for that. Next, we need to position the tree at its initial position."

"Good so far, Lisa. Who can tell me where the tree should initially be?" I asked.

"This is a boulevard, so the tree must be in front of the house, and further to the right so it will seem travel a greater distance," said Wes.

"Correct Wes. Would you like to carry on from where Lisa left off?"

"Sure, I'll give it a go." Wes replied. "Where were we?" Wes hesitated, "Oh yeah, position the tree on the first keyframe, and then insert a keyframe at frame 60?"

"Frame 60 is fine." I said, "All of the objects are going to be moving over the same number of frames, but their distance will be varied. Go on Wes."

"Then, on frame 60, or the second keyframe, move the tree to its final destination point. The tree will have to move further than the house, so I'd guess that the far left is a pretty good bet."

"We could be pretty mathematical about the positioning, related to scale I mean," said Deb.

"Deb is absolutely right." I said. "For now though, we are just getting a preview of the concept. So we'll be pretty rough and ready about it. Deb, would you like to carry on?"

Deb nodded. "Certainly. Once you have the tree positioned on the left side of the stage, select a frame between the two keyframes on the timeline and make it a tween."

"I can't remember how we did this," said Bonnie.

"Look in the Property inspector Bonnie!" Steve hinted.

"That's the idea Steve!" I passed out some handouts to the students, giving Bonnie one first. "This handout tells you how to make a motion tween – keep it handy while you're creating animations so you'll always have a quick and easy reference.

Making a Motion Tween in Flash MX

1. Convert the graphical object to be tweened into a symbol by selecting it and choosing Insert > Convert to Symbol, or by pressing F8.

2. Position the symbol instance on the first keyframe – this will be the start point of your tween.

3. Insert a keyframe at the destination frame using Insert > Keyframe, or the F5 key.

4. Position the symbol instance on the destination frame – this will be the destination point of your tween.

5. Set a tween by selecting any frame in between the start and end keyframes, and choose Motion from the Tween drop-down in the Property inspector.

"Oh yeah, I see it now," said Bonnie. "Now we press Enter to see it run, right?"

"That's right Bonnie." I said. "How does it look? If it doesn't feel right, then the tree may be traveling too far, or too short, or the scale might not be right. If the tree appears to be moving too far, simply select a keyframe and reposition it."

"What if the scale is all wrong?" asked Zed.

"Then you'll need to resize the tree on both keyframes using the Free Transform tool, otherwise the tree will rescale during tweening." I answered.

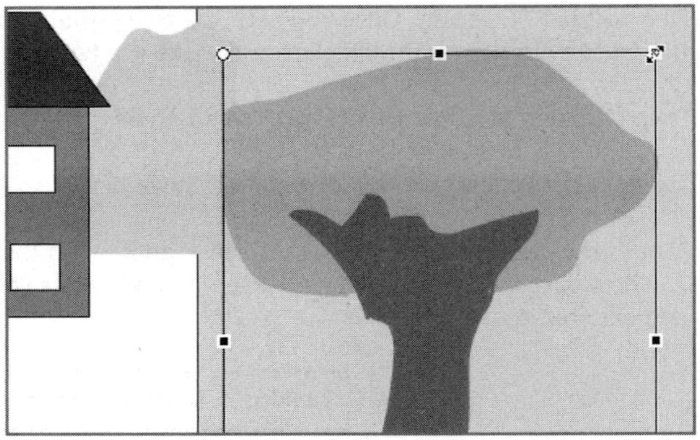

"You mean that the motion tween can also make things grow and shrink too?"

"Flash MX works hard for you doesn't it?" I said. "Finish the animation by turning the mountain graphic into a symbol and giving them a tiny amount of distance to tween over. They should hardly be moving at all".

"By the way, if you want to preview your animation frame-by-frame, click above the timeline where the frame numbers are and drag the little red playhead to the selected frame."

"It probably still needs a little tweaking," said Wes.

"Deb was probably right when she mentioned mathematics and scale earlier in class, and in a professional situation you might be better to use these to get a little harmony. For now though, it's just a quick introduction to tweening and basic animation in Flash – and achieving a sense of depth in that context."

"And it also helps define our point of reference." Said Zed. "Not only does scale apply here, but the movement creates space either side of the scene."

"I think I understand it all now!" Bonnie said.

"OK. Save your movie if you'd like to work with it later and we'll proceed." I said. "Let's cover one more attribute for depth perception, and then we'll take a break."

How position affects depth

"The last tool to help the viewer realize depth is the position of elements relative to each other." I interrupted their daydreams of time and space.

"When you place two objects of the same size in your design, the object that is situated lower down on the format surface should appear closer than the same object that's placed higher." I asked them to make a square in Flash MX, duplicate it, and place one at the bottom of the stage and one at the top.

"So, which one do you think appears closer... and why?" I asked.

"The bottom one appears closer," Deb explained, "Because it appears closer to my eye level."

"That's the answer I was looking for!" I smiled. "This form of perception has a lot to do with a real or imagined horizon line. I turned to look at Zed's monitor. He had three squares of different values with a toned background. "Everyone, take a look at Zed's monitor. Can you tell which square is intended to appear closer?"

The rest of the class gathered around Zed's monitor. "The one in the middle seems closer to me," Wes answered.

"No." Bonnie said. "The one in the lower right appears closer."

"You're both right," I said. "This image is similar to the ambiguous figure that Wes showed us last week. If you remember, some of you had trouble defining the profiles and some of you had a difficult time spotting the flower. If you place several objects of the same size and different values on a plane, you'll add to the viewer's visual confusion.

Zed jumped and turned to Wes, "I want to see that image again. It was so cool!"

Wes obliged, and went to pull the image from his pile of drawings.

I pointed at the image and said, "As you can see, Wes didn't use any of the depth tools we talked about earlier. His use of value, color, texture, and size gives us no indication of depth. This adds to the visual confusion."

Bonnie shook her head, "I still have a hard time seeing the profiles unless I really concentrate." The class agreed they had to concentrate to see either the profiles or the flower.

"There's no rule that states that you can't use this tool. You should just realize that you might add to a visual problem instead of creating a solution." I turned to the class. "Zed also brought up the issue of using gradients as a tool for depth perception. Which element of design are you using to portray this illusion of depth?"

"That would be value, wouldn't it?" asked Bonnie. "Unless, of course, the object was in color."

I asked them to return their attention to their computers and use the Rectangle tool with a gradient fill to create simple geometric shapes with changes in value.

"Select a shape tool as you have before, and choose a gradient fill from the bottom of the color palette.

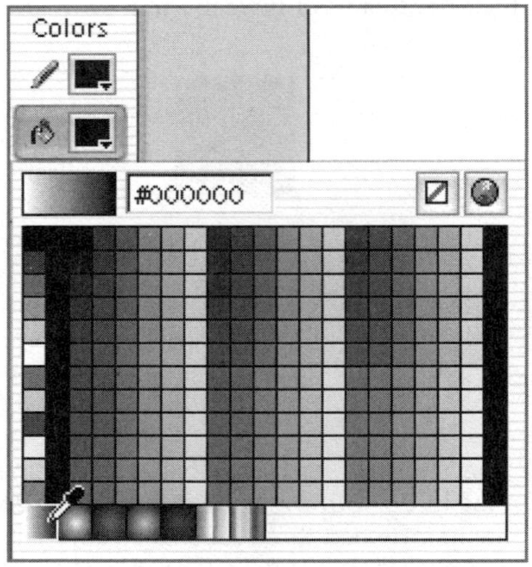

"Create one rectangle in gray values, and create another object with a color gradient."

I walked around the class, studying their work. "When you look at your objects, do they appear to contain three-dimensional shape and direction within your two-dimensional formats?"

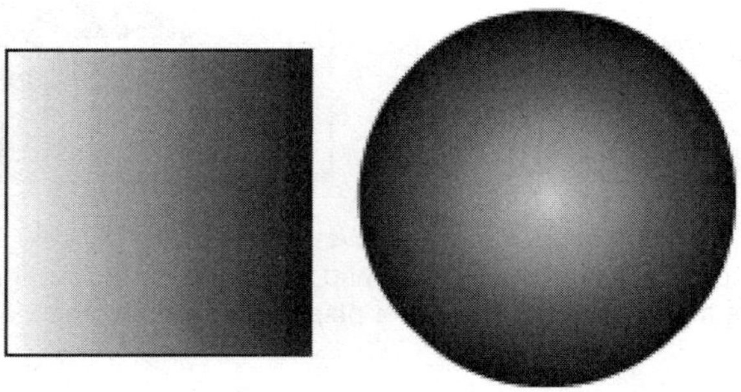

They all agreed. "The light part appears closer, and the dark part appears to be further away," Steve said.

"Yes," Deb agreed. "And my red ball appears to be closer to me than the gray ball with the same gradient."

"I guess this proves that some of these rules work," Bonnie sighed. "I never knew all these tricks even existed."

"You did," Wes answered. "We see these illusions so many times in our daily lives that we just don't question why they look the way they do. We just accept that something appears to be what it is because that's how it's supposed to look."

"Wes is right," I responded. "Until something appears awry – then we notice something's wrong. As designers, our aim is to help portray some images as they really appear, so we can pull the viewer into some safe visual environments. Our other job," I added as I looked at Wes, "Is to jolt the viewer into seeing our message in a different way. We can manipulate our viewers so they remember our images, and a slight distortion of depth is one way to handle this problem.

"One example is through amplified perspective." Several students looked at me with interest. "We'll cover this viewpoint next when we look at the design implications of linear perspective."

I reviewed the tools we'd used so far to create the illusion of depth within a two-dimensional format. "We just learned that size, texture, color, value, position, and movement all provide visual clues to depth in two-dimensional space," I said. "OK, why don't we take a break? When we return, we'll study linear perspective within a two-dimensional format."

Visual linear perspective

During this portion of class the students would become familiar with using simple line elements to draw various forms of perspective along a horizon line. These techniques can be used to enhance the illusion of depth within the two-dimensional format of Flash.

As the students came back to their computers, I asked them to return to the Flash MX authoring environment, and to prepare to use the Line tool for drawing and the Arrow tool for positioning lines. I then began to sketch out some examples of each case of linear perspective, and asked them to replicate the perspectives with Flash on their own computers.

"The first tool we need to use in linear perspective is the **horizon line**," I said. "This is the junction between land or sea and sky." I drew a line on the whiteboard. "Many times you won't be able to define the horizon line, because buildings or other objects will obscure your view of the meeting of land or sea and sky. But, you'll know this line is there, because you'll have tools to tell you where this line is located."

I continued to draw descriptions of these tools on the board. "You probably know what a picture plane is by now," I said. "The **picture plane** in this instance is vertical, and resembles the two-dimensional format of your authoring environment." I drew a rectangle around the horizon line. "The bottom of the frame is your **ground line**. This is a horizontal line that represents the junction of the picture plane and the ground plane. The **ground plane**," I added, "Is the horizontal plane where your viewer is standing. This is an imaginary plane that extends toward you from the ground line.

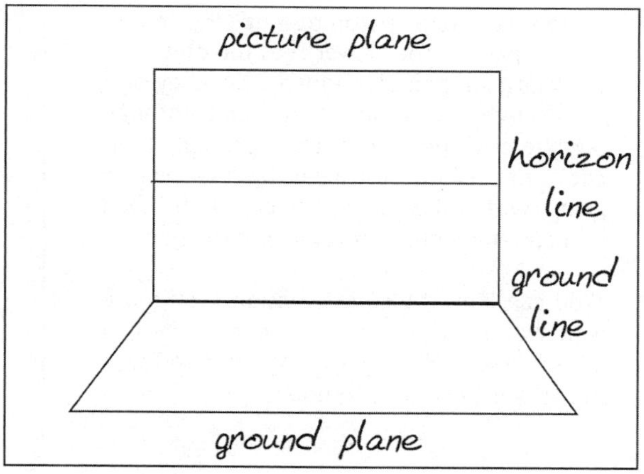

"The viewer is at a **station point**." I drew a shape to indicate the viewer standing on the ground plane. "This viewer is looking at a point on the horizon line," I said as I drew a line from the viewer to the horizon line. "This dot on the horizon line is the viewer's **vanishing point**, and the direction is indicated with an imaginary line from the pupil of the viewer's eye."

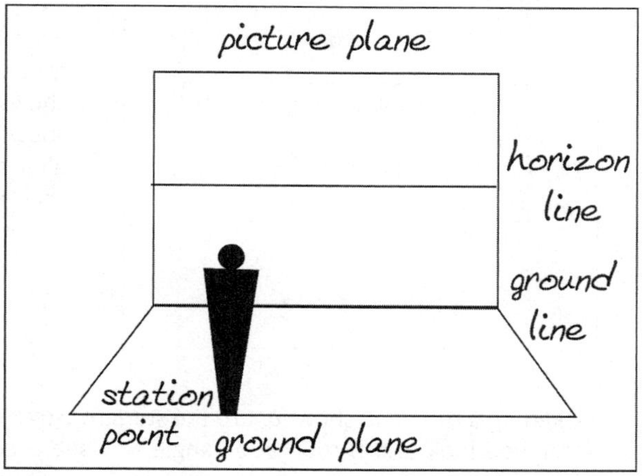

"Just like when you look at something that everyone else is looking at, right?" Bonnie asked.

"That's right, Bonnie," I replied. "When you notice someone looking at something, you follow the psychic line from that person's eyes to the object."

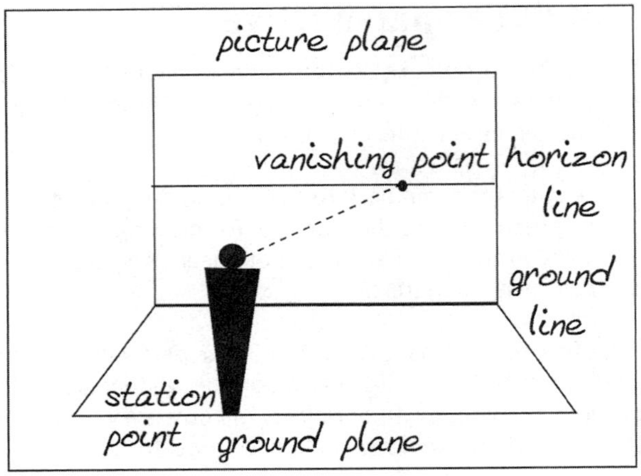

I drew a circle encompassing the entire picture plane. "The viewer sees the object on the vanishing point," I added, "But they also see everything around that point through peripheral vision. This circle represents their **cone of vision**, restricted by the picture plane. Within this range, objects can be seen in focus and without too much distortion.

"You can limit the cone of vision even more with the use of borders and more frames," I added, "Especially if you really want to focus the viewer's eye on one object."

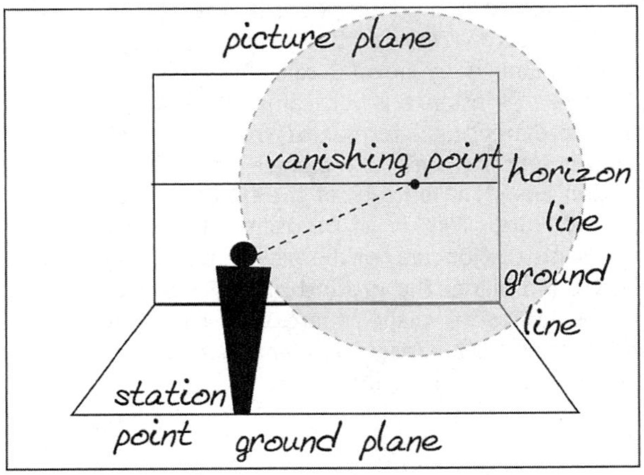

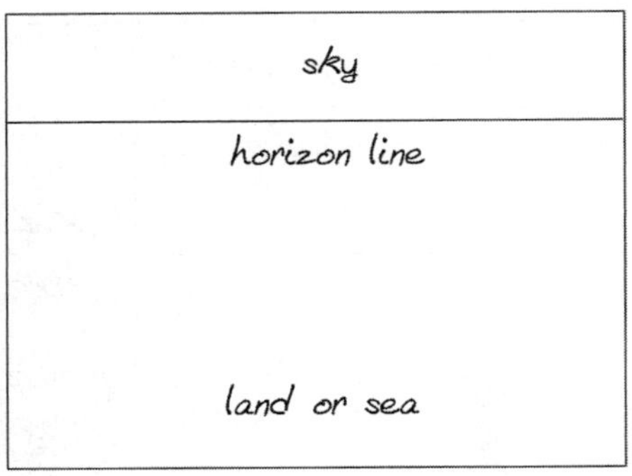

"Another aspect to this horizon line is your viewpoint. If you want the viewer to feel as though they're standing on high ground, you'll establish a **high viewpoint**. This viewpoint shows more ground. Alternatively, a **low viewpoint** will show more sky." I turned to the class. "Each viewpoint will alter the position of the viewer. Therefore, it will also alter their view of your subject matter."

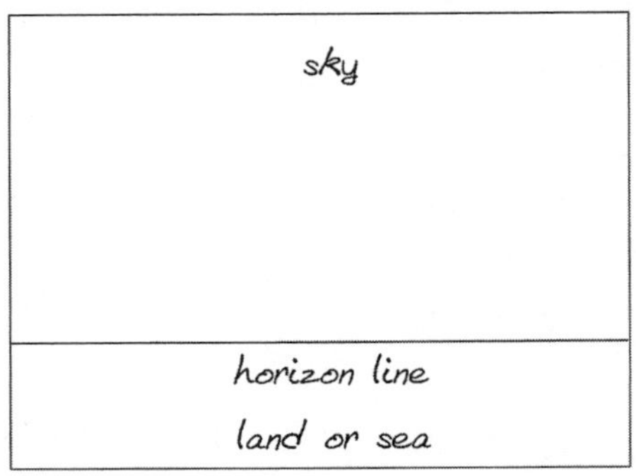

I picked up a ruler and showed it to the students straight on. "When you look at this ruler at an angle, you see each end as being the same distance from your eyes. As I pull the top end away from you," I slanted the ruler back toward my body, "You begin to see the end closest to me become smaller. This is called **foreshortening**.

"To mimic these illustrations, we can use the Free Transform tool, with the Distort option.

"If you hold down SHIFT the distortion will be symmetrical.

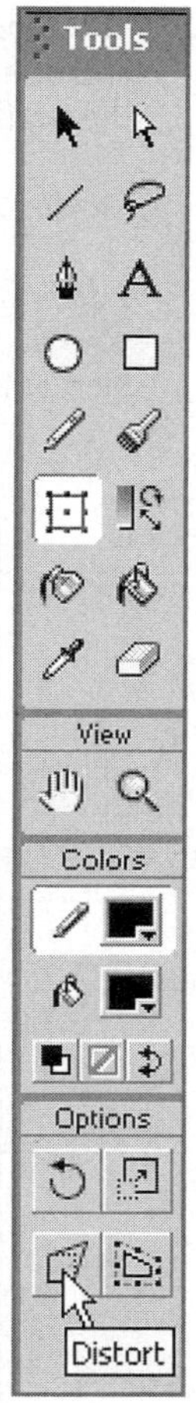

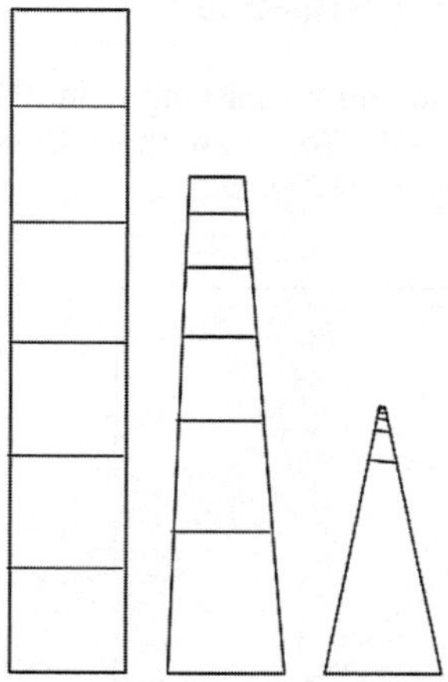

"This is the same principle as the image of the railroad track. Each rail contains the same height, width, and depth, but as the rails recede into the horizon, they appear to become smaller.

The point where these rails meet the horizon line is called the **vanishing point**, " I said, "This highlights what is known as the **principle of convergence**."

"It looks like the first inch of that ruler is longer when the far end is further from our point of view," Deb stated. "Even though I know it's the same size as it was when I viewed the ruler straight on."

"That's the other point of foreshortening," I added. "When you view objects in perspective, those that are closer appear to be larger than they are in reality. This is called **amplified perspective**, and it's one method we can use to distort an image to grab the viewer's eye. We see this when a hand, foot, or other object appears to be huge, and the rest of the body appears to be small - think of those stunning photos that your Mom takes, which include a huge thumb covering one corner! "

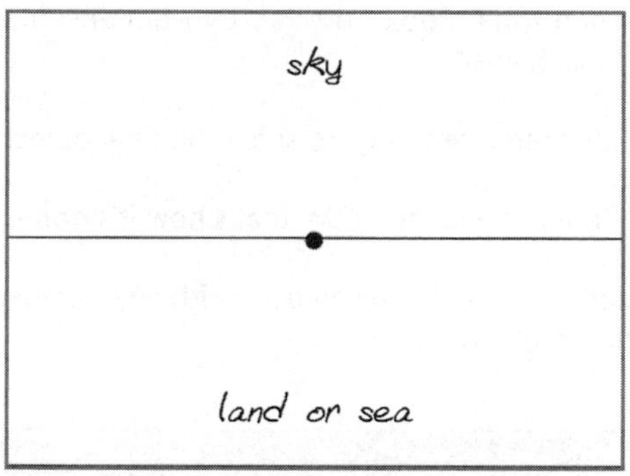

I continued, "The simplest form of foreshortening is **one-point perspective**. I turned back to the board and drew another horizon line and vanishing point within a rectangular plane. "This is the vanishing point on the horizon line. All objects in this area will recede in lines from the outer frame to meet at this point."

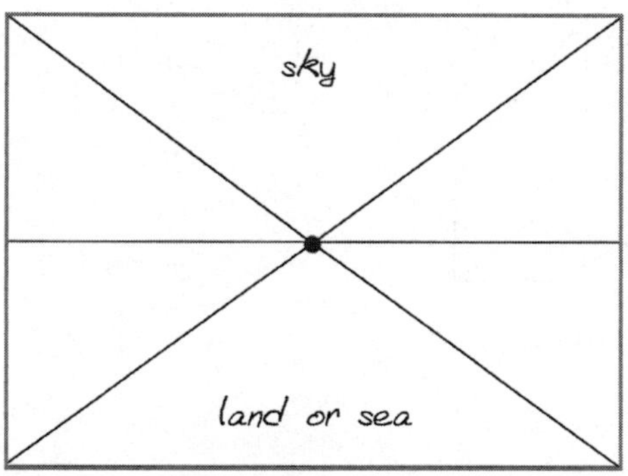

I drew several lines from the frame into the picture plane, all meeting at the vanishing point on the horizon line. "Your authoring environment is your picture plane. So is the stage. For the moment, we'll use the authoring environment to practice these linear perspectives. I want you to replicate what I've just drawn. Be sure to place the horizon line as close to eye level as possible, and draw your lines into the vanishing point from each corner of the picture plane. They should intersect at the middle, where your vanishing point is located.

"You can move the different elements around until you achieve the precise locations. This," I explained, "Is the direction and movement of objects to or from the vanishing point at eye level."

"The lines you drew in from the top corners of your horizon line to the vanishing point represent the size and direction of objects that would be above the viewer's head. The lines you drew in from the corners below the horizon line to the vanishing point would represent the direction and size of objects at the viewer's feet."

Moving on, I said, "Now let's see how we can create a 3-D box with this one-point perspective."

I drew a box in the top left corner of Bonnie's screen. I also drew a horizon line and a vanishing point. "If you want to create a box that appears to be over the viewer's head," I explained, "You draw these three elements. Then, you draw lines from all four corners of the box to the vanishing point."

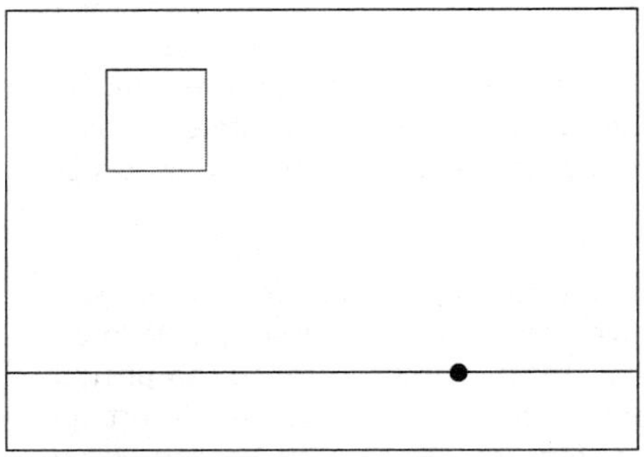

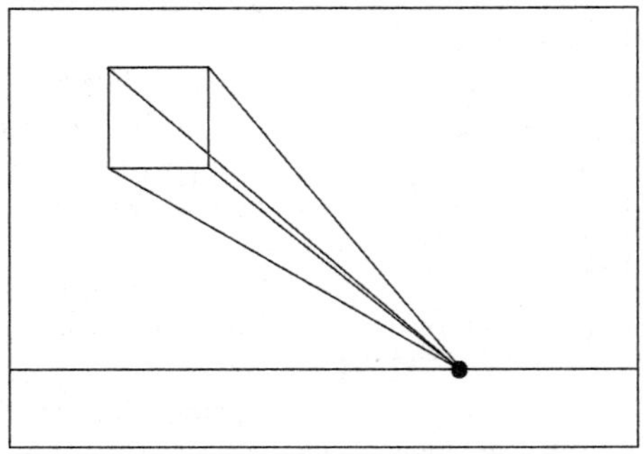

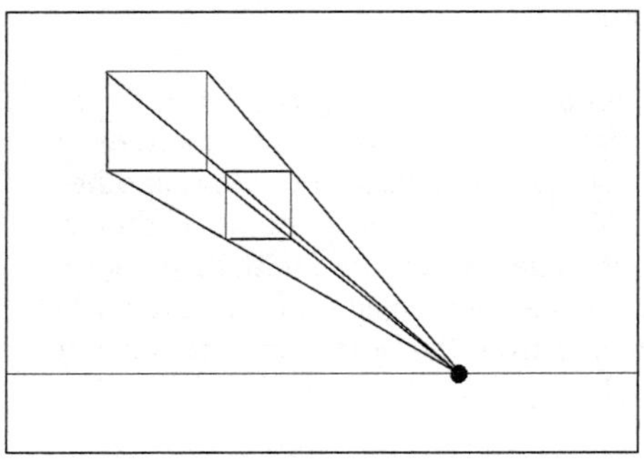

I drew these lines and then added another box. "This box could represent the end of the illusion of a three-dimensional box on a two-dimensional format," I explained.

Finally, I deleted a few lines to show the final object.

"Wow," Bonnie exclaimed. "So, that's how it's done!"

Wes added, "Yep, and you can do it with any number of geometric forms."

Zed interrupted, "How can we use this with animation?" he asked.

"Before you start playing about with animating such three-dimensional forms," I answered, "We need to cover at least one more angle on perspective. This is **two-point perspective**, and it's based on the same principles that I've already shown you."

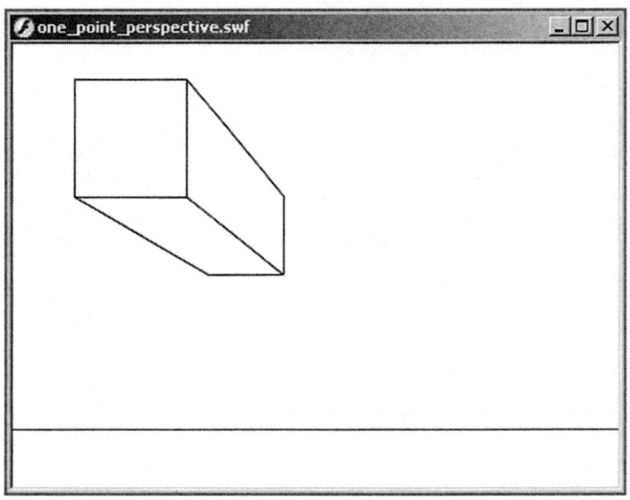

I went to the board and drew a horizon line, and two vanishing points. "With two-point perspective, we begin to display our objects in a more realistic fashion. This line," I pointed at the line I had drawn, "Is your horizon line. And this," I drew another line above the ground line, "Is a **height line**, and it's used to measure the height of your object."

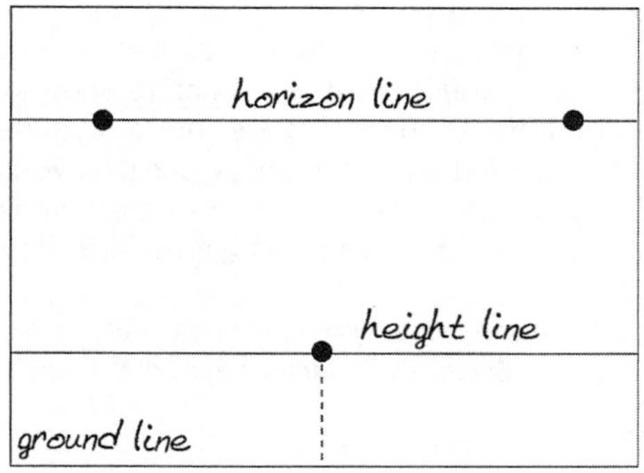

I started to draw lines between this dot on the height line and the two dots on the horizon line. "These lines indicate the angle of your box, meeting at its nearest corner." I said.

I drew some more lines to indicate the sides of the box. "Now I'll draw two lines that will indicate the ends of this box. These two lines must be vertical. Don't slant them, or you'll have a box with different angles. We're constructing this box along the vertical axis, so we're sticking with a box that has straight lines."

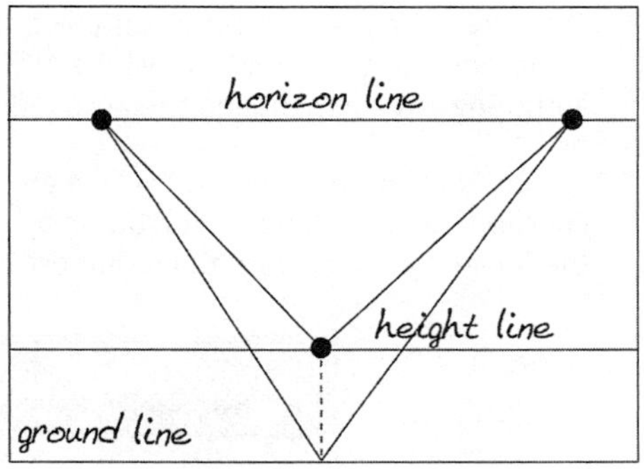

I turned to the class. "Now, can you tell me how we're going to close the top of this box?"

Wes volunteered. "Draw lines from the tops of those two new vertical lines to the vanishing points on the opposite sides. When you do, you've created the box top!"

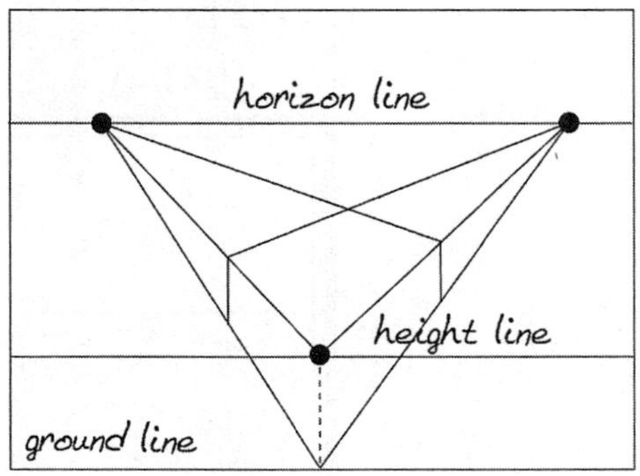

I drew the lines, and finished the box. I then removed the lines to the vanishing points to show the box. "Now you have a box seen from a bird's-eye perspective. This is a perspective that is used when you want the object to appear below the eye-level of your viewer. You would place your height line at the top of the picture plane, and the horizon level below the height line if you want the object to appear to be above the viewer's eye-level."

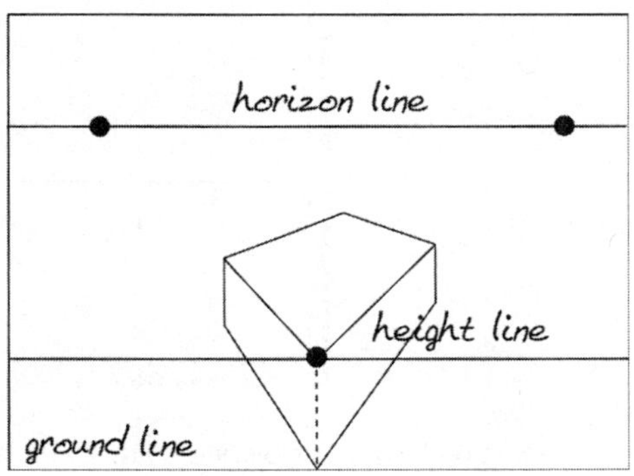

Next I reversed the drawing and showed them another perspective. "Of course, as we advance with our drawing skills, you'll eventually want to show various objects from different angles. These more complex objects can be rendered with the aid of perspective grids. This will allow you more flexibility with the object, and will help you render the object so it doesn't appear distorted."

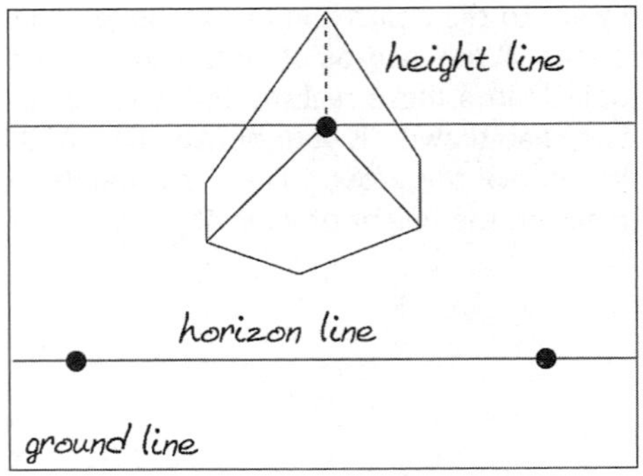

"I have a question," Zed was rubbing his forehead. "Can the horizon line be placed beyond the picture plane?"

"Yes, Zed." I answered. "You can place the horizon line and any vanishing points way beyond your picture plane. However," I added, "It will be difficult to render without first drawing a rectangular plane within your authoring environment and then expanding the size of the object when you're through rendering the image."

I pointed at the drawing on the screen. "You begin with this image in your format, then you delete all the lines, or use a guide layer for the imaginary lines, and expand the size of the object. You could even draw the image by hand, scan it, and import it into the Flash MX Library."

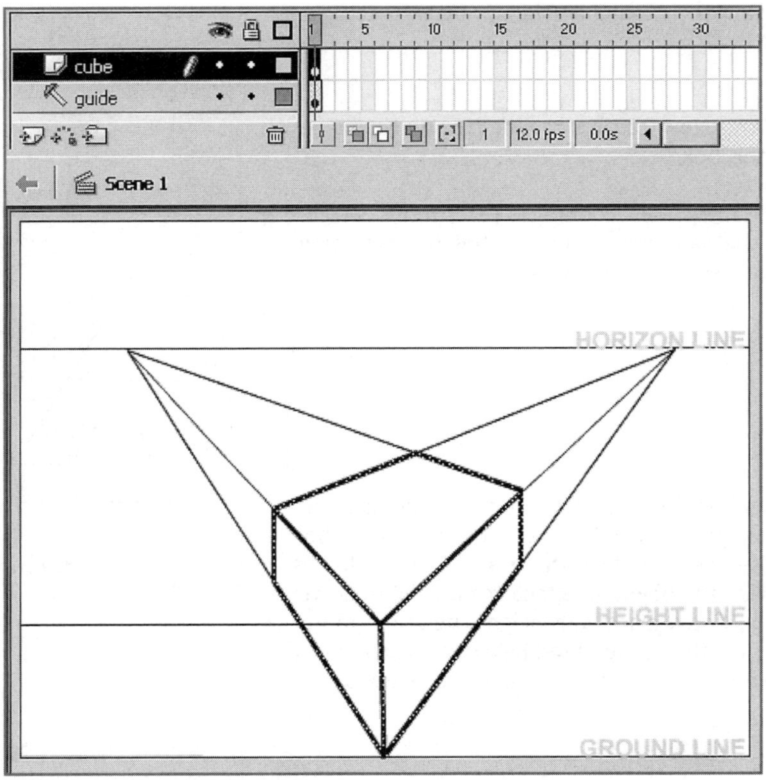

"Oh, sure," Bonnie frowned. "I'm going home to draw all week long!"

Lisa laughed, "At least you can use a ruler with perspective. I would be lost without my ruler."

"The ruler is indeed useful," I nodded, and then looked at Bonnie. "And you're not going home yet, Bonnie – we've got a few more important topics yet to cover in this class!"

I turned to the rest of the class. "You've just learned the very basic tools to draw simple objects in one- and two-point perspective. As you develop your skills, you'll learn other ways to portray the illusion of depth within your two-dimensional formats. For this course, however, these tools are all we'll need for the moment."

"How about a five-minute break, teach?" Zed asked anxiously.

I looked at Zed. He seemed anxious to be in another room altogether. I smiled, agreeing that a break was a good idea, and asked the students to meet back at the table. "When you return," I said, "We'll cover some basics of composition."

Composition concepts

As the students settled in at the table, I ask them to open their drawing pads to fresh pages and to retrieve their drawing supplies. The idea was that I'd get them to practice along with me as I explained some of the most basic concepts of composition. These techniques would help to define the placement of elements within a page or screen.

"Why are we using drawing pads instead of Flash?" Bonnie sounded a bit peeved.

"The designs I'm going to show you will be easier to remember if you sketch them in," I responded. "These composition principles are borrowed from fine art and commercial art practices. When you apply them to the Flash format, you'll understand why you're arranging your work along these lines."

I looked at Zed. "Plus, I think we need a break from the computer screen."

Bonnie seemed only slightly satisfied with my answer. "I just hate to draw," she admitted.

I turned to the board and drew a rectangle to simulate our chosen format. "Remember, your Flash format is two-dimensional," I began, as I turned back to the class. "Within this area, you need to work with composition, so you know how to align the elements of design. We just learned how to fool the viewer into believing your format has depth. Now, you'll use the tools of composition to lead the viewer's eye around your page. You don't want them to leave your page until you've given them as much information as possible within the shortest amount of time."

Zed smiled, "So we're getting into the element of movement again!"

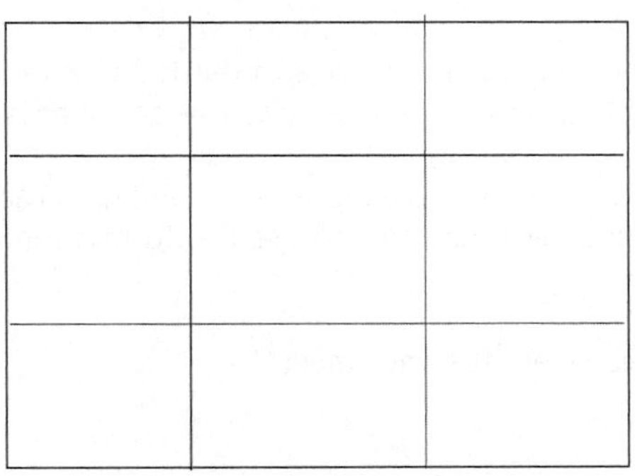

I smiled back at Zed, "The element of movement is much more than blurring an image or repetition of an element to show motion," I said. "You will use a composite of lines and planes to move the viewer's eye to a point of emphasis on your page."

I turned back to the board and drew four lines, creating nine blocks within the rectangle. I asked the class to draw the same image in their drawing pads. "You don't have to use your rulers," I added. "This practice is to simply reinforce the essential ideas of composition. We'll structure these more formally when we design our class project."

I continued explaining the grid I had just drawn. "Grids," I began, "Are controversial in the world of design. Some designers swear by them, and others scoff at those who use them. When you're first learning design principles," I added, "You really need to know about using grids – there's no way to decide whether you might want to use this tool unless you try it out first."

"It's also probably a good thing to learn if any of these folks want to go into print publication," Steve added. "From the time I started my career, I used grids for paste-up. Now I use them in software programs."

"Steve's spot on," I said. "Most magazines and newspapers use a grid to align bodies of text, pictures, and headlines."

Bonnie added, "That's what we did with our thumbnails and roughs, isn't it? And, that's what I do with tables in my web designs."

I nodded at Bonnie and said, "Computer design has brought the grid into focus of necessity with the use of tables and other design formats. The computer format is based on a mathematical system, and the grid is the logical solution for this format. When you encourage your clients to carry their look into a thematic progression from a computer-based design to business cards to letterhead to advertising, you'll repeat this design throughout each piece."

"Many artists use grids," Wes broke in, "In fact, many art movements were based on grids."

"OK," Zed seemed exasperated, "I want to know what you're all talking about. Is a grid just a bunch of blocks? Isn't this what we just used in our perspective exercises?"

"I'm sorry Zed," I said. "Yes, a **grid** is simply measured spaces on a two-dimensional format, designed to hold different elements in place. Each space is measured using horizontal and vertical lines. Your viewer won't see these grids unless you want to use them as an element in your final design," I added. "But you'll use them quite a bit as you structure the development of your design.

> *"Flash MX has the option of using grids if ever you need them. The Flash MX grid is switched on using* View > Grid > Show Grid, *and the size of this grid can be edited using* View > Grid > Edit Grid...."

I pointed at the board. "This particular grid is called **rule of thirds**. This grid is used most often by artists, but it's also a great way to compose your design."

Deb was punching numbers into a calculator. She looked up when I mentioned the rule of thirds. "That term came from the ancient Greeks," she said. "It was part of their infatuation with geometric spaces and shapes."

She continued, "The Greeks used this rule of composition for architecture, sculpture, and paintings. They basically divided the format into equal thirds both horizontally and vertically. We still use this format today for a lot of imagery, including photography."

Wes said, "I use that layout a lot." He looked at Zed. "Do you see where the lines meet?"

"Sure," Zed answered.

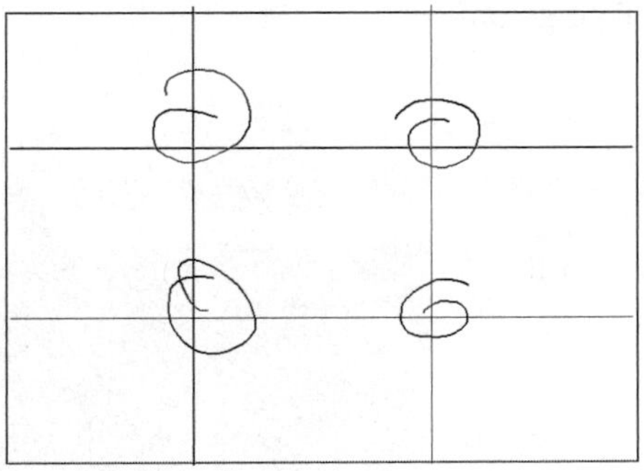

I drew circles at the junctions of the four lines.

Wes continued, "Those are called **points of focus**. This is where you want to place objects you want to emphasize."

"At any rate," Wes said, "It's where I place an object I want the viewer to see before they see anything else."

Steve seemed excited. "That's a great tip! After all these years, I never knew about that one!"

I added, "You may not need to use each point for emphasis. One point of focus would be all most designers need to send a message."

"I don't get it," Bonnie said. "Do you mean that we can only work within those four points?"

"No," I responded. "You can place images in any one of the squares, or along the horizontal or vertical lines. The point to remember is that a person's eye will follow whatever action you lay out for them in your format."

Deb interrupted, "So if we use the rule of thirds in the 550 x 400 pixel Flash format, we'll have nine compartments that are approximately 184 pixels wide by 134 pixels deep."

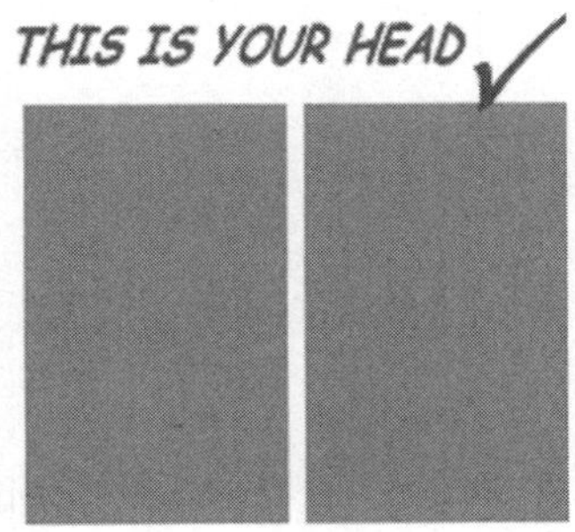

I agreed with Deb, complementing her mental arithmetic. Then I erased the grid and drew two boxes to represent type on a page. I added a headline and a checkmark. As the students drew this image in their drawing pads, I explained the problem of the English language and composition.

"When we read English, we read from top left to bottom right." I began. "Our eyes want to travel from the left, and you might think that if we don't have some element to stop our eyes, they'd go right off the page onto another object!"

Steve spoke up, "Placement of advertising on the top right of a magazine or newspaper will always demand top dollar, if it's even allowed in a publication. On newspaper front pages, you'll see the top news story go in that location."

"Steve's right," I said. "I'm glad you brought that up, since it just boosts the importance of this space."

"As designers," I continued, "You want the viewer to look into your page. So you will direct the their eyes with an element that will stop them heading off the edge of the page. But," I added, "You need to use the right element to stop them. Let's consider this simple example – if you use an italic typeface for a heading, and you stop the eye from going forward and off the page with a checkmark, you haven't really done the job..."

"What do you mean?" Bonnie asked. She insisted, "My eye stopped?!"

I explained further, "In this case, your eye has been told to follow the heading to the right, where you meet the checkmark. Your eye actually follows the line of the checkmark up and off the page again."

"Oh!" Zed looked up from his drawing pad. "I see what you mean. It's like taking the eye on a trampoline. I read the headline and almost bounced off the page along that checkmark."

"Do you see that now, Bonnie?" I asked. I could literally see the light go on.

"Oh, sure!" she said. "I see that now. That's tricky!"

"A better solution would be to use a finger pointing to the body copy instead of a check mark." I drew a hand pointing into the page. "Your eye will stop at that hand, and it will at least slide down the finger into the page."

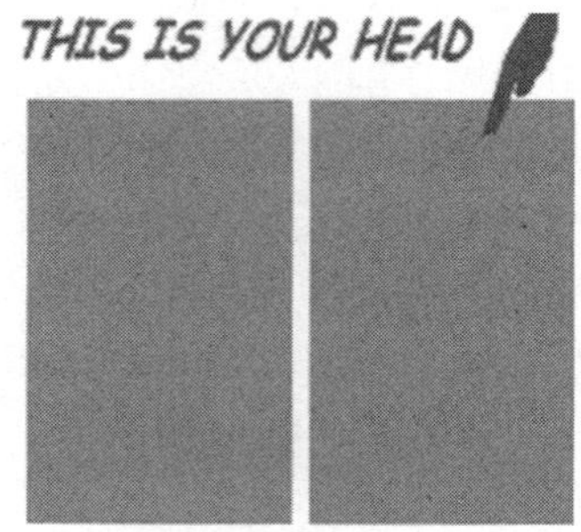

Wes laughed, "That's still lousy design," he stated.

"It is," I agreed, smiling. "But I have a point to make here."

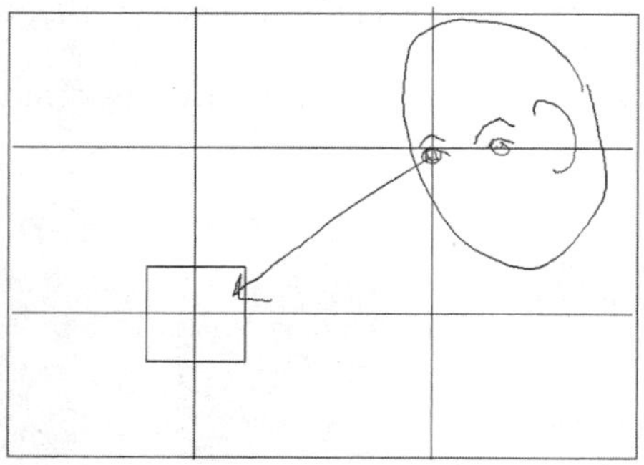

I erased the images, and drew another grid with focus points. "Remember the power of the psychic line," I said. I drew an oval slightly beyond the top right focus point." If you use the powerful image of a face, make that image look into the page at any one of your focus points." I drew one eye on the focus point. "Your viewer will follow the line of vision back into your page." I drew an arrow to show the psychic line of vision.

"You should avoid having an element that draws a psychic line off the page," I emphasized, "Unless of course you want the viewer to look off your page! In that case, make sure you point to the direction you want them to go."

"That's like the arrows used for people to go to another website, right?" asked Bonnie.

"Right, Bonnie." I answered. "That's precisely how we direct our viewers in that instance."

"Another tool playing on this format has been used in advertising for years..." I said as I drew another grid, this time containing a large *Z* over the grid lines, "Is the **Z-format** – this has been used for decades to pull the eye from top left to top right, down the page to bottom left and over to bottom right and ending with a logo or brand or leading the eye back up to the top right again."

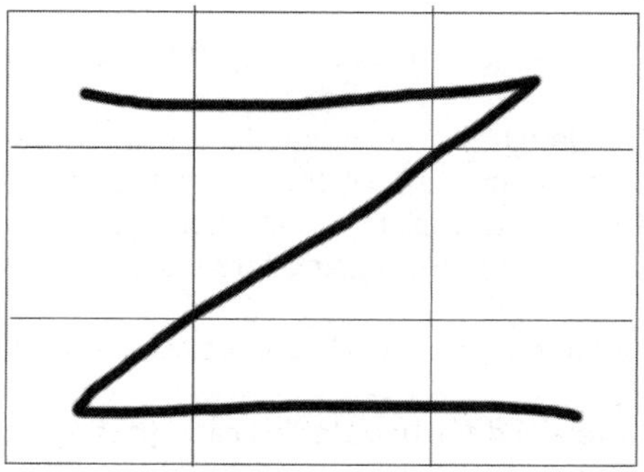

I drew a bone with two lines of copy. "With this simple illustration of the bone, you can see the Z-format in use. Think about your words and the typeface, as well as the layout. You can direct the eye with a letter. For example, with the **g** in **Dog**, your eye goes to the top of the bone, and the bone takes your eye straight down to the **W** in **Wants**. I could have written **Needs This Bone**, but the **N** in **Needs** wouldn't have *embraced* the eye sliding down the bone as well as the **W** does."

Steve paused and said, "When I do my layouts, I feel compelled to line up the letters to meet each other at top and bottom."

Deb and Bonnie looked puzzled. I drew lines along the elements to show them Steve's problem. "When we use grids, it's for a reason," I explained. "Steve's eye is used to seeing type aligned along a grid, and this type would meet along the grid lines at top and bottom.

"Isn't that really picky?" Bonnie asked. "I mean that's really obsessive-compulsive behavior."

Steve laughed. "Actually, Linda did a pretty good job freehand," he said. He turned to Bonnie, "Lining up type and other elements is a good rule to follow when using grids. It keeps the viewer from becoming disoriented with the line of direction."

"We can't have our viewers disoriented!" Wes hit the table with the palm of his hand. Bonnie jumped. "After all, control of our viewer is imperative!"

Lisa smiled. "It's imperative if you want to be paid well," she said. "The client pays to make sure the viewer pays attention to their product or service. If the designer doesn't grab and keep the viewer's attention, then the designer's failed at their job."

I looked at Wes. He was still scowling. "Wes, this is where you can use your experience as an artist to the max. You want to get your viewers to pay attention to your artwork, right?"

"Sure," Wes answered. "But I don't manipulate them!"

Zed laughed so hard he almost fell over backwards. "You lie!" he laughed. "You use all sorts of tools to draw attention to your product."

"But I don't do it to get them to buy commercial products." Wes seemed to be backing off his outrage. "I'm selling art, not a product."

Lisa waved her hand like she was brushing away some dirt. "Wes, that's a pretty pompous statement."

Wes looked at her with surprise. "What do you mean?"

"Either way," Lisa continued, "You're selling something, whether it's art or dog bones. Don't take this so personally. We're just learning tools that artists have used for centuries."

"Lisa's right," I agreed. "As artists, we might want to go over the edge, or push the envelope. As designers working in the commercial field, we need to remember that shock value, or *drawing outside the lines* is great for some formats and for some markets.

"But, when designers work to communicate to the mid-range market, they need to stick to some traditional methods to portray their message. The mid-range market is traditional and conservative, and they don't go for drastic change or confusing images.

"We'll discuss this more when we design for our client, " I added. "The first person we need to please is the client. If it works for him, it may work for his market." I looked at Zed. "We're meeting the client next week," I said.

Wes shrugged, sheepish. "I guess I see what you're saying. I'll save my debates until the right time," he added with a glint in his eye. "I'm still not sure I'm buying into this commercial manipulation."

"That's fine, Wes," I smiled. "I'll be up to the debate. We may all need to be convinced we're going in the right direction."

Steve laughed, "Yeah, it would be good to know if I've been going in the right direction all these years." He grinned at Wes.

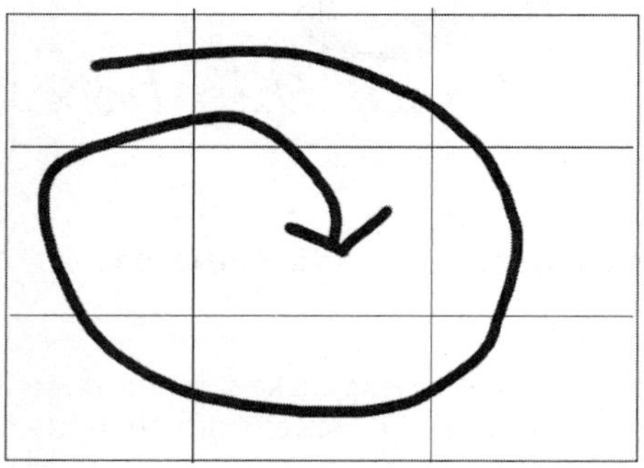

I turned back to the board and drew another grid. "Here's another compositional tool I want to show you using the rule of thirds grid." I drew a circle within the format. "This is very basic. This composition simply keeps your viewer's eye from going off the page until they force themselves to move on.

"You would lead them in from the top left, and actually spiral their eye deeper into the page. You can use various elements of design to do this, and they can be curved or angular. Just make sure they're pointing *into* the page, instead of *off* the page."

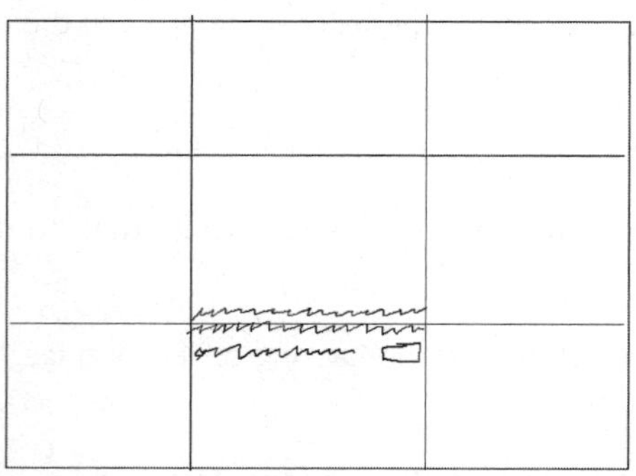

I erased the circled grid and replaced it with a grid and a few lines to indicate type. "This last compositional tool is one that uses white space as the ground," I said. "The type along the bottom third becomes the positive shape, or figure."

I turned to the class, "The type can be placed in the middle, too. Many of you may have seen ads that consist of a few words in the middle of the ad format with nothing else surrounding them. This can be very effective in grabbing the viewer's attention, especially on a page that has a lot of type. Many financial institutions use this composition for advertisements on pages of stock quotes.

I looked at Wes and reminded the class, "These are just the general rules, and they're obviously as flexible as you want. In fact, in some cases, they're made to be broken.

"We have a frame outlining the design area. Other dimensions to this frame are the client's market, and the client's budget. We'll tackle those along the way, and add these dimensions to our compositions."

"I'm sorry I erupted over these formulas," Wes shrugged. "They just seem so... stifling."

"In some cases, they are, Wes," I agreed. "But, they're heavily tried and tested, and known to work. When we design, we often don't have the luxury of time or money to test our compositions. These techniques can be used to our advantage, and they save us numerous headaches in formulating our designs."

"But, there are other compositions that work as well," Deb argued. "All of them are also based on mathematical formulas." She looked apologetically in Wes's direction. "Sorry, Wes. That's just the way it is."

Wes laughed, "I guess I'm outnumbered for the moment."

'You've got at least one other person on your side, Wes," Steve said. "I've worked with grids and mathematical formulas throughout my career. Now I want to break out of those boxes and try some new things!"

I sat with the students and addressed Steve and Wes. "I think part of your frustration is the fact that we're learning basic elements of design. You both understand how to move beyond some of these elements. I think the Flash format will give you both some problems that will occupy you beyond the grid."

I looked at the rest of the class. "We've just reviewed some basic compositional structures centering on the rule of thirds grid," I said. "There are many other compositions that can be used, and, as Deb mentioned, most of them are based on mathematical formulas. Before we discuss any complex compositions or any other issues, let's cover the principles of design."

The principles of design

The principles of design are just as important as the elements of design that we covered in the first two lessons. In fact, these principles help to define the use of all the elements. Accordingly, we've actually touched upon most of the principles during our discussions of the design elements and the composition of our format.

The important issue here is to help clarify the principles as tools separate from the actual elements. Returning to our architectural analogy, the principles of design are part of the architect's blueprints, where he defines how he will use his materials to build his house.

"Let's relax and go over the principles of design," I began. "As we begin to analyze each rule, you may realize we've already discussed some of these when we covered the elements of design and as we discussed basic composition.

"Make yourselves comfortable," I said. "I'm going to cover each principle of design in short lectures. I'll ask for questions when I'm through with each one. At the end of this session, I'll give you a handout that lists the principles of design with a brief definition. Is everyone OK with this?"

"Go for it, teach!" Zed said, stretching back in his chair. Even Wes and Steve seemed to relax.

Contrast

"The first principle of design is one of Zed's favorites," I smiled. "Contrast is an *inherent* principle of design. By this, I mean that you can't avoid contrast, even with one dot on a piece of paper.

I looked at Wes. "Can you tell us how, for example, this single dot on a piece of paper can create contrast?"

Wes nodded, "I think I'm up to the task," he grinned. "The spot creates contrast through the addition of another value, another shape, and another color against the original smooth and blank sheet of paper. You've automatically created a point of interest in contrast to the original unfocused large expanse of blank paper. You've also created a texture where before there wasn't any."

It was my turn to grin. "Wes went overboard," I said. "But he's right. We create contrast in a variety of ways with just the smallest point or line. The creation of a point or line on a page is not the most that can be done with contrast, though. Contrast is also leveraged through the use of every element of design.

"Remember," I added, "We're delivering a graphical message. The use of contrast is perhaps the one principle that needs the most care, since it could deliver the message with more impact than any other principle in graphic design.

"Contrast can be the muscle behind the message. Last week, we learned how high contrast alone could be used as a powerful message. If we leverage this high contrast with a low contrast border or frame, the message could be even more powerful.

"Another way to portray contrast would be with contradiction. If you decide to use just one word in your message, what is that word, and how would you display it? You could use the word *war* with a flock of lambs," I said.

"That's contrast, all right," Deb stated. "It could also be facetious or ironic."

"That's right, Deb," I agreed. "Sarcasm is a tool of communication, and there are many formats that would lend themselves to this structure. Contrast can also be very confusing, as we witnessed with the ambiguous figure Wes drew. High contrast isn't just visual, as Deb just mentioned. Any of these principles could be used as visual or intellectual guidelines."

"What do you mean?" Bonnie asked.

Wes responded, "Visual principles of design are based on what we see. Intellectual principles of design are ideas based on a theme. We can use both to push a point."

I agreed. "The point here is to be very aware of your power as designers. You can gain a lot of attention for your message if you use this form of contrast." I showed them a picture of a frightened carousel horse. "In this instance, we see contrast in value, and we also experience a contrast to what we perceive as normal. Most carousel horses are rather benign. This one appears to have a problem."

Bonnie squirmed in her seat. "Remind me not to ride that carousel."

"Exactly," I responded. "The artist wants to shake our world a bit, and it was shaken with visual and intellectual contrast."

I continued, "The use of color for contrast is common. The most common colors for Christmas greeting cards are green and red. In general, agents for this market discourage any other colors for depicting traditional scenes. Red and green, if you remember your color schemes, are contrasting colors on the color wheel that form a **complementary color scheme**.

"Size is another tool of contrast used to attract attention. Remember Danny DeVito and Arnold Schwarzenegger together in films? Together, they provide comedic contrast, as one was short and round and the other was tall and trim. Together, they appeared to be shorter and rounder and taller and trimmer due to the use of contrast.

"Once you begin to look for contrast in events and objects around you, you might not be able to stop. It can become an addiction.

"Any questions?" I looked at the class.

Zed looked around at everyone, and said, "I think we understand the principle of contrast. It's kind of hot and cold, sweet and sour, and the long and short of it all."

Even Lisa laughed at that comment.

"That's great then," I said. "Let's now move on to direction."

Direction

"As a designer, you have the ultimate control over your viewer's eye." I looked at Wes, who appeared to be calm. "This is certainly subliminal if your viewer is unaware of the elements and principles of design.

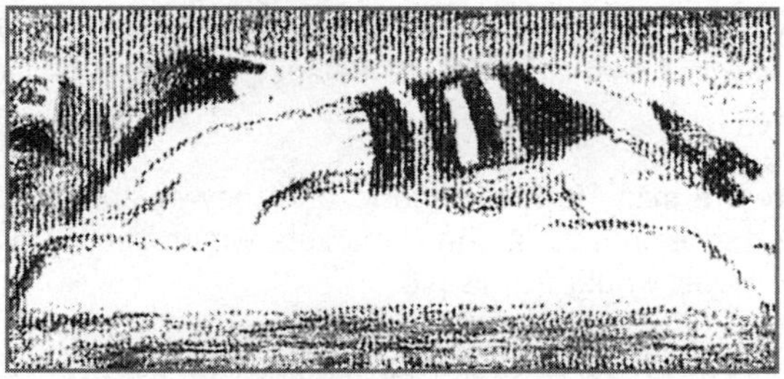

"We just learned how direction takes the viewer's eye into and around your piece of work. This principle of design involves every element within design, so you might say it's the summation of all the tools you use to deliver the message of your work." I held up an image of two greyhounds. "This image also shows a concept Steve mentioned earlier," I said. "The greyhounds convey motion, speed, and direction. They appear to come and leave the format, and this tells me they're running through the format, so to speak. They're also blurred, and this denotes speed, and they're all facing the same direction, so I know which way they're headed.

"The basis to all good design and artwork are the format and a great concept. Both are interrelated, since your concept will be modified by your format, and your format will display your concept. Many other factors, including budget and tools available will affect both of these elements. Once these have been decided, then you have a direction to proceed."

"Any questions?"

Bonnie shook her head. "Is that all there is to direction?"

I smiled. "Well, it's the main thrust of this principle. We'll discover many other reasons to use direction as we define elements for our client."

"I'd say your statements were pretty direct," Steve smiled. "What's the next principle?"

I answered, "After direction, we need to look at the emphasis of our work."

Emphasis

I looked at the students. "Have you ever known anyone who told a story, only to come the ending saying *And my point is this...?*" They all nodded. "Although the story might be interesting, the point could be made with less embellishment and more structure."

> *"The same logic applies to emphasis in graphic design - when everything is emphasized, nothing is emphasized!"*

"It's important to understand each element of design and how it can support your work with this principle. When you use the elements to tell your visual story, the idea is to build it up with structure, not embellishment. The emphasis, or dominant objective, in a design is often supported by a second or third point of emphasis called **accents**. Dominance contributes to unity, which we'll discuss shortly, because the main ideas or features are emphasized and other elements are subordinate to this central theme."

I continued, "The other way to remember which element to use as your emphasis is to stay focused on your target audience. A psychological emphasis requires thought, and its vision is swayed by perception. You may create what you believe to be a simple point, but your viewer may take a different stance, based on his or her own experiences.

"Music is a fine way to explain this principle, since there are many forms of music, and they all appeal to different markets. From a psychological point of view, the emphasis in some markets within the music industry is sex – maybe artists like Barry White and Isaac Hayes would fit this bill."

These references promoted laughter from the class, as Zed started to sing in an unnaturally deep voice, "*Who's the cat that won't cop out, when there's danger all about?*"

"SHAFT!" offered Lisa.

"Right On!" answered Zed.

Attempting to regain control of my class, I continued, "In other markets, the emphasis could be on sex and defiance. In yet other music markets the point is sex, defiance, and violence – and I don't want to hear your impression of any *gangsta rap*, thanks all the same Zed!"

Deb laughed, "And some areas of music actually place the emphasis on the music itself, like Bach or Beethoven!"

I agreed, "Absolutely, Deb. Hopefully, we'll base our designs with the emphasis on the visual message." I looked around. It seemed everyone comprehended the principle of emphasis. "Shall I move on to economy?" I asked.

They all nodded. "Is this about the client's budget?" Zed asked.

"Kind of..." I answered, teasingly.

Economy

I launched into my explanation of this principle, "Economy of design is perhaps the easiest principle to write about or to understand. However, it is perhaps the most difficult principle to execute effectively. Economy of design is based on the principle that *less is more*.

"The economy of time, motion, and skill are cohesive units in the world of design. The principle of economy in design is another form of consolidation, and it can be achieved with three simple steps.

"Whether you work alone or with a group, with or without a computer, the first step is to take everything you know about the project and throw it all out on the table. At this point you are going to sift through the ideas and visual images with the mental and physical process of elimination.

"Next, your goal is to focus on telling your story with the least amount of elements. Some of the many factors involved in this process are the client's budget, timeframe, format, and message. We will economize our design problem with the creative problem-solving process. Our format within Flash has already been decided.

"All we have left, then," I stated, "Are the bare bones of the design."

I leaned into the group and asked the questions we would need to ask ourselves with each design problem. "I would want to know if my message is clear. I need to ask myself if each element is utilized to its maximum advantage. Do the elements align themselves to the principles of design, or is my message confused by elements that don't make sense for my message?

"Sometimes it's good to walk away from a design and come back to it later with a fresh point of view. We can become so absorbed with our work that each part becomes too precious to let go."

I showed them a picture of a crowd of people surrounding a steam engine. "Someone tell me if you think any of the elements in this picture can be removed without taking away from the visual direction of the eye, and the total unity of the picture."

Lisa looked at the picture and began to explain her ideas. "This picture is set up like a stage," she explained. "The steam engine supplies the contrast and the backdrop to the people. Even though the people are standing in the way of what's happening, I know that they're engaged in something of importance."

"How can you tell that, Deb?" Bonnie asked.

"It's the way they're standing, like they're patient, but they're also attentive."

"But you can't see their faces. How can you tell that they're patient?" Bonnie insisted.

Steve interrupted, "It's the way everyone's standing, Bonnie."

Zed jumped in, "And, this time I see how the circle works in composition. Each person adds to the element of space and depth, and leads my eye around the center of the image."

"I can see what was left out," Wes offered. Everyone looked at him. "There's no trees, no sky, no gravel. The artist left those elements out and simplified the contrast and direction, and the illusion of depth."

They all sat back, satisfied with their answers. "You're all catching on quickly to the principle of economy," I said proudly. "You'll be art critics in no time flat."

Wes laughed, and I continued, "We'll learn, through practice, how we can pile on the elements and then strip them away to let the message shine through. We'll learn how to become clever," I added with a grin.

Deb chuckled. "I've always wanted to be clever," she said. "What a charming concept."

"Is clever different to intelligent?" Zed asked. He eyed Deb with suspicion.

Lisa said, "Clever is intelligent with a twist."

Wes and Steve laughed out loud. "I'll have to remember that the next time I order a clever," Wes said.

I grinned, "If there are no questions, let's move on to proportion."

Proportion

"In comparison to perspective," I began, "Proportion deals with size, or scale, and the relative size to the surrounding environment."

Zed laughed, "You mean like saying someone's head is out of proportion to the rest of their body?"

Wes laughed. "I'm not going to take that personally," he said.

I smiled and continued, "Actually, yes, Zed." I answered. "Proportion can be used to emphasize a message. Perhaps an example we all might understand is the story of David and Goliath. Goliath is portrayed as an element of fear that is totally out of proportion to David's real situation."

"So proportion can be used to define emotions?" Bonnie asked.

"Yes, Bonnie," I answered. "Actually, any element or principle of design can be used to define any emotion, as we mentioned earlier. But," I added, "Proportion is probably the easiest principle to apply to this concept."

Zed abruptly raised his hands in the air. "That's just like using an oversized creature in anime to show strength and to invoke fear in all concerned!"

I agreed. "Caricatures are examples of portraiture done with exaggerated elements. The artist might draw the nose bigger or emphasize someone's balding head. All of these elements are drawn out of proportion to exaggerate a person's actual features."

Wes had been busy scribbling in his drawing pad. "Here you go," he said. "Here's a caricature of Deb."

Deb laughed, "That's great, Wes. I didn't know my chin was that prominent, though. And, is my mouth really that big?"

"No, not really, Deb. I just exaggerated your features to give an example of caricature for Linda."

"I don't think caricatures are very flattering," Bonnie stated.

"I think it helps to have a sense of humor, Bonnie," Deb replied.

I brought up another art movement, to Wes's satisfaction. "Surrealism uses this tool to portray scale confusion, in addition to clarification of the focal point."

Wes nodded, "Dali did this with his melting watches; Escher is also famous for the scale and perspective confusion in his designs."

Bonnie sighed, "I'm going to take a course in art history. I recognize some artists mentioned, but I'm not sure about the art movements."

I looked at Wes. "Can you pull something together to help Bonnie and the rest of us understand some of these art movements?"

"Sure thing!" Wes stated. "I think it's important to understand art history, only if for the tools we can pull into our designs."

I looked at the rest of the class. "Wes is right," I said. "Later in the course we'll take time to cover some of these movements so you all can sense some of the heritage of design."

"Back to proportion," I continued. "This principle works closely with the principle of contrast to develop a focus or emphasis to your work. It's fun to play with scale, and we'll do this during our brainstorming sessions."

"Does anyone have any questions about this principle of design?" I looked at the class.

"Does scale or proportion have anything to do with confusion of depth perception?" Bonnie asked.

"Yes, it does," I answered. "We can confuse or enlighten the viewer, even amuse them with scale and depth perception. We can emphasize how small something is by placing the object in a huge environment. We can also emphasize how huge something is by making it much larger than it actually is. Does this help?"

"I think so," Bonnie paused. "It's like a cartoon I saw one time where humans were the bowling pins in a bowling alley, and a huge bowling ball was rolling down the lane toward them."

Deb choked, "Bonnie, I think you have the concept, but I don't want to know the punch line."

Zed said in a stage whisper, "I want to meet you after class!" We all laughed.

"Bonnie, I think you have the idea, like Deb said. Let's move on to the next principle of design."

Balance

"When using all the elements of design in creating a piece of graphic work, you will need to think about balancing these elements within your format." I held out my hands as a balance scale, and continued, "Actually, there are only two ways to think about balance – either you want to use it or you don't.

"The use of balance also requires two choices, since you can either use symmetrical or asymmetrical balance. The difference is simple: **symmetrical balance** is balance that is even in weight across the format. Right and left sides, as well as top and bottom, are equivalent. A perfect example of this would be the pattern or design used in gift wrap, textiles, or wallpaper. You saw samples of this when we talked about texture last week.

"**Asymmetrical balance** is more commonly used than symmetry," I added, "Simply because symmetrical balance can be very boring. This tool is used to emphasize contrast and direction, but you can use any element of design to build within this principle."

I showed them an image of legs wearing a pair of boots. "This is an example of asymmetrical balance," I explained. "The image is shown off to the left side of the format. Plus, the direction isn't vertical, so there's an element of movement within the lines of the legs and the hands pulling up the jeans."

"So the emphasis in this piece is on the left side of the rule of thirds grid, right?" Zed asked.

"It is, Zed." I answered. "This was an illustration for a boot ad. The copy was along the bottom right focus point."

"I can visualize that," Bonnie stated.

"Me, too," Deb said. "Even though it's asymmetrical, it's balanced all the same."

I put down the drawing. "There's always the choice of having no balance at all," I concluded. "This would be an **unbalanced** piece, and it is perfectly acceptable in any work outside of a client's presentation. This is a tool to create tension, confusion, and chaos. Within many art movements, this lack of balance was called **anti-design**. Whether the work was designed or not is the debate."

I looked at Wes. He was about to speak, and seemed to change his mind. "Wes, I'll be perfectly willing to debate these art movements with you, but we'll have to wait until later."

He laughed, "I was just going to open my big mouth, but I thought better of it. We'll have to talk about this at some point," he added. "Only because I'd love to debate the issue of anti-design with you, too."

I nodded. "Agreed, then. For this course, I'm going to ask you all to be careful not to let your desire for a certain balance, or lack of the same, overwhelm your concept. The use of symmetry might be pleasant to view, but if you lack contrast or even the subtle direction of line or texture, you might end up with a very bland piece on your hands."

Rhythm

I continued with the principle of rhythm in design. "Rhythm is as unavoidable as contrast in your designs. Rhythm is instinctive and could be classified as primal. We tap our foot to keep time with music. The poet organizes words into a flow of sound. The seasons are repetitious, and life cycles are based on the rhythms of our planet, which is based on the rhythms of our galaxy, based on the... well you get the picture.

"In a similar way, the designer creates rhythm with the repetition of elements. The question is not whether the designer is going to use rhythm, since this principle will happen with the use of any element. The question is how, why, and to what affect the designer uses this principle to achieve the mission of the message."

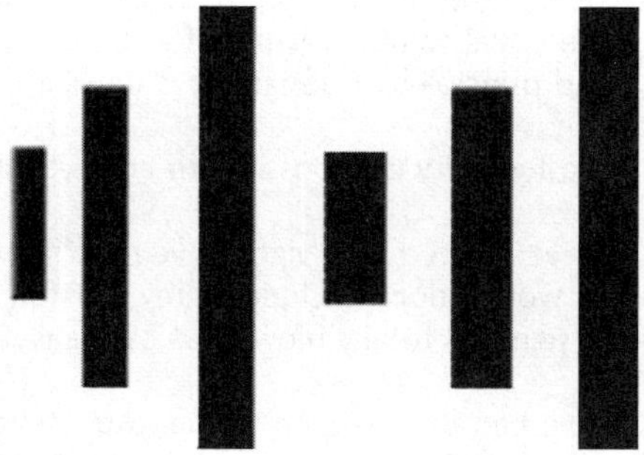

I showed them an image of repeating lines. "In this image, you can see how the rhythm of line adds to the illusion of depth. This is a simple example of rhythm, but you can see that the concept doesn't have to be complicated.

"Design, in its simplest sense, makes use of repetition as one element used in a repeat pattern. You can see this most often in wallpaper, gift wrap, and in textiles, as I mentioned earlier. This is the principle used by Andy Warhol in his paintings of Campbell's Soup cans. You might interpret his statement, based on the monotonous repetition, that consumerism allows no room for variety or creativity."

"You could equally interpret it as: *Andy Warhol really likes soup!*" suggested Zed.

Trying not to laugh, I continued, "A variation of rhythm is used to create interest. A brick wall will come to life if a window is installed. If three windows are installed, another problem is presented. If the windows are the same size, and if they all use the same window treatment, then we're back to the same problem of repetition and monotony. This may be the goal in some instances, but as a designer creating a message for a client, this is not the effect you want to achieve.

I looked at the class. "You'll develop your own rhythm in design as you progress with Flash. Timelines, moving images, and repetition of certain elements can all help create a suitable design for your message.

"Any questions?"

"I don't want to appear dense," Bonnie said, "But if I can't dance or snap my fingers in time to music, will that hinder me in the development of rhythm in my designs?"

"It's not such a dense question," I replied. "Many students worry about this, and they never say a word. In answer to your question, no, you don't have to dance to develop a sense of rhythm in design. Rhythm is one of those principles that add spice to our layouts. It's a principle that is either automatic, or added as a solution to a sterile design."

"Phew!" Zed said. "I was worried, because I can't dance, either!"

Wes was about to laugh until he realized Zed was serious. "Hey, Zed," Wes stated, "You'll be doing the Watusi when I'm through with you."

Zed grinned and waved his arms in the air. "I can dig it. But it will have to be a group dance."

"Good timing, Zed," I laughed. "We're going to wrap this session up with the principle of unity."

Unity

I began explaining this final principle of design in the context of fine art. "In fine art, the principle of unity is often called *advanced pictorial composition*. This makes unity sound like the crowning achievement of all the principles of design, but it's really no more important or relevant than emphasis or rhythm. Unity is, however, a principle that is based on the designer's experience. The result is judged on how well the message is communicated.

"A designer is defeated in sending an effective message when the form and content aren't appropriate to the visual solution. Unity of a design is also impossible when the designer is inexperienced in the elements and principles of design, or is unwilling to learn from experience.

"Lastly, unity is impossible to achieve when an inexperienced client edits a designer's work."

Steve nodded with vigor. "I've had that last problem happen numerous times," he said. "In fact, I have a ton of work I don't include in my portfolio, because the client demanded so many changes that the original design was totally blown out of the water."

"I've had that happen to me, too, Steve," I said. "In fact, it happened so many times that I figured half the world was nuts." Steve nodded again. "But I found that half the time, I just wasn't able to convince the client that my design was going to work.

"How can I do that when the client is so confident?" Steve asked.

"You have to be more confident than the client," I answered. "We'll cover this issue later in the course. I think you'll be interested in this part of the course, and I know you'll have a lot of experience to add to the subject."

"He's not the only one that has this problem," Bonnie said. "But, I realize now that I didn't know enough to defend my non-design," she laughed.

> *"If you want to be a successful designer," I said, "Just remember that this title really means a planner with a visual message that is clearly understood. When you can define your goals to yourself and to your client, with content and format that fit those goals, you're well on your way to success!"*

I handed out a list of the principles of design, and asked the students to look it over and ask any final questions:

The Essential Principles of Design

- **Contrast** – An *intrinsic principle*. Whenever an element is placed within a format, contrast is created. Can be emphasized with the use of size, shape, color, texture, and so on. Contrast offers variety within a visual format.
- **Direction** – Utilizing the illusion of movement to create the visual action of displacement. Direction and speed can be illustrated through the *actual* or *implied* movement of an object from one point to another. This is important to remember in both static illusion of direction and in animation.
- **Emphasis** – Also known as *dominance*. This condition exists when an element or elements within a visual format contain a hierarchy of visual importance. For instance, a headline might take precedence over an image. This headline maintains emphasis, and the image is the supporting accent.
- **Economy** – A principle operating *on the slim*. Can also be considered *precise* or *simplistic* design. This principle is used to create emphasis on a subject.

The Essential Principles of Design cont.

- **Proportion** – A two- or three-dimensional element defined by comparisons or relationships with other elements in the design, in context with the surrounding environment. This principle can create emphasis, direction, balance, or contrast.
- **Rhythm** – A recurrence or repetition of one or more elements within a visual format, creating harmony. Yes, it's just like music!
- **Balance** – The elements of design converge to create a design or arrangement of parts that appear to be a whole, incorporating all other principles of design.
- **Unity** – *Oneness, Harmony, Gestalt*. The condition of completeness with the use of all visual elements within a format, where the sum of elements is more important than any one of its parts.

After some quiet reading, Zed held up his hand. "Yes, Zed?" I asked.

"What does this word *gestalt* mean?"

"Ah, thanks for pointing that out, Zed. I need to go over the concept of *gestalt*." I turned to the class. "Anyone here know what this word means?"

Lisa answered, "It's a German word that roughly translates to the concept of the whole being larger than the sum of its parts."

"What?" Bonnie asked. "I don't get it."

Lisa explained, "It's like a play, Bonnie. One act in a three-part play isn't going to support the play. But, three acts may not support it, either. In order for the play to work, the costumes, scenery, lighting, atmosphere, and skill of the actors all need to work together. Otherwise," she added, "The play will flop."

"Thanks, Lisa," I was truly grateful for her input. "That's a perfect example of *gestalt*." I looked at Bonnie, "Did she help you understand this concept?" Bonnie nodded, and I looked at Zed. "Zed, do you understand it now?"

Zed shrugged, "Yeah. It's like life." We all waited for him to continue. "If you have money and a great car, it's not gestalt. It helps to have a good attitude, knowledge of the elements and principles of design, and a girlfriend."

After we stopped laughing, I reminded the class we still had a project for next week.

"Right," Deb replied. "What's the deal for next week?"

Preparing to meet the client

In this portion of the class I wanted to prepare the student to meet the client on a level beyond that of a person new to design. They learn to prepare themselves with the tools of research and a professional demeanor.

"Next week might a pain for some of you," I stated. "While some of you will feel quite at home with the prospect of meeting the client, others may feel anxious at the prospect.

"But before you get too nervous," I added, "The client isn't going to be a stranger – in fact, I'll be representing the client, so you'll should feel comfortable enough to experiment and not worry about making mistakes."

"I'm sure I'll make a lot of them," Lisa stated. "I'm not used to talking to other people on a professional level."

"You don't have problems talking with us, Lisa," Zed replied. He turned to the rest of us, "You should hear her outside of class. She's a regular chatterbox."

Lisa turned a bright shade of pink. "See if I say anything to you from now on," she smiled.

Zed apologized, "Oh, Lisa, I didn't mean to embarrass you. I just think you're a lot of fun," he said.

"Lisa has a point," I said. "Many of us don't know how to talk with a client. We don't have the first clue about what to ask, and how to ask it.

"So, for next week," I continued, "I want you to each come up with ten questions you would ask a client if you were meeting him or her for the first time."

"Do we get to know what this client does before we meet them?" Steve asked.

"No, you don't," I answered with a grin. "This is practice for developing a standard procedure that you can use in future real-life situations. Your clients will come from many different backgrounds, and they'll have many different products and services to offer. Your job as a designer," I added, "Is to find out the basics first."

"Will we have just one chance to meet the client?" Wes asked.

"No, you'll have two chances to meet with the client," I answered. "But the first meeting is the most important.

"In addition to the questions, I also want you all to come to class dressed like you would when you meet your clients."

"Oh, man!" Wes shook his head. "I don't know about this. I haven't dressed up in a long time. I don't have a suit and tie," he added.

Steve laughed. "I guess I'll have to help you out next week," he said. "I'm sure I have a clip-on bowtie somewhere in my closet," he laughed.

Wes smirked, "I'm sure you'd look great in it, too," he said.

"It's going to be interesting to see what you all come up with," I said. "Remember, ten questions from each of you, and no cheating. I want a variety of questions. And dress for the interview." I added.

Deb, Bonnie, and Steve left, laughing and appearing confident about their assignment. Zed, Wes, and Lisa sat and peered at me with a look bordering on disgust.

"Can't we get someone to meet the client for us?" Lisa asked. "I'm going to fall apart in next week's class."

I looked at the three of them, and spoke to Lisa. "Lisa, I promise you won't be singled out or ridiculed. We're going to learn this as a group, and it should be a lot of fun."

She sighed and picked up her tools. "I'll give it a shot. Come on you guys," she looked at Zed and Wes. "Let's go get some chocolate."

I smiled when they left. Chocolate must be the universal cure for stress!

Summary

In this chapter we learned to create the illusion of depth in static and dynamic two-dimensional formats. This included drawing and sketching, and working in the Flash MX format. We learned that we can create the illusion of depth in a number of ways:

- Using layers in Flash MX
- With the basic elements of design, such as value, color, and texture
- Through one- point and two-point perspective

Within Flash MX, we learned about layers, timelines, and basic animation. The importance of the use of overlapping images to portray depth was emphasized.

Within a static format, we saw that it is possible to portray movement through **repetition** of elements, **blurring** of lines or images, and with **multiple images** highlighting the **process of movement**. We also found that movement depends on the point of perspective, and we learned how to see objects as images with depth that move along a point of view within space and time.

Finally, after studying some basics compositional formats based on the rule of thirds, we got down to learning about the important principles of design:

1. **Contrast**
2. **Direction**
3. **Emphasis**
4. **Economy**
5. **Proportion**
6. **Rhythm**
7. **Balance**
8. **Unity**

These principles can be used as a methodology to visually align the elements of design. This combination of visual and intellectual properties of design will also be utilized throughout this book. In the next lesson, we'll be studying the relationship between the designer and their client.

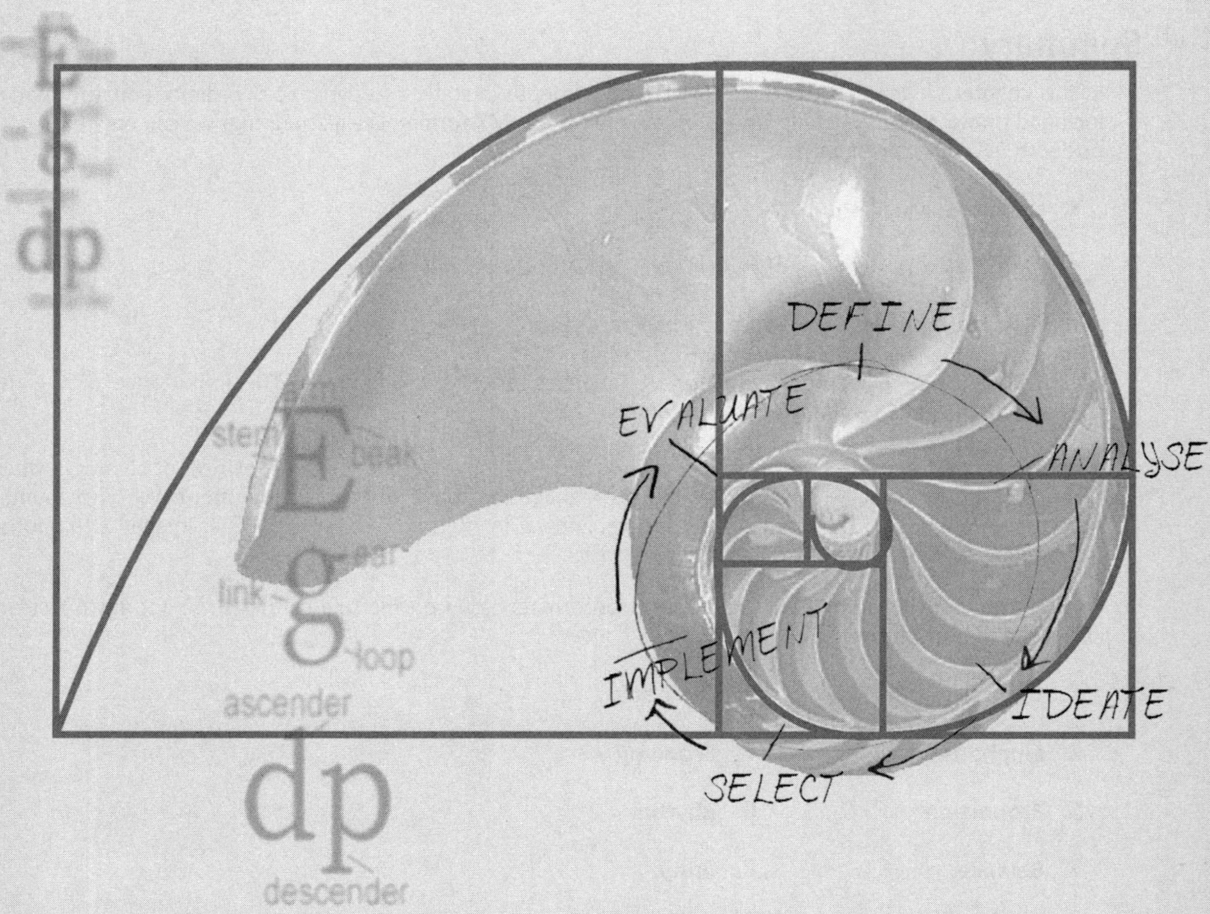
DEFINE
ANALYSE
IDEATE
SELECT
IMPLEMENT
EVALUATE
stem
beak
ear
link
loop
ascender
descender

Chapter 4

The Designer/Client Relationship

Objectives

In this class, you will learn:

- How the creative problem-solving process adds to a designer's skills
- Coming up with questions to help define a client's visual problem
- How to handle a client interview and gain a client's confidence
- Defining a client's image and preparing to write a client brief

Introduction

As I walked down the hall toward the classroom, I wondered how the students would handle their first meeting with the client. I was also curious to hear the questions they might ask a client when meeting them for the first time.

As I approached the door to the classroom, I heard what sounded like tap-dancing. When I entered the room, I was greeted with a bow from Lisa, and applause and laughter from Wes, Zed, and Bonnie.

Was it Lisa or was it Ingrid Bergman? Was this a classroom, or was I in Casablanca? I looked at Wes, and he looked strangely like Humphrey Bogart. Zed looked like a dashing aviator... or perhaps an extra in a scene from *The Great Gatsby*. Bonnie, fortunately, looked more or less like Bonnie, only with polish.

Lisa adjusted her hat and blushed. "I brought some regular shoes with me, too," she nodded at a pair of shiny black heels set side by side at the foot of the table.

I set my materials on the table and turned to inspect the dramatic trio. "Actually," I smiled, "You all look fabulous. But Zed," I pointed at my neck as I looked at his white silk scarf. "Isn't it a little warm for the scarf?"

Zed pulled a pipe from his pocket and stuck the stem in his mouth. "It's not warm at all, m'lady. It's quite comfortable. You should try one." As he tried to talk, the pipe wobbled and fell from his mouth.

"I think the pipe's a bit much," Wes laughed. "I guess we need to explain ourselves."

As he began to talk, Steve and Deb walked in, dressed in suits. They both stopped short when they saw the scene, and Steve burst into laughter. "I didn't believe you when you said you had a suit, Wes," Steve said. "It goes great with that clip-on bowtie!"

Everyone settled at the table. Wes looked at me from under the brim of his hat, "Well Linda, the three of us," he pointed at himself, and waved his hand at Zed and Lisa, "Didn't have anything suitable for an interview like those three." He swept his hand at Bonnie, Steve, and Deb.

"So Lisa let us rummage through the wardrobe department at her theater. At the moment they don't need their 1940s outfits, so we thought they'd be OK," he explained. "Even if they're a bit outdated." He brushed at his lapels.

Steve grinned so hard his face seemed twice as wide as usual. "You guys did great! Actually I'm jealous."

Lisa looked around, and then faced me. "I guess I need to explain, since this was my idea. We used the creative problem-solving process."

As she leaned forward to talk, I interrupted her. If she was going to explain this process in action, I wanted to reinforce it to the rest of the class. The instruction today incorporates the first two steps in the creative problem-solving process, and subsequent steps will be used to guide the remaining classes.

"Before you explain your thoughts," I looked at Lisa, "Let's talk about what we'll do today, and then you can lead us into your solution to this problem."

Lisa nodded, and I explained today's course of action. "Today, we'll study the potential solutions to the client interview," I said. "We'll cover the questions we need to ask the client during the first interview.

"Then, we'll meet the client, talk about how the first interview went, and see what we might have missed. We'll also talk about what the client might want to know from us, also. This is where we begin to define boundaries for ourselves.

"After the second interview, we'll analyze the client's answers to find their problem. Within this process, we'll also begin to define our boundaries for their design."

"So we'll get to *ideate* solutions today?" Zed asked. "I'm ready for that!"

I laughed, "No, Zed. At the end of this process, we'll begin to manufacture the design brief, which explains our viewpoint of the problem. This happens after the second interview with the client.

"We'll also highlight the limits of our visual solutions within our chosen format – Flash MX," I added. "We'll talk about optimizing Flash for the Internet and the World Wide Web." Bonnie perked up when she heard the word *optimizing*.

"These tools will help us make reasonable decisions during and after the ideation process," I looked at Zed, "When we meet next week."

Problem-solving revisited

The creative problem-solving process is a solution to many problems within and outside of design. Instead of reiterating this process to the class in lecture, I felt Lisa's first-hand experience with the process would help the class understand how they'll use these steps over the next few weeks.

"Lisa," I asked, "Can you go to the board and draw the creative problem-solving circle as you explain your solution?"

She nodded, and went to the board. As she began to talk, she drew a circle. "When Wes, Zed, and I left class last week, we went for an espresso so we could talk about our problem. Once we'd all complained a bit," she added sheepishly, "I realized this was a creative problem that needed a visual solution."

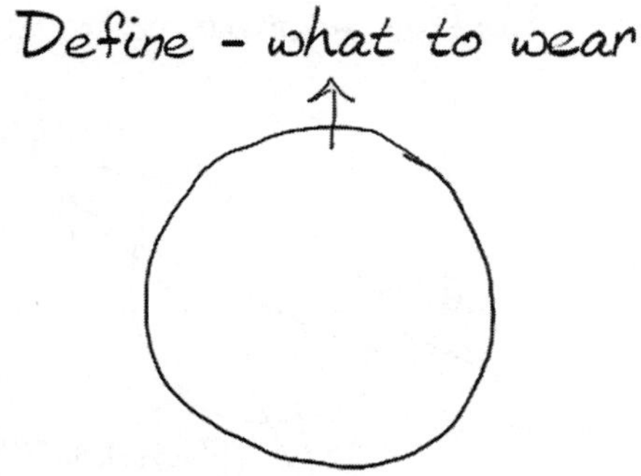

"We used the creative problem-solving process to see if it would work for this problem. First," she explained, "We *defined* the problem." She wrote *Define – what to wear* on the board, and turned to talk to the class. "We needed to dress properly to meet a client. None of us had suitable outfits," she shrugged, "Or what anyone might consider a suitable professional outfit!"

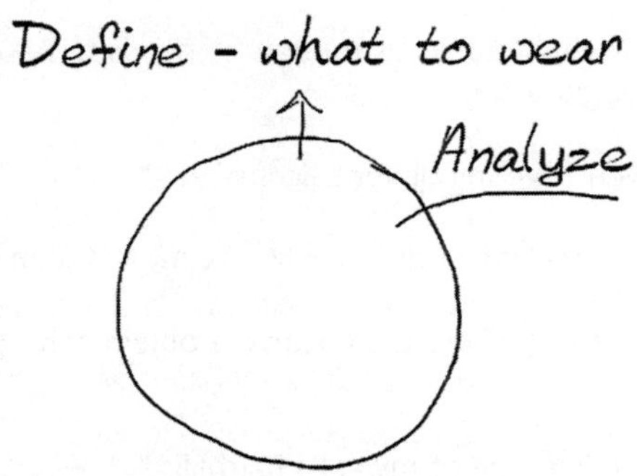

She turned back to the board as she talked. "After *analyzing* the problem and our finances," she continued, "We realized we'd have to brainstorm to come up with a solution." Lisa nodded at Wes. "Wes showed us how to loosen up with the brainstorming process."

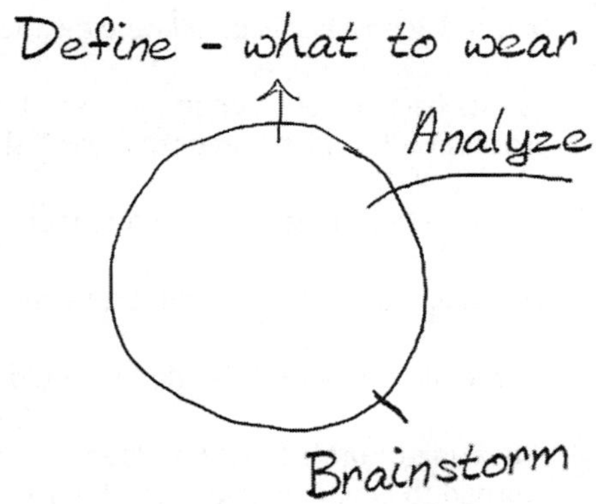

Bonnie interrupted, "Oh, I'm jealous! That would have been fun."

Zed nodded enthusiastically, "Yeah, it was. We came up with some really ridiculous solutions!" he grinned.

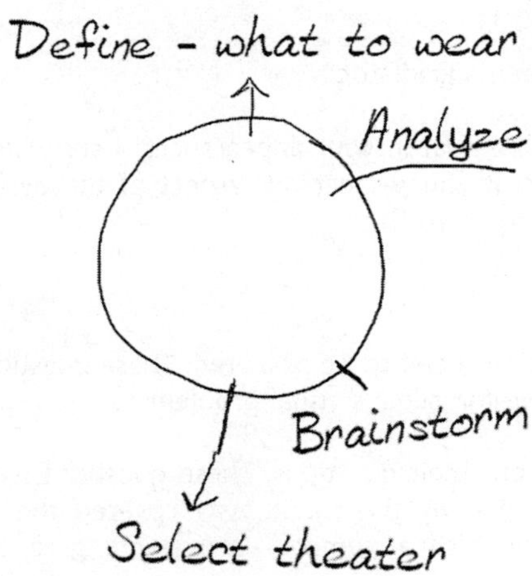

"Finally," Lisa continued, "I remembered the wardrobe department at the theater. I don't know why I didn't think of it before." She wrote *Select theater* on the board.

"That's the idea behind brainstorming," Wes said, "At least, it is for me. I begin to remember a lot of things after the brain garbage is out of the way."

"So," I said, "You came up with the this selection. Once you arrived at the theater, did you know exactly what you wanted to borrow?"

"No," Wes said. "We had to find out what was available and make our choices from the rack of clothes that weren't in use. Then," he added, "We had to find items that fitted us well."

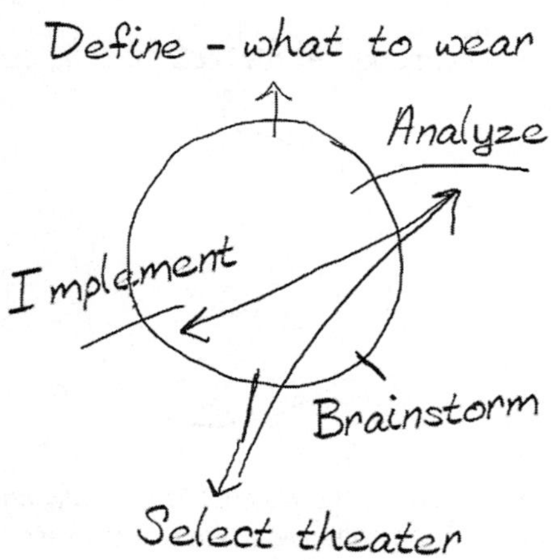

Lisa stated, "So, we had to go back to the *analyzing* stage before we could even implement the solution." She drew arrows back to the *analyze* stage, and then to *implement*.

"You're *implementing* the idea today, and I guess we need to *evaluate* your selections." I leaned back in my chair and looked at the rest of the class. "What do the rest of you think of their solution to the problem?"

Steve jumped in, "I think they did great. Lisa looks charming, Wes looks like he's in control..."

Wes interrupted, "As if I'm never in control!"

"...And Zed looks, well, he looks as though he needs to be a bit older." Steve laughed.

Zed grinned. "I can't meet the client anyway," he said. "I don't even have my driver's license yet."

Deb and Bonnie laughed. "If I were the client," Deb raised one eyebrow, "You would all certainly have my attention."

Lisa sat back in her chair and looked at her circle on the board. "I can see where the creative problem-solving process isn't always a smooth circle," she said.

Zed followed her gaze. "It isn't smooth," he agreed. "It looks more like one of my cat's hairballs."

Wes laughed, "Yeah, creative problem-solving is a lot like mental regurgitation!"

With that comment, I decided it would be best to move on to the development of interview questions.

"Speaking of problems," I nodded at Wes, "Let's get down to the business of resolving today's first obstacle." I turned to Lisa, Zed, and Wes. "I think you three did a commendable job with your solution to this problem. Your choices are creative. It appears that you've chosen the appropriate clothes to convey your creativity as well as respect for the client." After another glance at Zed's pipe, I added, "Well, perhaps Zed's gone a little over the top, but his intentions were all good!"

Zed sulked. "It could have been worse," he said. "I could have been a gladiator."

"If you don't have access to a theater wardrobe, try to at least be neat in your appearance," I suggested. "Even though you may be creative, your client is pure business. If you respect this aspect of the design business, your path into a designer/client relationship will be much smoother."

Questions for the client

Before the designer meets the client for the first interview, questions need to be prepared. These questions provide maximum benefit to the designer, as they begin to resolve the client's visual problems.

I took Lisa's place at the board, and asked the students to get out their questions. These questions were prepared over the last week, as each student thought about meeting the client. As I covered the six categories, I asked them to mark each one of their questions with a number corresponding to the appropriate category.

"Although many of you may write content for your clients, none of you are actually journalists." I began. "This list is a basic formula for most journalists. Actually this list becomes a litany, and then second nature for the journalist who covers a story." I wrote the following list on the board:

1. Who
2. What
3. When
4. Where
5. How
6. Why

I turned back to the class. "Number your ten questions according to each category, and we'll see how close you come to covering all six bases listed here."

Deb spoke up first, "I have all six, no problem. I had a gut feeling you'd go after these questions." She added, "Actually, my mother's a writer. I knew about these six categories before I learned to read."

Zed nodded, "I should know this list. My mother asks me these questions every time I leave the house!"

Steve and Deb laughed. "I really didn't have a problem, either. After being in the print world for so many years, I think this list rubbed off on me," Steve said.

I looked around at the rest of the students. "How did the rest of you do?"

They all agreed they were satisfied all six topics of inquiry were covered with their individual questions. "It seems I have more questions under *who* and *what* than anything else," Lisa responded. "Since I don't have the first idea about this client or what they do," she added.

"I want to hear some of your questions," I said. "We'll go around the table, and each of you will add a question to each category. I'll write them on the board. When you hear or see a question you don't have on your paper, I want you to add it to your list. This is an *ideation* session, so throw all your questions on the table."

Wes began to explain his questions, and we worked our way around the table until everyone had offered something to the list. Some of the categories, by their very nature, had fewer questions than others. Other categories had some information that would be obtained over a period of time working with the client, rather than information the designer would discover in a first interview. Some of the questions would also be answered indirectly over a period of time as the designer becomes more familiar with the client and the client's business.

By the time we'd finished, we had the following general questions to work with:

Who

- Who are you (this can be as personal as finding out about the client's family, present and past, hobbies, education, and so on)?
- Who do you work for?
- Who do you expect to hire for this job (more specifically, is this a bid, or is it a direct request for design help)?
- Who will maintain your Flash site?
- Who are your competitors, and how do they market their products/services?

What

- What do you do?
- What company do you work for?
- What product and/or service do you offer?
- What is your current image?
- What makes you and your business unique?
- What information do you already have for your business?
- What sort of marketing have you done in the past?
- What is your market?

When

- When does your business operate (is it seasonal)?
- When are you open for business?
- When do you work (as opposed to when your business is open)?
- When do you take time off?
- When do you expect this job to be done?

Where

- Where is your business located?
- Where do you plan to expand?
- Where are you from?
- Where do you plan to be in 5, 10, 15 years (personally or with business)?

How

- How do you plan to reach your market?
- How do you plan to maintain your communications?
- How have you reached your market in the past?

- How long have you been in business?
- How many years have you worked for your company?
- How do you plan to pay for your design work?
- How do you think a Flash site will make you more successful?
- How do you plan to market your Flash site?

Why

- Why are you planning to change designers?
- Why are you choosing a designer?
- Why did you choose to talk to me?
- Why are you choosing Flash MX for your business?
- Why do you need a website?

As we continued to write questions, the students came up with other ideas they hadn't thought about for their lists. Zed was excited. "This is almost like the brainstorming session Wes, Lisa, and I had the other day," he said.

"I agreed. "When you begin to eliminate ideas from the top of the pile, you make room for other ideas to come to the surface." I pointed to the board. "We could ask the client many other questions, but the ones you came up with today will get us on the right track."

I then asked them to decide which ten questions would be the most important ones to ask a client at the first meeting. "You have limited time, and you need to find out as much as possible from this client on the first go-round," I said. "So choose your questions carefully.

"I want you to do this as a team, and you have five minutes to decide which questions you'll ask this client," I added.

Bonnie sighed. "Do all designers wear this many hats?" she asked. "First we're architects and mathematicians. Now we're journalists and interviewers."

I smiled, "Bonnie, designers do have to learn a lot of diverse roles. Most designers I know crave this variety. However, I also know a few designers who wouldn't meet a client face-to-face if you paid them a million dollars!"

"Why are we learning this, then?" Wes asked. "I'm probably one of the latter designers."

Steve answered for me, "Even when I don't handle the financial part of the business deal with each client, I like to meet them one-on-one. That way," he added, "I save a lot of time. I can find out first-hand who this client is, and what they like. I can also find out more about their attitude and demeanor."

"Why is that important?" Zed asked. "If I don't meet them, I don't have to put up with any attitude!"

"I think you're hanging around Wes too much," Bonnie grinned. "I have to deal with my clients all the time, since I do it all – the books, the billing, the creating. But," she added, "I never thought to ask so many questions."

I nodded at Steve, "Steve has the right approach to the client. The more we know about the client, the client's market, and the client's competition, the more we can put into the final design of the client's site.

"The client's market will tell us how far we need to go with usability issues, and the client's goals will tell us how much we need to learn about the future use of their site design. If we stay on top of our client's interests, we can assure ourselves we have a better chance to keep working with this client."

Deb was wearing her watch today to create a good impression with the client. She looked at it and stated, "We just ate up two of our five minutes. Let's get cracking on those questions."

"Yes ma'am!" Wes laughed.

After a few more minutes and quite a bit of debate, the group decided on their ten questions. Before they told me what they were, I said. "You've just learned six categories of questions to ask your client," I said. "These categories can contain many different questions, depending on who your client is, and what they do."

"It sure would help if we knew more about this client," Bonnie complained. "Just the difference between a client who owns their own business and a client who represents a business can change the perspective on these questions."

"You're going to meet your client in a few minutes," I consoled her. "If you picked the right questions, you won't have a problem. Why don't you take a break, and decide who your spokesperson will be for the initial interview?"

They all leaned back and looked at Deb. "I don't think there's any debate about this choice," Wes grinned. "Tag, Deb. You're it!"

Deb sighed, looked at her watch again, and said, "I expect all of you back at this table in ten minutes."

I had to turn away and hide my smile as the students groaned under Deb's demands.

Interview scenarios

Before the actual interview, I'd give the students various scenarios for an actual first-interview situation. No initial interview is ever the same, and each one will add to the designer's experience.

I sat at the head of the table as the students returned from break. "Did you all agree for Deb to represent you?" I asked. They all nodded in agreement. "Before we begin, I want to present several interview scenarios for you. What you're about to experience is a skill you may or may not need in the real world, but it's always good to have this knowledge in your back pocket in case you ever need it.

"If you have your own design business, you will probably at least know what your client does before the initial meeting. Many times, they won't just knock on your door. They'll call in advance for an interview or consultation. At that time, you will at least get the person's name, contact information, and their occupation.

"In many ad agencies or design firms, you won't meet the client unless you're the senior designer or creative director. These people will brief and work with you and others as the design team develops the client's project.

"If you meet the client as a team, it would be a very unusual situation," I added. "It's not a good idea to meet a client with a table full of people. That would be a very intimidating situation for the client."

"Is it a good idea to use a tape recorder?" Bonnie asked.

"That's a good question, Bonnie," I answered. "In most cases, for the initial interview, I would advise against it. This could also intimidate the client, and it could defeat the purpose of helping your client feel at ease."

Zed seemed surprised. "You mean the client will be nervous, too?"

Steve laughed. "The client is hopefully about to spend a lot of money, Zed. Of course they're nervous."

I responded, "The client could be nervous or just very busy. Their design problems are probably just one of many problems. It may or may not surprise you that many people don't consider their design issues to be that important. This is why the first interview will be short and to the point. Unless," I added, "The client indicates they want the interview to be more thorough."

"How will we know that?" Zed asked.

"I'll bet it's through body signals," Bonnie stated.

Steve replied, "Usually the interview goes on when the client keeps talking."

"You're both right," I responded. "There are two other difficulties I want to talk about before our interview begins," I added. "First, you may meet your client on their turf, rather than in your own studio or workspace."

"Great!" Wes seemed relieved. "I don't want to clean my place up!"

Steve grinned, "I know what you mean, Wes." Steve looked at me. "I try to meet my clients at their offices. That way," he added, "I can pick up brochures and other materials they might not remember to bring with them on the first visit."

"That's a great point, Steve," I said. "You'll want to develop files on your clients, and these files will hold as much information as you can get your hands on during your relationship with them."

"You make it sound like we're spies," Wes grinned. "Do we need the client's fingerprints?"

Lisa looked at Wes seriously. "You are a spy, Bogie. Your mission is dangerous, but you'll be paid well."

Wes laughed. "What's the other issue, Linda?"

I continued, "You'll find there's a huge difference between phone or cyberspace relationships and the face-to-face relationship with a client. You'll be able to pick up on many visual clues that won't be apparent in a long-distance relationship. This long-distance relationship could mean difficult communications with each other. In this case, you'll want to be much more thorough with your interview processes than you would in real life."

Deb looked concerned. "Is the interview today a phone interview, or a real-life interview?"

"It's real-life, Deb," I answered. "This particular interview will give you the skills you'll need if you meet a potential client who has very little time. You have ten questions and about ten minutes to find out as much as you can about this client. I'm going out in the hall. When I knock, I want you to answer, greet me, and welcome me into your studio."

"I can't come to your office?" Deb asked.

"No," I smiled. "You'll find out why in a minute." I looked at the rest of the class. "I would like for the rest of you to hang back and take notes."

Deb looked at Wes, "Can you ask them not to interrupt?"

Wes laughed. "I think we all can keep our mouths shut for a few minutes, right?" He looked around at his classmates, and they all nodded.

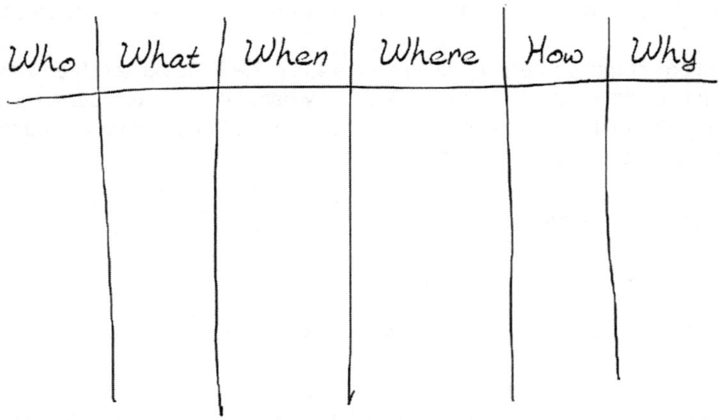

I stood and wrote a few notes on the board. "You all need a piece of paper. Divide it into six categories, like this. These are your *who*, *what*, *when*, *where*, *why*, and *how* answers. As I answer Deb's questions, write the answers down on your paper."

The students all lined their chairs up along the wall, and sat with pencils poised for our performance. I went out in the hall, and Deb and I began the interview process.

The initial interview

After I gave them various possible scenarios of the initial client interview, the students would now experience one of many possible cases. Each student in this class has a different focus for the use of design skills and Flash MX for their various careers and interests. This factor alone gave me reason to keep the client anonymous, so they could use their skills to devise creative solutions to this design problem.

For the client, I chose someone who, hopefully, would be in a profession that would place the students in unfamiliar territory. This would give them experience in research and in the development of their creative problem-solving skills.

I knocked on the door to the classroom, and Deb answered. As she opened the door, she asked if she could help me.

"I'm looking for a designer to help me develop a Flash website," I replied. "I found your address in the phone book, and thought I'd stop by on my break."

Deb extended her hand to shake mine, "Well," Deb responded, "You may have come to the right place. My name is Deb, and "I'm a freelance Flash designer."

"My name is Frieda Ray," I replied. "I'm a carpenter."

Deb seemed shocked, but regained her composure quickly. "Wow," she stated. "I don't meet very many female carpenters."

I laughed, "I'm sure. That's why I want to get my name out there. I want to expand my reputation. So far, my gender hasn't hurt me. I have a few big guys working for me, and that helps a bit."

Deb waved me into the room. "Why don't you have a seat over there at the table. Let's get to know each other a little better."

"Don't mind if I do," I said. I walked over to the table and relaxed in a chair. "I don't have much time today to spend with this," I stated. "I just wanted to know what's involved in this process and how much it might cost me. I don't know anything about this Flash MX stuff, but I know I don't want a site that just sits there, looking back at the viewer. I want some interactivity between my information and the viewer, and I want it to work without a lot of glitches. Can you tell me what's involved?"

Deb sat down with me, and opened her notepad. I noticed some questions written on the paper inside.

She began the interview with a simple question. "Do you have a business card?"

I smiled, "Yes, I do...somewhere." I dug around my pockets and came up with a plain card printed with Frieda Ray's name, an address, and a phone number. "This is all I have with me right now," I mumbled. "But, I have a brochure back at the office."

"I see you're located just a few blocks from here, and your business name is..." She looked up and asked, "Do you go by just your name, or does the business have a name?"

"I just go by my name," I answered. "But, I realize I might need to change this image. I've been tossing some ideas around in my head, but they all seem too corny or clichéd," I looked up at Deb. "Can you help me with a name, as well as a Flash site?"

Deb stared at me with a blank look on her face. She shook her head slightly and answered, "I'm sure I'll try my best to help you with your image," she stated, and continued with another question. "Can you tell me how long you've been in business?"

"Oh, I've been around this business for a lifetime," I said. "My father was a carpenter, and I hung around him while growing up. He quit a few years back, due to arthritis. I decided then to take over his clientele."

Deb looked sincerely concerned. "I'm sorry to hear about your father," she said. As I shrugged, she asked, "Who're your clientele?"

"Mostly homeowners," I stated. "I build new kitchens, for the most part. You know, sort of help them upgrade their homes." I added, "Lately, though, I've been receiving calls from larger contractors for help in designing and building storage for apartments and condominiums. I guess the word is getting around that I'm ethical, and that I do a good job."

"You sound proud of your work," Deb smiled. "It sounds as though you plan to expand your business, am I right?"

"I'd like to do that," I agreed. "But expansion can be tricky, with taxes and the cost of extra personnel. I'd have to expand rapidly to be able to justify my decision."

"How far would you expand your business?" Deb asked.

"I wouldn't go too far beyond the city limits I don't believe," I said. "But, I understand that having a Flash site would make me more or less international. How can I manage a site and still stay local?" I asked.

Deb seemed a little flustered. "I don't know," she stated. "I'd like to know more about you before I could answer that question." She regained her composure and asked, "Do you operate your business year-round, or is it seasonal?"

I thought for a moment and answered, "It's year-round now. It used to be seasonal. I used to have time off, but lately I haven't had a moment's rest. This is partly why I want to expand, and expand rapidly. If I have the business, I'll be able to hire supervisors to take on the heavy time commitments and grunt work. My real goal," I smiled and added, "Is to design environmentally sound living spaces for people."

Deb grinned. "That sounds like a great goal," she stated. "But, your focus at the moment is to expand the carpentry business, right?"

"Right," I answered. "That will get me where I want to go." I looked at my watch. "Speaking of going, I've gotta run. My break is just about over."

Deb asked, "Would you like to meet again when you have more time? I'm sure I'll have more questions for you, and I'd like to talk to you more about your market potential with a Flash design." Deb paused a moment, and added, "Plus, I need to know more about what you expect for your site, so we can align a goal and budget for your needs."

"How about next week?" I asked. "I have a lot more questions to ask you, too."

Deb made an appointment for a date and time to meet at my office. We shook hands, and I left the room. As she closed the door behind me, I could hear loud laughter coming from the classroom.

I opened the door and saw Deb sitting on the floor, shaking with laughter, tears streaming down her cheeks. Everyone was standing around her, giggling and hooting.

"What a riot!" Zed shook his head. "A female carpenter! That sure took me off guard." He turned to Deb. "You should have seen your face when you heard that one!"

Wes helped Deb up off the floor. "You two were something to watch," he managed to choke out.

"You bet," Bonnie grinned. She looked at Deb and starting laughing again. "You looked so lost when Linda – I mean, Frieda – asked about going global!"

Deb wiped her face with the back of her hand. She looked at me and stated, "I was so caught off guard!" She accused me of cheating. "Clients aren't supposed to ask questions!"

"Oh, I could have hit you hard," I said. "I was really easy on you because you were doing such a great job."

"I did a great job?" Deb looked at me suspiciously. "I don't even remember what happened!"

"We do," Steve grinned. "We wrote down all the information." He snapped his heels and saluted Deb. "You did do a great job, whether you realized it or not," he stated. "You're a natural!"

"All I need is five other people in the background taking notes," Deb sighed. "I don't think I wrote down anything." She picked up the business card and started laughing again. "Where did you get this card?"

Wes asked to see it, and he laughed and passed the card around to the rest of the class. "Good question! Where did you get this awful card?" he asked.

"I typed it up and printed it out last week," I said. "After you all left class."

"I know one thing," Lisa gave the card back to me. "Even I could do better than that."

"Hopefully, you all will be able to do better than this," I pointed at the card. "But before we begin, we need to process all your information." I asked them to sit at the table. "You just experienced a very short interview," I stated. "But, you saw how much information you can gather within a very short time. This will be useful if you meet a potential client at a meeting, on the bus, or at a very boring party."

Steve nodded, "One never knows where the next client lurks."

"I filled up my page with answers to a lot of questions," Zed said. "But, then again, I write really big!"

Steve leaned over to look at Zed's page. "I got a lot of information, too, Zed. Let's see what you have..."

I interrupted Steve and Zed. "Before we compare notes, give me a minute to review what you just experienced." I pointed at the categories listed on the board. "Those categories help us *define the client*. This is the first step in the problem-solving process. We're going to list what we just learned, and analyze the information to see if we're missing anything."

"I can't wait for this," Deb chuckled. "I can't wait to see what I missed!"

Defining the client

The students now have a basis to begin the creative problem-solving process. They already have a good deal of information about the client. The next step is to categorize the information for further reference. This process helps to **humanize** the client, bringing the core of the client's problems to light. Whether the client is a small business owner or a marketing manager, the designer needs to acquire, retain, and improve their relationship with them. The number of customers lost due to lack of interest is extremely high, despite the fact that the cost of attracting a new client is about five times the cost of keeping a current client happy.

As the students sat at the table, I stood to write answers to the six categories on the board. "I want you all to help define the client," I said. "We'll make a list in our notebooks, and later we'll use this information to prepare the client brief."

"You mentioned that term before," Bonnie said. "What's a client brief?"

"A **client brief**," I explained, "Is a short report to the client that states how you see the situation at hand. This brief – and it is brief, since it's no more than three pages long – will show the client you understand them and their design problems. It also states what you plan to offer if the client takes you on for the job."

I continued, "The client brief also helps the client define you, as the designer, as a person who is interested in them and in their goals. Frieda is a small business owner, so most of our contact with her may be organic, or casual. If you meet with larger businesses," I added, "This process will be more formal, but no different in content. Not only are you showing the client you understand them, you're also qualifying the client to see if they're worth your time and money."

Steve agreed, "Part of the independent designer's problem is doing business when they really want to just design. If we qualify the client from the beginning, we end up seeing if they are either *prospects* or *suspects*. The suspects are those businesses who have an interest in what we do, but they don't have the means or real intentions to buy.

"The prospects are what we want," Steve continued. "These businesses fall into three categories: *cool*, *warm*, and *hot*. Of course," he stated, "We want hot prospects."

Steve continued, "I also worry about a possible client that wants to know more about cost than they do about my expertise. That's a clue to me that they're more interested in a deal than a good job."

"Very well put, Steve," I said. "We don't know whether Frieda Ray is a suspect or a prospect at this point. That's why we want to get to know her, her goals, and her business. We'll also discuss how to approach the money issue in a bit."

"Now," I continued, "Who is this client? Bonnie, would you tell us who the client is?"

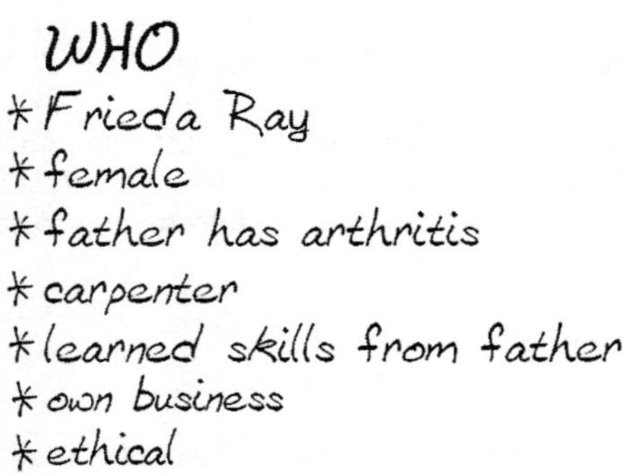

Bonnie cleared her throat and began with her description. "This potential client's name is *Frieda Ray*. She's *female*, and her *father has arthritis*. She's a *carpenter*, and she's *learned her skills from her father* and has been in this profession most of her life. She *has her own business*, based on her father's previous clientele." She stopped and looked up. "That's basically all I know about *who*. Oh, one more thing, she said she was *ethical* too"

I looked at the class. "Do we know anything else about this woman?" Everyone looked blank. "Let's move on to *what*," I said.

Steve spoke up, "Frieda's *business is carpentry*, and she has her *own business*, like Bonnie just said. She *builds cabinets* and other *storage spaces* for homes. She has *several men working for her*. She *doesn't have a name for her business*, but she's thinking about a more professional appearance. She may want to change her business name to reflect this need. Right now, she *goes by her own name*."

Wes began the *when* category. "The only thing I have down for *when* is the *next appointment date*," he said. "Frieda didn't state exactly when she took over her father's clientele," he added.

WHEN

* next appt. date
* worked seasonally in past
* works constantly now
* hours?
* when does she want site?

"I listed a few more things for that category," Lisa stated. "Frieda *used to work seasonally*, it seems. Now, however, she *works all the time*. She hasn't had time off for a long time. She *didn't state her hours*, but I'll bet she works a long day."

Deb looked at Lisa, "I got that feeling, too. But," she added, "I don't think we're allowed to make bets about our client." She looked up at me.

"You're right, Deb," I replied. "Don't take anything for granted with a client. A long day with little time means one thing to one person, and something altogether different with another client."

"I know one thing for sure," Zed stated with assurance. "If she wants to be a designer, she'd better get a new business card!"

Bonnie laughed, "I think that's a fact."

I grinned. "Before we discuss Frieda's propensity for bad taste," I said, "Let's finish with her descriptions. We also want to add *when do you want your site delivered* to the when category," I said.

"Deb," I asked, "Do you remember anything about where Frieda is located?"

She picked up the business card. "We have her address right here," she grinned. "But I can guess this address isn't real. Does that matter?"

"For this project, no," I answered. "Is she located in the same city as the designer?"

"Yes," Deb answered. "And she doesn't want to expand the business beyond the city." She looked up at me and asked, "What should I have said when Frieda asked about going global?"

WHERE

* 2022 Lumber Lane
  Cabinetville, USA
* doesn't want to expand beyond
  this area at present

I said, "That's a good question, Deb." I looked around at the class. "Does anyone have an idea of what Deb could have said?"

Lisa answered, "She could have told Frieda that this information could be stated on her site, right?"

"Correct, Lisa," I answered. "We can always state on the site that this client doesn't sell their products or services outside a certain geographic area.

"Did anyone get any answers for the *how* category?" I asked. "This is where we'd be able to answer questions like that."

Lisa answered, "The only thing I wrote down was that Frieda *got Deb's name from the phone book*."

HOW

* Frieda found Deb in phone book
* clientele generated from web site expected
  to support and expand Frieda's business
* wants to expand carpentry business rapidly

Wes added, "I also wrote that Frieda plans to use the *additional clientele generated from the Flash site to expand her business*. She *plans to expand rapidly*, and then begin to drop out so she can design, rather than build."

"Wes, that's a very good point," I said. "This will be a key focus to remember as we go along with this project. If she wants to expand rapidly, does this mean she'll want the site done quickly?" I turned to look at the list on the board behind me. "There's a lot of unanswered questions, aren't there?"

Everyone nodded. Steve leaned forward and asked, "How much more do we need to know?" He nodded toward the board, "Is it important to know her father has arthritis?"

"It may be important, Steve," I answered. "At the moment we don't know this yet. But, we're going to keep this information in our client file in case we need it down the road."

Bonnie spoke up, "I do know my client's birthdays," she said. "I always send them cards. They really appreciate the thought."

"That's one good reason to get to know the client, Bonnie," I said. "If we respect the client and honor their lives, they might remember us when another design job comes around," I stated.

"Other than the personal side of our clients, and how this affects our business," I continued, "The only category we have left is *why*. Bonnie, why does Frieda want a Flash site for her business?"

WHY
*wants an interactive site
*wants a 'slick' site that works
*wants to expand her business
*wants to stay ahead of competition

Zed jumped in, "I heard Frieda say she wants an interactive site."

Bonnie nodded, "She said she wanted a site with no glitches, too."

Steve added, "I think she wants the site because she thinks it will help *expand her business*."

"Good point, Steve." I wrote the reasons on the board. "What about other motives? Does she want to *stay ahead of her competition*?"

"That's implied, right?" Deb asked. "She didn't come out and state anything about her competitors, but it makes me wonder what their sites are like."

Steve agreed. "We don't have to be mind readers for that one," he said. "I think we can safely state she wants most of the business in this area."

"What other information would you like to know before we take on this client's design problem? Steve," I turned to him, "What would you consider important?"

"I'd like to know about that brochure she mentioned," he said. "Although the business card is a little on the ropey, the brochure might be slick."

Lisa looked up from her notes. "What if she had another designer before she knocked on this door?" she asked. "She might have tried some other forms of communication, too. She might have run newspaper ads. Another thing I want to know," Lisa added, "Is what kind of wood Frieda works with."

"How important is that?" Zed asked.

"Color, texture, and quality," Wes answered. He looked at Lisa, "Good question!"

Deb added, "I want to know what style she works in, too. Is she traditional or modern? She mentioned she wanted to design environmentally sound living spaces, but that didn't tell me anything about her preference in design."

"I see what you're saying now," Zed said. "As far as we know, Frieda might be into some heavy-duty sci-fi or lacy old fashioned stuff."

Bonnie tapped her pencil on the table. "Shouldn't we be concerned about Frieda's clients, too? What do they like?"

"They must like what Frieda likes, or they wouldn't hire her," Wes said.

"All we know is that Frieda said they like her ethics and top-notch work," Steve said. "Remember, we can't take anything for granted. I think it's important to ask her more about her clients during the next interview."

"I know one thing," Lisa said as she smiled at me. "At least we know where to find Frieda so we can get our answers to our questions."

I smiled. "You can get answers," I admitted. "But, first you need analyze the problem and finalize your questions. You'll only have one more interview with your client before you tackle the client brief. Then," I said, "You'll begin the brainstorming process.

"So far," I continued, "We know a good bit about Frieda. Now," I said, "Why don't we back off a bit and gather some answers for questions she may have for us?"

Deb agreed emphatically. "Yes, yes, yes. I don't want to get caught off-guard like that again!"

"Before we go there," I said, "Let's review this experience. What did you all see that worked really well here?"

Lisa said, "I liked how Deb asked for the business card up front. That sure helped to eliminate a lot of *where* questions."

"Yeah, that was cool," Zed stated. He looked at Deb. "The other really neat thing was when you said you didn't know the answer about going global. You could have made something up, but you were right up front about the answer."

I nodded, "Deb, that was a great thing to do." I addressed the rest of the class, "*If you don't know something, don't act like you do!* Otherwise, it will eventually come back to haunt you."

"No one will think less of you if you're honest," I continued. "We can't expect so much of ourselves that we're *willing* to have the answers to every question."

"Phew!" Bonnie slumped in her chair. "I was wondering if we'd have to wear perfectionist hats along with all those other hats."

I smiled at the class. "Let's find out what our boundaries are within Flash MX and publishing on the web. Then," I said, "We can give our focus some direction. We'll also be able to answer Frieda's questions with a little more authority."

Preparing for the client's questions

We continued to sit at the table as we talked about questions the client may ask us, as a potential Flash design team. Most of the questions would apply to any design job.

"Questions generated from the client can range from the sublime to the ridiculous," I said. "Most clients don't know about Flash, or how Flash operates. They may not know about the creative problem-solving process, and they usually don't have a clue about the elements and principles of design. Usually," I added, "Most clients are just groping in the dark, trying to find something solid to latch onto for direction. Hopefully, you'll be that something solid they can rely on to get them through this process.

"When a client hires an outside designer, these are some of the questions they might ask you. As I ask the questions, let's tackle them one at a time. These are the first two:

* Have you developed Flash MX sites?
* Who are your current and previous clients?

Bonnie immediately asked, "How do we handle the fact that we don't have previous clients for Flash MX?"

"Bonnie, you and Steve both have previous work experience in graphic design. Hopefully, you both have portfolios. If not, you need to work on pulling one together, and we can do this during the course. This will give your client some assurance that you've at least worked in this field for a time.

"Another way to build Flash clientele is to offer your services to non-profit groups. This may cost you a little money, if the group doesn't have a budget for a project with this scope," I said. "You may even find yourself buying the domain name and hosting space as a donation to the group. Needless to say," I added, "It would be best if you offer your time and money to a group with a cause you believe in."

"What about building sample sites?" Bonnie asked. "That's how I started my web design business. I built three sites for fictitious companies, and uploaded them to my business site as samples."

"Nothing wrong with that at all," I said. "In fact, that shows some creativity and initiative. As a client, I would be just as impressed with samples, since one of my interests would be to see your skill level." I added, "My other main concern would be with your business ethics.

"I would want to know if you're reliable, trustworthy, and capable of meeting deadlines. Bonnie and Steve probably have some reliable contacts for this information," I said. "Wes, you probably have clients who have purchased commissioned work from you. Can you get them to write testimonials?"

"I sure can," Wes said. "No problem."

Zed laughed. "I'm about the only one here that doesn't have any *real* experience. I'm probably going to have to count on you guys to back me up on my reliability."

"I'm sure any one of us will help you out when the time comes," I said. I turned to the rest of the class, "As you can see, there's a multitude of ways to resolve the issue of your credibility. If you get stuck for an answer, use the problem-solving process to see if you can think of any other ways to convince the client they need you for the job."

I continued, "The next question is:

* Do you have in-house graphic artists and copywriters?

"Wait a minute!" Zed stammered. "We are artists, aren't we?"

Bonnie looked at Zed with apparent annoyance. "Zed, your memory cells are fried. Lisa said she can't draw a straight line without her ruler, and I'm horrible at artwork."

"Oh," Zed said. "I forgot about that." He looked at me and held out his hands. "What will these two ladies do?"

"We can hire any one of the rest of you," Lisa stated.
"There's a variety of solutions to that problem," I added. "Lisa has one solution. Another solution is to use an artist the client may have in mind. A third solution would be to use art and graphics from a design house. There's a few really good photography and art stock houses, too."

"What's a stock house?" Zed asked.

Steve said, "It's a place where they keep art and photography in stock, and they sell it to folks like Lisa and Bonnie when they need it."

"Steve's right," I said. "Once again, we have a variety of solutions to this problem. The same holds for a copywriter," I added. "Copywriters and editors can be hired, if you feel you can't handle the client's writing job. If you do write for the client, be sure you have a professional follow behind you to cross those 't's and dot those 'i's!"

Steve added, "Some clients might not know to ask this question, especially if they're inexperienced. Sometimes it's good to ask them if they have copywriters or artists. Or," he added, "If you already have artists and copywriters on board, you can tell the client you're capable of handling all artwork and copywriting.

"Of course," he added, "These are all items you would add to the total bill to the client."

I agreed, "Good point, Steve. These points are crucial to bring up, so if the client forgets, make sure you ask the client."

Along these lines," I added, "The other question your client might ask is...

* Will you manage my project?

"Now that you've answered the previous questions," Wes stated, "This one doesn't seem so hard."

"What would you say, Wes?" Lisa asked.

"I'd say there's no one else for the job," Wes laughed.

"That's a good answer, Wes," I said. "But, the client is also asking if you are the art director and/or creative director. Are you ready for that position yet?"

Steve laughed. "After all these years in the design business, every day I find I'm far from those positions. There's a lot of responsibility that goes with those titles."

"I'll give Wes a star for his confidence," I laughed. I looked at Wes. "It's very difficult to take on jobs alone. Bonnie could probably tell you how difficult it can be to juggle client jobs, books, and billing as well as meeting with clients and..."

"Remembering their birthdays!" Zed said. "That would be the tough part."

Bonnie laughed. "I think the answer to that question will be more apparent as we learn more in this course."

"Good answer, Bonnie." Deb winked at her. "Spoken like a true pro."

"Let's move on to some other questions, and maybe you'll see how tough this position can be for a lone eagle," I said.
Noticing his instant confusion, Wes leaned over to Zed and whispered loudly, "A lone eagle is someone who prefers to work alone, and mostly in a remote location."

Zed looked at me with raised eyebrows.

"Wes is right," I assured him. "More and more designers, writers, and artists have followed the lone eagle route with the advantage of computerized communications. However," I added, "You all already know the problems this might cause with long-distance designer/client relationships. Success or failure depends on each particular situation, so don't let a cabin in some mountain ghost town remain a dream if that's what you really want," I said.

That last scenario seemed to send a few people off into daydream land. I pulled them back in with a few more questions from the potential client. "The following questions might belong together. They tackle the issue of site maintenance, and they are:

* How will I make future changes to my site?
* Is the site structured to grow with my business?
* What's the cost?

"These three questions probably won't be asked at the very start of your designer/client relationship," I said. "Unless you already broke the ice with the client beforehand. If the client asks you these questions on the first interview, you don't necessarily have to answer them directly," I advised. "The first question is an enigma. The client could be asking you if they're going to make their own changes, or if you will handle those changes. If you know that you want to have a long-term relationship with this client, then answer it immediately. Tell them that you would be willing to make the changes. If you don't know the client that well, you don't know if they mean monthly, weekly, or daily changes. This question needs more clarity. It's not a question that can be answered right there and then.

"The second question can't be answered until you know the client's goals. If you don't know how much or how fast the client wants to grow their business, you can't answer this question, either.

"The third question," I continued, "Isn't fair to ask at this point. You still need to know the answers to the first two questions and more. The cost might include building just one page, or it might include building a fifty-page site and maintaining it with daily changes and upgrades.

"These questions are for your business manager if you have one. If you don't have one, then wait to ask or to answer these questions during or after the second interview, when you know more about the client and how much it will actually cost you to design and maintain the site."

"Why is that?" Bonnie asked. "I've always been up front with my prices and with maintenance for my client's sites."

Steve looked at me and asked, "Can I answer that question?" I nodded, and he looked at Bonnie. "This is just from my experience, and it's just my opinion. I've learned that when I give up my prices on the front end, I usually shortchange myself.

"From my experience, when a client wants to talk money before they talk about design, I know what's important to them. It most likely isn't my expertise they're worried about." Steve continued, "Mostly, they're looking for a bargain, or they want a price to compare with my competitor's price.

"I don't know much about the maintenance end of a website," Steve admitted, "But my first thought is that I'd rather be designing another site rather than burdening myself with grunt work. I've seen so many designers sell themselves short by talking money on the front end. I think any businessperson would understand that a designer is a businessperson, too. We need to know our costs, as well as the cost of our time before we can even begin to quote a price to the client."

Bonnie looked at Steve with surprise. "If you don't know about web maintenance, you sure could fool someone. Maintenance *is* grunt work. At least it feels that way to me. My clients always want something done to the site, and I end up doing it for free."

"I hear some people pay exorbitant prices for site maintenance," Deb said. "What does it involve, anyway?"

Bonnie answered, "It's anything from making additions or changes to the site to optimizing the site for search engines. It may not sound like much, but hours can fly by taking care of all these little details."

"I think each of you will have to make this decision for yourself, when you get your own clients," I said. "One important thing to note with Flash MX is that not everybody in town will have your skills. You can make a good deal of money with site maintenance, or you can give your work away. Either way, it's your decision.

"Steve brought up a good point, though," I said. "If you'd rather spend your time designing, you might hire another source to maintain the site for your client. This can be added to the client billing, same as it would if you were doing the maintenance yourself.

"Shop around, and make sure you grill the potential maintenance crew the same way a client would grill you. It's your work and your skills on the table. If the crew doesn't have your skills, they may make a mess of your work."

"I assume you mean slight changes," said Bonnie, "As opposed to a complete overhaul."

"Sure Bonnie. From time to time most websites require a complete redesign or overhaul, but mostly require a bit of maintenance here and there. One thing that you might have to find out from the client is how often they intend to update their website.

"This might mean the difference between creating the client a **static** or **dynamic** website."

"A dynamic website?" puzzled Zed. "Is that just something with lots of animations and movement on it?"

"Not quite Zed," replied Deb, "A dynamic website is one that is updated frequently and regularly, like news websites for instance. The information and content is always changing whenever there is something new to report."

"I often get asked to make dynamic websites," said Bonnie, "But I often have to turn them down. The fact is that I'm not experienced enough to do them. Instead, I usually ask the client why it is that they want it to be dynamic."

"Dynamic websites are indeed complex projects." I said, looking at Bonnie, "They can involve all sorts of scripting languages and database storage. To make a dynamic website you have to be familiar with some of these scripting languages. We won't be covering dynamic websites in the classes ahead.

"Many external companies and website hosts are usually able to offer some dynamic technologies, but we have enough to worry about in just designing the Flash MX website, without looking towards working with a third-party."

"I don't suppose Frieda will want a dynamic website will she?" whispered Bonnie.

"Frieda didn't ask for a dynamic website. She wants an interactive site, which is quite different," Deb interrupted. "Interactivity is any activity that involves an immediate and reciprocal action between a person and a machine. In this case, the machine is the viewer's computer."

"Thanks, Deb," I said. "Although Frieda isn't here to answer," I replied, "I'm sure she won't require a website that is updated *that* regularly. I suppose a lot of it is down to what she wants to show on the website. That is what you need to determine."

"So the site might just need a little maintenance then?" asked Bonnie.

"Sure, but as I mentioned earlier, if you choose to sub-contract this out, you need to check out the company that will do it for you to make sure their skills are worthy of the task.

"There are a few tools in Flash MX to make handing over the work a little easier if you choose to do this, such as the ability to make templates."

"I use templates in my print design." Said Steve. "If I'm working with another designer's original work then it sure makes things easier as I know where to look for things."

"We would do the same thing, enabling someone else to work on our Flash files with as little trouble as possible."

"The aim might be to create a website which can easily be updated from the original Flash files," said Bonnie.

"That sounds about right. We also want to make the files easy to update ourselves."

"I suppose the next thing on the agenda is where the website is hosted," asked Bonnie. "I usually host all my clients' websites with the same hosting company. Not only do they offer a great service, but they also give me discounts because I use them regularly."

"What is a hosting company?" asked Wes. "What do they do with our website?"

Deb was quick to reply to this one. "A **host** is someone that stores your website for you on a web server, allowing people access to it via the Internet.

"A **web server** is basically a fancy computer which has been opened up to the World Wide Web."

"Opened up?" Wes asked. "This is Matrix stuff right?" Wes tried hard to contain his humor.

"Well, we're not quite that advanced yet Wes, but it might happen one day." I said. "The Internet is just a bank of interlinked computers which talk to each other. When someone accesses a website, they are looking at files that are stored on a web server. Just like the files on our computers here."

"You mean someone could be looking at the files on those machines over there?" asked Zed with a wide-eyed sense of paranoia.

"No, they can't Zed." I said. "A computer has to be explicitly told to allow access to itself via the Internet."

"That's good." Said Zed with a sigh of relief. "I don't want people to steal my Flash files!"

The students all laughed. When they all stopped, I continued. "A host specializes in letting their computers, or servers, be accessed via the Web. So they are ideal for hosting our websites files."

"Hosting can often be pretty expensive." Said Bonnie. "Sometimes the price can depend on the amount of visitors the site gets and how much file space it requires."

"These factors are usually important to consider," I said, "As they can sometimes mean that you will have to pay a lot more for better and bigger hosting. The amount of traffic a site gets is the usual thing to calculate, as this obviously varies from a family homepage to a large corporate website.

"Because we are using Flash MX to create our website, and the file sizes will be kept to a minimum, I don't think the file size issue is in question here."

"In which scenarios would you need lots of file space?" asked Lisa.

"Well, every file adds up Lisa, but video and sound files are usually the largest, and a lot of these will not only make the website load slower for the viewer, but it will also occupy a great chunk of the file space."

"How about we use the same hosts as you normally use for this project Bonnie?" I asked.

"Sure thing Linda." Bonnie replied. "I have a website which I use just for testing. We'll be able to use that."

"That sure gets us out of a deep hole!" said Deb. "I thought we were going to have to pay for hosting then."

"There are a number of services that offer free hosting, but these are really only suitable for small websites, and not clients' sites." I said.

"My website is hosted for free." Said Zed. "That's why it sometimes doesn't work though. It sometimes stops working for days."

"Not really suitable for a client's website at all then!" said Steve. "Imagine only being able to view a website on certain days. Sheesh! They would never do any business!"

"That's right." I said.

With little time until the second interview, I decided to bring the class back to the topics at hand.

"How you plan to host and maintain the website will be one of the key issues that the client will want to know. In many cases, the client may not be familiar with web terminology and procedures, and it is up to you to advise them with your knowledge and experience.

"On a minor note, it may also be up to you to register the domain for the client. This is sometimes offered as part of a hosting deal, where they register the domain on the client's behalf, but this might be entrusted onto you.

"The client will sometimes trust in you when it comes to these details, and it is up to you to make the most of this relationship and to do the best you can for them."

"That's a lot of stuff to remember," said Zed.

"These," I stated, "Are the most important questions your client will ask you. If you can't answer these questions, don't fudge on the answers. Be prepared to be honest, like Deb was earlier. State that you don't know, but you'll find out and contact them immediately with your answers. Or," I stated, "You can tell the client you don't have enough information to answer the question, and find out what you need to know to answer them directly."

"The client may have already checked up on you. You all saw that Frieda managed to keep her business going quite well up to this point with word-of-mouth advertising. Anytime someone is very pleased with your work, they will most likely tell at least one person about you. This," I emphasized, "Can bring you more work.

"And, of course," I added, "Anytime someone isn't pleased with you, you can almost bet the house they'll tell more than one person how rotten you are."

I asked if there were any more questions, and if they could think of anything else the client might want to know. When they all said they couldn't think of anything, I reviewed what we just learned.

"Now you have an idea of the questions the client may ask you. You can choose to answer any question with any answer at any time," I said. "However, be aware the client is hiring you for a job. If you want the job, you may bend your own rules just to get your foot in the door.

"Whatever you do," I added, "Just know you're responsible for your commitments. If you have a clear goal in mind for your work, you'll know how much you can take on, and how much you can give back in return. This is part and parcel of a designer's work ethics.

"Many times, we may feel the client is taking advantage of us and of our skills," I said. "But, if you define and analyze the problem, you may discover you set yourself up for that situation.

"Hopefully, this class will help you be more in tune with your capabilities," I said. "You'll also be more in demand, since you'll know more than the person who hasn't studied these problem-solving skills. Your work will show your thought processes and your skill level," I said. "You won't be able to hide what you know, because your skills will visibly improve with each job you take on."

The second interview

The students had more specific questions ready for their second interview with Frieda. They were also ready to answer her questions, if she had any. I set up the scenario by informing the students a little about Frieda's background. This information might have been obvious with an actual visit to her office. Since this office didn't exist, I needed to brief them on some physical characteristics.

The information I gave them included some actual physical characteristics of her office. Frieda likes modern Scandinavian design, and she incorporates these lines into her office environment and into her life. I told them Frieda is neat, punctual, and thoughtful. She doesn't make rash decisions, and she handles her own books.

I also told them Frieda was a very busy person, and wouldn't have time to deal with her own site. She was placing her trust in our design company, referred to as *The Students* in our role-play, to deliver a site that was clean, concise, productive, and interactive.

After I gave them this information, Deb once again interviewed me as Frieda. The classroom became Frieda's office. The other five students sat along the wall, and wrote Frieda's answers on a fresh sheet of paper, lining the answers up under the six standard categories.

Deb proved to be a natural interviewer, as she seldom referred to her paper to ask questions. She preferred to keep the interview on the level of a conversation. Since she conducted the interview in this manner, I found myself opening up to her, telling her things I might not have mentioned if I was being 'grilled.' I had based Frieda on a friend, and I knew quite a bit about this person. As the interview went along, I found myself becoming Frieda, which was interesting for me.

Deb also found herself involved in the process. She brought each issue up as a matter of course. When the interview was closing, she looked at her notes, "I want to make sure I have all I need to commit myself to this project," she stated. "I also want to know if I have all the information I need so I can construct a budget for you to approve."

"I'm quite pleased you were so business-like," I added, "Although I expected as much from you. I'm sure my business is in good hands, and I'll expect to talk with you when you have the budget and other information ready for me to review."

"Thank you," Deb responded. "I hope we covered everything. If not, I hope I'm free to call you for answers. Please feel free to call me at anytime if you have questions as well."

I let her know the best times to contact me. We stood and shook hands, and Deb saw me to the door. This time, I didn't hear any laughter from the other side of the door.

The interview took approximately forty-five minutes, and Deb covered just about every question in the six-category list. Each student was anxious to compare their answers, so they could define their new client with more clarity.

We gathered around a computer as Deb typed the client information into a word processor. The students took turns describing their information to Deb. This list was vital for completing the upcoming week's project, so great care was taken to gather as many details as possible. This list would not be clarified as to why or how we would use this information. This list would form a basis for the students to create their client brief. From information gathered in the two interviews, we created the following categorized information.

Who

Frieda Ray is a thirty-five year old female who was born in Cabinetville, USA. She's lived here all her life. Although she hasn't lived anywhere else, she's well traveled. She's been to Europe, and has traveled to South America and Mexico.

Her father has arthritis, and we learned her mother is active in the community. Frieda also has two brothers. One is a dentist, and the other brother is an attorney. Frieda likes camping, and enjoys physical activity. She learned the skill of carpentry from her father, and took over his clientele when he retired with complaints of arthritis. Frieda is not married, and has no children.

Frieda's local competitors include *The Thumb Brothers* and *Black and Blue Builders*. Both competitors have websites, but neither of them is built with Flash MX. Her competitors also advertise in the local newspaper. Both businesses have been around as least as long as Frieda has with her business.

Frieda's clients consist of homeowners and construction contractors. Most of the business comes to her through word-of-mouth. Some of her clients are the children of her father's older clients. The contractors are also from word-of-mouth. Frieda has a harder time contacting the latter in time to be included in the building design process.

What

Frieda owns her own carpentry business. She builds cabinets and other storage units for apartment buildings, condominiums, and homes. Individual homeowners, who heard about her by word-of-mouth, hired her in the past. Recently, Frieda has landed a few larger jobs with contractors, who also heard of her by word-of-mouth.

She works with whatever wood product the client wants for their home. Her designs are eclectic, since she designs for a wide variety of clientele. On a personal level, her style is very streamlined, with a modern Scandinavian appearance and appeal.

Frieda has three male employees, and will hire two more next week. She doesn't have a name for her business. She's been using her personal name, just as her father did.

She's done no advertising in the past, but she has a brochure made by a stock brochure company. She wrote the copy for the brochure herself. She also has business cards. Her market consists of personal homeowners who want to spruce up their homes. Her other market are contractors who build larger living spaces. Frieda's desire is to build environmentally sound living spaces, based on the expansion of her carpentry business.

Her current image is one of an ethical, honest, and fair businessperson. She's also known for her quality work. What makes her unique in this field is that she is a female carpenter. She's the only female carpenter in Cabinetville. Frieda seems to be very proud of this fact.

When

Frieda began her business when her father retired about three years ago. The business was, at that time, seasonal. She mainly worked during the winter, and traveled during the summer. Lately, she's been working year-round with the current increase in business. She works approximately ten hours or more per day, six days per week. Her actual office hours are from 9am to 6pm weekdays, 9am to 3pm on Saturdays.

Frieda has no office personnel. She carries a cell phone, and answers calls while on the job. She also maintains her own scheduling and billing. Her attorney brother handles her legal matters. She feels a further increase in her business will allow for more employee supervisors and new office personnel, freeing her to design homes.

Where

Frieda's office is located at 2022 Lumber Lane, Cabinetville, USA. Her phone number is 800-800-8000. Her FAX number is 800-800-8001.

Frieda plans to expand her business within the city of Cabinetville. Her current plans are to expand this business within the next five years.

How

Frieda plans to reach her current market with her Flash site, and with newsletters. Both instruments will communicate new materials available in the construction industry, as well as new ideas for home storage spaces. She plans to reach new markets with her website and with progressive marketing through newspaper advertising and mailings.

The Flash site will be marketed through her other advertising, so it's imperative the site is completed before other means of visual communication to customers. The images created within the site will also be utilized in other materials (especially her new business card).

Frieda is expecting a client brief this time next week. This brief will detail objectives of the website for her business. Based on this client brief, Frieda will sign a contract allowing The Students to design, host, and maintain her site. The Students will also prepare print-ready graphic images for her printer to produce other advertising material.

Why

Frieda Ray chose to use Flash MX for her business site, because she feels a Flash site will help portray her as a person who is concerned about her image, as well as the image of her clients. She also wants to stay ahead of her competitors, who only offer static sites. She wants a site that is interactive and produced professionally. She wants few upgrades, only those that add new designs or future directions for her business.

She chose The Students to produce her work because they're pretty hot!

As Deb finished the last sentence with a flourish, the students laughed. "We *are* hot," Wes said. They all high-fived each other with congratulations on a job well done.

"Not so fast with the champagne, folks," I grinned. "So far, so good. We still have tons of work to do over the next few weeks." I looked at the list, and asked them if they had any questions. All of them felt they had enough information to forge ahead with to the ideation step of the creative problem-solving process.

"I learned a lot," Zed said. "I never knew what modern Scandinavian furniture looked like. "It's awesome."

"I do have one addition to this list, and it's just a clarification for your own education," I said. "When business cards, letterhead, newsletters, or other printed material are developed to enhance the client's image, these printed materials are included in the client's **collateral design** package."

"Collateral design?" Wes asked. "That sounds like an accident waiting to happen."

All the students laughed. "What is collateral design?" he asked.

I smiled, "Collateral design is related material that runs parallel to the design you'll build for Frieda–print design, in particular. Her business cards, stationery, and other print material needs to reflect the design you'll build for Frieda's Flash site.

"We'll learn to create the printed graphic for the printer. Frieda's printer could be the local neighborhood service bureau, or a copier place at the corner. Whoever Frieda's printer is, this person is responsible, for the printed collateral material based on your designs." I looked at the class and stated, "This has been a great day. You all came to class with a willingness to do the job, and that counts toward your success more than you know.

"It's also been a pretty rough day for us creative types," Wes said. "Nothing like a good dose of business to make an artist want to hide in a cave."

Lisa looked at Wes. "I thought what we did today was very creative," she said. "I didn't realize this part of the job even existed, let alone how fun it could be."

"Remember that we were dealing with a make-believe client," Steve nodded at me. "Real clients can be a real pain."

"Oh, I don't know," I said. "Sometimes designers can be real pains, too."
As Wes pretended to pout over that last sentence, I reviewed the information we just covered. "Over the next few weeks," I said, "You'll find how much this research and work will help you in your ideation and selection stages. I hope you learned today that this part of the creative problem-solving process doesn't have to be stale and dry.

"The interview process can be completed quickly when you treat your client as a human being with interests and a life. When you get to know your client, you open doors to new opportunities," I stated, "And, you will complete the design job more quickly and with much more polish that you would have without this information."

I pointed at the client list description. "Now, you've gathered enough material for your client brief. Before we finish this part of the process, we have one more thing to do – we have to cover the material for this week's project," I said. "Let's go back to the table and plan our next steps."

Creating the client's image

After the students clarify their client's description, they need to add some more research to build the client brief. One of the few items missing is more information on the client's competition. As we sat at the table, I outlined the work that needed to be accomplished over the next week. This work would help us step into the ideation phase of the creative problem-solving process.

"Congratulations on gathering so much information today," I said. "Take a look at your list, and tell me what else you might need to know before we begin the brainstorming process next week."

They all sat silent for a moment before Steve spoke up. "I want to know more about our client's competition – *The Thumb Brothers* and *Black and Blue Builders,*" he said.

"And I want to know more about the construction business in general," Bonnie added. "I don't have a clue about how people market this profession."

"Two good points, Steve and Bonnie," I agreed. "Frieda's competition can be a real threat, or just a minor blip on her path to success. We need to learn more about their method of operations.

"Since they don't really exist," I added, "Let's find some real companies in the area, and do a little research on how they present themselves to their potential markets. Find out as much as you can about the *who*, *what*, *when*, *where*, *how*, and *why* of their businesses. We can use this information to help us decide how to present Frieda's business.

"This," I added, "Will also help you learn more about the construction business in general." I looked at Zed, "If there's anything within this list you aren't sure about, look it up. Modern Scandinavian furniture and architecture is a clue to one side of Frieda's personality. This clue might also affect how we present her site.

"You'll know if you're lacking information when you prepare the client brief," I stated. "Each one of you will prepare a brief and bring it with you to class next week. We'll combine the information to present a team client brief to Frieda."

"How do we make a client brief?" Lisa asked. She looked at Wes. "No jokes."

Wes sat back in his chair and grinned. I continued, "The client brief usually contains four sections. Some briefs are shorter than this. Others are much longer. If you align yours like this," I held up a list to show them the categories, "You'll be fine."

I gave the list to Bonnie to read out loud as I wrote the list on the board.

"First," Bonnie began, "We need a **cover page** with the client's *name*, and *date*. We need to add *our name* in smaller type.

Frieda Ray
date

your name
your contact information

"Then we need to outline the **client's history**, or profile."

Client Profile (history)

* Who is the client?
* What do they do?
* Some timeframes . . .
* Where are they located?
* How did they get to this point?
* Why do they do what they do?

I added, "This history can be very brief. You have all the material you need for this already." I wrote a list on the board. "Basically, each section is centered around your essential question categories. In this section, you'll state one or two sentences to fulfill this profile section."

Bonnie continued, "That seems easy. After we do that, then we need to state the client's objectives."

I interrupted her at this point. "The objective needs to be something more than the fact that Frieda thinks Flash MX is *hot*. This is where further research will help you. It will give you more information to flesh this part out."

"You mean we don't just state facts in this brief?" Wes asked.

Steve helped with his explanation, "We can add our opinions, based on our research," Steve stated. "This brief will help convince the client we know what we're doing. If we have viewpoints on what the client needs, we need to add these to the **objectives**."

Client's Objectives

* Who's the competition?
* What's the goal?
* What's the timeframe?
* Where's the geographic goal?
* How are they getting there?
* Why Flash MX will work

"Steve's right," I said. "The client brief tells the client we know and understand their goals. It also tells them we know how to reach those goals. Frieda will be impressed that you checked out her competition. She'll also have an idea of your realistic goals for this project, and why you believe a Flash site will work for her objectives."

Bonnie continued, "After we state the client's objectives, we need to define her **market profile**." Bonnie looked up. "This is where we talk about Frieda's market and her market potential, right?"

Market Profile
* Who's the current market?
* What's the potential market?
* When is the market hot?
* Where are the markets located?
* How do the markets reach the client?
* How does the client reach the markets?
* Why this client?

"Correct, Bonnie." I added, "You'll talk about Frieda's *current market*. This is also a good place to be creative, utilizing your further research. You'll find *new markets* as you look into Frieda's competition. Add these, and any others you might think of.

"You'll also discover *when the market is better* for Frieda's profession. Is it more active in winter or summer? When does she expect to be overloaded, and when can she take those few weeks off to go camping?

"Also, we need to state here *why this market will choose Frieda*. These aren't just stabs in the dark, folks. These are educated estimates based on our research." I looked at Bonnie to tell us the last part of the client brief.

"The next step," Bonnie continued, "Is the **anticipated outcome**." Bonnie looked up and she appeared to be slightly frightened. "How can we state an outcome? We aren't fortune tellers on top of everything else, are we?"

"Ah! I knew my crystal ball would come in handy one day," Wes laughed.

"The anticipated outcome is just a revision of what you already know, in addition to what you'll learn this week," I said. I shook my head at Wes, "Nothing psychic about it.

Anticipated Outcome
* Who will be affected?
* What will be accomplished?
* Anticipated timeframe
* Where impact will be felt
* How this will help client
* Why you can do the job

"This is where you'll state you know about Frieda's goals. You'll tell her this when you list how the Flash MX site will help her stand out above her competition in the local or regional market.

"This is also where you gain Frieda's confidence with your skills in organization. You can do this with a numbered list stating each result of your objectives."

"Oh!" Bonnie seemed relieved. "So we align our objectives with the anticipated outcome?"

"That would be the easiest way to handle this," I smiled. "We don't have to be oblique about our objectives or anticipated outcome. In fact, it helps tremendously to write intelligently, but in layman's terms. Don't dazzle the client with your specialized knowledge. Just keep it simple and to the point."

"How long is this client brief?" Zed asked. "It looks like a book!"

"Outside of the cover page, you shouldn't have more than two to three pages," I said. "This isn't a business plan. It's just a statement of goals and objectives for a particular project.

"This few pages will help you and your client keep an eye on the original goal. Although," I added, "Many a goal changes as you progress with the project. That's why this needs to be simple."

I looked up, "I did forget one thing. You need to sign this, and also have the client sign off on it. Make a copy for the client."

Bonnie stated, "I'm confused. Is this a contract?"

"Not at all," I replied. "This is the open door to a contract, and it confirms that both parties have consented to the information within the brief. When the client feels you know them well enough to tackle this job, they'll feel confident about paying you for your skills."

"So when does the contract come in?" Deb asked.

"It can be right behind the client brief," I stated. "This all depends on your initial relationship with the client, the client's timeframe, and a variety of other factors."

"What about an **NDA**?" Steve asked.

"Good point, Steve," I stated.

Zed looked up, "What's an NDA?"

"An **NDA** is a **Non-Disclosure Agreement**," I explained. "This document varies in content, but the basic gist is that you agree with the client that their work is confidential. You promise the client you won't talk about the details of their work, their objectives or their goals. Sometimes, it's good to promise you won't work with their competitors within a certain geographic area.

"This NDA is usually only one page long, but this one page helps increase client confidence in you, your work, and in your professionalism. After the client brief and an NDA, they can walk away, confident they've chosen the right person for the job."

"Then, we get the money, right?" Wes asked.

"That's everyone's hope, Wes," I smiled. "Contracts are beyond what we'll do in this class. However, if any of you have questions about contracts, we'll discuss them as we go along.

"Mostly," I continued, "Contracts are developed according to a client's budget, your anticipated time and effort, flat fees for certain items, and your geographic location. The variables are too wide to discuss here, but if you do some research, you'll find information on contracts in many places. One of the best sources of information for contracts and graphic designer information like pricing and legal guidelines, is the Graphic Designer's Guild, at www.gag.org."

"I think skill levels demand certain prices, too," Steve added. "Paying dues is one thing, being in the business for twenty years is another thing."

"Steve's right," I said. "Zed won't be able to ask as much as Steve for a while, even though Steve is just learning Flash MX."

"I get that picture," Zed sighed. Then he brightened up, "I'll just work with you, Steve. When you get arthritis, I'll take over your clientele!"

Steve groaned, and the rest of the class laughed. "Let's make sure no one has questions before you leave for the day."

"So you want us to type up a two-page client brief, add a cover sheet, and bring it to class next week, right?" Deb asked. I nodded in agreement. "What will we do next week?"

"We'll pull together a complete team client brief, and we'll begin the third step in the creative problem-solving process," I answered. "Be sure to bring your drawing pads and pencils."

"Can we go back to our usual grunge look?" Wes asked. "I've had fun today, but I'm itching in places I can't talk about."

Lisa laughed, "Wes, you're totally incorrigible. I think you look great today."

Everyone agreed. "And, you seemed to carry yourself with a little more dignity," Deb added. She looked at her watch, and gathered her papers together.

"Do me a favor," Wes responded. "Leave that watch at home next week." He grinned.

Deb laughed. "I promise! I've been going crazy today. I can't decide if I'm creative or a business person."

"I think designers are a little of both, so you're OK," Bonnie said.

After the students said their goodbyes, I sat and daydreamed about a cabin in the woods...

Summary

In this chapter we've gained experience with two client interviews. The first one was impromptu and informal. The second interview was more structured, but still organic in that the interviewer kept the interview on a conversational level.

We reinforced creative problem-solving process to begin with, and then moved on to learn how to structure questions for the client, based on the **who**, **what**, **when**, **where**, **how**, and **why** journalistic format. We talked about various interview possibilities, and it was emphasized that the interviews the students experienced today were just one of many possibilities. Even so, the questions typically remain the same. The designer's responsibility is to discover as much as they can about the client so they can deliver a product that fits the client's needs. This eliminates headaches for the designer, and may help to encourage a long-term designer/client relationship.

The students left with a list of questions to be answered in a client brief. This assignment is due for the beginning of the next class, where we will look in detail at how to write the ideal client brief. We will also look at the brainstorming process at length, and the symbolic graphic language. Along the way, we'll take an in-depth look at the toolbar in Flash MX.

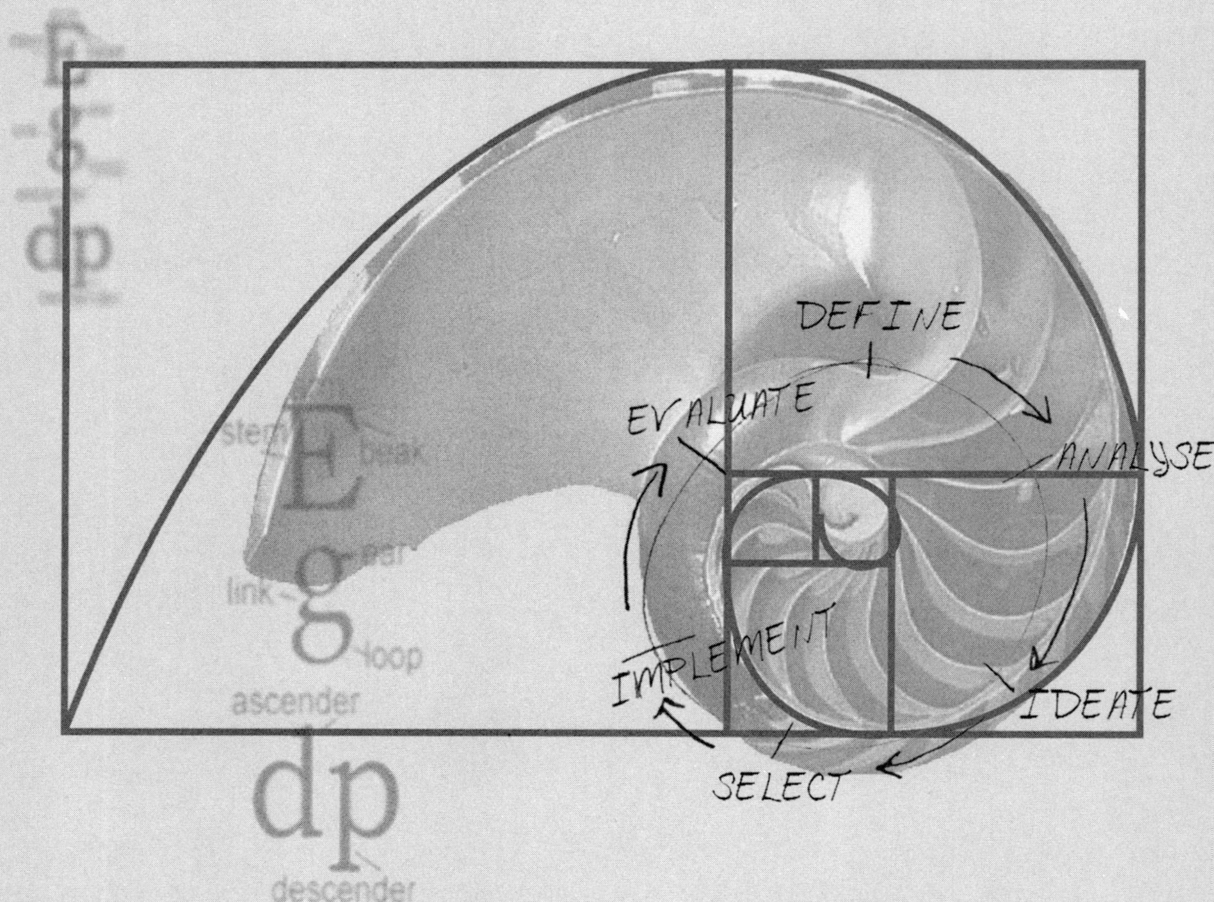

DEFINE
ANALYSE
IDEATE
SELECT
IMPLEMENT
EVALUATE
stem
beak
bar
link
loop
ascender
descender

Chapter 5

Learning Visual Languages

Objectives

In this class, you will learn:

- How to prepare a client brief and various other client deliverables
- The difference between identity and image
- Free association and other brainstorming techniques
- Utilizing the tools in Flash MX to create and manipulate your designs
- Symbolic graphic language and the power of object and abstract representation

Introduction

This week's session began on a casual note – as the students arrived and sat down at the table, everyone began to compare their client briefs with each other. These briefs were developed as a project between classes, so we could compile the information at the beginning of this session. After gathering all the information, the finalized client brief would open the door to the third step in the creative problem-solving process. As we learned in our very first class, this step is *ideation*, or more commonly, *brainstorming*.

Last week's lesson on defining and analyzing the client's problem or design requirements left more than just memories with the students. "I still have blisters on my feet from wearing those high heels," Lisa moaned as she rubbed her heels. "It's good to be casual again."

I looked around at the class. "It's strange to see you all back in your normal, casual clothes," I admitted. "You all looked fantastic last week, so thanks for getting into the spirit of the role playing."

I looked at Zed, who still had a white silk scarf around his neck. "When we give ourselves permission to try new things, sometimes we find that something works for us. Without this experimentation, we'd be stuck in a rut."

Zed grinned and fingered the scarf. "I couldn't keep the scarf that we borrowed from the theater," he said, "So I went out and found one just like it. It's part of my new image."

"And a dashing image that is, my good man," Wes stated. "Just don't get that scarf caught in a revolving door!"

"Outside of Zed's dangerous new image and Lisa's blisters, did anyone else gain anything in particular from last week's session?" I asked.

Bonnie nodded, "I've had clients ask me to sign an NDA, but I never thought to reverse that process. That's a very great tool to take charge of the designer/client relationship." She nodded at Steve. "Thanks for the idea!"

Deb agreed, "That was a good idea. I also thought the use of *who*, *what*, *when*, *where*, *how*, and *why* tools throughout the whole defining and analyzing phases was very smart. When I used these categories, it helped me stay focused with my client brief this past week."

"Speaking of focus," I said, "Let's pull these client briefs together into one final brief now. We'll assume the client approves of the final rendition, because I want to maximize our time with the brainstorming sessions today."

Zed seemed ready to jump onto the table, "Now we're going to have fun!"

Everyone looked at me, expecting me to deny the fun they would have today, but I surprised them, "I'll admit it, brainstorming can be fun!" I looked at Lisa. "But, in keeping with my image as dungeon master, I'll also add that this phase can be simultaneously frustrating and nerve-wracking.

"Brainstorming alone can be like working in a vacuum. It's often difficult to validate our choices when we don't have someone to listen to us and give us their own perspectives. However," I added, "Working as a team is tough, too. You might find conflict, jealousy, rivalry, and other factors come into play when a group of creative people work together."

Wes grinned, "Really? I would have never guessed a bunch of creative individuals could generate their own problems."

I grimaced at Wes, "Sarcasm aside, I think you'll find there's more bumps and twists in this phase than in any other stage of the problem-solving process. After we come up with some ideas, we'll learn to apply these thoughts to graphic forms."

Wes leaned forward and looked around at the class. "I promise to be good today." He noticed the looks of disbelief on all our faces, "No, really!"

Who is the client?

I asked the class to pass their client briefs to another student. As they looked at different ideas, the students circled what they thought were the best phrases and thoughts, and crossed out what they felt was irrelevant. We then spent another half hour pulling the best ideas together for the final brief.

Steve typed up the information with help from the rest of the class, and copies were made for each student. Before we began the ideation phase of the project, we looked the information over and discussed various terms used within the brief (the cover sheet was omitted from this final client brief).

The client brief

CLIENT PROFILE

Frieda Ray is a well-traveled entrepreneur, carpenter, designer, and businessperson based in Cabinetville, USA. She's incorporated a lifetime's experience working with wood products into her own carpentry business. This business and her skills were developed under her father's tutelage and from his previous clientele. She's operated this business on her own with the support of a limited staff for the past three years. She's the only female operating a carpentry business in this area.

Her specialties at this time are represented by a wide variety of styles incorporated in cabinets and storage spaces for existing homes and for apartment and condominium construction projects. Frieda's concern for the environment shows in her love of the outdoors. Her interest in the slim, organic, no-nonsense lines of modern Scandinavian design emphasizes this concern.

CLIENT'S OBJECTIVES

The current objective for Frieda Ray's business is to create an identity for her business, and a medium to communicate this image to current and future markets. The format is Flash MX and the medium is the Web. This goal will span over the next five years as Frieda expands her business in this area, based on fresh and consistent marketing with brochures, newspaper advertising, and other printed collateral material.

Her competition in this area consists of two other carpentry firms: *The Thumb Brothers* and *Black and Blue Builders*. Both these firms market their services and products through newspapers, letterheads, business cards, signage, and websites, although their sites do not utilize Macromedia Flash MX.

The final objective, which can be emphasized through implementation of a Flash MX site, is the creation of a design firm for environmentally sound living spaces based on the merits of the expanded carpentry business. Frieda's Flash presence will appeal to a high-end market interested in home improvements.

MARKET PROFILE

The current market for Frieda Ray's construction business consists of homeowners who desire upgrades to their homes. These modifications are used to increase the market value and appeal of their homes. The other current market is business-to-business, based on orders from contractors in construction of apartment homes and condominiums. Both markets are concerned with low cost, high levels of expertise, and aesthetics of the final product.

Future markets center on the expansion of current markets, and a new focus on storage spaces for businesses, including offices, schools, and other structures designed for public use.

Both current and future markets combined can increase the potential of a year-round carpentry business. Although construction can tend to be seasonal, based on weather conditions, Frieda Ray's work is concerned with indoor spaces. The work can be done on location, or in the current workshop at 2022 Lumber Lane, increasing the potential to expand this business year-round.

Both current and future markets can be tapped with the potential of a Flash site, and a marketing push that advertises the advantage of client access to the site.

ANTICIPATED OUTCOME

The Flash site will enhance and expand Frieda Ray's carpentry business to current and future markets. This site will accomplish this from a number of aspects:

1. The use of this form of visual interactive communication will appeal to the high-end homeowner and to business owners who want to increase the value and visual appeal of their commercial structures.
2. The focus on high-end markets will help expand business, and allow the use of high-quality products. This will appeal to customers wanting to increase the value of their properties.
3. The focus of immediate targeted market expansion will add value to Frieda Ray's business. This expansion will eventually create an outlet for anticipated design goals with the focus of a five-year plan.
4. The impact of a Flash site will be felt within the current market area. Frieda Ray's competitor sites will appear to be outdated and stagnant compared to her interactive, accessible, and highly usable site.
5. Although the current focus is local and regional markets, it's possible that Frieda Ray's business could garner attention from a larger geographic market due to the global format. This format lends itself to more possibilities as Frieda Ray's business expands.

The site design will be approved and constructed before other advertising venues are utilized, as the images and structure of the site will be the source of focus for targeting Frieda Ray's markets in other media. The anticipated timeframe for construction and activation of the Flash site is within two months, based on the completion of a contract and timeline and client approvals of the site's progress.

Thank you for choosing The Students as a potential design firm for your Flash site.

This client brief was finished, and I signed off as Frieda Ray. Deb was chosen to sign off on behalf of *The Students*. We sat at the table and began to review the final product.

"I want you all to hang onto your original client briefs, and the information we developed last week," I said. "You can use all the information for your client file. That way," I added, "You won't be scratching your head, trying to remember small details."

"I noticed we didn't add any of Frieda's family to the final client brief," Steve said. "I guess that isn't important in the long run."

Deb replied, "I don't know, it may be important. We won't know until we begin the graphic side of the problem, I guess."

"Deb's right," I said. "Although we didn't include it in this information to the client, let's keep it close in case it helps us decide on some small detail to the project."

Zed changed the topic of conversation by asking about a particular term we used in the objectives section of our finished client brief, "What do we mean by *signage* here?"

"**Signage** is just a general term for all sorts of signs," Steve explained. "Pretty simple, I guess. If these signs are for a business, they always contain the business name, and sometimes the hours of business and location, if it's a billboard or something like that. I guess Frieda will develop signage as we begin to develop images for her, right?"

"It's a safe guess that Frieda doesn't have significant signage," I agreed. "She certainly hasn't had the time to spend on her identity or her images. With a client like Frieda, it helps to think of what else she may need to promote her business. Whatever you design for her site should be carried out through all her other advertising design and promotion for a consistent image.

"On the other hand," I added, "If the client already has an identity and wants a site to enhance their business image, then you need to take the materials the client has on hand, and design the site to fit the look the client already has developed.

"Now that we have a client brief on hand," I stated, "Let's talk about other paperwork you may need for the client."

Other client deliverables

Between the client brief and the jump to the ideation phase of the creative problem-solving process, the designer often needs to deliver several other documents to the client. Even if the designer may not be the individual to generate these documents, the knowledge of their existence can help the designer and the client solidify their relationship.

"I'd now like to address some documents, or deliverables, to the client that you may or may not generate during your careers as designers," I said. "If you work within the environment of a design studio, an agency, or as a small cog in the large wheel of a corporation, you may never even touch these items," I stated. "But, if you work alone, you're typically taking on more than one role," I said as I smiled at Bonnie. "You are the creative design person, the identity strategy team, the technician, the project manager, the researcher, and the writer.

"Make a note of the following documents, since you'll never know when you may have to generate one or all of them during the span of a project. The first item would be the client brief, where you would sit down with the client and let them know you understand their goals. Even if you don't present the client brief to the client in person, you've developed a solid working document that will keep you focused on your own goals as you develop the look and usability of the site.

"Other such client deliverables can include a contract, a detailed timeline for the project, various progress reports, and knowledge of the client's own computer system and possible systems within the client's market. Let's talk about each one of these items briefly."

Contract

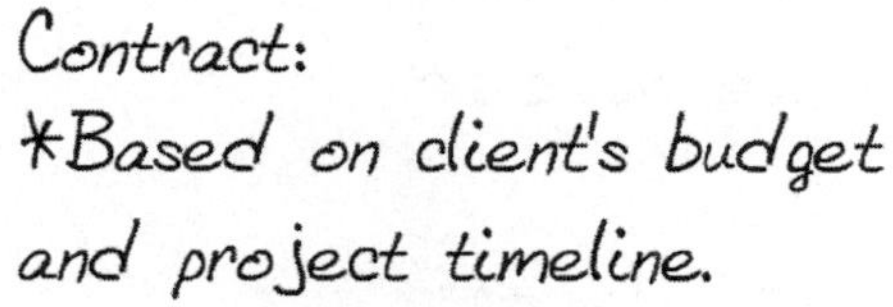

Turning to the whiteboard, ready to write about the contract, I continued, "At some point in the beginning of your work, you will present a contract to the client based on conversations between you and your client about the project's budget. The contract should include information about the timeline and required technology for the site to work."

Timeline

Next up, I wrote *Timeline* on the board, "The timeline defines when you'll deliver finished phases of the client's project. After presentation of each phase, you and the client will sign off on the timeline, indicating approval from the client as you progress through each stage to the final goal. This timeline also gives your client structure, so they don't waver and procrastinate with your own time.

Timeline:
*List all items due to client, and the date they're due.
*Designer and client signs off when each item is delivered and approved.

"However, don't make the timeline any more complicated that it needs to be," I warned. "You've been operating on a timeline with this course. Each week, you complete a project for the following week. You present your projects, and I approve or comment. The timeline for Frieda Ray or any other client would work in a similar way."

Progress reports

Progress reports:
*Due with each item delivered to client.
** Also due when there are problems with client's project timeline.

"With each phase of the timeline, you will also present a short report," I added. "This report is similar to the client brief, because you'll state why you executed that stage in that manner. You will justify your work, so the client understands why you chose each course along the way, including any problems that you come across, and how you expect to resolve them. This report is usually less than a page long, unless you have severe problems. In this case, you'll probably need to sit with the client to resolve any outstanding issues."

Platform or implementation technology

"You would also add an agreement between yourself and the client indicating the technology platform you intend to use for the client's project. In this case the technology required is the Flash Player 6 and any browser capable of running it.

Platform Use:
*Note any operating system the client owns.
*Note plug-ins or any other device needed to view site.
*Access current and future market platform use.

"In many web design scenarios it is essential to assess the client and their customers' browsing abilities and technology level, otherwise you risk alienating them from viewing the website.

"For this reason, Flash includes the functionality to detect the user's browsing capabilities, and can serve up a Flash or HTML site dependant on the results.

"For Frieda's site we will be assuming that the audience has the Flash Player 6 plug-in. If they haven't got it we can recommend that they download the very small plug-in, or can show them a plain *vanilla-flavor* HTML version of the site.

"The other deliverables to the client will be developed over the next few weeks," I added. "These include the identity project and images, navigation for the site, and storyboards for Frieda's approval. These items are included in your weekly projects, so you'll be working your timeline as we progress through this course."

"Is everyone comfortable with this situation?" I asked. They all nodded. "Are there any other questions or issues before we begin the next step?"

Everyone signaled they were ready to begin. Before we started the process, I thanked Zed for his research into modern Scandinavian design, and also thanked the students for researching local carpentry businesses. "This research will help us during the ideation process," I stated. "We'll rely on each other for our new expertise."

"Wow, expertise!" Zed appeared awed by his elevated status. "Now I can tell my parents I'm not too young to be an expert." He flipped his scarf over his shoulder and rubbed his hands together. "Let's start the show!"

What's the difference between identity and image?

The Frieda Ray case was developed to implement the process of identity design for the client. Although this wasn't expressed to the students in so many words, they were about to discover how the client's lifestyle, manner of business, and even the client's name lend credence to the formation of their identity and image.

The willingness of the client to change her business name left some students feeling unable or unwilling to begin the ideation process without resolution to this issue.

Steve began the discussion with a question regarding this problem. "I don't know about the rest of you," he looked around. "But I'm going to have a tough time moving forward unless I know if Frieda's going to stay with her name or if she's going to develop a new name for her business. Can we talk about this first?"

"I'm feeling awkward about this problem, too," Deb stated. "How can we focus on designing an image, when we don't have a name to put to that image?" Bonnie and Lisa nodded agreement.

I looked around at the class. "Identity design is actually a little different to the company image. A company's identity communicates a company's vision. This includes the company's message, products and services, and the way they do business. You're about to place Frieda's life into visual focus.

"We're going to use traditional elements and principles of design within the Flash format. This format is flexible and subject to constant change. Somehow," I continued, "You need to make Frieda's identity so solid that you can take it from this medium to other, more traditional media."

Bonnie seemed confused. "Do you mean we need to design Frieda's logo or mark first?"

Defining the logo and brand

Zed quickly looked in my direction. "I know what a logo is," he assured me. "A **logo** is short for logotype or logogram, and it usually consists of symbols that represent a name or phrase. A **brand**," he continued, "Actually represents the products or services that belong to a company, including each department of a company and how they handle these products or services."

"Whoa, gunslinger!" Wes held up his hands, "What have you been doing lately?"

Zed grinned, "I wanted to know the next step to this process, so I did a little research."

"Good for you, Zed," I commended him. I turned back to Bonnie to answer her question. "Bonnie, the logo and the brand are just small parts of a company's identity. When an identity is developed, everything from the typeface to the color of a background is decided. It's the feel of the company, portrayed through its individual parts. The company's identity is the company's *gestalt*."

I tried to put the definition of a company identity into focus...

> *"We can say that the company's identity is its foundation, while the elements and principles of design used to portray this identity form the structure. The way the identity and its elements are used will build the actual 'home'."*

"Oh," Bonnie said, "So the identity isn't just the mark of the individual or company. It's the *total vision*."

"Yeah," Zed emphasized. "It's like when the architect stands on the hill and waves that psychic line around to show his vision of a house."

I laughed. "Zed, I hope we do more than wave psychic lines around the room. I just want you all to understand your responsibility as designers in this process. We need to remember that the images we use for Frieda Ray's company identity aren't the vision. These graphic images only *represent* the vision for herself and her company.

"These images, hopefully, will change over time to keep up with her company's focus and with the times and lives of her market. Let's keep this in mind when we begin to alter Frieda's current images," I said. "You're about to make the invisible visible to a great many people, even though our current focus is on local markets."

I added, "You'll probably display Frieda's work on the site. When you do, you'll realize that Frieda has several lines of cabinet designs. These lines will be defined with product identity."

"**Product identity**," I continued, "Is any graphic representing an individual product within a family of products. For instance," I explained, "If Frieda has a line of cabinets that reflect traditional Victorian tastes – this is a **line** of cabinets. The individual designs within that family of Victorian designs are themselves products with their own identity."

Bonnie asked, "By *graphic* do you mean type or a picture?"

"A **graphic** implies any mark you make to identify a company, a family line, or a product in that line," I answered. "It can be type, art, photography, shapes, or lines. Each mark we make will be shaped by Frieda's vision, and how we portray that vision through the elements and principles of design.

"Frieda's identity will house her brand and product identities, which are all portrayed by their own individual marks. Once you make decisions on the feel of Frieda's vision, that feel needs to remain consistent so the images will be safe and free to do their jobs within that house.

"When we finish making Frieda's vision visible through graphic images, we'll also produce an image that will be used in the print process. This image will be used for Frieda's print collateral material, matching the site you design.

"I get it," Lisa said slowly. "That's a great metaphor. All her images are like live entities that reside in a house called *Frieda's Vision*. They may change, just like we do as we evolve over time," she said. "But, the vision doesn't change."

"It might need a new roof every few years," Steve joked. "I never thought of company identity that way before. I always thought it was a mark or a logo, just like Bonnie." He added, "I was feeling at loose ends about the lack of decision on Frieda's company name. I don't feel so awkward about that now. I think we need to find Frieda's vision and identity first."

"I agree," Bonnie and Deb stated in unison.

"I'm OK with this, too," Zed said. "I just have one question." Everyone looked at Zed. "What's a metaphor?"

Deb laughed. "I'll give you an example of a metaphor, Zed," she said. "I still think this creative process is mysterious. But I believe the heavens will open and angels will attend our brainstorms with roaring thunder and blinding bolts of lightning."

Wes stared at Deb. "I think Miss Business Lady has a poet hidden beneath her high-heeled façade."

"I thought you were going to be good, Wes," Deb blushed. "I can't help it if I think metaphorically."

Zed demanded. "What's it mean?"

I was thrilled to have an opening for the verbal process of ideation. "A metaphor, Zed, is a descriptive figure of speech where one thing is compared to another to give us a fresh look at the original idea. We use metaphors to suggest common qualities shared by both the original thought and the comparison. Metaphor also relies heavily on imaginary relations, rather than a direct comparison. This provides scope for original design ideas. Another example that some of you might recognize is the saying, *All the world's a stage*."

Lisa smiled and finished off the quote, "*And all the men and women merely players!* That's Shakespeare!"

"Well spotted Lisa!" I said, encouragingly.

Steve joined in the metaphor game with another, "Let's put the pedal to the metal and drive this baby home to look at ideation."

"Hey, I think we've opened a Pandora's Box of worms here!" Wes laughed.

Zed looked confused. "Wait a minute. There are cars, stages, babies, and worms all over the place," he said. "What are you all talking about?"

"You've just experienced **mixed metaphors**, Zed," I explained. "This is something you don't want to do in real life when you present visual ideas or write content for your client. When you pick one metaphor, it's good to stick with that image. But," I added, "It's a perfect way to wrap up this explanation of company identity and move into the ideation process."

I looked at Deb, "Didn't you say your mother is a professional writer?" Deb nodded. "Are you familiar with rhetorical figures for prose and poetry?"

"I guess so," Deb stated. "I float in a sea of writing when I visit my mother."

Zed announced, "That's a metaphor!"

"You're catching on now, Zed," I smiled. "Before we talk in any more riddles, let's take a break. When you return, we'll begin to lay the foundation for Frieda's vision."

Brainstorming begins

When the students returned from their break, I asked them to get comfortable, but to remain at the table. This way, they could face each other to ensure efficient communication of their ideas. They were also asked to bring their drawing pads and pencils to the table. They would use these tools to help formulate graphic images through written type and drawn sketches. We were ready to start the ideation and brainstorming process.

The verbal flow

Wes sat surrounded by pencils. He picked one up, pointed it at his drawing pad, and asked, "Where do we begin?"

"Let's put Frieda's vision into words," I answered. I asked them to use words to define Frieda's identity. As they said the words, they would write them in their drawing pads.

"Why can't we type the words in?" Bonnie asked. "It would be a lot faster."

"I want you to feel the pencil on the paper as you write," I answered. "Each letter is formed by a line, and those lines will begin to help you shape Frieda's identity. The words you type don't have the same feeling or fluctuation of flow as the written word. The tactile experience is important in the beginning."

I joined them as they began with one-word definitions. They began slowly, but the pace picked up rapidly. "*Wood, curves, lines, organic*," Lisa said.

"*Honest, hardworking, ethical*," Bonnie added her words to the growing list.

"*Artistic, brave, creative*," Wes stated.

"Can we use words that are actual places and things?" Zed asked.

Steve answered, "*Cabinetville, Frieda, Ray, storage*."

Zed grinned and added, "*Cabinets, homeowner, fragile*."

"Fragile?" Deb asked. "Where did that come from?" She turned to Steve and asked, "And why did you say Frieda's name as two different words?"

"I'll go first," Zed leaned over to look at Deb. "My dad had a friend who was a drummer, and he was the best drummer around," he said. "One day, he told my dad he had to quit drumming, because he had a form of arthritis. The constant pounding and vibration only hurt his hands more, so he had to quit.

"Frieda's dad reminded me of my dad's friend. They're both artists, and they both had to give up what they loved because of physical problems. It just reminded me how fragile our dreams can be."

"Wow!" Wes began writing again. "*Homes, dreams, clouds*."

The rest of the students wrote those words, and Steve looked at Wes. "I'll explain the thing with Frieda's name, and then I want to know about the clouds." Wes nodded.

"Frieda's name is interesting," he said. "If we go with her name as a graphic symbol for her identity, we could use the full name, her first name, or even just her surname." He looked at me and added, "I know her name is another problem past the scope of this process, but I wanted to explain why I suggested her name as two words."

** Frieda Ray's vision **

wood	homeowner	pound
curves	fragile	thumb
lines	homes	blue
organic	dreams	black
honest	clouds	night
hardworking	angels	stars
ethical	wings	production
artistic	fleeting	stage
brave	speed	curtain
creative	force	interior
cabinetville	fingers	window
Frieda	hands	frame
Ray	nails	picture
storage	hammer	elements
cabinets	steel	principles

Flash MX?

"That's alright, Steve," I assured him. "We'll get to her name by the end of next week, so any thoughts on this subject aren't premature."

Wes interrupted with another burst of words, "*Angels, wings, fleeting, speed, force, fingers, hands...*"

"Whoa, Wes!" Bonnie laughed. Deb quietly shushed Bonnie and kept writing. Wes continued to spout words, "*Nails, hammer, steel, pound, thumb, blue, black, night, stars, production, stage, curtain, interior, window, frame, picture, elements, principles, Flash MX...*" Wes looked up. "That's it on my run," he admitted. "I can't think of anything to go with that last word right now."

Deb applauded, "Wes, that was some excellent free association."

Wes grinned, and Zed looked at Deb, "What's that?" he asked. "What just happened?"

Deb looked at me, "Should I explain some of the tools writers use to overcome *writer's block*?"

I nodded, "We've got plenty of words associated with Frieda now. Deb can explain some writer's tools that can be used by designers, too."

Creative design borrowed from writers

Deb knew some literary tools used by writers to help overcome writer's block. Writer's block is a term used to describe a situation where a writer feels blocked from any creativity. Designers often have *designer's block*, where they feel they can't come up with ideas. Using the writer's methods of unblocking that creativity is one way a designer can also begin to break through to new ideas. Wes had just used one of these tools, which is known as **free association**.

"The tools that writers use to develop their work and to brainstorm new ideas are called **rhetorical figures**," I said. "These figures will help us develop ideas for Frieda's site. I'll let Deb explain the terms, and then we'll talk about how we can use these in our work."

Deb began, "Wes used free association to come up with his flood of words. Free association is a tool used to go past normal word associations in a given subject. Aristotle made the discovery that certain words sometimes trigger responses in people, like the word *fragile* did with Wes. This notion wasn't really pursued until Carl Jung explored the possibilities at the beginning of the twentieth century. Now psychologists and psychiatrists sometime use free association with their clients and patients, and professional writers use it on themselves to help loosen up the creative process.

"Usually," she continued, "You begin with a keyword, or a trigger word, and then you add a word that reminds you of the first word. You just keep going until you run out of words. Then," she concluded, "You take a look at the list of words, and pick the ones that stand out, or that make sense. These words, hopefully, will be more creative than the words you would have used if you didn't go through this exercise."

Bonnie looked at her latest editions to the list. "Oh, I can see that now. *Angel* made Wes think of *wings*, which then reminded him of *fleeting*."

"Why do we need to know these things?" Zed asked. "Why does a designer need to know about rhetorical figures?"

Wes answered, "For the same reason an artist needs to know rhetorical figures, Zed. I work in simile, metaphor, and personification all the time."

Zed looked at Deb. "You sound safer than Wes, Deb. Go ahead."

Deb laughed, and continued her explanations. "We already talked about metaphor. That's when we identify one thing with another, even though they may not be related. Another figure is called **personification**. This is a metaphorical figure where we give an animal or an inanimate object a human characteristic."

Lisa looked up from her drawing pad. "Oh! So Frieda's *vision house* is a metaphor, but the graphics became personified when I equated them with living beings, right?"

Deb continued, "Another rhetorical figure is the **simile**. This is when something is compared to something else, using the words *like* or *as*. For example, we can say that Frieda's an artist, because she approaches her work like a sculptor."

"So, if we approached Frieda's identity as a simile, then we would carry the idea throughout her graphics, right?" Bonnie asked.

"That's right, Bonnie. Consistency of rhetorical figures in design is a must. Otherwise," I added, "Our communications could appear confusing to the viewer."

"I have some other terms, but I'm not sure they apply to Frieda's situation. Do you want to hear them anyway?" Deb asked.

"Sure," Steve answered for me. He shrugged, "I'm sorry, but I'm fascinated with the application of writing skills to design processes."

"No problem, Steve," I responded. "Deb, what are the other terms?"

"One is the simple **pun**," Deb continued. "I think we all know this one as a play on words, where one word is understood in two different ways. This would include homonymic words like *see* and *sea*. Another way to use a pun is in a play on the concept of the use of words. One example is: *When the boy became a farm hand, he grew another foot.*"

Wes burst into laughter. "That's an old pun, but it always cracks me up. How about this one: A three-legged dog walks into a saloon in the old West – he sidles up to the bar and announces: "*I'm looking for the man who shot my paw!*"

Deb rolled her eyes and, after the rest of the group had stopped laughing, or groaning, she continued, "The rest of these terms are used to describe levels of meaning within rhetorical figures. An **analogy** is a structure that uses simile or metaphor throughout a work.

She looked up and stated, "Linda's been using similes and metaphors throughout this course with the comparison of building a house to the design process. The analogy would be that the designer is the architect, and the elements and principles of design are the architect's tools."

"Oh! You've caught me out there!" I laughed.

Wes grinned and leaned forward to ask, "What about irony and symbolism?"

Deb blinked, and said, "Well, irony is another tool, but I don't think it fits Frieda. **Irony** is used as an element of surprise. It's a bit complex, since various forms of irony are used for different situations. There's verbal, dramatic, and situational irony. Each one uses what we know as sarcasm, facetiousness, or double meanings. They can be tricky, and I doubt it would be a good tool to use for a client, unless they're in the business of irony."

"That's a good call, Deb," I replied. "Irony is very complicated. The global reach of the Internet makes it tough to use this form of communication and still be understood by the majority of people.

"Symbolism, on the other hand, is quite appropriate," I said. I asked Deb to describe this tool.

"**Symbolism** is a technique where one item is used to represent another idea or item. We've been alluding to Frieda with the symbols of words," Deb said as she pointed at her drawing pad. "In design, I'm sure symbols can be more than words."

Before I could respond, Deb added, "Oh! I forgot about paradox! A **paradox** is a statement contrary to perceived opinion. Frieda is sort of a paradox herself, because she's a female in a predominantly male occupation. This fact seems almost contradictory, but it's true."

"And all along, I thought Frieda's occupation was ironic," Wes grinned. "Oh, well," he shrugged, "So much for my hopes of surprising the public with my sarcastic wit."

"And charm, I might add," Steve laughed. He thanked Deb for the rhetorical figure definitions. "This has been a real education for me," he said. "Now all these words make sense. I can see where using the words *cabinet* and *angel* might form an evocative simile of '*her designs are like visions from heaven*'." He quickly added, "Yes, that's corny, but I just wanted to make my point."

"It's not that corny if you add wings to cabinets," Zed assured Steve. "That would be cool! They could fly into the sky when the customer clicks on the cabinet."

Everyone looked at Zed. He was scribbling away in his drawing pad. "Let's see what you've got there, Zed," Steve pulled Zed's pad out from under his pencil. "Is this wild or what?" Steve showed Zed's work to everyone. "I think we're a little too formal compared to this guy."

Bonnie looked at Zed's drawing pad and then down at her own. "I see what you're saying, Steve. My work looks so stilted compared to Zed's."

I looked at the difference between the two drawing pads. "Bonnie, we're not really into shapes just yet. Zed just seems to think in shapes more than words. But," I looked around, "Anytime you feel like creating images as well as words to mark your ideas, don't stop yourselves." I tapped Zed's drawing pad. "These pads are your resources into Frieda Ray's problem. She has little or no identity, but you're about to create one for her, based on the pages you develop in this book."

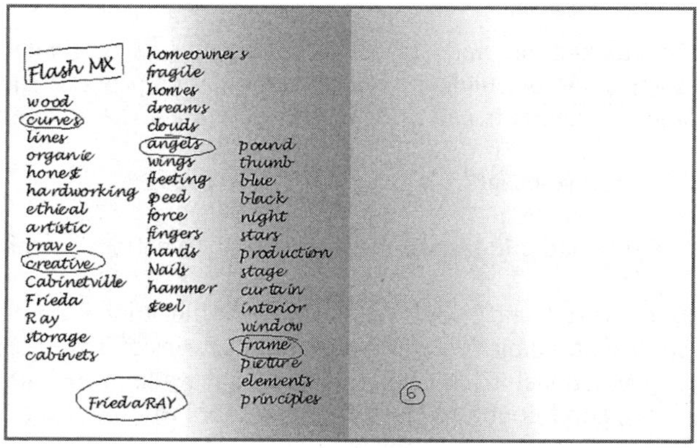

Bonnie leaned on the table and put her head in her hands. "I don't know if I can do this," she said. She looked up, "Everyone here has some specialty. Steve knows about science, Wes knows about art. Deb has a handle on technology, math, writing, and high heels. Lisa is an expert in additive lighting, and Zed's specialty is youth."

She looked at Zed, "You have the fortunate advantage of being young enough not to be worried what others think of your suggestions. Plus, you have this amazing skill to pick up new information like a sponge."

Zed grinned, "That's a simile."

"Oh, stop it!" Bonnie muttered. "I don't think I can do this. I feel so block-headed and dense. With every new term, I feel like I have to wade through mud to understand how it applies to design."

Steve jumped to Bonnie's rescue. "Bonnie, you have the skills that will help us with accessibility and validation. Your attention to these details will help us with color selection and legibility, too."

"I agree with Steve," I added. "You have a lot to offer the class with accessibility issues and validation. But I really can't help with your feelings – all I can do is offer to help you get through your confusion."

Zed had drawn a picture in his drawing pad. He showed it to Bonnie. "You're not a blockhead, Bonnie – you look nothing like this..."

Bonnie laughed, and stated, "At least I read you correctly. You have absolutely no fear."

"Why don't we talk about this," I said. "Bonnie's opened the door on a good topic. We often bring ourselves into the process of design development. The way we draw, or the way we develop ideas eventually becomes what is known as our *style*. This style will change over time as we learn new skills and techniques," I said "Sometimes, designers can come up with great ideas by looking at another designer's style or technique. Artist and designer sketchpads often carry notes as well as drawings. These are good tools for brainstorming."

I looked around, "How many of you know that you've incorporated your experiences and your knowledge into Frieda's identity so far?"

Everyone looked at their drawing pads. I continued, "It's not a bad thing to incorporate your personality and experiences with the client's identity. Let's talk about how we can differentiate between the two, and whether it matters if you bring your experiences to the table."

Bringing your experience to the ideation process

Often, a student will display frustration with the development of visual processes in design. This seems to happen most often in this phase of the design process, where individuals find their perceptions disturbing, or less important than the ideas of those around them.

"Let's put down our pencils for a moment, and take a look at each other's drawing pads." Each student passed their pads across the table to another student. "Go back to the beginning, and look at how the other student saw each element of design."

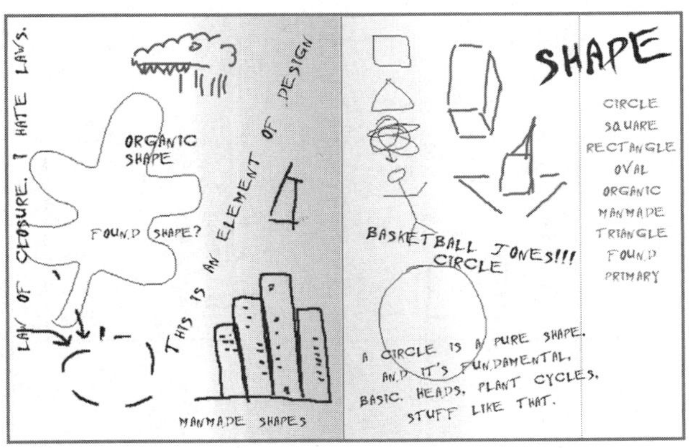

As they leafed through the drawing pads, I saw some smiles and some frowns cross the student's faces. "If you have thoughts about what you see, feel free to talk about them," I said. "If you become aware of something through another person's work, let us know what just happened."

Steve was the first to speak up, "Zed did something I didn't think about doing," he admitted. "He went back into his former assignments and added more images and notes when he learned new things." Everyone looked over at Zed's drawings and pasted down images. "This shows me that Zed isn't afraid to go back and change what he previously thought about some elements of design."

"Lisa did the same thing," Bonnie stated. She held up Lisa's line page, showing us how Lisa had modified her images and added notes. "I didn't know we were allowed to do that," Bonnie added.

"Wes didn't add to his pages," Deb stated. "He just added pages, period! There's very little room left in this drawing pad," She looked up at Wes. "It's about time to buy a new one, eh? I'm afraid to open it!" She held up Wes's pad, which looked like it was just about to burst.

Steve laughed. "I think we already know Wes and his propensity for images. I wouldn't open it either. It's a work of art as is."

Zed had Steve's drawing pad. He spoke up, "Steve's pages look like a magazine. He's got everything lined up just right." He pulled his hand down the page. "Did you use a ruler?" he asked.

Steve laughed. "No, I just eyeball the margin and lay things out along invisible grids."

"That's cool!" Zed stared at Steve's pages. "I guess you really know your grids, after spending so many years with them."

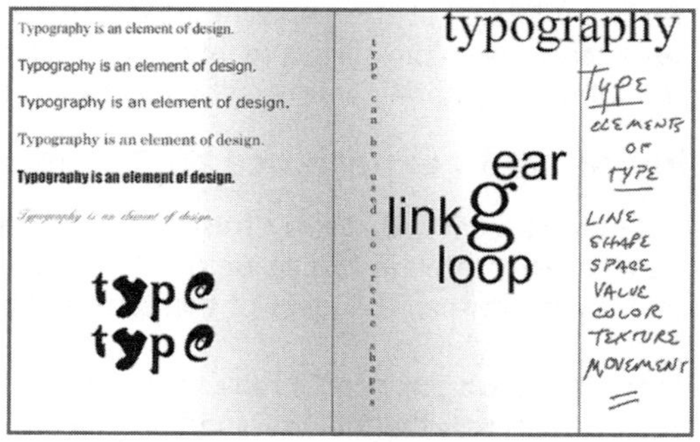

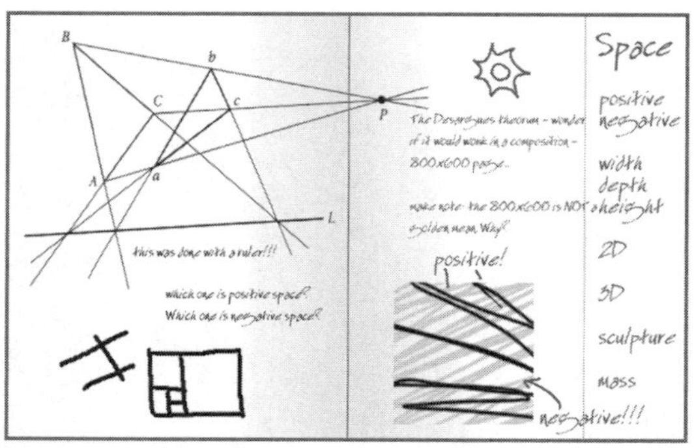

Wes looked at Deb and shook his head. "I didn't realize how analytical you were," he said. He held one of Deb's pages for everyone to see. "Look at this!" Deb blushed as everyone passed her drawing pad around.

I took Deb's pad and leafed through the pages. She had added mathematical formulas, line drawings of math theories for composition, and historical names with notes for additional research.

"I just wanted to fit this experience to my life," she said. "I didn't want to come to this class in the first place. Now, I see how it's expanded my own experience. Everything I've learned comes to play in design – I never realized the full complexity of this skill.

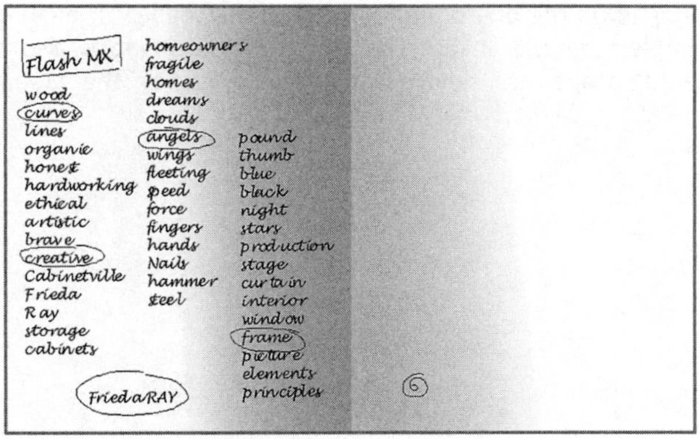

"I think that's why you're having trouble right now," Deb turned to Bonnie. "I've spent most of my life analyzing situations along the structures of mathematics and writing in the format of technology. I don't know much about your life, but I can guess you spent your time on other things."

"I certainly haven't spent it with complex formulas, unless you consider a couple of deadbeat marriages and two children to fit that equation," Bonnie stated. "I've spent most of my life scraping to pay bills. I love creating, and I really like dealing with clients," she added, "But I haven't had time to spend learning about things that are outside the *need-to-know* realm."

"Lisa, can you tell us what you get from Bonnie's pages?" I asked.

Lisa looked up at Bonnie. "Your images and the way you write are interesting. You use a lot of basic shapes, like circles, squares, and triangles. You even write in square blocks, and you use circles to emphasize things you want to remember."

Bonnie leaned over to look at her work. "I never realized that before," she admitted. "But you're right." She looked at me, "Is that wrong? Maybe my way of thinking is a little too straightforward?"

"Actually," I answered, "You've probably brought some much-needed simplicity to a rather complex team." I asked them to hand back the drawing pads to the original owners. "Visual thinking is a complex issue. When we work alone, we often find ourselves limited to what we know, and we have to trust our own judgment on what we learn."

I looked at Bonnie. "You just told us a limited version of your past experiences. This could be used to rationalize why you are drawn to simple shapes. You also use these shapes in your web design," I added. "Tables are a very structured, convenient, and widely accepted method to display visual information on the web. You haven't had the luxury of time to explore beyond this method, other than your concern for accessibility and validation of pages. Your focus along these lines is noble, and very necessary for a number of viewers of online information."

"But is that a bad thing?" Bonnie asked. "I felt I was doing all I could."

Steve reminded Bonnie, "Our ideas aren't good or bad. They're just a result of our experiences."

I smiled. "Steve's right. The fact that you found the time to come to this class tells me you're ready to expand the structure you've lived with so far. This is great, in my opinion."

"What's the deal with her circles and squares?" Zed asked.

"Remember when we talked about perception in the principles of design?" I stood and went to the board.

"Perception is how we see things," Zed said. "So does Bonnie see everything in circles and squares?" He looked at Bonnie with a hint of sorrow in his face.

Bonnie laughed, "No, Zed. Sometimes I'm so busy I don't see anything at all. I have a very narrow focus."

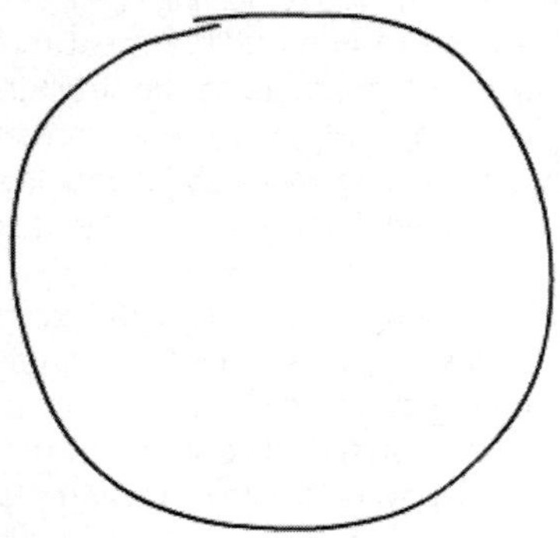

I drew a circle on the board and pointed to the shape. "The circle is the simplest natural shape. The fact that this shape is also a fundamental shape has never been abandoned by the global human mind."

I pointed at Deb's drawing pad. "Science and math have fought since the beginning of time against the circle's dominance in the human mind. According to the way we think, everything is supposed to go in a circle – concepts like electrons and atoms, the planets, the seasons, and wedding rings are just a few examples. The mind seeks formation, and the circle imposes itself on many of our explanations, forming bonds and relationships that, hopefully, make sense."

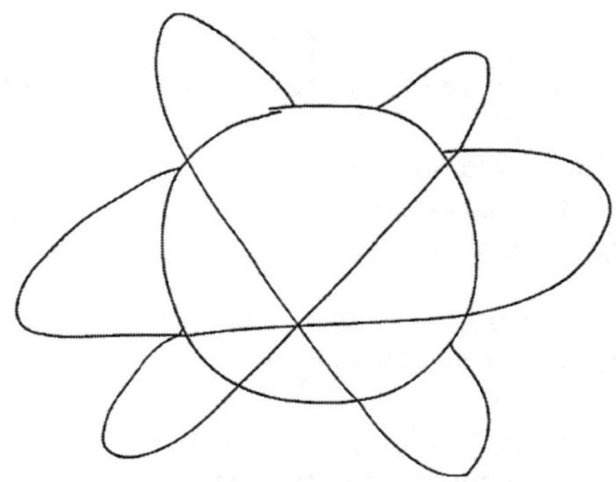

I drew several ellipses over the circular shape, and continued, "As our experiences expand, our perception also expands. We become aware that there is, perhaps, more depth to this circle, or more width or height. We're all aware the planets don't travel in the shape of a pure circle. But would we know this if our experience hadn't proven it to us? Would we even notice it at all?"

I drew a triangle on the board, and pointed at it. "Someone, somewhere back in prehistory fell on a sharp rock and was wounded or killed. The people around him realized that a sharp object would help them hunt animals for food, clothing, and shelter. This shape," I continued, "Represented danger for a long period of time. It's the shape of an arrowhead, a spear, or a dagger."

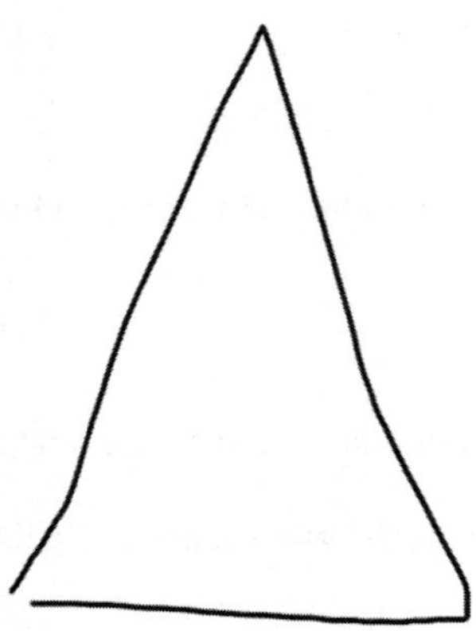

"It's also the shape of the pyramids," Deb offered. "The concept of danger represented by a triangle must have changed sometime around that period."

"Probably because it represented a pointed finger, too," Steve added. "Pointing upwards, it would represent pointing to an authority beyond the circle of earth."

"Oh," Zed said. "Just like steeples on churches."

Wes looked at Zed. "Let's keep it down to earth, kid."

"You're all on the same wavelength now." I grinned, pointed to the triangle, and then drew a square next to it, "The triangle could represent a number of things. Similarly, the square might have originally represented solidity. People discovered that square and rectangular shapes were better supports than circular objects. Stones might roll away, but a large rectangular piece of wood could be set into the ground. It could support much more weight, and distribute it more evenly.

"Monoliths are a good example of the development of the rectangle as a symbol of strength and power. But," I added, "What it all boils down to is that the triangle and the square were developed as contrasting elements to the circle."

"Oh!" Wes jumped up and grabbed the marker from my hand. He drew a circle containing two smaller circles. He turned and waved his arms, "I know where you're going with this now. When we first learn to recognize objects, it isn't by word. It's by shape." He pointed at the image on the board. "When we first learn to draw, we often draw the human face before the form, because it's immediate and most important to us.

He added lines for a body, arms, and legs. "When we get a little older and more observant, we give our pictures bodies, legs, and arms. We realize there's more than a circle involved in our relationships!"

He waved the marker around, "Once we become sophisticated in our perceptions beyond circles and sticks, we either become more fascinated with shapes, or we become more interested in other subjects. The person who becomes involved with other things keeps their focus on these primal shapes. Everything, subconsciously, relates to these forms."

Wes appeared to have over-exerted himself with his enthusiasm. He was breathing heavily when he handed the marker back to me. Steve laughed, "Wow Wes, that was brilliant. I remember reading about studies done with children and shape perceptions. I never thought beyond what happens when we progress beyond those stages."

I nodded at Wes, as he seated himself at the table. "That was great, Wes. You certainly don't lack passion in your discoveries." Wes laughed. I addressed the children's studies. "Steve, those studies proved to be a valuable resource for the study of visual thinking, and the intelligence of visual perception.

"For instance, the children who were asked to draw their perception of *the unknown* often drew organic shapes. Their experiences with these shapes were minimal, so that was, obviously, their *unknown*.

"The person who does go on to study shapes as a means of communication finds that they go deeper and deeper into theory, rhetoric, and pinholes of discovery. Eventually, they break away from detail and find themselves back at the point of origin. They begin to develop abstract images and symbolic forms, based on these pure shapes."

Bonnie laughed. "I'm sure I'm not abstract. I didn't even understand abstract until you placed it in this context." She appeared slightly puzzled. "But is all abstract art a simplification of shape?"

"By definition, yes," I answered. "However, abstraction can be as complicated as irony." Deb smiled, and Wes laughed.

"So, my life patterns have kept me from exploring beyond basic shapes, right?" Bonnie asked. Before waiting for an answer, she stated, "That makes sense. I don't feel so inadequate now. I just haven't pursued shape and visual imagery like some of you have in the past."

Deb said, "Algebra is basically pure shape, too. But the shapes have various meanings. It's a language, and that language is formed from shapes."

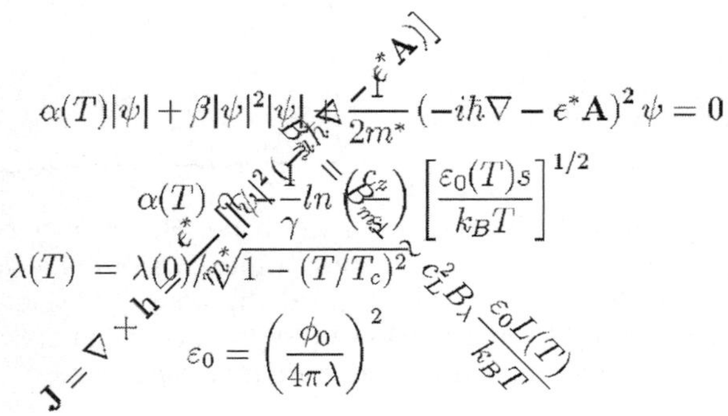

Steve nodded, "That's the language of physics."

"Our own language is a series of shapes," I added. "That's why I want you to combine words with images. Each stroke you make on the paper is a graphic mark, and each one is important as a representation of your perceptions."

"So, my perceptions really aren't bad," Bonnie sighed. "They're just sums of my experiences." She looked around at the rest of the class. "You all are teaching me so much. I'm sure I'll be drawing triangles in no time flat!"

Everyone laughed, and Deb patted her on the shoulder. "Bonnie," Deb said, "I guess that's why software companies use circles and squares for the basic icons on their toolbars. We're so familiar with those two shapes. Anything beyond those shapes is just a result of our experiences."

Lisa smiled. "I never noticed that, Deb. Now that you mention it, I guess you're right."

"Hopefully, you just learned that those simple shapes are the basis to all visual communications. This applies whether they're numbers, letters, or forms, so such simple shapes will be vital tools for communicating with a wide variety of people." They all nodded that they understood.

"I hope you understand, also, that each person in this team brings their own experiences with these shapes to the table. If we honor each other's experiences, we could expand our own perceptions of the world around us."

I looked at the computers on the other side of the room. "We haven't spent a lot of time brainstorming Frieda's site specifically yet" I stated. "But we have talked a lot about the brainstorming process in general. When we use the writer's tools of rhetorical figures, we can help ourselves reach deeper for more creative ideas.

"When we look at our own and other's experiences, and how we use these to write and draw our ideas, we also gain knowledge about how other designers work. When we develop these experiences, they eventually become our *style*. Each designer's style comes from their own experience and perceptions," I added. "When we remember that we have our own perceptions, as well as perceptions as a society in this place and time, then our visual language can be more focused.

"OK, we haven't spent much time learning how to utilize the tools in Flash yet," I said. "So I think this is a good time to take a look at how we can create and manipulate basic shapes with the various tools available to us."

Zed seemed torn. "Man!" he stated, "I was really getting into this brainstorming stuff. But," he added, "I would never turn down a chance to play with Flash!"

At that, I suggested a break before starting our study of the Flash MX toolbar.

The Flash MX toolbar

The class returned from their break and settled down at the computers and I familiarized them with the Flash toolbar.

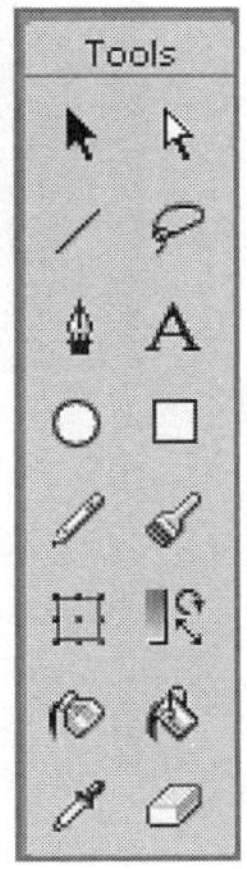

"We've come across several Flash tools already on this course, but we'll certainly benefit by looking at the capabilities of all of the tools in a single session. Let's get started by examining the use of the Arrow selection tool."

Arrow tool

"The chances are that you will use this tool more than any other when you work in Flash. Even though it is hardly the most exciting tool in the set, it has a number of different uses. Its basic functionality is for moving objects around the stage, but it also allows you to select and manipulate objects.

"The arrow tool has three main functions: **selection**, **movement**, and **manipulation**. Let's take a look at each of them."

Selection

"The basic mode of the arrow tool allows you to select objects on the stage. You might want to select objects to move them around or delete them." I drew a square with different fill and stroke colors on the stage.

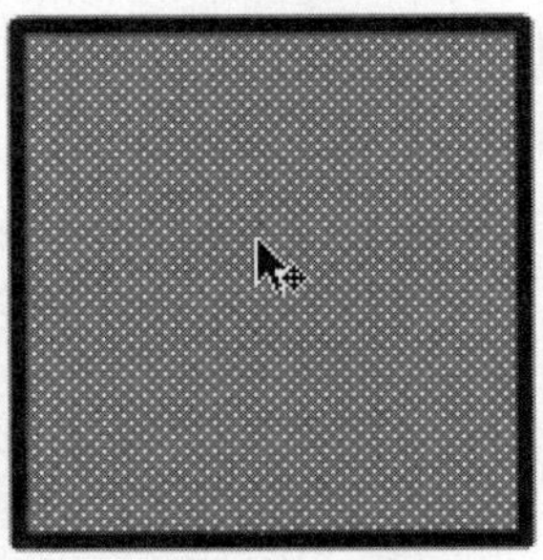

"This square, as with other vector shapes, is essentially created out of two pieces – the stroke and the fill. If you click once on the fill with the Arrow tool, it alone is selected." I clicked on the fill of the square.

"The fill can now be moved or deleted at will, leaving the stroke unchanged. However, if you want to select both the fill and the stroke of the square, you need to double click on the fill of the square.

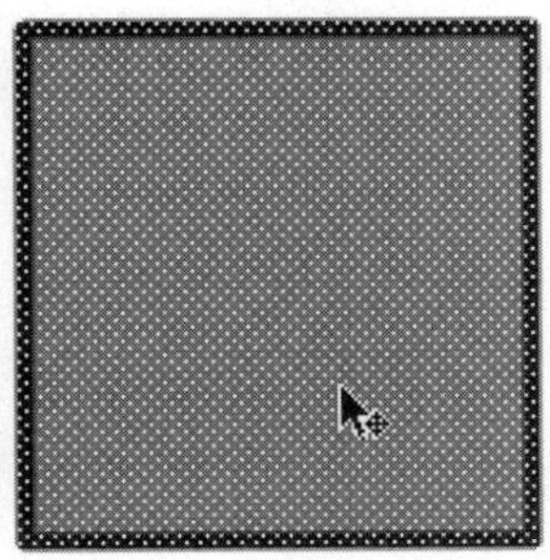

"Now both can be moved or changed at the same time. Even though this single and double click system is fairly logical, this is one of the first things that Flash users forget about!

"But after a little practice, you'll usually come to depend on it." I said.

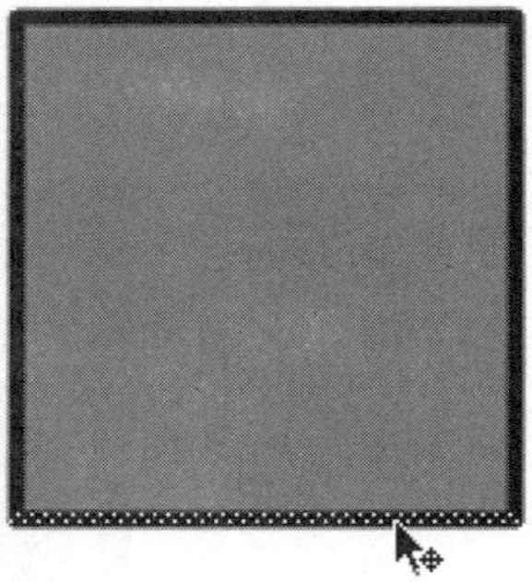

I continued, "When it comes to selecting the stroke lines of a shape, there is a different rule to remember. A single click on a stroke line selects that line alone.

"While a double click will selects all the joined lines – in the case of this square, all four boundary lines.

"Try and master this distinction between fill selection and stroke selection and you'll find that your work flow will become a lot more efficient.

"To select multiple objects, hold down the SHIFT key while you select additional items. For example, if I hold down the SHIFT key and select the fill and the top stroke line at the same time, then delete them, I turn a filled square into an empty bucket.

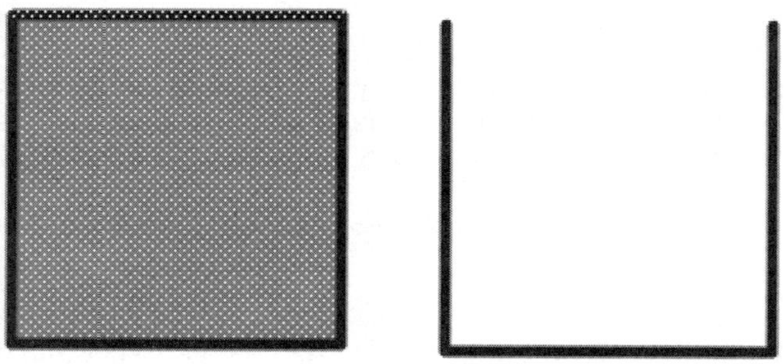

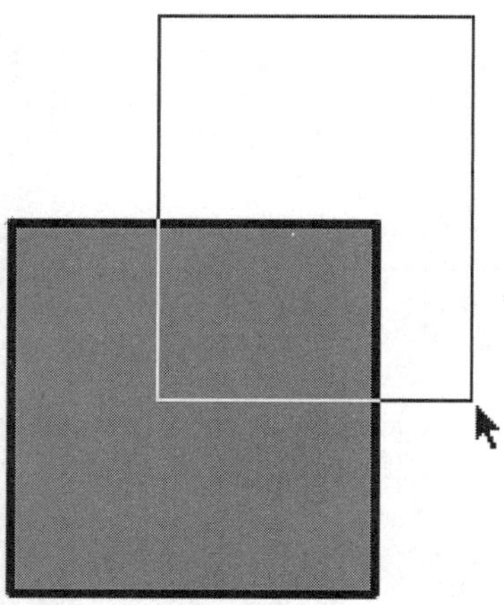

"The final mode of selection is the same as that commonly used to select files or folders on your desktop." I said. "That is, by forming a box over the required items, or in the case of Flash, over the required elements or objects.

"This enables you to select an area, or a number of objects in an area, by drawing a box with the mouse down and releasing the mouse to confirm the selection."

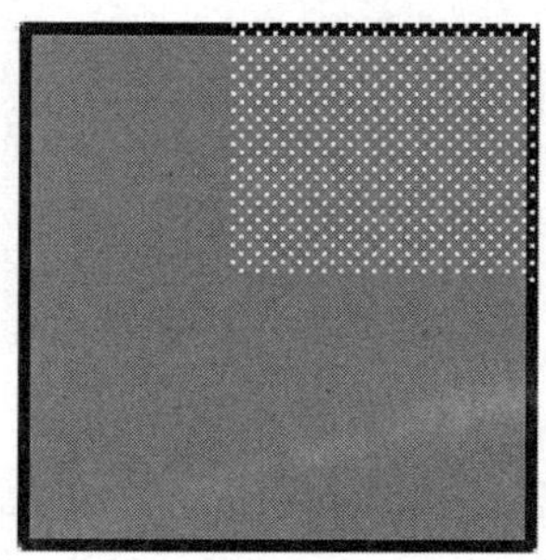

Movement

"The next mode of the Arrow tool is the ability to move objects around the stage." I said. "Firstly, you should select the object you wish to move. Once you've done this, a four-point symbol will be added to the cursor when you rollover the selected object.

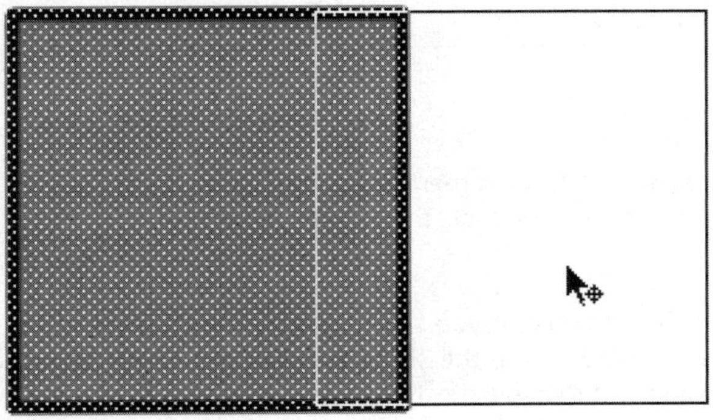

"Whenever you see this cursor, this means that you can move an object by clicking and dragging it. While moving an object or objects, Flash draws a ghostly outline of the changing destination point.

"With that, this function is pretty much covered. A final tip is that if you want to move an object in a straight line, just hold down the SHIFT key while moving it and the motion will be restricted."

"You can also move objects a short and precise distance," Deb said, "Using the cursor keys to move it a pixel at a time in the direction of the key press."

"Even though it isn't traditionally linked with the Arrow tool, that's a useful tip Deb." I said. Deb smiled.

Manipulation

"The last function of the Arrow tool is the ability to stretch, distort, and manipulate objects." I said. "For example, if the uniformity of the square bores you," I looked at Wes, "Then you might want to mess around with its edges.

"To manipulate an object, it must be unselected. This is another common problems that new Flash users seem to forget about."

"You're right Linda," Bonnie said. "I played with this during the week, and I couldn't work out why I kept moving the object, not changing it."

"It's a common mistake to make Bonnie." I said. "Once you're sure that the object you want to manipulate is unselected, then the cursor will change to resemble a curve when it's over the objects edge.

"You can pull and distort the shape from the edge by holding the mouse button and dragging. Release the mouse button to fix the shape."

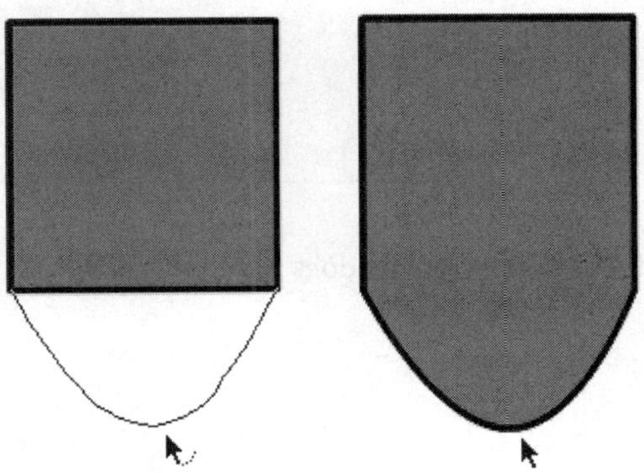

"That's pretty wild!" Zed exclaimed.

"It is if you can remember how to do it." Bonnie said.

"Just look for the different cursor states when you are using the Arrow tool." I said. "When the cursor has the four compass points, it means that you can move the object, and when it has a curve, it suggests you can change the shape of the object."

Subselection tool

"The Subselection tool is used to manipulate vector shapes. Although there are a number of ways to do this in Flash, from the Free Transform tool to the Arrow tool, the Subselection tool is arguably the most quick and easy.

"Vector shapes are made up of a number of points. For instance, if you take a rectangle, it has four points, situated at the corners, between which Flash draws lines to create the shape we recognize as a rectangle. With the Subselection tool, you can select these points and manipulate the shape.

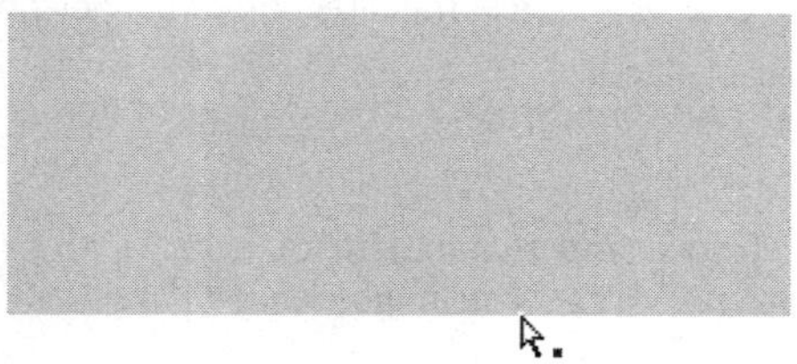

"Select the Subselection tool and rollover the edge of a shape on the stage. The cursor will change to show a point alongside it.

"Click when the cursor is in this state to select an object. Its vector points are now revealed.

"Drag any of the points to manipulate the shape, and release it to render the new shape.

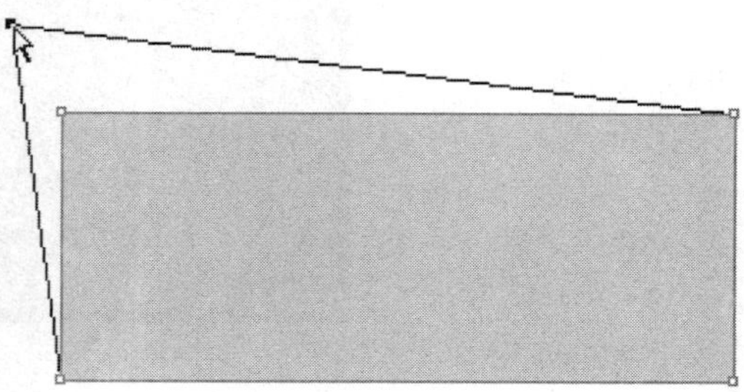

"If a rectangle is made of four points," Zed said. "How many points does a circle have?"

"Well Zed, when it comes to rounded shapes, Flash forms them with curves rather than small straight lines. A circle will be drawn with eight points.

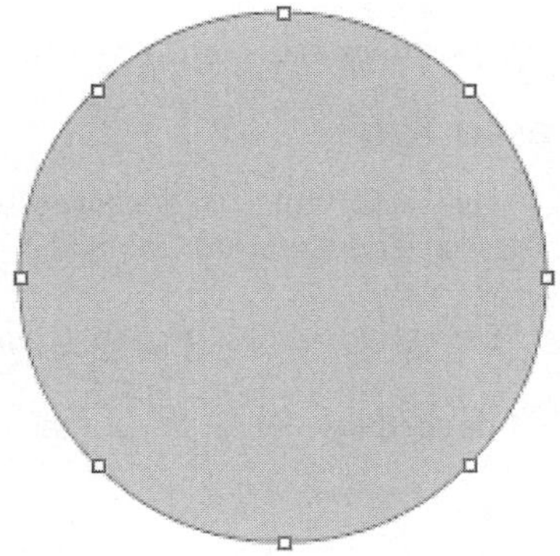

"These points link together to form the curves of eight 45 degree segments." Deb said.

"Very quick Deb," I said, "You certainly know your geometry. Lines and strokes are also made of vector points, and can be manipulated with the Subselection tool."

Line tool

Even though I assumed that most of the students were familiar with this tool, I decided to recap anyway for those of them that might have dozed off when we've looked at it before, or haven't had the chance to play around with the Flash toolbar in their own time.

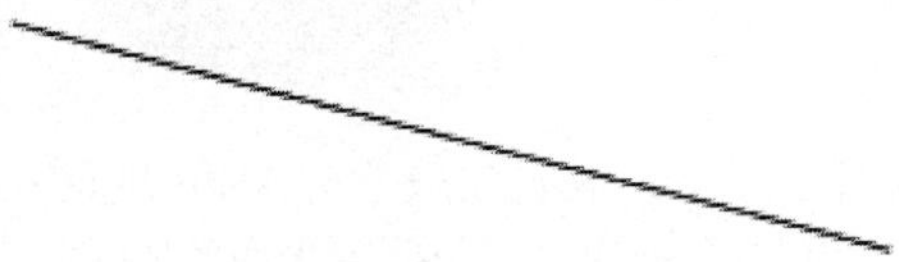

"The Line tool is used for creating a vector stroke between two points.

"The origin point is defined on the initial mouse press, and the destination point is changed as the cursor is moved around. A line is drawn between these two points when the mouse button is released.

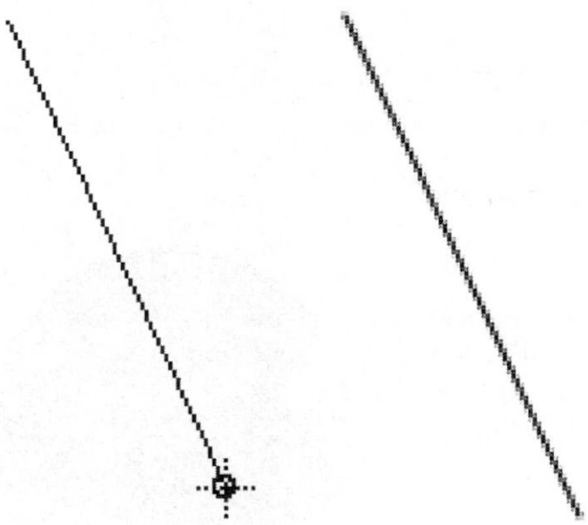

"Once you have a line, you have to start the process again and draw a new line unconnected to the last one. This tool does not support *rubber-banding*..."

"What the heck is rubber-banding?" Wes interrupted.

"Rubber-banding is a term used for line tools where each line picks up from where the last one left off." Bonnie said. "So you get a set of inter-connected lines. The Line tool in Photoshop is rubber-banded."

"In Flash MX, the Line tool doesn't work in this way," I said, "Each drawn line is started from the mouse position and is not connected to the previous drawn line. You can simulate rubber-banding with the View > Snap to Objects option switched on. When you then come to draw a new line, Flash will attach the new line to the end of the nearest one.

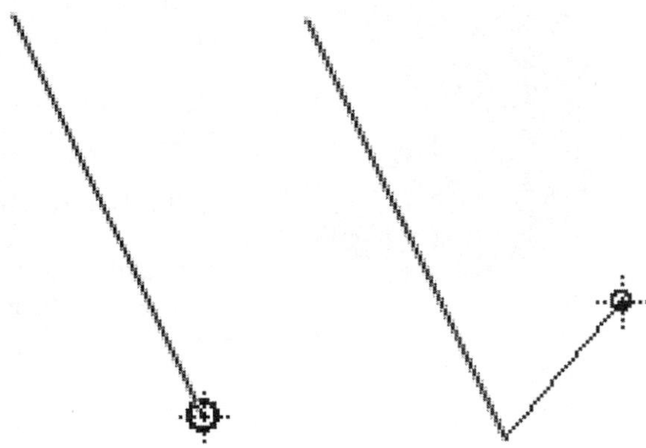

"Everyone got that?" I asked. The students nodded. "Snap to Objects is very useful for many things throughout Flash so it's best to keep it switched on all the time."

Lasso tool

"The Lasso tool is an advanced selection tool, allowing you to select an area by drawing with the lasso." Zed chuckled to himself. "Please keep all your cowboy jokes to yourself, Zed.

"Even though Zed is probably thinking of herds of cattle and buffalo, I'm going to use an apple to demonstrate."

I opened up a Flash file containing a representation of an apple.

"At the moment, this is a perfectly round and juicy apple." I said. "But now I'm going to take a bite out of it using the Lasso tool. When you select the Lasso tool from the toolbox, your cursor changes to a lasso rope."

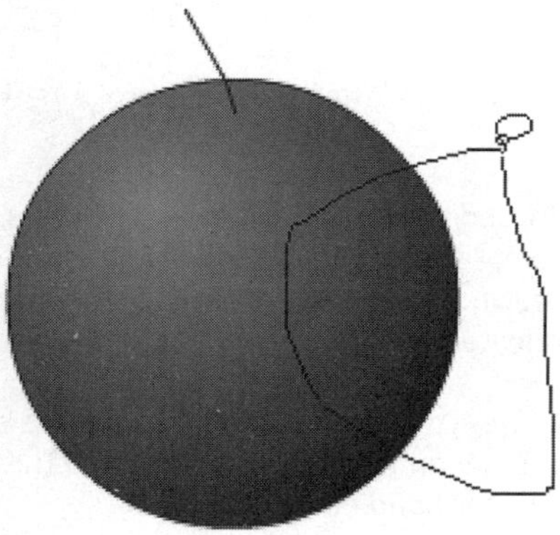

"Use the Lasso tool to draw the shape of a bite taken from the apple. Hold down the mouse button as you draw the shape.

"Once you've finished drawing the shape, release the mouse button and the selection will be highlighted.

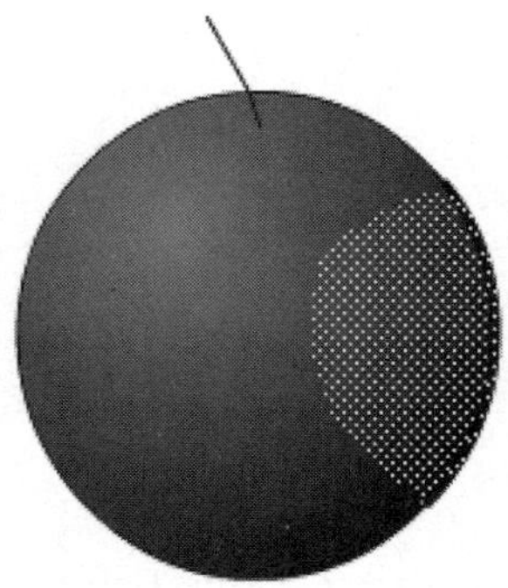

"You can then delete, move, or manipulate the selection as with any other selected portion. In this instance, hit the Delete key to remove the selected area from the apple."

"Cool! Someone's taken a bite out of my apple!" Zed exclaimed. Wes shook his head.

"Actually, it reminds me more of Pac-Man." Bonnie said.

"Oh, and remember, as with the Arrow tool just hold down the Shift key to select multiple areas." I said.

Pen tool

I could sense the students were getting a little bored with being lectured at, so I tried to make the lesson a little more interactive. "Steve, would you like to explain the rest of our group how the Pen tool works?" I asked.

"Sure, I'll try." Steve replied. "Feel free to come in at any point though Linda. I know how to use it, but I might not be the best at explaining it."

Steve took a deep breath. "The Pen tool is also known as the Bezier tool; both are based on the concept of the Bezier curve. This type of curve was invented by Pierre Bézier and is used to describe a two-dimensional shape using two anchor points and a control point."

Bonnie interrupted, "Uh... I'm confused already. Can you talk in English Steve?"

"OK, maybe the practical solution is best here Steve." I said. "Why don't you draw a Bezier curve on your screen and then explain?"

"Sounds like a good idea Linda." Steve said. "I wasn't sure where I was going anyway!

"Gather round my computer everyone." Steve said, waving his arm theatrically. The class gathered behind Steve.

"Although this is called the Pen tool, it really doesn't act like any traditional pen. Instead it draws curves. It is called the Pen tool because designers have used it by default since Adobe adopted it in their software, and I guess because it has become as useful as the pen is to designers working on paper.

"If I'm totally honest with you, using the Pen tool at first isn't that straightforward." Steve paused. "The first thing to do is to define the first **anchor point** by clicking the mouse button." Steve clicked on the stage and produced an anchor point.

"Now, we need to produce the second anchor point. When we position it this time, we need to press and hold down the mouse button:

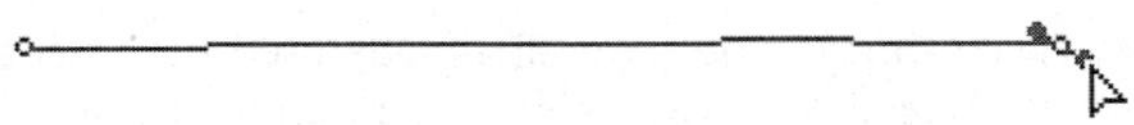

"This then allows us to position the **control point** by moving the mouse cursor.

"What is happening is that the curve is being defined by the *force* of the control point. The control point here is defined with solid points, and the anchor points are empty."

"But there are two solid points." Bonnie observed. "I mean control points..."

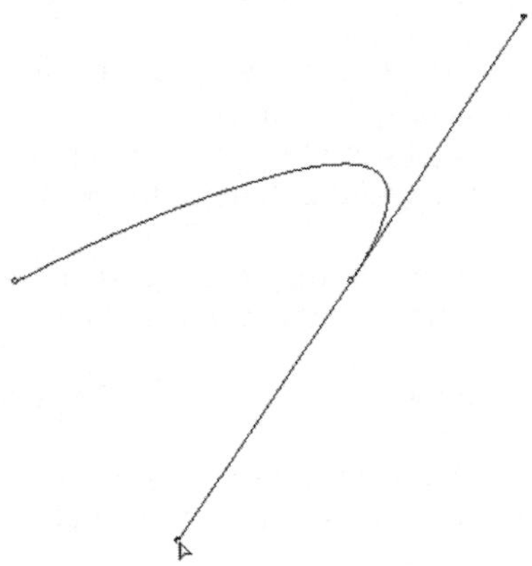

"No, there is only one control point, and that is the one that is the one at the top. The point that is being dragged by the cursor is used to change the position of the control point. The dragged point simply mirrors the control point.

"To see what's happening it's best if you imagine a line from the center point between the two white anchor points to the control point. Imagine that the line is magnetized towards the control point, forming a curve that reflects its attraction to this control point."

"Wow!" Deb exclaimed. "I wonder what algorithm the developers used to get that affect – that's math in action!"

"Before you go trying to work out the equation Deb, remember that Monsieur Bézier worked it out first, and I'm sure it's documented on the Internet if you'd like to look it up."

"Hmm, I'm still not sure I understand how you made it." Bonnie said.

"Bezier curves require a lot of practice Bonnie." I said, "The trick is to keep playing with them, until you feel comfortable enough."

"I'd never use anything else." Steve said. "The truth is that once you get it, then I doubt you'll ever use any other tool to draw curves."

"When you combine the Bezier curves from the Pen tool with the Subselection tool," I said, "You can create really organic looking shapes that you can alter any way you choose.

"You might not find it that easy to use initially, but once you are comfortable drawing a single curve, click some more anchor points to make complex shapes. If you want to create a filled shape, click back on the original anchor point.

I gave the class a little time to draw their own Bezier curves and experiment with this tricky but invaluable tool.

Oval and Rectangle Tools

Since we had covered the Text tool already, and were going to learn a lot more about it in a future class, I decided to skip it and talk a little about the Oval and Rectangle tools.

"Even though you have all already used the Oval and Rectangle tools," I said. "I just wanted to share one small detail with you before we go on to the next tool. First, I'd like you all to try and draw a perfect circle or square with each Respective tool." The students went ahead to try and create a perfect shape.

"The chances are that you can manage something close," I said. "But when the shape is measured, it will be inaccurate. The solution to this is to use the Shift key whilst drawing the shape. This will constrain the height and width to the same ratio and you'll get a perfect circle or square, as opposed to a rectangle or oval." I encouraged the students to try this out.

"Additionally, the Rectangle tool has another subtle hidden bonus – the option to change the corner radius of a rectangle shape. When the Rectangle tool is selected, the Round Rectangle Radius..."

"That's easy for you to say!" Steve interrupted.

"Ahem... thanks Steve." I said. "The Round Rectangle Radius appears in the Options section at the bottom of the tools panel.

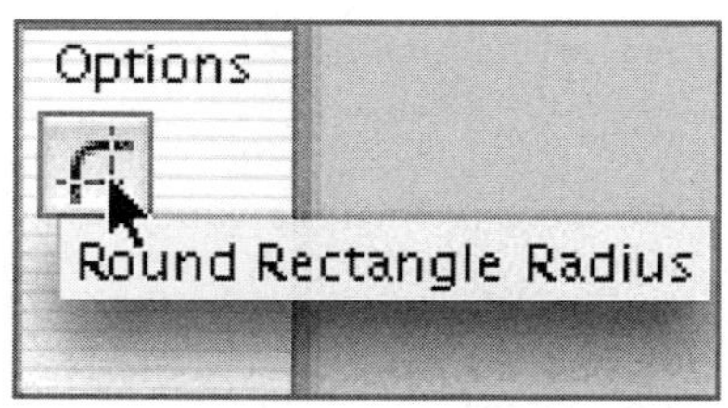

"When you click this, a dialog will request the radius of the corners. By default this is set as 0, giving you hard 90 degree right-angles. If you increase this, Flash will allow you to draw rectangles and squares with rounded edges."

I changed the corner radius setting to 30.

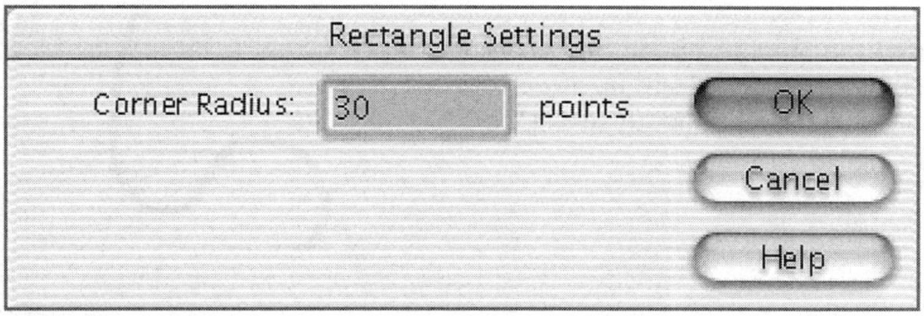

Next, I drew a rectangle on the stage.

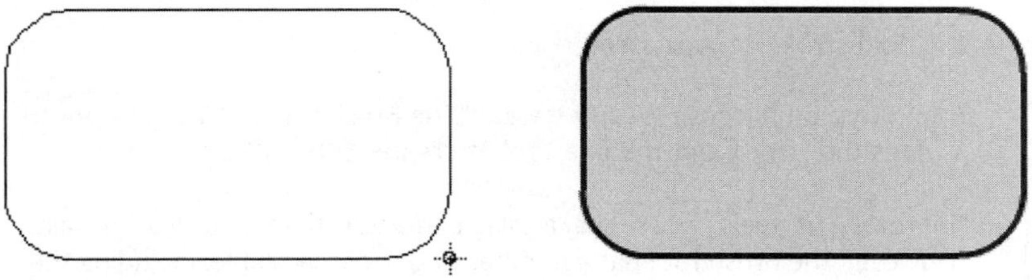

Pencil tool

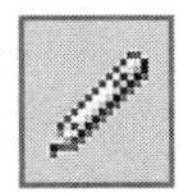

"The Pencil tool" I said, "Is the most basic of all the tools, allowing you to draw freely. I think of it more like a *squiggle* tool, because it always reminds me of doodling."

"Yeah, I guess it does have that effect." Wes said. "It's certainly not as pleasurable as the real thing though."

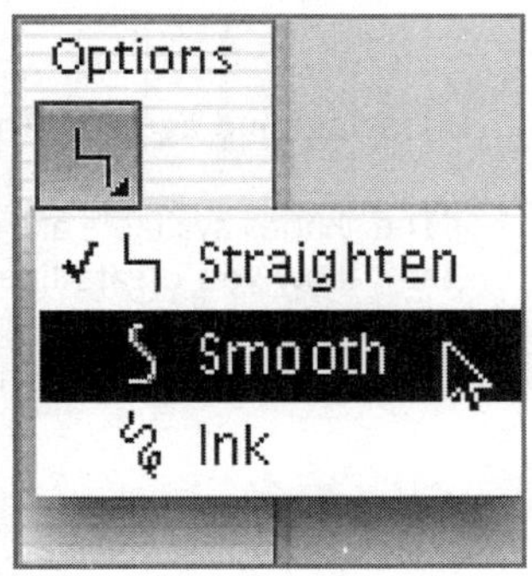

"Besides the standard doodling format, the Pencil tool allows you to place a certain computational order on your line sketches. In the toolbar Options area, you'll find a drop-down menu to set the mode of drawing.

"If this is set to Ink, what you draw is what you will get. This mode doesn't change your sketch at all.

"When set to Straighten, Flash will take your initial sketch and straighten the lines you have drawn. This is helpful if you're working with straight lines. For example, if I draw a rough four sided square, Flash will tidy it up for me.

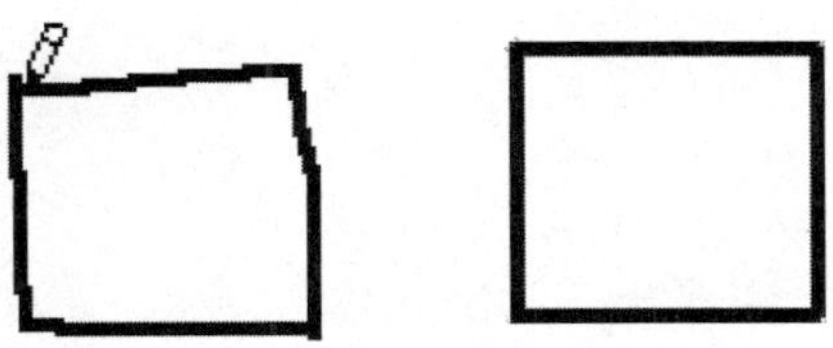

"The Smooth option does exactly what it says on the tin, removing any jagged areas from your drawing.

"Once you've used the Smooth option, the chances are that you will become hooked. It cleans up any errors that you make, ending with a lovely smooth stroke."

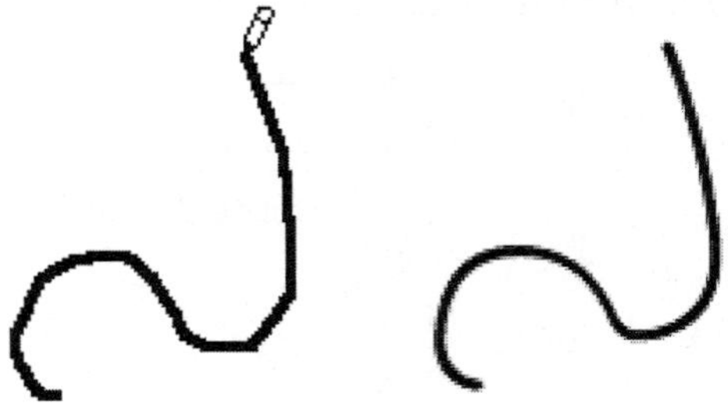

Brush tool

Next up was the Brush tool. "The Brush tool is the equivalent of a paint brush, allowing you to draw big bold lines," I began.

"Don't you mean big bold *strokes*?" Wes asked.

"I said that on purpose Wes." I stated. "The Brush tool in Flash MX doesn't produce strokes, as does the pencil and the line tool, it creates **fills**." Wes smiled.

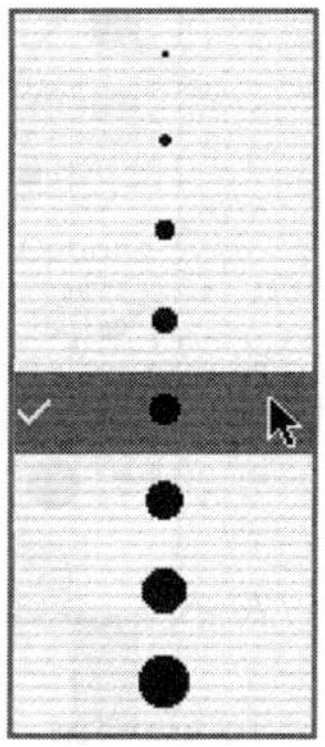

"In reality, it feels more like a magic marker than a brush." I said. "However, the Brush tool has a number of options available, including the option change the shape and thickness of the brush. The brush thickness is changed via the drop-down in the middle of the option area."

"This allows you to paint with a really chunky brush!" Wes said. "It's certainly a lot different to the Pencil tool. You can get much more depth and texture with this."

"Looks like Wes has discovered Flash MX as a new vehicle for his art," Deb said.

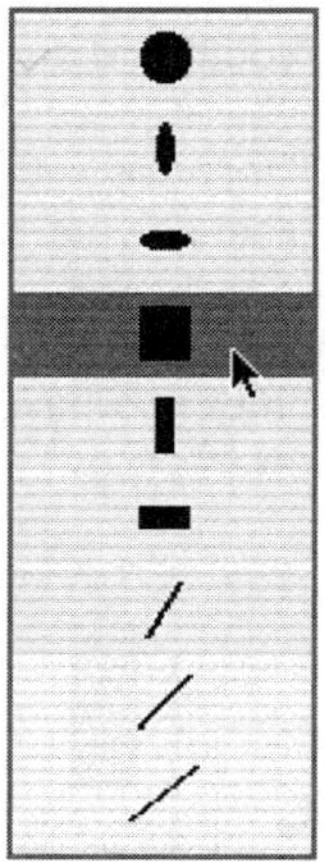

I laughed and agreed, "The shape of the brush is changed on the next drop-down.

"The shapes available are pretty diverse, and even though they don't look that impressive, they allow you create lines in all manners of calligraphic style. Give a few of them a try."

The students went on to create shapes with the brushes on offer.

Free Transform tool

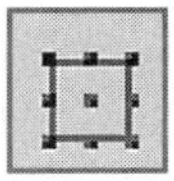

"Most of you have already worked with the Free Transform tool already," I said. "If not, then you'll generally find it useful for all sorts of graphic manipulating, from basic routines like scaling and rotation, to all sorts of weird and wonderful distortions.

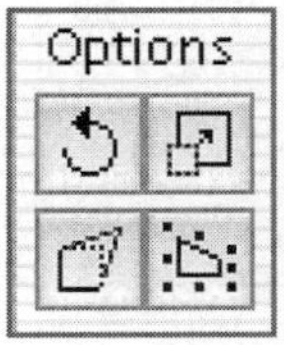

"When you select the Free Transform tool, a number of options appear at the bottom of the Tools panel. These are Rotate and Skew, Scale, Distort, and Envelope.

"By default, without selecting any of these options, Flash lets you rotate, skew, or scale an object. Firstly, select an object and choose the Free Transform tool. Then, depending on where you place the cursor in relation to the box around the object, you are able to perform the different manipulations – as indicated by the changing state of the cursor.

"Place the cursor over the corners to rotate the object.

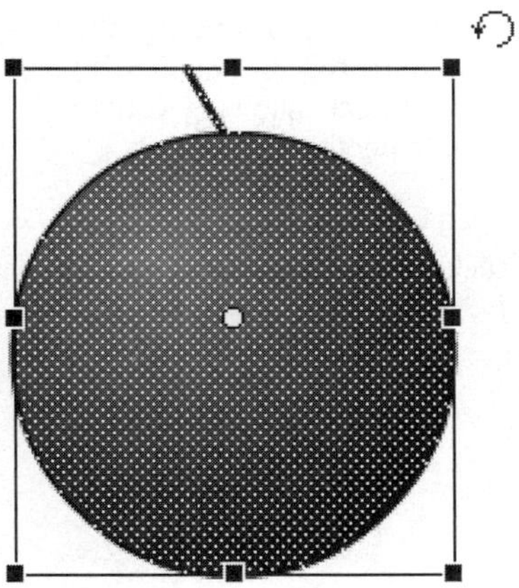

"In between the points, you can skew the object.

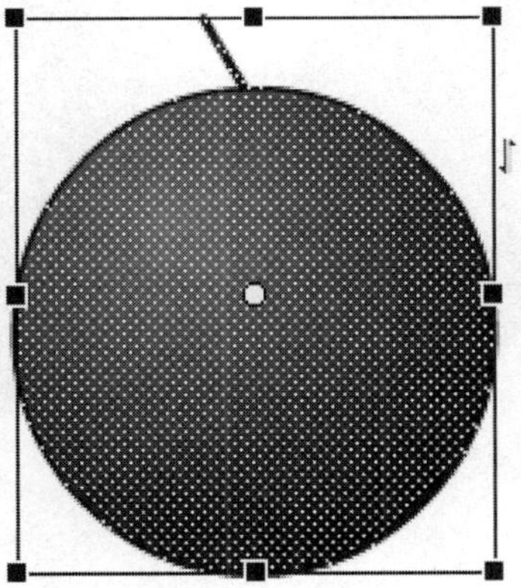

"And finally, on any of the points to scale the object.

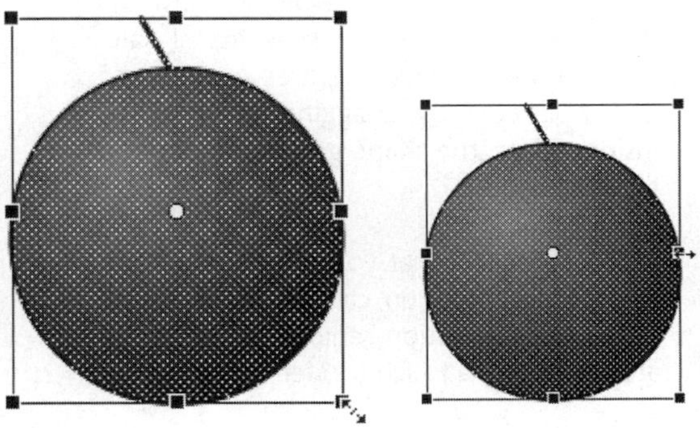

"To make a change in any of these modes, just drag and move the mouse, and release it when you are satisfied with it.

"The different options allow you to make greater changes." I said. "We've already covered the first two options here, but the next two are slightly more complex."

"The Distort option allows you to scale the object from the individual points, allowing you to distort it in any direction.

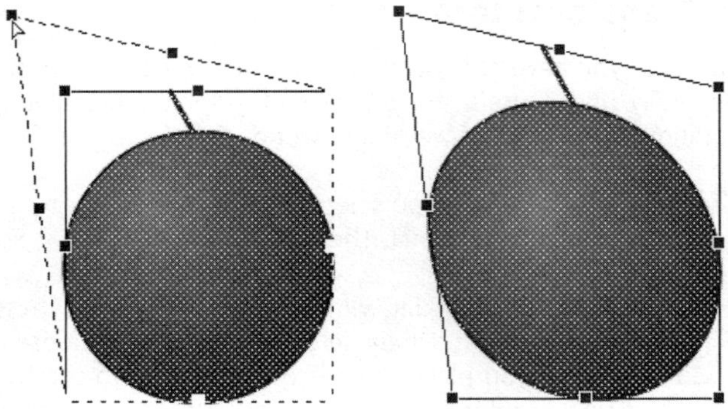

"If you hold down the SHIFT key while making a change with this option, the distortion will be mirrored and applied to both sides of the object, allowing you to create a simple perspective effect."

"That's cool!" Zed said, quickly returning to his studious clicking and dragging.

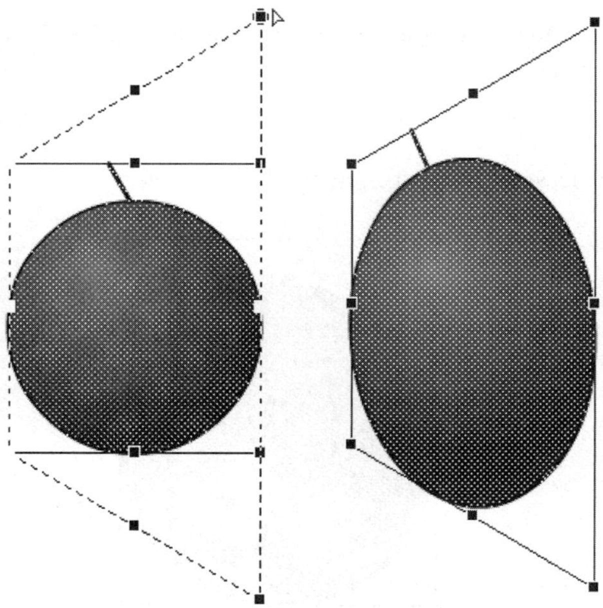

"The last manipulation available with the distort option is severe skewing," I said. "Or, for Zed's benefit, *extreme* skewing." Zed nodded. "By dragging one of the inside points, the shape gets highly skewed and distorted.

"I'd recommend that you play around with this to see what you can get from it. The next and final option requires a little more attention – it's a touch trickier than this one!

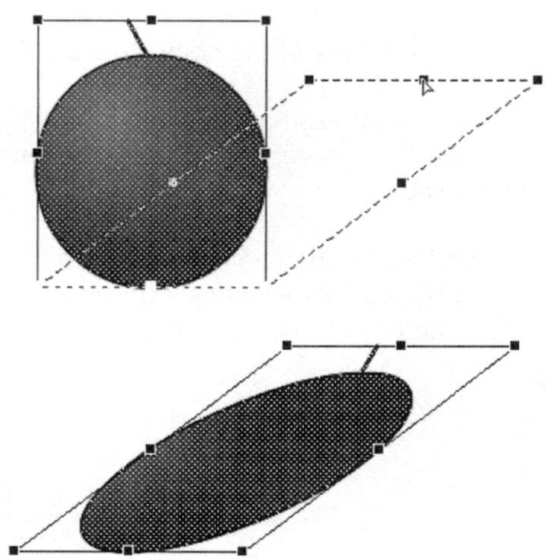

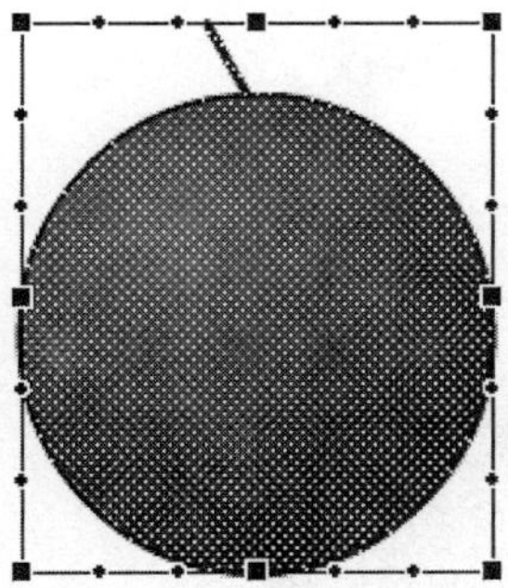

"The Envelope option is a little esoteric for my tastes, and produces some really wacky results. When you select it, you'll see a number of points are placed around the perimeter of the box.

"Each of these points is a Bezier anchor point, meaning that you can achieve some really organic manipulations.

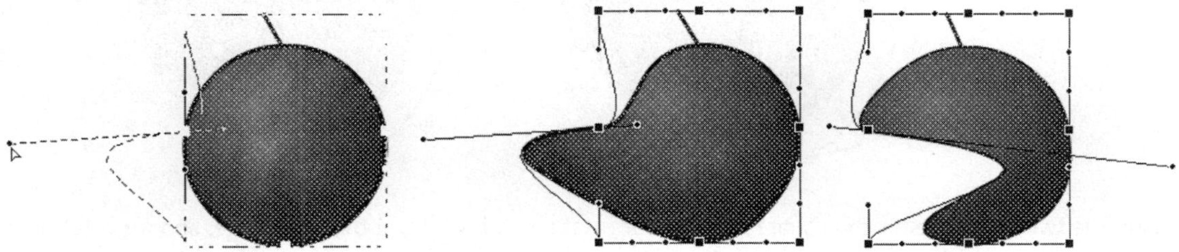

"Of all the Free Transform options this is easily the most addictive, but you will probably find that you use it less than the others. My advice is to experiment with all of these options, as you will certainly find a use for them in the future."

Fill Transform tool

"The Fill Transform tool allows you to change the appearance of gradient fills." I said. "Both radial and linear gradients can be scaled or rotated.

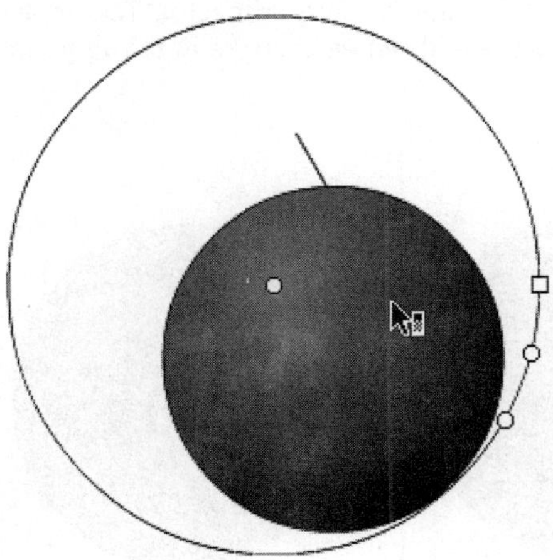

"To change the fill of a shape, make sure the object is unselected, and click on the fill. This will present you with a frame and a number of shapes. These shapes are the different modification options.

"The small circle in the middle of this radial gradient can be moved to change its center – with this, you're effectively changing the position of the imaginary light source that is creating the gradient effect.

"The square symbol is for horizontally scaling the fill.

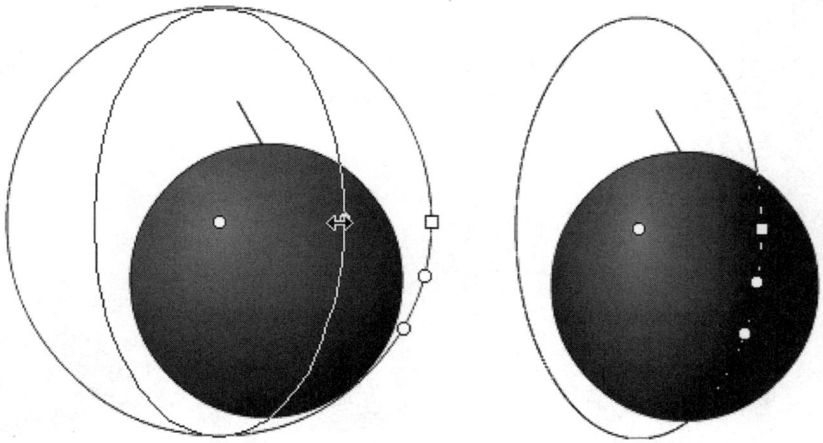

"And the two circles below the square icon are for rotating and scaling at the same time, and for rotation only.

"The options for linear gradients are quite similar, but in this case you are most likely to want to change the direction of the gradient."

Ink Bottle tool

"The Ink Bottle tool is used to give a stroke to any filled area if it doesn't already have one." I deleted the stroke from the apple. "This is extremely useful for objects created without a stroke, or fills that have accidentally had their strokes deleted.

"To use the Ink Bottle tool click on the fill that requires it. It takes the current stroke color and width from the Property inspector. The applied line is the same as any normal stroke and can be changed in the very same way.

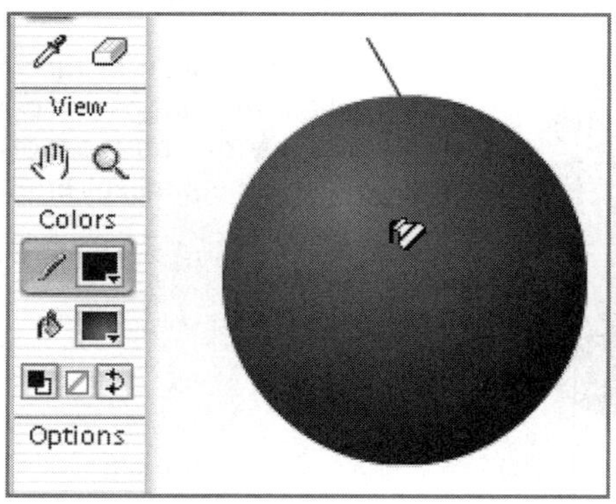

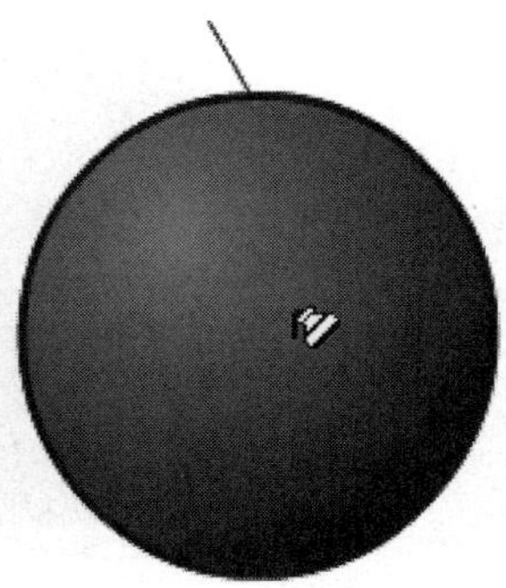

"This tool also allows you to give strokes to shapes drawn with the Brush tool."

Paint Bucket tool

"The Paint Bucket tool is used for filling an area, or changing the color of an existing fill." I said. "The basic idea of the tool is simple enough when it comes to existing fills, but is a little more complex when it comes to filling strokes.

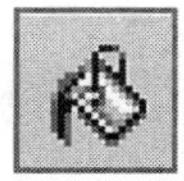

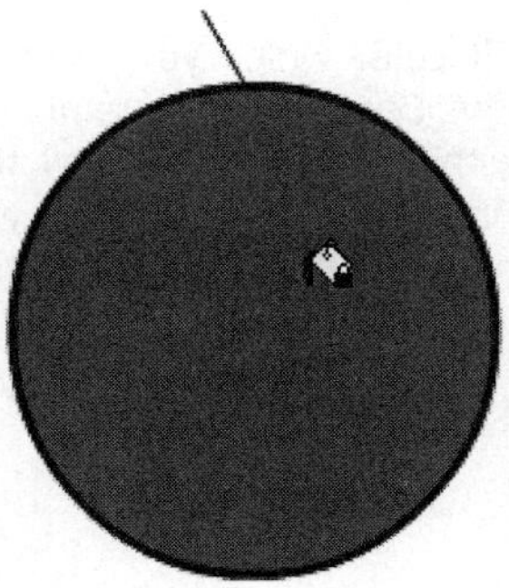

"You can chnage the color of an existing fill by selecting the new color, and clicking on the fill.

"Filling a stroke is a little more complicated, and depends on whether the stroke is a complete or broken shape or not." I drew two shapes on the stage with the Pencil tool, one a complete shape, and the other with a visible split.

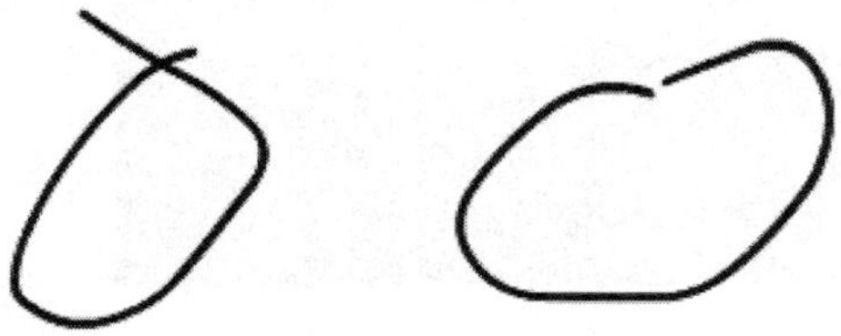

"The Paint Bucket Tool has four options for filling shapes:

- Don't Close Gaps
- Close Small Gaps
- Close Medium Gaps
- Close Large Gaps

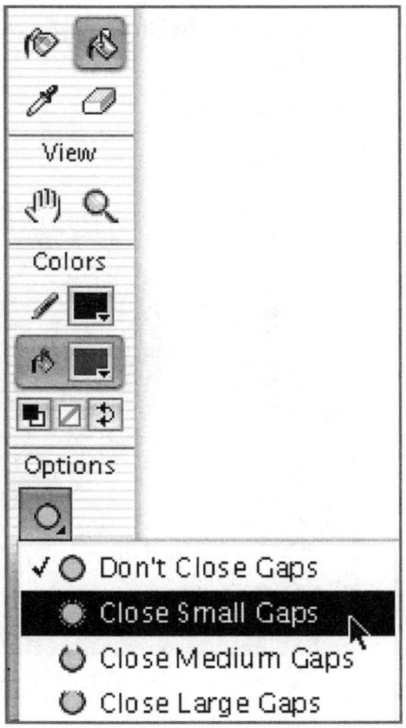

All of which are pretty self-explanatory.

"Flash has to be given permission to attempt to fill incomplete shapes. Of the two shapes that I've drawn, the one on the left is complete, so it can be filled with no problems and no special treatment." I set the Paint Bucket option to Don't Close Gaps and filled the stroke.

"The stroke on the right can only be filled if the Paint Bucket tool option is set to Close Large Gaps. Even though this doesn't look that large, Flash considers is to be a chasm." I changed the option to Close Large Gaps and filled the shape.

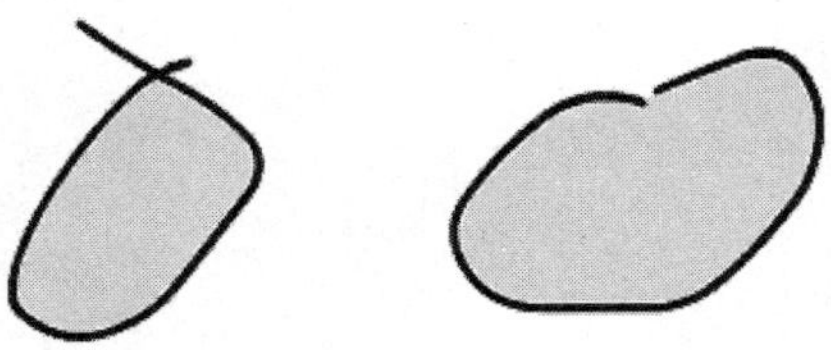

Eyedropper tool

"The Eyedropper tool is used to select a color from anywhere within Flash, and to change the stroke or fill color depending on which is chosen." I said. "It's useful for grabbing a color that you have forgotten how you created, or for choosing a color from an imported image that you want to match up.

"Select the stroke or fill color which you want to change, and then use the Eyedropper to sample a color from anywhere within Flash – note how the current color indicated in the Color Mixer panel will change to reflect the color that the Eyedropper tool has *sucked up*."

Eraser tool

"The Eraser tool is essential for deleting pesky and unwanted graphic elements." I said. "It also has some options allowing you to select what elements you want to be rid of and what you would like to keep.

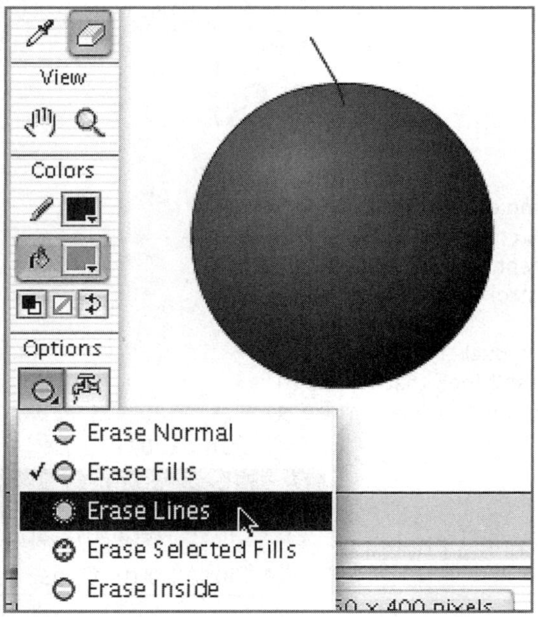

"The drop-down in the options section will allow you to specify what the Eraser will delete.

"These options let you to erase normally, erase fills only, erase strokes only, erase selected fills, or erase inside stroke lines. Most of these are pretty self-explanatory, so I'll let you experiment with them."

That was it for our tour of the tools in Flash. "These tools will be your allies over the next few weeks," I stated. "Let's now go back to our drawing pads and learn a few simple tricks to enhance your manual drawing skills – you'll then be all set to efficiently realize your ideas in Flash."

Improving your drawing skills

I decided that we should spend a brief period looking at some shortcuts to the drawing process. I asked the experienced designers/artists, Steve and Wes, to help with this part of the lesson, so the rest of the class could become more adept with their manual skills.

I turned to the class. "I'm sure many of you are anxious to get back into Flash again. But before that, I want to help you learn to simplify your drawing skills using the grid format.

"You'll find that many designers and artists might belittle using a grid for drawing. If you were all going to become illustrators or animators, I wouldn't suggest this process. But," I added, "Most of you either don't know how to draw, or don't plan on making a living with drawing or illustration."

"Using a grid can help you convey your ideas with more confidence. If you have to show roughs to the client, you'll want your work to appear more than amateur. This method will help you convey your ideas with a little more precision."

Wes laughed, "I know that for a fact. Some artists will declassify you as an artist if you can't draw by eye and motion." He waved one of his pencils around. "I'll admit that experience in drawing can help eliminate the need for some of the tools we use to form shapes, but it takes time."

Wes sat back and crossed his arms. "Every artist learns various drawing methods in the beginning of their career. Using a grid can be addictive, and some artists use it without telling anyone."

I laughed. "I wouldn't be as harsh as Wes in my opinion, but he's had his own experiences. We saw how Steve managed to keep his work organized in grids without drawing the actual grids. A person learns to draw just like they learn to expand their perceptions. Both skills expand through the experience of practice and time."

"Some of you still believe that the skill of art and design is learned through osmosis. Osmosis involves absorbing liquids, but in this context I'm referring to the unconscious process of assimilation.

"This sounds more like a Friday night on the town than learning a new skill – I guess I was practicing osmosis last weekend." Wes laughed.

Bonnie laughed. "I'm happy to hear I don't lack drawing genes, even without osmosis."

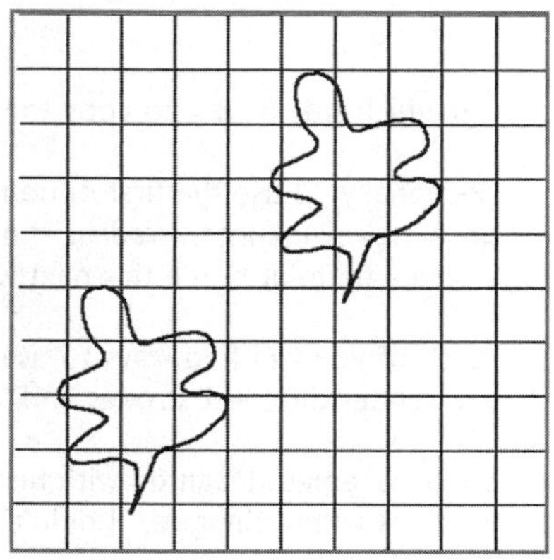

"None of us do, Bonnie. Some are just more skilled at drawing than others because they've learned to see objects with a different perception. I gave Bonnie, Zed, Lisa, and Deb a sheet of grid paper and a leaf. Each leaf was different. I asked Steve and Wes to help me show the students how to replicate the leaf using a grid.

"First, place the leaf on the grid paper, and trace it. Remove the leaf, and look at the height and width of the organic shape you just traced. Then, I want you to copy that shape, using the lay of the lines within the grid."

"Isn't this cheating?" Zed asked.

"No," Wes answered. "It's a shortcut to learn how to draw a shape."

"Wes is right, Zed," I replied. "We don't have the time or the space or supplies to get deep into the skills of drawing. There are plenty of books that can take you there. This," I pointed at the traced leaves, "Is just one method to get you further faster."

As Steve and Wes helped the students *see* where their lines had fallen on the grid, I watched how the students were holding their pencils. "Stop for just a minute and watch my hand," I said. I picked up one of Wes's pencils, and the pad of grid paper. "When I want to draw with restricted arm movement for short, controlled strokes,

I'll hold my pencil as I would if I were writing." I showed them this hand position, which seemed familiar to all of them.

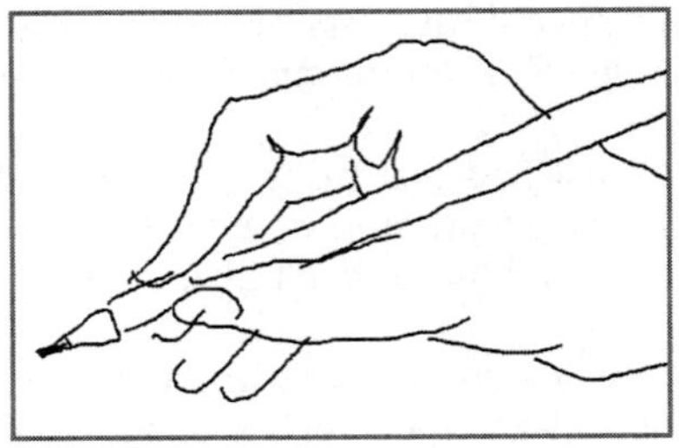

"If I want to draw free strokes that show rhythm, I would hold my hand like this," I showed them how to use the forefinger to control the pencil, with the hand at an angle.

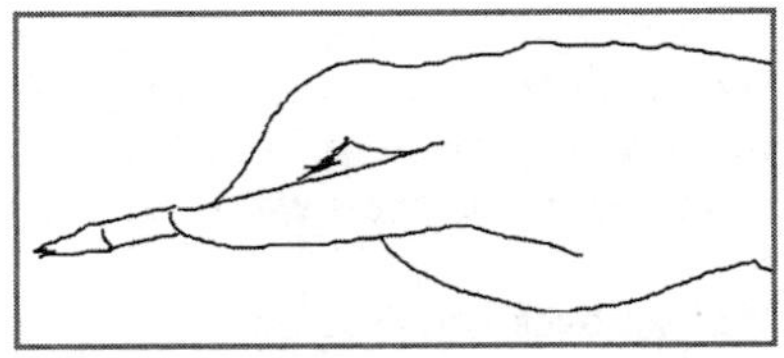

"Now, if I want to do quick motion studies," I continued, "I would use an easel or other support for my paper. This way I would have the full use of my arm to control the pencil." I held the paper pad up, and showed them how to hold the pencil, controlled by my thumb, and resting on my other four fingers. "This method is good for showing a figure in motion."

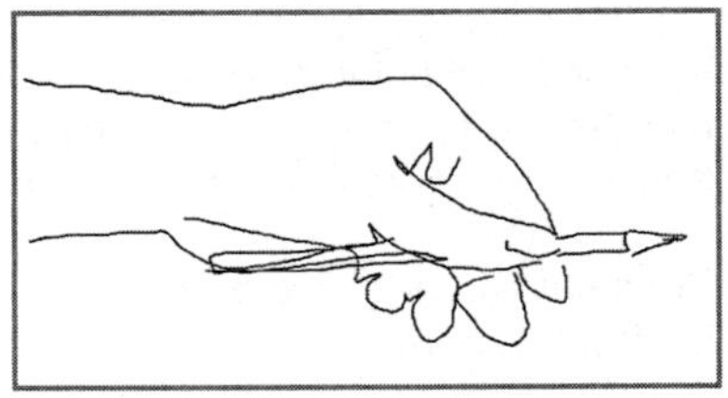

Zed seemed to study that method very closely. "The last method is for developing tone and detail." I moved my hand from an upright to a downward position. "You hold the pencil the same way as you would to show motion, but you've now restricted your arm to the movement of your wrist against the support of the table."

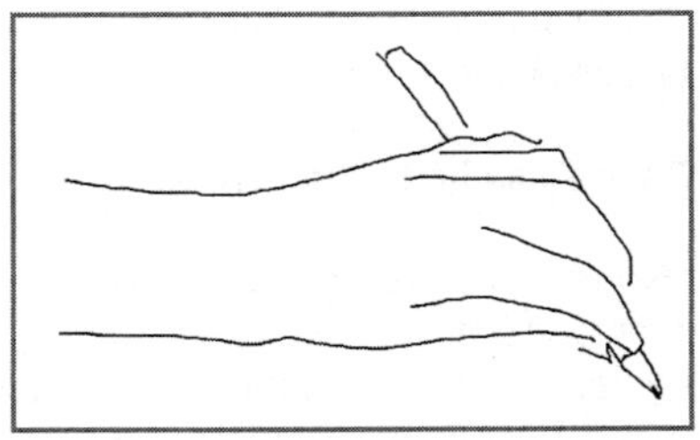

"So which way is best to copy the leaf?" Lisa asked.

"Personally I'd use the first option in this case, but I'd say we could use any one except the third technique, since we're not interested in showing motion." I said. "You should try all of the different methods, and practice them at home this next week.

"Each of you will find ways to use your hand and arm as an extension of the pencil. Each position will help you render different strokes and, eventually, different textures."

Bonnie seemed delighted with her copy of a leaf. "I can see how the lines fall now," she said. She pointed at the lines within the grid. "I didn't realize each line could be measured."

Wes nodded, "Measuring by a grid is a good first step. When you get used to drawing other shapes within a grid, you'll begin to see the relationships between the object and each line framing that object, just like Steve," he grinned, "Except you can expand your vision to include other shapes beyond circles, triangles, and squares."

"I get it," Zed said as he stared at his leaf. "It has something to do with positive and negative space, too." He pointed at the area outside of his leaf. "This space is negative, and it has a shape now, too."

Bonnie, Lisa, and Deb looked at their pictures. "Wow, it does!" Lisa said. "If you stare at it long enough, both positive and negative shapes almost lose their meaning. Both appear to come forward and go backward." She shook her head.

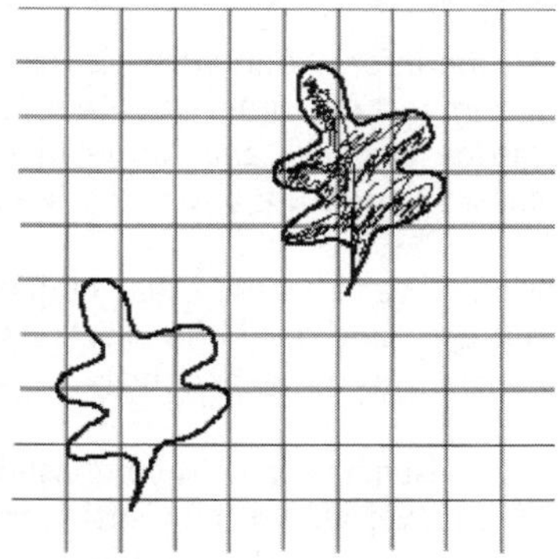

Wes and Steve laughed. "You need some tone or something to hold that leaf down," Wes said. He leaned over Lisa and added some value to her leaf. "There, is that better?"

Lisa grinned. "Sure is. I was getting very disoriented for a moment."

I asked for their attention, and began to explain the importance of the grid within Flash. "There are several reasons why we're staying with the elementary structure of the grid. First of all, it's a good way to simplify your layouts. I don't expect any of you to stick to the Rule of Thirds, as we discussed some time ago, or to restrict yourselves to a balanced and perfect symmetry within the grid composition. This is a structure that helps define your elements."

Zed added, "So if we use the grid for the layouts in our Flash designs, then it's a good thing to use a grid in our drawing processes too, right?"

"That's the idea Zed," I said. "We can use grids to help us visualize the relative scale of objects, so we can ensure they're true to proportion. We can also use the grid to draw shapes, scan them into digital images, import them into Flash, and utilize them in our concepts."

"Won't the grids show up when we scan them?" Bonnie asked.

Steve answered, "Not if you draw the grids in lightly, and erase them before you scan. You can also use tracing paper for the drawing. Just place the paper over the grid and go to town."

"You could also eliminate the grid after it's scanned in, using any combination of tools, like the Arrow or Eraser tools for instance," I added. "I'd encourage you to trace the object using the Pen tool, anyway. This will help increase your skills with vector shapes.

"You might find converting a layer into a guide layer will also make tracing it a little easier. To do this, just double click on the layer icon and select Guide from the Layer Properties dialog box. When the Flash file is published, the guide layer will not be shown.

"By the way, although I wouldn't suggest it, you can also cheat by getting Flash to automatically trace your imported image into the component vector graphics. This is done with Trace Bitmap... from the Modify menu."

"Why wouldn't you suggest it?" asked Bonnie, "It might save us some much needed time?"

"Well Bonnie, although the Trace Bitmap option allows you to set the parameters of the vector tracing, it generally produces shapes with more data and much larger file sizes. If you are going to use this, be sure to experiment first to see the output.

"Wherever possible, try and hand trace imported artwork using a grid. It is important to know how to draw shapes using the grid. You've also learned how to hold your pencils for different drawing purposes. This will help you give more life to your drawings and sketches. Remember," I added, "Learning to use our pencils in different positions will seem awkward at first, but with practice you'll soon get used to the various positions."

"Next up, get your wizard gear together!" I grinned. "We're going to learn about symbols, signs, and portents for the future."

Symbolic graphic language

All the information we've covered today leads to the development of symbolic languages. These languages are important within the Flash format, as with any online format. The use of symbols to portray messages can be powerful and can resolve identity relationships between corporate identity or images and product lines. Symbols are also often used for site navigation.

"Today we've learned that human communication is a process," I began. "We receive visual messages with our eyes, and our brain processes the images. Our perception works alongside our sight, giving us clues that conform to our experiences.

"This visual language is composed in layers of meaning, like the layers in Photoshop or in Flash," I continued. "Each layer within the visual language represents something different. One layer is language, another layer represents attitude. Another layer could be knowledge, and yet another layer could represent social and cultural influences. All of these layers can be operating simultaneously in any graphical communication.

"This form of communication is represented by objects and abstracts, and also with typography," I added. "I'm talking about the signs and signage you see everyday, and probably have become so accustomed to working with and around them that you may not even be aware you're reading a language other than what you normally speak."

Verbal and nonverbal communication

"In graphic design, this language is known as **semiotics**, or the study of visual sign making. Some of these layers are learned in childhood, and some are learned as we gain new skills," I added. "For example, the International Marine Code is known by sailors across the world. This language, or code, is created with signal flags. Each flag represents an action that needs to be taken by a sailor. This is a nonverbal communication that is understood by people who navigate by water."

"Nonverbal communication is a way to communicate to others without words," I added. I drew a marine signal flag on the board. "For instance, this flag is white with a red diamond. It means: *My vessel disabled, please communicate with me.*"

Zed asked, "So everyone across the world knows that flag stands for *help*?"

"Yes they do, Zed," I answered. "This flag doesn't have a nationality or a special verbal language. It's a nonverbal code that helps me understand you, even if we're from two different parts of the world."

Zed added, "I've been learning all the symbols drivers use to navigate roads. I didn't realize there were so many symbols until I had to use them for my *Driver's Ed* class."

Wes added, "The driver's signals aren't international, though. They're different across the world. For example, there's no international standard for a yield sign."

"Wes is right," I confirmed. "Another example of a nonverbal symbol or code used locally instead of globally is the little white blinking light we have at our traffic signals."

"You mean not everyone has those?" Bonnie asked. "I thought everyone had those lights."

"What white lights?" Lisa asked.

Steve laughed. "How long have you lived here, Lisa? Those lights signal that a fire truck or ambulance is somewhere near you, heading toward an emergency."

"Sheesh," Lisa admitted. "I never noticed them."

"This is a good example of specialized symbols," I looked at Lisa. "Don't worry. I didn't know about the white lights until I lived here for a year."

Bonnie shook her head. "I seriously thought those white lights were mandatory everywhere."

"Global communication is a tricky task," I said. "Outside of the International Marine Code, the Morse code, and a few other languages, each culture has their own set of symbols to represent their language."

Lisa asked, "Isn't sheet music a nonverbal code? I realize musicians are the only ones who can read the notes and understand how to convey the written code into music, but we all recognize it as an international code for music."

"That's a great example of an internationally recognized nonverbal code," I replied. "The language is music, and the notes and other symbols are the code used by the musician to decipher the sounds."

Wes added, "I know at least one place that's mad on using symbols to speak to all cultures. I traveled to the Philippines last year, and on the way, I had a layover in the Tokyo airport. All the signs use either Japanese language or symbols. If you don't know that language, you have to rely on the symbols to find your way around."

"Did you get lost?" Bonnie asked.

"No, I didn't," Wes said. "In fact, I found it easier and quicker to get around using these standard symbols." Wes looked at me, "Even though I know that each letter in the English language is a symbol, it seems more difficult to place all those symbols at once into a message than it does one graphic image."

"Wes has a point," I said. "The symbols we use need to be clear, and the fewer symbols we use, the more clarity we have in directional formats."

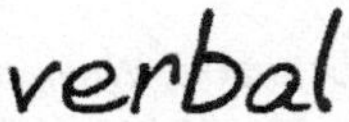

I went to the board, and began to explain the different types of symbols, or *codes*, used in our daily lives. "The first code is verbal," I wrote the word on the board. "This word is composed of six verbal code letters. You recognize these codes, and you use them to form a word that means something to you.

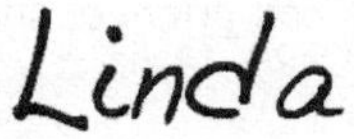

"If you didn't speak the English language, this code would make no sense to you at all. Another example is my name." I wrote my name on the board. "In English, this code word represents my name, because this is the verbal code I use to tell you who I am. In Spanish, this code means something else. It could stand for my name, but it also means *pretty*."

Wes smiled, "Your parents coded you well!"

nonverbal

Everyone laughed as I waved his comment aside and wrote *nonverbal* on the board. "This code is used to display something that means the same as a verbal code, but it's done physically. For instance, sign language is a form of nonverbal code. Unfortunately, sign language isn't universal. American Sign Language, or ASL, is based on signals that have layers of meaning within the verbal codes.

"ASL is considered difficult to learn, even among hearing impaired. Many of these individuals have developed local and regional slang to help them communicate among themselves," I stated. "For instance, if you sign the word *pizza* in New York, that same sign might confuse someone who lives in San Francisco. The codes have been altered to help ease communications within each cultural group."

"I knew that," Bonnie said. "My brother is deaf, and his group of friends has established their own form of communication that's really hard for me to follow. I studied ASL at a university, and I had to unlearn everything I knew and relearn the code with my brother."

"That's fascinating," Lisa said. "I always thought sign language was a universal language."

Representing the subject

"It is a problem to a degree," I agreed with Bonnie. "Much the same as the problem of various dialects within the English language." I wrote the words *object representation* on the board, drew an apple, and said, "This sketch represents an apple. **Object representation** is just that – a representation, or a symbol that closely resembles the real object or form. This is also called an **icon** or **iconograph**."

object representation

"So this is a code that represents the real thing, right?" Zed asked.

"Correct," I answered. "Names are also considered a realistic symbol to represent an object." I pointed at my name on the board. "The word *Linda* is a verbal code, but when I write it on the board, it becomes a visual code, as well as an object representation in the English language."

Bonnie sighed, "This is where I feel like I'm crawling through mud. Why don't things stay in just one category? How do I know when I'm using a visual code or an object representation?"

"You don't," I assured her. "The code can represent several different things at once. This is where we need to understand the implications of the variety of categories."

"Oh, I get it," Zed waved his pencil. "You're telling us we need to take responsibility for our marks. We can't just put a mark on paper and say we're done. We need to research the mark to see if it means the same thing to everyone we're trying to reach with our message."

I shook my head in disbelief. "Zed, keep wearing that scarf, you're really on form today!" Zed grinned, and looked around for more approval.

I smiled and turned back to the board. I wrote the term *abstract representation* on the board and drew a picture of a suitcase underneath." Bonnie, have you ever been in an airport?"

"No, I haven't," she answered. "I've never really had the chance to fly anywhere."

"Can you tell me what this code would mean if you were in an airport?" I asked.

She thought a minute and responded, "If I saw that symbol in an airport, I think it would indicate where I could find my luggage after I get off the plane."

Wes applauded. "That wasn't hard, was it?" he asked.

"What's the difference between an *icon* and an *abstract representation*?" Lisa asked. "They look the same to me. Both of them represent an object."

"The main difference," I answered, "Is that the icon, or object representation, is detailed and represents the actual object. The abstract representation is more symbolic." I drew a few wavy lines on the board. "What do these lines represent to you, Lisa?"

"It stands for water," she answered instantly.

"It certainly does," I answered. "And you knew this without the benefit of waves, beaches, and palm trees."

"Oh, I see," she stated. "So the simple abstract picture of a piece of luggage – the rectangle with a handle – actually means that this is where I'd find luggage in general, not just that particular piece of luggage."

"That's right," I answered. "Images used for abstract representational codes are very generic, and they're known as **symbols**. They're recognized by many cultures and have stood the test of time, because they're simple and clear. This symbol for water," I explained, "Was created hundreds of years ago by our ancestors. It still stands as a strong global code, or symbol, for water."

"Is this also a logo or a mark?" Bonnie asked. "I'm trying to fit these all into the right categories," she smiled.

"A logo or mark," I explained. "Is an abstract representation of a company or an idea." I drew a heart with an arrow through it, "What does this represent?" I asked.

Wes groaned, "A broken heart. A symbol I'm very familiar with..."

"Spare us the details, Wes." Deb said with a smile, and turned to me to ask, "A company logo can also become an object representation, if you use the company name, right?"

"That's correct, Deb." I answered. "It can also become a mnemonic device."

"Argh!" Bonnie growled. "A what device? Nemonic?"

"That's right Bonnie, Neh-mon-ic," I pronounced the word for her again. "The beginning *M* is silent. A **mnemonic device** is a code used to trigger memory. This code is applicable to groups of people who understand the meaning behind the code. For example," I drew a house on the board, "When you see this symbol on a web page, what does it mean to you?"

Bonnie answered, "It usually represents a link back to the home page."

Deb scratched her pencil on her paper, "I thought a mnemonic device was like a keyboard shortcut in certain programs." She looked up, "Like using the keys of CTRL+C on a PC or APPLE+C on a Mac means you've copied the material selected; although the codes are different, their meaning is the same. You avoid the long route of going to the top menu, and selecting Edit > Copy."

"Well, the mnemonic device is a shortcut of a sort, and it's known to those who learn this code for a specific task. Indeed, Flash uses all sorts of codes for you use it in the most efficient way." I added, "We know about the circle and square icon in the tool bar. These are abstract representations, but they're also object representations, since they are actually a square and a circle.

"The Pencil or Brush tool symbols are icons, since they don't mean you'll use an actual pencil or brush. But, these tools represent how these items work in real life.

"The Free Transform tool symbol is very close to an abstract *non-representational* symbol, which is the same thing as a mnemonic device. This kind of code relies on an image that has no detailed likeness to real objects – they're abstract. They could represent a concept, or represent an action to be taken, or act as a representation of another code. One example of the latter is the music Lisa talked about earlier. We all know the notes represent music, but unless we're musicians who can read music, it doesn't mean anything to us."

I drew some notes on the board, "This is a code, and it represents how another language – the language of music – is to be played."

"These are metaphors, aren't they?" Steve asked. "They're objects that represent actions through symbols."

"I think so," Deb answered. "More realistically, they're all codes within a symbolic language."

"Actually, mnemonic devices include just about everything we've just talked about," I added. "A mnemonic device can be an object representation, an abstract representation, and it's a representational code. Usually mnemonics don't include typography, as it uses symbols to create a language."

"I think I've got it!" Zed was horsing around with the different tools in the toolbar. "Now, tell me again why you want us to learn codes?"

I rubbed my hands together, "You're about to find out, Zed."

Wes laughed, "I smell a challenge coming on."

I grinned. "You've just learned about the various codes used to communicate with other people. You could draw a Pen tool symbol to a person in another country and, if they were computer literate, you would both discover you have something in common.

"If you drew an abstract picture of a fork in just about any country, they would know to bring you a fork. If you showed just about anyone a picture of a rose, they'd immediately recognize this flower too."

I looked around at some very non-attentive students. They were absorbed in using the various tools in Flash. "If I can get your attention for the next ten minutes," I said, "I promise to leave you all alone for another week."

"If that's a promise," Zed stated, "You have my undivided attention."

Symbols in context

The project this week would involve the creation of a series of symbols. Since the development of site navigation would take place next week, I set several goals for the development of these symbols.

"Over the next week, you will create a series of symbols for Frieda's site," I stated. That really got their attention.

"What site? We haven't even started creating colors or backgrounds," Zed complained.

"We haven't even discussed her name or the business name," Steve added.

Bonnie seemed smug as she reminded Zed and Steve about the identity problem. "We have to capture the vision first, Zed. Then, we can talk about color and backgrounds."

"Bonnie's right again," I stated. "We're still pursuing Frieda's vision. We're going to begin this process with shapes, and the shapes will become a language representing her vision."

"You can use the tools in Flash, or any other graphics software to draw your final images," I said. "But first, you have to draw them in your drawing pads. I want to see both drawn and digital images next week, but I don't want you to use color. I just want black and white line drawings or positive and negative shapes."

"But what exactly should these symbols represent?" Zed asked.

I wrote the assignment on the board as I talked. "I want you all to come up with three website navigation devices; one for **home**, one for **history**, and one for **gallery**. Each graphic you develop will fall under two categories: *object representation* and *abstract representation*. These symbols can be a combination of codes, typography, and any other shapes you want to use to get your message across."

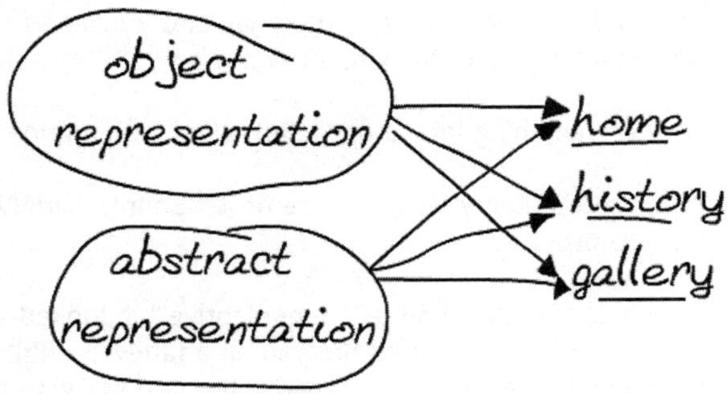

I started to write on the board on the board as I re-explained each category clearly, "**Object representation** is a symbol that resembles an actual object, like the suitcase sign at an airport. You can also use type with this form of communication."

"**Abstract representation** is a symbol that expresses the idea, without using the letters or sounds of the word that represent the idea. This would be like the wavy lines I drew that represented water. Typography usually isn't used with the abstract representation."

"Wait a minute, whoa!" Bonnie held her hand up, "You mean you want six graphics from us next week, and they're supposed to be drawn *and* computerized? That's twelve graphics!"

I agreed, "That seems like a lot, but the computerized representations won't take long, if you've done your work right." I walked back through the students and explained the process. "First, I want each of you to work alone." I looked at Wes, Zed, and Lisa. "No cheating." Lisa blushed, and Zed groaned. "I also want you to use the words we developed today in our initial brainstorming session. I'd encourage you to add even more words. Begin to make code relationships between the words and Frieda within these three categories.

"I hope to see at least three pages of sketches for ideas as you go through this process. This is minimal for developing a new language, which is essentially what you are doing for each set of navigation devices.

"The icons might seem easy, since you'll be tempted to use a picture of a cabinet for the gallery. Just remember that people might believe you're going to talk about a particular cabinet, rather than a full *range* of cabinets.

"You might be tempted to use the word *history* for the history icon, but you'll have to be conscious of your typeface, and the message it sends to the viewer. Does it fit with Frieda's vision, and have you conveyed this vision through that typeface?"

I looked around. "One final rule – please don't use a house to represent the *home page* button. Be more creative, OK?"

Wes spoke up, "Why do you want us to work alone?" He glanced at Lisa, who seemed forlorn.

"Because I want everyone to experience what you experienced today Wes." I addressed the class. "I want you all to work somewhere where there's no disruption. Put on some music, if you want. Start with some of the words you have listed, and when one of them strikes you, let yourself go with some free association. Don't censor yourself. Bring your own experiences, perspectives, and languages to the table next week.

"Today we covered a lot of material, and you've all developed a lot more confidence in your skills. You're now ready to begin thinking in symbols."

"Is there anything left to do?" Zed asked with a grin.

"Oh, there's plenty left, I'm sure of it," Bonnie said. "Anyway, we've only barely touched the third step of a six-step process."

I smiled. "Bonnie, you're so perceptive." I looked around at the slightly stunned students. "Any final questions? If not, then I'll bid you all a farewell until next week." I packed my bags and left the six student designers to start playing around with Flash MX with a lot more confidence than before.

Summary

This week's lesson was a pretty intense series of lectures relating to learning visual languages. We began by producing and analyzing a finalized client brief, which should always include the following details:

- Client Profile
- Client's Objectives
- Market Profile
- Anticipated Outcome

From there, we discussed some of the other client deliverables that we may come across –a contract, the timeline, various progress reports, and platform usage.

Next, we talked about the visual symbols used for a client's identity, including logo and brand image. The class began the ideation process using verbal clues that would lead to visual symbols and the overall look and feel for Frieda's site. As this brainstorming session progressed, the students discovered some techniques that would help them ease into the process of laying their ideas on the table. These techniques included:

- Rhetorical figures borrowed from literature
- Learning from their own and each other's experiences
- Learning to view things from another perspective

After this session, the students went to the computers and learned how to manipulate the tools available in Flash MX toolbar:

- Arrow, Subselection, and Lasso
- Line, Oval, and Rectangle
- Pen, Pencil, and Brush
- Free Transform and Fill Transform
- Ink Bottle and Paint Bucket
- Eyedropper
- Eraser

Finally, we studied the symbolic graphic language, incorporating the study of visual sign making, and verbal and nonverbal communications. Within this realm, the students learned about object representation and abstract representation.

In the next lesson we'll be looking at creating visually striking designs in Flash MX to refine the client's identity.

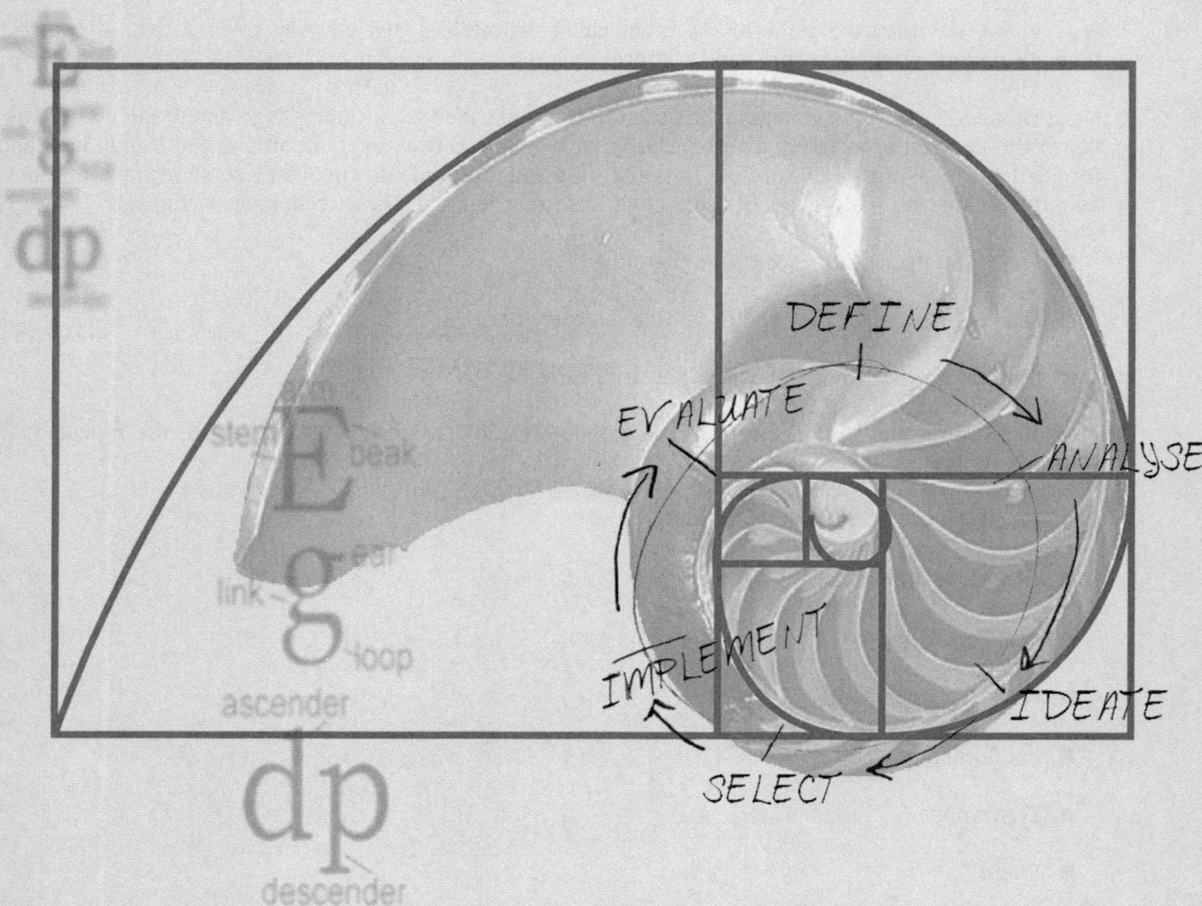
DEFINE
ANALYSE
IDEATE
SELECT
IMPLEMENT
EVALUATE
stem
beak
ear
link
loop
ascender
descender

Chapter 6

Dynamic Visuals

Objectives

In today's class you will learn about:

- The critical process of design
- Refining the client's name and identity
- Organizational models
- Creating a flowchart to represent the client's website
- Symbols in Flash MX:
  - Button
  - Graphic
  - Movie Clip
- An art history overview

Introduction

This morning, I walked in on five students who seemed highly motivated and absorbed in their work. They all stood around the table, bent over various projects, talking excitedly about the possibilities for Frieda's site.

I set my bags on the floor, "Everyone seems much more animated than last week. When I left, I thought none of you were coming back."

"I think you must really underestimate us, Linda," Wes said. He stood with his hands on his hips. "We've made some headway this past week."

I looked at the drawings and printouts scattered on the table. "Looks like everyone's done a great job," I smiled. "There are the beginnings of some interesting and inspirational work here."

"Beginnings?" Zed stood straight and looked at me with surprise. "Some of these are amazing!" He held up some illustrations of leaves with type. "Aren't these awesome? I never thought about using leaves, but look what Lisa did."

"So you all remembered to bring a combination of object representation and abstract representation? " I stated. "Nice touch with the organic shapes, Lisa! "

I asked them to have a seat at the table. "Let's go over what we'll cover today," I said. "Then, we'll take a look at the work you've all done. But wait a minute, we're one member down on our usual class..."

Just then, Deb straggled into the room; hair messed up, tools and art dropping out of her arms. As she dropped her bag to the floor, Wes and Steve picked up the trail she left behind her. "This is what I get for leaving my watch at work," Deb gasped. "I decided work was the only place where I really needed to keep track of time. I guess I've gone a little overboard on that decision."

Wes laughed. "Deb, I admire you more and more each week."

Zed smiled, "Nice to see you in sandals, too."

Deb grinned. "Before you know it, I'll be living in the warehouse district, splashing paint on canvas." She looked at me, "I'm sorry for being late, but I was buying some music and lost track of time. When you asked us to create a space for ourselves and listen to music to create new words and symbols, I realized I had nothing that reminded me of Frieda."

Wes placed her artwork on the table. "You're really getting into this, aren't you?"

Bonnie looked at Deb thoughtfully and asked, "Was the music supposed to remind us of Frieda?"

I grinned, "Let's just say that Deb seems to have been inspired by last week's class. We'll talk about this as we go over our assignment. Last week we went from business practices to creative ideation and then to symbolism. It's no wonder you all appeared to be in shock when I left – that's a lot of information for anyone to absorb."

I continued, "Today we'll streamline the process and focus on refining our client's image with what we've discovered last week. Accordingly, we'll spend more time at the computers today..."

"Yes!" Zed raised his fist in the air.

"...because we need to organize Frieda's data. We'll learn about some methods of organization. We'll refine some of our symbols as we learn to use the Library in Flash MX. We'll also learn how to organize content in Flash, so our elements won't get away from us. Additionally, " I nodded in Wes's direction, "Our resident artist will educate us briefly on some art movements. This will help us bring the art content of Frieda's site design into focus."

"Will we make a decision on Frieda's business name today, too?" Steve asked. "This issue is still bothering me, and I want to talk about it when we have a chance."

"Sure, Steve. We can talk about that bit of business today, too." I asked them to retrieve their drawing pads, pencils, and any other tools they would need to draw and sketch ideas. "Let's continue with the ideation phase of the creative problem-solving process. We'll look at a few ideas for navigation, and then we'll move on to the process of refining the client's identity and image, before implementing these ideas in Flash."

The critical process

For their assignment over the week, each student designed two sets of three different navigation symbols, forming a total of six different symbols. Since time was limited, I asked the students to spend five minutes choosing the best three for critique as a refresher to the elements and principles of design.

"Please understand these choices don't eliminate other possibilities. We'll just see what appeals to all of you right now, knowing what you know about Frieda," I instructed. "Let's critique these examples within the framework of the *elements* and *principles* of design."

Elements of Design	Principles of Design
1. Line	1. Contrast
2. Shape	2. Direction
3. Color/hue	3. Emphasis
4. Movement	4. Economy
5. Space	5. Proportion
6. Value	6. Balance
7. Texture	7. Rhythm
8. Typography	8. Unity

The students bent over the table and debated examples while I listed the elements and principles of design on the board. When I finished, I asked if they had made their choices. "This is a tough on-the-spot decision," Wes stated. He looked around at his classmates. "Do we have the finalists?"

Everyone agreed, and they presented their three examples. The first one was Lisa's leaf and type symbols. The second was Bonnie's, consisting of a series of three stars, one open, one with a circle in the middle, and another with a square in the middle. Steve created the third set of symbols. He had three circles textured with wood grain.

"These are very interesting, and they're all very different," I stated. "I'd like Lisa to talk a bit about her symbols, then we'll got through a constructive critical process them." I nodded at Lisa. She took a deep breath, and began to explain her choices.

"I saw a leaf in a magazine that was really graceful, and it reminded me of some of the words in our word list from last week. The photograph hit me, and I thought of more words, like *graceful*, *natural*, and *outdoors*. These words also seemed to fit Frieda herself.

"So, I scanned the leaf, imported it into Flash, dropped out all the color, and added a gray value." She shrugged. "I just got deeper and deeper into the shape, and then I decided to add type. My problem was that I couldn't find a typeface that seemed to fit Frieda, so I used a typeface that seemed to go with the shape of the leaves."

"Thanks, Lisa." I asked the rest of the class what they thought, as they compared the project to the design elements first. "We're not dealing with color at this point, so that leaves seven elements. Why don't each of you take one element and I'll finish with the seventh."

Wes spoke up first. "I like the line of the *y* in *History* and *Gallery*, because it leads my eye back into the leaf. It's almost circular, the way my eye follows the lines." He added, "The other thing I noticed was how the leaf seems to point. It could almost be used as a directional symbol on its own."

Bonnie said, "I like the connection between the leaf and Frieda's use of wood in her products. And the organic shape of the leaf is in contrast to the angular and man-made nature of here products."

"It moves me, Lisa," Zed grinned. "Seriously, Lisa indicates motion with the curve of the leaf. It looks like it's falling from a tree. I think that's why we made the connection between the leaf and the wood in the tree."

Deb nodded, "The space between the words and the shape of the leaf is interesting. Like Wes said, there seems to be unseen arrows leading our eyes around the shape."

Lisa smiled, "I didn't think I'd have to critique my own work." She looked at her symbols. "I decided to base my work on values. I chose the gray without outlines for the leaves, since the type needed some contrast. I tried several ways to portray the leaves, but the softer gray value seemed to work best, rather than a stark black and white."

"I see texture between the softness of the leaves and the hard, black type," Steve said.

"That's great so far." I was pleased at their thoughtful answers. "I'm glad you tried type with this, Lisa. It's interesting you chose the type to complement the leaves. Who knows – you might have stumbled across a typeface that will be part of Frieda's vision. Even though it doesn't incorporate stark angular lines, like we would expect for the shape of cabinets, it might be a nice contrast."

"Plus," Steve added, "It seems feminine. That might work for Frieda."

"That's an interesting point, Steve. I'm not sure how we classify typefaces as feminine or masculine, but it happens in many societies. We'll cover typefaces in more depth next week. Until then, Lisa, I have to say that you chose your type well to fit with the shapes of the leaves. Let's try a sans-serif typeface later for some contrast, to see how that looks."

"It would be great to have some other opinions as I try things out," Lisa said. "It was tough working on this alone. I guess that's what you wanted us to realize with this project, right?"

"That was part of it, Lisa," I answered. "The other part was to get your own stamp on the designs. I wanted to see what you would come up with on your own.

"You all mentioned several principles of design when you talked about the elements of Lisa's work. The focus, I believe, is in the nice use of contrast she used throughout each element. Anyone have any other thoughts?" I asked.

Zed volunteered, "I'll give this a shot. She uses direction when she leads our eyes around with the positive and negative shapes. Plus..."

Lisa interrupted, "Zed, you're talking about me like I'm not here. Can you talk to me directly?"

Zed looked at me, and I nodded. "Sorry, Lisa. Where was I? Oh, yeah... the emphasis is on the type, since it's darker. Your proportion of type to leaf is great, since the lighter value of the larger shape balances the darker type, too. Using the repetition of the leaf shape gives us rhythm, especially since it has movement, too. It all seems very unified." He looked at Lisa. " You've worked to achieve economy, but I wonder if even more can be left out, and we'd still have the same feelings about the symbols."

Lisa looked at her symbols, "How much more could I leave out?"

"Maybe just show a portion of the leaf, make it more abstract," Zed suggested.

"That's an interesting point, Zed," I said. "Let's see if we can push the limits on this a bit more, OK?"

Lisa nodded. "That is an interesting thought. I wonder how far I can take it before the whole essence of the leaf disappears?"

I looked at the class. "Lisa brought up an important point in the critical process. It's always nice to address the artist or designer if they're present. Their work is under the magnifying glass, and they often feel they're under that glass with their work. Anyway, you all did great job of critically analyzing the work according to the fundamental elements of design."

Lisa thanked the class, "I'm thrilled you all saw everything I was trying to communicate through the symbols. That's a great feeling!"

Wes nodded, "It really is an awesome feeling to know your art has been read as an understandable language."

We moved on to Bonnie's stars. When I asked the class why they chose these symbols, the reasons were varied. All of them agreed the continuity and rhythm of the shape was interesting. The addition of a circle for history, and a square for the gallery intrigued them. When asked, Bonnie explained her choices.

"I chose a star as the foundation for each icon because I felt Frieda was a star in her field. I was messing around with the tools that we learned in Flash last week, and came up with something that just spoke to me. While I made the star shape, I also selected the points and made the star a little different from the average star.

"I thought of other people looking into Frieda's past, and it seemed almost invasive, like being under a looking glass. Most magnifying glasses are circular, so that's the shape I chose to make this star different," she said as she pointed to the star in the middle.

"The square didn't take much thought. I just used it in contrast for the circle, and also because her cabinets are angular... maybe you could even interpret it as relating to the frames of pictures in an art gallery – the thing I really like about using such basic shapes is that they are so open to interpretation."

Wes noted that the smaller shapes within the star shapes were above the middle line of the shapes. "Did you use the Rule of Thirds within the stars to establish the location for the smaller shapes?" he asked.

"I did, yes. But more so because it just seemed right, rather than any strict need to conform," Bonnie answered.

"That's interesting, because most pictures are framed in mats that have a larger margin at the bottom than at the top," Wes replied. "This is an optical illusion that makes the picture appear to be more aligned to eye level."

"What do you mean by *mats*," Zed asked. "Are they like wrestling mats?"

Wes laughed, "No, they're the thin illustration board or hardboard that surrounds a picture in a frame, Zed."

Steve looked closer at the stars. "I didn't notice this before, Bonnie. It seems that the placement of the smaller shapes within the star shapes makes the star seem to bulge out."

"I thought maybe that was because of the shape of the star itself," Zed added. "Either way, it's really interesting. You seem to have added a kind of depth with the placement of the shape. Very cool!"

"Thanks!" Bonnie seemed proud of her effort. She sat back and added, "I still don't like the *home* star, though. Something's not right, but I can't put my finger on it."

"Bonnie, the only problem I have is the stark outline," Deb said. "For some reason that star doesn't seem to go with the others. I agreed to choose yours because the second two stars were really creative. I think these images could be pushed further, especially as a visual language for an entire site. Let's play with these some more, too."

Bonnie nodded, and we began to look at Steve's symbols. "What attracted everyone to these images?" I asked.

Zed laughed, "I liked them because they looked like knobs on a dresser drawer."

Steve groaned, "Is that the only reason you voted them in?"

"I liked the texture too. I could see these as different colors, representing the different woods Frieda works with," Zed replied.

"I agree, it'd be interesting to see what colors could do to these icons," I said. "Why did you choose circles, Steve?"

"I remembered what you said last week about the circle being a pure shape, supported by the shapes of triangles and squares. I also researched modern Scandinavian design on the Internet," Steve answered. "A lot of the images I saw were circular or organic in shape. The circles really stuck with me. Then," he added with a smile, "I went to the library, and checked out a few books on Scandinavian design..."

"Oh, so that's where those books went!" Lisa laughed. "I went looking for the same thing."

Steve grinned. "I guess I beat you to it."

"Ah, the true nature of competitive design rears its ugly head," Wes grinned. He looked at Lisa and said, "Don't bother to look for books on various wood types. I've got them all."

Zed groaned. "Hmm, so that's where those books went too! This is like detective work."

"We'll have to bring our books to class next week and share them," I said. "I didn't realize you all would take this project so seriously."

Wes shook his head, "Once again, you underestimate us." He turned to Steve. "I like how you added depth through value," he said. "And, I think you've made the circles organic by adding the texture of the wood grain."

Zed added, "Great movement with the lines in the wood grain. I like that you didn't use the same grain for each piece. That makes them a little different, event though they're all the same shape."

Bonnie asked, "But how can we tell which button is *home*, *history*, or *gallery*?

Steve said, "I wondered about that, too. Then I realized that we'd be using these in Flash MX, so I could make the look of these buttons change when a mouse cursor rolls over them, or I can use sound to say which is which."

He looked at me, "I realize we were supposed to create symbols without the direction of format. I just didn't know where to take them from here."

"You created an interesting situation for yourself, didn't you?" I asked. "How would you use these symbols in a graphics standards manual, where they might be used in print or some other medium?"

"I guess I need to push these a little more, too," Steve frowned.

"Don't take these first efforts too seriously," I said. "This exercise was constructed to reinforce the elements and principles of design, and to get the mental wheels rolling on Frieda's identity. One thing I want you all to learn from this is that your first idea isn't always your best idea.

"If you have an idea in the shower, keep that thought and write it down or sketch it when you've toweled off. Take your time, and develop another idea based on the first one. By the time you go around at least five times with idea developments, you might have an original and creative design."

Deb looked exhausted, "Learning to design is hard work."

Wes and Steve agreed. "But," Steve answered, "I've never had as much fun working at anything else."

I agreed with Deb and Steve. "Design *is* intensive work, but it's also exciting work. Especially as we learn more about how the process is structured.

"Most of you implemented the elements and principles of design in these samples. Although I didn't see much thought given to rhetorical figures or how you might carry these symbols through to the rest of the site, I did see some implications to Frieda's vision. But some of these ideas can be carried even further. That's why the first idea isn't always the best idea. There's so many items to check off in the process, there's no way we could utilize them all in the first sketch."

"Why does creativity have so many boundaries?" Zed asked. "I thought a free spirit was all we needed."

Wes looked sympathetic. "This is one thing I've found to be true," he said. "We can't break rules until we know what we're breaking. Otherwise, our work has no merit."

"Wes is right," I replied. "You also need to remember who you're speaking to – if your market doesn't understand you, they won't bother to listen.

"OK, let's get back to defining and enhancing our client's image and identity."

Refining the client's identity

The students needed a resolution to Frieda's business name, because they were about to take her identity to another level with type and color over the next few classes. They've already learned that the first idea isn't always the best idea, and they're very familiar with the creative problem-solving process. The combination of this knowledge will help them make a quick, yet very important decision.

As we sat at the table, I asked them how they planned to resolve the name problem.

Defining the problem

"We define the problem, of course," Zed answered. He drew a circle on his drawing pad and posed the problem to himself: *New business name?*

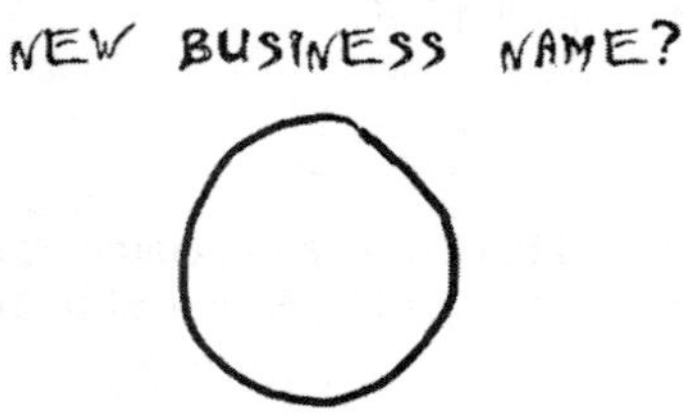

"Frieda's used her own name for three years," Zed stated. "She hasn't done a lot of marketing, so she could probably change the name of her business. I think that's the whole problem, isn't it?"

Steve nodded, "Her problem is whether or not to change the name of her business." He looked at Zed's drawing pad. "That was fairly straightforward. If no one else has anything to add, let's begin analyzing the problem."

Analyzing the problem

Zed wrote *analyze problem* further along the circle.

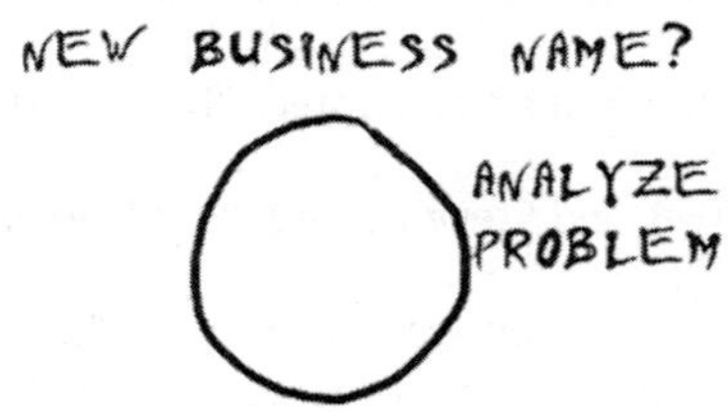

Lisa leaned in to talk, "The way I see it, Frieda's been in business for three years, using her own name. Even though she hasn't done extensive marketing, she's still known by her personal name."

"I agree," Deb added. "Plus, using her name is a very personal thing. It makes her feel approachable. After all, her competitors aren't known by their first or last names. If we keep her name, it might be a nice contrast to her competition's impersonal aspect."

"That's a great point, Deb," Steve agreed. "What about professionalism?"

Wes tapped his finger on his chest. "I go by my own name in my business, and I'm professional. I don't think using a personal name has anything to do with how someone does a job. I agree with Lisa and Deb."

Steve spoke up again, "One thing we might take into account is that Frieda and her father have the same surname. She took over his clientele, and they're familiar with the Ray name in quality carpentry. Should we use her full name or just the last name?"

Brainstorming

Wes leaned on the table. "I don't know about you guys," he said. "But, I'm partial to using her full name for the reasons already stated. Her current market already knows her by her name; any change might put them off. Plus, the use of her name indicates the continuity of a family business to this market.

"In addition," he emphasized, "I like the idea of her name representing her as an artist in her field. She doesn't mass-produce her cabinets. This, in my opinion, makes her an artist, since she oversees each line herself. This might appeal to the high-end potential market."

I saw Zed scribbling on his pad like a man possessed, "What are you writing, Zed?"

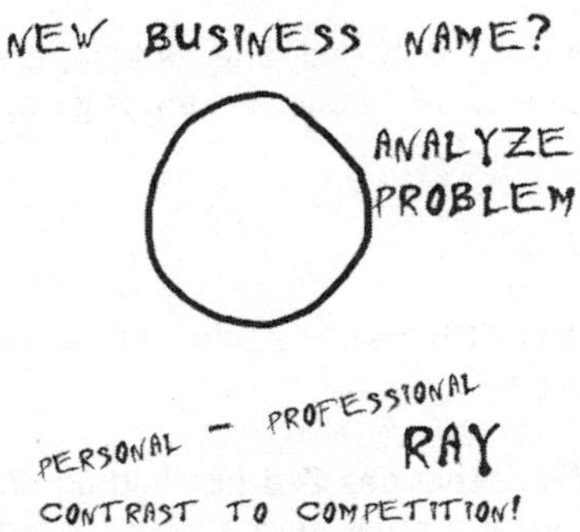

He looked up with surprise, "I'm taking notes. We need to justify our decision to Frieda, right?"

"Good idea, Zed." Steve added, "I guess this information should be included in a report to Frieda when we meet with her again."

Bonnie looked around at everyone, "Have we decided to use her name, then?"

Deb responded, "We haven't talked about what we'd name her business if we didn't use her personal name. Is that important?"

Lisa put her hands down on the table and looked at them while she spoke. "I don't know, Deb. I thought about names for her business all week long. I was having the same problem Frieda had herself. Every one of my ideas seemed corny or clichéd."

She looked up, "I think we'd be doing a disservice to Frieda to steer her away from the current use of her name. She's proud of being the only female in the business locally, and she's also proud of her work. To use anything else would hide Frieda behind a barrel, in my opinion."

Steve added, "Plus, we don't have the capabilities to test the market for a new name. It would be awful to implement a new name and have it fail after all our work. That would be a bit unprofessional."

Deb nodded and looked around, "Are we all in agreement?" Everyone nodded. "Good." Then she stopped and looked at Zed's drawing pad. "How are we supposed to brainstorm a problem that's already selected to implement?" She looked up in shock. "Wow – we just brainstormed Frieda's business name, didn't we?"

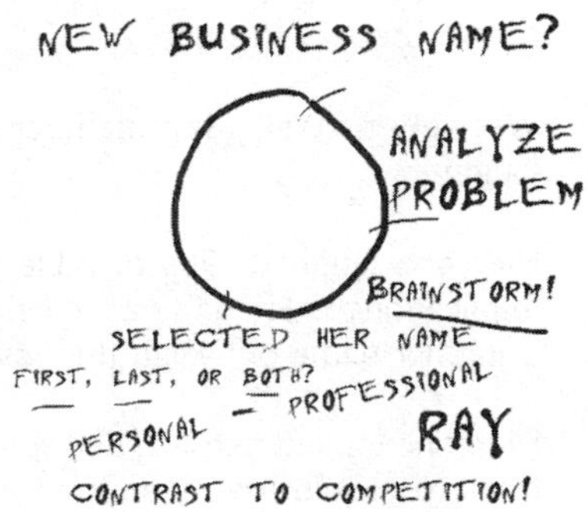

Wes laughed. "Pretty painless, wasn't it?"

"In the real world, this process could take months," I reminded them.
"Then again, it might take only one phone call or one day of research. Each problem is different. In the real world," I added, "You would also need to make sure her name isn't being used by competition. You might want to check to see if a domain name is available under her name, and you may even look into trademarks or service marks in case Frieda ever wants to incorporate her business.

"For now," I stated, "I appreciate your quick decision on this problem," I added.

Zed nodded with Deb and scribbled his notes. "Before I forget..." he wrapped up his writing and looked at the class. "I want to add that we didn't look at the idea of using her name as it sounds, and not as it looks."

I was floored. "Zed, that's brilliant. I wasn't going to approach this idea until we tackled the use of her name as an image next week. Since you've mentioned it, why don't you explain what you mean?"

"Think about what her name sounds like," he said. "Say her name out loud." Everyone muttered her name. Zed looked exasperated. "No, I mean really say it out loud and hear how it sounds."

Everyone said her name out loud, and Wes repeated it several times. "*Free-da-ray, free-duh-ray, free-daray.*" He stopped and looked amused. "That's interesting," he said. "We could almost make a new word based on the sound of her name."

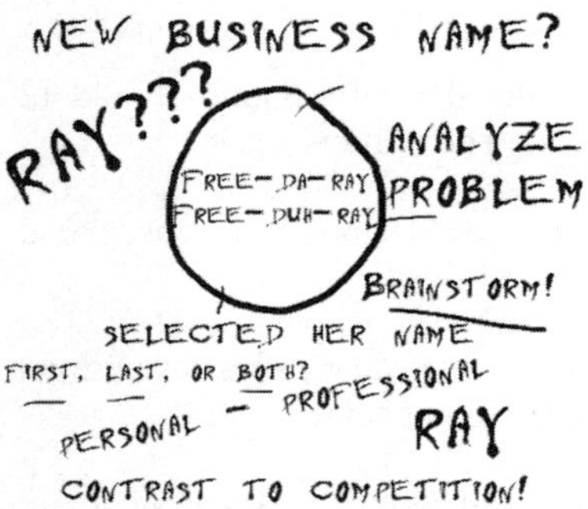

"I'll put a stop to this idea at the outset," Deb said. She looked very determined. "The first part of her name says *free* and we're not giving her work away."

Steve laughed. "You've got a point, Deb."

Zed blushed and shrugged his shoulders. "Oh well," he said. "I thought maybe there might be something there."

"There's no wrong idea," I assured Zed. "The idea Zed just had about using a name as a basis for a new word is a great device to use when you're looking at all the possibilities. I have to agree with Deb on her rebuke, though." I grinned at Deb, "We can't have the implication of *free* bouncing around with high-end clientele; this word has clear connotations that don't work for them."

Bonnie asked, "Well, wouldn't just the sound of her name hurt her, then? From now on, when I say her name I'll think of *free*."

"If we don't say *free* then maybe people won't think of that word when they say her name," Zed said. "I'm sorry I brought this up! "

Wes sighed. "Well just remember that her name is *Frieda*, not *free*." He looked like he was going to burst into laughter.

Everyone laughed. "It's possible to analyze a problem to death," I said. "I think we could overwork the implications to Frieda's name. One question I'd like to ask before we move on," I said, "Do the negatives with using her name outweigh the positives?"

Everyone looked pensive. Zed spoke up first. "I don't think so. If we hadn't talked about this last part, I don't think we would have seen it. I think most people won't even notice."

"Don't bet on that, Zed," Steve replied. "I think the solution to this problem is to present Frieda's name in a style that's as far as possible from the implications of *free*. Thanks for helping us see that problem."

"You're most welcome," Zed replied. He volunteered to wrap up this part of the session from his notes. "So far," he began, "We've decided to keep Frieda Ray's name for her business, because her current market is familiar with this name, and her potential market might perceive her to be personable, compared to her competition.

"There are several problems inherent with using her name," he added. "One of these problems is that the sound of her first name implies the word *free*. This problem might be overcome with the use of graphics that downplay this suggestion. There's also the possibility of using her surname alone."

"Good job, Zed," I said. "We've selected Frieda's name and arrived at the point were we're ready to implement it. You've covered the first four steps of the creative problem-solving process in a very short period of time, too. Great job!"

I added, "We really can't go any further until we begin to look at how we can arrange our client's information within a design – for this we need to spend some time studying the various organizational models and, more specifically, how we can make the best out of flowcharts."

Organizational models

The students have already gathered information on Frieda Ray's carpentry business. They've also spent time focusing this information into some basic symbols that may represent Frieda's identity. The visual indexing of information will help bring the work into focus.

"We need to make a flowchart for Frieda. This information will be included in our first report to her," I began.

"What exactly is a flowchart?" Zed asked. "And, why do we need it?"

I Looked at Wes and smiled, "Imagine Wes has created a marvelous painting. It's the most remarkable piece of work you've ever seen." Wes looked at me like I just arrived from another planet. "When you first walk up to this painting, it seems that the painting on that canvas is all there is to it. But," I said, "When you point your finger at certain sections on this painting, the canvas moves, and another picture takes its place."

Wes laughed, "Sounds like a rather special painting, too! Have you been drinking, Linda?"

Lisa smiled. "That's a good way to describe what happens when we go to a website. It looks like it should be static and just one page deep, but we've learned that all it takes is a click of the mouse to move through to something else."

"You've got it, Lisa. It's often difficult to tell how large a site is when we first see it on our screens. The site may have navigation, but we don't know how much information is held within each category represented by these navigation tools. It's not like a book, something we can pick up, weigh, and leaf through the pages. It's more like theater, where a designer's in control of what's behind each curtain, and where the audience reacts to the scenes.

"The site you'll design needs a navigational tool – you had some practice with creating symbols to represent directions within the site. The site also needs a **flowchart**; this represents the scheme of pages in a publication, whether it's in print or online. The flowchart is usually organized before any pages are designed, so the designer has a graphic model of how the site or publication will look."

"Is this like a table of contents in a book?" Zed asked.

"Similar," I answered, "But it's a graphical representation of each page. Some flowcharts use tree diagram, and others use matrices, or boxes. Let's talk about the different types of organizational models used for flowcharts, and we'll begin to design one for Frieda's site."

I stood and went to the board, "There are seven organizational models to consider." I began to tell them about these seven models as I wrote them on the board.

Organizational Models

1. *Linear*
2. *Hierarchical*
3. *Web*
4. *Overlay*
5. *Matrix*
6. *Spatial zoom*
7. *Parallel*

Linear

"The **linear** model is the easiest to describe – systems like index cards or the slides in a projector rely on a linear organizational structure. A good online example would be a gallery of images or products, perhaps organized the order of some criterion, like least expensive product first."

Hierarchical

"The **hierarchical** model is just like a traditional family tree. The head typically represents a welcome page that introduces the rest of the information. Each block of information that flows from this head has something to do with that top dog. Some websites use this tree when they include pages that aren't all connected with each other through links."

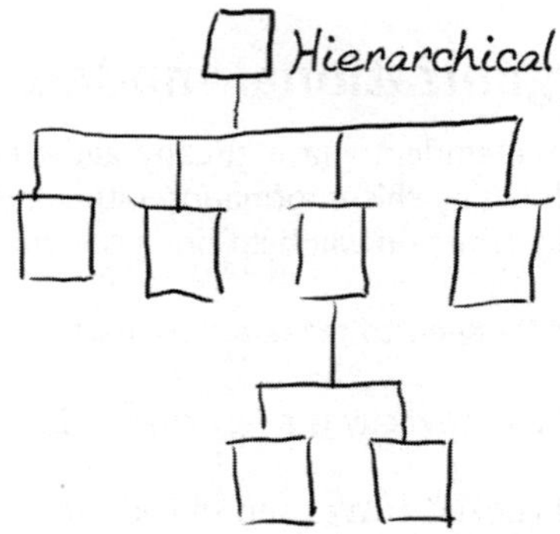

Web

"The **web** structure interconnects more like this..."

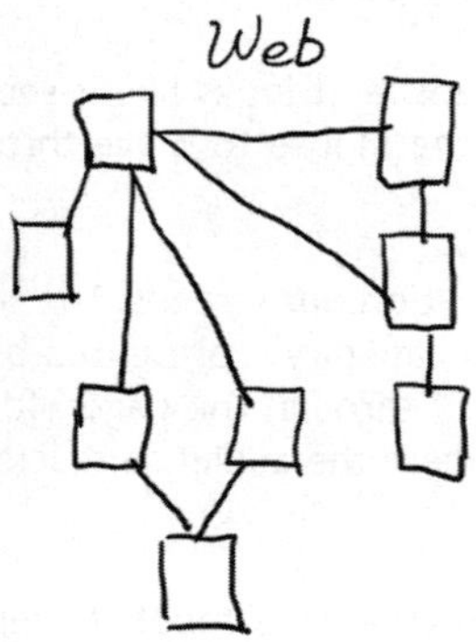

I drew a series of boxes with lines connecting various boxes to each other and continued, "This is similar to a dictionary or the index of a book – when you look up a word in a reference source, these resources will often indicate another place that will help you clarify the information. Each source is interconnected."

Overlay

"An **overlay** is another method to organize information. This is similar to the layers within the Flash authoring environment, where details are layered according to visual information. On the top layer you place the information that's most important. In this respect, it's similar to a hierarchical system. But," I added, "It's also like an x-ray in that you can visualize the relevance of each layer, and you have a clear structure holding these layers in place."

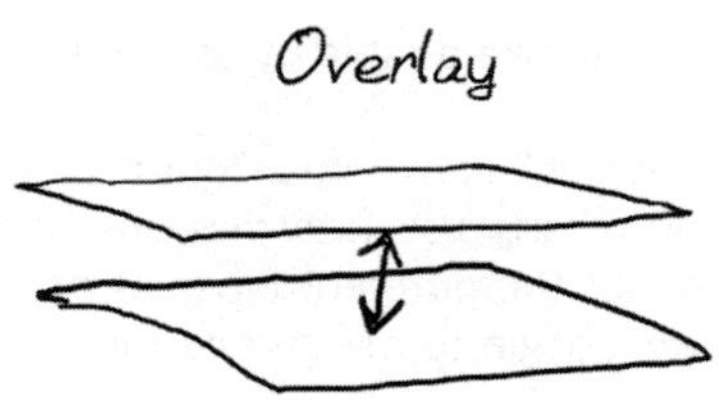

Matrix

"A **matrix** is a grid or container that holds information. In a matrix system for online information, each block may hold information. Using a matrix is a good way to align information in tables." I smiled at Bonnie. "Did you realize you were using an information system with the tables?"

"I certainly did," she replied. "A table cell holds all sort of data – images or text."

Spatial zoom

"Another tool for organizing data is **spatial zoom**. This is similar to a magnifying glass, as it picks up information and magnifies it for the viewer."

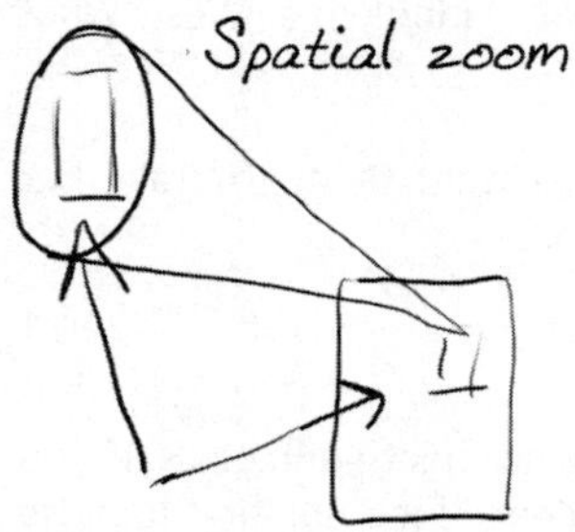

Bonnie added, "Just like zooming in on the screen in Flash!" Then she asked, "Is this the same as a pop-up ad on the web?"

Wes laughed, "If you want to magnify information no-one wants, I think that's the way to do it most obnoxiously."

I answered Bonnie, "Wes is just about right. A pop-up ad is hidden information that's been magnified. Merchants use these ads to optimize their available space. One reason many people don't like them is because they aren't in control of that activity, and they need to react to close the window or spend time checking out the advert."

Parallel

"The last technique for organizing information is the **parallel** method. This method portrays information that's shown in another medium, like a book, newspaper, or television. For example, a television schedule will tell you when and where something is on television, and a book review will often tell you what you can expect from a book."

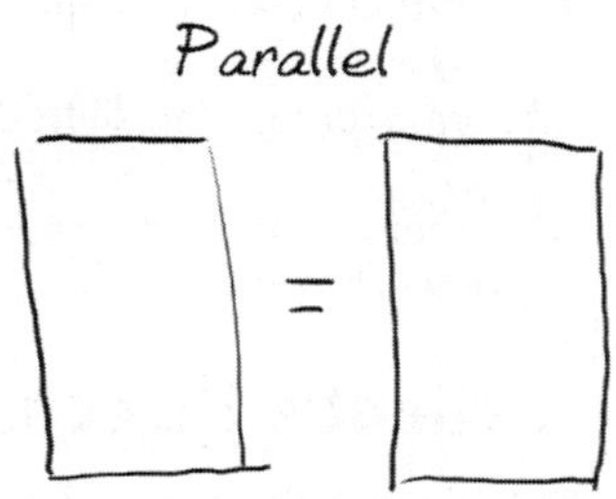

Bonnie spoke up again, "Oh! That's just like sign language, too. A signer signals nonverbal code to the hearing impaired while others listen to the same information presented in verbal code."

"Brilliant, Bonnie," I smiled.

Zed held up his hands. "I have a question. Do we use all these methods to build Frieda's site?"

"You can," I answered. "But, for this class, a simple flowchart will do. A flowchart eventually uses more than one method of organization. We'll probably end up with something that's a mix between the hierarchical and web organization models."

"One issue we need to keep in mind is usability. You know the markets that Frieda's going after. Have you thought about what they want or need?" I asked.

Bonnie answered, "I do know that the more confusing a site is, the less likely anyone will use it. Frieda's market will be very focused, and therefore usability, along with an amazing design, will be the overriding issue. The site will probably be a destination from some other form of advertising, rather than a site that will appeal to someone who just happens on it."

"I don't know," Zed said. "Why don't we design a killer eye candy site that'll win lots of web design awards? That way, Frieda will get attention for her product through competitions."

"I think the use of Flash will give us enough eye candy in itself," Steve said. "My concern is how well Frieda's customers will be able to navigate through the site."

Bonnie nodded. "You all know my main issues. I want to make the site as accessible as possible. Although this site isn't for the general public, I think it would be great if we ensure that anyone who wanted to could have a look."

"OK," I said. "I hear that some of you want a flashy site, and others are more concerned about usability and accessibility. I think we can meet both goals with careful planning, thoughtful design, and our tool of choice – Flash MX. The best thing to do is to start simple, and move slowly into complexity." I looked at Wes. "What experience would you expect to give Frieda's clients?"

Wes raised his eyebrows. "I want to show them the essence of Frieda's work. I want them to crave her cabinets with such a desire, they'll be drooling to have them in their own homes."

Steve laughed, "I think we're making a marketing manager out of Wes."

I smiled, and assured them, "The interactive format of Flash will allow all of you to meet your goals. If you dream it up, you can do it with this program. However, this can also be a problem, since our first impulse might be to go ape with all the toys!

"What you need to remember is that you are in control. Your mission is to put Frieda's customers at ease, and let them take the control from you. You give them tools and navigation, and they drive the site."

"Vroom, vroom," Zed shifted some imaginary gears. "Let's get this site on the road then!"

"OK, then," I grinned. "Let's create a flowchart for Frieda's site, and see where we're going to take her customers."

The client's flowchart

By looking at the client's flowchart, the students will be able to relate to the client's information flow. As the class sat at the table, I stood to draw the information on the board. My plan was to suggest that the students should each deliver their own project flowchart for the next class.

"Now that you understand some of the organizational models, let's start brainstorming over Frieda's flowchart," I told the students. I went to the board and drew our ever-popular creative problem-solving circle for them again. "Initially, we need to define what Frieda needs in her site. Accordingly, one of the first things we need to consider is the type of user who will look for and need Frieda's products. We'll use this information to help us build the organizational flowchart for her site."

"Generally, the flowchart would be done before any graphic symbols were generated," I stated. "However, the information flow within this class is centered on modules of information. Last week, we talked about graphic symbols and languages, and your assignment lent itself to that focus.

"Once we organize Frieda's information, you may or may not want to use the symbols you developed this past week. That will be your decision once we go over this material. Let's begin with the creative problem-solving process to help you get started with Frieda's flowchart."

Defining the flowchart

Wes began, "One of the markets for Frieda's product is the homeowner who is building or remodeling their home."

Steve added, "And we also want to reach construction workers and contractors who are about to design or build apartments, town houses, or condominiums."

I wrote *homeowners* and *contractors* on the board. "How often do you suppose these people will shop online for cabinets and storage space units?" I asked.

Lisa spoke up, "Not often, as I suppose that these people would want to actually touch and see the wood product in person."

"You're probably right, Lisa," Steve stated. "The biggest different between the two groups is that homeowners aren't going to know as much about the cabinets and how they're installed as the contractor or construction worker does."

"What about interior decorators?" Bonnie asked. "I think that's a huge market for Frieda."

I nodded, "Good point, Bonnie. Frieda will probably have to do a mailing when the site goes live, something to announce that she's online and has her work available to view."

"She has a current market, don't forget," Wes added. "If she lets folks know she's online, they'll probably catch on to her site pretty quickly."

I added *current market* and *interior decorators* to the list. "This makes four different markets we're trying to reach, and each of them can be divided into past and future markets," I stated. "If you feel we've defined her market, let's think about her product lines."

"Product lines?" Bonnie asked. "I guess she must have different lines of cabinets, but I was so focused on her love of modern Scandinavian that I didn't think about any other designs she might make."

"Good thought, Bonnie," Deb stated. She looked around at her classmates. "What are her lines, anyway?" They all looked dumbfounded.

I laughed. "I knew someone would catch on sooner or later. One of you needs to call Frieda and ask her which cabinet lines she would like to focus on."

"You mean we don't admit we forgot to ask?" Bonnie asked. "What a relief!"

Wes looked at Bonnie. "No wonder you've been struggling, lady. You're too honest." He raised his hand. "I'll call Ms. Ray and ask her which lines she wants to push. I'll tell her it would be reasonable to limit the lines to four, so she can begin to show off her love for the modern Scandinavian lines."

Bonnie shook her head, "I guess I'm not much of a business person." She looked at Wes. "That was really a great way to handle the situation. Thanks!"

Wes pretended to tip an unseen hat. "No problem, Bonnie. Before I hired my agent, I had to do my own sales for a number of years. I learned that an artist never apologizes, unless the customer complains."

"That was good, Wes," I agreed. "Every time you admit a mistake, the client loses a little confidence in your work. The ethic is that you remain honest, but the ways to procure the information you need don't have to be laced with apologies.

"Be straightforward, get what you need, and then let your client go about their business," I added. I turned to the board and wrote *gallery*. "Let's just say that Frieda has five lines of cabinets. These will be *Modern Scandinavian*, *Colonial*, *Victorian*, *Mediterranean*, and *Traditional*." I wrote these lines under the gallery heading.

"Is there anything else we need to define for Frieda's site?" I asked.

"How about the technical bits?" Bonnie asked. "We need to know about the computer capabilities for her market so we can design the site for ultimate usability and accessibility."

I wrote *computer capabilities* on the board. "Anything else?" I asked.

Deb tapped her pencil on the table. "I'm trying to think along the line of our '*who, what, when, where, why,* and *how*' questions," she stated. "We know who her markets are now, and what Frieda is selling. We need to add when she's open for business, where she's located, and why she's in a predominantly male business."

I wrote this information on the board. "I think we have the definition phase covered," I stated. "Let's move on to analyze this information."

Analyzing the flowchart

I continued, "So, tell me how you think the markets that we've identified will affect the site you're about to build."

Bonnie began with her analysis. "I think the site will have to be simple, fast, and clean," she said. "The people who will use it are busy people, and they're intent on finding cabinets and storage units for their homes and other living spaces. I think they're probably pretty focused, and they won't browse through the site unless they're purposely looking for this type of merchandise."

"I agree," Steve stated. "But, we need to remember that the sites of her competitors are almost too plain and seemingly outdated. We want Frieda's site to be eye-catching and interactive. In fact," he reminded the group, "Frieda stated specifically that she wanted interactivity."

"That doesn't mean that there will be tons of animation," I said as I looked at Zed. "Remember, interactivity can be as simple as the viewer just pressing a button. But," I added, "Flash gives us new dimensions to play with. I think we can add some movement and give the viewer the idea that they're about to see something special."

"I don't think the site should be cryptic though," Deb stated. "We need to be clear at the start where everything is, so the viewer can go right to their focus."

"Is this a complicated site or just a small *calling card* for her to get information to her markets?" Steve asked.

"That's a good question, Steve," I answered. "We can make this site as complicated as we want. However," I added, "We only have a few weeks to finish this project, so I'd suggest a simple site for pragmatic reasons.

"So the site will be direct, and it won't have anything beyond what is necessary for the homeowner or contractor to know, right?" Bonnie asked. "I don't see any reason for all the useless bells and whistles."

"We all know that Frieda wants to cater to people who have the financial means to remodel or build," Wes added. "We want to show that Frieda is savvy and up-to-date."

"What about the product lines?" Steve asked. "In following with the idea that she's a kind of *artisan*, I think we need to have a gallery for Frieda. This gallery would showcase her product lines."

"I like that idea, Steve," Lisa responded.

"I do, too!" Zed agreed. "We could show beaches for the Mediterranean line, and log cabins for the Colonial line!"

Wes laughed, "Zed, I think that might be carrying the themes a little too far." He looked at me. "Speaking of themes, shouldn't she have a theme for the site? Is there anything that would give us this focus?"

"That's a great thought, Wes. Let's deal with that in the ideation phase," I said. "Let's finish analyzing what else Frieda might need from her definitions first."

Deb spoke up, "She'll need a contact page for her hours and location."

I agreed, and wrote that information on the board. Bonnie asked, "Do you think she'll need any legal information? I mean, what if the homeowners and contractors want to know about her guarantees and that sort of thing?"

"Ah, good catch," Steve stated. "I think that a disclaimer and a few violators will help the viewers get the information they need."

"We're going to violate Frieda's viewers?" Zed asked. "I didn't know we could do that!"

Steve laughed. "I guess I need to explain a **violator**. That's a device like a circle or starburst that overlays a page. Within this shape, you would type what you want the reader to notice."

I asked Steve to draw a violator on the board, and he agreed. "They look like this," Steve stated. He drew a circle with the word *Guaranteed* inside the circle. In the starburst, he wrote *sale*. "Of course, Frieda wouldn't use something like the starburst. I think her clientele isn't looking for specials as much as they're looking for quality and reliability."

"We might use some other shapes to point out her focus on some pages," Lisa stated. "I guess we'd have to know if there's anything special she would want to say, like a link to a guarantee."

"This is all valid information, Steve," I said. "I think the violator might be used, but with restraint."

"I want to use violators, and I'd like to make them blink and roll around the page, but I guess I'll have to hold myself back," Zed pouted, "Right?"

Bonnie laughed. "I think Zed is beginning to understand that *interactive* doesn't always mean *overdone*."

Wes patted Zed on the back. "We might let you make a page with spinning violators. We just won't show it to Frieda," he smiled.

Zed perked up, "What about a splash page? Don't all Flash sites have those?"

"I'm glad you brought that up Zed." I replied. "Flash websites often have splash pages or screens. For those of you not already familiar with them already, splash pages are traditionally used before the actual content or website interface appear.

"Static HTML splash pages are often employed to show the visitor the required plug-ins and ideal browser for the website, before leading them to the website proper or to download the appropriate plug-in."

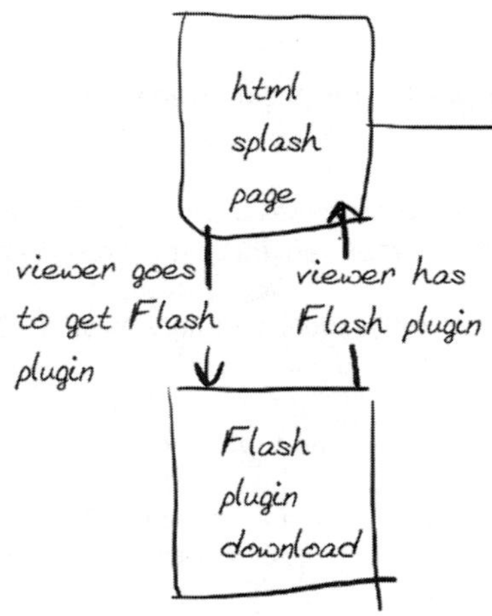

"I never have that problem," said Bonnie, "I make sure my websites are accessible through all browsers without using any plug-ins."

"The only plug-in we'll use for Frieda's website is the Flash 6 plug-in. This enables users to view the material authored in Flash MX. Frieda's site could have a splash screen warning the visitor of this requirement, but luckily, Flash MX has a built-in template to check the browser's plug-ins for us.

"The result of the check will either direct the user to the Flash site if they have the plug-in, or will display an alternative HTML version of the site in its absence. This alternative version of course will need to be created by you if you intend to use it as an option.

"So we don't really need a splash page then?" asked Steve.

"You do if there isn't an HTML version of the site available, Steve," I said. "Let's move on to the ideation phase, and brainstorm some ideas for our flowchart," I said.

Ideating the flowchart

"We've defined and analyzed the markets for Frieda's site, as well as her products and services," I reminded the class. "We also discussed the computer capabilities for the Flash site. Now," I added, "Let's throw some ideas around about how this site should be organized."

I drew a circle on the board. "Let's begin with Frieda's home page," I stated. "We know she has to have an entrance to the site."

Deb immediately added, "I think we need to add a history link and a link to a gallery, since we worked on these images already for our project this past week," she said. "Anyway, I believe those two links will be the most important parts for Frieda's site."

I added two boxes, one for *history*, and one for a *gallery*. "Before we go any further, should we connect these pages back and forth to each other, and should we connect the history and gallery pages together?"

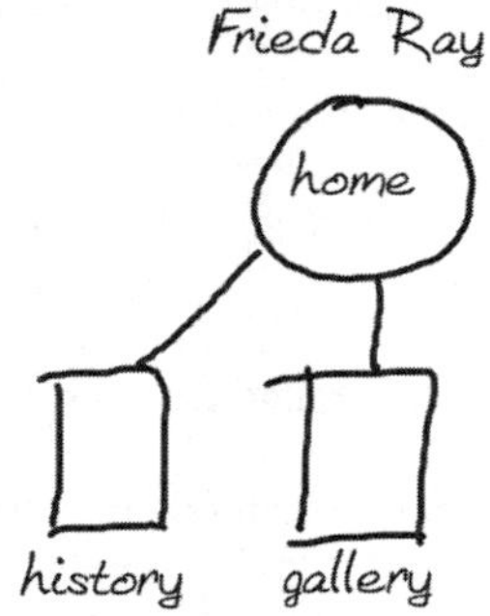

They all agreed, and I drew arrows to connect them all. I also wrote *exit*, and drew arrows from each page to that word. "Always give a person a way to go back to the main page or leave the site altogether."

"Let's add Frieda's legal information to her site," Bonnie said. "Even if it's just a *privacy statement* and a *disclaimer*, it'll help Frieda's market know she's not gathering information from them to sell to other vendors if they contact her for more information. It can also tell her markets she'll respect their privacy."

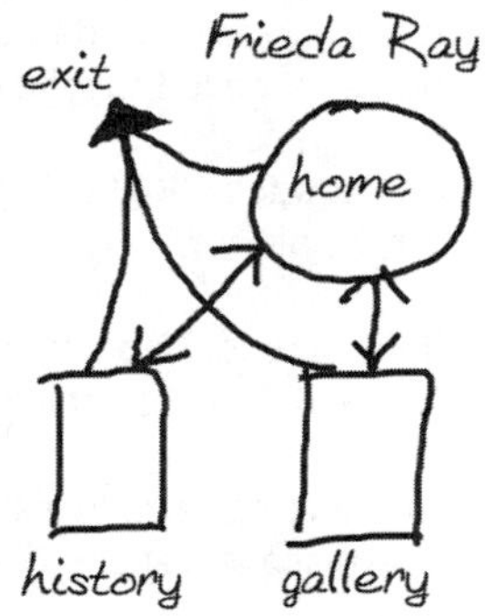

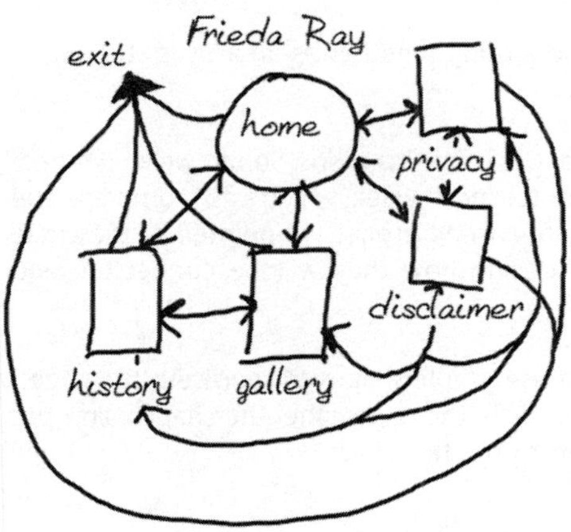

"Finally, let's add a location or *contact* page, with her address and phone number." Lisa stated.

I drew another box and labeled it *contact*. "Do we want to connect this box to any other boxes?" I asked.

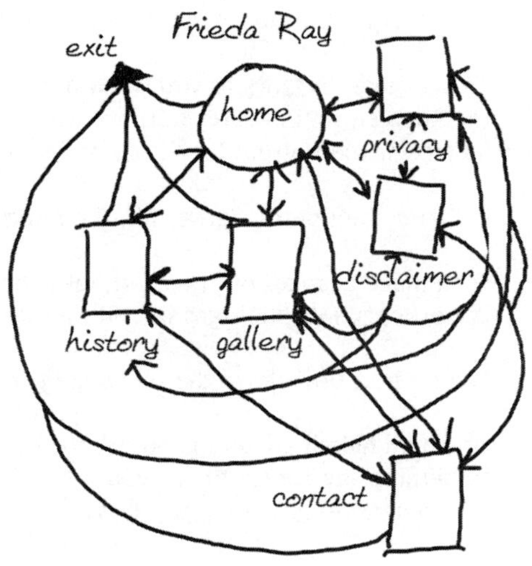

Zed looked thoughtful. "I would think a link to the contact page would need to be on every page, just like the legal information."

I drew lines to indicate the linking of these pages to the rest of the pages. "How big is her gallery?" I asked.

Zed almost fell out of his seat in his enthusiasm to answer that question. "She'll have five different categories that will lead off the gallery," he stated. "And they will all look like they belong to the site, and not have different scenes for each style of cabinet. I promise!"

Everyone laughed. "It would be hard to keep a beach and a log cabin consistent with a theme," Wes stated. "Speaking of themes, does anyone have any ideas whether Frieda needs to have a theme for her site?"

Wes looked around, and was met with a few blank faces. "C'mon folks, don't you know what a theme is?"

"I just have an image in my head of a theme park," Lisa giggled, "Something with roller coasters and huge cartoon characters. I think Zed would have a good time designing something like that."

Wes rolled his eyes, "I mean a theme as in a focus on a certain time period or a location."

Steve seemed confused. "I thought Frieda's location was in Cabinetville, and her time period is now."

Deb laughed, "Wes, I think you're having problems with this idea of yours. Maybe I can help." She looked around at the rest of the class. "I think Wes means that Frieda needs a focus for the *look* of her site. This focus would carry over from the actual look of the site to the flowchart. For instance," she said as she pointed at the board, "Frieda has a gallery. Wes wants to keep an emphasis on Frieda's artistic abilities, so we can include a page that shows Frieda's workplace and call it her *studio*."

Wes nodded, "Right! That's what I was trying to get at, but the theme evaded me. You got it, and it's perfect, in my opinion."

Steve agreed, "Now I understand what you're trying to say. I like the idea of the studio with the gallery. What do the rest of you think?" he asked.

Everyone agreed. "Great idea!" Bonnie said. "I think tying the whole thing together as an artist's studio and showplace is just the ticket."

"Hold onto those thoughts," I replied, "Because you're going to take it from this point. So far, we've defined, analyzed, and ideated Frieda's flowchart. One of your missions for next week will be to complete the flowchart. You need to do the other stages of the creative problem-solving process." I pointed at the circle on the board. "Now, you need to select the pages you want, decide how they will be connected, and implement the pages in your drawing pads.

"You can get as fancy as you want, but if you value your time, just use simple shapes to represent the pages. Use the Pen tool in Flash to draw nice curving lines to each shape. Title the page, label the shapes, and put a place at the bottom for Frieda and you to sign off in agreement to the flowchart."

"What if she doesn't agree with the information in the flowchart?" Zed asked.

"You make changes on the chart, take the chart with you, and make the necessary amends. Then you repeat the process until she signs off with her agreement."

"Won't that slow down the building of the site?" Lisa asked.

"It would help if Frieda signed off immediately," I answered. "But, the flowchart could help Frieda remember something she forgot to tell you in the initial interviews. In the meantime," I added, "You'll be working on her overall design during this class.

I looked around and asked if anyone had any other questions relating to the information flow on Frieda's site.

"I guess we don't know yet," Steve said. "Until Frieda signs off, this is what we have to work with."

"I agree," Zed said. "Let's go for it."

"Good enough," I said. I looked at Zed. "Now let's scratch your itch to get back on the computers and work with Flash."

"Great!" Zed jumped out of his chair. "What are we going to do?"

"We talked about visual languages last week," I reminded them. "Most of that lesson was centered on symbols and how they speak to us as a graphical language. Next we'll study the use of symbols in Flash MX."

Symbols in Flash

The students all understood the use of symbols as cultural and navigational tools. Now, they would learn that symbols form a major element of Flash MX. "You've all done a great job getting to grips with how and why we use basic shapes to develop symbols. In a similar context, the symbol is also an essential building block for Flash designs.

"We've already learned about the major drawing and design tools of this software. Now you should all be primed and ready to learn about Flash symbols." I didn't have to prompt Zed. He was already seated at a computer on the other side of the room, waving back at us.

I moved the rest of the class over to the computers, and they all started up Flash.

"Who remembers when we first used symbols?" I asked.

"Ah yes, that was when we looked at basic animation – the example of perspective in design, with the car moving past the tree and house." Steve answered confidently.

"That's correct Steve. And who can remember where we stored these symbols?"

"In the Library..." suggested Wes. When he realized there was a joke to be cracked, he added, "With the candlestick!"

The class was filled with laughter. "Thanks Wes." I said. "Flash symbols are indeed stored in the Library. Up until now, we've only briefly seen one type of symbol, the graphic, but Flash MX actually has three types of symbols." I turned to write on the whiteboard, "These three symbol types are **movie clip**, **button**, and **graphic**.

Symbols in Flash MX

* Movie Clip
* Button
* Graphic

"Each of these symbols behaves differently and is useful for different things. The graphic is generally used for **static** symbols, such as a simple square, whereas the movie clip is for **animation**. The button defines an object as being... well, a button! More specifically, buttons are essential for **user interaction**."

Buttons

"Let's start by studying the button symbol." I began.

Button States

* Up
* Over
* Down
* Hit

"When an image is turned into a button symbol, it is given four states – Up, Over, Down, and Hit. Each of these states define what happens at every one of the specified events.

"The first state, Up, represents how the button is seen within a design normally, without any user interaction.

"The next state, Over, shows what should happen when a mouse rolls over the button area. Steve, this is what you might use to implement your navigation icons that we saw at the start of this class." Steve nodded in agreement.

"The next state, Down," I said, "Is concerned with a mouse button press, and this state is shown after such an action takes place.

"The last state, Hit, is a little more complex than the others."

"There is always one!" said Wes.

"There nearly always is Wes," I agreed. "This last state defines the actual area of the button. This state will make more sense in a moment, after we've made our first button, but for now it's sufficient to say that the Hit state represents the area on the screen that the mouse cursor has to come into contact with in order to trigger any of the other states."

I made the class open up a fresh Flash document each, with the intention of them taking their first step towards interaction in Flash. I explained that we would make a button using the three rollover states, changing the color of the button from green to amber and then to red.

"Firstly, draw a green square anywhere on the stage and select it by double clicking on it. This will be our button.

"Now select Insert > Convert to Symbol... from the menu bar; you could also use the keyboard shortcut at this stage, F8. In the dialog that appears, select Button, give your symbol a name, and then click OK. The name you give it here is the name that it will be stored as in the Library, so give it something obvious:

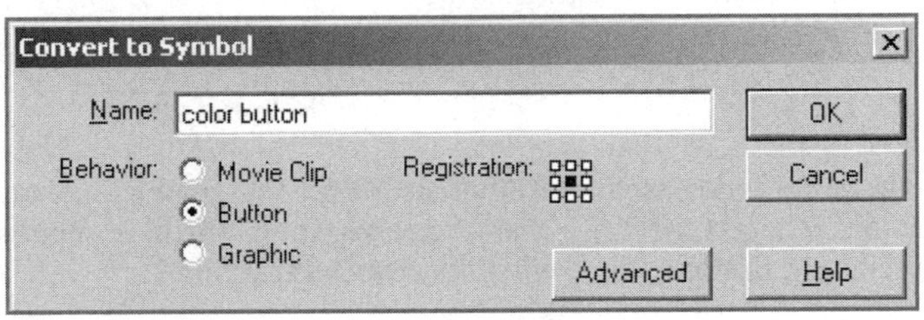

"Now select Window > Library, and you should see your new button symbol sitting happily in the Library:

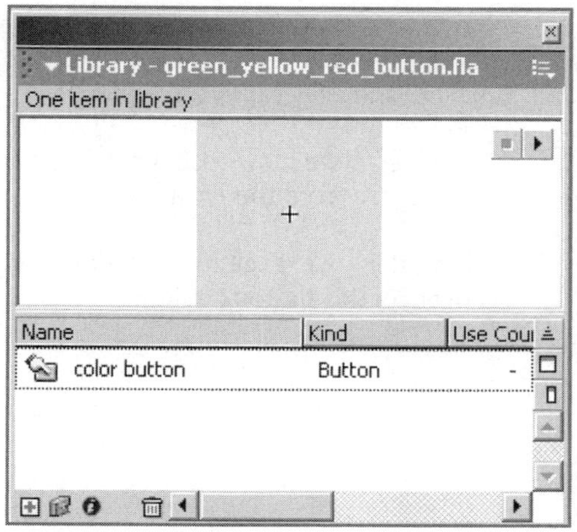

"Now we need to set the different button states by editing this symbol. To do this, just double click on the symbol in the Library."

"Hold on a minute Linda!" Zed exclaimed. "I've double clicked, and I seem to be changing the name of my symbol! "

"Ah, right Zed – I don't think you're the only one having trouble here either," I said, looking at some of the other monitors.

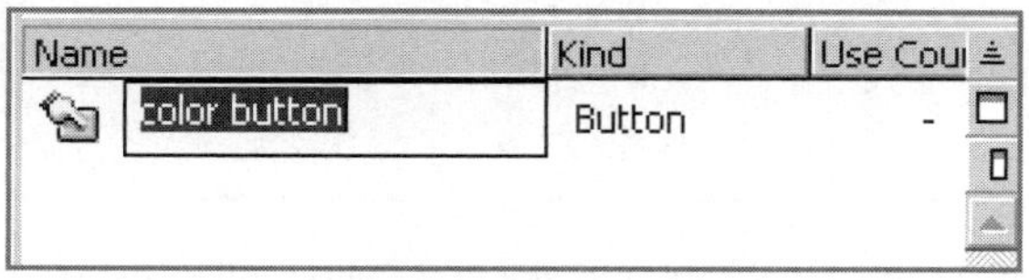

"Try double clicking on the little icon to the left of the symbol name, instead of the name itself."

"Oh yeah, that's a different result," said Zed.

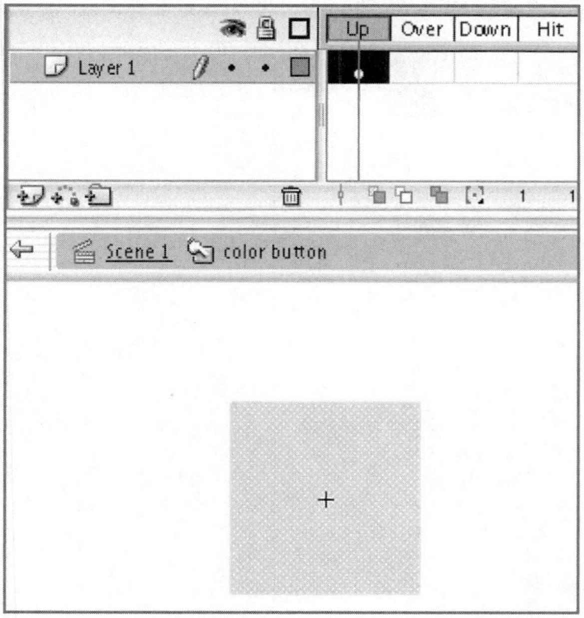

"What you all see now are the four button states that we've just discussed. They've taken the place of the standard timeline; in essence we are inside the button's own personal timeline."

"You mean we can have more than one timeline in Flash MX?" asked Steve.

"Yes you can Steve. Even though there is only one main timeline, movie clip symbols actually have their own timelines, which run parallel to the main one. We'll get onto this in a moment when we look specifically at movie clips.

"For now though, let's set our different button states. As you can already see, the Up state is already inhabited by the green square. If you click on any of the other states in the timeline, the state is highlighted, but nothing else happens. This is because the Up state is the only frame that has content right now."

"It's worth noting that the original image that we choose to convert to a button symbol always forms the Up state of the button."

"Right, let's now add an Over state. Start by clicking on the empty Over state on the timeline, and select Insert > Keyframe:

"The Over state now also contains the same green square from the Up state."

"I don't think we'd see much action if we did a rollover on this button." said Zed.

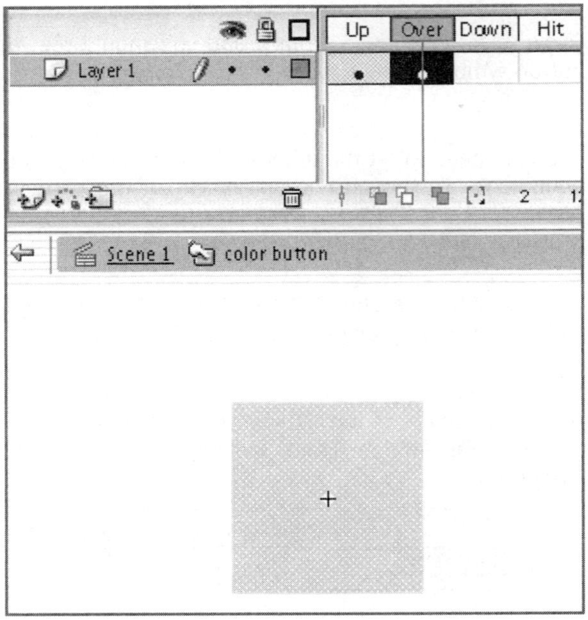

"Not yet anyway, Zed," I replied. "Select the square with the Arrow tool and select a yellow fill color from the Colors selector in the Tools panel. This will change the color of the selected object."

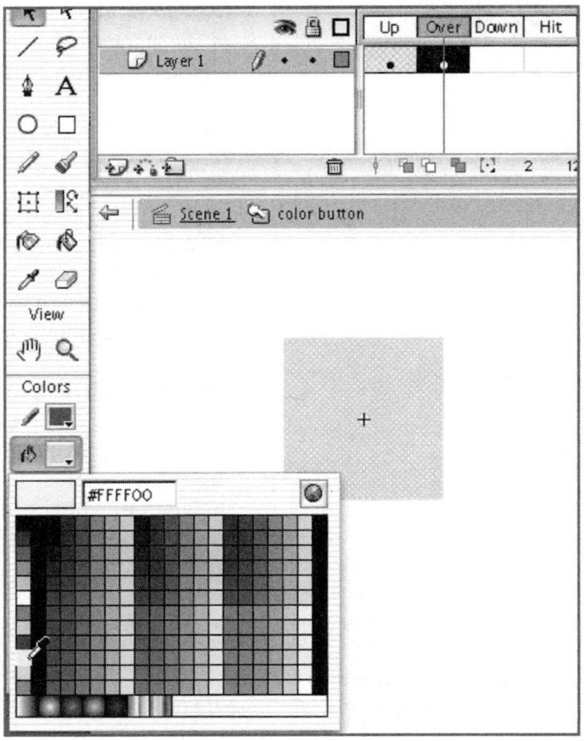

I made the class try their first button rollover by testing the movie, even though we weren't yet finished. I showed the class how this is done, by selecting Control > Test Movie, or by using the shortcut keys Ctrl+Enter on a PC or Apple+Enter on a Mac.

"It might not be the most exciting thing that you've done on a computer, but it signals the way towards full Flash interactivity."

"I think it's pretty neat," said Zed, moving the mouse cursor on and off the button like he was trying to break some world record for rollovers-per-minute.

"I think a rollover without any scripting is very cool," said Bonnie. "Look at all the time I've saved from making two separate images and hand-coding the rollover in JavaScript."

"Before you both explode with enthusiasm," I said. "Let's finish the button states.

"Close the preview movie, and you should all return to the Flash authoring environment ready to continue editing your button symbol. Now insert a keyframe on the Down state, and change the color of the square to red.

"Test the movie again and try pressing the button. It should now change color from green – the Up state, to yellow – the Over state, to red – the Down state.

"Although we have only covered buttons on a visual level here, sounds can also be added to the different states if necessary. We won't cover that here, but you can imagine all manners of bleeps and boings occurring when the user rolls over or presses a button.

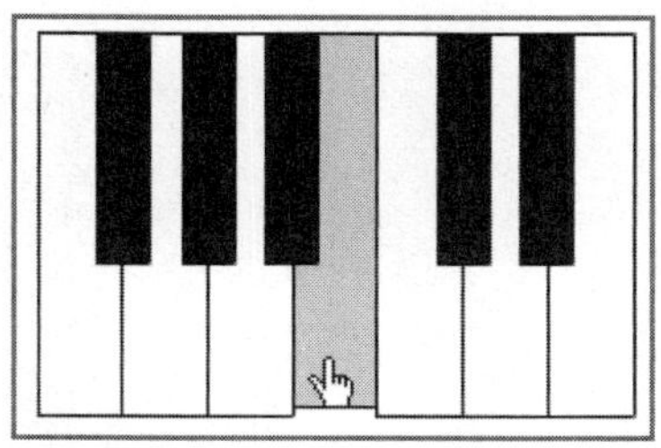

"Many people use this concept to make simple musical instruments in Flash. If you assign a different sound to a number of buttons, you instantly have a basic instrument."

"That's a pretty cool idea! But can you now tell us more about the elusive Hit state?" Steve asked.

"As I mentioned earlier, the Hit state defines the button area, or the area where the cursor must be over to activate the button.

"At the moment, because the Hit state isn't defined, it is using the Up state by default.

"OK folks, close the preview movie again and insert a keyframe on the Hit state of the button. For this we'll use a smaller area, so you all have to try and find out where the Hit area is.

"Select the square on the Hit area, and reduce its size with the Free Transform tool or the Transform panel. Make it around half the size, and center it on the original square."

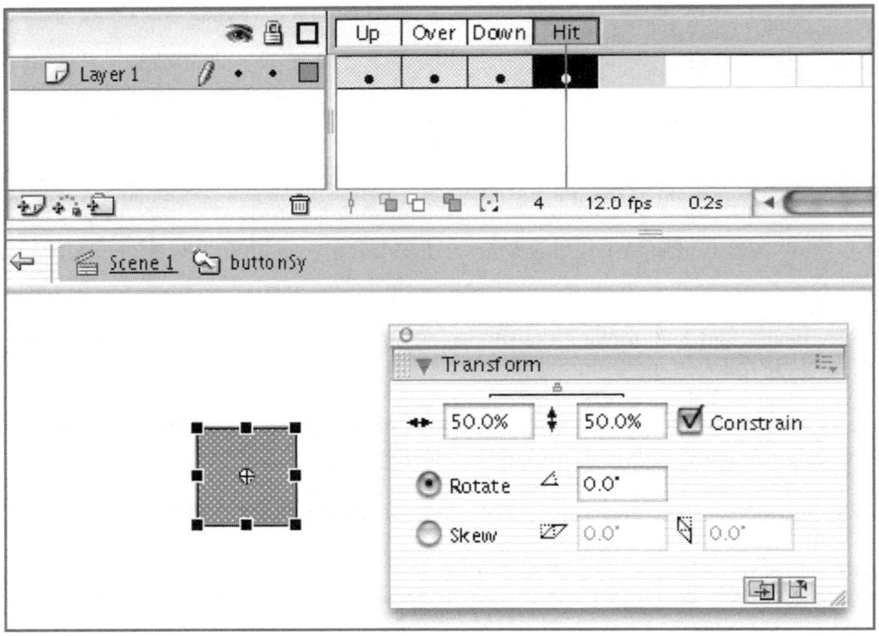

"Do we need to change its color too?" asked Zed.

"No Zed, the Hit state is actually invisible in the finished movie, and it is only used to define an area, not a visual state – that's what we have the other three states for.

"Test the movie again and try your button this time. You'll notice that the button states only change when you place the cursor over the center of the square – where the Hit state is hiding.

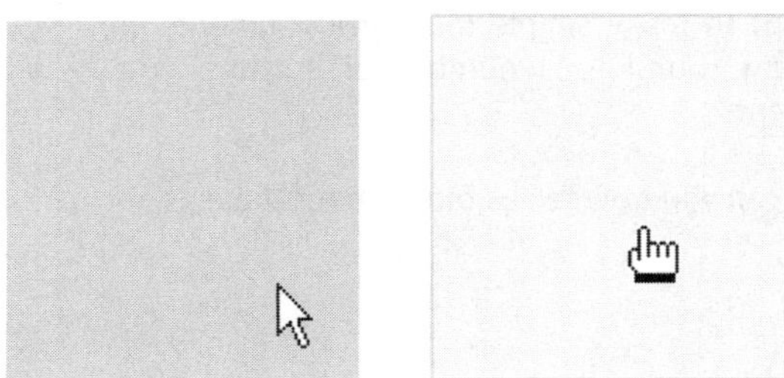

"This is because the Hit area has been redefined to only make the button functional when the cursor is over it."

"That's pretty freaky," said Zed. "Can we move the Hit area away from the other states of our button? Like, could we hide it in the top left corner of the stage?"

"You can Zed, but it would hardly be practical if the user had to hunt down an invisible Hit state!" I warned.

"I don't think your visitors would enjoy facing that challenge, when all they want is content or information," said Bonnie. "That would be commercial suicide!"

"It might be useful for a game though!" said Zed.

"A pretty nasty game by the sounds of it," said Steve.

"Why don't you try it out Zed? Move your Hit area, and let one of the others try to find it." I said.

After the complexity of the button symbol, and a bit of fun, I decided to move the class onto something easier – the graphic symbol.

Graphics

"The next Flash symbol to consider is one that we've already seen – the graphic symbol. Luckily, this isn't as complicated as the button symbol – it's simply a container for vector graphics, shapes, or pretty much anything else that can be drawn or imported into Flash.

"One of the reasons we might use graphic symbols is to save file size. Each time a shape is drawn loose on the stage, it adds to the file size of your final SWF movie. If a recurring shape, like a square, is turned into a graphic symbol and then this symbol is used numerous times in the Flash movie, then Flash only has to load that symbol once, making the overall file size smaller.

"Turning shapes and elements into symbols also enables you to organize your movie a little better, because you know that you only have to look in the Library for something."

"I think I get the idea," said Bonnie, "But I'd feel a whole lot better if we could make a graphic symbol ourselves."

"Bonnie's right – let's create a graphic symbol. Keeping it simple as usual, I want you all to draw a circle with a red fill and a black stroke.

"Once you've done this, select the basic graphic and again choose Convert to Symbol... from the Insert menu, or just hit F8. As before with the button, a dialog will appear asking you which symbol type you want and what its name will be. Go ahead and select Graphic this time, and give it a suitable name."

"Why bother with a different name?" asked Wes. "Flash seems to offer a name."

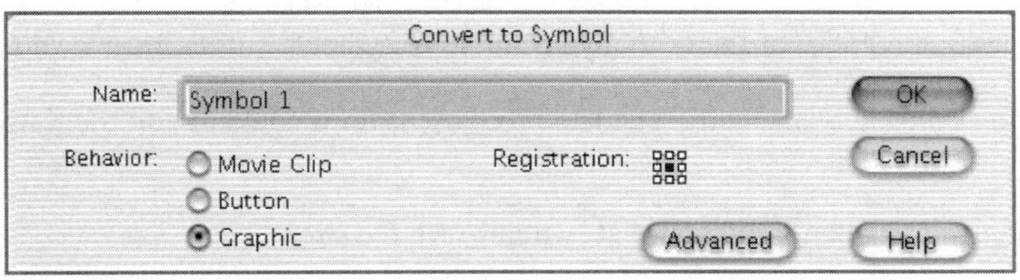

"Yes, but Flash only offers a generic name. The problem with this is that it doesn't make navigating your Library that easy when you come to have many symbols. The Library would quickly become unusable."

> *"Giving your symbols logical names will make your workflow quicker all round."*

"I suppose that seems to make sense. I'm forever trying to organize myself a little better," said Wes.

"When you're working on a small Flash file, the temptation is to leave all the symbol names as they are, but you never know when you will expand a Flash file, and then you'll have to spend a little time renaming the symbols in the Library. It's usually best to organize your file from the outset.

"Now, your symbol should now be located in the Library. Open it up, and double click its icon to edit the symbol as we did with the button."

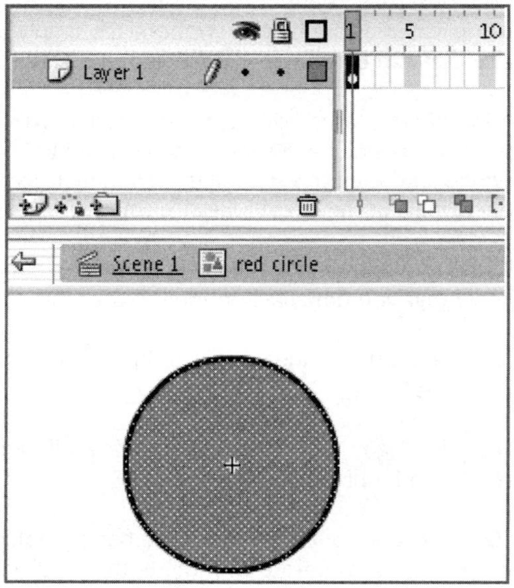

"Wow, this looks just like the main timeline," said Zed.

"It might look that way Zed, but it is the timeline of your graphic symbol. Generally graphic symbols are used to hold a single frame of content, even though they have a timeline. In most cases you wouldn't do anything else to this timeline, but this is where you make any changes to the shape if you need to.

"Click on the Scene 1 button from the navigation bar below the timeline. This will return you to the main timeline.

"If you changed the appearance of your shape, then it will look different here, because you've changed the content of the symbol."

"I can't edit the symbol anymore," observed Bonnie. "Why can't I change it?"

"This is because you're trying to edit the symbol from the main movie timeline – you need to be within the symbol's own timeline to be able to edit it. This is done through a double click on the symbol in the Library, or by double clicking on the symbol on the stage.

"There are, however, a number of things that you can do to symbols outside their own timeline."

"Like what?" said Bonnie, looking a little puzzled. "You just said we couldn't edit them from here – I'm a bit confused now."

"Well Bonnie, remember when I told you that symbols save file size?"

"Yes. Symbols are stored in the Library and are only loaded once. So you can pull as many copies as you like from the Library, and you won't pay in file size for it."

"That's right." I stood up to get the attention of the class. "I want you all to drag a copy of your symbol from the Library and place it on the stage."

I wanted to show the class how a symbol in the Library could be reused on the stage with different instances of itself.

"Next, open the Property inspector. If it's not already visible, you can do this through the Window menu. Then select the copy of the symbol. As you do this, you'll see that the Property inspector changes to show the properties of that copy of the symbol.

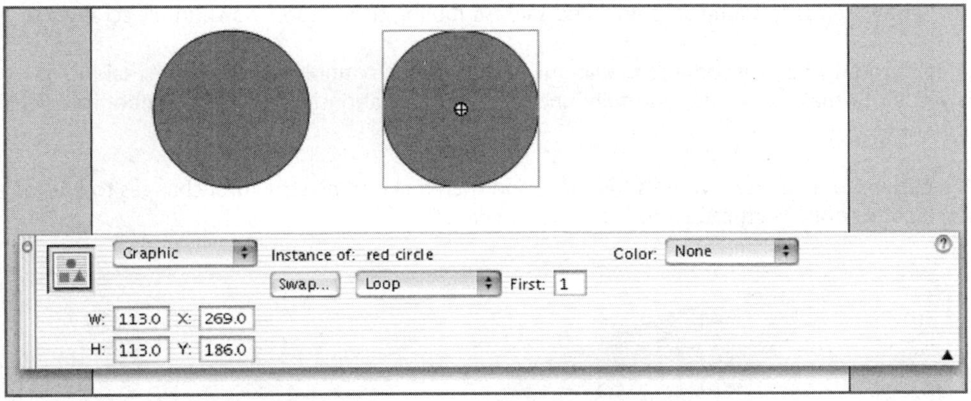

"Each version of a symbol is called an **instance**. As you can see in the Property inspector on Steve's computer, his second circle is an instance of the symbol that he named red circle.

"Every instance is independent. Let's prove this by changing the color of your new instance using the Property inspector."

I showed the class how to change the Tint value of an instance using the Property inspector. I then wanted to tell them about all the other options available.

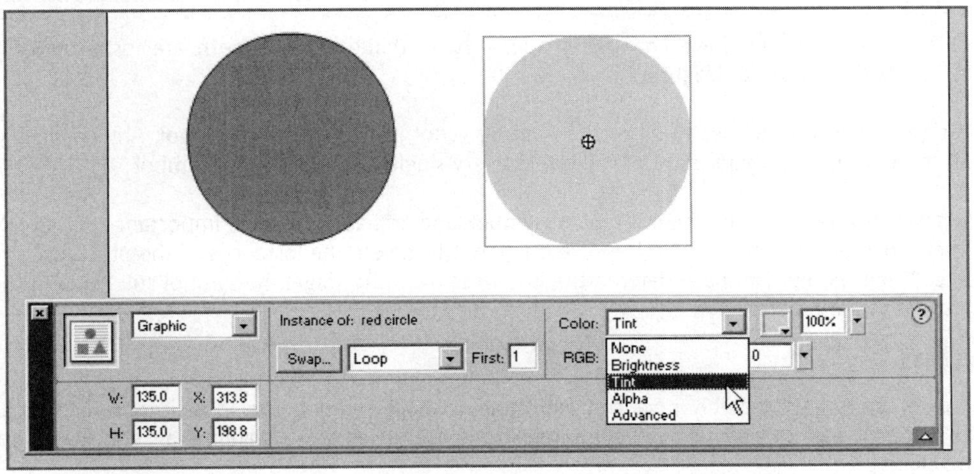

"The options of the Color drop-down menu in the Property inspector allow you to change the brightness, color, and alpha (or opacity), of your symbol instances. The most significant and useful of these are the Tint and Alpha options. I'll not go through these with you now, but you should experiment with them to see what each does and how it can be useful to you for a certain task."

"Wow, the alpha setting is cool!" said Zed. He then moved his hands in animated fashion. "I'll be able to make mysterious and ghostly figures come out of the darkness... before fading away into the background again..."

"Technically speaking," I said. "Zed is talking about performing an alpha-in and alpha-out motion tween. The opacity, or alpha, of the sinister figure that Zed describes would fluctuate from zero to maximum, and then back to zero again."

"You make my creativity sound so cold." Zed said, scribbling some notes down in his scrapbook.

"We'll indulge Zed when we come to talk about the movie clip symbol in a moment," I said. "For now though, I want you all to make sure that you fully understand the relationship between symbol instances and their parent symbol.

"Double click on one of your symbols to edit it, and then make some structural changes to it using the Arrow or Subselection tools. Then return to the main timeline."

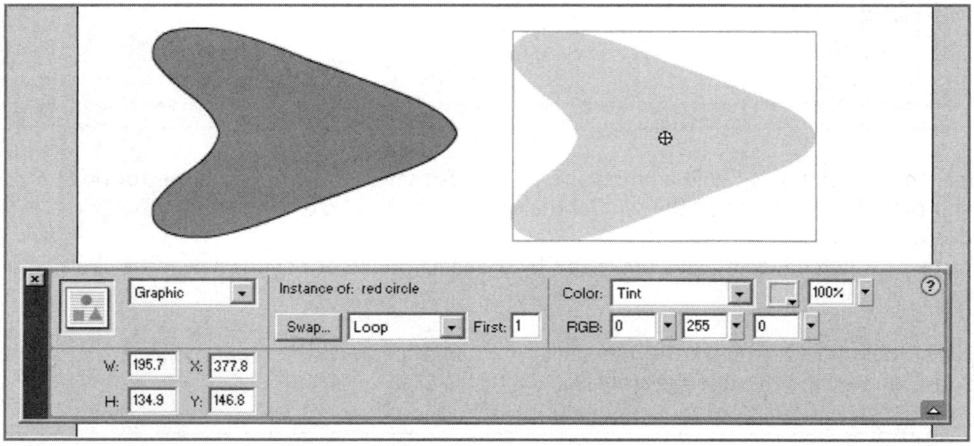

"Whoa, both of my circles have changed shape! I guess that's because both are instances of the same symbol," suggested Steve, as bright as ever.

"That's right Steve. This applies to all of the symbols – not just the graphic symbol. Any changes you make while in the edit mode of your symbol will affect every single instance of that symbol."

The class was now ready to see the last type of symbol, and arguably the most important in Flash MX designs. I told them to keep their current Flash movie open, but to delete the instances of the previous symbol from the stage. "Even though you have deleted the instances from the stage, the symbol still exists in the Library; we'll reuse it in a moment."

Movie clips

"The movie clip is an incredibly powerful and multi-purpose symbol. The most important fact about this symbol is that it has its very own timeline, making it useful for storing animation and keeping the main timeline clean.

"Many first-time Flash developers make the mistake of storing all of their animations and items on the main timeline, cluttering it up and making it difficult to change or extend. When you store different elements of the Flash movie within movie clip symbols, you then only have to change the individual symbols."

"I think I'm going to benefit from learning about movie clips," said Wes. "Otherwise I'm likely to make a bit of a mess of the main timeline."

"I think you'll find them most useful Wes." I said. "In fact, I know you all will. Let's give Zed a thrill and make a small animation within a movie clip."

"Woohoo!" cheered Zed.

"You are too nice to him," said Bonnie.

"This time," I started, "Rather than drawing something on the stage and converting it into a symbol, we're going to create a blank symbol and then give it content.

"Select the Insert menu and choose New Symbol.... This time, choose the movie clip symbol and give it an appropriate name." I turned to look at Wes, "What's your symbol name Wes?"

"My movie clip is called *circle animation*," said Wes confidently. "How does that sound?"

"Sounds perfect," I replied. "

"Once you've clicked OK, you'll be transported inside the new movie clip symbol. The only thing you'll see is a cross. Would anyone like to guess what this cross is?"

"I think I already worked it out when I was playing with the other symbol – it's the center point isn't it?" Bonnie said.

"That's right Bonnie. We refer to this center point more accurately as the **registration point** in Flash. This point is not only used for positioning elements correctly, but it also defines the point from which symbols are rotated or scaled."

I used Bonnie's computer to show the principle.

"For example, if you have a square with its top left corner touching the registration point, then the square will rotate around that corner. Here's a square rotated by 45 degrees:

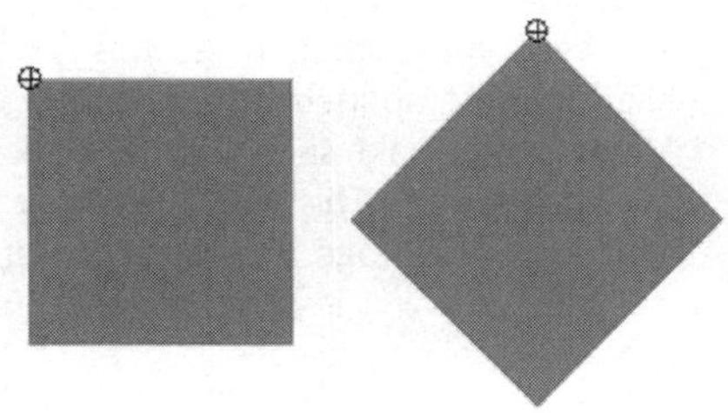

"But if you have the registration point at the center of the square, then it will rotate around that axis point. This one is also rotated 45 degrees:

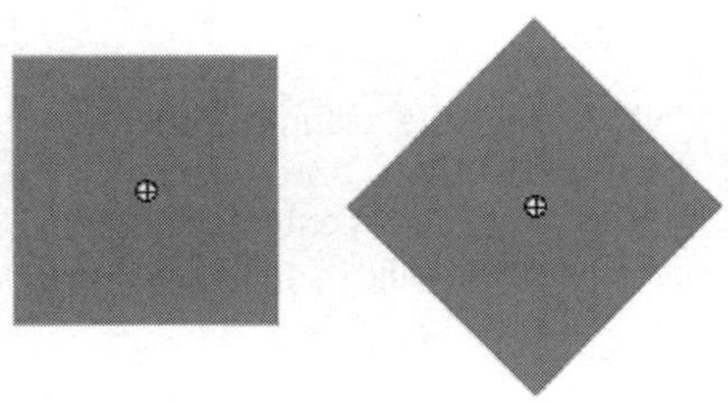

"Although both examples show a 45 degree rotated square, if you were to animate a full rotation, then you'd see why the top-left registration point is not quite right. If you want to experiment with this idea, try scaling a symbol from different registration points."

"For now though, let's work with the movie clip we've just created. As with the main timeline, frame 1 of the existing layer has a blank keyframe. The animation we are going to perform will involve moving and changing the alpha of the graphic symbol you just made.

"Drag a copy of the circle graphic symbol out of the Library into the new movie clip symbol.

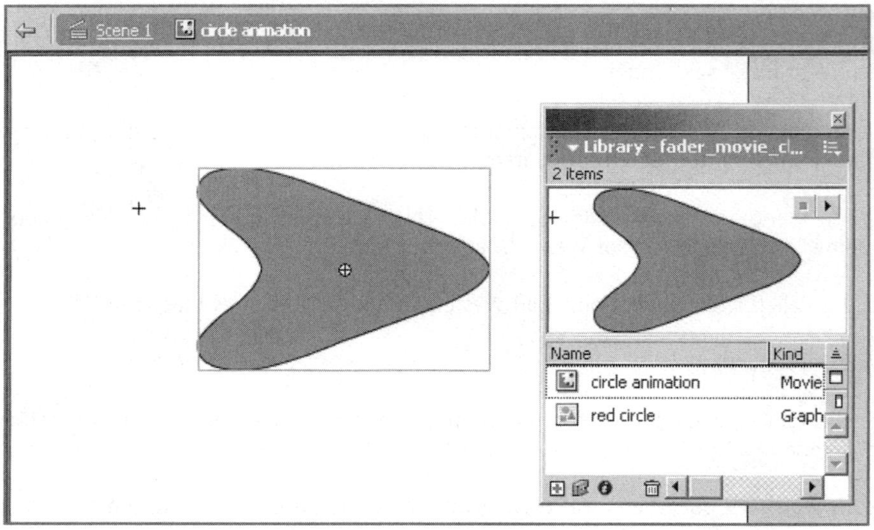

"Wow, so we can put symbols inside other symbols?" asked Steve.

"That's right Steve – this is how we can slowly build up highly complex designs out of simple building blocks. Remember to note where you are within a symbol hierarchy using the navigation bar just below the timeline.

"Now we want to centre our distorted circle to the registration point. To do this we can use the Align panel, opened by selecting Window > Align. Firstly, make sure that the To Stage: button is switched on. This will align any objects in relation to the stage and the registration point.

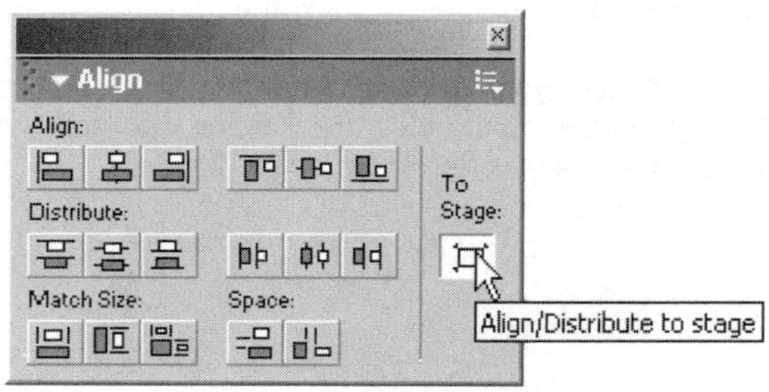

"Now select the graphic and press the Align horizontal center button to center the circle horizontally:

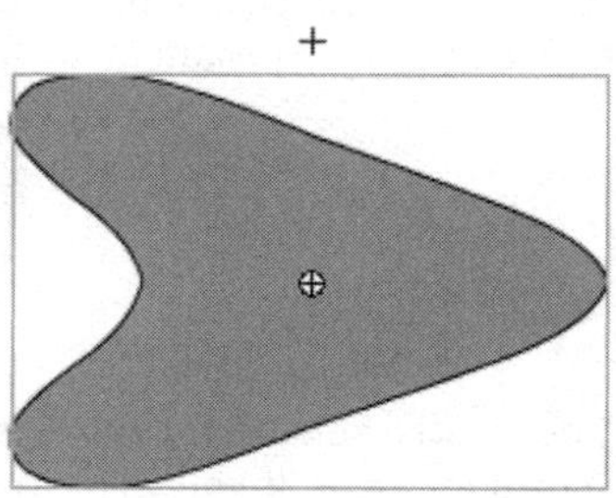

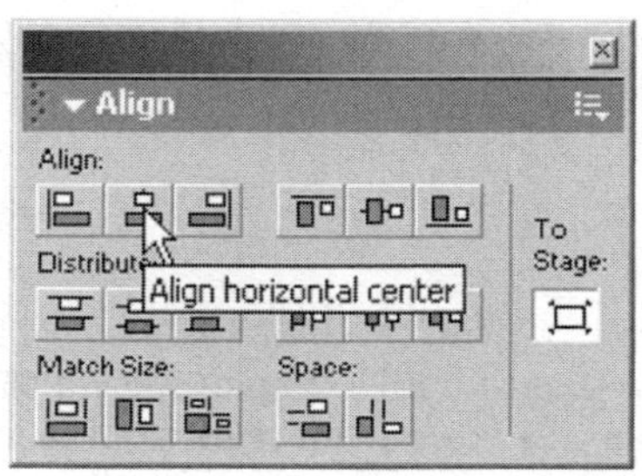

"Follow this by pressing the Align vertical center button. Your distorted circle graphic symbol is now centered on the registration point of the new movie clip.

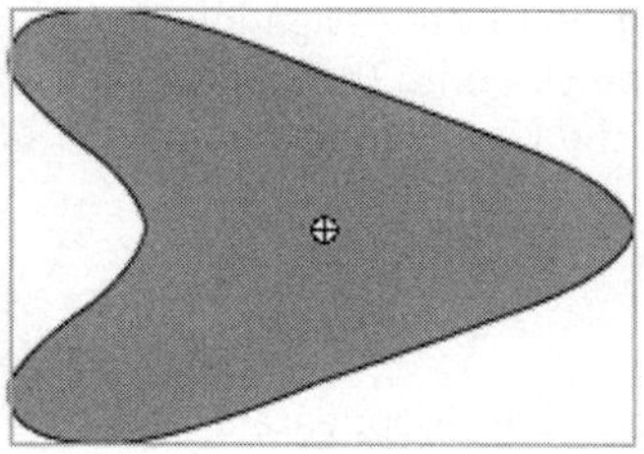

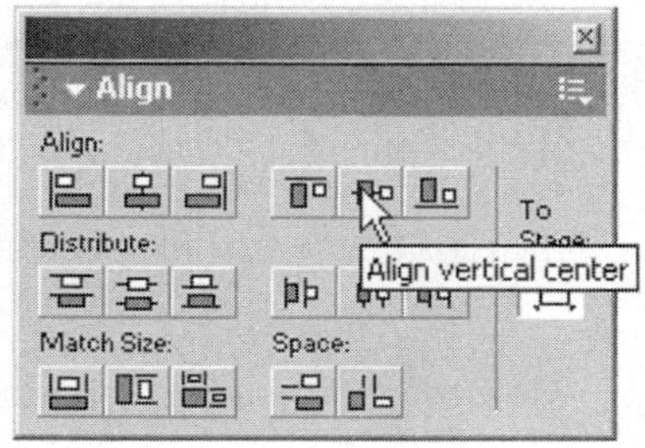

"Now we have a centered symbol on frame 1. This is the start point of our animation. The animation will simply involve this shape moving from its stage position on keyframe 1 to a different position on a later keyframe. The next thing we need to do is to define this destination keyframe

"So, insert a keyframe at frame 50, and move the symbol on this frame a distance away from the registration point. This will define the destination point.

"Now insert a motion tween by selecting a frame anywhere in between the two keyframes and clicking on Motion from the Tween menu of the Property inspector. If you run the playhead along the timeline, you'll see that the symbol moves from the one keyframe to another."

"Didn't we do this with the house and the tree?" asked Zed.

"Yes we did Zed, but this time we're not only making this animation within a movie clip symbol, we're also going to make the instance fade out.

"On the final keyframe, select the symbol and look in the Property inspector."

"Oh, I get it!" exclaimed Zed. "The symbol will lose opacity as it moves!"

"You mean *alpha* of course, Zed" Wes said with a mock scolding. "The Flash term is *alpha*."

"Now select Alpha from the Color drop-down of the Property inspector," I continued, "And lower it to zero. This will make the symbol fade out to nothing."

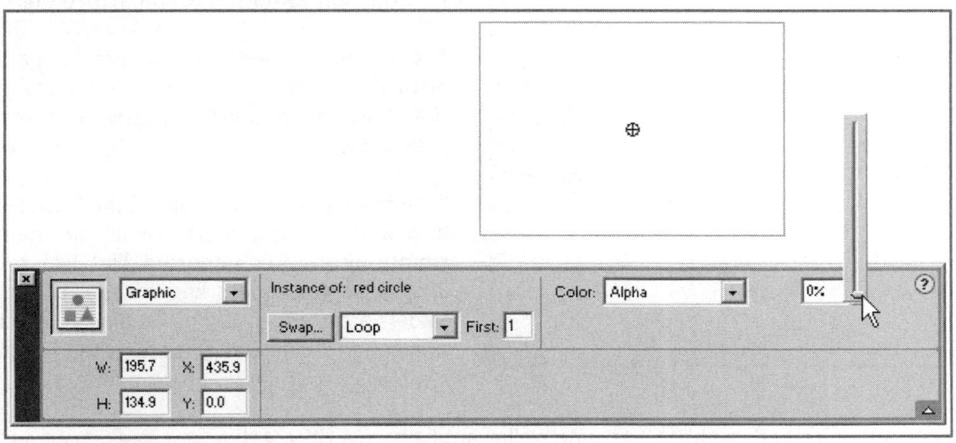

"I guess we test the movie now?" asked Bonnie.

"Well, almost Bonnie. Firstly, you need to return to the main timeline by clicking on the Scene 1 button of the navigation bar. Then drag an instance of the movie clip onto the stage. At the moment it exists exclusively in the Flash Library."

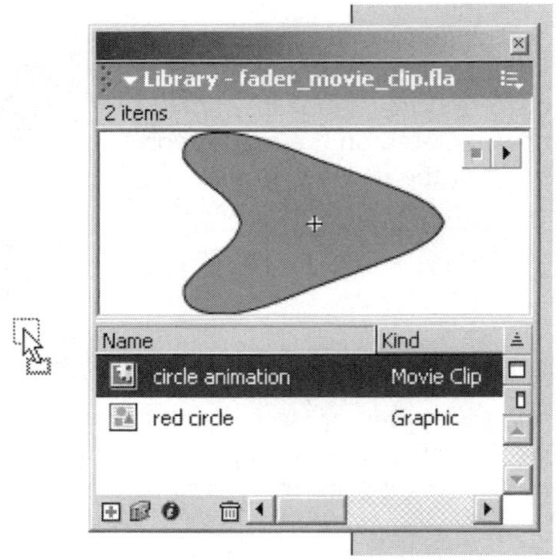

The class then tested their animations, watching it loop over and over.

"How come my symbol reappears after it has disappeared?" asked Zed. "It's not a great loop is it?"

"That's right Zed, movie clips loop by default," I replied, "Unless they are told not to. If you wanted to tidy up the loop, you could add another keyframe and animate the symbol back to its original position and alpha value."

I got the class to close their preview movies so that I could tell them a little more about movie clip symbols and instances.

"You can create instances of movie clips just as you do with graphic and button symbols. If you were to drag another copy of the movie clip symbol onto the stage, you would have two animations, both animating from where you positioned them.

"If you want to try something cool, Zed, try placing two instances of the symbol at the center of the stage and flipping one of them horizontally.

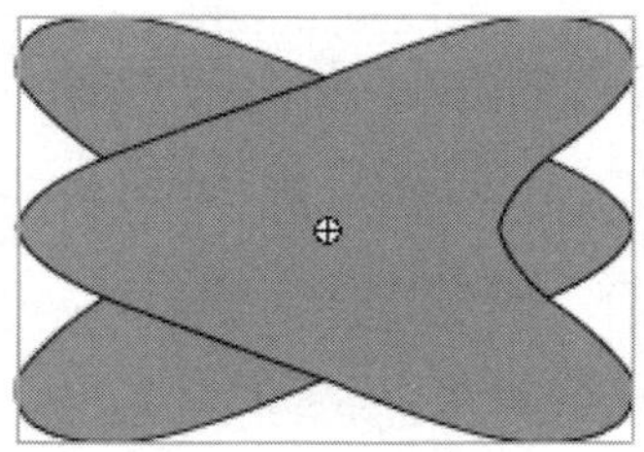

"The result would be the same animation, but mirrored. The power of instances is that you don't have to create another animation – the content can be reused."

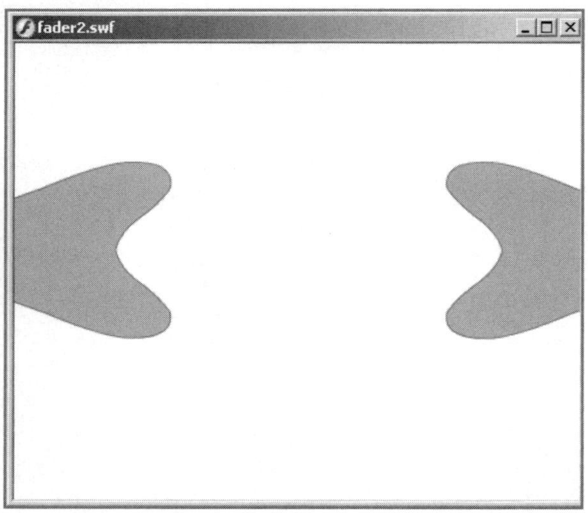

I decided that the class had practiced enough Flash for now, and so started to summarize the key points.

"As you've all seen, symbols are incredibly useful elements which help Flash movies maintain a low file size. They also promote a degree of organization in your designs.

"You have all also learnd about the Flash Library, and how it is a central store for all our symbols. The Library also stores imported files like sounds and images, so you always know where to look. Library folders are another way of keeping your Flash movie organized; they are very useful when the number of symbols in your library grows a little out of control."

"When we work on Frieda's website, I assume we'll want to have a Library that we can all share and add to." Said Lisa. "Which is the best way for us to do this?"

"That's a very good question Lisa. When your Flash file is saved, the Library is saved with it, and all of your symbols are stored.

"In a scenario where you want to work with a fresh Flash file using the Library from an old file, you can use File > Open As Library... to load it without the contents of the stage. Moving symbols between two Libraries is also very easy; in fact, you can just drag and drop items – we'll look at this a little later in the project."

"I think it's time for a break," I said. "When we come back, Wes will give a short lecture on some art movements that might be relevant to our design needs."

"This should be enlightening," Deb winked at Wes. "Are you going to wear that suit while you lecture?" Wes smiled as he walked out the door.

History in the making

Wes asked his classmates to sit at the table. He said that his lecture would be quite succinct, and they may find it useful to take notes. He'd try to cover various art styles and introduce the students to the most important movements of recent art history, but they were on their own to discover details and follow up this introduction with their own research. He began to walk around the table as he talked.

"The reason Linda wanted me to talk about recent art history, and art historians, is simple. She wants you to understand that you are part of art history in the making."

He cleared his throat, "The time period I want to talk about coincides with what most art historians consider to be the beginning of graphic design history. This is about the mid- to late-1800s, along with the Industrial Revolution and the introduction of typography and images on posters to announce events.

"Personally, I'm of the opinion that graphic design history began before fine art history, with drawn symbols found in caves. But," he grinned, "I'm not one to argue with the experts. So, without any further ado, I'll introduce you to some of the major recent art styles and movements, and why they affect what we do today.

"First," he said, "The art historian studies visual and tangible objects that humans make and use. They also study the structures we build. Frieda's work, for example, would be classified as architecture, since her objects are built into a structure. However, her work would also be considered a craft art, since she makes her products by hand, rather than by mechanical assembly line.

"Some other arts are sculpture, pictorial arts like paintings, drawings, printmaking, photography and film, and now... computerized art forms." He looked at Lisa, "In the past, theater, music, and dance were considered outside the realm of art, since they were thought of as temporal, rather than static. Lately, this concept has changed with the label of *performance art*, which incorporates productions on the stage, in the street, and even within computer-generated media.

"In fact, a new school of thought counts anything with form and function to live within the realm of art. Of course," he added, "Each art form carries the weight of applying elements and principles of design.

"You might ask why historians relegate art to categories," Wes said.

"Why do historians relegate art to categories?" Zed asked. Deb and Bonnie both shushed him.

"I'm glad you asked that question, young man," Wes continued. "Art historians relegate art to categories because it helps many people consign our own social history to categories. This, my friends, makes history easier to study."

Wes waved his arms, and continued...

> *"Nothing influences art like society, and nothing influences society like art. Artists are historians, prophets, manufacturers, architects, mathematicians, mapmakers, psychologists, and poets."*

"We knew that already," Bonnie and Deb said together. It was Zed's turn to ask them to be quiet.

Wes smiled. "OK, so one of the major things art historians look for – other than age of an item, subject matter, who made it, and who paid for it – is *style*. Since the mid-1900s, art has been generated at such a rapid pace that many historians don't have logical names for the most recent proliferations, but they do have names for specific movements within the various regions and timeframes.

"One name for a style is called **period style**. This simply refers to the style of a certain period, like ancient Rome, or the style of Early Italian Renaissance. Period style is hard to pin down after the mid-1800s," Wes said. "Maybe a thousand years down the road, art historians will call this the *eclectic period*, but for now, there's no way to put all these varied styles into a handy catch-all phrase."

Wes took a seat and faced the students. "Another classification is **regional style**. This is a style tied to a specific period of time in a specific location. One example is the pyramids of Egypt, built about 3200 BCE. Another example is the Great Wall of China, which was built about 221 BCE. Here we have two different times, and two different locations, producing two different regional styles.

"One problem with regional style is that there can be quite a bit of variety in one area in a given time frame. Another problem with regional styles is the names. The Hudson River School, for example, was named for landscape styles of artists in that area during the 1800s. A great many artists beyond the area of the Hudson River adopted this style, making no sense of the regional aspect. After some time, the use of the name results in a *movement*, rather than a true regional style.

"The next style," Wes said, "Is my favorite. It's called **personal style**. Personal style incorporates a distinctive manner of individual artists, like Frank Lloyd Wright, Cézanne, Dali, Escher, Hannah Höch, and Frida Kahlo, to name but a few of my favorites."

Wes crossed his arms. "Books have been written by scholars on visual metaphors present in cross-cultural studies. Psychologists are interested in feelings represented through the visual mediums. Anthropologists study the methods of cultural *gestalt* represented in regional works. Mathematicians study the construction of composition in every form of art.

"In other words," he said, "A specific artist who makes waves in recent art history does so because that person has personified their culture in art. Or, that artist projects where a particular culture is going, based on the expansion of every element and principle of design."

He waved his arms at the computers on the other side of the room, "You all know how to use the Internet. Some of us just became recent library addicts. Both tools can introduce you to various movements in recent art history." Wes jumped out of his chair and began walking again. "You may not realize that realism didn't give way to many other forms of art in America and Europe until the late 1800s. That was just a little over a century ago. Realism, in this sense, means portraying images as they appear to the eye. Since there were no cameras in use until about the late 1850s, the paintings and sculptures were often used to depict life. This realistic mode of painting and sculpture changed drastically, and when it did, it happened pretty quickly."

"The Avant-Garde movement began in Paris in the early twentieth century, when Leo and Gertrude Stein provoked debates and encouraged artists to invent new realms of vision. Both these folks were born in Pennsylvania, but they moved to Paris to seek a more stimulating environment.

"*Modernism*, *Impressionism*, *Pointillism*, *Expressionism*, *Cubism*, *Fauvism*, *Futurism*, and *Dada* were all born between the late 1800s and the 1930s. The Western world went from grand realism to complete rebellion of artistic structure within fifty years! Can you imagine how exciting that time must have been for the arts?

"During this time period," Wes explained, "Chemistry took hold on the world, and the language of physics was fully developed. Trains and stagecoaches gave way to automobiles. International communication was established, and world wars were fought.

"Not surprisingly, art reflected all these changes and more. Art became surrealistic, more abstract, and simplified all at once. Space-time relationships were studied, and color psychology was developed, based on color theory developed in the late 1800s.

"The Bauhaus and De Stijl Schools were created, developing an economy of style." Wes thought for a moment and added, "If you don't know the following name; write it down. This man, more than any one person in the 1900s, influenced the way we perceive art and design today."

Everyone sat, poised with their pencils ready and waited for Wes's dramatic announcement. "**Walter Gropius** once said that art and life are one, and that both elements express truth. This man was a major influence as director of the Bauhaus School. He pulled various artists and art skills together to produce a period of design. The successor of Gropius was Ludwig Mies van der Rohe. Rohe's famous aphorism *less is more*, is a quote from Browning's poem *Andrea del Sarto*, written in 1855. I would strongly suggest studying this movement and the philosophy behind each art form generated from that school." Wes went to one of the computers and quickly typed this URL into the web browser so that the students could read the poem he mentioned: http://www.library.utoronto.ca/utel/rp/poems/browning12.html.

He got up again and contiued pacing. "The rest is history, so to speak. The 1930s marked the beginning of American consumerism, launching the age of commercial art. Plastics were developed, everyone *turned on*, *tuned in*, and promptly *dropped out* in the sixties, Vietnam turned everyone on their heels, music became a major form of international communication, and man walked on the moon.

"This era marked the beginning of the Post-Modernist era. We moved from Art Deco constructions like the Chrysler building in New York City to the organic architecture of Frank Lloyd Wright. The super-realistic styles of Edward Hopper came to light and, at the same time, Jackson Pollock took us to the other extreme with his lack of compositional focus."

Wes looked at me. "I don't even know where to go from here," he said. "There's so much to talk about, and all of it influences how we work in this medium today."

I prompted him, "Well, there's *Pop Art*, *void sculpture*, *conceptual art*, *modernist formalism*..."

Wes continued with a smile, "*Environmental art*, *deconstruction*, *Neo-expressionism*, *Punk*, *Grunge*, and whatever's going to happen tomorrow." He held up his hands. "Does anyone have any questions?" I don't know what else to say, except to study the movements so you know what's been accepted, and what you have to draw from for your own work."

Everyone was silent for a second, and Zed began the applause. "Man, I learned more about art from you in twenty minutes that I've learned in my whole life! That was intense."

Bonnie agreed, and asked, "Wes, I'll look up Walter Gropius. Other than all these other suggestions, do you have any other specific directions for us?"

Wes thought, and answered, "I'll tell you what. I think I can direct each of you to certain artists and movements, so you can learn more about your own personal choices and history."

"What do you mean?" Deb asked. "I don't have an art history!"

Wes laughed. "I wouldn't bet me if I were you. I think a good choice for you would be some reality beyond the tangible world. I have a gut feeling you're stuck between Greek geometry and the never-ending fractal. In the late 1800s, there was a European movement called Symbolism. The poet Rimbaud was a great influence on this art community. Let me know what you find," Wes grinned. "I'd be interested in your thoughts."

Deb scribbled the information down in her drawing pad, and Wes turned to Zed. "You should check out Roy Lichtenstein, Zed."

"Will do, captain," Zed saluted.

"Bonnie, I think a good place for you to begin would be with Piet Mondrian. After you've studied his work, move on to Hannah Höch. She was one of the first women in the Dada movement. This should give you a clue to the wide range of styles developed during the twentieth century."

"Steve, what don't you know?" Wes asked. "I don't know where to point you, since I'm sure you're familiar with the graphic arts."

"I guess I am," Steve admitted. "I'm very familiar with many of the names you mentioned, plus Johannes Itten, Steven Heller, Philip B. Meggs, and Milton Glaser, among others. I haven't paid attention to Punk or Grunge movements, though. I'll have to look into them."

"Good choice – check out David Carson, Neville Brody, and anything from Émigré magazine " Wes looked at Lisa. "I think you'd love Josef Albers' work. He was a teacher who concentrated on the elements of design, with a significant focus on color. You'd probably love Christo's work, too."

Lisa nodded. "I've heard of Christo, but I never seen his work. I'll check it out."

Wes looked at me. "Good choices?"

"Great choices," I said, nodding at Deb – in turn, she was peering at Wes with suspicion. Before Wes could laugh, I said, "Right then, we need to talk about Frieda's business name and next week's project, but I want to make a few suggestions myself.

"Mostly, women have been recognized in regional art styles with textiles and with craft movements. Although these aren't minor contributions, they still don't speak a woman's name to us. Wes mentioned Höch and Kahlo. A few other women have made their art *heard* by the Western world. Among them are Georgia O'Keefe, Diane Arbus, Margaret Bourke-White, Audrey Flack, and Judy Chicago, to name a few. However," I added, "Women are making headway, so you men now have more competition than ever. I think it's important we look at women's artwork, since we can relate it to the fact that we're building a site for a woman in a male-dominated field."

Steve nodded, "The commercial and graphic arts have historically been dominated by men, too. I'm happy to see women become more visually vocal. It's exciting to have new voices in the fray." He smiled at the women in the class.

The women all smiled at Steve as I wrapped up Wes's performance. "OK ladies and gents, I hope you've gathered new material for future reference. It's good to know your history. You're becoming part of an ever-expanding international design team dedicated to refining this medium. The problem is local, regional, national, and global communication, and the format is the computer.

"It would be nice to see your work reflect some of the artists you've been asked to research. Notice," I emphasized, "I said *reflect*, not copy. Please don't just gaze at the artist's work and replicate what you see. Find out why the artist produced the work, what materials they used, and the social climate of the time. Critique their work along the elements and principles of design. This information might help you answer your design problems in the future."

They all agreed. "Are you all up to talking about Frieda's business name?" I asked. "I think we're ready to deal with the identity of this female architect and craft artist."

Moving beyond the first great idea

The class has now spent six weeks learning structures and tools of design and Flash MX. Beyond this point, they'll begin to utilize their knowledge as they advance through the brainstorming process. Both stages – ideation and selection – often work simultaneously to bring a design into focus.

As the class sat at the table, I asked Lisa, "How long does it take before a play hits the stage?"

Lisa looked surprised. "It depends on the play and the actors and actresses," she answered. "If the players are experienced, and they know the play, it may only take a few weeks to polish the work for public viewing."

"What if they don't know the play and this is their first public performance?" I asked.

Lisa grinned. "I know where you're going with this. To answer your question, it could take months."

Zed slumped in his chair. "I knew where that was going, too," he moaned.

"I could carry this further, and ask Wes how long it takes before an artist lands their first show," I said.

Wes nodded, "Some artists never get their first show. For others, it may take years. For sure, it doesn't happen in their first year of instruction."

"I don't mean to discourage any of you," I said. "I just wanted to point out your excellent progress as a group. All of you are becoming extremely professional. You've done your assignments, you've attended every class, and you've been proactive in your involvement with this course. Some of you have excelled yourselves to create solutions to your problems."

I continued, "Today we learned to critique each other's work using the structure of the elements and principles of design. We also settled on Frieda's name as a symbol for her vision. We learned how to organize our information, both on- and off-screen. Then we learned how to create basic symbols in Flash MX, and their associated benefits.

"We even learned a little about art history, with the aim to start applying those lessons to our learning process.

"What you've gained so far is similar to the builder who learns the lay of the land, studies his blueprints, gathers his tools, and is ready to build his house with a lot of scattered elements within the structured principles of design."

"Now you have the format, the blueprints, the tools, and the structure, you're ready to pull the elements together and construct your house." I went to the board and prepared to write a list. "These are the scattered elements you have to work with. I call them *scattered*, because they haven't been refined yet.

Frieda Ray – the name
Navigation – 3 levels
symbols
film
music
sound
illustrations
photographs
content

"You have Frieda's name, a set of navigation devices – those three symbols, and you've no doubt got some other elements that we haven't fully discussed in class – these could include illustrations, photographs, and any other general content."

I turned back to the class. "You also need to keep the problem of expansion in the back of your mind as you develop the composition of the site. This house may be small at first, but you'll need to plan for more rooms to be added. This job is going to need more than one person to tackle all the problems," I said.

"Bonnie mentioned last week that all of you had different strengths. You'll need these this week as you develop the next project together. It's now time to form a composition for these elements. Some elements will remain the same throughout the site, and some elements will fluctuate.

"Use the elements and principles of design and rhetorical figures. When you have a problem, resort to the creative problem-solving circle."

Steve asked, "What do we do when we can't agree on some of the elements?" I'm concerned, since we haven't decided our typefaces or what content we need or anything..." He continued, "Do you want these drawn or computer generated with Photoshop or Flash?"

"Steve, I know you might feel at loose ends, so I'll answer your question. When you can't make a decision, at least block out an area for the information. I would draw a sample on the board, but I don't want to give you any preconceived ideas." I held out my arms. "You're free to develop whatever you feel is right for Frieda's site. I'm letting go of the reins, to see how much you've learned from this course.

"All I want from you is a one-page composition that you might use throughout the site. Pull together any other elements you might use," I pointed at the list on the board.

They all looked at each other with apprehension. I stood and walked around the table. "I want to commend all of you for your rapid progress. You're in much better shape this week than when I left you last week. Now," I added, "We need to take what we know and go beyond that first great idea."

I rested my hand on Zed's shoulder, and nodded at Bonnie. "Can you two get together this week and work on this project?"

Zed and Bonnie looked at each other with surprise. "Sure, Bonnie said, "Zed, I'll get with you after class to compare schedules, OK?"

"Sure," Zed agreed.

I looked at Lisa and Steve, "How about you and Steve find some time to get together?"

They both shrugged and nodded. "I didn't realize you were going to pair us up," Steve grinned. "This'll be fun, Lisa." Lisa smiled.

Deb's eyes widened as she realized my plan. "Oh, no you don't," Deb stammered. "I don't think I can work with Mister Art Critic."

Wes laughed, "C'mon Deb, I'm not an ogre! Besides, I'm fascinated with your composition theories. Please?"

Lisa grinned, "You really need to check out his studio. It's a great place to be creative."

Deb sighed. "I guess I can stand working with you for one week. Worse things have happened. But," she added as she pulled her things together, "I'm wearing my watch."

"I'm not trying to punish any of you," I grinned. "I think you'll find working with another person on this problem will be helpful."

"Oh, I almost forgot," I said. "You also need a flowchart, and a report about why you decided to keep Frieda's name for the business. You can produce these as a team, so I'll need three flowcharts and three reports."

I began to gather my own things together. "When you all get stuck, study some art history. Use free association. Do whatever you need to pull an idea together. Bring your library books with you next week, too."

When I looked up, Zed and Bonnie were already talking about their schedules, and Steve and Lisa were walking out the door. Wes was sitting next to Deb with an exasperated look on his face. Deb laughed, looked at me and asked, "You know you just put the two most volatile people in the class together in one team, don't you?"

"I realized that," I agreed. "I also knew this combination of art, words, math, and symbolism might just produce the best design." I winked at her and left the room.

Summary

Today's lesson covered a wide variety of topics from Flash symbols to art history. Using the assignment set in the previous lesson the students started by critically examining each other's work, picking their favorites and discussing what each set of images conveyed to them a how it was accomplished.

The class then went on to look at how to refine the identity of a client, and a solid process for doing so: *defining*, *analyzing*, and *brainstorming*. We then went on to discus the seven different organizational models:

- **Linear**
- **Hierarchical**
- **Web**
- **Overlay**
- **Matrix**
- **Spatial zoom**
- **Parallel**

After that we looked at how we could structure Frieda's website with the use of a flowchart showing how we wanted to relate all the different pages to each other.

Next we used the computers and investigated the three different symbols in Flash MX – how to use them to create different effects and to create simple animations:

- **Button**
- **Graphic**
- **Movie Clip**

Finally, Wes gave a brief art history overview, mentioning some of the famous names that changed the course of art, as well as a number of styles and periods. Finally the class was paired off and sent away to complete this week's project.

In next week's lesson we'll look at the importance of formatting, and the fundamental concepts relating to typography.

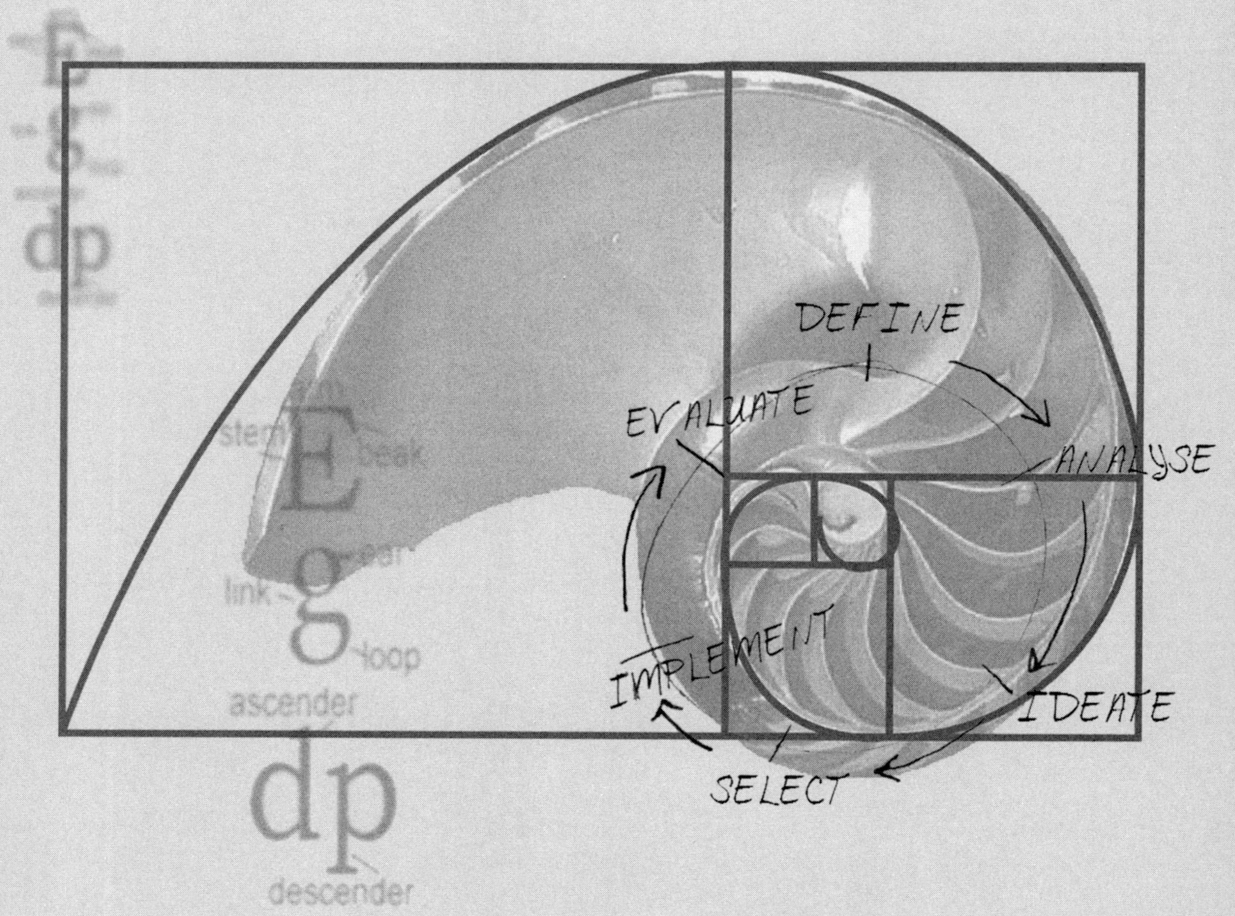

DEFINE
ANALYSE
IDEATE
SELECT
IMPLEMENT
EVALUATE
stem
beak
ear
link
loop
ascender
descender

Chapter 7

Typography in Design

Objectives

In today's class you will learn about:

- Critical assessment of compositions in line with the principles and elements of design
- The fundamentals of typography:
  - Size and width
  - Emphasis and weight
  - Kerning, tracking, and leading
  - Formatting and justification
- Manipulation of text and creating dynamic text in Flash MX

Introduction

I hadn't heard from any of the students over the past week so I was keen to hear how well they'd worked together in teams, and how productive they'd been with their projects. Overcome with curiosity, I arrived in the classroom early, before any of the students.

Zed was the first person to arrive. He was wearing his white scarf round his neck, and a frown on his face. "Have you seen Bonnie yet?" he asked.

"Good morning Zed, and no, not yet" I answered. "You're the first person here today. As soon as that sentence left my mouth, I heard Steve, Bonnie, and Lisa as they walked toward the classroom. They were laughing, and Steve was drawing a square in the air with his finger as he entered the room.

"I'm telling you," Steve chuckled, "Lisa almost had to beat me with a stick to get me thinking beyond square grids. I'm a primal circle man today."

Bonnie saw Zed, "Hey Zed. I've got those drawings, in case you were missing them."

"Phew!" Zed wiped imaginary sweat off his brow. "I was worried; I looked everywhere for them this morning. I tried calling, but you'd already left."

About this time, Deb entered the room alone. Her hair was done up in braids. "Wow, Deb!" Lisa said. "Your hair looks fantastic."

"I'll say," Bonnie added. "How are you getting by with that at work, though?"

Deb grinned, "I quit."

We were all stunned with her announcement. "What the heck are you doing now?" Steve asked.

"I've stashed a little cash," Deb grinned. "I paid the boss for the money he spent on this class, and we parted amicably enough. He told me my job was open if I ever wanted it back."

"This didn't have anything to do with Wes, did it?" Lisa asked.

"Good heavens, no," Deb stated with conviction. "I'm just through with all the insane pressure at work. This is so much more fun. I've got a million ideas running around in my head, and life is short." She laughed and set her supplies and project materials on the table.

Just that minute, Wes walked in. "Howdy, folks!" He set a briefcase on the table and clicked it open. "Am I late?" He glanced at a new watch strapped to his wrist. "No, I don't think so. Five minutes early, actually." He sighed, and sat at the table.

Zed, Lisa, Steve, and Bonnie looked at each other and burst into laughter.

"What's so funny?" Wes asked. He tapped the face of his watch. "I've decided my time is valuable. Nice, huh!"

We all agreed it was a good watch. "Let's get started then," I said. "No sense wasting time. You all have some compositions to share this morning, correct?" They all agreed. "Great! Last week you learned how to critique design work within the parameters of the design elements and principles. We'll continue that practice this morning with a compositional critique.

"You've also learned varieties of information models, and how to structure your client's work within those parameters. You also began to play with the symbols and organizational information in Flash.

"Wes gave a marvelous lecture on art history, cramming as much as he could into a rather short time period," I grinned at Wes. "I hope you all did a little research on your suggested art periods and artists of interest, because we'll talk about more art history today."

Deb grinned from ear to ear, "Oh, I learned something about my choice, all right," she said. "I'll be glad to share later with the rest of the class."

I remembered her topic, chosen by Wes. "I'm sure you have some interesting information," I was glad to see she took the subject with a sense of humor. I looked at the rest of the students. "You all did a great job with the choice of Frieda's name for her business. I'm proud of your utilization of the creative problem-solving process to accomplish this task."

Steve nodded, "I feel much more relaxed since we made that decision." He looked at Lisa. "We also learned to go beyond that *first great idea*, too."

"OK then," I said. "Let's do some compositional critiques, and then we'll spend the rest of the day on typography. We'll learn fundamentals of type and how to implement these ideas effectively in our Flash designs. Accordingly, most of the day will be spent at the computers."

Zed flipped his scarf back over his shoulder. "Let's do it!"

"Oh!" Lisa stopped me. "We have permission to use the theater next week if you'd like."

"Yeah!" they all said together. "We'd love to! " Steve added.

"Alright then," I said. "Let's meet at the theater next week. I'll remind you all at the end of class."

Client reports and composition evaluations

The students had been working on compositions for Frieda Ray's site this past week. They'd also prepared a flowchart, and a report on the continued use of Frieda's name for her business.

As the students settled at the table, I asked them to prepare their work for critique, starting with the flowcharts and business reports. As I glanced through the papers, I asked Steve and Lisa if I could show the rest of the class how they managed their project. Steve agreed, but Lisa cringed, "I guess you can show them. I'm not sure if it's right though," she said.

Steve retorted, "What? You don't trust me, Lisa?" He laughed and added, "I guess I wouldn't trust me, either. The execution of material flow for the web is a lot different than it is for print."

I agreed, "The main reason for this difference is because of the *linear* nature of printed material. Designing a site for the Internet would be tough to do in a linear fashion, unless you used a format that takes the viewer forward and backward with no other links. You might use something like this in a presentation, or in an art gallery format. However, ideally you'd also include a way to get back to the home page, or a way out of the site, just as you would give a person a way to close a magazine or newspaper.

"What you have here with your flowchart is one of *hierarchical* organization. We learned about linear and hierarchical levels of organization last week." I showed the class how Steve and Lisa drew their flowchart for Frieda's site.

"I see you also finalized the flowchart with some graphics program," I stated. "Is this the flowchart you would give to the client with the progress report?"

Steve nodded, "We felt it would look a little better to make the flowchart less formal, since we wanted Frieda to understand the flow of her site. We also added legal pages, like the disclaimer. But, instead of making the flowchart into a web organization, we decided to add that the disclaimer and other information would be included in a footer in all pages."

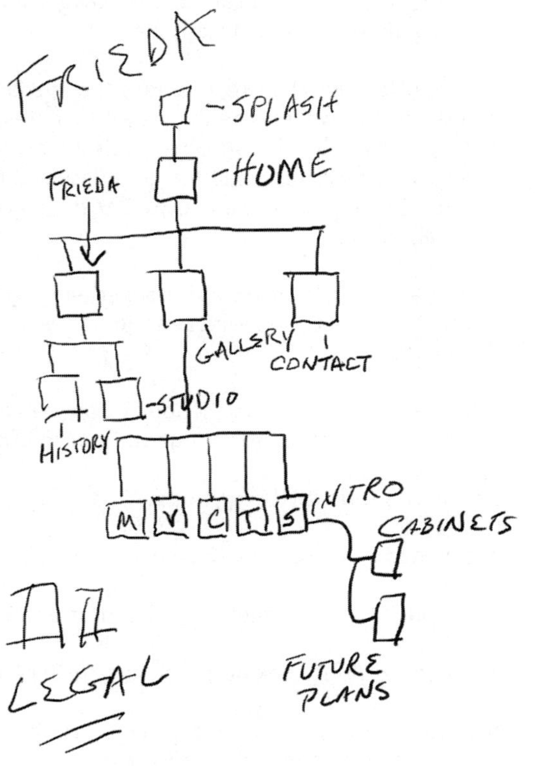

Lisa added, "We thought a web organization would look confusing, so we kept the hierarchical organization. Plus, we just initialed the cabinet designs on the hand-drawn flowchart. But we spelled these out in the final version."

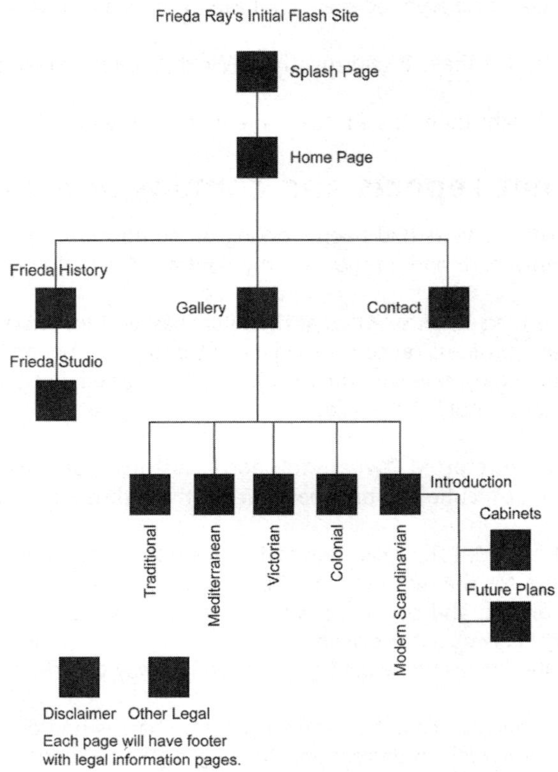

I passed the flowchart and the report around to the rest of the students. "You all basically completed the same report, with a front page entitled *Frieda Ray's Flash Site*, including your name and contact information.

"Each of you also kept the report to one page, which is great," I added. "And you also stated your progress very succinctly. I'm pleased with this, as it tells me that you all got together this week to hash out all the relevant information. Let me read Wes and Deb's statement, since I still have it in my hands." I continued to read their report out loud.

"This week, we decided to keep Frieda Ray's name for her business. It's yet undecided whether the full name will be used, or just the surname. We felt this would help keep the current market comfortable with the upcoming changes to marketing plans, including the addition of a Flash site.

"Included is a flowchart representing the Frieda Ray Flash site. The splash page is simple and will be instantly accessible. This will engage the viewer in a preview to the homepage. The home page will direct the viewer to three pages. One is concerned with the history and skills of Frieda Ray. Another page is a lead-in to the gallery, which will showcase the lines designed by Frieda Ray. The last page will be the contact page, which includes hours of operation, as well as the physical location of the shop, telephone and FAX numbers, and an email address.

"Each page will also carry a disclaimer and any other legal information required to protect the customer's privacy. The site is also developed with an eye to future expansion, especially within the modern Scandinavian design area.

"This week, we'll work on the look of the name and overall feel of the site. We'll report next week on our progress. If you have further questions or information, please feel free to contact us at any time."

Bonnie was furiously taking notes. "That progress report sure is written better than ours," she stated.

Zed agreed. "I don't think Bonnie and I are natural writers."

Steve laughed, "I can guess Deb did most of the writing on the report we just heard?"

Wes nodded, "Deb took over that part, for sure. I think she did a great job, and it only took her five minutes."

Deb waved her hand. "Well, actually I was thinking about the report for two days before I actually wrote it. I just wanted to state very quickly what we did and why we did it."

"All the reports are good," I stated. "You don't have to be Shakespeare to write a concise report that is understandable by the client. All of you covered the '*who*, *what*, *when*, *where*, *why*, and *how*' questions on your flowcharts and progress reports. I think Frieda Ray will sign off on these reports without a worry."

Steve laughed. "Phew, I'm glad Frieda likes our work. We all got together for a little brainstorming over the weekend."

I smiled, "Well, two heads are better than one when working on a flowchart. At least you all made the same progress."

Zed looked at the chart he and Bonnie created. "What if we want these for a portfolio of our work? Will you sign off on a copy for me?"

I laughed, "Zed, if you included a flowchart signed by an imaginary person in your portfolio, someone might think you're a bit too creative. This flowchart is a nice inclusion to your work, but leave it unsigned. If you had a flowchart for a real client, it would be best not to include that client's architecture in your portfolio," I explained. "Especially if you signed an NDA."

Zed grinned and shook his head. "Sometimes I forget that Frieda isn't a real client!" He added, "So we just make up a flowchart like this one for our portfolios," he pointed at Lisa and Steve's finalized chart, "Only without the signature and we include this to show we know what we're doing?"

"Right," I answered. "You might also include a hand-drawn sample to show your skills in that direction. We'll talk about portfolios later in the course. Keep your work, and make copies. We'll see what's best for each of you by the end of the course.

"I'm eager to see how well you managed your problems this week," I stated. "I didn't hear from anyone, so I assume everything went well?"

"It did for us," Steve said. "Actually, I think it went fantastic." Lisa nodded.

"Why don't you all sit with your partners," I suggested. "We'll start with Lisa and Steve, and work our way through to the rest of you."

The students rearranged themselves, and we began the critique.

Lisa and Steve

Steve began their presentation with an explanation, "When we all got together last weekend to talk about the flowcharts, we discussed the presentation of projects," he said. "We debated how to present our work, and Lisa had a solution." He looked towards Lisa.

"We decided you would want to see hand-drawn solutions," Lisa began. "But we were also worried that some of our drawings might not fully depict what we wanted to say."

She brought their work to the table. "So," she continued, "I believe that most of our work will include sketches, as well as some computerized representations. We also avoided color, since we haven't delved into that element in depth yet."

"That's great," I said. "As long as you've utilized hand-drawn skills first." I addressed the rest of the class. "Brainstorming and sketching go hand-in-hand. However," I added, "Sometimes you'll have additional discoveries when you take the sketches to the computer. Let's see what you have."

Lisa held up a board with several pages taped at the top. The top pages were hand-drawn on marker paper, so the images were slightly transparent. "Steve and I wanted to show the class how we decided on our layout," she said. "So we bought some marker paper, and drew our composition to show the placement of our elements using overlay organization. We used Flash to help us visualize the final look of the front page, which you'll see in a minute," she said.

Zed looked at the lines drawn on the overlay, "That's pretty trippy!" he said. "What did you base it on?"

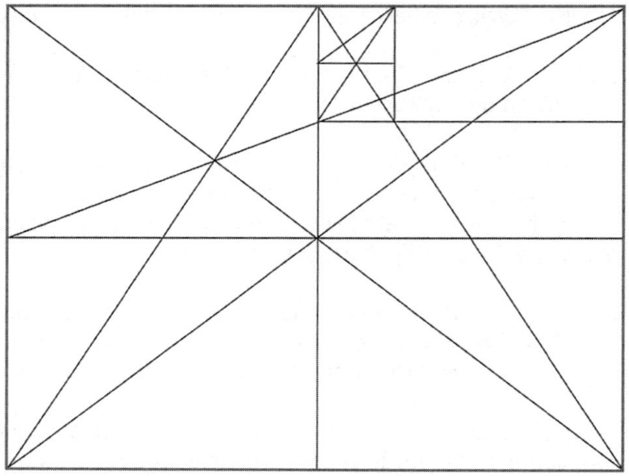

Steve answered, "We wanted to stay with the *Rule of Thirds* layout, but we also wanted to expand on this. I had a book at the office written by Jan Tschichold. He was a twentieth century German typographer, calligrapher, and teacher. He wrote about book structure and design, too. His studies on medieval book layouts were the basis for this design."

He continued to describe the layout. "One of the layouts he discovered was based on dividing a double-page spread into twelve sections. You don't even need a calculator for this one, since the page is divided by connecting the lines." He ran his finger along the lines they had drawn. "The neat thing is that a double-page magazine layout is almost the same proportion as the default Flash screen size that we've been using through out the course – 500 x 440 pixels. So we took this idea and ran with it."

"Isn't that plagiarism?" Zed asked, "It seems that you just imitated the idea."

I answered Zed's question, "It's not plagiarism when you use layouts as a study device, Zed. Plus, many print layout artists use these formulas. Utilizing them for the screen is a wonderful idea," I added. "If any one of you took this formula and added your different elements, each one of you would come up with a different look and directional approach.

"Steve used his experience to add to the development of their layout, and he's also teaching us a new device with this time-tested layout tool." I nodded at Steve and Lisa to continue.

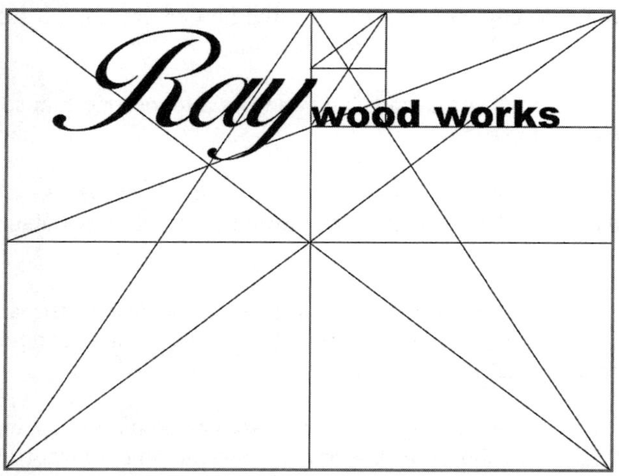

"Steve sure taught me a lot," Lisa added. "I never knew about Tschichold. His life and works are fascinating."

"There were several other layout ideas in this book," Steve said, "But we chose this one because it helped us see how we could utilize the page for navigation and for her name." He showed us how they used the top area for Frieda's surname and a description of her work.

"I notice you two went with her surname, instead of the full name," Wes stated. "Any particular reason?"

"Steve and I debated this subject for two days," Lisa admitted. "I finally agreed with Steve on the surname only, since it worked better within the layout. Plus," she added, "We wanted to use the rhetorical figures of paradox, with a touch of irony." She grinned and shrugged, "The curves in the text of her name certainly seem less construction-oriented than a bold sans-serif type like Helvetica or Arial."

"Well," Steve interrupted, "I compromised on the grid and the angular structure, too." He pointed at the next overlay, which included circular grids. "Lisa convinced me the structure needed a little softness, so we added ellipses. One is over Frieda's name, and the other once circles the entire format space."

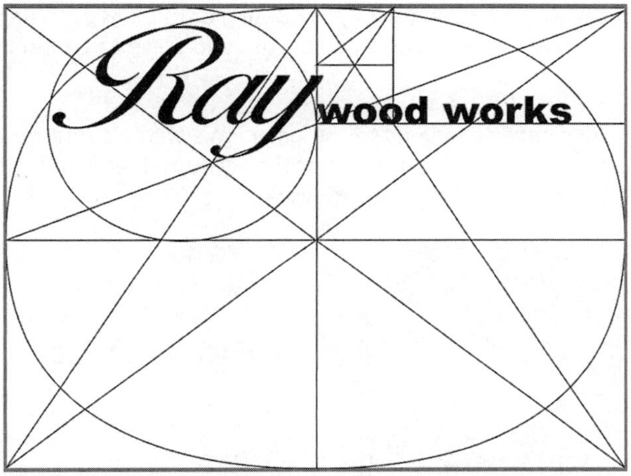

He pointed at the circle around Frieda's surname, "We didn't actually use this circle, but we left it there to utilize secondary and tertiary navigational tools."

Lisa added, "I wanted to see how our elements would flow along these lines, in addition to the angles. We knew we had four navigational elements to add in the beginning, but we left off the home page link. We'll add it to the other pages, so that additional element will stand out.

"We also wanted to include pictures of her cabinets, and possibly some text. I wasn't going to sit and figure how to lay these out along straight lines all week."

Steve laughed, "Actually, it worked out pretty well, and Lisa helped me move beyond the square grid." He showed us the next layer, which explained how they laid the navigational elements along the rim of the format ellipse.

"You kept your wooden buttons," Bonnie stated. "But, something about them seems different." She looked closer. "Ah! You changed the grain of the wood. It's moving diagonally, in line with the ellipse."

Steve grinned. "Neither of us could decide how to modify the wood buttons to clarify their purpose. But," he added, "You're right. We managed to change at least this much. We thought the deeper grain and the movement of the texture would help lead the viewer's eyes around the page, but we still haven't decided how to let the viewer know which button leads where yet."

"That's really interesting," I stated. "You've used the ellipse to create a psychic line that leads the eye from the name around to the buttons. I like the way you included the buttons within the framework of the circular grid, too. That was pretty insightful."

Bonnie stated, "I didn't know grids could be circular. I guess that's another way to think outside of the box, isn't it?"

Steve replied, "Grids can be square, circular, rectangular, and organic, Bonnie. Any shape that we've discussed in previous lessons is game for a grid. The trick to a grid is to remember to repeat it throughout a site or a publication. Once your grid is designed, be consistent."

"I couldn't have said that better myself, Steve," I said. I looked at Bonnie, "Start looking at magazine layouts, especially magazines that take more risks with their layouts. See if you can recognize grid layouts that use anything other than rectangles or squares. If you want, you can make up an *ideas* file that will help you with future designs.

"Once again, the use of someone's grid isn't plagiarism, if you modify the original design or use it as a starting point for your own original brainstorming and idea formation processes." I asked Lisa and Steve to continue their presentation.

Lisa turned that page over to show us how they added other elements to the page. "We weren't sure how to handle the text within this framework, so we just laid it out between some of the sections. It ended up as a shape that drew the eye down, but also seemed to point back up to **wood works**."

She pointed at the circle on the left. "This is where we'd put the photos of her cabinets, within a circular shape. We thought this shape might be a nice contrast to the rectangular cabinets, but we're not sure yet."

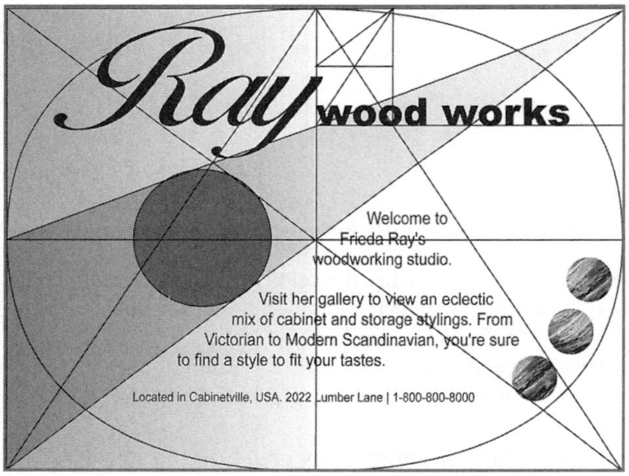

"It'd be hard to tell without the actual photos," I said. "But you can sometimes modify the photographs to work within that space. If you can't modify photographs or artwork, or simply don't have access to any," I added, "It might be a good idea to talk about this with your client. See if they have any current photos of their product, like Frieda does, or what they can afford in their budget for additional art and photos. If there's no budget, you might have to be really creative." I wanted her to lift the layout overlay so we could see the final image. "Tell us about the gradients."

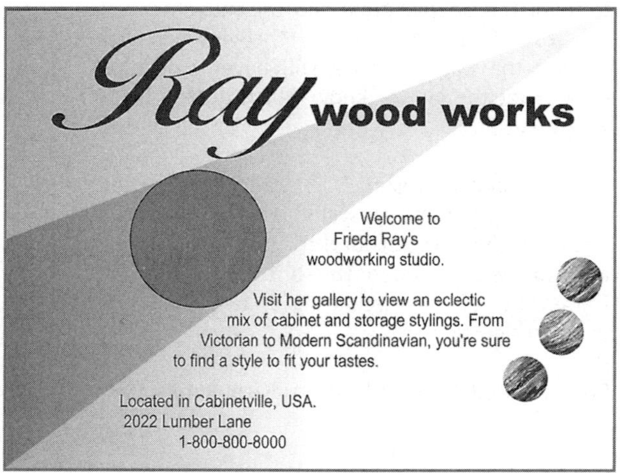

Steve sighed, "The space looked so empty without some sort of color or texture for the background. We took the triangle that was coming from the top right, and used it as a gradient background to focus on the circular space for the photographs."

"That's not a bad idea," Deb said. "Why do you seem so frustrated?"

"I can't think beyond flat two-dimensional space," Steve explained. "I can't imagine how this will look in Flash, with elements moving and changing on me.

I don't know if everything will pull together well or not. I'm not happy with how the body copy looks, either."

"The gradients are interesting," I said. "Especially if you're planning to add color or texture to the value gradations. Just remember not to use gradients to just fill a space. This is a design element that needs to be there for a specific reason, like all design elements. Don't worry about thinking in three-dimensional space or the body copy for the moment, Steve," I assured him. "You'll get there soon enough, and these are changes that are easily remedied."

"I hope so," he said. "Lisa has an easier time thinking about moving objects around in Flash. If I think along the lines of physics and sci-fi, I do OK."

"Keep thinking that way," Zed grinned. "That's how I do it, only I think about animated cartoons."

The class laughed. "Before we get to Bonnie and Zed, does anyone else have anything to add to Steve and Lisa's work?" I asked.

"The gradient that covers the whole page bothers me," Wes stated. "I like it, but I think it might work better if the white area were smaller. Maybe if you pull the gray values a little further to the right hand side of the page it would help."

"Oh, I see what you mean," Lisa said. "Thanks! That was bothering me, too, and I wasn't sure why."

Bonnie said, "I like how you used the triangle *ray* to repeat Frieda's last name in a symbolic image. I think you could have done more with that," she added.

Steve and Lisa looked at each other, "I never thought of that," Steve admitted.

"Neither did I, Steve; I didn't even realize we were repeating her name that way." She thanked Bonnie, and turned to me, "We also realized we'd take this page further into the site – we were thinking ahead."

"Would you use the same layout for the rest of the pages?" I asked.

Steve answered, "I think so. We can use this circle for other pages, and it would work well for images or any other media." He pointed at the circle under Frieda's name.

I turned to Bonnie, "Your idea of the *Ray* name and the shaded *ray* of light going through the page was very astute, Bonnie."

"What happened to Lisa's leaves?" Zed asked. He was referring to Lisa's navigation symbols from the previous week.

"Oh, we haven't forgotten those," Steve responded. "We're going to use them for our other tiers of navigation."

"Great idea," I stated. "I can't wait to see how those will work with the rest of the elements you have in place."

"Yeah, me too," Lisa laughed.

Elements of Design

1. Line
2. Shape
3. Color/hue
4. Movement
5. Space
6. Value
7. Texture
8. Typography

I stood to write the elements of design on the board, as a reminder. "How did they do along the elements of design?" I asked the class.

They thought for a moment, and Bonnie answered, "I think the elements of design are really well represented with this composition," she began. "They included *line* to direct the eye, various *shapes*, *values*, and *textures*. They also used *movement* with the ray gradient, and in the way the navigation symbols were laid along that ellipse. The *type* looks fine, in my opinion, but I'm sure I'll learn more about that today." She looked thoughtful and added, "I'm not sure how well the *space* was utilized. I guess that could use a little more work. Of course, I can't say anything about color, since we didn't use that element yet."

I looked at Steve and Lisa, "Do you agree with her assessment?"

They nodded, "I feel a little unsettled about the space we've created in some areas, but I'm very happy about how we managed to direct the eye around the page," Steve said. Lisa agreed.

Principles of Design

1. Contrast
2. Direction
3. Emphasis
4. Economy
5. Proportion
6. Balance
7. Rhythm
8. Unity

I wrote the principles of design on the board as they talked. "What about these?" I asked, pointing to the list.

Wes spoke up, "In my opinion, there could be more use of *contrast* on your page, but I can't tell until you add images. The *direction* is great, but I still don't get a strong feel for *emphasis*. It seems you can't decide which element is more important. The name has just as much weight as some of the other elements on the page."

He continued, looking at both Steve and Lisa as he talked, "*Proportion* seems good, but then again, it depends on how you place the hierarchies of importance with each element."

Steve nodded, "I felt totally bewildered when we added the circular grids. When I tried to think beyond the essence of two-dimensional formats, I lost every sense of hierarchies."

Wes nodded, "I think you'll be able to take this further. It's got a lot of *rhythm*, but I'd like to see some playful elements in there; it still seems so formally structured at present. You managed to lay out the elements with asymmetrical *balance*, even thought the format lent itself to symmetrical balance. That was a significant feat, in my opinion. The design has a certain *economy*, too. If you add more elements, I'd keep that principle in mind."

"Some excellent constructive criticism and appraising there, thanks Wes." I spoke to the rest of the class, "Notice how Wes cushioned his dislikes with plenty of positive feedback. He addressed Steve and Lisa directly, and he made his statements as a matter of opinion, not as factual demands."

I noticed the rejected look on Bonnie's face. "Bonnie, you did well, too. You just had less to talk about, and most of the information you imparted was very familiar to us. You just reaffirmed what this class already knew – a valuable contribution in itself."

I turned to Steve and Lisa. "You both still have some tweaking to do," I said, "But most of this can be done within Flash and any graphic software program. I think you have a working model on your hands."

The class applauded, and we moved on to Zed and Bonnie's work.

Bonnie and Zed

Bonnie and Zed explained their concept, and then I asked the class to assess the design according to the elements and principles of design that we were now quite familiar with.

Bonnie and Zed each held up a copy of their work. One page was the opening home page, and another was a simulation of an inside page. "Zed and I really didn't work long on this," Bonnie began.

"No apologies, Bonnie," Deb reminded her.

Bonnie waved her hand in front of her face. "Let me start over. Zed and I worked together on this project, and we happily combined his experience with comics and my experience with tables and structure."

She pointed at the opening page in her hand. "I liked the idea of using a series of cabinets in a regular structure, similar to a table or grid. Zed had the great idea of foreshortening the cabinets and laying them along a 45-degree angle. Once we did this," she said, "The rest was easy."

"Yeah," Zed added. "We just used the *Rule of Thirds* to lay out the name and the navigation buttons. We used Bonnie's images of stars, because they lent themselves to the natural and organic feel of the Scandinavian designs. That's a bit of a hint as to what's coming."

He showed the class the other page. "We decided to use the star image as the format within the page for all other information. This is as far as we got, though," he admitted.

"Wow, that's really eye-catching," Lisa said. She glanced at the board. "I'll try the elements of design, and someone else can do the principles."

She continued, "You used a variety of *lines* to bring the focus into the page. You both have *movement* with the 45-degree angle of the cabinets. I think the cabinets could carry a little less *value*, maybe so the name and other information could stand out. You've incorporated *texture* with the wood of the cabinets, and the *type* stands out pretty well – simple and clean.

"The *shapes* are interesting," Lisa added. "Although you said they remind you of the

Scandinavian design, they also remind me of the images in comic books... for some reason I'm think of words like *Kapow!* and *Shazam!* written within stars. But," she added quickly, "I don't think that's necessarily a bad thing here – the star's certainly focusing my attention. This composition has a futuristic look, like *cabinets from space*. I think the space aspect is pretty complex here, just like the universe..."

The class started to laugh, and Lisa stopped talking, "Did I say something wrong?"

"No, not at all," Steve said. "I was thinking the same thing, that's why I laughed."

"Me too," Deb said, and added, "If you're finished, I'll tackle the principles next."

Lisa grinned and nodded, Deb leaned in to have a closer look at the work, and then sat back. "Nice *contrast*, but I agree with Lisa – I think you can back off on the *value* of the cabinets. *Direction* is obvious and nicely accomplished with the angle of the cabinets. *Emphasis* is evident with the focus on Frieda's name on the front page, and with the large star format on the following page.

"There's definitely *economy* here," she continued. "I don't think you can remove anything without a problem with navigation or identity. *Proportion* and *balance* are great, but I'd like to see what you're going to put in that formatted star. Whatever you do, I would be careful about overwhelming the page with a lot of unnecessary elements.

"The *rhythm* is apparent with the repetition of shapes, both with the star and the cabinets. To summarize, I think this is a great, simple design that tells us a lot about Frieda."

Bonnie and Zed looked pleased. "We were happy with how easy this was for us. We just kept working with the elements and principles of design notes next to us," Bonnie said. "Plus, it didn't hurt that Zed is an addictive note taker. He had a bunch of great ideas."

Zed looked at Bonnie and added, "I don't think Bonnie knows it yet, but our analogy throughout the site is to the comics, modified by some reality and streamlining of images and type."

"I'm surprised you didn't personify a cabinet," Steve said.

"She wouldn't let me," Zed answered, pointing a thumb at Bonnie.

Bonnie grinned, "No way. Frieda's not into comics."

"You two did a great job of simplifying Frieda's vision without the complication of personification," I said. "You may want to work on that text a bit more after today. Plus," I added, "I also really want to see how you both handle information within that star format. Otherwise, you've got a great working model on your hands. I'm very happy you both combined your learning and your experiences to produce this work. Congratulations on a very economical design."

The class once again applauded, and Wes and Deb prepared for their presentation.

Deb and Wes

Deb seemed amused at the onset of their presentation. Wes seemed a little mystified, not the usual demeanor for this man. We were all curious to see what this team had to offer.

Deb began by telling the class about her art history research. "This week has been quite an experience for me in more ways than one. When I began reading about the Symbolist movement, all I could see was that the poet Rimbaud insisted artists must become deranged to achieve the insight necessary for this style of painting!"

Wes looked miserable as the rest of us tried not to laugh. Deb continued, "But I read further into this movement. These artists considered themselves seers, with the ability to see beyond reality. Although they were reverent toward their subject matter, they also exaggerated aesthetic sensibilities. They became more esoteric, exotic, visionary, and dreamlike with their representations.

"It's important to note here that these artists came into this movement at the same time that Sigmund Freud began the age of psychiatry with the publication of his *Interpretation of Dreams*." She picked at the edge of her artwork. "The insight into this movement provided me with the impetus to be *insane* myself. This is why I quit my job."

Everyone looked at Wes. "Well," he stammered, "She didn't have to go overboard like that. It wasn't my intention, I assure you."

Deb patted Wes on the back. "If I were poor, it would be a different matter, Wes. I'm fine, trust me."

He sighed, and stated they needed to present their work. "I'll begin," he said. "We had a few differences of opinion until about two days ago. This was when she quit her job," he added. "Then, it all fell into place. Since we were rushed to provide images, we have yet to complete the rest of the content."

Deb added, "This piece shows the images we might use, including the windowed cabinet face, which is the navigation device."

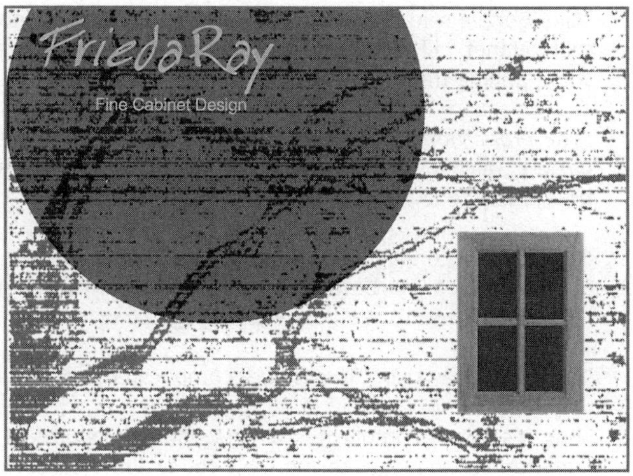

"That's clever," Bonnie said. "It looks like a window, and the wood grain makes it seem like it's on a house. But the tree in the background really isn't in the background, it's on the house, and..." She stopped and looked at Wes and Deb. "This is really quite esoteric."

Wes nodded, "I know. Before we get too deep in the meanings behind everything, why don't we just address the elements and principles," he requested.

Deb shrugged, "I think the meanings are important, but if no one sees them, then they'll just stay subliminal. The rhetorical figures are a bit of metaphor, and there's a whole lot of symbolism."

I assured Deb, "Don't worry about whether we *get it* or not. I'd rather hear how people feel when looking at these pieces."

Steve nodded, "I get it. This is wild. I can almost feel the movement in both these pages." He looked at me. "How about I address the elements and then we'll go from there?" I nodded, and he continued. "The organic lines of the tree are nice, and I like the additional horizontal lines of the wood grain."

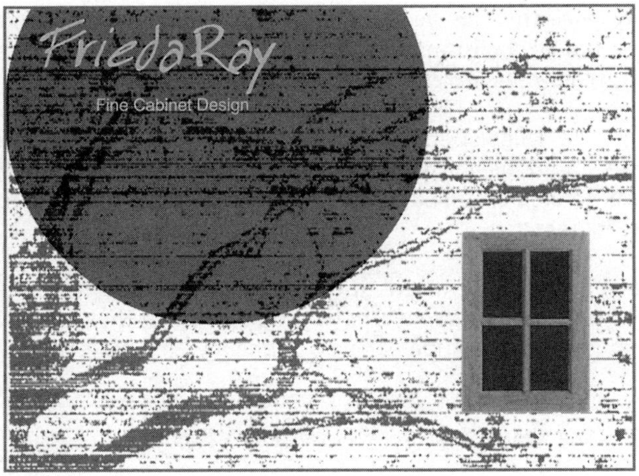

"You both used primal *shapes*, and that really helps with the space disorientation in the layers. I wish I could know the *colors* you're going to use, because there's something about this that says Oriental to me, rather than Scandinavian." He shrugged, "But it could be a northern winter environment, too."

Steve kept staring at the piece, and continued his critique, "The *movement* of the tree branches brings me into the piece, and the circle keeps me going. The cabinet face is definitely a stopper – keeps me from going off the page. There's tons of *value* and *texture*, and the *type* is really unusual. Her name's really artsy, but I can still read it. The feeling I get is dreamy, or surreal. It's definitely high-end."

Lisa nodded, "I get the high-end message, too. You both applied all the principles of design. There's *contrast* in between the illustrated images and the photograph of the cabinet face, and in the *contrast* between the artsy name and the description of what she does.

"Like Bonnie said, the tree limbs give me *direction*, and the circles hold me on the page. I'm not sure how that cabinet will work as a navigational tool once you add more information," she added. "It might be too stark, pulling the eye away from the information.

"The *proportions* seem right. The asymmetrical *balance* is wonderful, in my opinion. I can feel the *rhythm* between all the elements, with the repetition of shapes, and with the branches. It seems they'll nod in the breeze any second."

"It seems to me that your *values* need a little tweaking," I said. "The name is hard to read, but I'm not turned off by the *type* you both used. I think you both worked hard to bring this image to life in black and white. I'll be interested to see how you manage *color* down the road."

"So will I," Wes said. "This is very complicated, not as simple or economical as Zed's and Bonnie's work."

"But, it's not as complicated as Steve and Lisa's project, either," I added. All of you brought your own skills and graphic languages to the table today. I'm pleased with all the work."

"Does that mean we get a stamp of approval?" Wes asked.

"It certainly does, Wes!" I grinned.

After the whoops and cheers from the class, I offered them a much-needed break, "When you return, we're going to tackle typography in design."

The fundamentals of typography

Since Frieda Ray's actual name was crucial to her developing identity, the typefaces used to render her name would be an important element. As the class returned from break, I asked them to go to their computers and open up Flash MX. "A few of you may be familiar with typography," I said. "But these essential basics will be a good refresher for you, and an important lesson for the rest of the class.

"The fundamentals of typography include the design and function of alphabetic and alphanumeric symbols in any given language. There's so much information available on typography that we can't possibly cover all the nuances in this course. My suggestion," I said, "Is to utilize other resources to learn more. This is even more important if you want to go on to design your own typefaces."

I reminded them about the information I gave them during the second week of class. "We covered typography briefly when we talked about the elements of design. During that class, I mentioned that some type was commonly used for readability.

"You learned that sans-serif is often good for headlines, and that serif is good for body copy. The theory being that the serifs in text tend to help the viewer's eye go from word to word." I paused, and added, "But, within the past decade, many typefaces have been developed specifically for the monitor. These faces are designed with pixels, and they've been designed specifically for readability on the screen.

"Suddenly, the theory of using only serifs for body copy has been thrown out the window. Now," I explained, "There are sans-serif typefaces that have been tested online and shown to read as well, if not better, than some serif typefaces. One, in particular, is the Verdana font designed for online viewing."

"That's interesting," Steve said. "I was weaned on the '*serif for copy, sans-serif for headline*' rule."

"Just keep these thoughts in mind, Steve," I said. "Print and onscreen viewing are two different animals. Although some concepts and structures haven't changed, you'll discover a lot more creative room designing with Flash MX. It can be liberating, but the many choices can be a little daunting, too."

I turned to the rest of the class. "Using the Text tool, I want you to type Frieda Ray's name in Arial, and below it, type it again in a Times New Roman typeface. Left-justify your type, using the justify buttons in the top right of the Property inspector." I showed a few students how to justify the names.

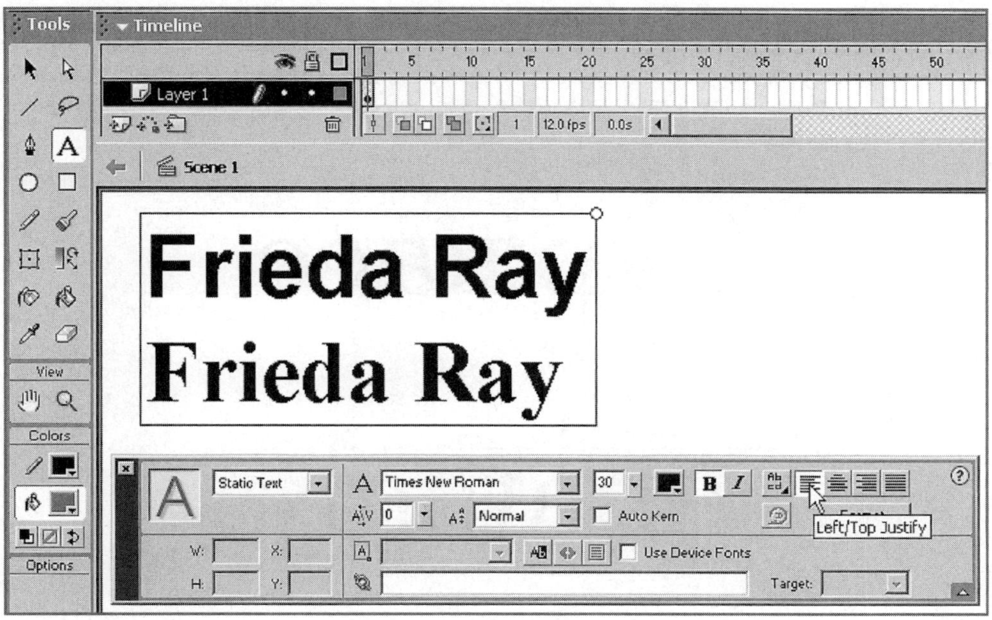

"We're going to learn about the various elements within the element of type first, then how a body of copy can be refined. The top line that you just typed is one of many sans-serif typefaces; the bottom line is one of many serif typefaces.

"As we briefly mentioned in an earlier class, Flash isn't limited to using the standard web fonts – it embeds the fonts in the published Flash movie so the user doesn't need to have the same fonts installed on their system."

"Hearing you emphasize that is a relief!" said Bonnie. "Using the standard web fonts for HTML websites can sometimes make them look a little tired."

"So what's the difference between Flash MX and HTML when it comes to fonts?" asked Wes.

"Well Wes, when an HTML document is displayed, it displays text using the computer's system fonts. If the HTML document uses a font not installed on the system, then text is displayed using some other default font.

"Because of this cross-platform problem, a few basic fonts are recognized as being standard web fonts, which are used across the board. Standard web-fonts include Arial, Courier, Helvetica, and Times New Roman."

"Whenever I build web pages in HTML," Bonnie started, "I'm limited to this basic font set. If I want to use any other fonts, I have to render the text in Photoshop and display it as an image."

"Flash MX embeds the font within the Flash movie and displays them as vector graphics. It therefore doesn't rely on the system fonts of users. This means that you and other Flash developers have a free rein on which fonts you use in your Flash websites.

"For the moment though, let's stick to using the serif font Times New Roman and the sans-serif font Arial."

"If we must." groaned Bonnie.

"So," Deb said. "*Sans* means *without*. Arial is obviously minus a serif or two."

"You've got it, Deb," I replied. "Both typefaces have a few things in common, though." As I talked, I passed around some visuals showing the named descriptions for the various elements of a standard typeface. "Take a look at the type on your monitor, and compare it to these definitions. And note that although this uses a serif typeface as an example, the terminology is also applicable to sans-serif fonts."

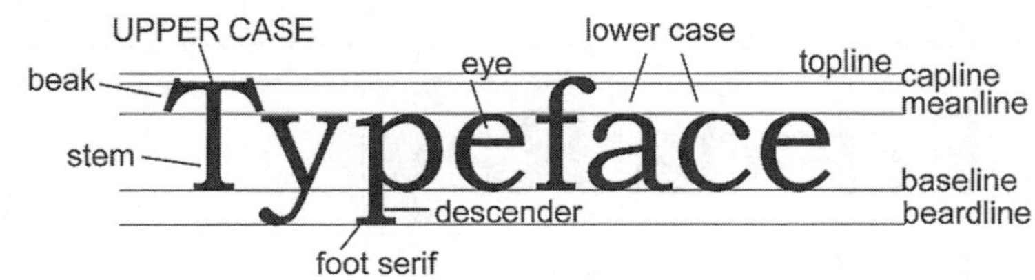

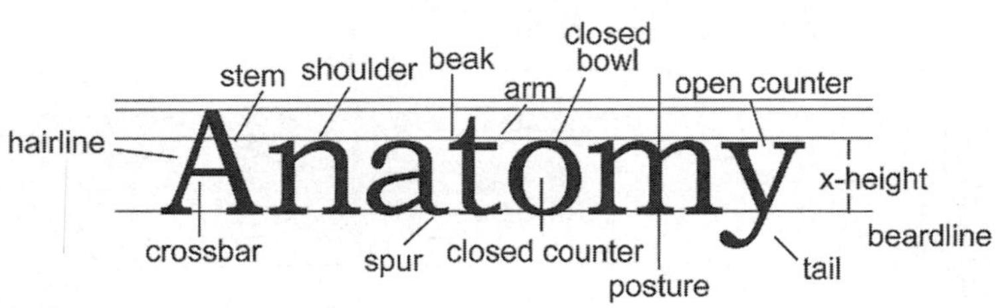

"These are definitely some creative names for the anatomies of type," Deb said. "It's interesting to see a *tail* resting on a *beardline*. It's goofy, but it makes sense, too."

"We'll get into some stranger names as we go along, Deb," I replied. "But, the very strangeness of the names can make them easy to remember. That said, I don't expect you to memorize every description listed here," I continued. "However, it would be a good thing to practice using these terms as we talk about type. This is common terminology among designers and printers. If you modify typefaces, you'll especially need to remember the terms so you can make notes for yourself or others to follow down the road.

"Although a designer creates a typeface to be used *as is*, there are certain things you may need to apply to a typeface for it to fit a line of type, or for it to look just right within your designs. We'll discuss these shortly," I stated.

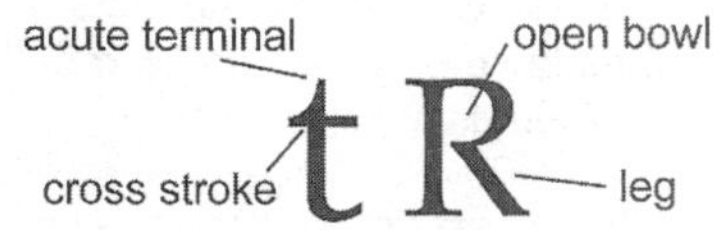

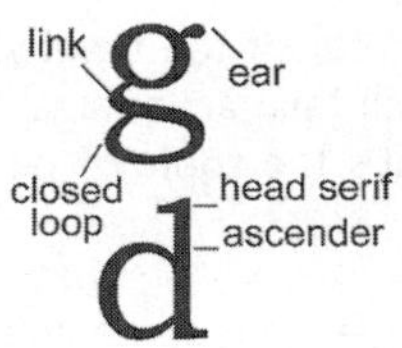

"Another point about modifying a typeface, while we're on that subject," I added. "Many typefaces were designed based on the modification of another typeface. Baskerville is one serif typeface that has seen popularity over the years, but it wasn't that way in the beginning. John Baskerville was a stonemason and had mastered the art of lacquering until he became interested in printing in his early forties. These skills kept him afloat financially, as his typeface creation was unacceptable to type designers and type foundries of his time – 18th century England.

"When it was created, the Baskerville typeface had straighter lines and flatter serifs than ever used before. Since then, many faces have been developed based on John Baskerville's mechanical approach to lettering. Many type foundries today even have their own versions of Baskerville, and each one is a little different, including the addition of cupped serifs.

"Today, type designers are leaning more toward protecting their typefaces, mostly because people modify them without any sense of how a typeface is designed. Baskerville spent many hours studying his type, and he kept these skills secret until they were revealed many years after his death. Many hours of work go into type designs today, and new designers might take that face and modify it with little regard to how or why each face was developed in its current form.

"Anyway, it's worth remembering that most typefaces were designed with no alterations or modifications in mind. So if you want to make changes, you should ensure that the type you're about to modify isn't protected with copyright or trademarks. And don't modify a typeface unless you've decided beyond any shadow of a doubt that your design needs this modification.

"Later today, I'll show you how to modify type within Flash. My concern is that you understand that type doesn't need to be modified unless your design calls for the modification. Although typography is an element of design," I concluded, "It's a *designed* element of design. Study the various type families and faces, and use what fits your design, with little or no modification unless absolutely necessary."

Steve agreed. "Some typefaces are really beautiful, if you take the time to look at them, and understand why they're designed in a specific way. On the other hand," he added, "There are plenty of new faces today, and a lot of them are available free of charge, or as *shareware*, on the web. These faces usually are fun and a little different from most regular fonts we're used to. However, the spacing and design in these fonts can be a mess sometimes. Most of them aren't handy to use if you want to develop body copy from them. They can be great for a new effect with headlines, though."

Size and width

We continued on with the students typing Frieda's name into text boxes in Flash. Steve waved his hand for attention, "Does the size of type matter in Frieda's name?" Steve asked.

"That's a good question, Steve." I asked the students to use a size that was comfortable for them, one where they could see the lines of type clearly. "Pretend you're using her name as a headline." I said. "Whatever size you choose, use it for both lines."

As I walked around the class, I noticed each student had chosen various sizes for Frieda's name. Zed had already colored her name red. "I'd like for you to keep the type black for the moment," I said as I tapped his shoulder.

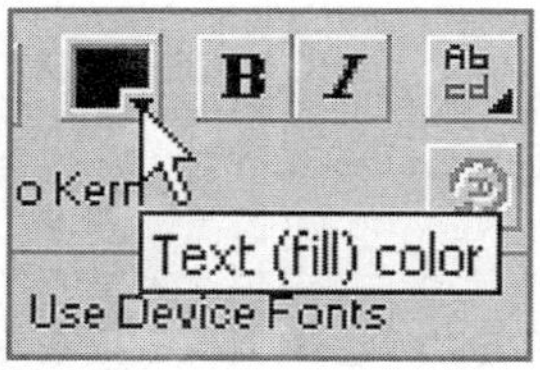

Zed grinned, "You're no fun, teach."

Addressing the class, I said, "We can indeed change the color of the typeface from the options in the Property inspector, and you can all take advantage of this after we've covered the use of color in design – that's the topic of next week's class, as it happens.

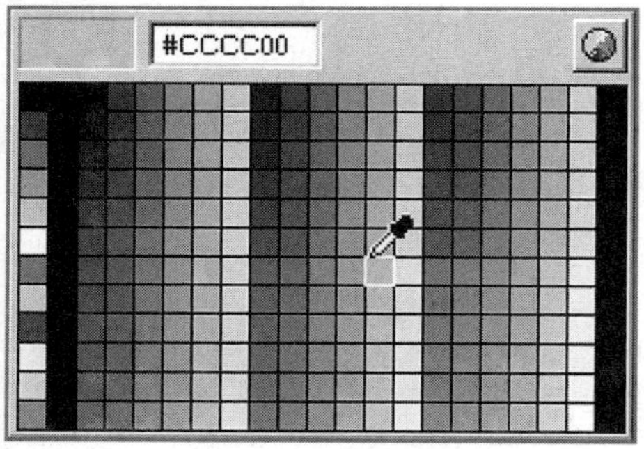

"For the moment, however, just remember that some color combinations can create what is known as **vibration**. When you place some colors of type against another color background, the type seems to vibrate."

"Is that anything close to the element of movement?" Zed asked.

I smiled, "Type vibration created from incongruous color combinations is a form of movement, but I would say it isn't exactly a positive step toward the element of movement. We'll cover some of these combinations next week. Right now, let's continue with the typography fundamentals.

"When type was first manufactured, it was carved or cast into the face of a three-dimensional block. The size was determined by the size of the block, rather than on the character. This measure is still used today in digital type. The point size is determined by the highest ascender and lowest descender in each typeface."

I asked Steve to tell us what he knew about hierarchies of type and how point size indicated the breaks. "Well," Steve began, "Headlines usually dominate the hierarchy. Traditionally, in print, the sizes range anywhere above 12 point. This is also called **display type**. The size of the format would help decide the size of the type.

"For large formats," he continued, "72 point type is often used for headlines, and something smaller, like a 36 or 24 point typeface is used for subheads. Anything below 12 point type is used for body copy. The size often indicates the importance of information."

He stopped and then said, "I can't forget columns and margins. These tools help keep the type in shape. **Columns** are usually vertical blocks of visual matter, and **gutters** are the spaces between columns. **Margins** are the spaces around the copy, at the top, bottom, right, and left side of a single page."

"Would 72-point type be too big for the Flash MX format?" Bonnie asked.

"Not necessarily, Bonnie," I responded. "Once images and content are added, a 72-point size typeface may or may not be too large, both visually and in file size. We'd have to decide according to context, especially when we get into type in motion and additional elements in the page."

I pointed to their screens. "One thing I do want you to notice is that, although you initially chose the same size for both faces, one is longer than the other."

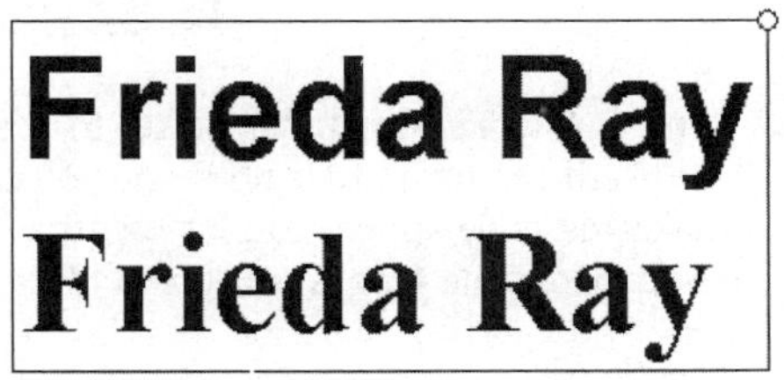

"Wow!" Zed peered at his monitor. "I didn't notice that until now. I mean, I saw it, but it didn't register."

Steve sighed, "If you've spent a lifetime fitting text to a specific space, you'd know how important type sizes in various faces can be. I've spent many long hours trying to fit different typefaces into a predetermined space, only to have a client decide they'd rather have a serif type than sans-serif."

I laughed, "I can relate to that, Steve. The rest of you will find out what Steve means when you begin to fit your copy into various slots in Frieda's site. What you're dealing with here is the **width** of the type. Each character has a different width in each typeface, and the accumulation of characters to create a word adds up to the width of the word.

"Various styles of character width include **condensed**, **regular**, and **extended**. Each style will carry the interval of space between the vertical strokes and counters. This," I added, "Is different to character spacing. The width of a character involves only the letter or character itself.

"For now, just remember that there are spacing issues with regular type, and even more if you decide to modify the face. Every change you make will change the look of your site, so experiment early and often in the rough stages of layout."

I asked them to type a paragraph into the Flash format, using a sans-serif typeface. "Use anything you want, and make it about five sentences long," I instructed. Most of them typed in copy they were working on for Frieda's site. Wes and Deb had typed the following:

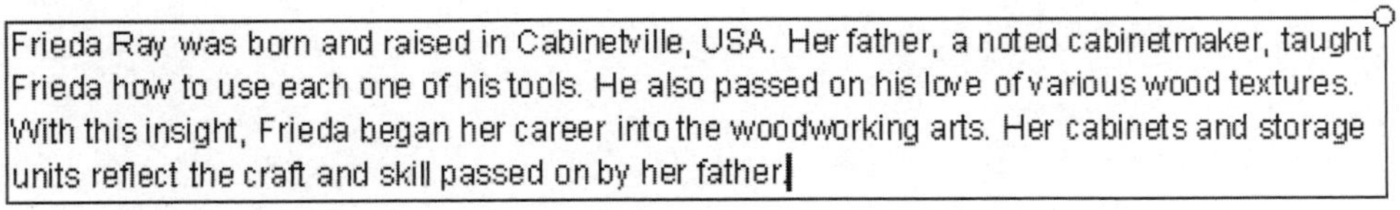
Frieda Ray was born and raised in Cabinetville, USA. Her father, a noted cabinetmaker, taught Frieda how to use each one of his tools. He also passed on his love of various wood textures. With this insight, Frieda began her career into the woodworking arts. Her cabinets and storage units reflect the craft and skill passed on by her father.

After they had typed in this paragraph, I asked them to change the font to a serif typeface, but keep the same paragraph space, and the same type size. The paragraph promptly shrunk in size. "That's wild," Wes stated. "I never realized there would be so much difference between the two styles of fonts."

Arial - sans-serif

Frieda Ray was born and raised in Cabinetville, USA. Her father, a noted cabinetmaker, taught Frieda how to use each one of his tools. He also passed on his love of various wood textures. With this insight, Frieda began her career into the woodworking arts. Her cabinets and storage units reflect the craft and skill passed on by her father.

Times New Roman - serif

Frieda Ray was born and raised in Cabinetville, USA. Her father, a noted cabinetmaker, taught Frieda how to use each one of his tools. He also passed on his love of various wood textures. With this insight, Frieda began her career into the woodworking arts. Her cabinets and storage units reflect the craft and skill passed on by her father.

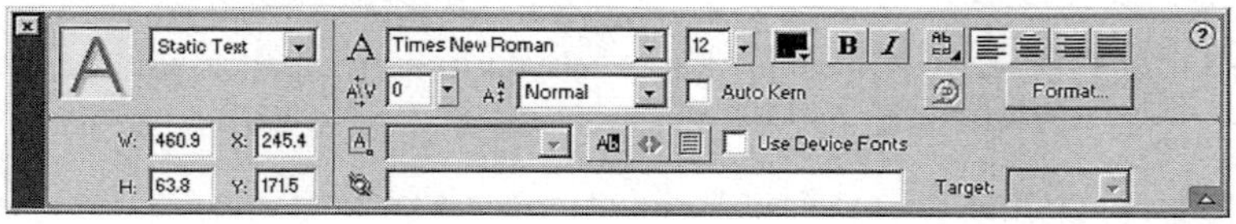

"This is why it's sometimes better to use a sans-serif rather than a serif for body copy online," I stated. "The sans-serif can be more legible, and you can also shrink it without all the confusing serif appendages that would make the copy appear to blur together. Take a look at some sites, especially their small print for legalese," I continued. "The type is small, and it's in a sans-serif, which makes it easier to read at that small size."

"OK, moving on, size lends a hand to emphasis and weight – let's tackle these topics next."

Emphasis and weight

I gestured at their screens, "Look at how the letters stand. This is called **character posture**. The upright position of these letters is referred to as **Roman**, after the Romans, who used vertically upright letters until the fifteenth century."

"What happened then?" Bonnie asked.

"Back in 1499 CE, a typefounder named Francesco Griffo created a typeface that resembled cursive handwriting," I answered. "He wanted a type that would fit closer, so he could put more words on a printed page. Griffo invented the first **italic** letters. Letters that resemble Roman letters, but slant to the right are known as **oblique** or **sloped Roman.**" I asked them to highlight Frieda's names with the mouse and make them italic using the italic button of the Property inspector.

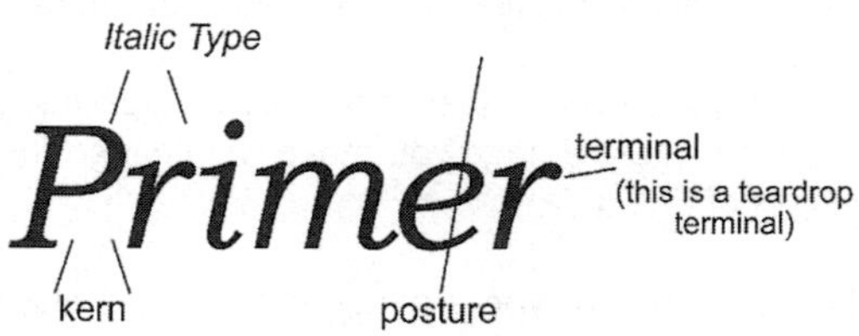

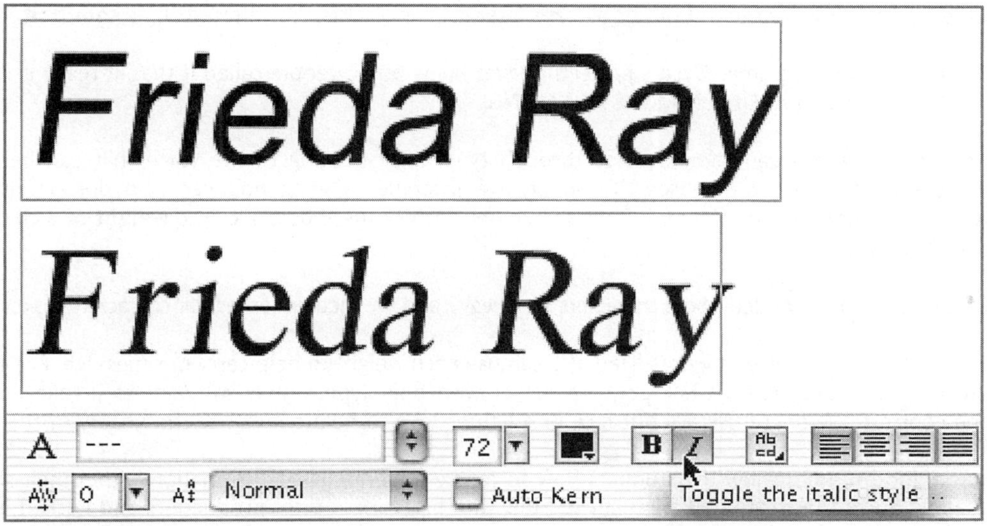

"Usually, we would use italics to emphasize a word in body copy, or to portray motion in static type," I said.

Steve added, "For sure, you don't want to use it in a whole block of copy. It can be irritating to read that way, because it's not the usual way we read type."

"That's right, Steve." I asked them to remove the italic styling and then make the names bold in a similar manner to before.

"It would be just as irritating to make all your words bold," I said. "Does anyone have a clue why this doesn't work well in large blocks of copy?"

Deb answered, "I imagine it has something to do with the hierarchies Steve mentioned earlier. If everything's bold, it can be confusing to the reader."

Zed added, "When folks write in bold or all caps in emails or on lists, it's referred to as **shouting**."

Wes laughed for the first time, "That's perfect! I never knew other people called it that; it really irritates me – ALL BLOCK CAPITALS ARE EVEN MORE ANNOYING! "

I added, "You certainly can carry a voice through type, and shouting is one voice that can be used to advantage for attention. If overused, it can be like listening to an announcer who doesn't quit. Bold characters are in contrast to regular or light characters. Each of these describes the **weight** of a character in any given typeface."

"I can see that," Deb responded. "Bold characters look heavy, and the medium or regular characters looked lighter."

"That's an interesting choice of words, Deb. We can use each weight to help carry our message. For example, it might not be appropriate to talk about a flower with bold type, unless we want to invoke irony with extreme contrast. We might use a script face or a lighter type to help emphasize the beauty of the flower."

This was a good time to show the students how to create a hierarchy of information within their sites with type. I asked Steve to explain how he managed this with his work in print production, and I asked everyone to join him and Lisa at their computer. "We usually use a sans-serif for headings and serif for body copy, like I said before," he began. "I'd like to try showing how we do this using all sans-serif for each one."

He wrote a heading in a sans-serif type: *View The Gallery*. The size was 42 pt and bold. The subheading went directly under the main heading, and it read: *Five Styles To Fit Your Needs*. This was in 24 pt and it was also in bold.

Steve began typing a few sentences below this in the same sans-serif face. The body copy was 14 point and he kept the type in a regular face, with no bold or italics. "Normally, we wouldn't use a 14 pt type for body copy," Steve stated. "But it seems right here. It's easier to read."

Wes agreed. "I think anything smaller would make the headings seem too large, too."

I asked Steve to change the body copy to 12 pt. "See?" Wes pointed a finger at Steve's screen. "The headings look to heavy, like they're ready to topple over on the body copy."

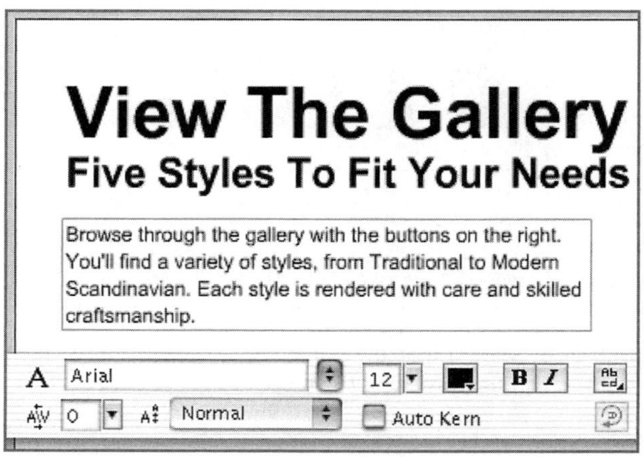

"I guess size is really important in creating information hierarchies in type," Bonnie stated. "I haven't been careful with this in the past. I'll pay more attention to it in the future."

I looked at the copy Steve wrote on the screen. "If you'll notice, some of the letters seem close together in the heading and some of them seem too far apart in the subhead." I pointed at Steve's screen. "Take a look at the *r* and *y* in the word *Gallery* in the heading."

"They look like they're kissing," Bonnie stated, and everyone laughed.

"They do, don't they?" I showed them the capital *F* and the small *i* in the words *Five* and *Fit* in the subheading. "These letters seem to be too far apart, don't they?"

"They do," Deb agreed. "How do we fix that?"

"Let's talk about that now," I said. "This problem can be remedied with a little **kerning** and **tracking**."

Kerning and tracking

I continued, "We obviously need to concern ourselves with letter size and weight. The other thing we need to notice is the space between letters." I asked them to return to their computers, and I pointed out the spaces between the letters in Frieda's names on their screens. "When a designer creates a typeface, they leave room for spacing between letters. Each letter in this alphabet has a width determined by its structure. When letters are placed together to form a word, the space between them is known as **differential** or **proportional spacing**. "The type designer does their best to make each letter fit with all the other letters and numbers in this language. It's almost impossible to make each space seem just right for every occasion, though." I asked them to look at the difference in space between the *F* and the *r* in the Arial version of Frieda's first name.

Frieda Ray

"There seems to be a lot of space there," Lisa said. "I noticed that, but I wasn't sure if it was supposed to be that way or not. Plus, some of the letters look like they're crowding each other."

"You're right," Steve answered. "Each typeface has its own difficulties with spacing, like Linda said. Usually you can take care of most of these problems with kerning or tracking."

"OK, I'm stumped," Wes said. "Tell me what kerning and tracking mean so I can add these terms to my design trivia knowledge."

Steve laughed. "It's a great way to make copy fit or look right," he said. "**Tracking** is used to modify a whole word, a sentence, an entire paragraph or a whole story. It's the space across a range of letters, and it's very important to keep an eye on this space. If the type is tracked too loosely, the reader's eye will slow down, because the words don't hold together as well."

I agreed, "Remember, we can treat the alphabet as a code; this code is comprised of letters that form words. We've also learned how to read these words in *clumps*. If the tracking is too loose, the code seems to fall apart.

"Although Flash doesn't explicitly allow you to change the tracking of text, using the character spacing slide bar in the Property Inspector on a block of text comes close." I took Steve's paragraph and increased the tracking drastically.

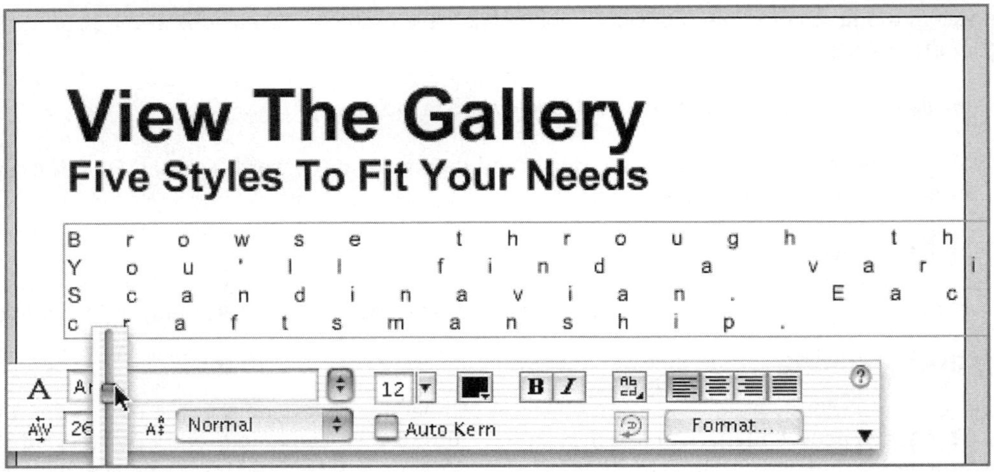

"See how the words seem to become just a series of letters?"

"It's hard to read," Zed admitted. "What happens if we kern it tightly?"

I had them tighten the tracking on the paragraph. "Yikes!" Zed jumped back. "I've just created a blob!"

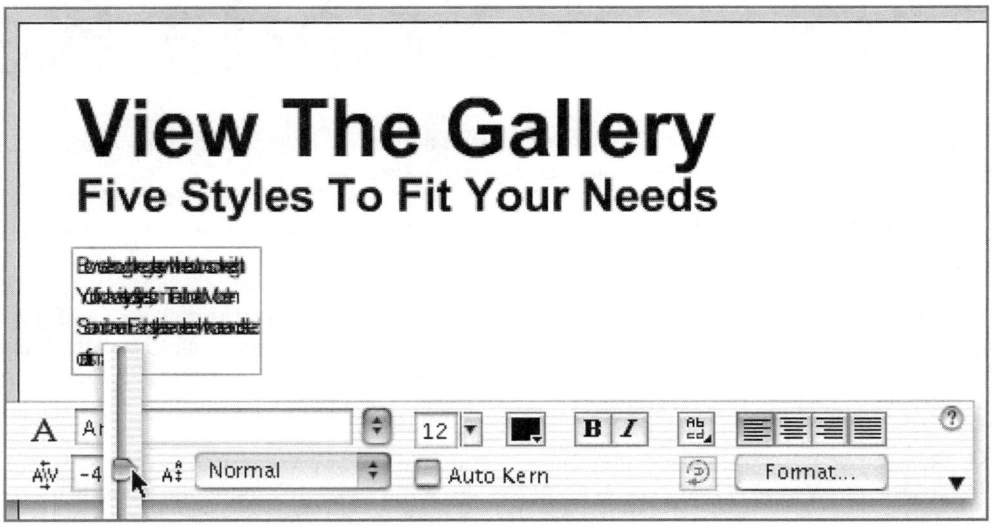

"Once again, the reader will have a tough time with your words, because their energy is spent on deciphering the code you just wrote," I stated.

After the students had played with the character spacing slider for a short while, Bonnie was first to speak up, "We adjusted the tracking across the paragraph, but some letters are still *kissing* and some are still too far apart," she complained. "This just isn't working!"

"Tracking is entirely different from kerning," Steve replied. "Tracking is used for spacing across a range of words or letters, whereas **kerning** refers to the space relationship between two specific letters or characters."

"By default Flash will render the text without kerning, but if the spaces are wrong, like with the Arial *F* and *r*, then you can alter the kerning and spacing. Flash has an Auto Kern option which will attempt to correctly space the characters according to how the designer made them in the typeface design."

"How do you know how much space to place between letters, if we're not happy with the Auto Kern?" Bonnie asked.

"You just have to use your best judgment," Steve answered. "I once had an instructor who told me that the space was right only when it *looked right*."

I agreed. "**Positive** kerning or tracking values move characters apart, and **negative** kerning or tracking moves characters or words closer together. Although kerning and tracking values are measured in units that are a thousandth of an *em space*, this space sometimes still doesn't work when you eyeball the type. It's especially noticeable in headings and subheads."

"What's an *em space*?" Wes asked. "Is that the space that the letter *M* takes up?"

I answered, "That's the idea Wes – the width of an **em space** is therefore relative to the type size you use, not the type of font. In a 1-point font, 1 em space corresponds to 1 point; in a 10-point font, 1 em corresponds to 10 points. Because kerning and tracking units are a thousandth of the em space, 100 units in a 10-point font are equivalent to 1 point.

"How do we change the kerning of text in Flash?" asked Bonnie.

"As we've just see, we can alter the spacing of the text in Flash MX via the Property inspector." I answered.

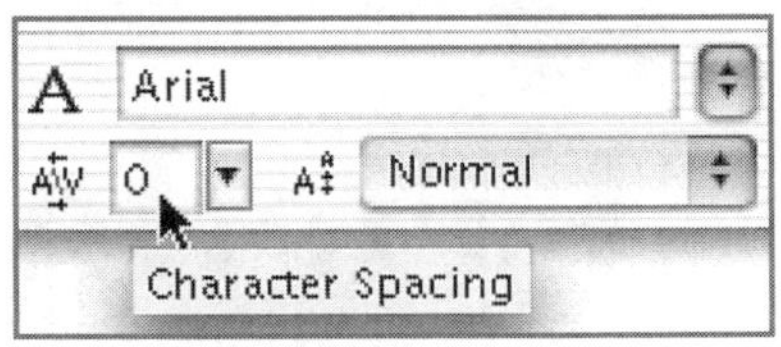

"So, we can also alter the kerning of individual characters." I told the class to follow my instructions to get a feel for kerning.

"Select the Text tool and then highlight the *F* character in Frieda's name. Then drag the character spacing slide bar downwards."

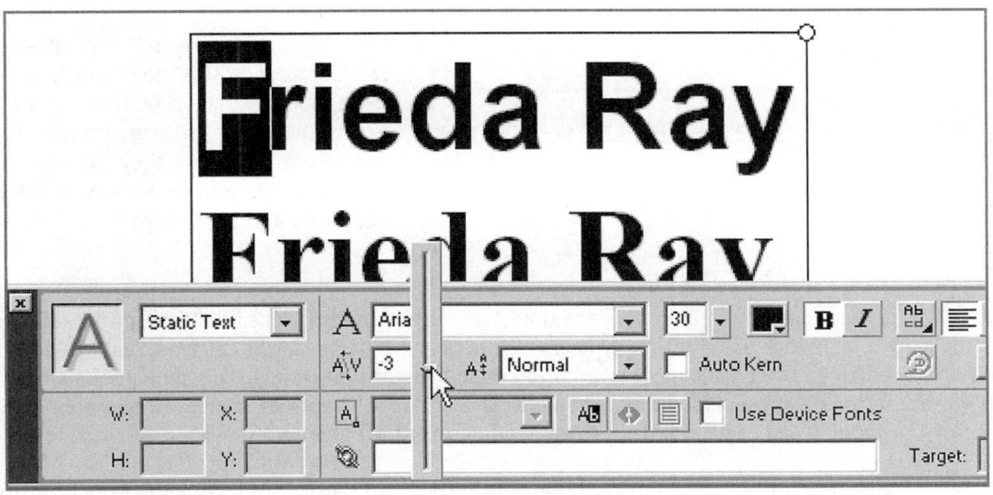

"Dragging the slider downwards, or entering minus numbers down to ***-60*** in the character spacing box moves the non-highlighted text – *rieda Ray* – closer to the *F*. Moving the slider upwards, or entering positive numbers up to ***+60*** in the box moves the other characters further away from the *F*.

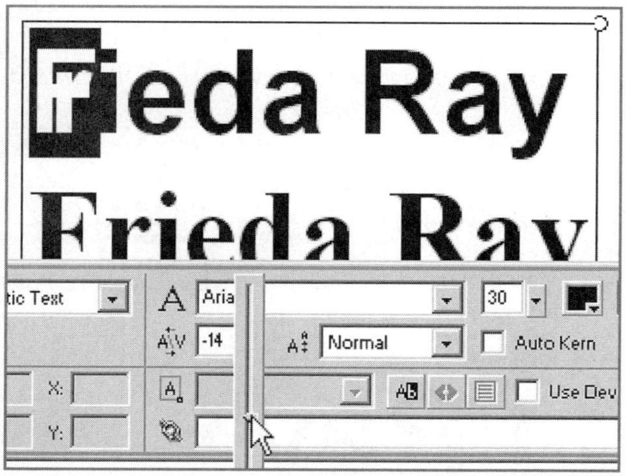

"This is where your eyeballing skills come into play, so experiment with it until you are happy. It takes some practice, and you can drive yourself mad by perfecting each word."

"Oh, yeah," Steve laughed. "I've been driven mad more than once by letters that just don't sit right with other letters in headline and subheads. That's where they matter most in some cases. Capital letters are really hard to fit together, too."

"All block caps are actually rather hard to read," I added. "The next time you pick up a newspaper or magazine, notice how the type is set. Check out the size and how the letters are kerned. Notice if they use all caps, and if they vary the serif or sans-serif between the headlines and body copy."

Leading

"Another sort of spacing we need to concern ourselves with is **leading**," I said. "Typesetters originally used a strip of lead to separate each line of type blocks, hence the name. In digital type, leading describes the vertical space between the baselines of two consecutive lines of typesetting. This space equals the type size and any predetermined space allowed between baselines. Usually," I added, "It's about two points more than the size of the type. If you use 9 point type, the leading may be 11 point."

"Leading is automatic with text boxes in Flash, but the setting can be changed trough Format... button in the Property inspector."

"Flash works a bit differently to standard layout applications, by using relative point values between -360 and +720, rather than the total point value for the line spacing. The way we control leading in Flash is basically the same as how we controlled kerning."

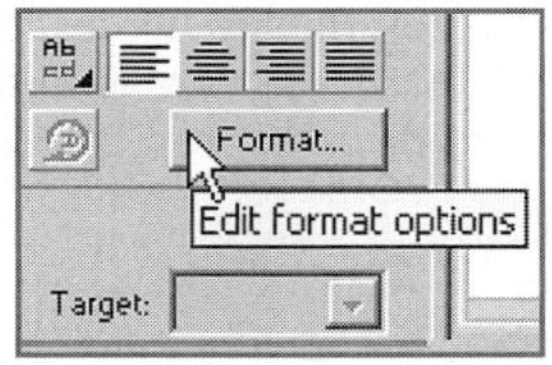

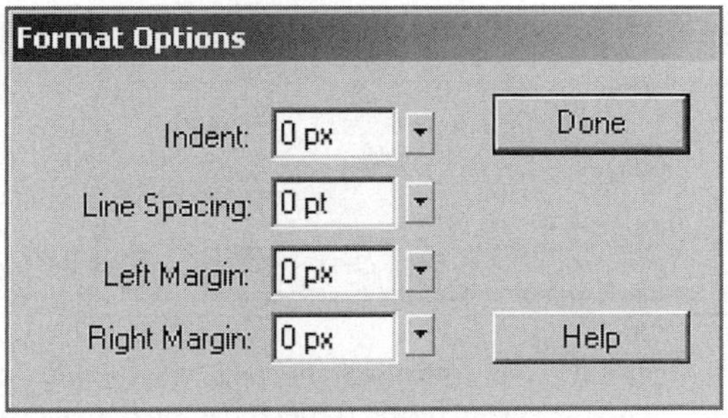

I then gave the students some more instructions "In the Arial version of Frieda's name, use the Text tool and add a line break between her first and last name. Then highlight her entire name and use the Line Spacing slider in the Format Options window to change the line spacing. Drag the slider down, or enter a minus value to tighten the line spacing, and drag the slider up or enter a positive value to increase the value."

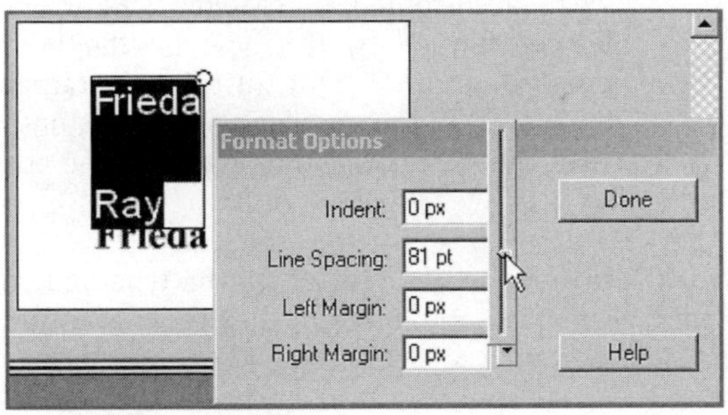

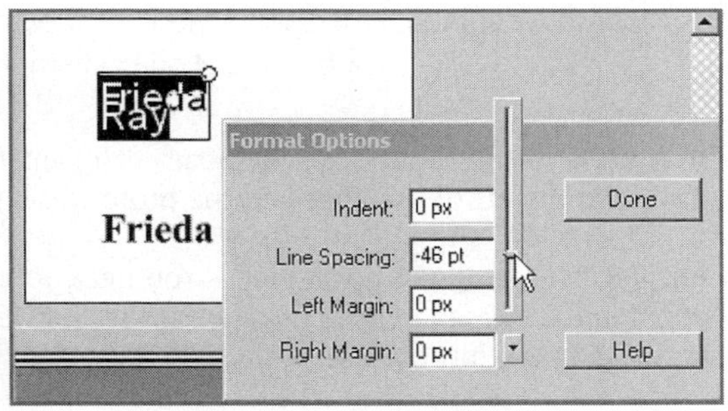

"The options here also allow you to alter the indentation and margins – we'll take a look at this in a moment," I said.

Formatting and justification

Next up, I asked Steve and Lisa if I could use their computer, and asked the rest of the students to watch how justification could alter the way we read a chunk of text. "Steve mentioned hierarchies created through columns, separated with gutters and margins. Columns of type are justified, and they can be flush left, flush right, or centered. They can also be fully justified, or full flush – this last justification is often used in newspapers.

"In fact, when your type is fully justified, you need to watch for huge spaces between your words and letters, especially in the final line. These **rivers**, the white spaces between words, can flow through an entire page, leading the viewer's eye right past the printed word." I pointed at the screen where I'd just typed up a sentence and justified it in a number of different ways. "See how the words are justified end to end of this column? The first line makes sense, but the second line looks like a riddle!"

Watch your justification for problems with rivers, widows,
a n d o r p h a n s .

Watch your justification for problems with rivers, widows,
and orphans.

Watch your justification for problems with rivers, widows,
and orphans.

Watch your justification for problems with rivers, widows,
and orphans.

I returned to the text that Steve was using earlier, and centered the paragraph. "We can center this paragraph by clicking the appropriate option in the Property inspector. Type that's centered is supposed to be more difficult to read because there's no consistent margin to stop the eye."

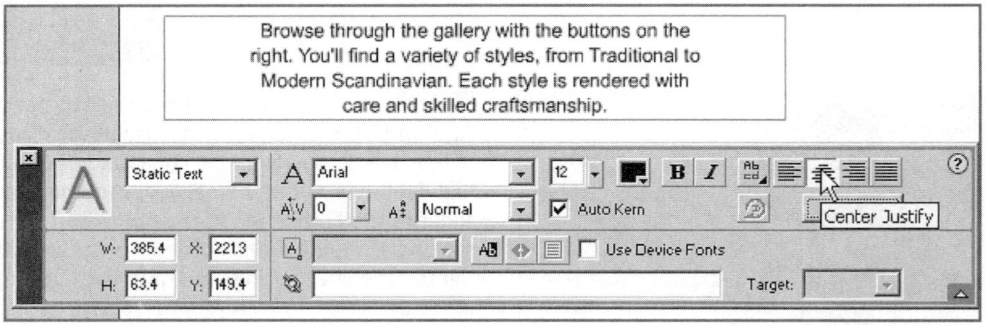

Browse through the gallery with the buttons on the right. You'll find a variety of styles, from Traditional to Modern Scandinavian. Each style is rendered with care and skilled craftsmanship.

Next, I right-justified the text, "Right flushed text is even more difficult to read because we're accustomed to reading with a linear border formed by the type on the left." I pointed at the right justified paragraph. "However, if you're talking about buttons on the right, and these buttons are square, it might be OK to leave the paragraph flush right, so the space between the ends of the lines and the buttons is a smooth line."

I justified the paragraph to the left. "You need to look at the positive spaces created by the type and your images in each case, and the negative spaces between each type shape and image. If they seem awkward – try changing the justification."

"We would decide most of this in our hand-drawn roughs, right?" Deb asked.

"In most cases, yes. But," I added, "Sometimes we might find the type isn't as we portrayed it in hand-drawn images. In that case, make adjustments within the Flash format as you render your designs.

"Additionally, be mindful of how your type sits on a page. When you have a leftover word at the end of the paragraph, this shows neglect of your type. These leftover words are called..." I looked towards Steve.

"Widows and orphans," Steve grinned. "**Widows** are leftover words that form a short line of type at the bottom of a paragraph. **Orphans** usually mean one word that's sitting alone on a line, usually at the top of a page. Both of these should be eliminated as much as is possible."

Deb stared at Steve, "You sure know a lot about typography, don't you?"

Steve laughed, "I learned from my boss many years ago as a magazine layout person. He taught me about line length, and about how to make the type more legible with layout."

"What about line length, Steve?" Wes asked, "How long can a line be before it's regarded as being too long?"

Steve shrugged, "I don't know how it works on a screen. In print, a line length typically couldn't be more than four inches, because that's all a human eye can keep on focus while reading."

I nodded, "It has to do with the blinking of an eye, and I'm not making a joke. The eye blinks every few seconds, and within this time, we need to get keep the viewer's eye focused on the words within the line, the end of the line, and the beginning of the next line.

"This means that a line of type on a screen, which is hard to read anyway because of the backlighting, needs to be no longer than four inches wide, as Steve said. You also don't want to make the lines in your column too short, as this will make the reader's eye move down the page too rapidly – keep them longer than about one and a half inches. If you have items you want the reader to see on both sides of the typed column, they may miss them due to reading down the thin column too quickly."

Steve nodded, "Yep, that old boss of mine was a stickler for what he called dangling words, widows, orphans, and four-inch line lengths."

"So I guess we need to avoid making widows and orphans, right?" Zed chuckled to himself. On that note, I knew it was time to move on to another topic... manipulating text with Flash MX.

Manipulating text in Flash

I asked the students to return their attention to the text box containing Frieda's name, "Constructive movement in static type can be created by altering the visual plane of the text."

"I assume this means using the Free Transform tool or the Transform panel in Flash?" asked Steve.

"They would do the trick Steve, but note that when text is retained in its original text box format, it is limited to being manipulated by scale, skewing, rotation and flipping." I demonstrated these manipulations on Steve's computer.

"However, when the text is *broken apart* into vector graphics, there are no limits to what you can do. That said, it's worth remembering that text is of a smaller file size in its original format, so wherever possible you should try to retain it in this format."

"This is the same rule of thumb used for web pages," stated Bonnie, "I only ever use graphic text when I can't get away with displaying it as normal HTML text."

"So, if your ambitions are beyond the options available with normal text boxes, then you'll want to break the text apart. Can anyone remember how to do this?"

The class frantically looked around the Flash user interface for the answer. Deb was the first to respond.

"With the Break Apart option from the Modify menu, or using the keyboard shortcut CTRL+B. You have to perform this twice to make the text into a vector graphic; the first time this is done it simply separates all the individual characters." She said.

"Well done Deb, that's the answer I was looking for!" I wanted the class to see how the text could be manipulated to a one-point perspective. "Now, open a new Flash file and type Frieda's name in large type." I said. "Center this text box vertically using the Align panel – first, make sure that the Align/Distribute to Stage option is switched on, and then use Align vertical center to center it vertically."

"Now select the textbox and place it close to the left edge of the stage. We place it here because we are going to use the center of the stage as the vanishing point.

"Draw a very small circle on stage and center it on stage with the Align panel, using Align vertical center and Align horizontal center.

"Now select the text box and use Modify > Break Apart twice on it. This will break the text into individual characters firstly, and then into vector graphics.

"Make sure all of the text is selected, and use the Free Transform tool with the Distort option – we studied this a couple of weeks ago." I reminded the students where to find this tool and its options.

"Now select the top left corner of the framing box, and drag it upwards." Zed turned around to face me. Before he had a chance to say anything I continued, "Firstly, only one corner of the text will be distorted, but we want to increase the top and bottom corners accordingly." Zed turned around again.

"To manipulate both the top and bottom left corners at the same time, start again by pressing CTRL+Z/APPLE+Z, and this time hold down the SHIFT key while dragging the top left corner."

"Aha!" Steve exclaimed. "Instant depth of field is achieved."

"Use the Free Transform tool with the scale option to stretch the text to the vanishing point, and there you have it!" I said.

"Essentially, this technique alters the plane and line of type. It alters the shape, and it also alters the viewer's perception of your message," I explained. "When you alter a baseline of type, you're creating a psychic line along the bottom of the word or sentence. The viewer will follow that baseline to the end. Hopefully," I added, "You'll have something for their eye to follow, or else..."

"You may lose your viewer!" The class finished my sentence in unison.

Value, texture, and space in type

"OK, let's talk about value in type. Value," I continued, "Can be created with grays, with various color values, or with alpha. All of these effects can stand alone, or you can create them in layers within the same design.

"Converting text into a symbol provides you with an easy way to build up some alpha layering. As we saw in the last class, each instance of a symbol has its own individual alpha property that can be changed using the Property inspector.

"Take this image for instance," I pulled up a file in Flash,

"This is made of many duplicated instances, each of which is pretty randomly positioned on stage around a focus point. The alpha, or opacity, of each of the background instances is very low, and as they are positioned over each other, the alpha increases in certain places.

"A final instance is placed at the center of the mass, and is given a much higher alpha to make it stand out over the others."

I asked them to type Frieda's name again, break the text apart twice, and convert the vector graphics to a graphic symbol by pressing F8. "When you use type at 100% of any color or value, that's referred to as *opaque*. If you decrease the alpha or color, you can begin to use subtle layering of type to increase value. You can also use this concept for color mixing.

"The Advanced Settings... option of the Color drop-down menu in the Property inspector allows you to change both the alpha and the color of symbol instances."

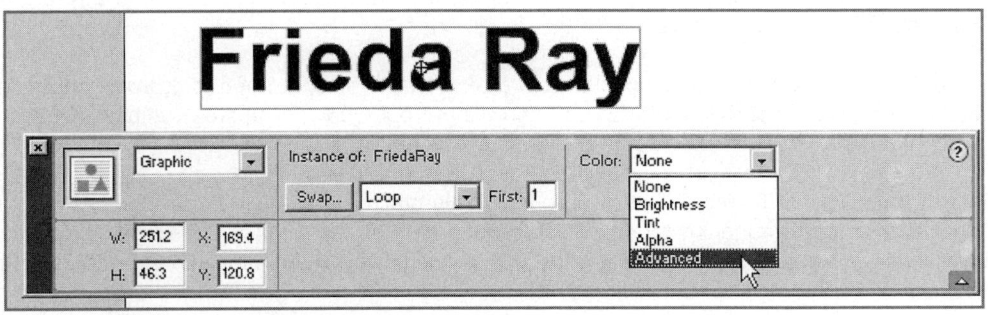

"Yow! That's wild," Wes said. He had combined a translucent layer of yellow type with another layer of translucent red type. This is just like using watercolors, only with light instead of paint."

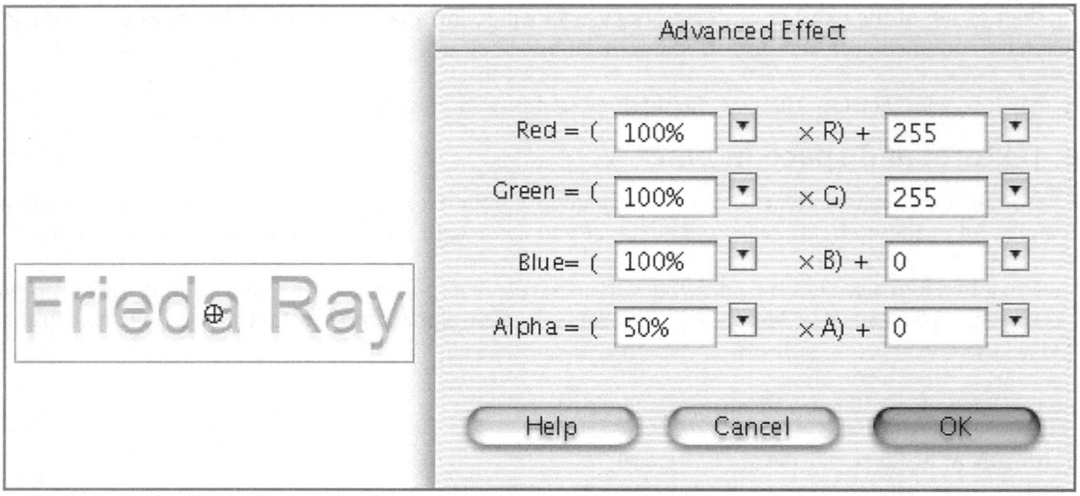

Wes's effect involved one symbol instance given a red color in the Advanced Effect window and a 50% alpha value, and the other being given the same with a yellow color.

"You can take it to the limit with transparencies, too," I said. "This is when layered elements of type appear hollow or outlined. You've seen the gradients at work. Try those with a layer of transparent type."

"So this is another way to add texture to type, too?" Bonnie asked. "I'm beginning to get mixed up again. Tell me that it's OK to feel like the design elements are constantly overlapping."

Wes leaned back to look at Bonnie, "The elements of design are everywhere. Type is just a little more complicated than most of the elements of design, I think."

"It's like a fractal," Deb muttered. "The elements are self-replicating..."

Wes dropped his head into his hands and moaned, "Please, please, let's not go there."

Steve laughed, "Deb, I understand. I've been trying real hard to keep physics out of all this. It amazes me how much physics and geometry mesh with the design arts."

"There's been a few books written about that very topic, Steve," I said. I turned to answer Bonnie's question. "Bonnie, the elements do seem to self-replicate throughout our work. Fortunately, we have the principles of design to help us sort through the various elements."

I returned to the topic of texture. "Texture is found within our type, and type in turn creates texture on the page. You saw how justification created texture. When we used left justified lines, the right side of the column is uneven. This is a result of uneven line lengths, and it's called **rag right**. Similarly, when the text is uneven on the left due to a flush right, it's called **rag left**."

"OK, now I just want to address space quickly, and we'll move on to text in motion."

Steve looked confused, "But we've covered character space, kerning, tracking, and leading... what's left to do with space?"

Zed answered smugly, "Steve, I'm shocked that you've forgotten about negative and positive space already!"

"Thanks, Zed," I responded. I asked the students to type in Frieda Ray's name again, once in Arial and once in Times New Roman. "Look at the open areas created by the lines in the *e*, *d*, *a*, and *R*.

These open areas are called **counters**, except for the *e*, which is called an **eye**. Usually," I continued, "The letter will be counter-balanced by a leg, or a spur, or stems." I asked them to look at the difference in the counters and eye between the two typefaces.

Frieda Ray

Frieda Ray

"They're a lot different," Bonnie stated. "Each letter's like a little face."

Zed laughed, "I guess that's why they call them typefaces, Bonnie!"

I continued to explain the positive and negative spaces created by lines in the letters. "We talked about kerning, tracking, gutters, margins, and other spaces created by letter lines. If you look at the letters as individual shapes, you can begin to see how they take up space, and create space."

"I see what you mean," Wes shook his head. "After a while, the letters don't seem like letters anymore. They seem to become images that make no sense whatsoever, except to take up space as shapes."

Bonnie muttered, "I just never slowed down enough to see how beautiful these letters are. A word is just like a little crowd of people, waiting to be organized with a touch of kerning and a little tracking."

Wes looked serious. "Linda, I think we need a break... we're in danger of losing our minds from thinking so much! "

"Good idea, folks," I said, "Take five."

Typography in motion

The class has covered the fundamentals of typography in design. Type in motion, however, is another concept altogether, with further implications to design and communication. When the students returned from break, I asked them to return to their computers so we could look at some examples and uses of dynamic text.

I sat back and relaxed as I reminisced to the class, "When I first began my graphic design career, I was hired by an agency that specialized in the design and production of national television ads. My job was to produce photographic images of white Helvetica type on a black background. These large two-line headlines were then pasted to 9" x 12" black illustration boards.

"The boards would leave the workroom, dozens at a time... then just week or so later I'd see my work on television! But a wonderful thing had happened to these static headlines somewhere along the way," I said. "Suddenly, the type would change color, spin, or fade-out and reappear. The words would emit rays of light. Someone in the television design studio had taken my headlines and performed a little magic with them."

"Actually, at the time I craved to do that in my own designs," I added with a small smile. I nodded toward the computer screen in front of Steve. "Be careful what you wish for, because it might come true!

"Film and television were the first media to involve type in motion. Like a design created for Flash, film and television type involves recording, editing, and transmitting information, whether live action or static. This creates a direct path between the content and the viewer that is strictly linear. The viewer receives the information, and they have no control over the response."

"Well, they can turn off the television or walk out of the film," Steve stated. "But I understand what you're saying – with Flash MX, we can apply motion, and the viewer can respond in kind. We can involve the viewer in ways film and television can't, because they can *interact* with the Flash site."

"OK, let's look at movement in typography," I said. "You've already learned the basic skills required to put type into motion in Flash MX. We learned the basics of the motion tweening early on in this course, and we'll combine this with your recently found knowledge of Flash symbols. So this section will be largely practical, putting your Flash skills to the test."

"I have *the skills to pay the bills* alright!" said Zed.

"I'm sure you will do very well here Zed." I said. "You must have absorbed something from all that anime and Manga you're interested in!"

Simple dynamic text

"For the following examples, we'll use Frieda's name as usual, using the Arial typeface. This first exercise will demonstrate how to create text that grows or expands over time."

I told the students to open a new Flash movie, use the Text tool to write Frieda's name at 50 point, and then to convert it into a graphic symbol by selecting the text box and clicking Insert > Convert to Symbol... from the menu bar or by pressing F8.

"Click the Graphic radio button and set the symbol to have a centered registration point by clicking the central square to the right of Registration."

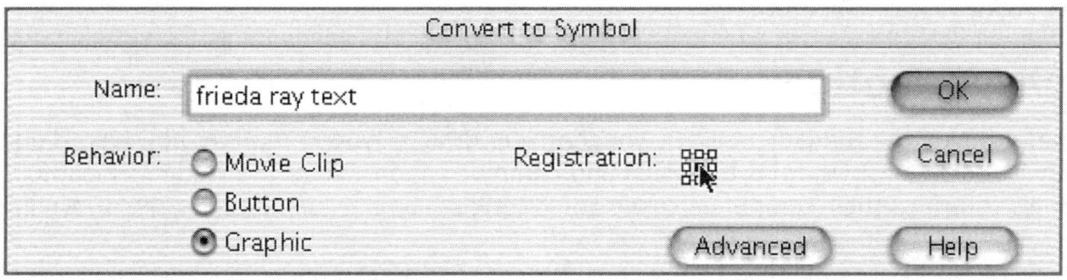

"We need to set the registration point centrally because we want the text to grow from the center and to be equally proportioned as it is scaled.

"Give the symbol a suitable name, such as frieda ray text, and click OK.

"Open the Align window by clicking Window > Align, and use the Align horizontal center and Align vertical center buttons to center the text instance on the stage."

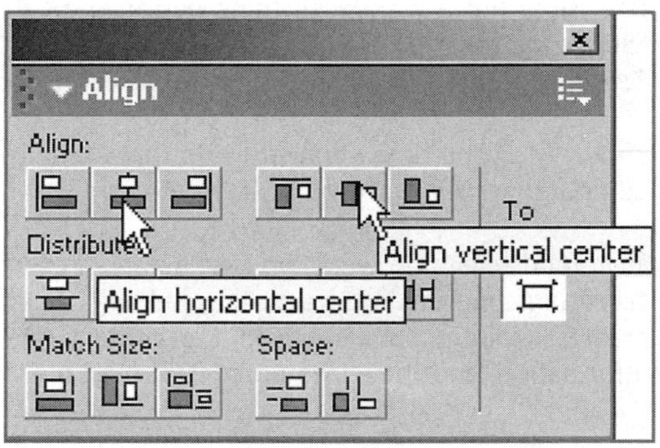

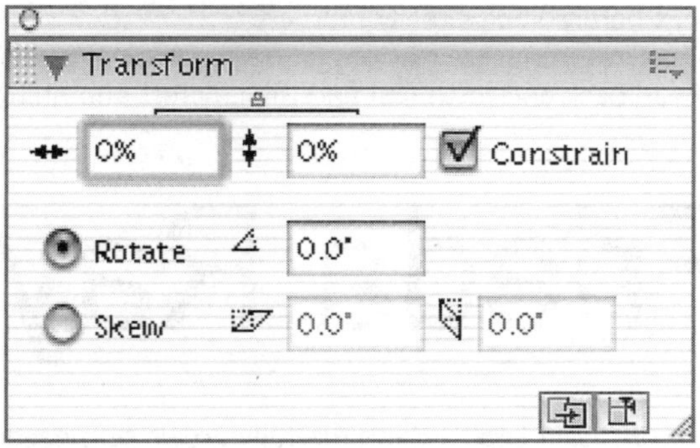

"Then click frame 60 of the timeline and insert a keyframe with Insert > Keyframe. Next, return to the keyframe in frame 1, alter the size of the instance to 0% using the Transform panel, which you can find by clicking Window > Transform or by pressing CTRL+T/APPLE+T. This is the size that our text will grow from.

"Then in the Property inspector, select Motion from the Tween drop-down menu."

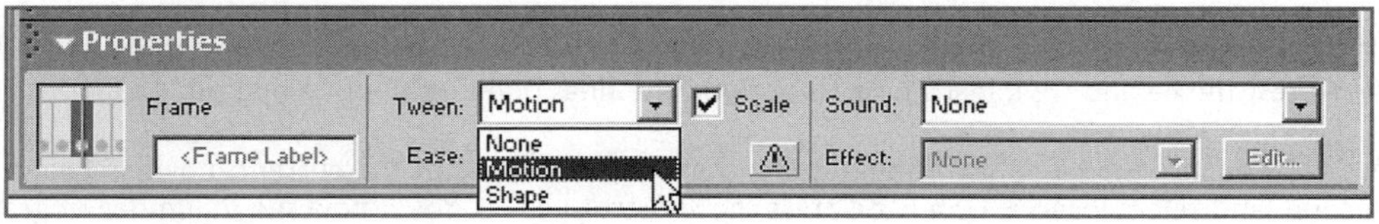

"Now set the size of the text on frame 60 to roughly cover the width of the stage using the Free Transform tool or the Transform panel."

"That's it?" asked Steve.

"Well, almost Steve. You should always test or check things before you're really finished."

I made the class check their tweens by dragging the playhead back and forth first and then by test publishing a movie, by pressing CTRL+ENTER.

"I think it's effective, but it returns to the start a little quickly," said Lisa. "I think the fully grown text needs to be shown a little longer."

"That's not difficult to do Lisa. Flash allows you to place extra frames where you need them in the timeline. Close the test movie and we'll learn how to prolong the final frame of your animation.

"Select a frame in advance of 60, remembering that the frame rate of the current movie is twelve frames-per-second, and select Insert > Frame, or press the shortcut key F5. You'll now see a number of gray frames after the keyframe. These are normal frames that will continue to show the content of the keyframe for a few more seconds.

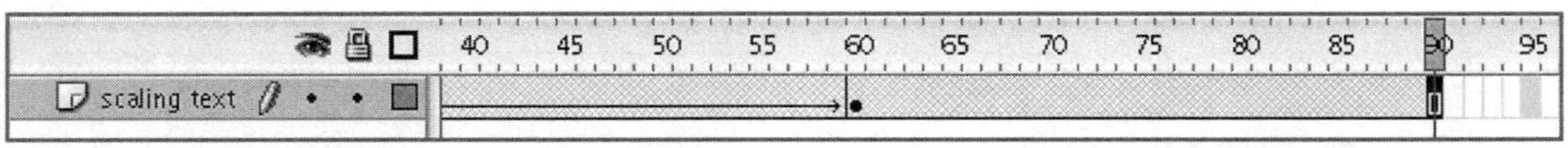

"If you test the movie now, your fully grown text will stay on screen for a little while longer."

"This text effect is cinematic," said Zed. "It reminds me of the opening titles of a movie."

"It's certainly an attention grabber," I replied, "It places real emphasis on the text instantly."

"I don't think it's suitable for Frieda though!" said Deb. "It's a little too dramatic and might scare off the visitors to the website."

Real movement

In the next exercise, I'd get the students to use value and moving type to create emphasis.
"This exercise will use two text symbols, both of which will move into place to show Frieda's full name. Both text elements will also appear from zero alpha and grow in value as they move towards their destination."

"Who'd like to suggest how we might start this animation?"

"I think I can," Answered Deb. "Firstly, we need two graphic symbols, one for each word of Frieda's name. These symbols will be used to create two motion tweens with elements of movement and alpha change."

"I think that's pretty comprehensive teach," grinned Zed. "I've nothing to add."

Deb laughed, "It's not like you to admit when you are beaten," she said.

"Not beaten. I'm just approving your suggestions!" Zed responded.

"Maybe Zed would like to lead the class from now on." I joked. Zed shook his head. "OK, you're off the hook Zed, I'll carry on then."

I instructed the class to open a new Flash movie, and to insert a new layer, by clicking Insert > Layer. "Both layers will house the different text motion tweens, so we should give them appropriate names. Double click the mouse cursor on the layer names to change them.

"On each layer, insert the appropriate text in 50 point Arial, and press F8 to convert it into a graphic symbol. Then use the mouse to drag the symbols to where you want their final point to be.

"We place the destination point first because this is the most important composition of the animation. Now, on each layer insert a keyframe at frame 60 of the timeline. This copies the information from the first keyframe to this one, meaning that the end of the animation is already set. Now, let's reposition the text at the start of the animation.

"On the first keyframe, frame 1, of the frieda tween layer, reposition the text Frieda to be at the top left of the stage. Next, select the first keyframe, frame 1, of the ray tween layer and move the Ray text to the right of the stage.

"As you move these instances, hold down the SHIFT key to lock the axis that they are moved on. This will help you get straight lines in your tweens.

"Now on any frame of each layer select Motion from the Tween menu in the Property inspector. Hit ENTER to watch your hard work in action. It might look OK so far, but it isn't finished yet – we need to change the values to give it emphasis and lightness.

"Select frame 1 on the frieda tween layer and then click on the Frieda text. In the Property inspector select Alpha from the Color drop-down menu, and using the slider or the text box, reduce the alpha value to 0%. Repeat this procedure with the Ray text. This makes our instances grow in alpha as they are moving."

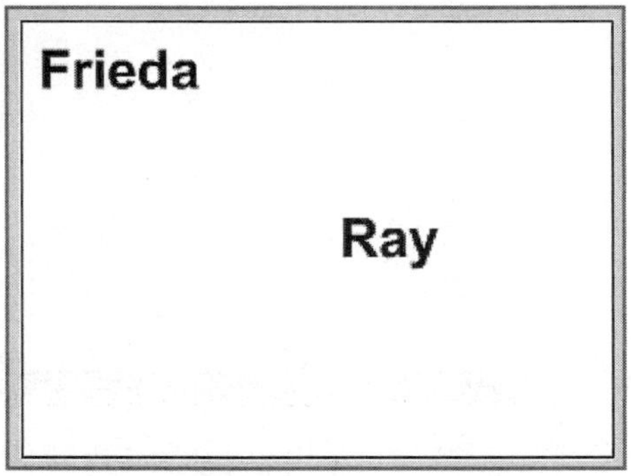

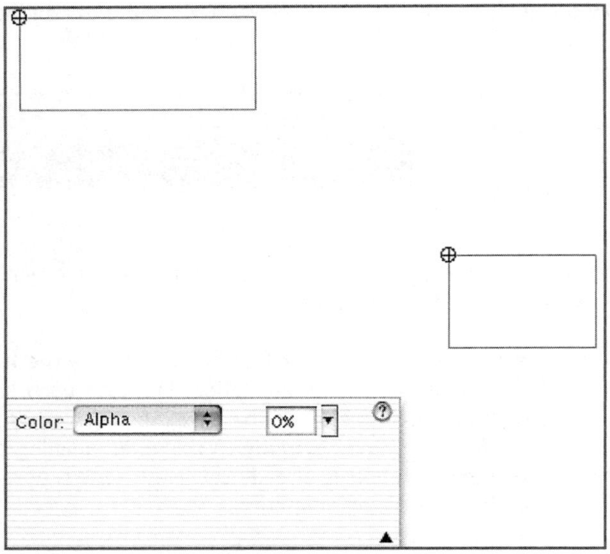

I made the class test the movie again. Many of them were impressed with it, but felt that it lacked finality.

"It needs something else when the tween finishes." Started Deb. "How about the text *Cabinet Designs* appearing at the very end?"

"Sounds good Deb. Why don't you finish off the animation and show the rest of the class?"

Deb went ahead and completed the animation. The rest of the students were impressed with her efforts.

"That's cool Deb," Said Bonnie. "I think you've polished it up nicely!"

"I decided to animate the Cabinet Designs text too. It's a simple alpha tween, but it's effective because the name still stands out as the highlighted element."

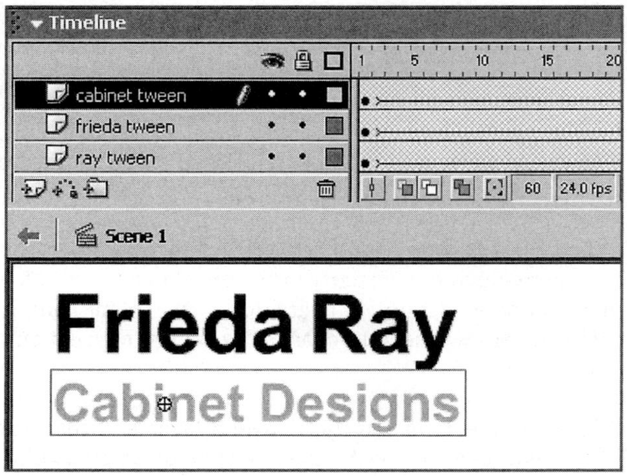

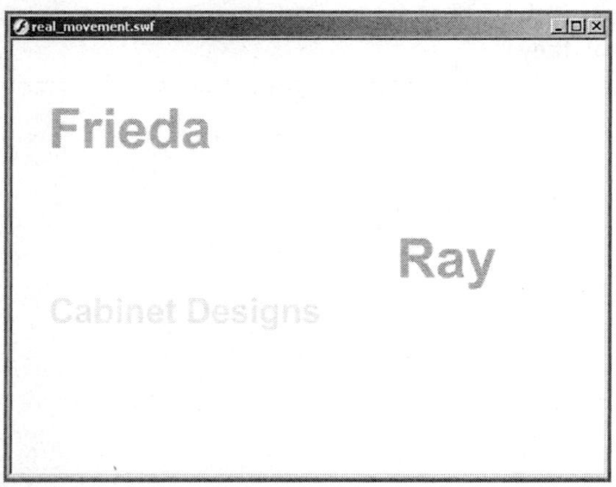

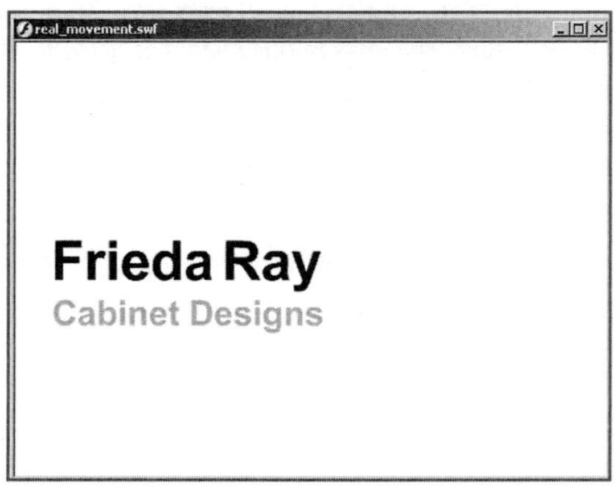

"You also used a little value too to keep the name in the foreground." I said. "The whole thing looks finished to me, even down to stopping the animation at the end. Great job Deb!"

"Thanks Linda," replied Deb. "I've really enjoyed this practical work."

"OK, I think we've had enough experience with Flash for today. Just remember that *form* and *function* of the Flash site is paramount. The *form* refers to your object, or text, in motion, and the *function* is the obvious use of the object. Don't animate anything unless you have a direct reason to animate within the design. The use of kinetic movement creates energy, and you don't want to waste energy on the viewer when you have a more specific goal in mind.

"Usually that goal will be to direct your viewer to the client's products and services for sale, not to direct the viewer to how *cool* you can be with your Flash skills." I pointed at their screens. "You've all learned a lot today about type, but really we've just scratched the surface of this expansive design topic. I sincerely suggest that you read more about the history of typography, and how it's developed and designed, especially for the computer. Every time you use a typeface, look it up on the web or in a typography book. Then, you'll become more intimate with the designer, the face, and the reason why they designed the type that way." I stated.

"A couple of good typography reference books are Type and Image: The Language of Graphic Design by Philip B. Meggs (ISBN: 0471284920), and A Typographic Workbook: A Primer to History, Techniques, and Artistry by Kate Clair (ISBN: 0471292370)."

"You may find that the type you choose isn't right for the design, just based on your knowledge of the typeface. These details are what makes a designer skilled in their craft." I said.

"Speaking of being *skilled at our craft*," Bonnie moaned, "What about the actual content of our sites? My copy writing stinks, for lack of a better word!"

Everyone laughed, so I had to comply, "I think now's a perfect time to touch upon writing content for your designs, Bonnie. Let's do that before we wind down this session today."

Perfecting your copy

"I'll keep this brief and simple, just like your copy needs to be for Frieda's site," I said. "After all we've covered today, can anyone tell me why most computer viewers scan, rather than read copy on the web?"

Bonnie said, "I would think it's because they're staring straight into a light source, and that's hard on the eyes."

"That's right," I said. "This is one of the main reasons people won't sit and read long lines of text and large bodies of copy. When they run across information they want to read, most often they'll print it out to read it in the reflected and diffused light of print."

"So we either need to be generous or succinct with our text," Wes said. "Either way, we'd better have something interesting to say, right?"

Deb nodded, "I think it probably boils down to the '*who, what, when, where,* and *why*' questions again. If we can cover all this in less than two paragraphs, I think we'll be safe."

1. Who
2. What
3. When
4. Where
5. How
6. Why

I wrote the six categories on the board, "OK, let's use this as a framework to help you fine tune your copy."

I pointed at each category on the list, "If you remember to include a sentence about each one of these items, you'll be safe. This way, you'll have answered the viewer's questions about each page on the site, no matter whether it's Frieda's history, or her gallery.

"If you want to embellish the text, don't make your paragraphs too long. The typical paragraph online consists of no more than four sentences. You can either indent the first line of the paragraph and not include a space between paragraphs, or you can leave the first line with a left flush and create an extra space between paragraphs. But don't do both, because it will slow the reader's eye down too much."

"What if we have absolutely no skills with writing?" Lisa asked, "Do we hire a copywriter?"

I agreed. "A designer might be an architect, physicist, mathematician, and magician, but the designer doesn't need to be a writer. The client may have a copywriter already hired. If not, you might want to develop some relationships with writers who specifically write for the web."

"The main reason web writers write a bit differently from writers who develop prose or poetry is because of writing on the web is, in general, intended to be *functional*," I said.

Zed looked thoughtful, "And with the web, the viewer is in control of the attention span. Even though some people spend hours in front of their computers, they don't stay in the same place too long; they move on very quickly in many cases."

Deb seemed confused, "Hmm, so if we only have a short time frame, why do you tell us to use economy of design? Surely high contrast and lots of movement is the way to capture viewers?"

Steve answered, "In fact, with our productions in Flash, and writing to advertise the client's products, we need to strike a balance. People will slow down long enough to read anything we write on the screen – *if it's important to them!* If the copy is the focus, then movement and high contrast – like white copy on black backgrounds – needs to be kept to a minimum. Everything we talked about today is important, like hierarchies of type into headings, subheadings, and copy. Plus, we need to be mindful of line lengths and short paragraphs. We also need to incorporate answers to all of the '*who*, *what*, *when*, *where*, and *why*' questions within our paragraphs, or within lists that stand out from the rest of the images."

"That's right, Steve," I said. "Plus, your copy needs to be proofed for spelling and grammar errors. You can have an award-winning design, but one misspelled word will knock you out of the running. Nothing spells amateur faster than an error in spelling!"

"Won't the spellchecker do that for us?" Zed asked.

Bonnie grinned, "I know from experience that a spellchecker doesn't do everything for us, Zed. It can pass by words that appear normal, but they're not in the correct context. Plus, it's not ideal with grammar. That's why I have so many problems with writing."

Deb responded, "Bonnie, probably the best thing for you to do is to use the categories up on the board. Don't use a lot of adjectives, because these are often a matter of opinion or personal perspective. If you use one, make sure you back it up with a reason why you say something is *strong*, or *valuable*. Otherwise, the viewer will think you're *full of hooey*, at least subconsciously."

Wes laughed, "I certainly don't want to be full of that!"

"Deb's right," I said. "Copy is great, especially when it's a learning device. For a client, it's best to keep it at a minimum. Just make sure you cover all the categories on the board and in your client brief, and utilize everything you've learned here."

"I would think that it would be best if the copy didn't move, right?" Deb asked. "Unless we move it into place, so the movement will make it a point of focus."

"That makes sense," Wes nodded. "I wouldn't do it with a whole page, but important words, or other short copy could combine with other static objects on the screen, right?"

"Wes, I don't remember the last time you asked a question," I grinned. "Moving type is fine, as long as it's one sentence, phrase, or word that's legible and clear. If you need to move the type, make sure you have a good reason, and that it fits within the scheme of your design."

"Don't fret over copy for this class project," I concluded. "If what you have to say is important to your client, then you have to say it. You can defend your short copy with all the information we just mentioned."

Refining the roughs

Today's work seemed to take the air out of some students, and breathe life into others. A little rest from the intense atmosphere would probably be good for the class, myself included. To wrap up this the session, I began to review what we learned today and let the students know about this next week's project

I walked among the students as they sat at the computers. "You've all worked very hard this week," I said. "There's nothing due for the client next week – you did very well with the flowcharts and compositions for this lesson. You also did great with your presentations and critiques. In fact," I added, "I'm very impressed with your growing perceptions of design."

"The only thing I felt growing today was my frustration," Wes said. "I don't know what's wrong with me."

Lisa grinned, "I think it's just a little artist's block, Wes. Maybe a break will help?"

"Nah," Wes shook his head slowly. "It's something else, but I can't put my finger on it."

"Take that watch off," Deb laughed. "It's probably stopping your blood flow." Wes looked at his wrist with sorrow.

"I'm sure that many of you still have frustrations and questions about your site. So, over this next week I suggest that you meet with your team member when you have time and refine your sites together. Begin to imagine what *type in motion* would do for your site. Add the possibility of motion to your images."

I continued, "Portray your ideas the way Steve and Lisa did with their project earlier today. Use layer organization, and use paper that will be easy to sketch on and see through. Use marker paper, vellum, or tracing paper."

"Does every sheet need to represent a keyframe?" Steve asked.

"Not at this point, Steve," I answered. "Although some of you may have a very clear vision of the movement through space and time within your sites. If you do, then feel free to add more sheets to the home page frame and another frame within the site."

"Don't we need to begin to pull more elements together, like our copy and photographs or artwork?" Bonnie asked.

"Yes, that's a good plan of action." I answered. "Thanks, Bonnie."

Lisa looked up from her screen, "What time do you want to reserve the theater for next week? I need to let the manager know today."

I looked around at the class, "Are you all happy to meet at the theater first, and then come back here for class?"

They all agreed. "Good then," I said. "Next week, we'll meet at the theater entrance, and Lisa will show us the ropes – we'll tackle additive color head on."

Deb rubbed her hands together, "I'm going to love this!"

"Just don't change too much more, or we won't recognize you," Bonnie jested. "After all, consistency, simplicity, and stability are paramount!"

Deb smiled as she logged off her computer, "I'll remember that tonight at my first drumming lesson."

Wes groaned, but the rest of us didn't say a word.

Summary

In this chapter we started with the class presenting the work that they had done in pairs during the previous week. They started off by presenting their flowcharts and short reports before moving on and critically examine each other's projects. In each project they looked for the different applications of the elements and principles of design:

We then studied the fundamentals of typography: the different **types of font**, **size** and **width**, **emphasis** and **weight**, **tracking**, **kerning**, and **leading**; before looking at **formatting** and **justification** of text.

Next up, we learned how to manipulate text in Flash MX, and the use of value, texture, and space in typography. Then we turned our attention to creating striking dynamic designs with text in Flash, with the emphasis on the *form* and *function* of the animations – we saw that textual animations should be utilized only when there is a clear need for them. As a close to this week's class, I set the students the rather general task of investigating how they could improve their designs with motion, type, and images.

In the next lesson, we'll begin class with a trip to the local theater to learn how additive lighting can work to our advantage, and how this relates to the computer and our Flash designs.

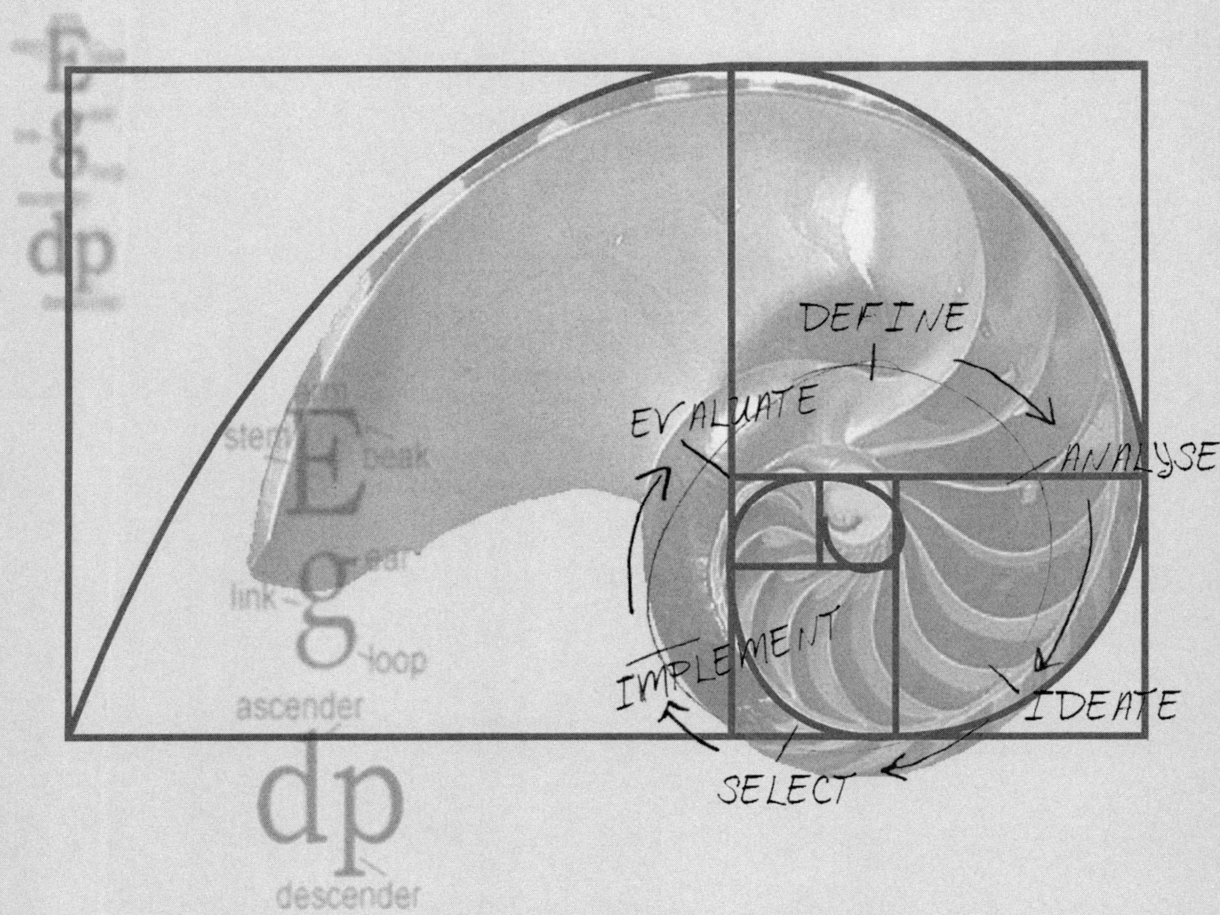

DEFINE
ANALYSE
IDEATE
SELECT
IMPLEMENT
EVALUATE
stem
beak
ear
link
loop
ascender
dp
descender

Chapter 8

The Color of Communication

Objectives

In today's class you will learn:

- The difference between additive and subtractive color
- The hidden meanings of different colors
- How light and color affects a design
- The properties of light, and how it affects your artwork
- Color spaces and palettes
- Usability and accessibility issues

Introduction

The theater where Lisa once worked as a lighting technician was just a few blocks from the classroom. We met there today to talk about color and its applications in a design context.

Lisa and I waited at the front entrance as the rest of the students straggled in. Zed, Bonnie, and Steve joined us, and we talked about what they'd been working on with their designs this past week. Shortly, Wes and Deb walked up, both holding cups of coffee.

"What's up?" Wes pulled at Zed's scarf.

"We're talking about typography," Zed answered. "I was telling Linda that type is really starting to talk to me. I'm getting all sorts of ideas when I watch the way they play with type on movie titles and television shows."

Deb laughed, "I can relate, Zed. I spent the better part of a day playing with Frieda's name in Flash. I only really touched a small fraction of the possibilities." She looked at Wes, "I did manage to narrow it down to a few choices, based on the focus of Frieda's vision."

Bonnie agreed. "I never realized how important or special type can be," she said. "Or, how complicated our verbal code can be."

"Type is a huge subject, and we only really scratched the surface – but it was a solid introduction," I stated. "This week, we'll be studying color, which is also a large topic to learn, so we'll spend the entire class on this element of design. We'll play around in the theater for a bit, and then head back to the classroom to learn about light movement and the various color palettes and color spaces. After we finish up with color, we'll cover a few pointers on usability and accessibility and how it affects the use of color on your sites."

"Last week was a bear for me," Wes confessed. He dug in his pocket for something. "This week, I had more fun with the typography and learning how to create copy from Deb."

"Good for you, Wes," Lisa said. "You look a lot better this week, too."

Wes retrieved a toy from his pocket. "Look what I have," he announced. "The eye of light!"

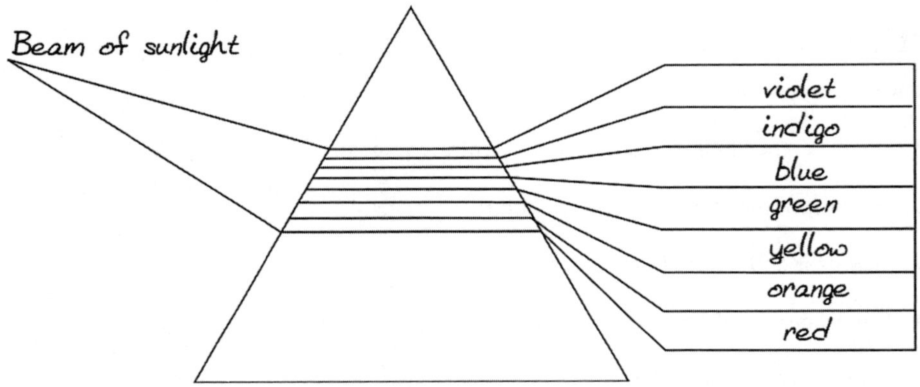

We all looked at the glass prism he held between his thumb and forefinger. He moved it around until a rainbow of light shot from the side of the prism onto the brick wall of the theater.

"Wow!" Zed bent forward to get a better look. Steve ran his hand through the rainbow of light.

"Hard to believe this little prism can capture so much energy," Wes stated. "Waves of light are bombarding this glass at a speed of 186,000 miles per second. The light waves are captured, bent as they enter the prism, and then bent again as they leave the glass. The energy is converted into visible color. "

"Thanks for bringing in that prism, Wes, that's the perfect intro for today's lesson." I talked as the students passed the pyramid of glass around. "The discoveries Isaac Newton made with his studies of prisms and light in the late 1600s formed the basis of modern physics," I added. "However, color theory now has its own place within the arts, and that's what we'll focus on today at this theater."

Bonnie shivered, "If I'd known how much science and math played a part in design, I'm not sure if I would have come to this class."

Steve put his arm around Bonnie, "Aw, don't let it worry you – I'll bet you didn't know that if you sent those beams of colored light through another prism, the beams would turn into white light again."

Zed arched his eyebrows, "Don't let her play that game on you, Steve. She's mad about this kind of stuff. Every time we meet to work on our design, she's got some book or other about physics and art with her."

Steve grinned, and Bonnie looked flustered, "Well, don't we look silly, out here on the street passing a prism around. When are we going to see the theater lights?"

"Let's get in there then!" Lisa grinned. She unlocked the front door, and we entered the lobby, ready for our adventure with color.

What's light got to do with it?

The class entered the theater, and I asked them to all take a seat in the front row. Before Lisa began her portion of this session, I talked to the class on the expansive topic of color and color theory.

"You're all probably pretty eager to begin working with color," I walked in front of them as I talked. "In fact, I know some of you are probably wondering why we've avoided adding color to our projects so far."

Wes spoke up, "I can guess why we haven't added color, Linda. When we use color in roughs, especially in tight roughs, we're going to be disappointed when we take the final roughs to the computer screen. The roughs are subtractive color, and the screen images are in additive color. It will take some work and a lot of tweaking to get them to match, if at all." He added, "Two different animals altogether, you might say."

"You're somewhat right, Wes," I replied. "I'll show you how to manage some of that later today." I paused and leaned back against the stage. "You've actually learned a lot about color so far. You've learned a little color theory, some color schemes, and some properties of color. You've worked with values and gradients. But, we've actually worked a little backwards to get where we are today. What we haven't covered is how we sense and perceive color. This perception is affected by everything we experience in life.

"The most basic sensory experience of color is our biological reactions to a color stimulus. This response is innate – you could almost say it's just like breathing," I added. "As we learn more about color through our various experiences, we begin to understand color as symbols, as cultural influences, and as fashion trends. Eventually," I said, "We begin to have our own personal relationships with color. As individuals, we all have our own perceptions and reactions to color." I looked around at each student, "As designers, we learn to speak to our audience with color."

Bonnie asked. "Will you also talk about colorblindness and other accessibility issues?"

"I'll do my best to cover the basics, Bonnie," I answered. "But it's up to all of you to research beyond what you've learned so far, and what you'll learn today.

"Today, Lisa will give us some color sense." I smiled at Lisa and continued:

> *"Although it's important to understand how light works, our concern as designers is to know how light and color affects our viewers. When we understand how color works, we have more control over our final effects."*

I walked toward my seat, and added, "The lighting effects you'll see today are the effects of additive lighting. This is the same lighting that is used on the computer, therefore it's the same lighting you'll use in your Flash formats. Lisa will show us how this color works, so we can apply the affects as designers."

Bonnie asked, "This is part of the house metaphor, isn't it? We've plotted the land, drawn the blueprints, gathered our tools, and built the foundation and framework. Now we're going to design the lighting for the house."

"Good thinking, Bonnie," Deb grinned. "Let's keep this house analogy going."

The class laughed, and I waved for Lisa to take control. Lisa climbed the stairs to the stage, and ducked behind the curtain. Wes pulled out his drawing pad. "I'm going to try to capture some of this performance in sketches," he said. "Hopefully, she won't do this whole thing in the dark!"

Lessons with light

After a minute, the house lights dimmed. As we sat in total darkness, we heard the curtain opened. Although we could sense Lisa, we couldn't see her. Her voice seemed to be coming from the left hand side of the stage.

"While you're sitting in what you believe to be total darkness," Lisa began. "In fact, you're really sitting in a field of electromagnetic energy. This field transmits energy in the form of undulating waves. Most of the waves bombarding you right now are either too high or too low in frequency to be seen by the human eye, but you're reflecting, absorbing, and radiating them as I speak."

At that moment, a rainbow of light fell over her, ranging from purple to blue, green to yellow, then orange to red. The theater went black again. "What you just experienced," Lisa said, "Was the range of electromagnetic light visible to the human eye, which is only a minute proportion of the electromagnetic spectrum. This is the same visible spectrum you saw with Wes's prism."

Zed leaned over and whispered, "Was she wearing a white robe there?"

"Yes, I'm wearing a white robe, Zed," Lisa answered. "Now, let me get on with it!"

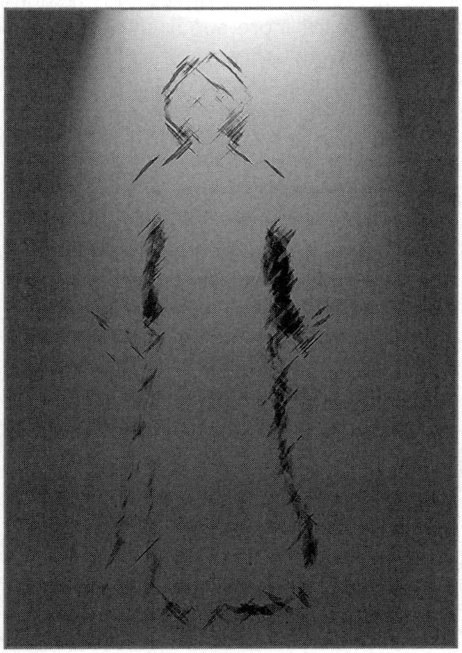

The students laughed, and they all turned to see who was operating the lights. When they realized it would be impossible to tell, they turned back to the stage. A light began to shine on Lisa, slowly illuminating her. Her robe appeared dark purple. The background was black. She began to stand out, but only vaguely.

"First, we sense shape, then we sense color. We learned this in our early lessons on the elements of design. When this light came on, your ability to recognize me was your first concern. You probably squinted your eyes to help pick out my shape from the background. Then, you perceived purple as the color reflected back to you. This was a biological reaction, based on your body's response to defining my shape by light. When we create images in the Flash format, we need to be concerned with shape first. The shape can be perceived by the viewer with various colors of light."

She added, "You may still have difficulty seeing me, since an object viewed in the dark has low saturation and contrast. In a Flash design, the same thing would happen. If you had a purple flower showing against a black background, the contrast and saturation would be low, and the viewer might have to strain to see the object."

Another purple light was lit, and it reflected on a table on the other side of the stage. She raised her arm to point at the table, "I'm representing a point of light, and the table is another point of light. We're both different shapes, but similarities between our lighting create a connection between us. In your mind, you know that my figure and the figure of the table are important, and that we have a relationship. When you create a design in Flash, you can create a bond between two objects by making them the same color or value."

The light on the table faded. "Purple, or violet, is the shortest wavelength of light visible to the human eye, but it also has the quickest vibrations. Blues and purples are known to lower human blood pressure. Many designers know this, and they design with this color to produce this effect."

The purple light dissolved into a red light. "Red is the longest wavelength of light visible to the human eye, but it also has the slowest vibrations. Colors can be used to produce a specific response in the viewers; the color red, for instance, can raise our blood pressure in some situations, and many designers understand this and use it to their advantage. Red is often used to grab the viewer's attention."

The theater went dark again. "Artificial light is created with energy from lamps. There are hundreds of different kinds of lamps, each providing light of a slightly different color, quantity, and direction."

The white stage lamps slowly illuminated Lisa from all angles. "White light is the standard by which all manmade lamps are constructed. These manmade incandescent lamps are not perfect, since they don't emit equal amounts of red, green, or blue. If you could imagine the bulb as a prism, some bulbs emit more of one color than another. This alters the *purity* of the white light. Our computer screens are also lamps – they backlight our images and type. Some of our computers send out more red or blue or green light than others. Sometimes, we need to adjust our own screens so we can achieve equal amounts of the red, green, and blue light. However," she added, "We have no control over the viewer's screen, any more than you have control over the lighting that's on this stage right now."

Suddenly, she was bathed in bright white light. She held up both arms at right angles to her body, and we could see the white light change. One half of her body appeared warmer than the other half. "Although both lamps are white, one emits more red waves, and the other emits more blue waves. Light sources that emit bluish light or white light are the hottest, while red or yellowish light sources emit less heat.

"This temperature is not the same as spectral distribution," she said. The lights changed, and she was drenched in light from above, tinted light blue. "**Spectral distribution** is a term used to determine and describe the quality of a general light source, but not its amount, or saturation." As she talked, the light changed to a light red. "These qualities include the light's warmth, coolness, or the neutral value of white."

The light changed to what appeared to be a neutral white. "As designers, we talk about *warm* and *cool* colors. This is how we refer to the **visual color temperature**, which is different from measuring it in degrees Fahrenheit or Kelvin. In fact," she added, "It's almost the opposite!"

Lisa was now fully lit, and she seemed to glow. "As individuals, and as designers, we use the energy of the visible spectrum to convey emotion and meaning. In Western culture, white represents purity; in India, white is the color of mourning. So our perception of color as a cultural language can vary too."

She held up her left hand, and a green light played on her palm. "Color can also be an icon, since it represents the name it's called. For instance, the word *green* means the color green, in all its various values and intensities. Green is also a mnemonic device, representing emotion and various other elements. In our culture, green means safety.

It can also symbolize nature, the environment, or money." She held up her other hand, and a pinpoint of red light shone danced on her palm. "Red means danger. It's a warning color. It can also symbolize passion, heat, love, or blood."

The lights dimmed again, and when they came back up, Lisa had moved to the center of the stage. The backdrop behind her was white. As we watched, the lights dimmed until one white light reflected off the backdrop at an angle. All we could see was the soft white outline of her robed figure.

She waved her arm toward the backdrop, and we could see particles of dust waving around her arm. "When a light is angled against an object, that object will reflect the light. This is called **luminosity**. You can see me only because the light is reflected from the background to reveal my shape. You can do the same thing within Flash. If you outline an object with soft white or tinted light, you've made that object luminous." She stood still for a moment, and said, "Just remember to put a light reflecting on something in the back of the object, so the viewer knows it's reflected light. Otherwise, the object will look like it's glowing on its own. Reflected light and glowing light are two different things!"

The students stifled a laugh at that last remark. Lisa moved about a foot to the left, and her shape was harder to define. "If I move from the angle of reflected light, my image becomes less distinct. Light bouncing off a reflective surface does so at an angle, and it exits the surface at the same angle it enters. If I move from this angle of reflection, my image will dim. This bending of light off a background surface will also create a shadow along that same angle."

She continued, "Notice that when light is reflected, it becomes scattered; it's *weaker* than direct light. This means that my outline will be more diffused, and my shadow will be less stark. Although the light reflecting on me is not as strong as direct light, you can still tell it's white light."

The light changed to green. Lisa moved to stand in the reflected light. "Now you see me through the green light reflected against the background. If I were wearing any other color than white," she said, "I would appear to be framed in a dark brown or black." She pulled a scarf from inside her robe and placed it around her neck. "What color is this scarf?" she asked.

The students muttered something, but none of them were bold about their answers. "The scarf is red," Lisa answered. "The green light is a filter used on a white light. The color reflected on the red produces a dark brown or black."

The light changed to red, and the scarf seemed to disappear. Everything was red. "Sometimes we use filters to color light," she said. "A filter is similar to using paint, or subtractive color."

She appeared darker. "A blue filter was just added to the red filter." She appeared a shade darker again. "A green filter was just added to the red and blue filters. If these filters were darker, I would eventually disappear, since the blend of filters would appear almost black, like the result of mixing subtractive primaries. This is opposed to the combination of all additive primary color, which equals white."

She stepped forward, and was bathed in white light again. This time, the lights shone from her feet, directly at her face, from overhead, from behind her, and equally from both sides. She appeared to be flat, like a paper doll. The red scarf appeared to be a thin bloody river against her body.

"When a person is lit from the front and all sides, the sense of depth decreases," Lisa stated. "All shadows are washed out by direct and indirect light, and the figure appears to be flat." The lighting fell, and she was lit from a 45-degree angle on our right side.

"Lighting from an angle on one side increases the depth and drama of a figure." The light changed slowly to a warm glow. "When the light changes from a bright white to a warm color, the lit figure also appears more realistic and human, but still dramatic. We can use these same techniques in Flash, when we use filters and lighting of our objects and type."

Another light slowly lit her from an angle on her other side. She appeared to be standing out, as if she were a statue. "When this warm light is countered by another light, the figure appears to be normal. What you may not realize, is that this light," she lifted her left arm on the side that was lit by a darker shade, "Is a cool color."

The light changed to dark blue. "When you view this lighting from a distance, a warm color countered by a cool light gives a figure more depth." The lights lightened, and she appeared almost normal, as though she was standing in sunlight.

Once again the theater went dark. As we sat quietly, we heard some whirring and clunking noises.

Slowly, the lights came up until the whole stage was lit. Lisa had removed the robe and was dressed in her jeans and sweater She was standing on the left side of a stage set. There were so many objects scattered around the set, it was hard to fixate on Lisa. She seemed to blend in with the carpet, sofa, tables, chairs, and paintings hanging on the walls.

"Stage sets are similar to any web page, or our Flash designs," Lisa stated. She stood very still. "Before, when it was just my figure on the stage, you were focused on me and nothing else. This was like looking at me through a microscope. We don't look at reality through a microscope; we take in large chunks of visual information at one time. When I surround myself with a clutter of objects, like we might do with our Flash designs, then we're taking away from our focus. We're losing the focus and the principle of economy in our designs."

She stood and began to walk across the stage, "Unless I move, it would be difficult to understand I was the center of attention. Your eyes would be drawn to other elements on the set. It's the same with our elements and objects in Flash. If we have too many objects scattered on a page, like type, images, and colors, it would be hard to make out the object that was the emphasis. There would be no *hierarchy* of information, whether through type or image."

She added, "Adding animation to make the object obvious isn't going to help the fact that you have *clutter* within the site design. Simplicity, or *economy*, is the key to elegant design."

She stopped and pointed at her head, "I'm a thinking person, but thinking takes so much time!" She turned to face us. "Some information is automatic, and it's hardwired into me. I can recognize primary shapes and colors without thinking. I can recognize movement. I can even perceive where the moving object came from, and where it's going.

"But, beyond that, I have to *think*." She emphasized that word, and suddenly the lights dimmed. All we saw was Lisa standing in front of a chair.

"Sensory input needs time to travel to my brain, and I need time to react. Obviously, it would help your viewers if you offered information in segments, rather than all at once." She sat in the chair. "Offer simple shapes and harmonious color. Offer emphasis on the important subject, with hierarchy created through values and hue. Let the viewers know what your point is, and where the focus is in the site. Give your designs a mood!"

There was a roll of thunder, and a lightning bolt appeared to light the sky above Lisa's head. She calmly crossed her legs and leaned back in the chair. "Utilize contrast." The lights shut down. Suddenly, a strobe lit Lisa, who had moved to stand in the center of the stage. She said, "But if you use too much contrast, and not enough continuity, your viewers may miss the message. If you animate an image, don't make it jerky." She began to dance while we sat mesmerized by the highly contrasted jerky motion of her body under the strobe light.

The strobe dimmed, and we could hear the set clink and clunk back into place. After a long pause, Lisa whispered, "You don't always have to shout in your designs."

We heard her walk from the stage. Everything was quiet. Slowly, the house lights came up, and we all sat there, stunned. Wes began clapping, and the rest of us followed suit. Zed whistled, and we cheered. "Great job!", "Bravo!"

Lisa emerged from the wings, and she took a bow, looking a little embarrassed about the ruckus. She sat on the edge of the stage and asked if we had any questions.

Zed leaned forward and raised his hand, "Lisa, that was awesome. I never realized filters acted like subtractive light. Do they work that way in computers, too?"

Lisa nodded, "Yeah, computer software can simulate a variety of color mixing techniques, but it's an illusion. I'm sure we'll talk about this more back in the classroom."

Steve said, "That strobe was interesting. I hadn't seen one for a long time. Watching you was like watching the jerky motion of an object before it's been tweened in Flash."

Deb laughed, "That's what it is! I was trying to connect it with that kind of animation, and couldn't figure it out."

Lisa grinned, "It's interesting how our brains work. You still knew, logically, how I got from one movement to the next, even though some of the sequences were missing. But," Lisa added, "It takes longer for our brains to make that connection. So, if we want motion in a client's site, we need to make sure the motion is smooth and sequential, and that it follows form and function, like we learned with type in motion last week."

"That's a good point, Lisa," I stated. I stood and faced the students. "Another demonstration of how to create emphasis is to move an object against a static background. You all saw this when Lisa moved in front of that crowded set. Within the format of Flash, this also creates a sense of depth. Just don't clutter up your sites like that set, and you won't have to use excess motion to make your focus known."

"I thought the color connotations were interesting," Deb stated. "Can you tell us more about how color affects us emotionally?"

"Sure," Lisa said. "I'll just go through the colors in the visible spectrum in order, and give you some idea how they can affect us physically and emotionally. I think we can probably use these colors and their connotations as designers for our clients."

The emotional impact of color

She began with red, the longest wavelength on the visible spectrum. "**Red**, as I mentioned before, has the tendency to raise our blood pressure when we view this color, especially as a red light, rather than a reflective or subtractive red. Red is also associated with anger. Sometimes too much of this color can be irritating and uncomfortable for some people.

"According to Hebrew tradition, the name of Adam means *red* or *alive*. The ancient Egyptians used red to symbolize Ra, their Sun God. The ancient Romans used it to symbolize Mars, their God of War.

"In China and India, red is a color for celebration, and women often wear red at their weddings, instead of white. Red is also a danger sign, and it's used as the color of the stop sign in Western culture. It's also the red heart for Valentine's day, and used for the red and green symbolism of Christmas celebrations."

Lisa crossed her legs and continued. "The next color is **orange**. This color is just as stimulating as red, but without the extreme emotions. It's a more joyous color, and it's thought to stimulate the mind and renew interest in life. So," she stated, "It's like a form of antidepressant!"

She laughed and added, "In Western cultures it's a symbol for Halloween, I guess since it's the color of pumpkins. This color sort of blends into yellow, since both orange and yellow represent happiness and love to the Chinese and Japanese. Buddhist monks consider orange to represent humility. Overall," she stated, "Orange is a color that seems a little more humble than red."

Lisa continued with the color yellow, "**Yellow** is a happy color, according to most cultures and traditions. This is probably because it reminds us of sunny days. Bright yellow can be almost too bright, especially when we view it on the computer. Like red, a little yellow goes a long way for emphasis.

"Yellow is considered a sacred color in Asia. In the animal world, it's a danger color. Bees, and some of the most poisonous snakes and fish have yellow and black markings."

Wes broke in, "In my travels, I found that many southern or tropical places have buildings that are painted yellow. I often thought that this would be a great color to use on buildings up north, where it's often cooler. It would make a house seem warmer."

Deb looked at Wes oddly, "Your brain works in mysterious ways, Wes."

He laughed. "Thanks, Deb."

Lisa grinned and continued. "Before I forget, yellow can also be a sickly color, especially when green is added to a certain degree. These green-yellows are hard to balance. Some yellows are also dull, and these yellows don't have the same attributes as the bright yellows. Dull yellow doesn't stimulate the brain like a bright yellow does.

"**Green**, as I mentioned before, is the color of money, nature, and the environment. It also means safety, since the green light means *Go*. In European and Chinese tradition, green is associated with spring and new growth. It's also a huge color in mythology, associated with the four-leaf clover, elves, and the Jolly Green Giant."

We all laughed at the last reference to green. Lisa continued, "Green is also associated with many religions as a sacred color. Islam, especially, holds green to be the color of Allah, since Allah is present in nature, but never in any human form."

Lisa shifted and seemed a bit uncomfortable, "I'll say this, but don't laugh at me. Some people think they can actually feel the vibrations of the wavelengths of the visible spectrum. Since green is in the middle of this spectrum, it's thought that this color is the most balanced color"

"I don't think that's odd," Zed said. "I think they're right – I mean, red seems to *vibrate*, doesn't it?"

Deb replied, "I think so, Zed. It seems to vibrate more than blue."

Lisa sighed, "Good, I'm glad you don't think that's crazy. Colors can be pretty powerful. Take blue, for instance. **Blue** is soothing, calming, and very cool in visual temperature. It's supposed to represent night, which may be the reason why it's so calming and peaceful. Many of the ancient gods were represented in blue, because blue represents truth and cooperation. It's considered one of the safest global colors to use, since it represents just about the same thing in every nationality. It's used for the flag of the United Nations, and as the background or part of many other national flags."

"That's interesting," Steve stated. "I never realized that."

"**Dark blue** or the blues that go into **indigo**, **violet**, and **purple** are often used on psychiatric patients to help calm them from various emotions and nervous disorders," Lisa continued. "Violet is supposed to suppress hunger, too."

"I guess that's why I hate eggplant," Zed stated.

We all laughed. "I don't know of many purple foods, or companies that use purple in their food packaging," I said. "The hunger suppression is probably the reason!"

Lisa grinned, "But too much purple can cause depression with some people. So if you're not a psychiatric patient, don't surround yourself with too much of this color, or you'll be depressed and skinny!"

"What about other cultures?," Deb asked. "Do people the world over react the same to purple and dark blue?"

Lisa thought a moment and responded, "Not really. Purple is the color of royalty, too. Combined with yellow and green, it's the color of Mardi Gras. That celebration is hardly depressing... unless you drink too much."

Wes grinned, "All along the Gulf Coast in the U.S. they decorate cakes with green, yellow, and purple icing. It sounds gross, but it's really festive. And," he licked his lips, "It's far from being an appetite suppressant!"

"Oh!" Lisa stated. "I remember now why purple and indigo are so prevalent for royalty. These colors were some of the first dyes ever made, and they were coveted by the ancient royalty, who paid well to have these colors."

"What about white, black, brown, silver, and gold?" Steve asked. "I realize they aren't part of the visible spectrum through the prism, but we use these colors too. Any connotations to them?"

Lisa nodded. "Yes, without a doubt. I'll start with black. **Black** was a sacred and fertile color to the ancient peoples of Mesopotamia. This included Egypt, where black represented the Goddess Isis, who symbolized the fertile earth around the Nile.

"Black cats were considered sacred in Egypt, but Western cultures now see black cats as a sign of bad luck in a certain context. Black is associated with death in some cultures, and in others it represents the infinite and mysterious...

"**White**, on the other hand, represents purity in some cultures, and mourning in others," Lisa continued. This color can be cold and isolating, like snow. Or," she added, "It can represent space and peace. It became the color of weddings in ancient Greece, where the color represented the goddess Athena and virginity."

"**Gray** is another color that has associations. These can vary from independence and self-reliance to depressing states caused by the color of fog and smoke. Most often, gray is associated with aloofness and isolation."

"**Silver** represents positive change," Lisa stated. "I guess because it represents the moon in some cultures, and Mercury in others. Both the moon and Mercury symbolize movement and liquid attributes."

Lisa took a deep breath, "I'm going to wrap it up with gold and brown. **Gold** is like yellow, and it's associated with the sun. In fact, this color is more powerful than yellow, as it also represents wealth. It's also associated with royalty, and with wisdom and power.

"**Brown** is considered a natural color. It's the color of many natural fabrics, and it's also the color of the earth. Brown can be uninhibited, but if muddy it can represent being bogged down with insecurities."

"I could go on, but there's so many colors, and so many different attributes from different cultures that we could spend all day on this topic. The human eye can discern over 10 million different colors, and each one means something different to us all."

"Lisa, you did a great job," I stated. "In addition to your expertise in light and color, you show an excellent grasp of the concepts relating to the emotional, psychological, and physical powers of color."

"Colors are powerful," Lisa stated. "The fashion world revolves around color, as do many other color trends. I think we need to know that a consumer will sometimes judge a site based on color alone, and how that color is represented according to fashion trends and seasons. Everything from automobiles to interior paint companies pay attention to color trends. I guess we need to pay attention, too."

"How do we learn about color trends?" Wes asked. "Honestly, I never paid much attention to trends. I'm not a slave to fashion."

Deb laughed, "I hate to tell you this, but the best way to find out which color trends are hot for the next year is to look in interior design and fashion magazines."

Lisa nodded and grinned, "If you can't stand to look through these, you can find websites devoted to color trends. One example is www.colormarketing.org; this group concentrates on color trends and how color is used to market products to consumers."

I added, "Just be aware that trends are just that – often fleeting trends. If you base your designs on colors that are predicted to be the craze for the next season, you're gambling with your client's budget and time. It's sometimes best to work with current color trends, and leave the future to prove itself before you make any major changes."

Lisa smiled, "I think Frieda is probably not that much of a trend-setter anyway. I picture her as classic earth colors, with a touch of gold for royalty."

Steve laughed, "I guess we've decided the colors for our version of Frieda's site," he stated.

"Speaking of Frieda's site," I said, "Let's head back to the classroom and continue this talk about color there, where we have access to some tools, and to our computers. We just learned a lot about additive lighting, but we have a lot more learning yet to do!"

I bowed to Lisa, "Thank you for an inspiring and memorable performance on color. When we return to the classroom, I'll need your help to summarize everything you taught us this morning."

The class applauded, and stood to gather their belongings. They all thanked Lisa for her performance and the learning experience.

"Wait," Wes shouted above the turmoil. "I have one more question." He had a sly grin playing on his face as he faced Lisa. "Who was operating the lighting system for you?"

Lisa pushed herself up off the stage floor and dusted her hands. She looked up to the operating booth, which was still dark. "I think you know who was operating the lights, Wes."

Wes grinned, and the rest of us looked at each other in confusion. "You got a secret?" Bonnie asked.

"I guess I do," Lisa replied, and turned to walk off the stage.

Bonnie looked at us and shrugged. We slowly filed out of the theater, listening closely as Zed bugged Wes to tell us who was in the booth. Wes wasn't talking, but he was still grinning...

How light affects a design

We arrived back at the classroom within minutes. I asked the students to settle themselves at the table as we recapped on their recent experience at the theater. We just experienced firsthand the possibilities and effectiveness of additive lighting, thanks to Lisa's theater display.

"While you all are settling in," I stated, "Let's go over what we've just learned this morning about using additive lighting, and I'll make a list here on the board. I also want you to apply what you learned to how you would represent a client's product or services."

"First off," Zed stated, "We learned that we see shapes before we see color. This is a biological reaction that can't be helped..."

* Shapes first, color second

** Client - make sure that the product is recognizable before any color effects are added

I started to write on the board, "OK, but how's this apply to your design for a client?

Deb answered, "I would guess that we make sure the client's product is recognizable before we add any color."

Wes nodded. "That makes sense. Why would we add a rainbow of colors if the viewer doesn't even know what's for sale?"

I wrote that reason down on the board. "What's next, Zed?"

"Well," he glanced at Wes's sketchpad. "We learned that if you want to make a connection between two objects on our site, we can make the link through light by using matching colors or values."

"How would this information affect a client's site?" I asked.

* Similar color or value
- Use similar colors/values to make connections between the product and the message.
- Also use this to create connections between product and logo.

Steve answered, "Well, I guess it would be good to make a connection between the client's product and the message with the same colors or values. We could also make a connections between the product and the logo or mark with color or value, too."

"What if the client designed their packaging totally different from their mark or logo?" Bonnie asked.

"You can always create a background shape for the product that reflects the colors in the mark or logo, Bonnie," I answered. "Whatever you do, always look at the colors in the client's logo or mark, or any other artwork they want or are required to use. These colors will affect what you use throughout the site, because you want them to be imprinted on the customer's mind."

I asked Zed to continue. He responded, "We also learned that things look really flat if we don't use light and values to give them more depth. Similarly, we can make something that has a lot of depth appear flatter if we use a lot of light and very little value on it."

* Create depth with color/value
- Use colors and values to create hierarchies of information.
- Don't use drop shadows unless absolutely necessary, and only to emphasize a product or headline.

As I wrote this information on the board, I asked the students how this information could affect a client's site. Bonnie answered, "We can make the client's product or other information stand out by using color and value to give it more depth. We could also make other information flatter, so it doesn't compete."

"So," Deb mused, "We're creating hierarchies of information based on depth created by color and value."

"That's right," I answered. "This is just one of many ways to create hierarchies of information. Last week, we learned how to create hierarchies with type, using headings, subheads, and body copy. You can reinforce these messages by using depth to make either the product or the message the primary focus. Don't use depth, like drop shadows or perspective, unless you want to make something stand out. If you have to use drop shadows on text, don't use it on body copy. The drop shadows make body copy too hard to read."

I turned to Zed. "Can you remember anything else?"

"The last think I remember learning, besides the colors, is to remember to tween any action in Flash efficiently, so it doesn't look like Lisa's dance. All jerky and hard to follow."

* No jerky motion?
- Maintain a smooth, fluid continuity throughout the site, unless jerky motion is intended.

"That's great, Zed," I responded. "Keep everything fluid within your site, with no jerky motions. This includes your text, color, values, motion, texture, space, lines, and shapes. Continuity is important, as it helps economize the site."

"You just mentioned all the elements of design," Lisa stated.

"I did, didn't I?" I winked at Lisa and looked around. "Anyone else have anything to add before we get into the colors Lisa talked about?"

"Don't clutter up the site with lots of junk!" Wes exclaimed. "Actually, that stage set looked like my studio on a good day."

I asked the students how this information would affect a client's site.

Wes answered, "I'll take a cue from what you just wrote. I'll bet this has to do with all the principles of design. If we clutter the site up with pop-up ads, lots of little bits of information, no clear direction, no clarity between images and text, and a lack of rhythm, we'll have a site that has no unity."

"Don't forget that we need to maintain a focus on emphasis with our images," Deb responded. "All of this creates **unity** in our designs."

I finished writing on the board. "You've all learned your elements and principles of design well," I stated. "Anyone remember anything else?"

* No clutter!

- Remember economy.
- Balance images and text.
- Contrast for emphasis.
- Keep things in proportion.
- Maintain a flowing rhythm.
- Simplicity of direction.

** Create unity!

Deb laughed. "I remember the part about thinking... if the customer has to think too hard while looking through a client's site, they may just leave and play online bingo instead, or something as trivial."

I wrote *K.I.S.S.* on the board. "I know what that means!" Zed stated, "Keep it simple, stupid!"

K.I.S.S.

Keep it simple, sweetie!!

"Ouch!" I responded. "Is that any way to treat me? I prefer to say, keep it simple, sweetie. I tend to catch more bees with honey, Zed."

Wes laughed. "I can hear Zed calling me a sweetie now." Zed grimaced.

"What about the warm and cool colors?" Steve asked. "I thought it was wild that we see reds and yellows as warm colors, when they're really cool in temperature."

"That was interesting," Deb replied. " I didn't think to compare colors to temperature."

"I think this is a good time to talk about the colors Lisa mentioned, and what they can imply" I stated. "Lisa talked about cultural values with color, as well as how they might make us feel. Can we apply this knowledge to our client's site?"

"I think so," Bonnie answered. "But, let's write the colors down, and I'll be able to remember them better."

I looked at Lisa. "I think I'll need your help with this one."

"Sure," Lisa nodded. "I'll simplify it and give you what is considered the safest use of each color on a global scale. Let's start with red again. Red has two opposing meanings. One would be vitality, warmth, power, sensuality, determination, friendliness, and happiness. The other side of red is danger, warning, anger, and impatience."

* Red
- vitality
- warmth
- power
- sensuality
- determination
- friendliness
- happiness

or
- danger
- warning
- anger
- impatience

I held up my hand to stop her flow for a moment. "Lisa, let's talk about red and marketing a client's product. Can any of you tell me which products would use red to promote an image?"

Wes answered immediately, "Sports cars!"

Steve nodded, "I would add red to promote some music labels or CD covers for some musicians."

"Good one, Steve!" Deb stated. "How about lingerie?"

"And bathing suits," said Bonnie.

Wes laughed, joining the game, "Boxer shorts!"

I grinned, "Obviously, red is used to promote excitement. As Lisa mentioned before, red seems to raise our blood pressure, especially when we view red light. When we see red on the computer screen, we're looking at red light. So, if we want to raise the viewer's blood pressure, we use red, right?"

"I guess so," Zed answered. "That's pretty powerful stuff."

I agreed with Zed, "If we use red, let's not overdo it, or the viewer may experience an overload. We want the site to maintain focus on the product or the purpose of the site, and the color red can easily distract us from that purpose."

* Orange
- warmth
- security
- creativity
- laughter
- joy
- humor

I nodded at Lisa and she continued, "Orange represents warmth, security, creativity, laughter, joy, and humor."

"I can't think of too many orange sites or products," Bonnie muttered. "I really don't remember that color being used that much online. Have the rest of you seen it much?"

Lisa stated, "It could be that orange is considered a seasonal color, representing fall. Leaves turn gold and orange and brown, and – of course – pumpkins for Halloween. I also remember one study that mentioned that people think orange packaging represents a cheap product."

"Those are all good reasons for the lack of orange in product development and packaging," I stated. "Although, I remember orange as being a major color used in a lot of children's sites."

"If we go to rust, which is a form of orange, then that might be the adult orange," Lisa stated. "There's a lot of rust colors used for various things, like clothes, and backgrounds on websites. Rust is a great color to represent aging or maturity."

"That's a color used on lots of gaming sites," Zed stated. "Especially sites that use a lot of metal textures."

"Good points, all of them," I stated. "Is this a color we would use for a client's site?"

* Yellow

- uplifting
- happy
- light
- stimulating
- warmth
- intelligence
- optimism

or

- sickly
- fearful

"Not very often, obviously," Steve stated. "Unless they sold pumpkins. Maybe this is a good thing, since orange is hard to duplicate from screen to print."

"Fair point, Steve. What about yellow, Lisa?" I asked.

"Yellow is uplifting, happy, light, and it's a mentally stimulating color. It also represents warmth, intelligence, and optimism. The other side to yellow is dependent on the shade of yellow. It could also be a sickly or fearful color in that respect."

"Watch your yellows," I reminded them. "Yellow, when placed next to a color like black or dark blue, can be very striking and create good contrast. If you place it next to various shades of green or lighter blues, it can take on the cast of the green or blue and appear to be sickly."

Wes nodded, "I know we haven't covered color combinations here, and I doubt we'll have time. But," he added, "It's important how we place our colors."

I agreed. "The scope of this course will limit our lessons, but your point is solid, Wes." I looked around at the rest of the class. "We'll talk about color palettes later today, and we'll also talk about some artists and instructors who can help you with color matching."

"Good enough," Deb stated. "I can see where we'd use yellow for a client. The first product I think of is laundry detergent. When I see blues and yellows together, I think of fresh, clean, sunny days, and laundry hanging on a line."

"Wow, that's ambitious," Steve laughed. "Yellow reminds me of sports cars again."

Wes nodded, "My laundry is yellow, but it's not because it's clean. When I think of a cheerful yellow, I think of fast-food restaurants and food packaging."

"Yellows, reds, and blues are used for a lot of food packaging," I agreed. "I think there are even studies that prove that these colors are stimulating to the appetite.

"OK, what about green, Lisa?" I asked.

"Green is a stable color, and it represents money, nature, and the environment. Even magic and sacred objects! It's a peaceful color, and it can bring about calm, security, balance, contentment, and generosity."

Zed asked, "Would we use green for a bank client?"

I laughed, "I guess you could, Zed. It would depend on the shade of green. I think many of the connotations listed here would rely on the shade, tint, or intensity of this color."

Lisa agreed, "Emerald green is the color for the sacred objects. Army green, on the other hand, would represent something else altogether. Green can also represent jealousy."

"And the army," Wes nodded. "Oh, and avocado green is a great color for refrigerators."

Steve laughed, "Only if you want retro! I grew up with an avocado refrigerator, and I hate that color. It's definitely not appetizing to me."

* Green
- money
- nature
- environment
- magic, sacred
- calm/content
- peaceful
- balance
- generosity
- security

"Steve brought up an important point, folks." I turned to the class. "You're not going to please everyone with the colors you choose. Event though Lisa is giving us psychological relationships to these colors, there are always going to be some people who don't see things the way many other people do."

"So we just go with the flow, and hope not too many people dislike the color?" Bonnie asked.

Steve responded, "If you were going to push a product to folks my age, the almost-over-the-hill-gang, I would avoid avocado green."

"That's good to know," Deb stated. "All those pop colors, like avocado green, orange, and yellow were just recently a fad in fashion."

"Yeah, I grew up with that stuff, too," Steve stated. "I kept having flashbacks every time I saw an advertisement with those colors." Everyone laughed.

"Fashion fads can be transient and fickle," I stated. "Even though they're good to get a sense of what's to come, as mentioned earlier at the theater, it's still a good idea to stay away from them until they're proven to stick around a while. The exception would be promotions for music, or other trendy products. Then," I stated, "You'd definitely look at the fashion trend colors to push immediate sales."

"Pine green reminds me of air fresheners," Bonnie added. "Although I'd rather be reminded of walks in the woods."

"That's sad," Deb stated. "But, I agree. I think we both need to go for a walk in the woods to change our attitude about pine green."

"Green is a powerful color," I stated. "If you're going to use green, think very carefully about how each tint of green will affect the viewer's attitude toward the client's product." I turned to Lisa, "How about blue?"

"Blue is also a peaceful color, but it appears cooler than green. This color can represent calm, tranquility, wisdom, and spaciousness – like in the sea or sky – and acceptance. It's the most trusted international color."

"I don't think we'd have trouble coming up with products or services that use blue," Wes stated. "Blue is an ideal color for websites, too. I don't have a problem with it. It's a great, safe color to use, I think."

"I agree," Deb stated. "I don't think many people have problems with blue, obviously. I didn't realize it was tried and tested to be the safest international color."

"Remember that you'll be using blue as a blue light when displayed on the computer screen with your Flash sites," I noted. "This blue can get pretty intense sometimes, depending on the value or shade of blue. Some of the brighter blues may overshadow your client's product or message."

* Blue
- calm
- spaciousness, sky, sea
- tranquility
- wisdon
- acceptance
- trust

* Violet, Purple, Indigo
- dramatic
- soothing
- regal
- overly calming/tranquil

I asked Lisa about purple and she was happy to continue, "As I said earlier, indigos, purples, and violets are dramatic, and they can represent royalty. At the same time, these colors are used as tranquilizers for people who are mentally distressed."

"I've seen a lot of psychic websites that use that color," Zed stated. Everyone looked at Zed. "What? I was researching the psychic line, and I got into a lot of the mind-reader websites... they use a lot of deep blues, purples, and golds."

"That's interesting, Zed. I'm glad you took note of the colors," I responded. "What else would you use purple or violet or indigo for?" I asked.

"I keep thinking of velvet," Deb stated. "But I didn't realize these colors could put a client to sleep. I don't think I'd use a huge amount of this color in any site, unless that was my purpose."

Lisa laughed, "Maybe the psychics are using it to hypnotize you, Zed."

We all laughed. "If we combine purple with gold, that would be another matter," I stated. "These are the colors of royalty. Color combining does make a difference, as it changes the context of the color message."

Lisa stated, "Golds and silvers are just like grays and yellows, but they're both a little more intense. I guess that's because of the metallic connotations.

"Grays are aloof, cool or warm, depending on whether they're mixed with blues or reds, and they represent either a business-like demeanor or an aloofness.

"Blacks are mysterious, sensual, and comforting, or they can also represent mourning. White can represent mourning, also, but it can also represent purity. I think that the connotations of white would depend on the context."

"Don't forget brown," Deb said. "I remember that one. Brown represents earth, and it's also used for a lot of natural connotations, like natural fabrics."

Lisa nodded. "Brown also can be used to stimulate security, but it can also represent a lack of self-worth."

Bonnie looked up at the notes on the board. "So if our client sells organic products, we'd want to use greens, browns, and maybe gold or yellow. If our client wants to sell their psychiatric care, we'd want to use purples and blues, with a highlight or contrast of orange or yellow."

"Cool!" Zed looked at the board too. "This is fun. Let's see... if the client sold wedding gowns in India, we wouldn't use white. We'd use red, and maybe blue for trust. If our client sold jewelry, the color of the jewelry would be silver and gold, so we'd use black to set them off, and because black is mysterious and sensuous."

Wes looked at Zed, "Do you know what sensuous means?"

Zed turned his head slowly to peer at Wes, "I may not drive yet, but I know what sensuous means."

Wes laughed, "OK, I'll play this game. If I had a client that sold bathroom cleaner in the western hemisphere, I'd use white for purity, blue for freshness and spaciousness, and a darker blue for peace, knowing that my toilet bowl was clean."

Steve laughed, and Deb rolled her eyes. "If I had a client that sold computer services, I'd use blue for trust and gray for a business-like demeanor," Deb stated.

Steve leaned in to look at the board, "OK, I'll try next. If I had a client who sold pumpkins at Halloween in the U.S., I would show a picture of the pumpkins, so they would bring orange to the site. The orange would be festive, warm, and joyful, so I'd contrast that with cool colors like blues for a crisp autumn sky, and greens for a natural feel."

"OK, thanks again for a great show Lisa, and for sharing so much information," I stated. "This information should help all of you narrow down colors to use for specific purposes."

While the students talked among themselves, I drew a sample of the visible portion of electromagnetic field on the board, and two squares, one white and one black.

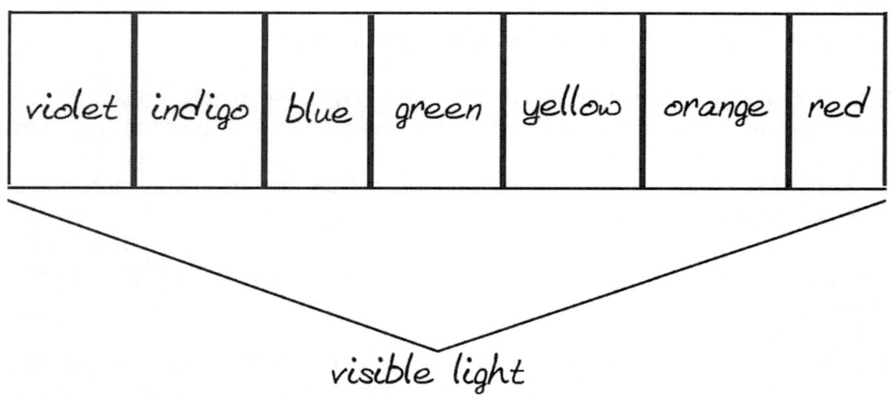

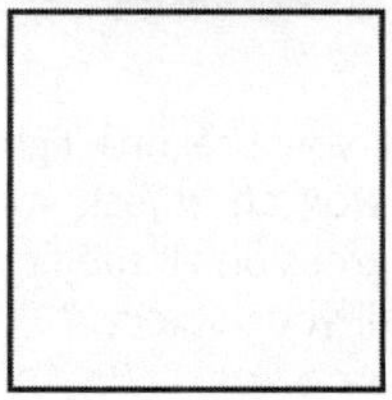

"Lisa talked about the visible portion electromagnetic spectrum at the theater," I pointed at the board. "This is the basic range she spoke about. The region of visible light ranges from violet with a wavelength of 400 nanometers to red at 700 nanometers. **Nanometers** are one-billionth of a meter, and the measuring stick of the visible portion of the electromagnetic energy spectrum," I explained.

"By the way, there's an old English mnemonic for remembering the order of these colors: ***R****ichard* ***O****f* ***Y****ork* ***G****ave* ***B****attle* ***I****n* ***V****ain*. The initial letter of each word represents the first letter of each color," I added.

"So, we know by now that white reflects all light, and black light absorbs all light. It's worth noting that when black absorbs light, it generates heat."

Zed looked confused. "I know that colors reflect light, but what happens to the ones that aren't reflected? I know they're absorbed, but that's a lot of energy. It's like every color outside of red for a red apple, right?"

"That's a good question, Zed. Let's talk about reflective light and its properties."

Reflective light

"When light strikes a surface, say an apple," I explained, "There are three things that could happen. First, the surface of the apple modifies the wavelength of the light. Some light is **reflected** from the skin of the apple, this is called **specular reflection**. Light that isn't reflected is either absorbed or **refracted** and scattered, exiting the apple from various angles. The absorbed energy stays in the apple and can heat it up slightly."

"Wow," Zed mused. "So when I eat an apple, I'm probably eating some absorbed light energy?"

"Right Zed," Steve affirmed. "The absorbed light changes to heat and, in the case of the apple, it probably changes into something the apple needs to survive. In some cases, it translates to vitamins for us."

"Thanks, Steve," I said. "Another example would be a black car. The energy is absorbed, and the energy that isn't released turns into heat."

I continued, "Light can also bend and flow around an object, like water flows around bends and corners. This is called **diffraction**."

"Another movement of these waves of light is called **transmission**," I said. "This is when light enters a transparent object and goes through, like light through a filter or a window."

"Can't we just play with filters and light to get what we want?" Zed asked. "The colors are right there, in the palette. Why do we have to know all this stuff?"

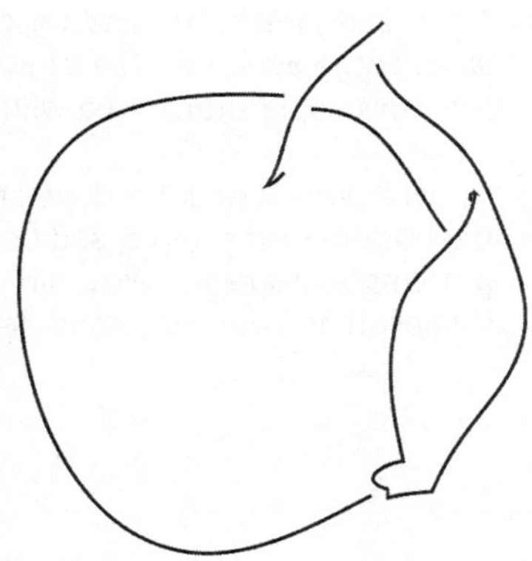

I turned back to the board and drew an apple with a leaf. "Zed, it has a lot to do with how we communicate our visual messages to our viewers." I turned back to the class, "Lisa said it very clearly when she asked for simple shapes and colors. When we communicate a visual message to the viewer, we don't want to confuse them with our own ignorance of the world around us."

"Yeah, that would be a bummer," Wes laughed. "No sense in talking if we don't know how to talk."

"You're right, Wes," I grinned. I asked him if he'd like to show how light movement would affect the apple I drew on the board.

"I'd love to," he said. He came to the board and began to show the students why our knowledge of light movement was important. "First," Wes began, "If you have a light source in your format, make sure every object in your format displays light and shadow the same way and in the same direction."

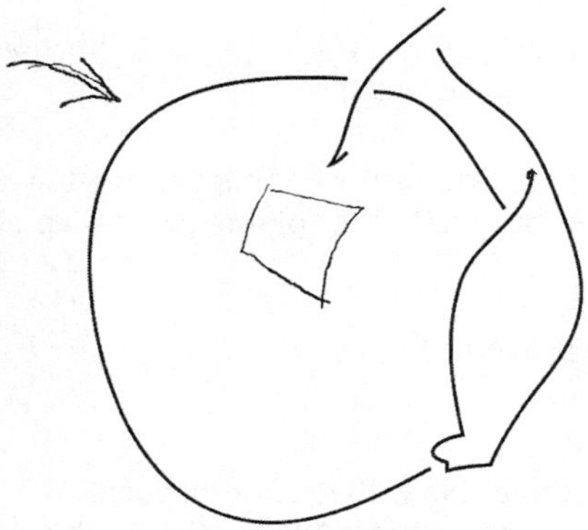

He waved the marker around the room, "If you use one light source, and you have it angled at 30 degrees on an object, you need to make that light source angle at 30 degrees on all subjects in your format, if you use a light source for all your objects."

He turned to the board and drew a square on the apple and an arrow. "Before I direct a light source on this apple, it appears to be flat. Now, I've directed a light on the apple, and it's hitting the apple right on that square," he said, "That's the brightest part of this apple."

He turned to the class, "You can let it go at that. You've already told your viewer there's light coming from the top left with that one little square, drawn to fit the curve of the apple. But," he added as he turned back to the board, "If you want to tell your viewer more, you can begin to add shadow."

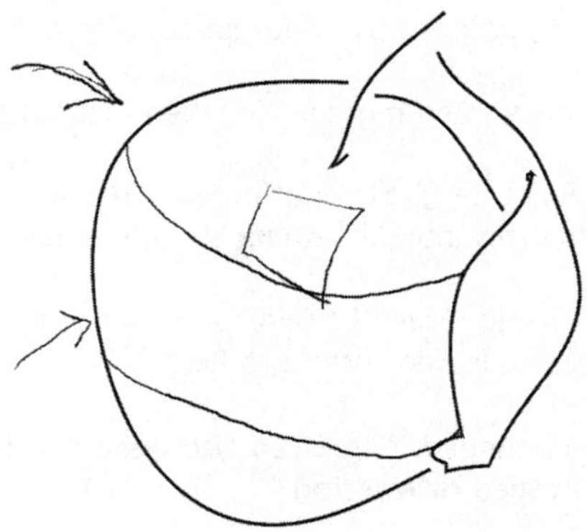

He drew a band around the apple, "You wouldn't draw the shadow like this, of course, but I wanted to show you where some of the darkest shadows would fall."

"Wouldn't the shadows be at the bottom of the apple?" Bonnie asked.

"Only if you had the apple sitting on black material," Wes answered. "If you listened to all your lessons on light, you'd know why."

"Oh!" Zed jumped up and raised his hand, "I know why. Black absorbs the light, so none of it would reflect on the apple. You have this apple sitting on a white or light surface."

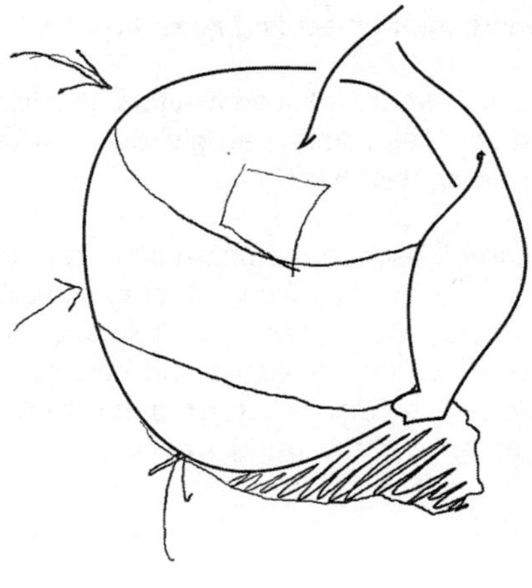

"Bravo!" Wes stated. He drew an arrow to the reflected light at the bottom of the apple, and began to draw a shadow. "The leaf presents a problem," Wes said. "Obviously, we need to draw a shadow that would accommodate the leaf."

He turned and faced the class again, "When light diffuses, or bends around this apple, it means that light will interfere with the shadow. If you've noticed, most shadows don't have hard edges, unless they're under intense light, creating hard line contrast."

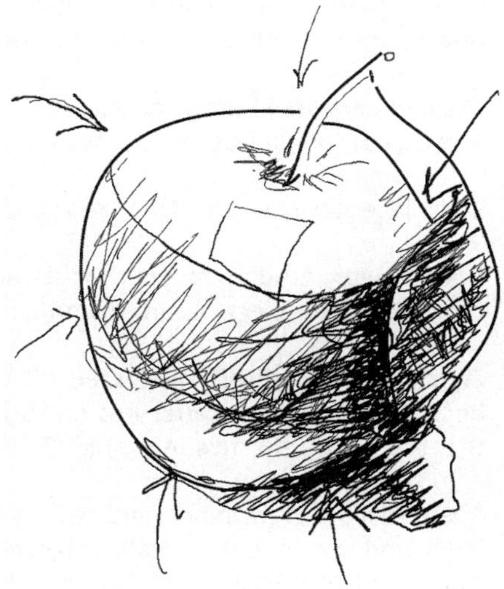

He turned back to the board and scribbled on the apple, "The darkest shadow might be here, under the leaf, and right beneath the apple, in a small space. From there," he said, "The shadow begins to dissipate, as light interferes in the space. This is where values come into play."

He stopped and then drew another arrow at the top of the apple, "Light would also reflect from the top curve of the apple," he said. "The color of the apple would also change if I placed a banana next to the apple. The light reflecting off the banana would also bounce off or be absorbed into the apple, and vice versa."

He handed the marker back to me and concluded:

> *"Nothing has shape, volume, or the appearance of mass without light. Values shape our world. Color adds to our sensory experience."*

Steve said, "Thanks, Wes. I knew that an apple or any other object isn't flat, but I wasn't sure how to add the values to shape the object in a two-dimensional format. You sure make it look easy."

"It is easy," Wes assured Steve. "Mostly, it takes thought and observation. If you take time to watch the light around you and how it reflects, refracts, transmits, and diffuses, then you can do anything."

"Wes has done a great job showing us how light moves on and around an object, and how we can mimic this movement," I said. "Another point to consider is when you use light on *moving* objects in Flash – think first where your light source will come from, and then observe how the light will play on your objects. Static objects will stay the same, unless you're showing a passing of time. Then, your shadows will move."

I continued, "Light on moving objects will change. Sometimes, it's good to set up a model of your object and shine a light on it. Have it move in the direction your object on the screen will move, and observe how the light changes."

"So, we're basically making three-dimensional objects to conform to our observations for a two-dimensional space, right?" Deb asked.

"Right Deb," I answered. "You can trust the light sources available in most software drawing and design programs," I added. "Although their calculations are usually spot on, it does get a little strange when you add more than one light source. Do a few tests on your objects in real life to see if the lighting is correct. Then, you can rest assured that your scene appears normal."

"What if we just want to use flat objects, like anime?" Zed asked. "I know there are tricks to show depth and movement, but a lot of the cartoons and Flash sites I've seen show simple flat shapes."

Deb laughed, "Zed, you just told us that you know how to show light movement without value. If you know how to show depth and movement, then you know how to show light movement." Zed looked confused.

"Remember when I drew the square on the apple and told you that's the direction of my light source?" Wes asked Zed. "I didn't use value, but I used line and shape to show the direction of the light."

Zed's face slowly lit up, "Oh," he said, "I see what you mean now."

I continued, "Study how your artists portray light. See how they handle the movement as it reflects and moves around objects. Learn from their experience."

"What about texture?" Deb asked. "It seems logical that suede or leather would appear softer than metal, because light would scatter less on surfaces that are smooth. It would also have more contrast on surfaces that are more reflective. Am I right?"

"Deb, that's a great point, and yes – you're right," I said. "You'll find that the computer renders metallic objects with much more clarity than any other kind of object. This is because the computer is a light source, and light appears to shine on metallic surfaces."

"I have some new images," Wes stated. "If you want, I can show you how light works on different textures, at least on paper."

"That would be great, Wes," Deb stated. "I didn't know you were working on these. They're super!"

Wes showed his sketches to the rest of the class, "I have new textures for cloth, bark, glass, and water," he said. "As you can see, the fabric doesn't reflect light as much as bark in sunlight. The glass is a filter I used in a graphic arts program," he stated. "The water is just an image that I scanned in and put through a ripple filter.

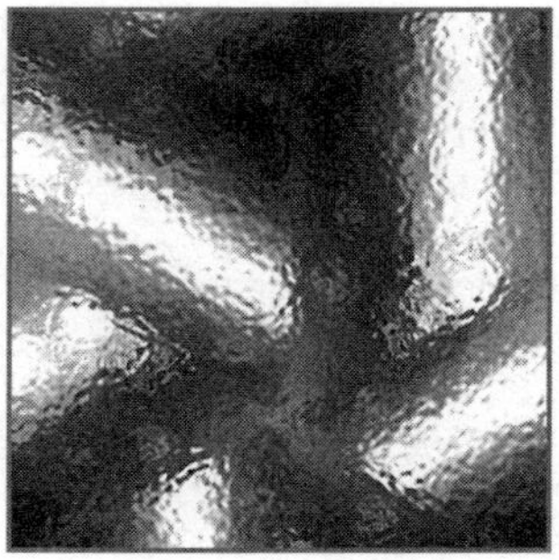

"As you can see, the water and glass appear to reflect light in different ways than the bark and the fabric," Wes stated. "I kept this in mind when I rendered the images, too. I knew that the bark would reflect a lot of light, but not as smoothly as the glass, or as brightly as the water. But," he stated, "The water and the bark have a lot more contrast than the fabric, too."

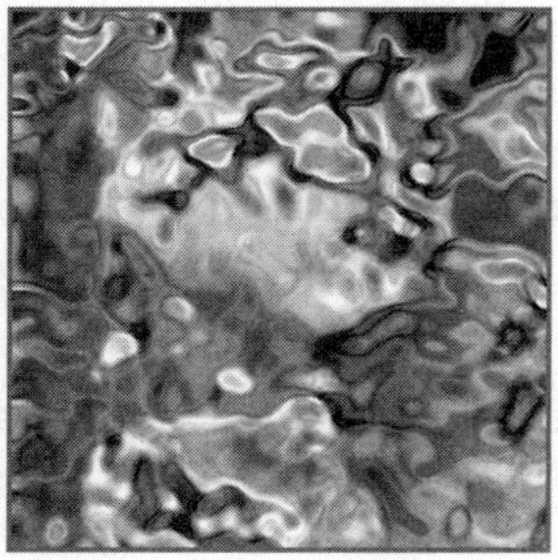

"These are great examples, Wes," I stated. "If we had these images on the screen, the reflections would be even more noticeable than they are here on paper."

Wes nodded, "I know. When I printed them out, I realized I had lost some of the brilliance, especially in the reflective glass and water images."

I turned to address the rest of the class, "Use some patterns and play with some of the filters in your graphic arts software. Try it in Flash, too. See how the computer makes your reflective surfaces appear even brighter than when you print them out."

I asked the class if they had any other questions. No one did at this point, so I reminded them:

> *"Just remember that we're dealing with time, space, and light in Flash. Light, even seen as achromatic values, is a powerful tool. When you add color, you've also added emotion, cultural values, and a language to your message that may not be understood by all viewers.*

"Make sure your message is clear in black and white," I said. "Then, add your color as needed. Along those lines," I added, "Let's move on to the computers and the designer's color palettes and color spaces, so we can understand the color we use in various designs."

Color spaces and palettes

A designer learns about many color theories, applications, palettes, and color spaces throughout their career. Not all of these are available in Flash MX, but they're all necessary to round out the designer's color experience. During this session, I explained these systems to the students.

"Let's deal with color palettes and color spaces," I said. "We already know that choosing colors for our work requires more than just naming them, or determining their wavelengths. If I asked you to choose green, every one of you would probably choose a different color green. If I said you need to choose an energy wave of a certain length and vibration, you would think I was nuts."

They all turned to look at me, "OK, so I'm already nuts. In which case," I said, "It's even more imperative to lock our choices into various palettes and spaces. This way, you and I both know what we're talking about when we say *green*.

"We already know about the traditional subtractive color wheel. We learned about this when we studied the elements of design. Let's now learn about computer color models."

The RGB cube

"One of the most elementary color spaces in digital design is the **RGB cube**," I said. I opened up a Flash file containing a simple diagram of the cube, and asked Bonnie to tell us more about it.

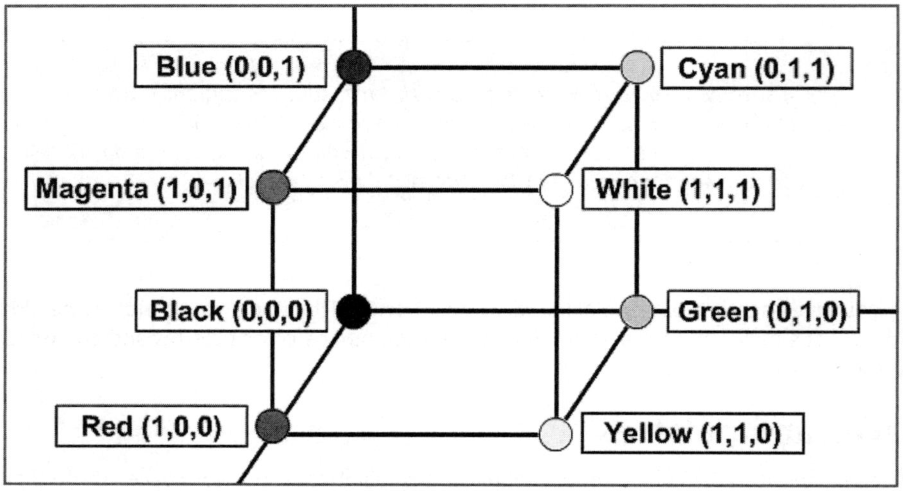

Bonnie began her explanation, "It's simple," she said. "The RGB cube is based on the primary colors of light, and is limited to the 256 colors between these primaries."

"Thanks, Bonnie," I started to write on the board, "Notice the binary numbers of each primary and secondary color. When you do the following vector computations, you'll see how you can end up with white light, which is at position (1,1,1) on the cube:

red (1, 0, 0) + cyan (0, 1, 1) = white (1, 1, 1)
green (0, 1, 0) + magenta (1, 0, 1) = white (1, 1, 1)
blue (0, 0, 1) + yellow (1, 1, 0) = white (1, 1, 1)
red (1,0,0) + green (0,1,0) + blue (0,0,1) = white (1,1,1)

Bonnie sat with her chin in the palm of her hand, "At the beginning of this class, I thought RGB was what computer color was all about. Now, I'm not so sure. It seems the RGB color palette is actually pretty limiting for design purposes."

"Well, as you know by now, Flash operates with the RGB web-safe color palette. This is the default palette, and it's the one you're familiar with by now," I said. "However, if you want to create your own custom colors within Flash, you can!

"I'm sure you've all seen the Color Mixer and Color Swatches panels during your sessions in Flash. If you haven't, open them now from the Window menu.

"With the Color Mixer you can add custom colors. Firstly, ensure that this panel is fully expanded by hitting the little triangle. Next, you need to select a color to add. You can do this by entering specific RGB values at the top of the panel, or by simply picking a color from the palette area below it.

"Once you have a color that you'd like to add to the main Flash color palette, as seen in the Color Swatches panel, select Add Swatch from the Color Mixer panel options."

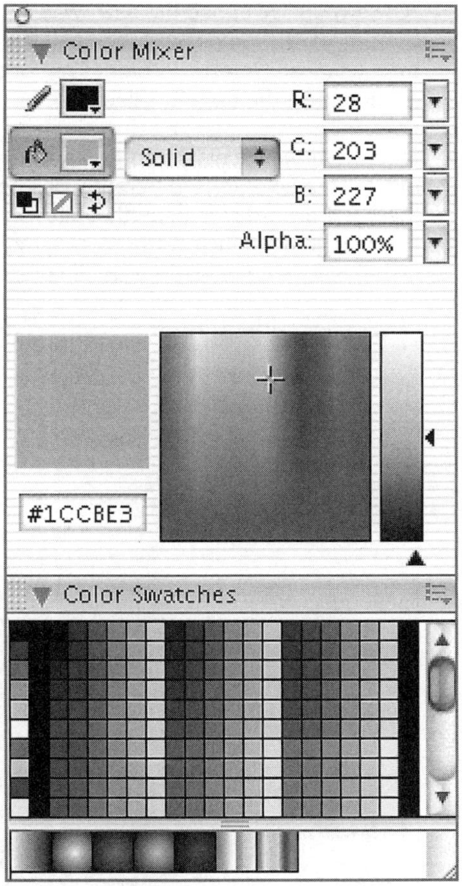

I showed the class where to find these options.

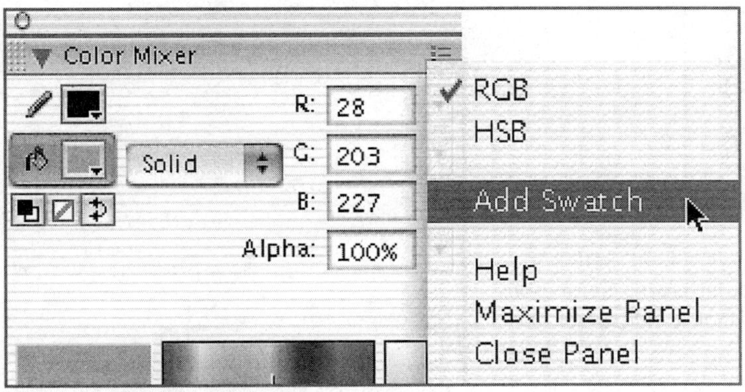

"I've never seen that menu before," said Bonnie, "Now I can see that every panel has one."

"Sure Bonnie, each panel has a set of options like this, so feel free to check them out when you can."

Wes groaned, "Even more options to learn about..."

"Once you have added the new swatch, you will find it at the bottom of the Color Swatches palette, and anywhere else that you can select a color. Every new color swatch is appended to the current selection.

"A customized gradient can be added in the same way, but this is created a little differently. In the Color Mixer panel there is a drop-down menu that allows you to select a radial or linear gradient. Select the Linear gradient option from the menu and we'll create a quick fill color."

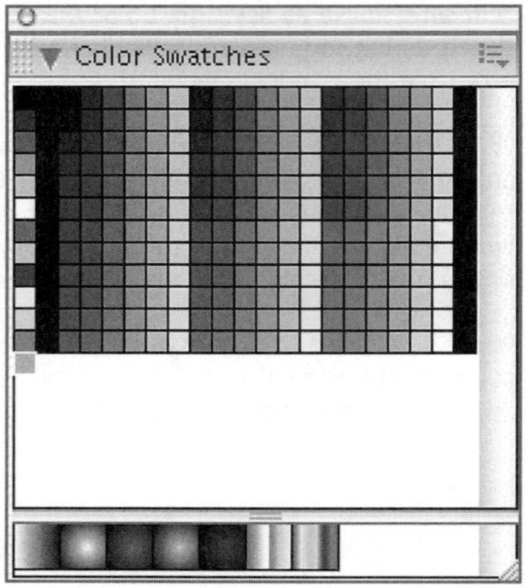

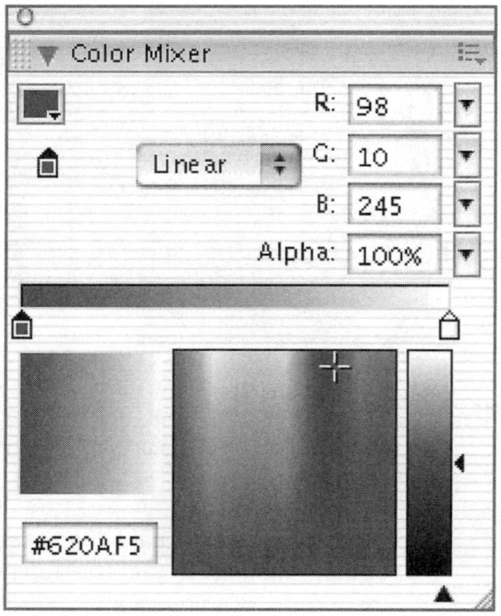

I wanted the class to see beyond the standard two-color gradient, to give them the option of more color depth if they need it.

"The bar at the center of the Color Mixer panel shows the current gradient in progress. Below this bar on the left and right are the two color pots, showing the mixing colors. Any changes you make to these colors are immediately reflected in the gradient bar above, allowing a lot of flexibility when mixing.

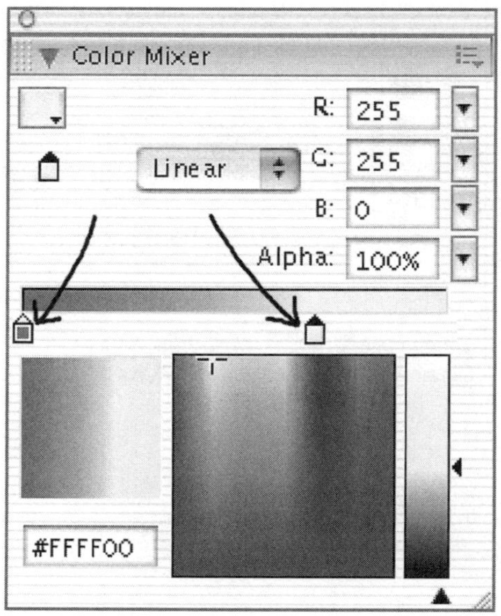

"Firstly, let's select the first color for the gradient. Select the color pot on the left and look in the palette area below for a color. Choose a red for now, and select a yellow for the other paint pot.

"The result is a warm range of colors, with an even spread of yellow and red. If you want more yellow, you can drag the yellow pot a little more the left."

"How about adding the third color?" asked Zed.

"To add an extra color pot to the gradient, just click below the gradient bar away from the other pots. This will add another pot that you can move and color as you wish. You can add as many pots to the gradient as you like, but the more colors you add, the more confusion you are likely to create. You can also remove by them by simply dragging them away from the gradient.

"Finally, add the gradient as you did the previous color, and it will appear alongside the other gradients in the Color Swatches."

"Are these custom colors saved by Flash or will they disappear when we restart the application?" Bonnie asked.

"A very good question Bonnie. You beat me to it! If we were to quit Flash right now, these custom colors would be forgotten and we'd have to remix them in the next session. Flash allows you to save colors using the Color Swatches options.

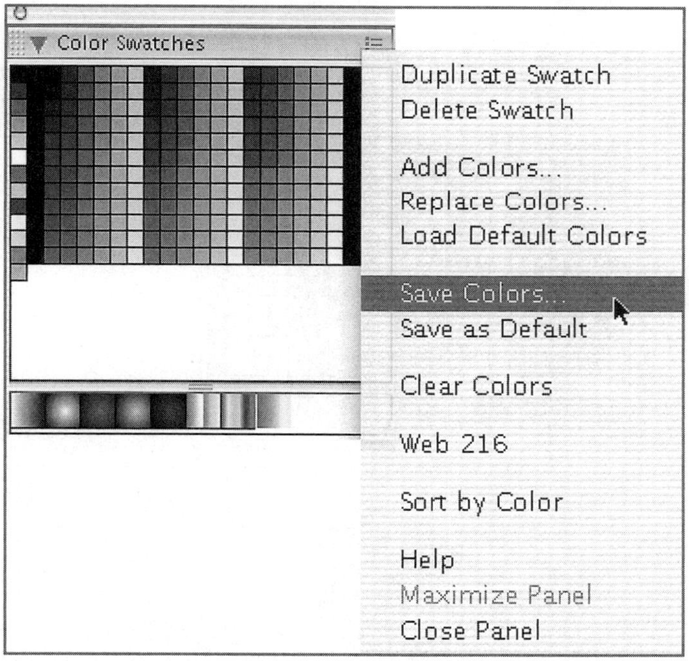

"The standard Flash color files are typically saved in the Flash MX\First Run\Color Sets folder of your installation directory, but you can save your palette anywhere. I recommend that you save a color palette for each different project that you work on.

"When you want to load in your colors in future sessions, use Add Colors or Replace Colors from the Color Swatches options menu.

"If you are all ready to move beyond the restrictions of the RGB cube in Flash, let's do it," I said.

HSB color space

"**HSB** stand for **hue**, **saturation**, and **brightness**," I explained. " We should note that the term HSL is also used interchangeably to refer to this color space (Hue, Saturation, and Luma/Lightness). In this space, hue is your red, green, and blue color sensations. These can be modified by the saturation, which is the amount of white light you apply to these hues. Remember," I added, "That your white light is equal amounts of red, green, and blue.

"Mostly, you can modify your colors with value or lightness," I said. "This is different from saturation, since it indicates how much red, green, or blue is present in your color."

I told them how the HSB space still confuses designers who are accustomed to traditional color mixing, "It helps if you remember that to make a color whiter, instead of adding white pigment, you must de-saturate the color and fully brighten it. The other problem," I added, "Is that HSB de-saturation leans toward middle gray rather than white."

Deb asked, "I've seen this color space before somewhere..."

"You probably did, Deb, while messing around in Flash," I replied. "Flash MX allows you to work with the HSB format – the Color Mixer allows you to work in the HSB format rather than the default RGB. You can change this mode by selecting it from the Color Mixer options menu that we saw earlier.

"HSB is a fairly simple tool. You pick your hue, and then decide the saturation, and the brightness. This is a good tool for flat, matte-looking surfaces."

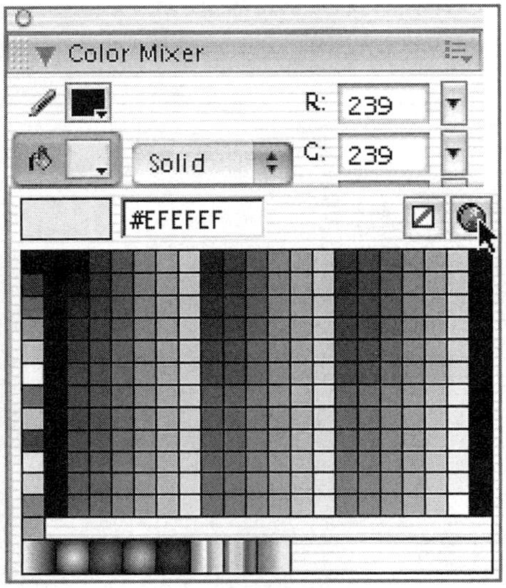

"In Flash on a Mac, you also have access to HSV color (Hue, Saturation, and Value). If you would like to work in a more visual manner with the format, you can use the HSV color picker – select this from the top right of the traditional colors palette.

"The HSV picker looks a little different to the standard RGB slider bars, allowing you to select a hue from the wheel, and then to alter the saturation and value as necessary."

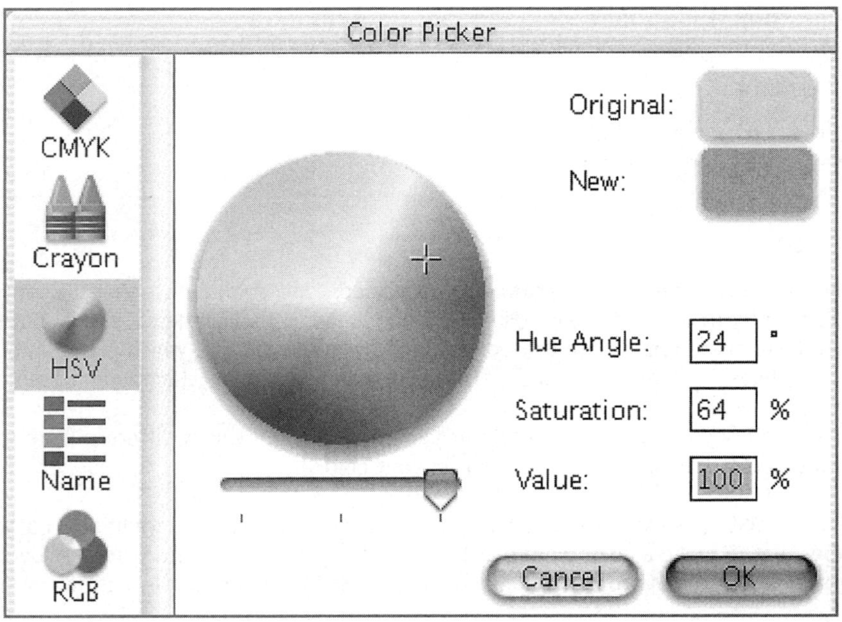

Wes leaned back in his chair and stared at his screen. "If this can do what I think it can, then I'm totally psyched," he said.

"What do you mean, Wes?" I asked.

"It's impossible to mix colors like this traditionally. If you add white to any variety of pigments, like oil or acrylic, you can't make it dark again without the hue becoming muddy. If you add black, it always has a gray value stuck in there somewhere. There's no way to go back to the original hue."

He looked at me, "With these color options, I can change the saturation without changing the hue or value. I can also change the hue to gray by completely de-saturating the color. I can add hue and saturation to gray to colorize it. This, my friend, is quite awesome!"

Steve grinned, "I didn't realize all the problems inherent with traditional media, Wes. You're going to have a great time with this. A lot less waste of canvas and paper, I imagine."

"You bet," Wes replied. "This is a lot like impressionist and pointillist painting, because it concerns the application of subtractive color with the concept of the additive mixing of light. I think I'm a computer color convert."

Bonnie looked up, "I guess we need to look at those art movements, too, right?"

I laughed, "Only if you want to learn something!"

CIE space

I asked Lisa to tell us about the CIE color palette. She began, "Linda and I both talked about wavelengths, starting with purple at 400, and ending in red at 700." Lisa said. "The CIE color palette shows these wavelengths, and all the wavelengths in between."

"What does CIE stand for?" Zed asked.

"It's the *Commission Internationale de l'Eclairage*, otherwise known as the French International Committee of Illumination," Lisa said. She grinned, "I'm sure I just butchered the pronunciation of that name. This commission works on international standards on all matters relating to the science and art of lighting," she added.

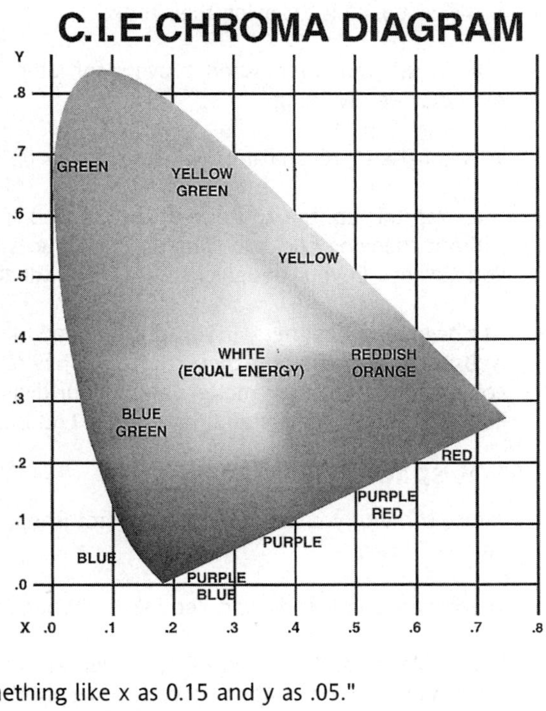

"You did pretty well, Lisa," I said. I held up a visual of the CIE chromacity diagram. "Actually, this device can't be used as a color-naming tool, since it focuses on wavelengths. Each wavelength, as we discovered earlier, is perceived differently by different individuals. The CIE color spectrum displays the entire spectrum of light, from purple to red, with green, the middle-sized wavelength, shown at the top of the curve."

I showed them how the x and y coordinates worked to determine the color as I pointed at the coordinates on the diagram in Wes's hand. "If x is 0.64, and y is 0.33, we have red. If we wanted a blue, what x and y coordinates would I need?"

Wes peered at his diagram. "It seems you would want something like x as 0.15 and y as .05."

"Good going, Wes," I stated. "That's about as close as you can get with this diagram."

"Anyone familiar with the Photoshop color picker will notice the impact of CIE – this is the LAB space," I said. "Where *L* stands for lightness and is achromatic, ranging from white to black. The *A* stands for redness/greenness, and the *B* stands for yellowness/blueness. LAB allows for specifications in terms of a three-dimensional space."

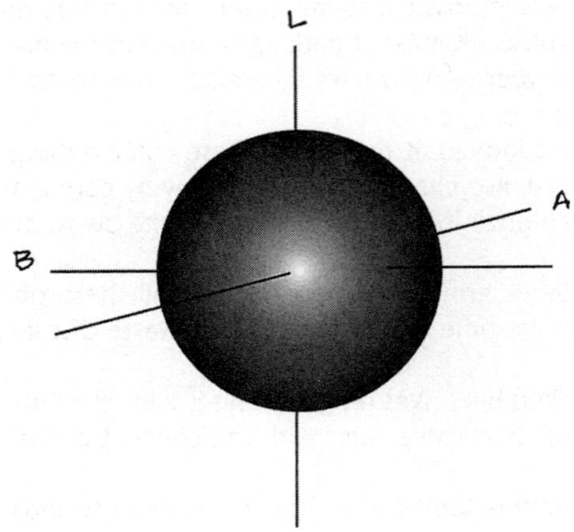

"This space isn't used in Flash, but one of the reasons we're discussing it is because the CIE spectrum shows us how we view color," I said. I pointed to the top portion of the palette, "This is green, and it's right in the middle of the color wavelength spectrum. What does this tell you?" I asked.

Steve said, "I guess it means that green would be the color that's easiest for us to see, since it's right in the middle of the full visual spectrum of wavelengths."

"Yeah," Zed nodded, "That sounds logical. Lisa mentioned this at the theater this morning, too."

"You're both right," I said. "But, we need to be careful about what exact shade of green we use. Some have been known to cause physical nausea, like yellow-green. Others, like army green, also have connotations that might not be useful for a client, as we discussed earlier."

"This is a great tool to see the whole expanse of color," Wes said. He was already at the CIE website, www.cie.co.at/cie/, viewing their tools.

"OK, Wes," Deb admonished. "Save it for later. If we're not using this in Flash, I want to move on and find out what we *are* using."

Wes coughed, "Yes ma'am!" He hid a grin as he turned off the browser.

"To wrap this up, the aptitude of the CIE LAB space gives the designer more room to work with brightness without changing hue, and sometimes produces better results for printing collateral material," I said. "When you advance in your design skills, this tool will aid you greatly."

"As beginning designers, if you don't already know about CIE, do as Wes just did," I said. "Look up their website, and read about their research. They're very involved with communications that relate to additive color, and that includes matters about your digital designs." I added, "But don't worry too much about it for now, you should understand that the CIE LAB is a color space that's rather beyond the scope of this course."

CMYK space

"Since some of you are familiar with Photoshop, you may have seen the CMYK color space within their color palette," I said.

There were some nods, and Zed asked, "What does CMYK stand for?"

"Cyan, Magenta, Yellow, and Black," Deb answered. "It can be confusing, because CMYK are the different screens used in the printing process. Since printing is a subtractive color system, it seems odd they use colors relative to mixing the additive primaries."

"It is odd, Deb," I agreed. "But, it makes our life easier when it comes to converting colors to the printing process. It's not the exact science we'd like it to be, but it comes close."

"Although Flash only renders work in RGB, it will allow you to pick a color using the CMYK picker on a Mac, as we saw earlier. This is then converted to HSB or RGB, depending on what mode the user is working in."

"In order for us to make an image for Frieda's name and use it for printing brochures or other collateral material, we need to comply to CMYK standards for her printer. Applications like Adobe Photoshop and Illustrator allow you to work in CMYK mode, as well as RGB.

"However, since you're developing most of your images within Flash MX, we'll avoid going into the finer details of CMYK right now. Suffice to say that whichever color space you're working in, Flash will try to carry that color across to all the other color modes.

"Let's move on to two more color palettes. These are devised with subtractive colors, but both are important to understand." We moved on to the **Pantone** and **Munsell** color systems.

Pantone palettes

The use of the Pantone color system is vital to designers, especially if computer generated designs will be used in printed material. Although this isn't used within Flash, the understanding of the system is useful for color generation within any computer design software.

"There are color systems available to designers that come close to matching hues between additive and subtractive color. These are **commercial color systems**, and they're limited to certain color ranges. These are useful when you prepare digital work for a client that will flow into print design as a collateral development.

"The CMYK printing process is a headache for digital designers," I said. "Oranges, and subtle variations in color gradients and tints are very difficult to reproduce from the screen to print. Can anyone tell me why this happens?"

Steve swung his chair around and said, "I can answer that one. Once again, we're dealing with a design that was generated using the medium of light. Printing uses flat color, even though the color screens seem to be based on the additive color system. The product coming off the press is subtractive color, and it's impossible to precisely replicate the light and color we see on the screen. Unless you've had some experience with printing, you're probably going to be terribly disappointed with what comes from the press."

"Steve's right," I said. "Often a client will ask you to design a site, and then also ask you to make a copy of their logo or other work for their printer. If you use oranges or light tints, you might be in trouble."

I pulled out a thick narrow book of color swatches. "This is just one of the many swatch books available from the Pantone Color Libraries at www.pantone.com," I said. "Before you ever design a new logo or artwork for a client on screen, ask the client if they think they'll ever use the images for print. If so, you'll probably need to use a commercial color system like Pantone."

Steve asked to see the swatch book, then he passed it around to the rest of the students. "Pantone has really kept up with computer generated design," he said.

"You mentioned earlier that oranges and very subtle color gradients are tricky to reproduce – does this mean we should stay away from oranges and these kind of tints?" Deb asked.

"Not at all," I answered. "You can usually find something in the Pantone libraries that will match your work. But," I added, "If you know you're going to go to press, work with the printer to make sure you don't have any surprises down the road."

"It would be awful to spend so much time tweaking colors when the printer can't reproduce them," Bonnie said. "I didn't realize this could happen. I was thinking about adding print services to my web design work, so I'm glad I learned about this now before wasting time and money."

"Adding print services to your computer design services is a logical progression, Bonnie," I said. "But, you really need to understand the print process. Hopefully, this is one step in that direction for you."

Steve added, "They have some neat metallic inks available, too. That's great, since metallic surfaces reproduce so well on the screen."

"That's good to know," Wes said. He looked at Deb, and they both nodded. "We were thinking about adding some metallic contrast to Frieda's name in our design."

"There are other commercial color systems available," I said, "But we're covering this one, because it's available to use in some of your design software, like Adobe Photoshop.

"We've got one more color system to discuss, and this one isn't found on any software," I said. "But, it's still an important color system relied on by many designers."

Munsell color system

This color system was developed by an American, Albert Munsell, and is based on the **perception** of color. Although it uses an alphanumeric library system like the Pantone system, it also uses a base of psychological associations and a geometric space to display the data.

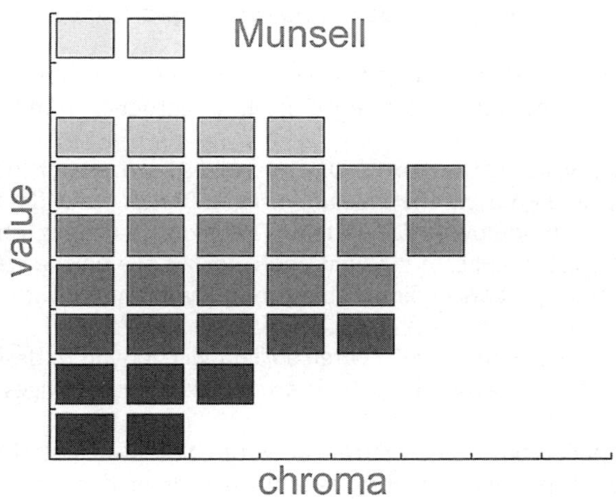

I went to a cupboard and pulled down a large wood and Plexiglas structure splattered with tiny flat rectangles of color. As I placed it on the desk, I began to explain this color system to the class. "This is the Munsell color system in a nutshell," I said. "These color swatches are aligned according to hue, value, and chroma, or saturation. Each color is assigned an alphanumeric value, and it's also given assignments of psychological data.

"Although Munsell died in 1918, a number of his colleagues formed the Munsell Color Company and published his work. Today, you can find them on the web at www.munsell.com."

The students left their computers and stood around the module. "This is pretty confusing," Bonnie said. "It doesn't seem right to me."

"Why not, Bonnie?" I asked.

"Well, for one thing, there seems to be a wide range of everything but tertiary colors. Plus," she added, "It just looks like a lot of pastels."

"It may seem that way," I explained, "Because Munsell developed this system on hues, values, and saturation leading to grays of equal value. This eliminates the grays based on chromatic neutrals, like the mixing of red and green or blue and orange."

"I remember those," Zed said. "We talked about those grays when we talked about the color wheel."

"Right, Zed," I replied. "Munsell based this system on association of colors and perception, which leads to a few flaws. Remember, this scheme was developed in the 1920s, a time of revolutionary change in the world of art.

"Obviously, Munsell felt there needed to be some order, at least in color," I said. "His system is based on social and psychological perceptions of that time period. For instance, Munsell felt that quiet color was a mark of good taste." I looked at Bonnie. "This is why you perceived pastel colors, rather than a mix of brilliance like you'd see on a traditional color wheel.

"Munsell used pure color first, then modified it with tint and shade to reach the whites and blacks. He used tone to modify the pure color to reach the equal grays."

Wes added, "This is a good system to learn just to know how to break out of it." He grinned, "I had a little taste of this early in my art career. It was before I learned about the Bauhaus school and their color masters, Itten and Albers."

I nodded. "The problem with this color system," I explained, "Is that so many people learn this, and they don't go beyond it to learn about the color theories of Itten or Albers. Or," I added, "They study Itten and Albers, and they don't learn about the theories of Munsell's structured color."

"Oh dear," Bonnie said. "Please explain!"

Wes sat on the edge of the desk, "Itten based his color harmonies on his **observation** of color," he said. "Albers based his theories on **human intuition**. Both theories work when color harmonies are in question, since these theories are based on each individual's perception of color. Even Munsell's work is a matter of perception, especially in his psychological meanings of each color."

"So we're right back where we began this morning," Lisa said. "With all these palettes, color spaces, theories, and subtractive and additive color mixings, it all boils down to how our audience perceives the colors we use. In the long run, we have no control at all, do we?"

"It appears we don't," Steve agreed. "But, isn't it wonderful? It would be terrible if everything in the world were black and white. I think, for simplicity, we need to follow Linda's advice of economy. This way, we can use color with power, and we can also be sure that the largest number of viewers comprehend our messages."

I smiled, "I'm sorry this is all so frustrating, Lisa. It seems even worse when we've studied a certain science of color for a long time, like you have with theater lighting. But, we can help our viewers with simplicity, as Steve said, and with color consistency.

"OK, it's probably time to move on. If you want to find out more about any of the color spaces and palettes we've studied today, the Adobe website is a good place to start. Check out:
www.adobe.com/support/techguides/color/colormodels/"

Accessibility and usability simplified

Lisa's short performance was still in the student's minds – she'd used limited color to express her messages effectively. When the students returned from break, I asked them to sit at the table, and Bonnie was first to say something.

Bonnie stated, "I noticed you didn't use a huge range of colors to show us how color affects us in your performance this morning, Lisa. I think this makes an important point."

"What's that?" Lisa asked.

"Well," Bonnie continued, "I'm going to stick with this subject of accessibility with Flash until I have some answers."

I sat with the students at the table and said, "Now's as good a time as any to address your questions about accessibility and usability with color and other issues, Bonnie. Fire away!"

Bonnie leaned forward and said, "I know there are a wide range of accessibility issues. One of them is the availability of color on a monitor. The others are about vision and hearing impaired viewers. How can we address these issues within Flash?"

"Bonnie, we can accommodate many people with Flash MX," I said. "The main reason I've avoided the use of color in your sites until this point in the course is because you need to know how to design without color first. If you can't achieve a balance of elements and principles of design within a composition without color, then something's wrong with your design."

I continued, "No amount of color will help your work if it's not unified. If you don't utilize competent text, contrast, values, textures, line, and all the other elements within the framework of the principles, your reader won't be able to follow you, even in black and white."

I looked at Lisa, "When Lisa talked about the inconsistencies with manmade light, she also described certain forms of colorblindness. Some people see more red than green, or more green than red. This is how some people view the world every day of their lives.

"About one in twelve people will be unable to see many of the colors you use within your design. If they do, the colors won't be close to the ones you picked for the site. So if 1,000 people connect to her website, Frieda may be dealing with 83 people who won't be able to see colors the way you intended."

"Wow, that's a hefty percentage," Steve commented.

"It's certainly worth taking note of, Steve," I answered. "And if you want to cater for this segment of your potential customers, you need to check your design against various sources relating to accessibility on the web. Macromedia has pages devoted to accessibility – for instance, take a look at www.macromedia.com/macromedia/accessibility/, and also www.colormatters.com or www.visibone.com. There are more and more sites today that offer color palettes to compare your colors against the sight limitations of the vision impaired. And don't count on one color-deficient friend to tell you what's wrong, since there's more than one form of colorblindness."

"So, you're saying that it's better to design sites in black and white?" Deb asked. "Isn't that a bit dull for the rest of us?"

Wes smiled, "It would probably be dull for you these days, Deb. I think what Linda's saying is that if we design first within an achromatic value system, we'll know if our design works regardless of the color added. When we do add color, we need to add it only to enhance any one of the elements or principles of design," he said. He added, "Of course, since color is a language, how do we avoid talking in reds and blues?"

"You're not going to please everyone, Wes," I answered. "Including ourselves. I think we would address your question in the framework of a personal or cultural sense of color, and how it's perceived.

"If you're designing for a company that wants to stay local, like Frieda's company, you're probably going to be pretty astute when it comes to color connotations. If you're designing regionally or nationally, I would think you're still going to be OK with your own perception of what works on an emotional or stylish or psychological level."

I continued, "But, if you're concerned about international appeal, I would carefully research each color you use, so you don't give anyone the wrong message. I would research color combinations too. By color combinations, I mean putting red and white together or green and red. Red and white in some cultures means loyalty. In other cultures it might stand for the enemy's flag. Red and green might mean the Christmas holiday, but it could also stand for hearts and leprechauns."

Bonnie spoke up, "We have limited choices anyway. The web safe colors are paramount. Some businesses don't buy into sites that haven't passed W3C standards."

"What's the W3C?" Zed asked. "Is that a government organization?"

"Not quite, Zed," Bonnie said. "The *3* means you repeat the W three times for World Wide Web. The *C* is for Consortium. They have a website at www.w3c.org. They're responsible for developing common protocols that promote its evolution and ensure its global interoperability. They work on code and upgrades to codes so that each new set of programming follows standard protocols."

I shook my head, "Thanks for that information, Bonnie, but I don't know if I agree with keeping to such strict standards on color. That may have applied ten years ago, when monitors and video cards limited our color capacities across operating systems. Since that time," I added, "The range of colors available on new systems, and the larger range of high-bandwidth connections have made many of these issues moot. A person who owns a computer that's ten years old won't be able to access many websites anyway."

"I don't know," Bonnie muttered, "I feel so responsible. The accessibility issues are real, with so many guidelines and compliancy issues."

Zed asked. "Can we be arrested for not complying to accessibility issues?" He looked up at me.

"No," I answered. "Basically, Frieda is selling her wood working skills, but the site is separate from this proposal. When Frieda's site goes live, it actually becomes one of her products, and it could fall into the realm of usability and accessibility, and she may have to – eventually – comply with these issues. It's best to think about these problems at the start of a design, so you can build them into your work.

"Simplicity is the key. *Economy*. That's one of the principles of design, anyway. It's always a good rule to test your site on as many operating systems as possible. Flash MX also has built-in accessibility options available to PC designers and developers."

> *"Accessibility and usability in general are covered comprehensively in The Flash Usability Guide, available from friends of ED (ISBN: 1-903450-25-X). If the issue of accessibility arises in a client brief, the advice found in this book is certainly worth noting."*

"You won't go wrong using all the elements and principles of design, and design according to usability guidelines," I continued. "Use a variety of textures instead of color. Don't name something *green* unless you label it green. For example, if you tell people to press the green button to complete a specific task, then you might want to label that button with the word *green* for those who can't see the color. Ask people to use your site, and report any difficulties back to you. These are some of the many ways to avoid problems with these issues," I concluded. "Any other questions?"

Zed looked sad. "I didn't know our sites would be so much work. I just wanted to have fun!"

Wes laughed, "Zed, your idea of fun is running without boundaries. Design does have a lot of structure and boundaries. The fun part is learning to push the boundaries, and still be understood."

This week's session covered color in depth. The complexity of this topic can't be narrowed to any particular software or any specific task. However, it's information that most professional designers know and implement in their daily work. As the students settled in to hear about this week's project, I asked each of them what they got out of the day's lessons.

"It seems color is the most complex issue we've dealt with in this course," Deb said. "To understand color, we really need to go beyond what's available in Flash MX. But," she added, "Everything I've learned has helped me understand the simplicity of this software."

"I agree," Bonnie said. "I didn't realize how much more I *could* simplify my sites. Instead of worrying about color matching for vision-impaired viewers, I can use textures, contrast, and values. I can minimize my colors, and save a lot of time."

Zed looked thoughtful, "I never worried much about colors in the first place. I'm more into lines, and what I can do with them. I know color is important, but I really like what I've learned about light movement today. I can't believe I'm being bombarded by energy right now. That's awesome!"

Wes laughed, "I already knew about a lot of what we learned today, especially the bits about subtractive color models. I've had my work printed before, and had to work closely with a printer to calibrate the colors from my work to the final print. Mostly," he grinned, "I was thrilled with Lisa's part in the class, and I'm fascinated with how she pulled that off." He winked at her, and we all waited for Lisa to say something.

Lisa laid her hands on the table and looked up at us, "I thought I knew a lot about additive color, but *painting* with light – like we do in Flash – is another thing altogether. I know it appears simple, and I have a fair grasp of it, but today's lesson has really added some deeper layers to my knowledge."

We waited to see if she'd add more information. She added, "No, I'm not telling who operated the lights today. You'll find out soon enough, I'm sure." She grinned, and turned to Steve.

Steve leaned back and crossed his arms, "I knew about the printing processes, and I know about working in digital design. I wasn't aware how much more I needed to learn. I guess I took color for granted. I've been working in black and white for a long time. It's just a whole lot easier, especially when I'm in a hurry."

"It sounds like you all learned something today," I said. "We learned about the importance of light, and how it affects what we see. We also learned about some of the designer's color tools, including the ones you'll use in Flash MX. Finally, you learned about some accessibility and usability issues.

"Next week," I said, "We'll spend more time working on your final drafts to show the client. We'll process the individual components for your sites, and we'll learn how to present these sites to the client."

"Do we have an assignment this week, teach?" Zed asked.

"Of course we do, silly," Deb tapped her finger on her forehead. "Let me guess what it is. I'll wager it has something to do with color."

I smiled. "Actually, the only thing you need to do this week is finalize your site components. But," I added, "You can also do some research on various issues that interest you, or topics you want to know more about. In three weeks, I'll have each of you talk about something you've researched. This way," I added, "We'll make sure we haven't missed anything along the line."

"That sounds great," Steve said. He looked around, "Anyone up for a coffee and some brainstorming on topics?"

Zed agreed, if he could stick with water. The rest said yes, except Deb. It seemed she had other plans. "I'll pass, Steve, but thanks. I'm going to get a tattoo in just a little while."

As they left, they gathered around Deb to find out what she was getting, why, and where. Wes looked at me, shrugged and grinned. "I don't have anything to do with this," he stated as he waved goodbye. I sat and wondered about Lisa's secret and Deb's tattoo, and then realized that I'd have loved a cup of coffee too...

Summary

In this chapter we've learned how additive lighting can affect the viewer's interpretation of the focus point, or emphasis, of a design, and the various connotations that color can bring. More specifically, we've learned:

- How to use color and value to emphasize a product or message.
- How we recognize shapes before we see colors.
- How to use the same color or value to connect a product and a message.
- To use elements consistently and sparingly, especially color.
- How color has underlying social, psychological, and cultural meaning.

We've also studied the different properties of light, especially reflection, learning that color appears more reflective on the screen than on the printed page. We then reviewed a few color spaces and palettes, including:

- RGB – Red, Green, and Blue
- HSB – Hue, Saturation, and Brightness
- CIE Space - *Commission Internationale de l'Eclairage*
- CMYK – Cyan, Magenta, Yellow, and Black
- The Pantone Color System
- The Munsell Color Scheme

Finally, we presented an overview of the issues associated with accessibility and usability in website design, emphasizing that the best method to create a site for maximum use by a large number of people is to keep to the elements and principles of design, and to practice the principle of economy with diligence.

In the next class we're going to take a step closer to finalizing our sites – by *selecting* and *implementing* our designs.

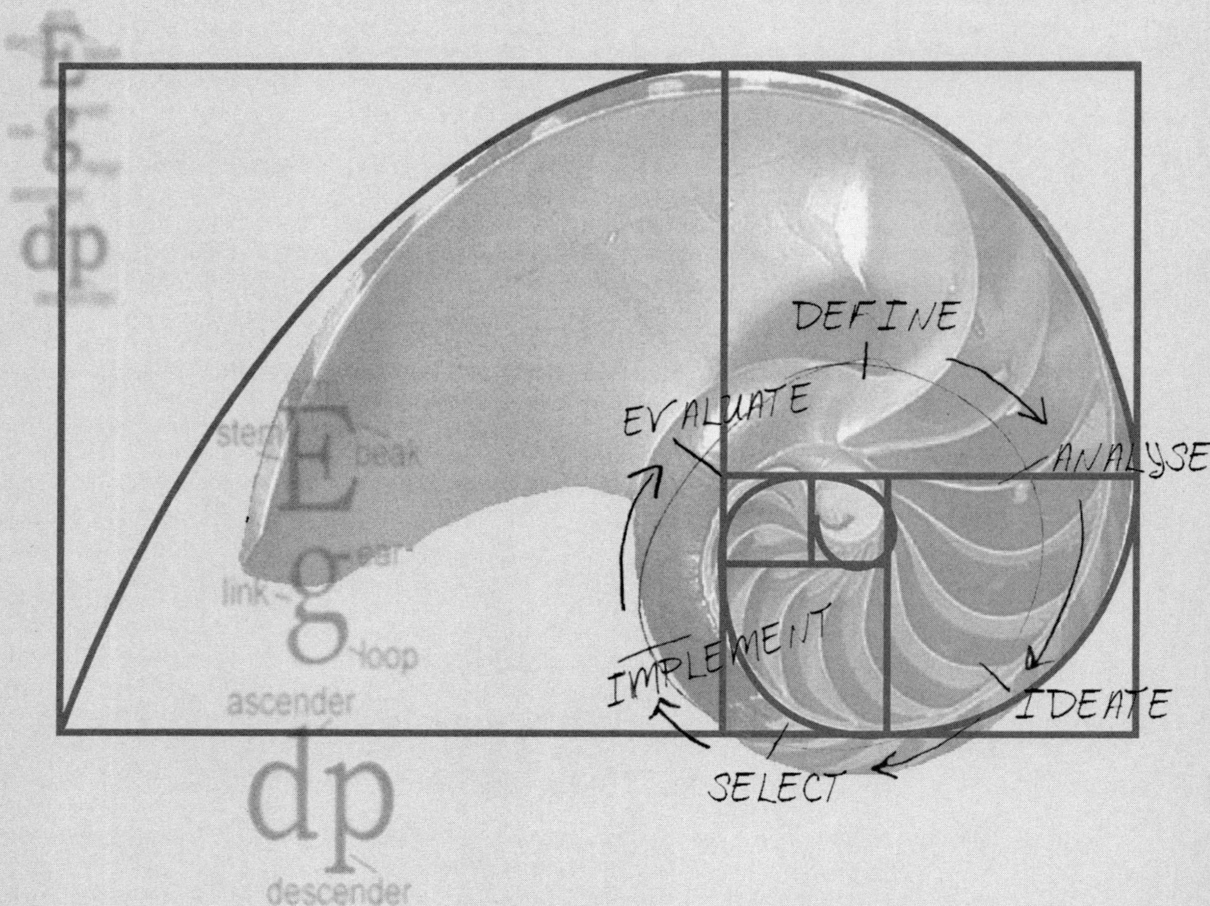

stem
peak
ear
link
loop
ascender
descender
DEFINE
ANALYSE
IDEATE
SELECT
IMPLEMENT
EVALUATE

Chapter 9

Select and Implement

Objectives

In today's class you will learn:

- About using guide layers
- How to import images and text
- How to optimize images
- About hyperlinks
- To use basic ActionScript code
- About storyboards for the project and presentation
- About the Dog and Pony show

Introduction

I was a few minutes late for class this morning. When I arrived, everyone was gathered around Deb, who was seated at the table. I plunked my materials on the desk, and walked over to see what the excitement was about. Then I remembered – Deb left class last week intent on getting a tattoo.

Wes stood behind her. He held her braids aside so I could get a good view of the body art. She rolled up the sleeve of her t-shirt to show off the image. When I looked at her shoulder, I couldn't keep myself from laughing. Deb looked up at me with a grin, "You recognize this, don't you?"

She had taken the creative problem-solving circle, reduced it to a symbol, and reproduced it on her shoulder in red, green, and blue. "Deb, that's really creative." I said. What was your motivation?

Deb replied, "I'll save the full explanation for later. Let's just say I needed a permanent reminder about this time in my life. It's the beginning of a truce between the left and right sides of my brain."

Bonnie wasn't saying a word. She sat next to Deb with a smile on her face. Steve settled in at the table. "I have to admit it's a clever way to remember what we've learned so far," he said. "But I put my tattoos in my drawing pad."

Lisa laughed, "I'll also admit the design is memorable. Thanks, Deb. I'll never forget that image. I have it tattooed on my brain now."

Zed was about two inches from Deb's shoulder, peering at the mark. Deb shooed him away. "You're breathing on me, Zed, and I can tell you had doughnuts for breakfast. Go sit down."

Wes laughed, "Deb brought her dumbek drum to my studio last night." He pointed at her shoulder. "She's not only got nerve, she's got great rhythm, too. Rhythm is a principle of design. I don't know about the nerve part."

Lisa looked up and asked, "How are you getting along in those drumming classes, then?"

Deb nodded, "Wes and I bought some filters for his studio lights. We combined light with the rhythms. While I drummed, he played with some lighting patterns on the wall." She shook her head. "Lisa, you'll have to give us some direction. Most of the stuff Wes tried ended up looking like mud, and I wasn't any help at all."

Wes shrugged, "I'm just an amateur at additive lighting. Seems Lisa and I have been schooled in two different types of color palette – additive and subtractive. She glows, and I reflect!" He stopped talking, apparently puzzled with his own remark.

Lisa grinned, "At least I've learned how to use a ruler!"

"You have, Lisa," I said. "Plus, it seems you've managed to gain a lot of self-confidence in just a few weeks. I'm really pleased with your progress."

Steve agreed. "She's been a great partner for this project. She's not afraid to tell me if she doesn't agree with my ideas."

Lisa blushed and fanned her face. "I just wish I could stop blushing! I'm afraid I'll blow it if I ever need to meet with a client."

I assured her, "You'll learn more about how to present your work to a client today, Lisa. We'll talk about storyboards, clients in cyberspace and real life, and how to professionally present your initial work. The culmination of these elements equals what is often called the *Dog and Pony Show*. This will prepare you for next week's presentations to Frieda."

Steve laughed, "Do they still use that term for presentations?"

"Dog and pony?" Zed asked. "What's that all about? Do we have to train animals, too?"

Bonnie shook her head, "Zed, I'm sure this doesn't have anything to do with animals. By the way, where's your scarf?"

"I'm having it cleaned for our presentation next week," Zed answered. He shrugged, "I guess I'd better keep my mouth shut today, since that scarf seems to carry my brains with it wherever it goes."

That last remark concerned me. "Zed, you are brilliant with or without that scarf." I stated. "I don't expect you to understand ancient advertising metaphors, and the Dog and Pony Show is just that – a metaphor. We'll talk about the implications later today. In the meantime, I'll let you show me just how smart you really are."

I asked the class if they had all the components for their sites with them today. "This morning, we're going to learn how to pull all these components together. We'll process all this information to finalize your three site designs."

I pushed myself out of my chair and went to the board. "These are the elements for your sites that you'll need today." I wrote the list on the board.

I continued, "These are the items that are necessary for your site. If you don't use photographs, that's fine. However," I added, "Your background images will be either photographs or illustrations. Even if you decide to just use a color for the background with the word *Enter*, you've created images. Can anyone tell me why?"

* the mark - Frieda's name
* background images
* navigational images
* sub-navigational images
* photographs/illustrations
* copy - who, what, when, where, how, why

Steve answered, "Because the formats of Flash and the browser are rectangular, the color presents itself as a shape. The use of type is basically a symbol – in this case it's an icon, an image consisting of verbal code representing a direction. This is our directional image."

Bonnie looked puzzled. "If we just use a word, shouldn't we also use an image that means *Enter* for those who don't understand this verbal code? Something like an arrow?"

"Ideally, yes," I answered. "Remember, Frieda's site is currently intended for local audiences only, and you need to state this somewhere prevalent in the beginning of the site. All you need for this project is a simple statement to tell your audience this fact. If she wants to expand her site in the future, you'll need to be more specific with your symbols. This is part of your vision for her site expansion."

"If we're all set, let's go to work," I said. "Grab your team member, and share a computer. This way, you can learn to manage your sites together, and save time."

Everyone gathered their materials, and we began to process the components for their sites.

Building the sites

This session would take up the better part of today's class, as each team worked on photographs, and other components for their sites. Some of them had developed images and copy in other programs, so we also needed to learn how to import these elements into the Flash authoring environment.

Before we began, Deb rolled up her sleeve and glanced at her tattoo. "So, we're now at the stage where we've selected the elements for Frieda's site, and we're about to implement them, right?"

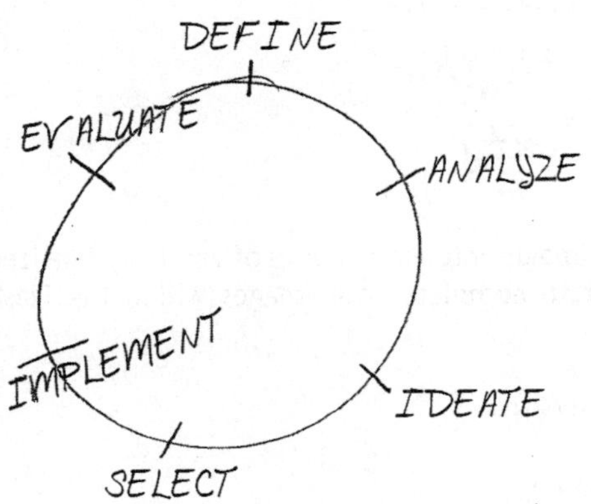

Zed and Bonnie and Lisa and Steve leaned around to see Deb's shoulder. "I'll draw the circle up here, so you all have a better vantage point of your progress to date," I said. I drew the creative problem-solving circle on the board. I then indicated where they were in their progress.

"Deb is right in her assessment," I said. "We're now at the *selection* and *implementation* stages for the design of Frieda's site. But remember, we'll constantly repeat steps in this cycle for every move you make today. If you run into a problem with your components, go back to the top of this circle. *Define* your problem, *analyze* it, *ideate* your possible solutions, *select* the best choices, *implement* them, and then *evaluate* your success."

"If you need help with your ideations or evaluations, ask your fellow students what they think. You've all advanced to the point where you can help each other out," I stated. "I'll be here to help you begin the process and to help you through the technicalities with Flash. When it comes to personal decisions about placement of the elements along the principles of design, you're on your own."

"Why?" Zed asked. "I'm feeling kinda lost today!"

Steve replied, "Don't be scared, Zed. We're all in this together. After all," he grinned, "We can't ask Frieda how she feels about our designs until next week."

Zed asked, "Are we going to present our designs as teams?"

I nodded, "You are, Zed. By working with a team member, you're able to come up with your own individual styles. Each team will pitch their ideas to Frieda, and this also helps your with your sales skills."

Wes looked at Zed, "I'm feeling as freaked out as you are right now, Zed, but I think that this team approach is better than coming up with one design for the course. I've learned a lot from your team's design and from Steve and Lisa's design, too."

Zed agreed, but with a lack of enthusiasm. "At least I'm not alone in feeling lost today. Maybe after I get started, I'll feel better."

I wrote the elements and principles of design on the board to remind them all. "This will help you with your progress today," I said. "If you run into any snags, just refer to these lists."

Elements of Design	Principles of Design
1. Line	1. Contrast
2. Shape	2. Direction
3. Color/hue	3. Emphasis
4. Movement	4. Economy
5. Space	5. Proportion
6. Value	6. Balance
7. Texture	7. Rhythm
8. Typography	8. Unity

Let's get started with learning how to compress and import our images into Flash. Some of you have finalized images you've created in other programs. Some of you want to complete your images within the Flash program. We'll do this as I help you transport your images."

"Rev your engines," Wes said. "We're ready to run our Flash software!"

At that announcement, the class prepared to import their images.

Building sites in Flash MX

"Now that you all have your current drafts of the website design, the first thing you need to do is to work it all into a Flash format. This can include taking the essential elements from renditions in Photoshop or similar and importing them into Flash.

"The main elements that you'll need to import are any images you have chosen to use. These can include background images and any other bitmaps that you've created for her mark or name, navigation images, photographs, and any of the other items listed on the board. Don't worry too much about shapes and text because these can be created within Flash."

"How do we go about bringing these images into Flash, Linda?" asked Wes.

"Well Wes, the first and most important thing to do is to make sure the images are no bigger than they need to be when you import them, otherwise you will pay in the final file size. If your images are bigger than they need to be, reduce them in your image editing application and export them."

"Should we compress them before importing them into Flash too?" asked Bonnie.

"Well, there are two approaches to this Bonnie. The first is to compress all your images before importing them into Flash, and the second is to leave them at the best possible quality.

"Flash has a number of built in compression options, so you can work with the high quality images from within Flash. In most cases, I would recommend doing this and keeping the original images as pristine as possible. This way you can decide what is best for the image when it has been put into its intended context and change the settings accordingly in Flash.

"It would be a good idea to keep the original graphic on your hard drive or backed up on disk, in case you feel you need to start over," I said. "This way, you won't bang your head on the table when you realize you've ruined your one and only uncompressed image.

"Images imported into Flash also need to be finalized, as Flash is unable to trim them. If you intend to use transparent images, only PNG transparency is supported on import. GIF transparency is not supported and your image will be flattened.

"Does this answer your question Bonnie?"

"That's obviously different to how I was taught to do things when working with HTML web pages," answered Bonnie, "But if Flash does some compressing for us, then it seems to make sense."

"One rule that applies to all website content, whatever the format, is to only use image files where necessary. Image files always add to our final file size whether they are highly compressed or not. In Flash, it is always best to use vector shapes and primitives, like circles, squares, and triangles wherever you can."

I showed the class Wes and Deb's design from the week before last. I turned to them. "Which of these elements will you have to import into Flash?"

"As far as I can see, we'll only need the tree and cabinet images." Said Deb. "The rest of the shapes, like the circles, can be drawn in Flash. What about that weird font? Can we use that in Flash?"

"You can use fonts in Flash as long as you have them installed on your machine during authoring. The viewer of the web page will not need the same font to see it displayed. You'll have to do some kerning and tracking of the font, but you can do this in Flash," I added.

"I think your evaluation is correct – the only images we'll need to import are the tree and cabinet door images, because we can't reproduce them in Flash." I turned to Zed and Bonnie. "In your design, the only imported data needs to be your background image. The text and star can all be redrawn in Flash."

"And Bonnie took so long drawing that star too!" said Zed.

"Steve and Lisa, " I said, "You can fully recreate your design in Flash, can't you?

"Well..." Lisa began. "We can, but I was hoping to use the images we had so we wouldn't have to spend so much time recreating them. I guess the images we have will add to the file size, though." She looked at Steve.

Steve looked back at Lisa. "I'm game for recreating most of the images." He looked back to me. "We may want to import Lisa's leaves for the sub-navigation images. Maybe the wood textured buttons, too. Other than this, I think we're fine.

"In circumstances where you need to trace over previous artwork – this might be relevant to Steve and Lisa – import the image into Flash, turn the layer with the imported image into a *guide layer* and trace over it. Guide layers aren't exported when the Flash SWF is published, and are therefore only present during authoring."

Lisa looked relieved. "I was just worried about our layout. Can you show us how to use the guide layer?" she asked.

Using a guide layer

Using my laptop and the projector I showed the class how to change a layer into a guide layer.

"It's really very simple," I said, "First we need to right click on the layer icon of the layer that you want to change into a guide.

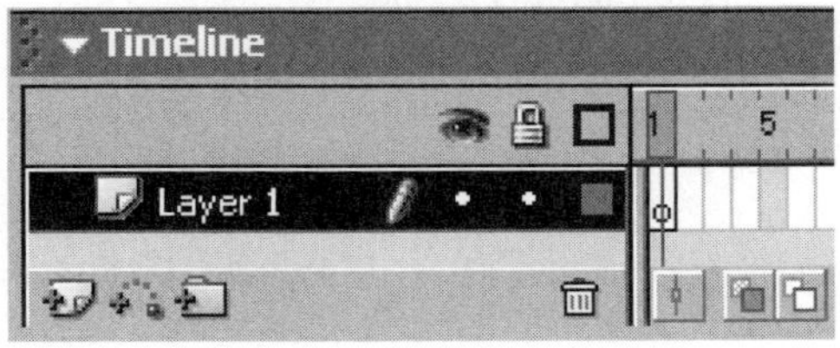

"And then we need to select Properties... from the options available. After some experience of using guide layers, you might find it easier to simply select Guide at this point.

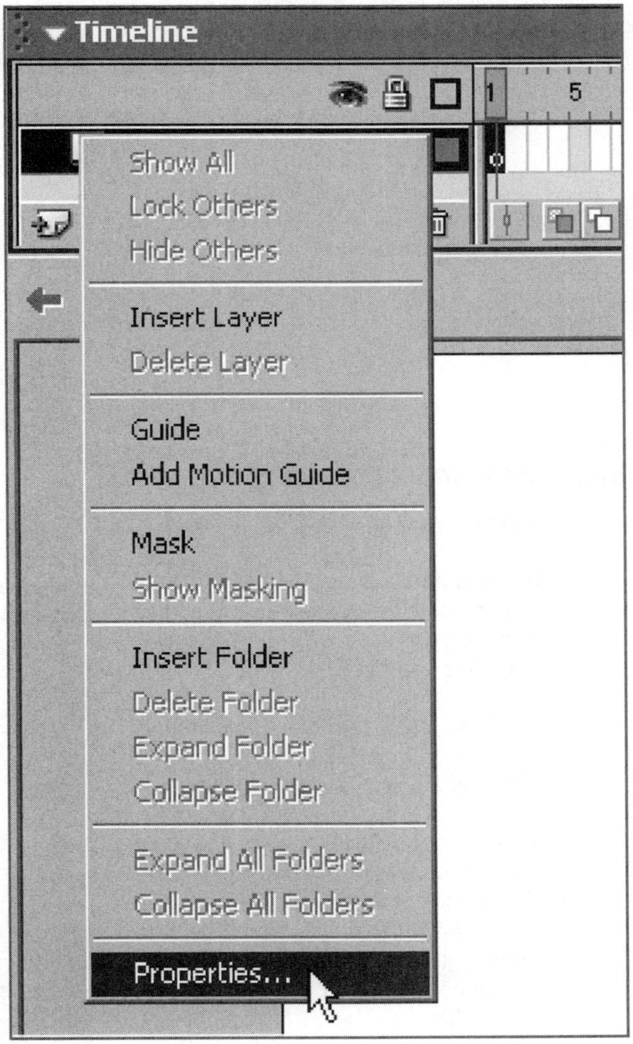

"The Layer Properties panel will then pop up. We then select the Guide option. It's always a good idea to change the name of this layer to reflect that it is a guide layer.

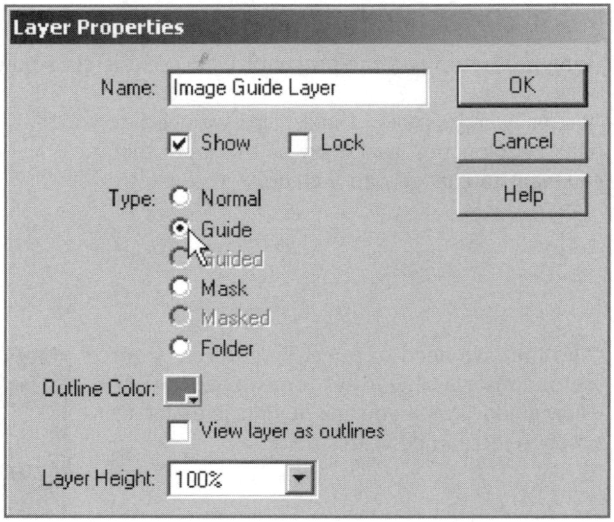

"Finally, we just need to click OK and the layer icon and name will change accordingly, as you can see."

Importing and optimizing images

I then began showing the students how to import and optimize their images in Flash.

"Flash can import a large number of image file formats, and as we mentioned earlier, it's always a good idea to import the best quality images you have."

I showed the class the two basic import options for any importable files – Import... and Import to Library... in the File menu:

"Both options are virtually the same, as they both import the file or files into the Library. However, Import... places the item on the stage as well. From experience, I'd recommend Import to Library..., as it lets you determine where you put your content without any fuss."

Turning to one of the Macs in our studio, I showed the class the typical import dialog window that pops up after selecting the Import to Library... option.

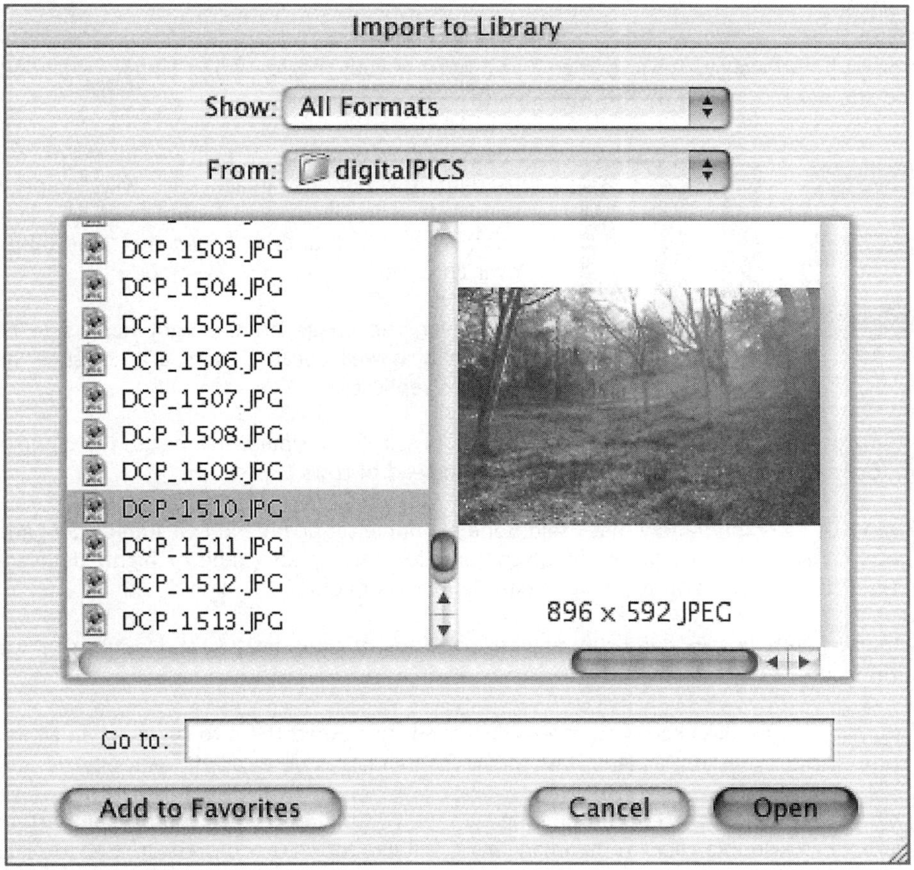

Next, I described how to import multiple files, "If you wish to select more than one file for import, press APPLE or CTRL and use the mouse to select the required files. Then just click Open. The files will now be in the Library, from where you can pull them onto the stage or wherever you want them."

"Linda, can you tell us about the optimization options in Flash MX?" asked Deb. "I think the file size of our image," she thumbed Wes, "Might be a little too large to be practical."

"Sure Deb, having an image which covers the Flash stage is a little on the risky side, but you might be able to compress it considerably because it's being used as a background and isn't a main point of focus.

"Flash has two forms of compression – **Photo** and **Lossless**. Photo is just a fancy name for JPEG compression, while Lossless is GIF or PNG-style compression. Bonnie, would you like to talk briefly about the differences between these compression formats?"

Bonnie looked a little shocked at my request, but grinned a little with pride. "Sure Linda! JPEG compression is best suited for photographic images. The way the compression works is by looking at an image and reducing the detail of it. This results in lower file sizes, but when the compression is too great, it can result in blocky images."

"Lossless compression is best suited for images with flat color. This compression doesn't affect the overall quality of the image; it just looks for patterns of similar colors and groups them together. Traditionally, GIF compression works by reading an image from top left to bottom right, row-by-row, and duplicating colors wherever possible. "

Bonnie stood up and walked towards me. "Can I borrow your magic marker Linda?" I handed the pen to Bonnie and she began drawing on the white board.

"Because GIF compression replicates blocks of colors from left to right, the leftmost image here will compress very well. Bands of color will simply be duplicated over and over, until another color is found, and then the same thing is repeated over and over.

"However, the image on the right hand side here will not compress as well because there are not such large areas of color to replicate."

"The right image shows how PNG compression reads." I said. "In a similar manner to GIF compression, PNGs read from top left to bottom right, but in columns instead of rows."

"I never use PNGs so I didn't know that." said Bonnie. Bonnie sat down and concluded, "So I guess the basic rule for compression is to use **Photo** (JPEG) compression for a photograph or highly detailed image, and **Lossless** (GIF/PNG) compression for images with flat areas of color."

"Thanks Bonnie. With this in mind, I'd suggest you look at your images and determine which type of compression to use."

I wanted the class to experience compression first hand, so I asked them to import a small image suitable for both compression types into a blank Flash movie. These images were called `peacock.bmp` and `star.bmp`.

After showing the students where to find the image files, I continued, "Once you have imported the images, open the Library and double click on the image most suitable for JPEG compression, `peacock.bmp`. This will open the properties for that image."

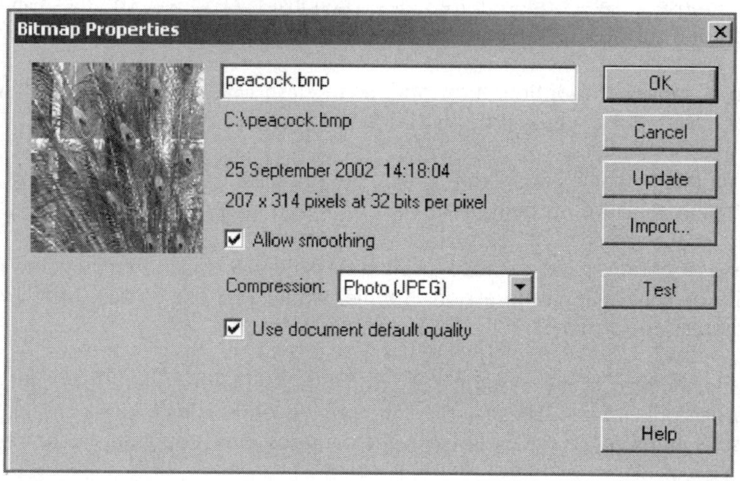

"At the moment, your images are using the default quality setting for this Flash movie. This is 80%."

"Oh, I forgot to mention something, " said Bonnie, "JPEG compression is measured in percentages. The higher the percentage, the better the quality of the image and the less compression is used. For instance, an image exported at 80% will be high quality, but also high file size. An image with a JPEG quality of 60% will still be of a good quality, but will have a considerably smaller file size."

"Thanks Bonnie, you've saved me another explanation!" I turned to the class. "As Bonnie just explained, 80% JPEG quality will give us a pretty hefty file size. Luckily, we can override this in one of two ways – by changing the overall quality used by the Flash file, or by individually setting the compression amount.

"I'd recommend that you set the compression of each image in your movie individually. This way you can squeeze as much out of each image, and be sure that each is of an acceptable quality."

"How do you know if an image is good quality or not?" asked Deb.

"It's not easy," said Bonnie. "Sometimes an image will look fine, until you realize that you have to compress it a little more and then it will look awful!"

"It's all about balance Deb," I said. "If the client needs the website to be under a certain file size, then you have to see what you can fit in that space." I turned to Bonnie. "If the client, say a photographer, requires high-quality images on their website, then they'll pay for it in file size, but you can usually get around this by reducing the physical size of the image.

"In most cases, you can check your quality and change it accordingly."

I asked the students to un-tick the Use document default quality checkbox, to allow them to set the quality of the image.

"Lower the value in the Quality box, and click Test. This will update the quality of the preview image at the top left, and shows the size of the compressed image, compared to the original, at the bottom of the panel."

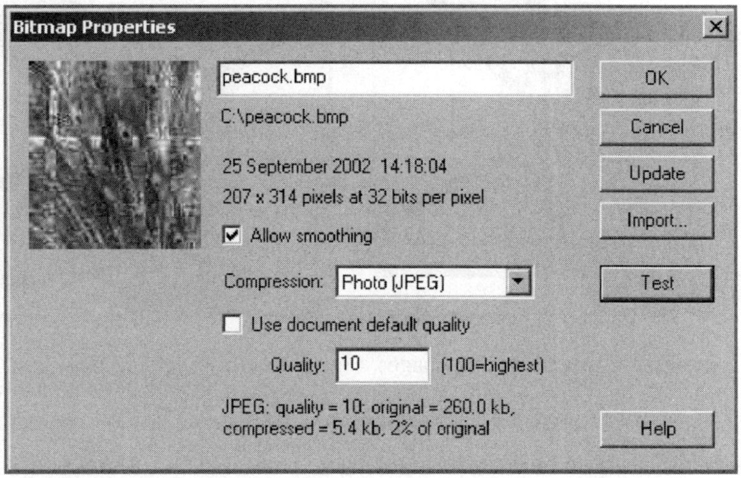

"This is where you should scrutinize both the quality and file size. You can move the image around by dragging in the preview pane. Then change the value if necessary and retry it. Once you are happy with the degree of compression, click Update and then OK."

"You can change the quality of the image at any time in this way. Flash will only show you the set quality of an image when you publish the movie."

Now that the class had seen JPEG compression, I wanted to quickly cover Lossless compression. "Lossless compression in Flash is less complicated because there is no quality setting as with JPEGs."

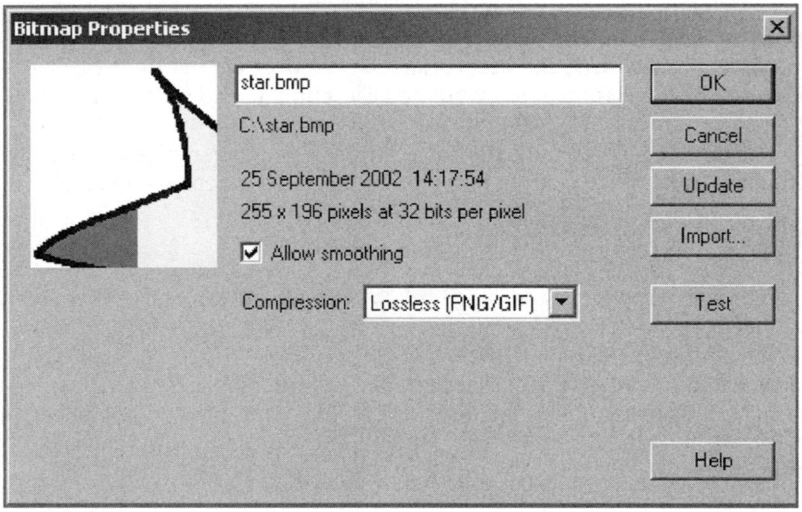

I showed the students the difference between JPEG compression set at a quality 10% and Lossless compression. Although this wasn't really a fair match, as the image was clearly unsuitable for JPEG compression, it showed the effects of JPEG deterioration.

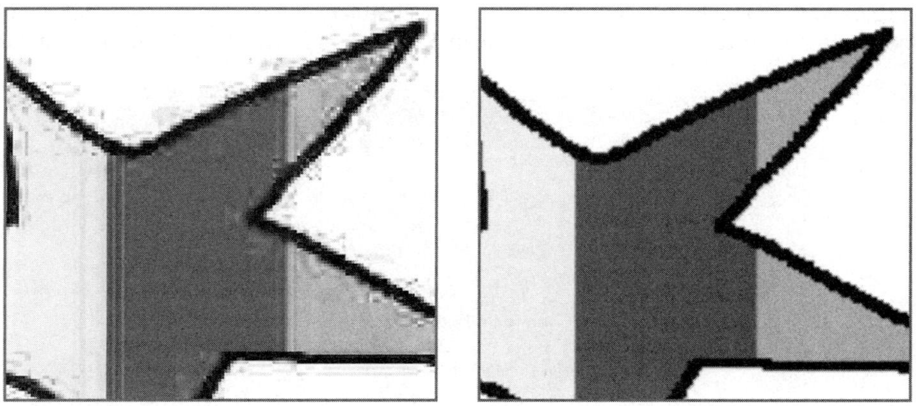

After looking at compressing and importing images, I moved onto importing text.

Importing text

"Bringing text assets into Flash isn't exactly rocket science." I said. "In fact, it's more of a *cut and paste* affair! Select the text that you wish to import from your text application and click Edit > Copy."

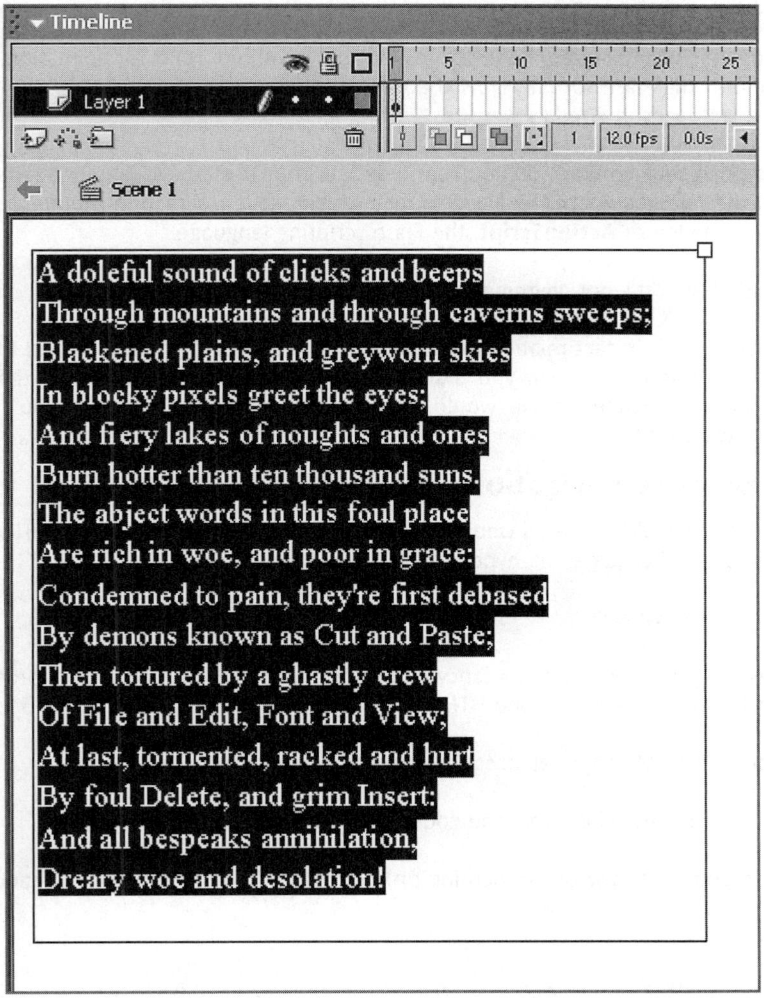

"In Flash, create a new text box of whatever width you want using the Text tool from the toolbar, and then click Edit > Paste."

"Does Flash capture styles or fonts?" asked Bonnie.

"No it doesn't Bonnie. When Flash imports text it usually renders it in a uniform style, so in most cases you'll find that you'll need to reformat the text considerably."

I made the class import a little text to make sure that they were all familiar with this, as they would need to do this to import the copy for their site designs.

The next part of the class would cover an essential element of Flash site creation – timeline navigation.

Navigating the timeline

The timeline is the basis for all good Flash designs; not only is it important for animation, but it's also crucial for site navigation in the Flash format. Now the class had their basic designs in place, they would need to learn how to change pages in Frieda's website.

"So far you've all had time to work on your basic designs, but these have largely been static and have not fully considered the interactivity of the Flash format. Making true interaction requires a little effort, not to mention some knowledge of **ActionScript**, the Flash scripting language."

"Ooh, scary!" said Steve. "It's not anything like the PostScript language is it?"

"Not at all! ActionScript is in fact relatively easy to learn." I replied. Wes groaned and I turned to face him. "Don't worry! I'm not going to teach you that much ActionScript, only enough so that you can navigate between frames on the timeline. Bonnie, would you like to explain to the class how you create links between the pages in your websites?"

Hyperlink vs. timeline navigation

Bonnie nodded. "In most HTML sites, a website is made up of a number of individual HTML pages. Each page is selectively linked to other pages via hyperlinks."

Wes interrupted. "Hyper what?"

"Hyperlinks, Wes. A **hyperlink** is a just a fancy name for a link from one page to another. What happens is that the user clicks on a hyperlink in one HTML page, and a new HTML page is loaded into the browser.

"This means that each HTML page replaces the previous page."

"Bonnie, could you show the class what the code for a hyperlink looks like?" I asked.

Bonnie nodded, stood up and wrote something on the board. "The code, or HTML markup, for a link looks like this...."

```
<a href="http://www.friendsofed.com">click here</a>
```

"This produces a link in the HTML document, something which is familiar to all of you. It's most commonly seen as blue underlined text," Bonnie turned to Wes, "And is more technically known as a hyperlink. It's just like the links we learned about last week for the different sites to reference color resources."

"Ah," Wes said as he scribbled his notes, "I remember now. I was too embarrassed to ask what the heck you were talking about last week."

Bonnie handed me the magic marker and sat down.

"Bonnie has just shown us one form of code, otherwise known as HTML markup. When our browser sees a file with the HTML extension, it knows to interpret the text as HTML markup, and to display and use it accordingly. So when the browser sees Bonnie's hyperlink code, it shows us '*click here*', which is linked to *www.friendsofed.com*."

"Recapping on what Bonnie just said, hyperlinks load a new HTML page into the browser each time, replacing the previous content. Flash movies works quite differently in that they can contain all the necessary pages of the website in one SWF file.

"So rather than replace the current Flash file with another document, we simply fetch the required page from the same movie. Essentially, this translates into moving around the keyframes of our timeline, within our Flash file."

I opened up a figure from my laptop that I'd already prepared, and turned on the projector so that the class could all see it:

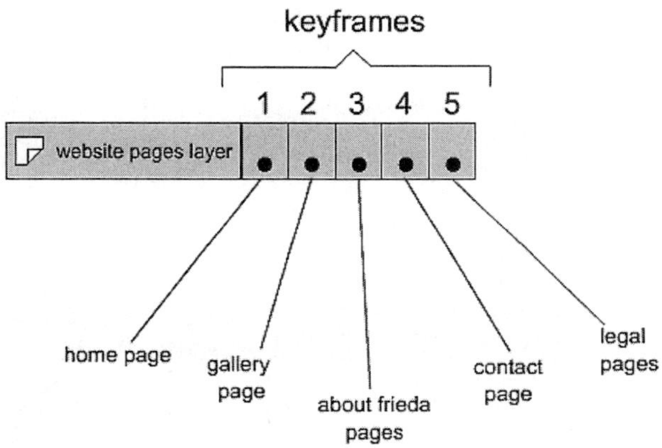

Using this diagram, I started to explain how the timeline is used for site navigation, "If you envisage each frame of your timeline as a different page of the website, then the general structure of your timeline might look like this picture. When the user selects a different page of the website, the playhead in Flash is sent to that frame and the required content is displayed.

"Given the content flow chart that you created a few classes ago, this number of frames is essentially all that you will require for Frieda's website."

The class all nodded, except for Bonnie. "I can see that this represents the fundamental pages of the site, but what about sub-pages within each category?" Bonnie turned to the flowchart in her workbook.

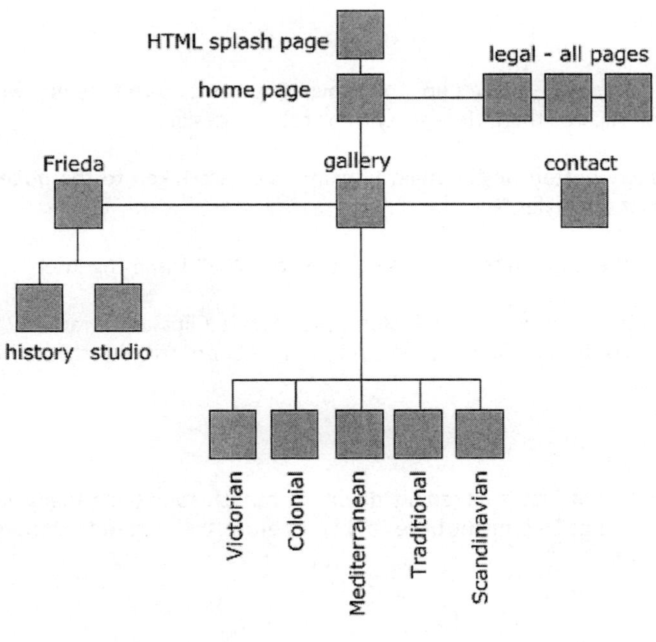

"Bonnie, this is really no different to HTML. Each main page – such as the *gallery* and *legal* pages – provides a route to the required sub-pages.

"For example, if a website viewer accesses the *gallery* page, then they will be taken to a page providing links to the different styles of Frieda's work."

Bonnie looked puzzled. "But if we only have one timeline, how we do we send the viewers to sub-pages?"

"Does anyone remember the assets of the Movie Clip symbol type that we covered a couple of lessons back?" I asked.

"It has its own timeline." Deb said confidently. "We can use a movie clip timeline for each page that requires sub-pages."

"Excellent Deb!" I said. "This next diagram will show the rest of you what Deb has just described." I opened up another image:

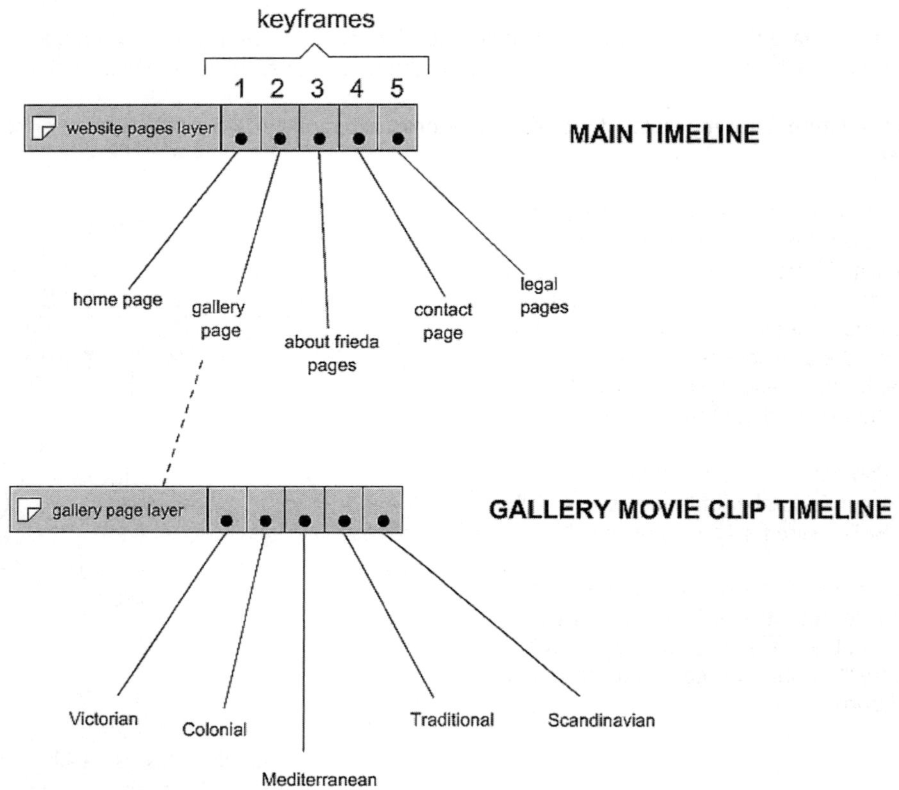

"Frame 2 of the main timeline here houses the *gallery* Movie Clip. This Movie Clip has its own timeline, with an initial introduction frame and a frame for each of the different styles of cabinet design.

"When the website viewer clicks on the *gallery* button on the main timeline, they are taken to the *gallery introduction*, from which they can view any of the styles."

"OK, so far so good." said Zed. "But there is one thing missing – the buttons to pull all these together."

"Well Zed, do you remember the Button symbol that we covered, along with Movie Clips and Graphics?" I asked. Zed nodded. "These are the key to navigation in Flash. When some basic ActionScript is attached to the Buttons, they can be extremely powerful."

"You're talking jargon again!" said Wes.

"Don't worry Wes. Learning any kind of scripting at first is incredibly daunting, but it's something that I had to learn too. I'm from a design background, and as Deb might have told you before she started this course – design and programming don't necessarily mix."

"Boy was she stubborn!" Steve said.

"Watch it Steve!" Wes whispered. Deb nudged Wes and grinned.

"Although learning programming isn't an essential part of design," I said. "When it comes to Flash and other website design, it helps to know a little. The possibilities that ActionScript opens are massive."

Starting to use ActionScript in your designs

"I think it might help you all if we get used to working with ActionScript, so you can see that there is nothing to be worried about Wes."

I made the class open up a new Flash movie, name it `buttons.fla`, and draw a red circle on the stage. They were also told to rename the existing layer as buttons.

Looking over Wes' shoulder at his Mac, I said "Convert the circle into a Button symbol by selecting it and clicking Insert > Convert to Symbol... and following the Convert to Symbol dialog. Next duplicate the button twice on the stage using Edit > Duplicate, and change the color of each instance so that they are all different by selecting Tint from the Color drop-down in the Property inspector.

"These are our navigation buttons, so place these three circles in a row at the top left of the stage – you can use the Align panel to align all the buttons precisely. Now create a new layer called pages and insert two blank keyframes after the first using Insert > Blank Keyframe.

"These three keyframes will hold changing content, to represent the different pages that are being accessed through the Buttons. Before we give these any content, we need to extend the length of the buttons layer, so that the buttons will be present whichever page we access."

I told the class to select frame 3 of the buttons layer, and extend the frames with Insert > Frame.

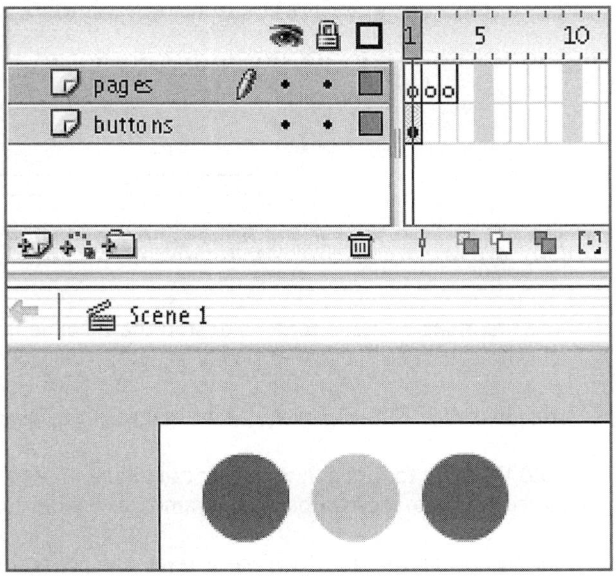

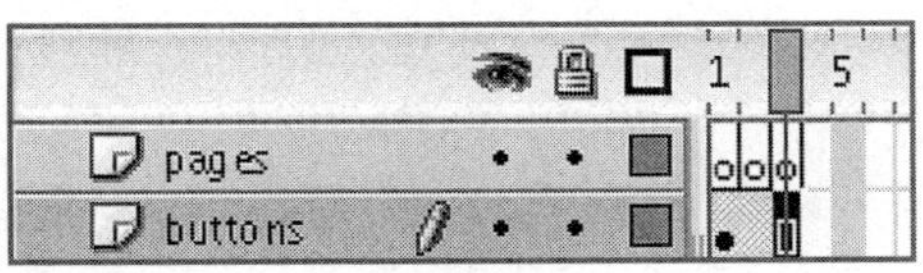

"Now to give the keyframes on the pages layer a little content." I said. "The first thing we need to do is to associate a button with each frame. The easiest way is to make the leftmost button link to frame 1, the middle button to frame 2 and the rightmost to frame 3. This is how our navigation will work."

"Given this rule, select each frame on the pages layer in turn, and use the Text tool to create a text box in which you type in the name of the relevant button's color on the blank keyframes.

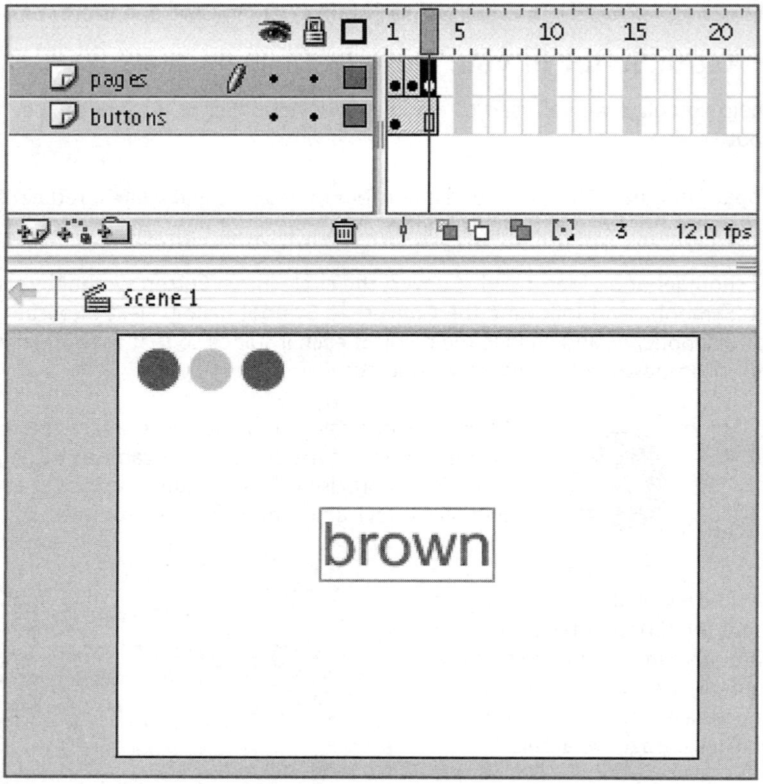

"Now that we have our movie ready, we need to add a little ActionScript to glue it all together, and to make the buttons function.

"The first thing we need to do is to stop the timeline from playing through every frame. This is done with an ActionScript command called simply `stop`."

"Ah," said Wes, "The simplicity of it! I might get to grips with the ActionScript after all."

I told the class to insert a new layer called actions and to place it at the top of the layers list. On this layer, I asked them to add two blank keyframes, as we did for the pages layer.

"It's a Flash convention to place a layer named actions at the top, because it is easier to locate should changes need to be made to it. These three keyframes will all be given the same code, but we have to do it for each one individually.

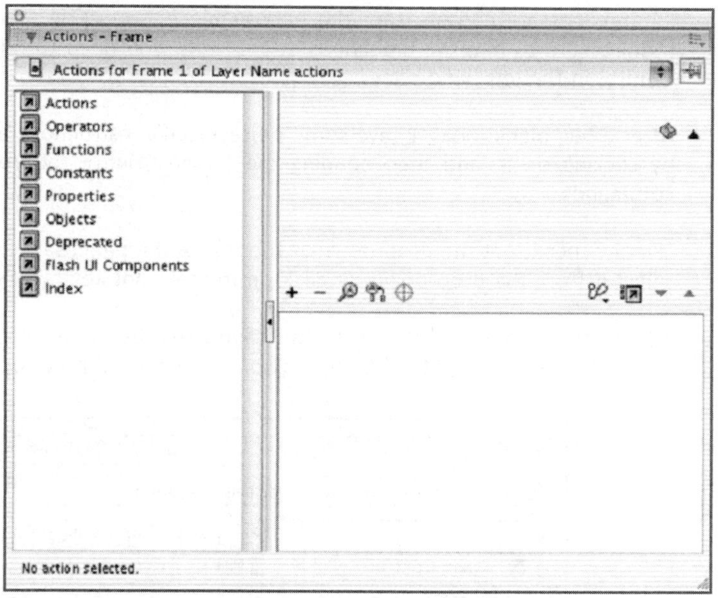

"Programming within Flash is done through the Actions panel. So, select the first keyframe on the actions layer and then open this panel by clicking Window > Actions."

"Entering ActionScript code into this panel can be done in one of two modes – *Normal Mode* or *Expert Mode*. You can switch between these two modes using the drop-down menu in the top right corner of the Actions panel."

"**Expert Mode** is similar to a text editor, and allows you to type freely. When you become familiar with ActionScript you might find this mode quicker to work in. **Normal Mode** however, is easier for ActionScript beginners. It uses drag and drop functionality and has many more user hints. Accordingly, we'll stick with Normal Mode for the moment.

"Returning our attention to the Actions panel, it's clear that there's a whole bunch of information here, and the panel is very well designed – you'll soon discover that it is really simple to use." I then started to point out the main features of the Actions panel to the class....

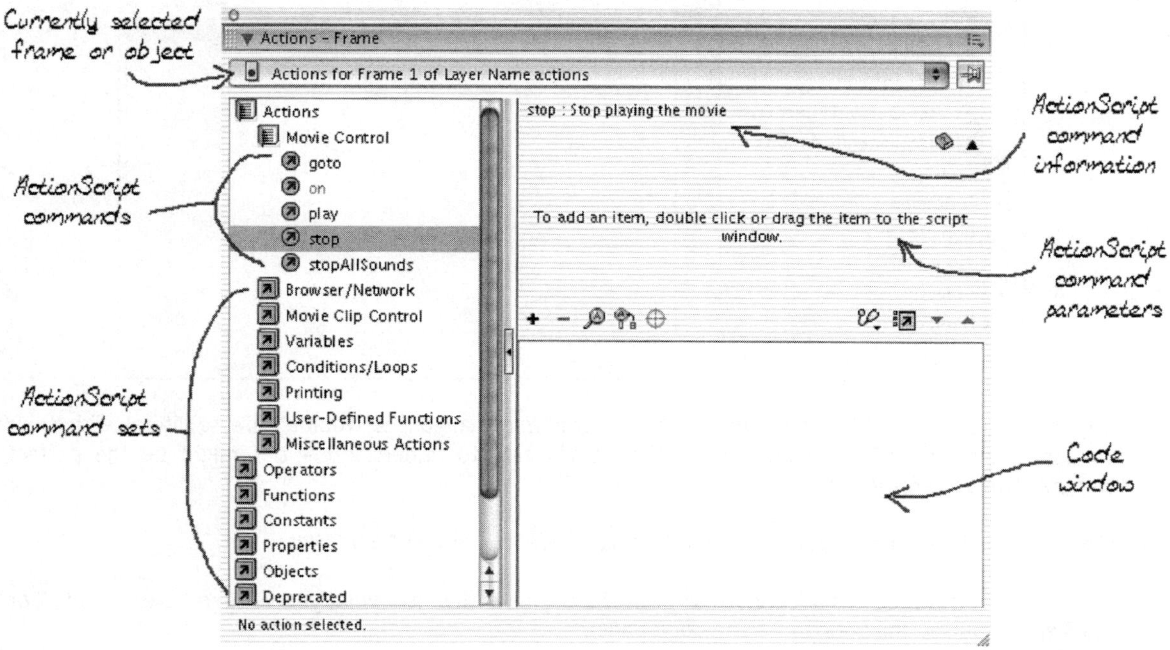

"Commands are chosen from the browseable ActionScript **sets** on the left hand side. The command we require here to halt the timeline is `stop`. Firstly you need to find it – you'll find it under Actions > Movie Control in the left hand pane."

After a few blank looks, I gave some more specific instructions and asked the class to open the Actions set by clicking on it, and then opening the Movie Control set from within it to reveal several ActionScript commands.

"Firstly, check that the drop-down at the top of the panel says Frame 1 of Layer Name actions. If it doesn't, select it from the drop-down, or click on the relevant keyframe in the actions layer.

"Now add the `stop` command to the code panel by double-clicking on it, or by dragging it into the code pane – the bottom right area. The `stop` command will now appear in the code panel."

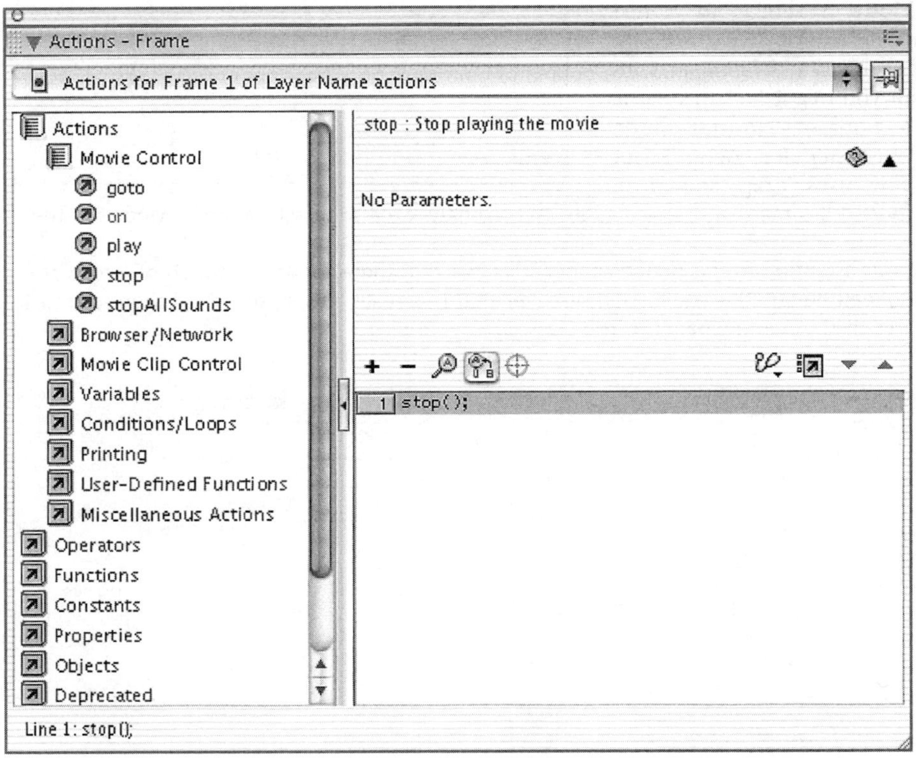

"Not too scary eh Wes?" asked Deb. "Some programming languages wouldn't be so literal with their commands, but ActionScript commands are generally easy to understand – this might be the perfect computer language for you!"

"Maybe – I think I'll have to play around in Normal Mode a little first." Said Wes.

"As I said, Normal Mode has a lot more to offer the beginner than just what you've seen here." I said. "For instance, do you see the area above the code panel?"

"Where it currently says No Parameters?" asked Wes.

"Right. When a command requires certain input from you, this area has a number of text boxes for the required information. We'll see this in use when we come to add code to the buttons.

"By placing the stop command on frame 1, we have told the playhead to halt on the frame. This means that our Flash movie will remain on frame 1 until something tells it to move elsewhere."

"That what the buttons are for!" Said Bonnie. "I bet they'll send the playhead to the different frames."

"In this movie, yes. Before we add any code to make the buttons do this, we need to add a `stop` command to the remaining keyframes on the actions layer. Before we do that though, if you look at the keyframe on frame 1 of the actions layer, you'll notice that it has a small a has appeared above the keyframe circle."

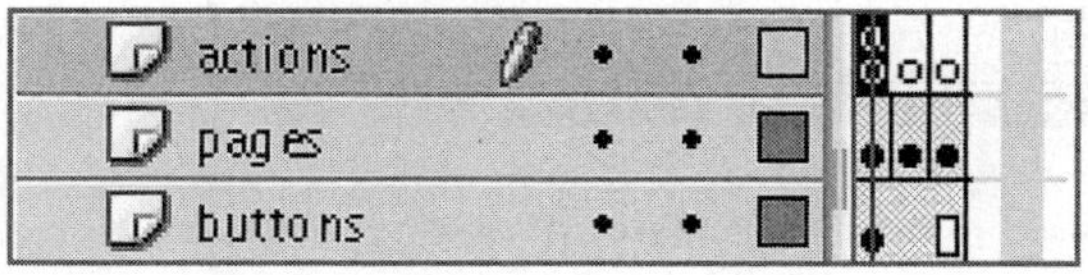

"This is an indicator to show you that the frame has some actions attached to it. If you ever wish to see the actions attached to the frame, select the frame and the ActionScript will appear in the Actions panel. You can them edit it from there."

Next I asked the class to select frame 2 and 3 of the actions layer and to add a `stop` command to each of them.

"You should now have three blank keyframes with a characters above them. The ActionScript to halt the timeline is now firmly set. Now we need to add some ActionScript to the buttons to give them navigational functionality.

"ActionScript commands can be attached to symbol instances as well as frames. This is especially true for buttons, where ActionScript makes them come to life. Each button can tell the Flash playhead to go to a particular frame of the timeline." I quickly typed up a bit of code on my laptop, and displayed it through the projector onto the board for all to see. "The code for our red button will look like this."

```
on (release) {
    gotoAndStop(1);
}
```

"Now you've got me spooked." Said Steve. "That's a little more than just a `stop` command!"

"It looks perfectly simple Steve," said Deb. "Because the code is attached to the button, this simply sets the `gotoAndStop` action to work when the mouse button is released. This looks a little like JavaScript."

"Not bad Deb." I smiled. "ActionScript was originally based on JavaScript so there are a number of similarities in the syntax or code style. The content within the curly brackets here runs whenever the event occurs – the pressing and *releasing* of the associated button by a mouse button click. I won't bog you down with programming terminology here, but most programming languages make things happen at certain events – like a mouse press, or when a certain time has passed.

"So, let's see how we can do this in Flash – select the first button, and double-click on the on command in the left hand pane of the Actions panel. The space above the code area now displays the parameters for this command."

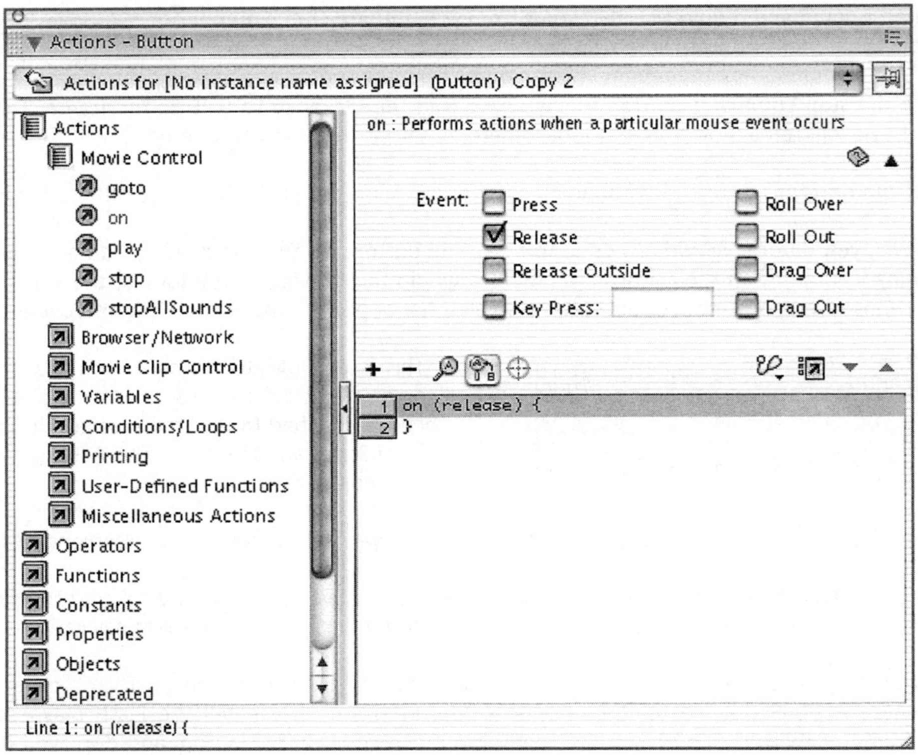

"The default is set as Release, which corresponds to a mouse button *press* then *release*. This is not to be confused with the Press event, which signifies just the initial *pressing* of the mouse button. The Release option is generally better to use because it is more final than a press, and suggests that the user has decided on that option."

"Now select goto from the Movie Control set of commands on the left hand side. This places the command within the brackets of the button event we just set."

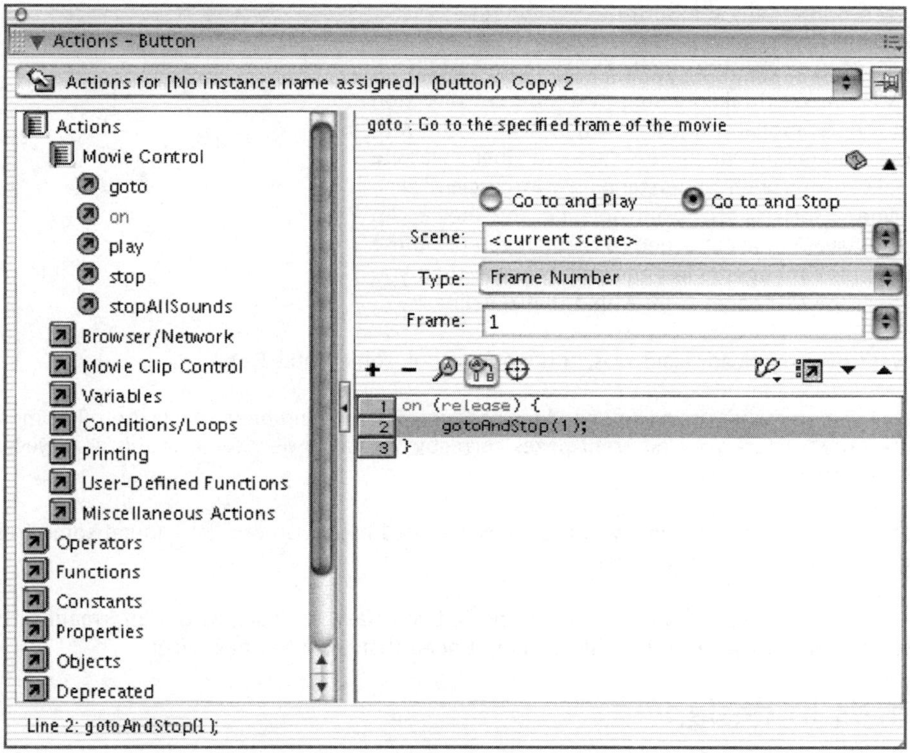

"In the parameters for this command, select the Go to and Stop button. This will tell the timeline to go to some set frame, and pause on that frame. Even though we've placed `stop` commands on each frame, it's still good practice to do this because Flash sometimes likes to run on. The default frame for this command is frame 1, which is, luckily, exactly what we need for this button.

"And that's all the ActionScript for this button! To make the other two buttons functional, add the same actions, but change the `goto` frame to 2 and 3 so that they will direct the user to the associated content page. Once you've done this, your first navigational movie is complete!"

I decided the class needed a quick recap of the essentials of what we'd just learned, so, pointing at the typed code projected onto the screen, I concluded, "Let's make sure we all understand how this chunk of ActionScript works – remember, it's attached directly to the Button Movie Clip that we created earlier, so the first part, `on(release)`, refers to the pressing and releasing of that particular button. Everything that follows this specified event within the curly brackets is the action that will be performed when the event takes place."

At this point, Zed butted in, eager to prove that he understood these potentially confusing concepts, "So I can translate this code like this: when we press and *release* the button that it is attached to, the Flash playhead will *go to and stop* at whatever content is on frame *1* of the timeline. That's pretty straightforward!"

"Looks like you're well on your way to understanding the use of ActionScript, Zed", I offered, encouragingly.

Next, I suggested the class preview their Flash movies by clicking Control > Test Movie. The class tested their Flash movies, and I could see Zed was having a great time clicking between each frame using the Buttons.

I continued to talk them through some more details of scripting in Flash. We'd taken a step in a different direction from our more traditional study of design principles, and with these basic commands being essential to their website building skills, a thorough understanding was crucial. "Each Flash timeline – such as the main timeline and movie clip timelines can have Actions attached to them. If you use these basic commands for pages – like the gallery page, then you can lead to all the sub-pages from within that timeline."

"That all went over my head," said Wes, "I hope you took some notes Deb."

"Wes, those two commands are all you need for basic interactivity and movie navigation. The most important thing to do is to structure your different pages correctly; we can review some of this next week so you can apply the code to your movies.

"After that intensity, I think it's time you took a well earned break. Go outside and get some fresh air! After the break we'll talk about your presentations."

The students quickly ejected from their seats and left the class. As much as the information they had just learned was complex, I was sure that they wouldn't need that refresher next week.

Storyboards in design

After the students returned from break, we sat at the table to talk about their project presentations to the client. First, we would talk about the storyboard and how this tool plays a huge part in their roles as Flash designers. I asked them to take out their drawing pads and drawing tools as we began this session.

"To date, you've all been using thumbnails and roughs to visualize your ideas," I began. "Each sketch in your drawing pads brought you closer to realizing your goals for this project. Whether you realized it or not, you were already in the process of creating storyboards for your sites. The final roughs were panels that told your story."

"Why didn't we call them storyboards in the beginning?" Bonnie asked.

I answered, "Because I wanted you to understand the processes of drawing and sketching before I asked you to project these images onto a format. If I had asked you to formulate storyboards for your sites during the first class, some of you might have walked out."

"I know I would have," Lisa stated. "It was hard enough for me to believe I had to draw in the first place. I thought I would just sit at the computer and begin to make shapes."

"Oh," Bonnie responded sheepishly. "I guess you're right. I had no idea we would be drawing and sketching, either."

"Let's talk about storyboards, then," I said. "There are two types of storyboards a Flash designer uses for their project. One is your project storyboard, and the other is a storyboard created for your presentation to the client. Let's talk about the project storyboards first."

Project storyboards

When the students began their projects using roughs and thumbnails, they were also effectively creating rough project storyboards. They created images that were used in the final processing of their components within the Flash format.

"Steve and Lisa created a project storyboard to demonstrate how they created their first design, or final rough," I said. "This format consists of a layout, and several overlays made from tissue paper, or other semi-transparent paper. These overlays showed the progression from the initial format to the final image. This allowed us to see how the stages progressed on one page of their site."

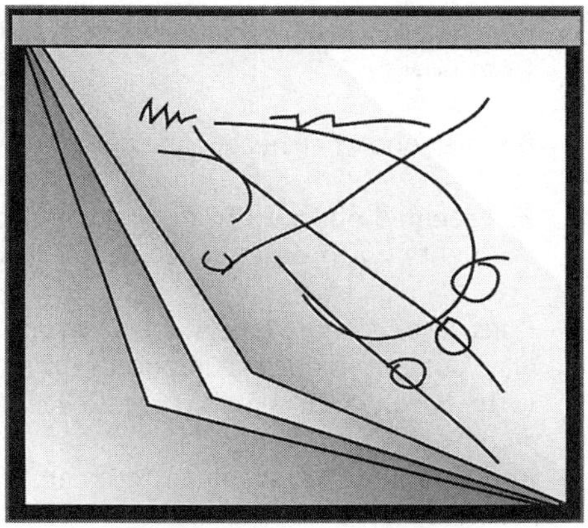

I asked them if they had their project available, and Steve pulled it from his portfolio bag. "As you can see, they mounted their original design on a mat board, and then taped overlays on the original to show us their thought processes."

"I used some materials from the studio," Steve said. "The mat board is useful, because it's sturdy, and it also gives a great framework to the piece. You might also find it called *illustration board*. It's about the same thing. Just make sure it's sturdy!"

"I'll bet it helped you see where you were going along the way," Wes said. "But, did you do it this way at the start when you began to develop the site, or did you create a lot of images before you created this board?" he asked.

"Oh, we created tons of images first," Lisa answered. "We must have used a whole drawing pad to arrive at this point."

I nodded, "They did create a lot of visual ideas to finalize this process," I said. "But, this final piece helped them today, when they processed the components to their site."

Zed interrupted, "Bonnie and I did ours differently. We used the final rough, and wrote all over it so we could see our ideas." He showed us their final rough with all their notes.

Bonnie grimaced, "It was a bit more difficult to tell what we were going to do, because we couldn't read half of what we wrote."

Wes and Deb looked at each other and laughed. "I don't think we went that far," Deb chuckled. "We just wrote our ideas down, and it was horrible trying to pull it all together. Even with detailed notes, we had no idea that we both were thinking different visual thoughts. We're living proof that verbal code doesn't always work when it comes to personal visual interpretation of this code."

Wes nodded and sighed. "Without a doubt, we needed more thumbnails and roughs. It's the only way to decipher visual ideas, especially when you work with another person."

Steve looked puzzled. "I'm surprised, Wes. You're so visual, I'm amazed you didn't use more sketches."

Wes raised his eyebrows and shrugged. "Just wanted to keep the partner happy. She's verbal and I'm visual. I let her have her way."

Deb frowned. "Don't be so accommodating, Wes. I didn't realize you were backing off to make me feel comfortable. If we had combined our strengths, we'd be better off right now. I can't believe you let me run over you like that."

"Ouch!" I said. "Wes, I'm surprised with your behavior and your logic. Teamwork means working together as a team. Individual quirks are put aside to improve the team's *gestalt*. Your input is valuable, whether it's verbal or visual. You'll never have a fully functional team unless everyone puts their ideas on the table."

Wes held up his arms in defense. "I'm used to working alone! I'm learning, OK? I promise to assert myself from now on."

Bonnie shook her head. "Imagine that. Wes having problems asserting himself."

Zed seemed oblivious to the conversation. He leaned forward and crossed his arms on the table. "So, what's the right way to develop project storyboards?"

I answered, "There's no right or wrong way to create a project storyboard. You and Bonnie worked it one way, but you found making notes on final roughs might not be all you need. Wes and Deb definitely worked it the hard way. It's vital to create visual images for your site, especially for transitions."

Bonnie asked, "Do we need to create a thumbnail for each movement we make on the site? Is this how we create a storyboard?"

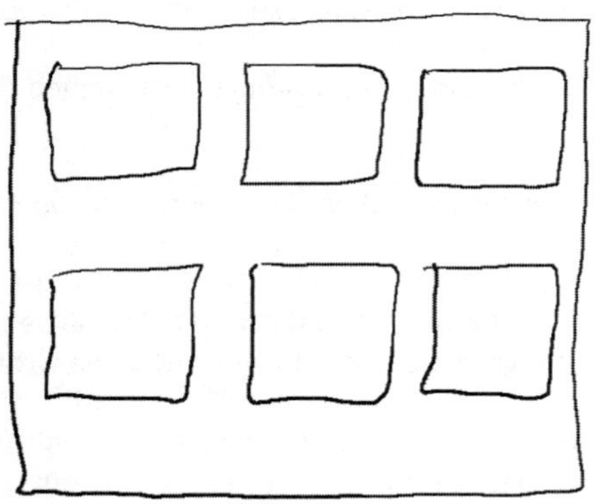

I stood and went to the board. I drew a rectangle, and drew several smaller rectangles within the first, larger image.

"That looks like an image you drew the first day of classes," Zed said. "It's an image from the lesson on thumbnails and roughs."

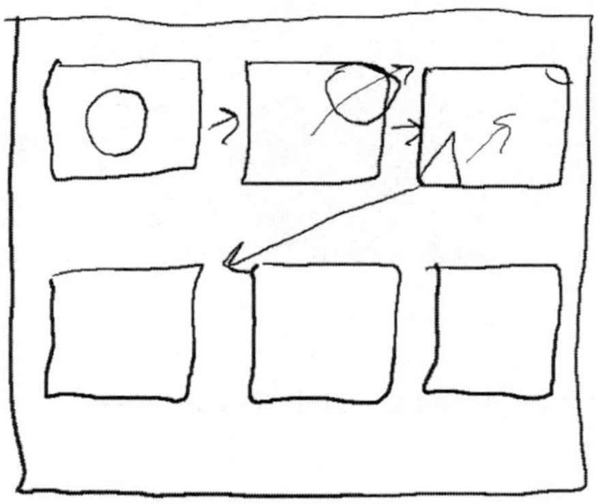

I nodded. "But this time you've selected a final rough and you're going to implement it to show movement within that page on the site." I drew a circle in the first square. I then drew that same circle in the second square, only in a different position. In the third square, I drew the circle leaving the rectangle, and drew the beginning of a triangle entering the shape from another angle.

When these images were finished, I turned to the class and pointed at the board. "This is, by no means, the end product of my visual idea," I said. "The first rectangle with the circle is the final rough I've selected. I want to make transitions from the final rough stage to the next stage. Even though I know how I want these images to move, I still need to add some indication of how I want them to move." I drew some arrows and various looping lines.

"Oh!" Zed almost leaped out of his chair. "You're drawing cartoon frames! That's how some comics show action without showing every single movement. It's just like watching Lisa under that strobe light at the theater, too. We knew she got from one movement to the next, and we knew how she got there, even if we couldn't actually see it."

"See how smart you are without that scarf?" I asked. "If you want, you can add detailed notes to these images. This will help you remember how you want to utilize other elements other than line, shape, and movement. It will also help when you want to make sure you've covered the principles of design as you move from one frame to the next.

"Even more importantly," I added, "Notes help if you work with other designers. This way, they have various visual images and verbal codes to decipher your message."

Bonnie sulked. "I still don't understand why you didn't teach this in the beginning of the course," she said. "This is fairly straightforward. I think we could have managed storyboards on the front end, even with the fear of drawing."

We leaned in to look at Bonnie. "My dear fellow student," Wes began. "If you were drawing storyboards instead of thumbnails and roughs, you would have expected yourself to draw every single detail of movement in your site. You would still be back on page one, in my opinion."

Deb responded, "Wes, don't be so hard on Bonnie. She's got a point, but I also understand why we went this route." She looked at me and said, "Let me understand this clearly. You're telling us we need to do what we're doing, but to improve on our methods to clarify our ideas. You're also telling us that we've been storyboarding all along, but you just didn't name this process as storyboarding."

I nodded my head, and she added, "Well, I'm more than OK with that. You've given me several names to this process. I can walk out of here saying that I know how to do thumbnails, roughs, *and* storyboards."

Wes and Steve agreed. "I never understood my napkin scribbles were thumbnails, roughs, and storyboards," Wes stated. "I just thought they were just chicken scratch. Now, I can see how these disciplines overlap. You've taken us from fine arts to commercial applications over the past few weeks, and I didn't even realize it."

"Smart move, Linda," Steve added. "If Wes knew he was diving into commercial arts, he would have dug his heels in like a stubborn mule."

Wes laughed. "It's hard enough to work on a commercial project. I really would have balked if you hadn't served it up from the fine art perspective."

Bonnie smiled. "I guess you had your reasons, Linda. I certainly couldn't imagine a class without Wes."

Wes apologized to Bonnie with his statement, "I couldn't imagine a class without you, either, Bonnie."

Zed asked, "So we work our project storyboards like Steve and Lisa, with mat board and overlays? Is that the professional way?"

"No," I answered. "You don't have to go that far on project storyboards. You can do them just like this, but keep them in some semblance of order." I pointed at the board. "You need to find your own way of expression, but you also need to realize that other designers may need to use these project boards."

"Communicate your ideas as if you were explaining them to someone who was listening to you for the first time," I said. "The trick is to explain them as though you were going on vacation, and some poor sucker had to take over from these boards. This is how you create successful project communications."

Steve laughed and added, "Lisa and I worked our project boards this way to save room at the computer. We felt it would be easier to mount them on the board with rubber cement and add the overlays so it was all on one page. The mat board gave it support. That way," he said, "We could prop it up against a wall or against the computer monitor, and flip the overlays over to check our progress along the timeline in Flash."

Zed asked another question. "Are these the storyboards we present to the client?"

Steve answered, "No way, good man. We don't want the client to know how we struggled to get to the final images. We want to appear magical, like we pulled the final project from a hat."

I laughed. "Steve, you've got public relations for designers down pat." I looked around at the unsettled class. "Now you know about project storyboards," I stated. "You select a final rough, and you implement this rough with visual and verbal notations to show movement along the timeline in Flash. This is a tool that helps you and other team members work through the implementation to the client presentation.

"If you don't have any more questions for project storyboards," I added. "Let's move on to presentation storyboards."

The students looked at me expectantly. I took their silence as my cue, and moved on to the development of the final presentation.

Presentation storyboards

The presentation storyboards consist of visual and verbal representation of the client's project. There are certain guidelines the designer can use to make digital images more appealing to the client. These guidelines help the designer look and feel more competent and professional during formal presentations.

"Next week," I began, "You all will present your work to Frieda as separate teams. As usual, I'll play the part of Frieda, and each team will present their projects to me. To do this, you need to know how to construct formal storyboards so the client understands your intentions.

"When you prepare formal presentation storyboards," I added, "You give yourself a chance to go over your work one more time with a fine-toothed comb. You're also preparing a product to leave with the client. This assures the client that they didn't leave out any last-minute information."

"Wouldn't it be a bit late to include more information?" Lisa asked. "We've already done all this work, and we still need to be open to changes?"

Steve glanced at Lisa. "We need to be open for changes all along the process, Lisa. This is just the first round of what may be a two- to fifteen-round project. This taxes our flexibility, to be sure. But, the client is almost always right."

I laughed. "I'm glad you included that word *almost* in your last sentence, Steve. The client doesn't know the elements and principles of design. You do. But, the client also knows their business better than you do, even with all your research and brainstorming. If you miss something within the client's vision or information along the way, the client will certainly let you know."

Lisa muttered, "Fifteen rounds with the client?" She appeared to be in shock.

Steve replied, "I've been to as many as twenty presentations to the same client for a one-page black and white print ad layout, Lisa. No telling how many times we'll have to sit with the client for formal presentations before their Flash site goes live. Some clients like to get their money's worth, I guess."

"You might not need to go as many rounds if you present your work along the lines I'll show you today," I said. "Then again, I can't predict how your client might react. Some people are impossible to please." I grinned, "Let's just say Frieda will be pretty easy-going."

Steve added, "These are the first boards the client will see. These are the toughest to get approved, I'm sure. Once they're approved, we can move into building the rest of the site before we need to present again, right?"

"You're right, Steve," I said. "Once the original boards have been approved – unless you have a very complex site – you don't need to go back to the client until you have the site completed and you've tested it. Then," I said, "You might need to bring the client to your studio, or upload the site to a space reserved for testing, so they can see what you see. This way, there are no mistakes in communication for the final product. We'll talk about uploaded projects in a minute."

"What does the presentation storyboard contain?" Bonnie asked. "And what does it look like?"

I asked Steve and Lisa to pass their project around so the other students could take a close look at the mat board. "This is the board you'll use to mount your images for the client presentation," I said. I drew a rectangle on the board. "This is how your storyboard should look."

Within the rectangle, I drew twelve other rectangles. "I'm about to give you measurements, so please take notes."

"Wait a minute," Zed said. "You're asking us to make twelve images per board? How many boards will we need to make?"

Wes laughed, "That's an odd question for someone who wants to produce animations. You'll be expected to make tons of storyboards for your projects down the road."

I grinned, "Sorry, Zed, but Wes is right." I added, "Not all these rectangles are images. Let me finish my explanation, and then I'll be open for questions." I dug out a television commercial storyboard from my materials. "This will give you a better idea of what I expect from you next week," I said. I gave the board to Wes, and he passed it along to the rest of the students.

"The images were rendered in marker pens," I explained, "Because that's how television images are often portrayed in professional storyboards. Your images from Flash will be digital, but they'll be laid out in the same way."

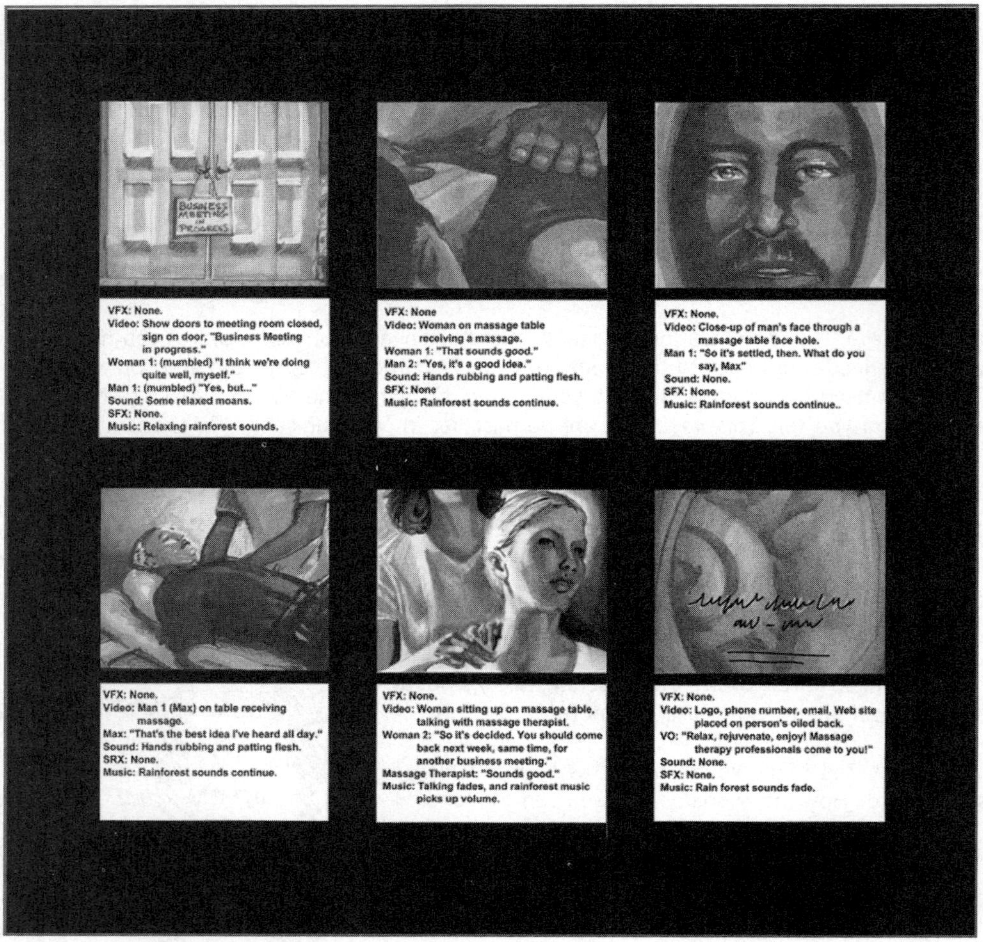

"If you'll notice, this layout is an obvious grid, and each panel is aligned with the panels above and below, and to the right and, or left. Each panel on this board also symbolizes a change in the commercial. This was a 30-second commercial and the images changed about every five seconds," I said. "This is about normal for a low-budget commercial. Every time the scene changes, lighting and camera angles need to change. Every move the camera team makes costs the client money, so changes are kept to a minimum in a low-budget production.

"Your Flash sites will change every second if you add objects that move across the screen. You can't possibly portray all these images to the client. Therefore," I stated, "You will use words to explain what's happening throughout that page in the panel below the image."

I pointed to the image on the board. "In your case, the first panel will represent the splash page," I said. "The next two or three panels may be needed to show how the splash opens to the home page. What you want is a beginning panel, a middle panel, and an end panel to the splash page, where the end panel will represent the home page. Depending on your final designs, some of you may need two middle panels to clarify the visual transitions."

"How many panels will we need after that?" Steve asked. "It seems that we'll have very few, since we're only presenting the splash, home page, and an inside page."

You shouldn't have to use more than one presentation board for Frieda's project," I answered. "This will equal five or six panels. The top panels will represent the splash opening to the home page. If you need to go into the second row for splash presentation, that first panel will be the home page."
"Then the other two panels will show the inside pages, right?" Lisa asked. "I know we might have changes on the inside page, one for a static page, and one for how the page appears with a mouse button clicked, or some other interaction from the viewer side."

"You've got it, Lisa," I said. "And, you also need to write how this transition takes place in the panel below the image. All you need to say is something descriptive and succinct like: '*This is how the inside page will look when the viewer clicks on the navigation image*'. Then, you also describe the changes. You'll say something like: '*When the viewer clicks on the navigation image, a light will appear behind the image, making it appear to glow*'.

"Let's get to the measurements," I said. I set the television commercial panel on the eraser tray of the whiteboard for all to see, and drew arrows and measurements to each area. "Your mat board will be 21" wide by 20" deep. Your borders will be 2" all around, except for the bottom, which is 2.5". The images are 1" apart, and each row is 1" apart. The distance between your image and text areas is 1/4".

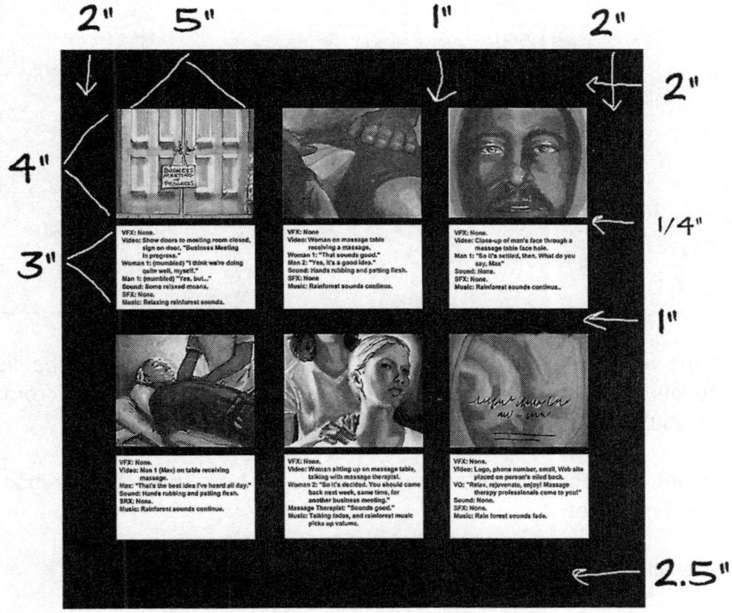

"Your text area is 5" wide by 3" deep. Your images should be proportionate to the Flash page, rather than the browser size," I said. "The default Flash format is 550 x 440 pixels in size. This means your printed image size at 72 pixels per inch, which is a little over 7.5" wide by a hair over 6" deep.

"You want to reduce this image to be 5" wide by 4" deep to keep the same aspect ratio as our format," I continued. "The image reduces to a 5"x4" printed version perfectly when you make it 360 x 288 pixels. You also need to remember to print the image at 300dpi. This will modify your measurements in pixels. Your image will now be 1500 pixels wide by 1200 pixels deep."

"But this doesn't change the printed image size," Steve commented.

"I know we went over this before," Bonnie said, "But why do we have to change the dots per inch on the printed version?"

"The answer to that question is print quality," Steve answered. "When you show the client a fuzzy image – which is what you'll get at 72dpi – the client will think his site looks fuzzy, too." He offered, "I have access to a great printer at work. It prints up to 600dpi. You all are welcome to use it for your storyboards this week. And if anyone has trouble with their calculations, I can help you with those, too. But just this once," he grinned.

Steve turned to me, "Speaking of capturing our Flash image, how do we do this, and what program do you want us to use?" Steve asked.

"Flash can export to a number of formats to provide you with suitable print quality. If you wish to render the content of your Flash movie as a bitmap ready for printing, use File > Export Image... and select the BMP format. This will allow you to set the output dpi quality to 300 or above, making it suitable for quality printing, or for working with in Photoshop."

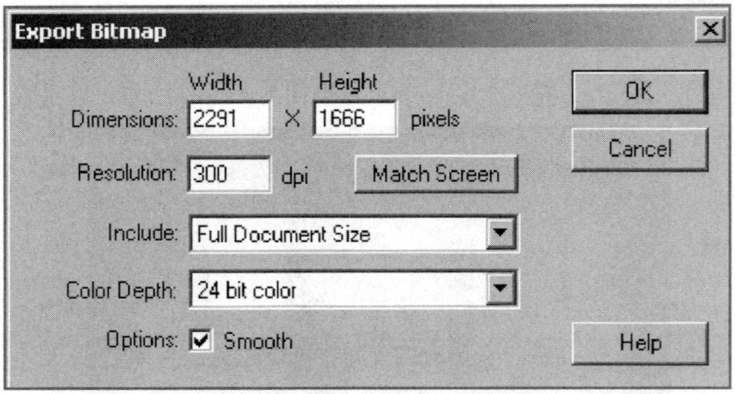

"If you wish to retain the vector format of the Flash file, export the image as an Adobe Illustrator image, with an `.ai` extension. This will allow you to convert the image into CMYK and to export from Illustrator at a high resolution. Either way, you'll have suitable images for printing."

Wes grinned. "I notice you left more space for the mat along the bottom of the storyboard," he said. "That's a great way to balance the images."

Bonnie said, "Didn't we talk about this already?"

"Do we always use black mat for the background?" Lisa asked. "It seems to me that the images would fade into the mat if the backgrounds of our Flash projects are black, too."

"Good point, Lisa," I replied. "If your Flash site background is black, use a gray mat board. But, please get a gray that's attractive to your images. You already know there are chromatic and achromatic grays, and this applies to mat boards too. If you get a gray mat board that's a cool gray – that has been mixed with a blue – it might look horrible if your images are green or violet. If you found a gray mat board that's a warm gray – mixed with a red – it might be overpowering to other gray images within your storyboard.

"Don't add borders to your site images to make them stand out against the mat board," I said, "Otherwise, the client will think they have borders on their site. When it comes to clients, what they see is what they believe they're getting."

"Is there a particular typeface you want us to use for the type below the images?" Steve asked. "I would assume it wouldn't be anything fancy, but I want to know if you prefer a standard."

"There's no standard, Steve," I answered. "You may want to stick with Arial, Helvetica, or some other recognizable sans-serif, simply because the type needs to be large and bold and easy to read. This is a display type, 12pt or larger, with *leading* between the text lines that's two points higher than the type size."

"These images won't be any larger than a photograph," Wes stated. "How can the client tell how detailed our pages will appear on the screen?"

"The image shots will be enlarged on extra panels," I explained. "This way, the client can see all the gory details." I pulled out another board with measurements drawn on the white paper pasted on the black mat board.

"These are the measurements for your home page, and for the inside page. You'll need two boards like this," I said.

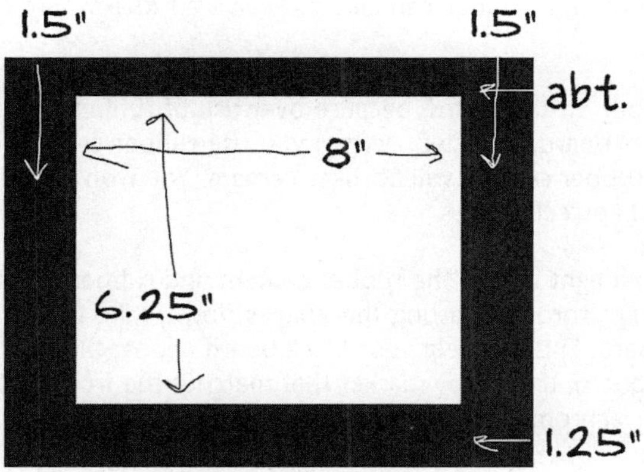

"Increase the pixel size of your image to 300 dpi, and then increase the width inch size to 8" wide. This will give you an oddball size of a little over 6.25 inches for the depth." I pointed at the mat board. "This is why you want to measure your border from the bottom first. When you place the image 1.25" from the bottom of this 8.5" x 11" mat board, you'll be left with a little less than 1" at the top. Both side borders are 1.5" wide."

"How do we cut the mat board?" Lisa asked. "I would think we'd need a large size board, and we can cut our pieces from that."

"It would be less expensive to buy a large board and cut your own," I said. "Cut the board with your scalpel or X-Acto knife and a metal ruler. Cut on a surface you don't care about, because you'll cut right through whatever's underneath. Don't use the dining room table! You can get cutting mats that are intended for quilters. These have measurements printed on the mats, and they're self-healing to a degree."

"Will you write down what we need, so I don't forget anything?" Bonnie asked.

"Sure," I answered, starting to write a list on the board.

I stopped and turned to the class. "When you print out your images and your type, cut them with the a sharp bladed knife or scalpel. Paste them down with rubber cement, and make sure the stray cement is picked up from around the edges of your images and type. When you paste them

Supplies for presentation storyboards...

* black or gray mat board enough for one 21"x20" board and two 8.5"x11" boards
* your x-acto knife and ruler with cork backing to cut the board
* if you can get one, a cutting mat for cutting the board
* a black marker
* tracing paper, marker paper, or vellum
* masking tape or invisible tape (no drafting tape)

down, use rubber cement on both the image and on the board. This way, they won't peel up after a period of time."

"Why can't we use a spray mount?" Steve asked. "I'm only asking because I know that some of these folks might want to use it once they discover it," he grinned.

I laughed, "Thanks for bringing that up, Steve." I looked at the other students. "You can use spray mount, which is a spray adhesive. However," I added, "Both forms of adhesive – the spray mount and the rubber cement – are toxic. Limit your contact time with both adhesives, and use proper ventilation.

"The reason I ask you to use rubber cement is because it's more forgiving than spray adhesive. Spray adhesive will also be less forgiving to your paper if you decide it's not mounted properly. When you try to move your paper on the mount board, you'll discover it's permanently sealed with spray adhesive."

I added, "Spray adhesive is also an aerosol and will go into the air and land on objects in the surrounding areas where you decide to mount your project. At least with rubber cement, you have an idea where the glue lands, as you'll see or feel it immediately."

"Be careful about the amount of rubber cement you put on the board, because over use of rubber cement will actually alter the black or gray ink dye on the mat board." I added, "When you use rubber cement on both your mat board and the back of your image, the rubber cement will act like...cement. You won't be able to remove the image, so be sure you're laying it down correctly.

"If you mark the areas where your images will go with a light pencil, the rubber cement and rubber cement pick-up will erase the pencil lines," I said. "When you're through pasting the images down, take the black magic marker, and go around the edges of the mat board. This will help your black board appear black from all angles in a frontal viewpoint. If you have gray mat board, use a gray marker that matches the front of the board. This means you'll have to find a warm, cool, or achromatic gray to match the board.

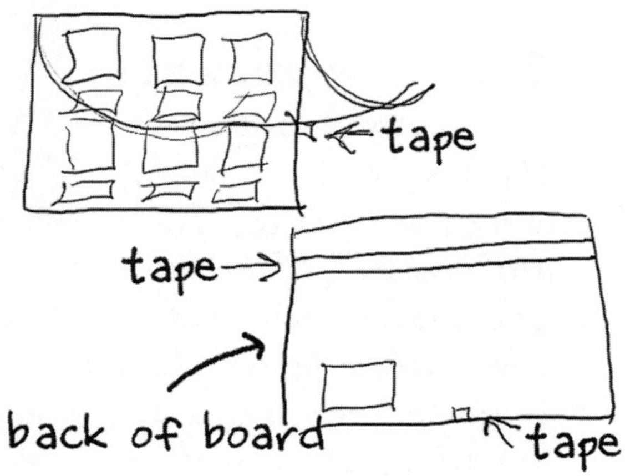

"Then, I want you to cut some vellum or tracing paper that's 21" wide by 24" deep. Vellum is not the skin of some poor animal," I added. "It's a white semi-transparent paper that's similar to parchment. You can use vellum, marker paper, or tracing paper, as each one serves the same purpose – that of protecting your images." I drew some examples on the board. "Place this paper over the front of the storyboard, and place a small piece of tape at the bottom. Carefully smooth the vellum or tracing paper over the board, and bend the top over to the back. Tape the edge of the vellum across the back neatly. Make sure you don't catch any cat hairs or other stray filaments in the masking tape. This will help protect your images, and will keep the protection secure. It can also be used to make alterations to the images per your client's suggestions, if you don't want to mark up the storyboard," I added. "This way, if the client wants to keep the storyboard, you can remove the cover and take it back to the studio with you."

"Why do you want us to use masking tape instead of drafting tape?" Bonnie asked.

"Simply because it's less expensive, and because it sticks better for a longer period of time," Steve answered. "You can also use invisible tape." He looked at me, "I remember doing boards this meticulously years ago. I haven't seen a board done like this in a long time."

I smiled. "Because this procedure isn't taught in very many places anymore, Steve. If you do your boards this way, you'll be noticed. This presentation preparation will mark you as a professional, even among professionals."

"What's that rectangle on the back of the storyboard?" Wes asked. "I'll take a guess and say that's our name and other information so the client can contact us."

"You guessed right, Wes," I replied. "For Frieda, put your team member names on the board."

"One more question," Lisa asked. She was busy writing in her notepad. "Do we also cover the two 8.5" x 11" boards?"

"Yes," I answered. "The vellum will be..."

"The vellum will be 11" wide by about 11.5" deep," Zed interrupted with a grin. "And I promise not to catch my cat *or* my cat's hairs in the tape. I want to show the client I care about my work for them."

"This is really, hmm..." Bonnie started to say something. "This is really kind of overboard, isn't it?"

Wes dropped his head to the table and muttered, "I can't believe the queen of perfectionism is stating someone else is going overboard!"

Bonnie shot Wes a look of disgust. "I just want to make sure I don't have to do anything more than what I already have to do."

Steve responded, "Bonnie, Linda's right. This is a great way to protect your images, and it's also a super way to show the client you care about your work."

Deb nodded, "I'll go for that." She tapped her pencil on her drawing pad and stared off into space. "So when we present these images, we'll pull the tape from the bottom, and wrap the tissue or vellum back over the image. Do we need to bring a prop for the image, or do we just hold it in our hands?"

I answered, "This is where we can talk about your presentation with the Dog and Pony Show, or we can table your question for a moment and talk about client presentations on computer."

Everyone voted to cover the computer presentation first. "OK, then," I said. "We just covered the two forms of storyboard. One is for projects, and one is for presentation. The project storyboard is less formal than the presentation storyboard, but both receive detailed attention. This way, your viewer won't ever doubt how you want your work to be perceived. Any more questions?" I asked.

"I have one as soon as we move into the next topic," Steve stated.

Well, then," I said. "Let's move on."

Clients in cyberspace

In this portion of our session today, we talked about computer presentations for the client. The plan was to cover both clients that live right next door as well as online clients, offering reasons for what does and doesn't work, and how we can maximize our presentation information.

Steve began this session with his question, "Can't we just use laptops to show how the site will work?" he asked. "That way, we don't have to go through the work of preparing formal storyboards."

"Steve, that's a good point. More designers now use laptops to present their work, especially in programs that portray moving images. But," I added, "What do you do when you take the project to the client on the laptop, and all they have is a phone modem? This phone modem may be the only line they use for their business, and you set the appointment during work hours."

"I doubt we'd run across that scenario," Wes said. "How many businesses today have just one phone line, let alone a phone modem? I would assume most businesses – at least businesses that are interested in a Flash MX site – would have cable or broadband lines for Internet connections."

Bonnie shook her head. "I hate to disappoint you, Wes, but you'd be surprised at the number of smaller businesses that don't have access to some of these tools. One phone line may be a bit severe, but phone modems are still in operation in many areas. These clients may be located in areas of lower population concentration, or they may not make the time to connect themselves at all. They're more focused on their own product manufacturing or services, not their web connections."

She continued, "When Linda talked about the designer as a lone eagle, I was tempted to head for the woods. But," she added, "I realized that many remote places aren't wired for some of these capabilities yet."

I nodded, "Bonnie's right. In spite of our advancements in digital communications, there are still many remote places left in the western world. These places are considered *stepchildren* to the communications industry, and they don't provide them the accessibility reserved for larger areas of population concentration. Although," I added, "Hopefully, wireless communications will help us reach more people."

"We'd know in advance whether the client had capabilities to show them the project on a laptop or by computer during the analyzing stage of the creative problem solving process, wouldn't we?" Deb asked. "That way we could prepare the laptop presentation or leave it alone."

"Right, Deb," I answered. "Plus, you might have the option of bringing the client to your studio or office. This way, you could prepare both the formal presentation storyboards and the laptop or desktop presentation."

Steve said, "I have one other question. The client is viewing the storyboards in subtractive colors. How can we show the properties of additive colors for the site if we don't use computers?"

"This is a drawback, Steve," I admitted. "There's no way to overcome this problem. If you have a client who has appropriate conditions to view the site on a laptop, then you have an ideal situation. You can connect if possible to see how their connection will handle the Flash site. Or, you can just take the laptop and not connect. Otherwise, you just have to describe what goes on the best way possible – through printed digital images and words."

"I guess this is why it's really important to calibrate the computer to the printer," Bonnie stated. "Now I get it. I've never printed out my web designs for clients before, I used to just point them to a place on my site where I'd upload their pages. They could view the pages there before they went live."

"That's a great way to handle web pages, Bonnie," I said. "But, when it comes to Flash, you're dealing with moving images. The client – who doesn't own your designer's vocabulary – will have a tough time telling you what they want changed on the site."

Wes laughed, "I can see it now, *'I want that doohickey to go to the left, and this thingamabob to move over that what's-it'*." Everyone laughed.

"That's about the gist of it, Wes," I said.

"One way to counteract this is to provide the content in easily linkable pages, so the client can refer to each page and asset. If the pages of the website are clearly marked out then the client can simply send their comments about individual pages."

"Now," I stated, "If everyone is satisfied with their answers for their project presentations for next week, I'll move on to how you present yourselves with the Dog and Pony Show."

"I'm ready for that," Zed said. "I want to know who's the dog, and who's the pony."

The Dog and Pony Show

The designer's presentation of their project to the client is a form of sales presentation. The designer hopes to sell either him or herself, once again, to the client, and they hope to sell their initial work on the client's project. Showing the first draft of the client's site is important. If the client is happy, then the designer has much less work to do in the long run.

First, I answered Zed's question, "Zed, I have no earthly idea who's the dog and who's the pony in the Dog and Pony Show. I do know this is an archaic advertising term, but it's still in use. Advertisers coined this term based on the trained animal acts at circuses. Performing the Dog and Pony Show can be demeaning or fun, depending on your attitude about showmanship."

I sat with the students and relaxed as I spoke. "Today, the term is used to describe an elaborate presentation made for approval. Reporters use the term when they write about politicians and their policies. Stockbrokers use it when they talk about a business going public for the first time. Basically," I concluded, "The Dog and Pony Show is the same as a road show."

"Oh," Deb sighed, "So we need to get easels and pointers and other tools to present the storyboard to the client."

"You would," I said, "If you're presenting to a board of a nonprofit group or corporation. The rule of thumb in this case is the more people you present to, the more formal your presentation needs to be. But, this won't often happen," I said. "If you work as part of a larger organization or agency, it's unlikely you'll do the client presentation." I added, "You wouldn't have had much to do with the design concept or marketing, either, unless you're part of the management team."

I nodded at Steve. "If you work for a smaller agency or studio, or if you work on your own like Bonnie, then it's doubtful you'll land a huge corporate job. Most of the presentations you'll handle will be with clients who have smaller budgets. The atmosphere for this sort of presentation is a lot less formal, but no less important.

"We've already established that as a lone designer, or with a smaller agency, you'll wear many different hats. The client presentation will become old hat after you do a few of them. Some minimum guidelines would be to make sure you at least appear to respect yourself, your work, and your client. You can include the props, like easels and pointers. That's up to you. Most likely, the client will want to hold the work, and look at it closely. That's why neatness is paramount."

I glanced at Bonnie, who seemed absorbed in her notes, and continued, "The designer needs to be aware these days. We need to be aware of our professionalism, our ethics, and our demeanor when we present work to clients who spend their hard-earned dollars on us."

Bonnie looked up from her notes and asked, "So what do you suggest we do when we present to the client? Do we play it according to the client's standards? When they're in blue jeans, do we go in blue jeans?"

Steve answered, "I'll add my two cents. Our clients have been won by a work ethic that shows them we're serious about what we do. We don't play artsy, and we don't go out on a limb." Steve nodded at Wes. "I wish we would sometimes, but our current clientele expects what we've given in the past.

"I think the point I'm trying to make is that the design world is really cutthroat. Designers come and go. So do businesses. If you really love this work, and you want to maintain a thriving business, you must be flexible. If you can't be flexible, then find a niche and hide out."

"Ouch, that's rough, Steve," Zed said. "But I understand what you're saying. I just don't think I'm ready to be as old and mature as you are yet."

Steve and Wes laughed, "Don't worry, buddy," Wes said. "You'll get here eventually. Steve's point is that every day is a Dog and Pony Show for a designer, even when they're not doing a client presentation."

Steve nodded, "I compare myself to other designers. If I can be more professional and more attentive about my client's needs than the designer down the road, I'll do it. That's one way to stay ahead of the younger and more energetic competition." He looked around at the other students. "Some of you will go out there and compete against me. I'm going to support you every way I know how if you show initiative, consistency, reliability, flexibility, intelligence, awareness, talent, and skill."

"That's a huge list to fill, but why would you do that, Steve?" Lisa asked. "Isn't that taking money out of your own pocket?"

Steve grinned. "I didn't say I'd hand the job to you. If I feel the client might benefit from your perspective or your experience, I'll call and ask if you want to work with me."

"That's an interesting take on working as a designer, Steve," I said. "Instead of losing the client altogether, you'd take on another designer to help you out. That way you won't lose the client, and you'd also make a percentage."

Steve kept grinning. "I'm not cutthroat, just smart!"

Wes laughed. "So what do you do when you present to clients?"

Steve answered, "For the first and second interview, I always wear a suit. When I get a handle on the client, I always dress just a touch better then they do. If the client's style is jeans and sweatshirt, I'll wear jeans and a jacket. If they dress in a tuxedo, I'll wear an evening gown."

The class laughed. "If you took on another designer, would you bring them with you to the Dog and Pony?" Deb asked.

"Never," Steve answered. "I don't want the client and the other designer to recognize each other on the street. They may hit it off better than I do. That wouldn't be to my benefit."

Deb glanced at Wes. "We're working in teams of males and females. How should we operate? Should the women talk during the presentation or should the men talk? I mean, we're giving the presentation to a woman, so I would think women-to-woman would be best."

Lisa interrupted, "I don't know about that. Frieda's used to working with men. Plus, I would be scared out of my wits to present to a client."

I grinned, "Lisa, I think you and Steve make a great working team. Whatever you both decide will be fine." I turned to Deb. "You, on the other hand, might have a problem on your hands. You have a finely tuned professional mind, but you've managed to present yourself as an esoteric free spirit over the past few weeks. How are you going to manage the presentation? You might scare Frieda with all the changes you've made recently."

Deb blushed for the first time during this course. "I forgot about that," she admitted. "I forget what I've done to my appearance sometimes. I feel so comfortable this way."

Wes looked at Deb with a small smile. "I think we can work this out."

Deb nodded. "I know." She grinned and looked at Wes. "We can work on this, I'm sure of it. We'll win the client, hands down."

Bonnie sighed and tapped the end of her pencil on the table. "And what do Zed and I do?"

Zed asked, "We bribe the client?"

After the laughter subsided, I let the students know my own criteria for the first client project presentation. "The first thing you need is **confidence**. You have this now, because everything you've done, you've done for a reason. You can defend your work. By this, I don't mean you need to get belligerent about every points, line, and plane in your design."

Wes laughed, "I probably would. That's why I send my agent out to talk to galleries."

"Uh-huh," I nodded. "I understand. Your design is supposed to work for your client, not for you. You'll need to be able to tell the client why you chose to do what you did without bringing your personal story into the picture."

I stood to go write a list on the board. As I did, I kept talking. "The other point to remember is to **be yourself**. If you try to be something other than who you are, it will show." I turned to Deb, "If you want to keep your braids and put a ring in your nose, it doesn't really matter. But, it may matter to the client. Be aware of changes you make to yourself when dealing with current clients. You may shock them into letting you go without any consideration of your work if you haven't been with them that long."

"You'll need to remember the items on this list for next week." I wrote a few items on the board:

Supplies for presentation
* presentation storyboards one 21"x20" and two 11"x8.5"
* body copy for site, typed neatly in folder, no typos
* props, if needed (easel, pointer, laptop, etc)

"These are the items you need," I said. "The body copy is laid out just like your client brief. Include a flowchart, and number the pages. The body copy will also be numbered, to correspond with the pages in the flowchart."

"Does the type of folder matter?" Bonnie asked.

"It doesn't," I answered. "The criterion is simply to be *appropriate*. Use a clear binder if you want to portray an image on the front page, like Frieda's name. Use a colored binder, but be aware of which color you chose. Coordinate it with your work. Be creative!"

I called attention to the fact that there were no formal projects this week. "Just get yourselves together for the presentations next week," I said. I asked if there were any other questions.

"Can I bring a dog and pony next week?" Zed grinned. "I'll leave the cat at home."

Wes laughed, "Just make sure Frieda doesn't have any allergies."

I smiled, and dismissed the class. They slowly wandered out, talking among themselves about next week's presentation. I was intrigued to see if Zed would really wear that scarf, and how Deb would manage her changes.

Summary

In this chapter we've focused on the selection and implementation stages of the creative problem solving process, and we looked at how we can use this tool to help us with any design problems. We looked at how to process components into site designs in preparation for a first client presentation.

We next looked at how to build a site in Flash MX; more specifically we looked at:

- Using a guide layer
- Importing images
- Optimizing images
- Importing text

Before moving on to look in more detail at how our different pages sit on the timeline. The main things we looked at were:

- HTML hyperlinks
- Flash timeline navigation
- ActionScript for timeline navigation

We rounded this off by creating a working FLA using what we'd just learnt.

In the following section, we saw how storyboards consist of thumbnails and roughs. We also learnt that storyboards are used for both projects and presentations:

- **Project storyboards** – used to portray ideas for selection and implementation into the Flash MX timeline
- **Presentation storyboards** – used to present projects to the client.

Finally, we looked at the Dog and Pony Show, where we learnt about client presentation, and how we – as well as our work – need to be presented professionally for the ongoing designer-client relationship.

In the next lesson we're going to look at presenting initial work to a client for approval, and finalizing projects with corrected and completed components.

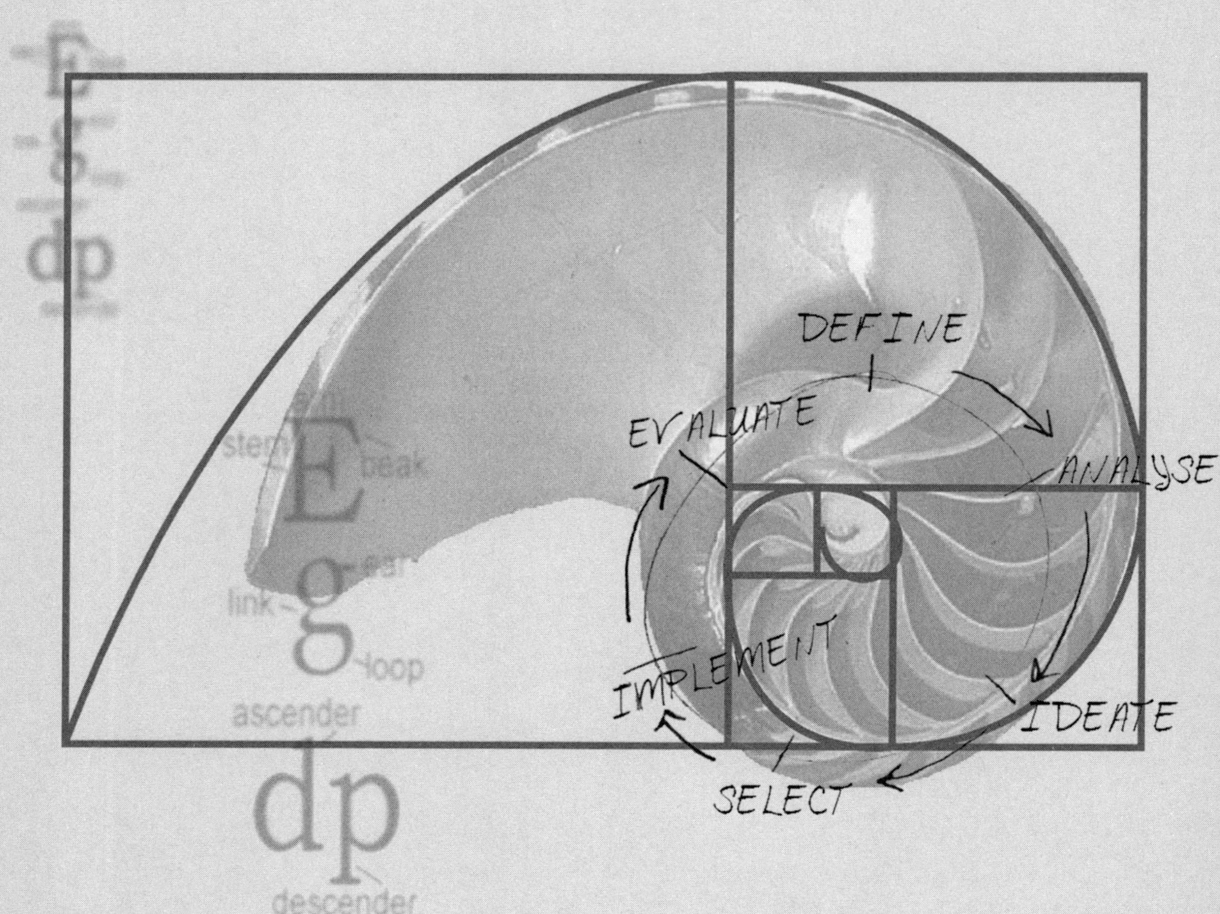

DEFINE
ANALYSE
IDEATE
SELECT
IMPLEMENT
EVALUATE
stem
beak
ear
link
loop
ascender
descender

Chapter 10

Unifying the Design Concepts

Objectives

In today's class you will learn about:

- The principles of intellectual and visual unity
- The unifying attributes of proximity, repetition, continuation, and variety
- Presenting the final roughs to the client
- Evaluating the presentations and processing client feedback
- Improving your designs: dynamic transitions made with masking in Flash

Introduction

I knew the students would be anxious about their presentations this morning, so when I tried to arrive early I was surprised to see that Wes and Bonnie had beaten me to it. They stood outside the classroom door deep in conversation, and barely noticed me as I swept past them into the room. I settled at my desk to prepare myself for today's class.

As they entered the room a few minutes later I looked up from my work and Bonnie began to speak, "I have to apologize for my behavior over the past few weeks," she said.

Wes smiled, "Bonnie's reached a point of saturation. I think she had an epiphany!"

Bonnie agreed, "I apologized to Wes too. The antagonism between us keeps me awake at nights. The other morning, I realized this was my problem. The only reason I pick on Wes is because he has an attitude about my penchant for keeping things in boxes, both in life and in design."

Wes grinned, "Yeah, I avoid boxes like the plague!"

Bonnie continued, "I'm still having problems thinking *outside of the box*, so to speak, but this class has really opened my eyes to the way other people operate. Nothing is ever going to be as ordered as I'd like it to be, but I'll try to be more open to other points of view."

Wes put his arm around Bonnie's shoulders, "We're like night and day, Bonnie. But, I appreciate your efforts to understand and respect how I think and act. I'll try to do the same for you."

Zed had entered the room on tiptoe. He stood right behind Bonnie and Wes, "Aw, ain't this sweet!" Bonnie jumped, and Wes laughed.

"I see you're still wearing your scarf, Zed." I nodded at Zed's neck.

"Just to class." He whipped the scarf from around his neck and flung it over a chair, "I think it looks cool!"

"Oh, it's very cool," Deb entered, dressed in a business suit.

"Where did your braids go?" Bonnie asked. "You look just like you did during that first interview."

"I decided to give Frieda a break," Deb laughed. "Besides, Wes and I really need this job."

Wes nodded, "Nobody's even mentioned my suit." He turned so everyone could get a look at his Armani.

Steve and Lisa walked in just as Wes finished turning round. Steve let out a low whistle, "Wow, take a look at that!"

Lisa laughed, and Zed spoke up, "So what's up for today, teach?"

"As if you don't know!" Lisa stated, "Last week we learned about the process of selection and implementation with our projects. This week is evaluation time in the creative problem-solving process."

I grinned, "This week is more than just evaluation – it's presentation, evaluation, and then returning to the creative problem-solving process to take your sites further with whatever feedback you learn."

"Yes!" Zed slapped his hands together, "I'm ready for this!"

Steve looked puzzled, "Are all of us going to continue with our sites, or are we going to work on just one project chosen by Frieda?"

I tried to look serious, "Well, Frieda won't be in until a little later, so you'll have to talk to her directly."

"Oh, man," Wes slumped in his chair. "I can't wear this suit for a whole couple of hours. I'll have to pay for it if I start sweating."

"Take the jacket off, Wes," I said. "Because before Frieda arrives we're going to talk about unity and why it seems to stand alone amongst the principles of design."

The principle of unity

The principle of unity is the foundation of the creative problem-solving process.

"You've already learned the definition of the principle of unity," I said. "Unity is the **condition of completeness**, accomplished when all the elements and principles of design work so well within your format that the sum of these concepts is more important than any one of its parts."

Zed nodded and pointed at the last three words I wrote on the board, "So we need to achieve oneness, harmony, and gestalt in our work."

"But how do we know when we've created something like that?" Bonnie asked.

"Evaluation by a colleague or peer," I answered. "This is difficult when you work alone, since you'll be evaluating your own work. If you have someone you trust to critique your work, you'll be in much better shape," I added. "This person doesn't need to be a designer, but it helps if they're schooled in the elements and principles of design."

Steve nodded, "I sure learn a lot about my work from my partners at the studio. It's tough to see problems in your own work."

I agreed, "It's important to watch your evaluator as they look at your piece," I said. "Sometimes, you can tell immediately if your work comes together as a complete visual message, rather than in bits and pieces."

Steve laughed, "I've been told that some of my work seems to be written in an unknown code."

I asked Steve why he felt it was important to achieve unity in his work. He thought for a moment and responded, "I never really thought about achieving unity, only because I hadn't actually identified it as what I was after in my work. However," he added, "After some of the things we've talked about on this course, I've realized how important unity is in creating design. If the viewer isn't able to see a whole picture from the various objects we use in our designs, then we haven't achieved unity in our work."

"Thanks, Steve," I responded. "So, we need to have unity in our work, or the viewer won't understand what we're trying to say."

"I know that I have to follow a theme, especially when I work on a magazine story or a brochure," Steve added. "But, I also need to become more aware of the how the work looks overall."

Bonnie seemed perplexed. "Are you talking about *intellectual* unity or *visual* unity?"

Intellectual and visual unity

"That's a great question, Bonnie," I said. "A designer is concerned about both forms of unity. I wrote the words *visual unity* on the board, and highlighted the fact that it is intrinsically related to the fundamental elements and principles of design.

* visual unity
* elements and principles of design

"The last critique we did, we concerned ourselves with the **visual unity** of your message," I said. "The critique was centered on how well the elements and principles of design worked in your project."

* intellectual unity
* theme

I wrote the words *intellectual unity* on the board, and underneath that term, I wrote *theme*. "Even though we didn't critique the **intellectual unity** within each project on the last go-round, you've been working towards this goal all along."

"We did that when we prepared the client brief," Deb stated. "We defined the message Frieda wants to send, and we made decisions on how to send that message to her market."

"That's right Deb," I replied. "We also learned about how to create a theme by using rhetorical figures, like metaphors and analogies. The difference between intellectual design and visual design is similar to the difference between your work in your drawing pads and the projects you'll present today."

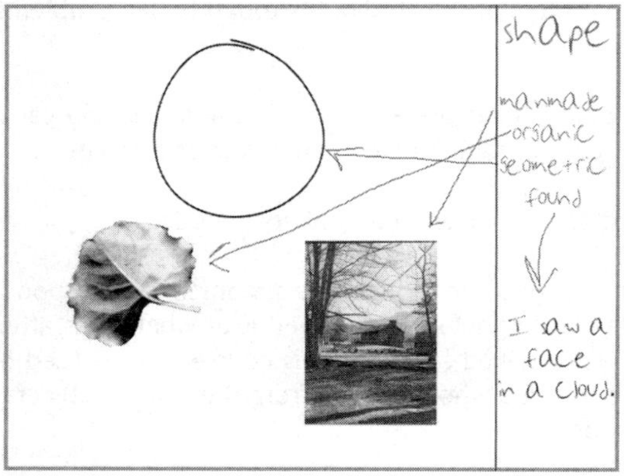

"I didn't know our drawing pads were designed," Lisa stated. "I guess they are, since we planned them to show a visual message."

I asked Lisa for her drawing pad. I opened it and showed the class one of the pages, "I'm not picking on you, Lisa. Every one of you planned to use your drawing pads as a tool for learning. Based on that theme, your work within these drawing pads is designed based on ideas."

The students shuffled around to retrieve their own drawing pads, "Wow," Bonnie said. "I didn't realize I was designing when I pasted photos into my drawing pad."

"Your drawing pads are similar to scrapbooks. When you open a page, you look for shapes within the overall pattern. The visual pattern may not be obvious, but the shapes are quite obvious because you've aligned them and titled them by subject."

Steve said, "So the intellectual unity within these drawing pads is based on the theme of the elements and principles of design. We titled each page, and each page is a topic within this theme. The visual unity is achieved when we practice the elements and principles of design."

"That's right Steve," I pointed at Lisa's page again. "Once a viewer notices there's no rhyme or reason to the overall pattern, they begin to look at each individual piece within that page design. They begin to see that each element on this page in particular, has something to do with shapes."

Lisa interrupted, "Now that I see the page as a design, I would be concerned that a person looking at the page for the first time wouldn't realize the page was about shapes unless I labeled it with text." She added, "How would I know that a leaf, a circle, and a photograph of a building had anything to do with each other unless I added the labels like I did?"

Wes laughed, "I wouldn't know, and I'm trained to see the images as shapes."

Lisa scowled at Wes, "We're all trained to see images as shapes first, Wes. That ability is wired into us."

Elements of Design

1. *Line*
2. *Shape*
3. *Color/hue*
4. *Movement*
5. *Space*
6. *Value*
7. *Texture*
8. *Typography*

Deb interrupted, "I wouldn't know that those shapes were related. I guess that's why type is an integral element of design."

I nodded, "That's right, Deb. Intellectually, we look to type to help us create a theme for the images. Especially," I added, "When a viewer looks at something that doesn't contain visual unity."

"All the *elements* are certainly there," Steve said as he looked at Lisa's page. "I see line, shape, color, movement, space, value, texture, and type." I wrote the elements down as he spoke, "What I don't see are the *principles* of design at work," he added.

"OK then, who wants to remind us what the principles of design are?" I asked.

Zed chanted in a monotone, "Contrast, direction, emphasis, economy, proportion, balance, rhythm, and unity."

We all laughed, and Wes said, "I guess if there's one thing we're sure to remember from this class, it'll be the elements and principles of design."

As I finished writing the principles of design on the board, I asked, "So what principle of design is Lisa missing in that page of her sketchbook?"

There was complete silence, until Steve attempted an answer, "I guess none of them are missing if you look at the page with the concept of intellectual unity."

"Why doesn't it work along the lines of visual unity?" I asked Steve.

"Because the elements and principles of design work within each individual item, but not as a whole."

Principles of Design

1. Contrast
2. Direction
3. Emphasis
4. Economy
5. Proportion
6. Balance
7. Rhythm
8. Unity

"Do you all see this?" I asked, pointing again at Lisa's page. "Lisa created a page that contained individual items. The only element that ties the page together is type. If we couldn't read English, the page would lose unity altogether. There would be no visual or intellectual unity.

"Lisa made an important point earlier," I said. "The viewer automatically looks for shapes, and they also look for organization among those shapes. When we look at something chaotic, what's our first response?"

"I don't know about anyone else here," Bonnie said, "But I move on when I'm confronted with chaos. I figured that was just because I'm so particular about organization."

Wes grinned, "I don't think you're the only one who would choose to look at something else, Bonnie. We all probably have an affinity for organization in one way or another."

"That's the reaction your viewer will have if you don't achieve intellectual and visual unity within your client's site," I said. "The site will appear chaotic, and the viewer will move on to a simpler, easier to comprehend site."

> *"To summarize, we can say that* **intellectual unity** *is achieved when we strive for a theme; this idea is the driving force behind the design.* **Visual unity**, *on the other hand, is achieved when we use the elements and principles of design along the lines of unifying acts."*

I continued, "Let's talk a little about how the visual and intellectual unity of design is affected by other attributes," I said. "The ultimate goal of good design is to use each element within the framework of the principles of design to achieve unity. Unity is also affected by four other attributes – *proximity*, *repetition*, *continuity*, and *variety* – and each of these attributes affects the overall visual unity."

Proximity

I began with the visual attribute of proximity, and how it affects visual unity. As I wrote the word, *proximity* on the board, I began to explain how the students could use proximity with various elements of design.

Proximity

Concerned with state of closeness - positive and negative space. Overlapping.

Can be achieved with elements of design used within principles of design.

"One of the ways we can achieve visual unity in design is with proximity. Proximity, or the state of closeness, is how we can train our viewer's eye to see what we have to offer as a whole unit. With this attribute, we're concerned with the positive and negative spaces in our designs, and with how each object relates to each other as a visual language."

I continued to make notes on the board. "Proximity within visual unity is similar to overlapping your objects. It could also be connecting two objects with value and color, like Lisa showed us at the theater a few weeks ago."

I turned to talk to the class. "You can also connect objects that have similar line, shape, texture, movement, or typefaces."

Wes stated, "I guess we really need to focus on proximity within Flash MX, don't we?"

I nodded, and asked Wes if he could explain why this was so important. He was eager to start talking, "Well, proximity is the state of closeness, but it doesn't always mean that the objects need to be physically close, as you mentioned. Proximity can also apply to time and context, as well as place. Within Flash MX, we have to be concerned about proximity of visual elements along the timeline, and we need to focus on how all these elements play together within the context of the message. If we use an element of design, we need to relate it somehow to the intellectual unity as well, because visual and intellectual unity will play off each other in a client project. If our objects don't fit a theme, then they're not worth keeping in the design."

I agreed with Wes, and went to my computer and opened up Flash MX. I quickly created three different shapes on the stage using the drawing tools, "This is like Lisa's page in her drawing pad. I have three different shapes here, and they don't seem to relate to each other."

I added the same texture to two of the shapes, and turned to the class. "What have I just communicated to you visually?"

Wes answered, “You've just told us, through the addition of texture, that two of the shapes are in some way *connected*.”

“That's right, Wes. So which of the principles of design did I use to unify these elements of line and shape?”

Deb answered, “I think you used *rhythm* and *direction*. You added the rhythm of the gradient texture, and you directed them towards each other.” She thought a moment and added, “I guess that would also mean that you used the element of movement, and the principle of direction.”

I smiled at Deb, “You guessed right! “I said. I went back to the colors and textures of my original shapes, and then dragged them closer together so that they touched each other. “Now they appear to be related because of their close proximity – this is *overlapping*.”

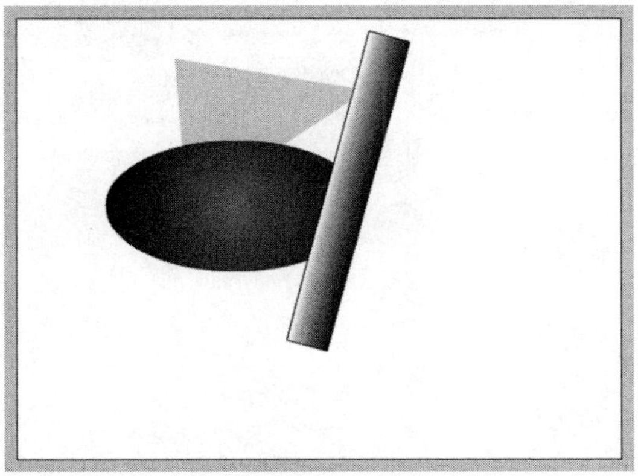

“They do seem related, even though they're different shapes,” Lisa admitted. “I don't know why they're related, but you're effectively telling me they are, because I see them as a group.”

“Oh,” Bonnie stated, “I see now. This is visual unity, and it has nothing to do with intellectual unity. The shapes belong together, but I'm with Lisa. I have no idea why the shapes are together because there isn't any theme.”

I added words to the picture, “If I add words, and tell you explicitly that we have a triangle, oval, and rectangle here, then we have a form of intellectual unity as well. As basic as it is, the theme here is *shapes*.”

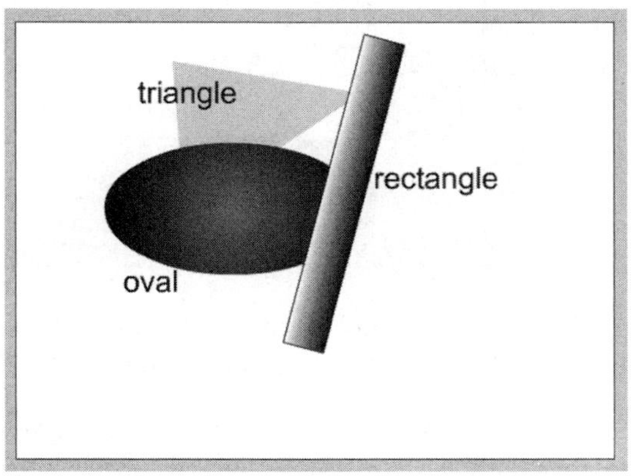

“Words really are important, aren't they?” Lisa said. “You just added the element of type, and it single handedly created a theme. How do we achieve intellectual unity without words?”

“With the proximity of symbols, I guess,” Zed said.”

I nodded in agreement, “If we train our viewers to see a shape as a symbol, then we can speak to them without words. These are the mnemonic devices we talked about a few weeks ago. You can speak to the viewer with icons, ideograms, and other graphic codes and symbols.”

"That's like the navigation buttons on our sites," Steve added. We place them close together, so the viewer knows that the symbols belong together."

I agreed, "If you use symbols for navigation, you usually place them together, so the user doesn't have to hunt all over the page for them." Proximity is a visual tool to help you create unity. When you place items together, whether it's with overlapping, or through any of the elements of design, then you've helped the viewer see the design as a whole."

As I spoke, I started to work in Flash. I selected Window > Common Libraries > Buttons, and started dragging a number of different buttons from the Flash Library onto the stage, and strategically arranging them with the help of the Align panel. "For example, when we layout our navigation buttons in our design, their positioning is always worth some care and consideration. Obviously, you'd never have this many controls in your designs, but this demonstrates nicely how easy to create themes with your design elements in Flash."

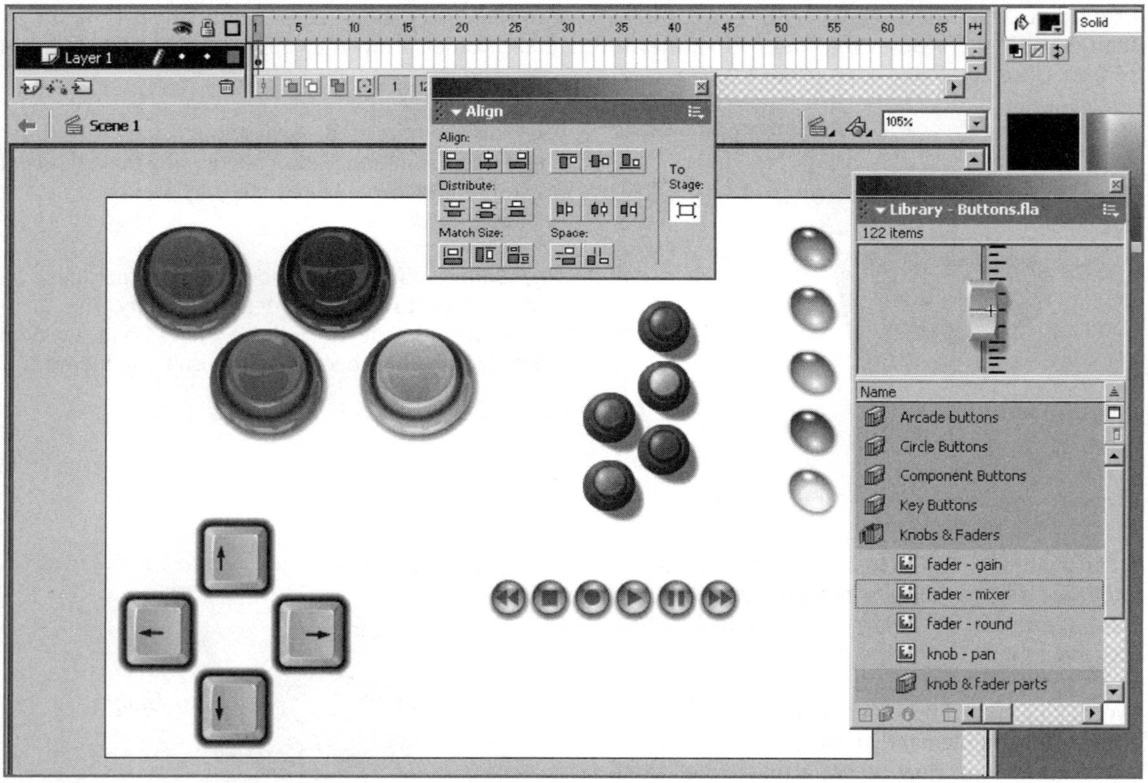

Bonnie stated, "Looking at that, I think unity must have a lot to do with the repetition of objects, too. Notice that the objects in each group, or theme, are the same shape, so we know they're related."

"Aha, very good observation Bonnie! Let's move on to the next attribute of visual unity," I said. "Since you're heading there anyway..."

Repetition

"One of the best ways to get your viewer to understand your project as a whole unit is repetition of any element used within the principles of design," I said. "For instance, your navigation shapes are basically the same, and this assures the viewer that these images belong together."

"Steve and I also used repetition of texture in our navigation buttons," Lisa said.

I agreed, and looked at Deb. "I hope you don't mind me using your hair style as an example of visual and intellectual unity," I said. Deb grinned. "We were used to seeing Deb with a certain hair style. Then," I stated, "She changed her style dramatically. She discontinued her repetition, and began a new cycle of repetition.

"These cycles of repetition kept us going, because we became used to each change both intellectually and visually. If we see Deb as a format with items that tell us who she is, we connect with Deb visually. We see her as a composite of these items, like her hair, her clothes, and her way of carrying herself.

"When she changes any one of these items, we become confused. Our idea of Deb changes when she changes any visual aspect of her format."

She patted her head, "I guess I messed up yet another cycle of repetition," she smiled. "I'm glad I didn't dye it red. You guys would have had it with me!"

"Chaos can be curbed with the next attribute of unity," I grinned. Wes shook with silent laughter, and Deb cleared her throat.

"Repetition is a great way to communicate visually," I added. "When you repeat an element of design on a page, you help the viewer learn how to visually *read* your site."

Deb looked at me, "So visual unity with repetition is like using similar navigation buttons, and keeping them in the same place on each page of our site. We're using the elements of design, whatever we might choose, with the principles of direction, balance, and rhythm. We give direction with the navigation, we balance the design with whatever element of design we choose, and the rhythm is created with repetition, like drum beats."

I agreed, "The attribute of repetition affects mostly visual unity," I stated. "But, when the repetition of ideas is carried through the site with your theme, you've also used repetition to create continuity, which affects the intellectual unity of the site."

I turned to write more notes on the board. "Let's talk about how continuity can affect the visual and intellectual unity of your design."

Continuity

"Repetition and proximity are two easy ways to show unity on a single page," I said. "Continuity, however, is a little more subtle – it's how we carry the elements within the principles of design *throughout* the site."

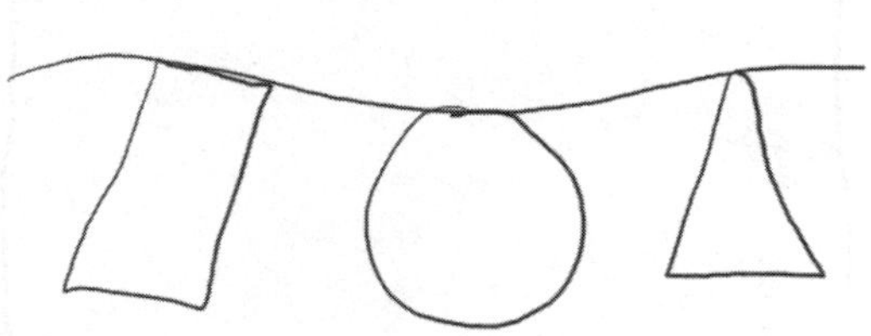

I drew three shapes connected by a wavy line. "I don't have overlapping shapes here," I stated, "But I've connected them with a line. Do they seem unified to you?"

Wes nodded, "They look like clothes hanging on a line during a storm."

"This isn't an inkblot test, Wes," Deb laughed. "But now I can't see anything but clothes hanging on a line!"

"The power of suggestion is an incredible tool," Steve laughed. He continued, "I assume that the continuity in our Flash designs includes the need have some similarities and consistencies from page to page?"

I agreed, "Each object on that line means something different. On Frieda's flowchart, you have a page for her history, a page that introduces her gallery, and a page telling viewers how to contact Frieda. Each page has different information, but you want to unify them with visual images. This would be like that line holding those three shapes together on the board," I added.

"When you design your pages, the navigation tools need to always be in the same place, unless you design the pages to be different. If you design for a client, continuity is good, because that's what most of them automatically want for their sites, whether they state it or not."

"What about continuing color, texture, and all the other elements and principles?" Bonnie asked. "Wouldn't it be good to continue the whole look and theme throughout the site?"

"It's certainly good to keep the whole look and feel, and especially the theme going throughout the site," I agreed. "You can change a few things when you come to certain sections in large sites," I added. "This would indicate to the viewer that they're in a section containing different subjects from what they were viewing before."

"How can we do that and not throw the viewer off?" Lisa asked.

Wes answered, "If you use different shapes for your navigation, you could use repetition, and repeat those particular navigation button on those pages."

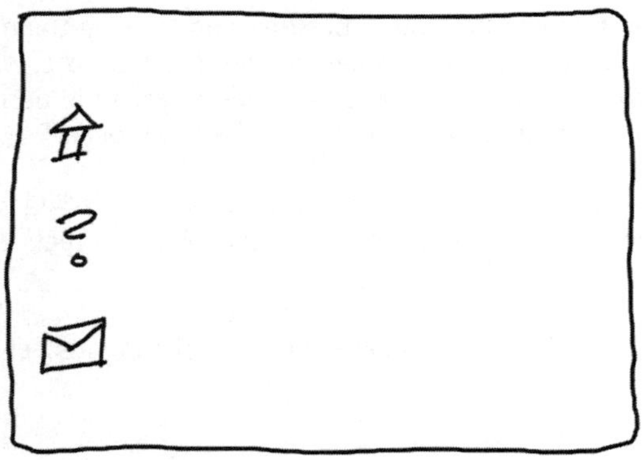

I laughed, "That's an interesting way to handle page changes, Wes. I think I know what you're trying to say." I drew a rectangle on the board, and added several different navigation icons. "Let's say this house indicates *home*, and the question mark indicates *information*, like an FAQ page. The envelope would indicate how to *contact* the site owner."

"Your other pages wouldn't look like this, since they have nothing to do with contact information. But, you could change your pages and still keep unity, since you're continuing the practice of placing the navigation tools on each appropriate page." I drew another page for the information question, "When you click on the contact page, it could have little envelopes in the background. Although each page is different," I added, "We've created unity throughout the site with the running design idea, and we've continued it throughout the site."

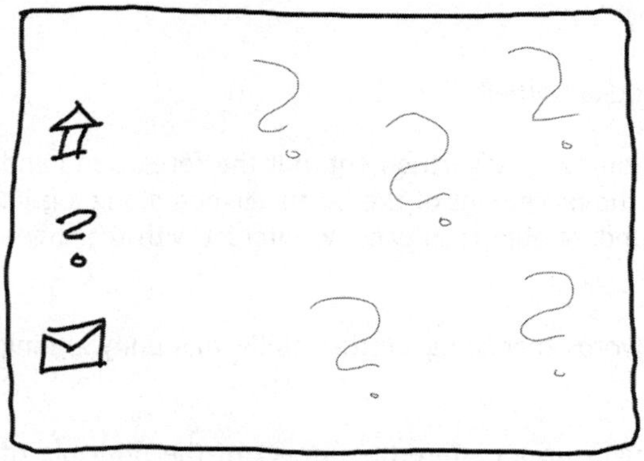

"Plus, the viewer already has repetition and proximity," Deb stated. "We give that to them with the repetition of the navigation devices and the proximity of their placement throughout the site. Even though the navigation symbols on the left of the page are different, they remain the same on each page, and the symbols are reinforced with the background images."

Deb continued, "So we can use any element of design to get our message across as long as we repeat that element to create continuity."

I agreed, "Another way to create continuity throughout a site is with type," I added. "We've talked about how we can create hierarchies of information with headings, subheads, and body copy. When you create these hierarchies, you need to continue them throughout the site. And," I insisted, "Be sure to use the same typefaces throughout the site, too. If you use Verdana for headings and copy on one page, use it on all the other pages, too."

"Using a logo or mark throughout the site helps, too," Lisa stated. "That way we know who or what we're studying as we look through the site."

I agreed, "Think about some other products and how they carry the colors and shapes of the logos or marks throughout their visual communications. The use of repetition to create continuity is a great trick to create memorable designs."

"Theme is important," Steve agreed. "Maintaining a singular goal is crucial for client sites." He looked at Wes, "I imagine it would be important for you to maintain a site that has a single focus, but how would you do that for your artwork?"

Wes thought and answered, "I think I'd have a different section for each *style* of artwork."

"We've already seen how to plan for this using a site map or flow chart for Frieda's site. This would be our clue to continuity," he stated. "I'd utilize the same tool, a flowchart, to build my own site – this would be the map of my design. I could also use it on a page as a site map for the viewer, if the site was very big."

Steve nodded, "Great idea, Wes!"

"You're all on a roll this morning," I said. I looked at Steve, "How would you achieve visual unity with continuity in a magazine article or layout?"

Steve answered immediately, "With grids. I would align elements along a grid," he said, quickly sketching a rough grid on his pad, "Each article would have its own look, but the magazine as a whole would be pulled together with some element of design that would be used throughout."

"Doesn't that get boring?" Deb asked. "Especially if you have to use the same grid month after month?"

Steve grinned, "Not exactly. Even though we use the same grid, there's room to move within that grid. The possibilities are limited only by our imaginations."

"I'm not sure what you mean," Deb stated. "Do you mean you can have variety and still have continuity?"

Steve asked, "Are you familiar with the *Absolut vodka* ads?"

Deb nodded. "Sure. The ads all contain the shape of the vodka bottle."

Steve nodded, "They use a grid to place that bottle shape on every advertisement, but the foreground and background change on every ad. They use continuity with the placement of the bottle aligned along a grid. They also use repetition and proximity, because the surrounding objects in each ad interact with the shape of the bottle."

"That's a good example," I said. "They also use a play on words that brings in the intellectual unity among the ads. Everything is *Absolut* something..."

I nodded my head in Deb's direction, "Deb's actually brought up an interesting aspect of the principle of unity. She wanted to know if you could have variety and still have continuity. Let's talk about variety as an attribute of unity."

Variety

"Steve's example of an ad that maintains continuity, in spite of a number of changes to the information in the ad is ideal. So how can you change your sites so they don't becoming repetitive to the point of boredom?" I asked.

"I thought our sites were supposed to stay the same throughout," Bonnie stated. "Now, you're saying we need to change them so they don't get boring. What can we change, and how much?"

Zed shook his head, "That's what Linda just asked us," he said. "I'll take a stab at the answer. Can I use the board?"

I agreed, and handed him the marker. He began to explain his thoughts as he drew. "I'm drawing a grid, like the ones we can use in Flash," he said. "It's pretty boring, right?"

Everyone nodded. "Now, I'm going to take this grid and erase a line here, and add a line there." He made adjustments to the grid. "We can do this with layers in Flash."

He drew more rectangles with a variety of information in each square. He then drew another grid with the same rectangles, but each one held different information. "These grids aren't perfect, but I hope you all catch my drift," Zed said. "Each layer can contain something different in each page. This way, we have unity with our grid layout, and we have variety with the type of information that we put in each rectangle on each page."

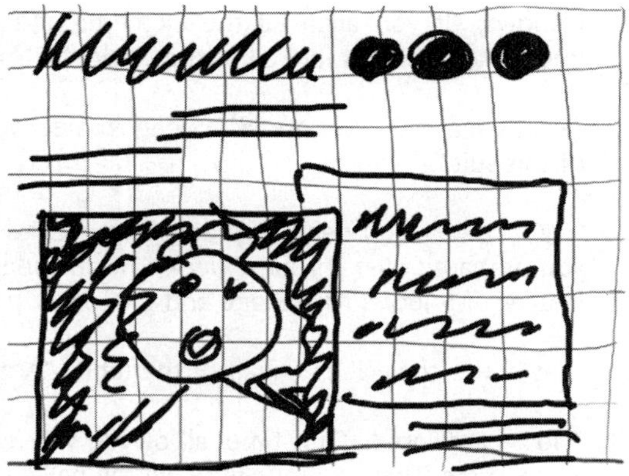

He added, "Of course, you notice that the navigation didn't change places, and the heading and subheading also stayed the same. I want the navigation buttons and header and subhead to stay together to create proximity. Within the first page, I've also created repetition, since the navigation buttons are all the same, and we can assume that the type in the heading and subhead are the same, too. I've continued this repetition and proximity to the next page, and I've also created continuity by creating the same grid spaces, too. But!" he dramatically pointed out, "I've moved the copy and the images within the grid. Therefore," he concluded, "I've also used variety.

"I could use this technique throughout the site to create unity with the attributes of proximity, repetition, continuity, and variety!"

He bowed, and everyone applauded. He slung the scarf over his shoulder as he made his way back to his seat.

"So if we use variety within the sites, then we aren't boring," Bonnie said. "Why do we need variety? Can't we survive with repetition and proximity?"

"If you appear perfect, everyone's going to look for that one fatal flaw, Bonnie." Wes crossed his arms, "I ought to know."

"Actually, Wes has a point," I said. "We're fascinated with pattern, and we're even more fascinated with flaws in patterns, because they provide interest. The Amish actually sew in flaws to their quilts, because they believe anything manmade is imperfect."

"So you want us to create flaws?" Bonnie asked. "I know that's a silly question, but I'm confused."

"It's not a silly question, Bonnie," I answered. "What I'm saying is that you need to create some visual interest so people don't go looking for flaws."

"Oh!" Bonnie sat back. "How far do we go with variety?"

Wes said, "I think I can answer this one. You can go as far as you want, but you might alienate a wide variety of viewers. Plus, most clients won't go for a site that doesn't display any unity because of wide variety. The point is to create a happy balance between boring static sites and a site that goes against the grain so badly that it's difficult for anyone to find anything useful. I would think the best way to handle variety is the way Zed just showed us. Or," he added, "The variety can be created when we add new body copy to the front page on a regular basis, or add new merchandise to a site."

I agreed, "Another way to supply variety, other than changing your information, is by using contrast and/or movement. You all know about movement in static sites as well as in animation. Flash provides you with the means to create variety. As long as you align your focus along the elements and principles of design, you'll have visual unity. And," I added, "As long as you keep the principle of economy in mind, and don't overdo the contrast and movement. Too much variety, as Wes just stated, can create confusion."

Bonnie agreed, "Nothing like confusion to mess up a site's usability and accessibility."

I added, "If you align all the elements and principles of design along a theme, you'll have visual and intellectual unity," I looked at the students. "Are there any questions?"

"Am I sweating?" Wes asked. "I need to meet with Frieda like there's no tomorrow, because I need to get out of this suit."

"OK," I said. "You need to prepare yourselves for your presentations. You'll need your matted images that you prepared over this past week. This includes the large storyboard with the six images, and the two single images of Frieda's homepage and one other page."

I sat in the chair at the head of the table. "Aren't you going to leave?" Zed asked.

"No," I answered. "This time, all of you will leave, and each team will enter one at a time to present their work to me. There's a lounge down the hall to the left. You all can wait there while each team presents their work.

"The first team should arrive in five minutes, and each team has fifteen minutes to present their work."

"We won't get to hear what you tell the other teams!" Deb complained. "I was anxious to hear what you'd have to say about all of our work."

"Not this time," I stated. "You all are bidding for the client's approval, and you're competing against other design teams for the job. When you compete in the real world, you very seldom hear how the other teams were evaluated."

"Well, this sure raises the anxiety level a bit!" Steve grinned, "Actually, I think I'll do better without the rest of you sitting in the corner giggling."

"I'll just go down the hall and giggle," Zed retorted. "C'mon Bonnie. Let's go rehearse."

With that, I knew Zed and Bonnie had opted out of first place. I sat back as the students left, wondering who would knock on the door first.

Presenting the final roughs to the client

The students were ready to present their finalized roughs to the client. As discussed in the previous lesson, these roughs consist of six panels of various pages from the site on a mat board. This storyboard is accompanied by two other matted images: one is a final rough of the home page, and the other is a final rough of some other page in the site.

Confident, self-assured, knowledgeable, and well prepared

Steve and Lisa

After just a few minutes, I answered a knock at the classroom door, greeted Steve and Lisa, and showed them into the room. After we shared a few perfunctory pleasantries, they settled at the table with me. Steve pulled the storyboard and the other two final roughs from his portfolio bag, and began talking about their work.

"Ms. Ray, we've completed some final outlines for your approval. This is what we envision for the general flow of your site." Lisa handed me a flowchart and pulled her chair closer to help me see which pages they chose to show on their storyboard.

"Lisa will show you the pages you're about to see on your flowchart," Steve stated. "We chose the homepage, and a history page. The history page tells a bit about your past, and how you came into the carpentry business."

I nodded, "That's important to me. I'm proud of how I managed to grow this business from my father's previous clientele."

Lisa responded, "We thought you'd be happy with that addition." She pointed at the flowchart. "Here you see we have the homepage at the top, under a splash page, and each subsequent page branching off from the homepage will be linked to and from that page.

"What's a splash page?" I asked.

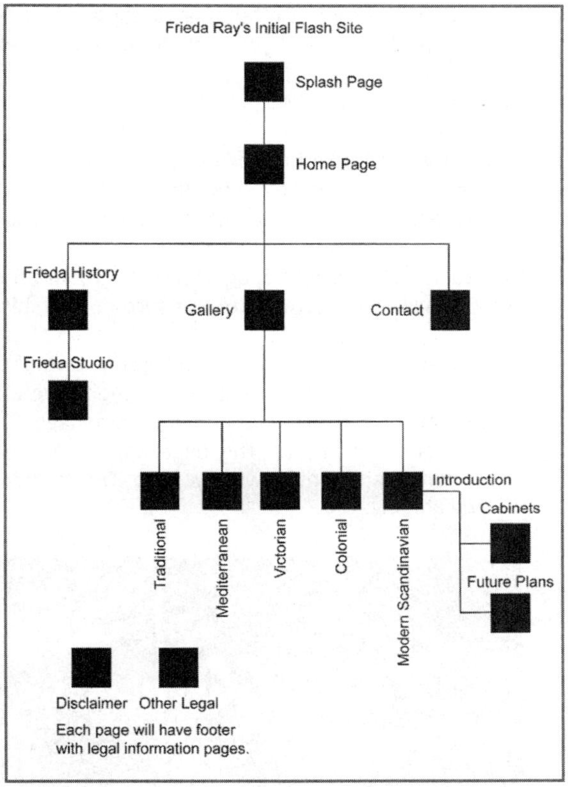

"It's a basic page stating the Flash plug-in requirement for the site," Lisa replied. "If the viewer doesn't have the plug-in they can click on a link to get it. This is just in place to make sure that we can accommodate all of your viewers. The information will be presented along with your logo, as seen on the main page."

I looked at their flowchart, "I see you have a contact page and a gallery of my work."

"There's room to add more, as you see fit," Steve added. "We've left you room to grow on the homepage and within the site itself." He held up the homepage that he and Lisa had designed.

Steve pointed at the ray of light color coming into the page from the upper right corner of the page. "We played on your last name," he explained. "We felt it might be important to you to keep the family name in the business, since you took it over from your father."

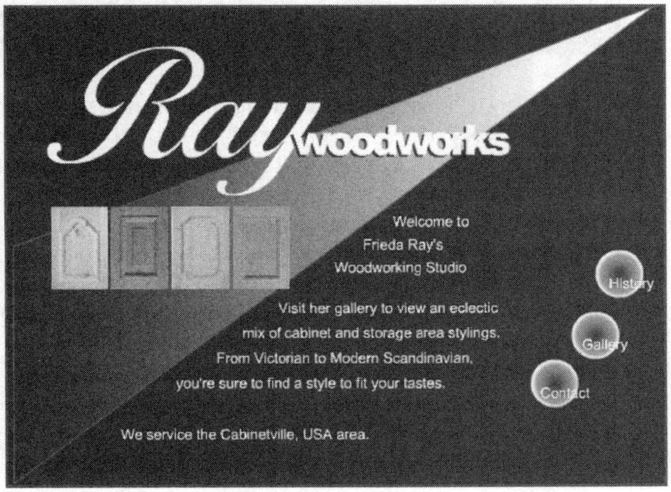

Lisa added, "And, we also felt many people might not take a female carpenter seriously until they got to know you. So we downplayed your role as a female, and honored your role in the family carpentry business."

I grinned, "Tell me more!"

Steve and Lisa looked at each other, Lisa nodded, and Steve continued, "We played off your last name and this ray of light color. You could look at this as a subtle metaphor for being a *ray of light* that will make every homeowner and contractor happy they chose you for their wood storage units."

I asked to see the homepage final rough, and Steve handed it to me. "I like the colors," I said, "But the buttons have me worried. I'm not sure I understand."

Lisa explained, "The buttons are a combination of spotlights and door pulls. We wanted to keep them simple, but we also wanted people to notice them. We didn't want the buttons to compete with the artwork." She pointed at the cabinet doors on the homepage. "This is what's important," Lisa stated. "We wanted to draw the viewer's eye around the page and back up the cabinets. They sit under your name, and act as an underlining statement of what you do. The roundness of the buttons is a nice contrast to the angular nature of the cabinets, too."

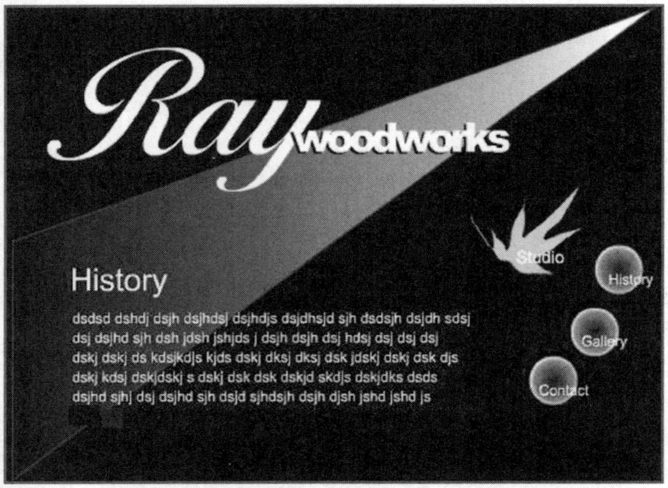

Steve handed me the history page, "Of course we'll need to go over the copy with you, if you approve of the site," Steve said. "We just indicated the copy on the boards until you approve. If we need to make major changes in the copy, it may change the look of the site. This part of the site will be very important, since we feel it will help gain more clientele based on the long history of this business."

"What's the leaf about? It looks like it's falling. I like that," I looked at the images again. "Won't it be hard to read this light type on this dark background?"

Steve answered, "Those images will be the sub-navigation throughout your site. Since we have a studio page under the history page," he referred to the flowchart, "We thought it would be handy to have this link next to the history button. We'll place the leaves for the gallery page in a different place, since we'll have at least five of them," he stated.

Lisa nodded, "We kept the type simple, and laid it out on the leaf the same way it was on the primary navigation images. This way," she added, "Your viewers will know that the leaf is a navigation device." She added, "We're going to lighten up the background a bit. I'm glad you pointed this problem out for us. If it bothers you, we know it will bother the viewers."

I looked at the homepage and history board together, "I'm glad to see that you're going to stay consistent throughout the site. I was a little worried you might design one page to look one way, and another page a different way. I really like consistency."

Steve stood and held up the storyboard so I could see it from where I sat, "We kept the consistency throughout the site," he explained. "As you can see, each page maintains the same colors and layout. The only things that change are the copy and a few bits of artwork."

Lisa then explained to me which images were represented compared to the flowchart. "We felt this would be enough for you to get a good idea of where we'd like to go with your site," Lisa finalized.

"Where will the Flash go?" I asked. "How will things move around, or how will it interact with the viewer?"

Steve explained the rollover buttons, and he talked about how they wanted to work with fading images, "We want to create motion and intensity, but we also want to keep the files sizes small so the site will download quickly and move smoothly for your viewers." He continued to explain how they wanted to keep an elegant style with just enough movement to keep the viewer's interest.

Lisa finished their presentation, "We want to represent you as a solid business-person who's been in business for a long time," she said. "We also wanted to play up your wood work, since that's what you're all about." She pointed out that they noted her business as being located in the Cabinetville area at the bottom of the homepage, and that the contact page would display her business phone, address, and work hours. "We'll also add a footer to each page that will lead people to a disclaimer and privacy statement," Lisa said. "Your customers will be assured that their information will be private, if they contact you for information about your woodworking skills."

When she was finished, they asked if I wanted to keep the boards to take a closer look at them at my leisure. "I don't think I need them right now," I responded. "But I would like to go over some copy with you soon. I want to make sure we include everything, including cabinet woods, sizes, and prices."

Steve stopped and thought a minute, "Ms. Ray, I hope you don't mind if I make a suggestion."

I nodded for him to continue, "If you were a much larger business with a huge inventory, I would suggest you list prices on your site. Since you're a smaller business catering to a very specific area, I really don't think prices are necessary."

"Why not?" I asked.

Steve sat back in his chair and began to explain his reasoning, "Because your work is dependent on the amount of work you do, and the type of wood you use. Your designs are custom-made, and susceptible to price variations. I think it would suffice to include a blurb about calling for quotes, rather than to state an actual price for each cabinet."

"That's a fairly reasonable explanation, and a good reason for me to keep prices off my site. Thanks, Steve," I said. I looked at my watch, "Look at that! Fifteen minutes has already come and gone."

The student designers both stood, and Steve held out his hand to shake mine, "I hope you approve of the site, Ms. Ray." He nodded toward Lisa, "We're enjoying the work."

I asked them both to sit back down for just a minute for a little bit of feedback, "I just wanted to tell you both that your presentation storyboards were immaculate. They were mounted perfectly, and the images were sharp. I was able to visualize everything you told me, and you raised some interesting points during your talk.

"The point about downplaying Frieda's role as a female was interesting and well-made," I added. "She might take offense at this decision, but you put it so well that I wasn't about to debate the issue with either of you. Plus," I added, "This point came from Lisa. Did you both plan this?"

Lisa blushed, "I insisted that I would be the one to say it," she said. "I thought the point might be better taken coming from a woman."

"That might not be the case," I replied. "Sometimes women will trust a man's opinion far more than another woman's thoughts. But, we'll say Frieda Ray respects anyone who's spent time on her site."

Lisa blew out a breath, "I was worried about that one. Thanks." She looked at Steve, "You sure pulled the pricing issue out of your hat. That was interesting."

I agreed, "Good point on the pricing on the site, Steve. Frieda may choose to keep the pricing, but your argument for flexibility was good. You don't want to change her site every time her prices change, too. But you don't want to tell the client that one."

Steve grinned, "I never tell clients how I make my life easier."

Lisa and I laughed. "I think we'd better send you back to the lounge," I said. "The others are probably wondering what's going on in here. I'll have more to say to you both when we resume class. Do you have any questions?"

"Is this where we ask you to sign a contract?" Lisa asked.

"Good question Lisa," I answered. I noticed Steve slapping his forehead with the palm of his hand, and I laughed. "This is where you'd pull out the contract, yes."

Steve laughed, "I forgot all about the contract. I hardly handle the business end at work, even though I make quite a few presentations. It just slipped my mind."

Lisa smiled, "We may love our work, Steve, but it sure would be nice to be paid, too."

Steve agreed wholeheartedly, and he and Lisa gathered their work and prepared to leave. Before they left, I commended them on their short presentation, "You both seemed confident, self-assured, knowledgeable, and well-prepared," I said. "Although we hit a few rough spots, like forgetting to ask for the signature on a contract, I think you both defended every element you put into this site. You both were also very sensitive about the gender issue, and you offered advice based on your experiences. You also took my criticism well. Excellent job!"

As they left, I made some notes about their presentation:

- Be knowledgeable about your designs
- Act self-assured in presentation
- Be confident about design choices
- Have well-prepared images and presentations
- Offer advice based on experience
- Be sensitive about gender issues
- Don't forget to ask for a contract
- Take criticism with grace

Inflexible, nervous, and over prepared

Zed and Bonnie were next up, and I answered their knock on the door. I noticed Zed wasn't wearing his scarf, and he was standing behind Bonnie. I asked them to come in, and I sat at the table.

Bonnie set up an easel, and placed their storyboard on the lip. Zed pulled out the two other images. One was the homepage, and one was a history page. Zed placed them carefully on the table in front of me, and he continued to stand, holding his hands in front of him.

Bonnie produced a pointer from her portfolio bag, and proceeded with her presentation, "Ms. Ray, we'd like to show you how we envisage your site." She pointed to the first panels in the storyboard.

"We incorporated your cabinets as a background on the homepage. This is the page you have on the table to your left."

I picked up the image and began to study it. "This is nice and simple. I like it," I stated.

Bonnie smiled, "When people come to your site," she stated, "They won't get the wrong impression about what you do. They'll also notice where you're located, and how to contact you immediately."

She pointed to the other panel on the table with the pointer. "As you can see, we pull back the cabinets on the Flash site to allow more room for copy and for other images."

"Won't it look a bit busy with this image constantly in the background?" I asked. I noticed Zed had shifted on his feet.

"Not at all, Ms. Ray," Bonnie continued. "We'll fade the background back and make sure the site appears unified throughout." She turned her pointer to the storyboard, "Each page will be similar throughout the site, as you can see.

"We included a page about your history, and why this is important to you and your clients. If you notice, we just indicated the type until you approve of the copy. We have a gallery, and we also included a map to your office on the contact page." She continued to point at each page on the storyboard as she explained what they had to offer.

"How will the Flash work on this site?" I asked.

Bonnie pointed at the cabinets on the homepage image lying on the table. "The cabinets will slide back to reveal a space with text and images. Plus," she added, "The buttons will be what we call *rollovers*. As the viewer rolls the mouse over each button, some text will reveal where that button will take them."

I nodded, "Are the buttons clear? I mean, will the viewer intuitively know where to go?" I noticed Zed was rocking back and forth on his feet. He seemed uncomfortable.

"Why don't you both sit for a moment?" I suggested. They both sat on either side of me, and I asked them the question again. "How will the viewer know where to go with these buttons?"

Bonnie answered, "The text will show to the left of the buttons when the viewer rolls the mouse over each button."

I pointed at the history page, and then leaned back, "I don't know. It seems my eyes are jumping between the buttons and the text, and then up to the text on the left top of the page. The page doesn't seem unified. Maybe you can work on this?"

Zed seemed ready to reply, but Bonnie interrupted, "We sure will, Ms. Ray." She paused for a moment and continued. "We thought that using your name would add a personal touch to the site," she said.

I looked at the homepage again, "I hope you don't mind, but I'm not sure if *fine cabinets* means I'm a carpenter or an interior designer. Although I'm a mix of both, I want the viewer to be sure that I build cabinets."

Zed reached into his pocket for a small notepad and pen. He began to write notes.

I continued, "Is my name this big throughout the site?"

Bonnie nodded, "We left it that way, yes. Your name in this instance is the logo. This tells the viewer that they're on your page, and it imprints your name in their minds."

I nodded, "I'd like the name to be a bit smaller, just the same." Zed jotted this down in his notes.

I turned to Zed, "Young man, what are you doing?" I smiled as he fumbled with the notepad.

"Just taking notes on your comments, Ms. Ray. I hope you don't mind?"

I looked at Bonnie and back at Zed, and went back to being Linda, "Just what kind of setup do you have here?"

"What do you mean?" Bonnie asked. "We're presenting our work to you."

"Bonnie, you are presenting the work, but I think it's a little too formal for a small audience. I thought you were going to hit me with that pointer a few times!"

Zed stifled a laugh and Bonnie looked angry, "But we want to appear professional. I thought this would be the way to go."

"This would be the way to go if you were presenting to a boardroom full of people," I stated. "But it's just me, pretending to be Frieda Ray. Although you're full of good intentions, I'm going to make a few suggestions that might help you both relax."

I held out my hand and asked for their presentation storyboard. Bonnie handed it to me, and I looked at the quality of their work. "The presentation storyboard and the other two matted images are well done," I began. "Don't be afraid to hand them to the client if you're not afraid of them seeing the images closeup." I looked at the history page again. "We've got some work to do on this page, but we'll get to that when we go to the computers after this process."

Zed leaned back in his chair, "I was ready to tell you, when you were Frieda, that we could overlap the text and the cabinets so the page would look more unified. But," Zed said, "I was afraid you wouldn't be interested in the solution to the problem." He looked at Bonnie. "Plus, I was told to be quiet."

Bonnie looked flustered, "I asked you to be quiet back in the lounge. I didn't mean to be quiet here. I felt like I was floundering without your input."

"Oh!" Zed leaned forward and snatched the pointer off the table. "I'm sorry. I thought you were going to whack me with this thing if I opened my mouth!"

I laughed, "Well, that's one mystery solved. I couldn't figure out how you managed to keep Zed so quiet, Bonnie."

"I usually talk with my clients on the phone while wearing my robe," Bonnie stated. "I think I've presented work to a client in person only once. That was with someone I knew fairly well, so the presentation was more informal."

"This is fairly informal, too, Bonnie," I stated. "Try to think how a client feels when they're sitting and you're standing. If it's two to one, like the odds between you two and Frieda, this can be pretty intimidating to the client."

"Oh," Bonnie nodded, "I didn't think of that."

Zed sighed, "I didn't feel we were ready to show to a client anyway. The site is so... unfinished."

"That's OK, Zed," I replied. "You're showing the client final roughs, not a finalized site. This gives the client a feel of what you intend to do, and how you plan to utilize the site. You both have continuity throughout the site, and with just a little tweaking, I think you have a great presentation on your hands."

Bonnie asked, "Would we go through another stage of showing finalized roughs to the client if they didn't like the first set?"

"That's completely feasible," I answered. "In fact, it doesn't hurt to have up to three ideas to show the client at this stage. No more than three, though," I added. "More than three ideas will make the client think you don't know what you're doing, and they will have too much to choose from."

"Gosh, just one idea was hard enough," Zed stated. "Three ideas would kill me!"

"Once you get the elements and principles of design ingrained in your mind and hand, the ideas won't be so hard to render," I responded. "In fact, there will be many times when you won't be able to choose just one idea yourself, and you'll need the client's input."

I looked at my watch – twenty minutes had passed, "I hate to break this off, but you both need to send Wes and Deb in for their presentation. Let me say your storyboards were perfect. If you relax, and allow the client to become part of the process, then you'll both do well," I said.

I added some more compliments and critique to their presentation, "Be prepared to talk about more than one idea, and understand these are *finalized roughs*, not the actual site. Let the client hold them and look at them closely. Also, be yourselves." I smiled at Zed.

Zed breathed a sigh of relief, "I think we could have done better, but I sure learned a lot." He looked at Bonnie, "How about you?"

"Oh sure," Bonnie laughed. "I learned how to use that pointer without poking anyone's eye out."

We laughed, and Bonnie and Zed gathered their things and left. As I waited for Wes and Deb, I made some more notes about their presentation:

- Be relaxed during your presentation
- Sit if possible - try to not intimidate the client by standing over them
- Be prepared to talk about more than one idea
- Let the client touch the presentation images
- Don't be afraid to talk about site changes if needed
- Be yourself, but be respectful to the client

Team bickering, over anxiousness, and poor attention to detail

Wes and Deb

The third and last team of Wes and Deb were about to arrive. The knock came on the classroom door, and I welcomed them into the room. They immediately engaged me in idle chatter, and as I sat at the head of the table, they joined me, one on either side.

"We're excited about our design for your business," Deb stated. "We've researched your competition, and they have nothing compared to what we've designed for you."

Wes nodded, "Your competitors' sites are static, and they seem to be outdated." He pointed to their homepage image. "This site will be pleasing to the viewer and will let the viewer interact with the images as well."

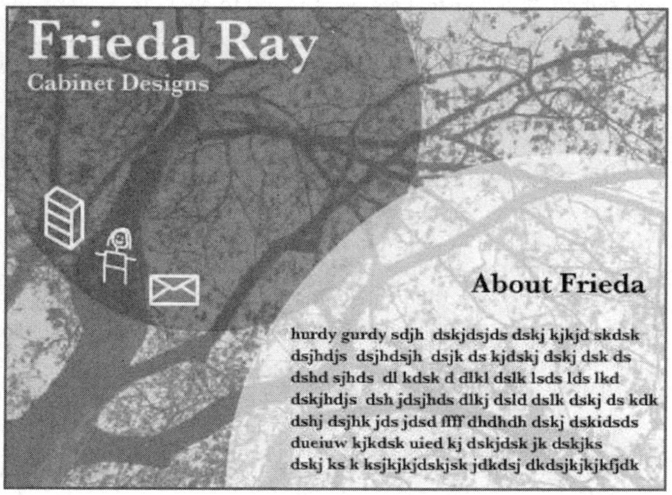

Deb showed me the *about* page, "This is really our history page; it talks about you and how you came into the business. We felt this part of your life was important to present to your future potential clients."

"I like the general organic feel of this image," I stated. "Is this my logo?"

Deb smiled, "We wanted to present you as a natural artist. These navigation logos give an informal feel to the site, and the tree in the background brings in the natural elements."

"I like that idea," I said. "My only complaint is that I don't see any of my work or the idea of my work on any of the pages outside of the gallery."

Wes looked at Deb, and she answered, "Well, the tree represents your love of natural products, but I guess we didn't make that statement clearly."

Wes nodded, "I think we can remedy this situation, Ms. Ray. I have a few ideas that may help the viewer understand what your site is about."

I leaned forward, "Tell me what you have in mind."

Wes took a deep breath and ignored Deb, who was glaring at him, "Well, I feel that we need to have more of a wood grain image, something that will bring the tree closer to the viewer. This way," he added, "They will feel that they're coming as close to nature as you do with your work."

He continued, "Plus, I would probably use a green circle instead of this red one. The green would be calming, and would remind the viewer of nature. I would also remove these frivolous buttons and replace them with images that would better represent your interest in shapes and lines within the modern Scandinavian line of design."

I glanced at Deb. She was listening to Wes with interest, "I like those ideas," I said. "Why don't you take the work and make these changes and come back to see me when you have them finalized?"

Deb shook herself and looked at me. "I'm sorry we weren't better prepared, Ms. Ray. Before we leave, I'd like to ask you if you like the idea of the site. We've included a gallery, this page about you, and a contact page. We felt this was a good start for your site, and it allows room for expansion as your business grows."

I looked at their homepage storyboard, and rubbed off a piece of rubber cement along the edge of one of their images.

"I like the continuity throughout the site. It seems very unified, except for the button images. They just don't seem to belong to the elegance of the tree and the simple circular shapes. But, I'm happy with the work so far."

Deb asked, "Would you be willing to sign a contract with us? We'll be happy to leave the paperwork with you and return in a few days with the finalized design."

"I'd be happy to look over the contract," I said. "But right now I'm going to leave Frieda behind and give you both some feedback about this session."

Wes sat back and Deb dropped a pen she was holding in her hand. The clatter of the pen falling to the table startled Wes. "I'm sorry!" he said. He leaned on the table toward Deb, "I like this design, but some elements are going to kill it for us."

Deb shrugged, "You're the artist."

I held up my hands, "Whoa, both of you." I looked at them both. "Obviously there's been a little tension about this design between you two, and it shows. You can't walk into a presentation with a client without some unification between you, because the client will smell the discontent a mile away."

Deb sighed, "I know. I feel I can't have any input, because Wes seems to think he's always right."

"About design issues, yes, I'm right," Wes stated. "But that's the only thing I feel competent with. You're the one that's got the writing and business experience. I feel we can both learn from each other, but you seem to get so defensive when I criticize any of your ideas. They just don't work for this site."

Wes leaned down to pull a notepad from his briefcase, "I have something to show you," he said. He flipped the pages of his notebook and showed Deb his sketches. "I've taken notes and drawn sketches on every idea you've had. Although they aren't appropriate for this site, they may work for another job down the road."

Deb looked at Wes's notes and sketches, "I had no idea you kept track of all my ideas," she said. "I wish I'd known you were doing this. I feel a little more important with this process now."

"Deb, don't forget that Wes has many years of art training. He truly understands the elements and principles of design. You, on the other hand, have many years training in writing and programming. I thought you two would be a great combination for this project." I leaned back in my chair, "This is a perfect time to be learning from each other, rather than be worried about how much input you have in the project," I added.

Deb smiled. "Wes just drives me nuts," she said. She looked at him. "There's something about you that makes me want to do the exact opposite of what you want."

I laughed, "Deb, I think you've been working around competitive situations far too long. You've quit your job. This is supposed to be a learning experience, not a contest."

"Thanks for that, Linda," Wes said. He looked over at Deb. "Now, can we work on this design together?"

"I'll try," Deb grinned. She turned back to me, "I have a question about the contract. Would it be better to get the signature right away or is it OK to leave the contract with the client?"

"Good question, Deb," I said. "It varies on the situation. The preference would be to get an immediate signature. But, if the client isn't happy with the design I would suggest leaving the contract out of the picture until you return with the revisions."

"We didn't discuss hosting or any of the management issues with you, either," Wes stated. "I think we jumped the gun on the contract issue."

Deb nodded in agreement, "I guess you both are right."

"You can leave the contract with the client, but it's best to be on hand to discuss the issues with the client, and have them sign it in front of you. This way, you both are assured the client understands each point in the contract," I said. "I'll bring this topic up again when we're all together, so all of you will hear the questions and answers on this subject." I added, "You're not the only team with questions about the contract."

I looked at their presentation boards, "These could be in better shape," I stated. "I rolled some rubber cement off the edge of one of your images. I'm not sure I noticed it because I'm trained to notice these things, or whether it would have caught my attention anyway as a client."

Wes sighed, "I hate rubber cement. It stinks, and I can't seem to get it all off."

"Did you use the rubber cement pick-up block?" I asked.

"No, because I couldn't find it in all my junk at the studio," Wes admitted. Deb's smug look crept onto her face, and Wes noticed. "Like I said, I'm only good at art, not at anything else."

Deb laughed, "Don't play martyr, Wes. I saw the rubber cement pick-up block on the floor by your desk at the studio." She looked at me, "I didn't look at the boards because of some little argument I had with Wes. But I won't let that get in the way of my professionalism any more, I promise."

Wes rolled his eyes and then focused on me, "What's an artist to do?"

We all laughed, and I asked if one of them would ask the other students to return to the classroom. Deb left, and Wes caught my attention. He whispered, "How does a guy make a girl like that relax?"

I shrugged and grinned, "That's your problem, Wes. To be honest, I think she might ask the same question of you."

Wes looked shocked, and then laughed, "Maybe you're right, Linda. Maybe you're right."

Deb returned with the other two teams in tow as I wrote down my notes about this last presentation:

- Be prepared with clean images and presentations
- Be confident about your design before you present it
- Ask client for feedback and input
- Be honest about problems
- Don't present a contract if client isn't happy

If presenting as a team:

- Don't bicker in front of client, present a unified front
- Don't be defensive in your presententation

Processing the client feedback

As the students settled down, none of them seemed comfortable with their recent experiences. This would be the time to talk about how to process the client's feedback so their designs and plans with the client could solidify. In particular, I wanted to talk about a concern of everyone's – when to enter into a contract with the client.

"Before we begin," I said, "I want to heap praises on you all for a very interesting experience. Each team took a different approach, and I was happy to see some diversity among you. I made some notes about each of your presentations, and I'll type them up and give you all a list of *do's and don'ts*."

"We could have done better," Bonnie stated. "I really botched things up."

"I'm not surprised to hear that for some reason," Wes laughed. "What happened?"

Zed hooted, "Bonnie's pointer got out of control."

Everyone laughed as Zed began waving his arm in the air like Zorro, "She was the queen of out-of-control!"

Bonnie blushed, "It was a misunderstanding, believe me."

"Oh, we believe you," Lisa grinned. "I think we were all out of control."

"You all did great," I insisted. "It's hard to role-play, and I'm sure you all would have acted a bit differently with a real client. When we're faced with difficult situations, we tend to find out our weaknesses in a hurry. That's why we went through this process." I spread my arms to encompass the group. "You all had the same questions on the contract issue. Let's talk about this subject, and then we'll discuss anything else that comes to mind."

contract - timing

I went to the board started to write, "The contract timing is a very important issue. You want a client happily signing the contract with few or no questions beyond a few clarifications here and there," I said. "I'm not going to discuss what you need to include in the contract, because that will vary with each client. You will know what you can offer the client. If you can't offer something, say hosting the client site, hopefully you'll have access to information or sources that will help you do this for the client."

I pointed at the two words on the board, "The timing of the contract is the important issue. All of you knew, either through instinct or experience, that the contract issue would come up at this point in your relationship with the client."

I held out my hand toward Wes and Deb, "Deb wanted to leave the contract with the client. How do the rest of you feel about this?"

Steve immediately answered, "Unless the client is someone who is at a distance, I wouldn't do that."

"Why not, Steve?" Lisa asked.

"I would prefer to be with the client to talk about the contract and answer any questions. Then, I would hand them the pen to sign in front of me." He thought for a moment and added, "I only had to do this one time, and it scared the pants off me. I felt so pushy, I guess that's why some of the other guys at the studio handle the business affairs of our clients."

"They taught you well, though, Steve," I responded. "It's best to sit with the client, and it's even better to hand them the pen. This way," I added, "They feel they need to respond by taking the pen from your hand. Once they have that pen, it's hard for them not to sign."

"That sounds pretty pushy," Wes stated. "In fact, it sounds downright manipulative."

"It is," Deb agreed, "But it works. If it makes you feel any better, most business people know this tactic, and they're often highly amused at the gesture. But," she added, "They also know that you're one of them. They see you as a person who is well-versed in business and sales procedures."

"Oh," Lisa muttered. "I see how that works. If you do these business tricks, the client will see you as one of them, and that will help create a bond."

"It's purely hypothetical, but yes," I replied. "This is why many design companies separate the business side from the design departments. There are those who don't mind putting a pen in a client's hand, and there are those who feel very uncomfortable doing this. When you have your own business, you can't have a problem handing the pen to the client, or you'll starve."

Bonnie laughed, "Thank goodness I do my work over the Internet. I couldn't stand handing the pen to the client."

Zed asked, "How do you get the client to sign an online contract?"

"I state the urgency of signing the contract before any other work is completed," Bonnie answered. "I tell them I'm available to answer any questions, and that as soon as I receive the signed contract, the work will be done according to the timetable in the contract. I've never had any problems," she added. "If they don't sign and return the contract after three days, I contact them to ask if there's any questions. If not, and they hesitate to sign, I remind them that they approved of the design, and I ask why they haven't signed."

She continued, "If it's a time issue, I remind them that they need to sign in order to get the design online. If it's any other issue, I give them reasons why they should sign. If I spend too much time on the contract, I figure they were just pulling me around, and I move on to jobs that will bring in money."

Steve nodded, "I think that's why we need to qualify the client before we even begin any work for them. If we complete a client brief, and they're willing to sign an NDA, then I would think they're serious about doing the work."

I agreed, "Once you get a client's signature, whether it's on an NDA or a contract, you know they're serious about the work. A signature isn't frivolous. It's a commitment for most people."

"So we shouldn't ask a client to sign a contract if they're not happy with our work, right?" Deb asked. "I think I jumped the gun on our deal."

Zed looked confused, "Frieda didn't like your design?" he asked. "That makes me feel a little better!"

"Thanks a lot, Zed," Wes laughed. "I have a gut feeling we all have a lot of work cut out for us yet."

"Let me answer Deb," I grinned, "And then we'll start to think about getting that work done." I turned to Deb, "I wouldn't leave a contract with a client, especially if they're hesitant about the design. If you can push them over with a few more visuals, I would wait and return with the visuals and the contract."

I added, "You might also work with clients without a contract. These are known as *handshake deals*. The client commissions the work, and you accept the work without a contract, NDA, or anything that will secure the money for your time."

Bonnie shuddered, "I haven't been paid for any of the handshake deals I've made over the past two years," she stated. "Unless I know the client well, or I've experienced their reliability in the past, I insist on a contract. If they don't want to sign, then I feel I've saved myself time and effort."

I nodded at Bonnie, "There's another side of the issue though, where you *want* to trust the customer. When you don't get a signature, it's not a matter of whether the client will trust you, it's a matter of whether you will trust the client."

Steve agreed, "We have clients that date back for years. I don't know that they sign contracts for each job, but I do know that we can trust these clients, because they pay. I think the guys at the office don't take on new clients unless they sign something. It doesn't matter if they're little guys or corporations," he added.

"Sounds like you both have had some experience with contracts," I said. "Especially, you, Bonnie. I think it's a personal decision, if you work alone. If you work for a larger company, someone else might make that decision for you."

"It was hard presenting the work to you today, Linda," Bonnie said. "A regular client that wasn't versed in design wouldn't see what you did. They would either like the work or not. Sometimes," she added, "They would want to make their own changes. That's the hard part, especially if I have to tell them why their ideas won't work."

Wes looked at Deb. "Tell me about it," he commented.

"The client is always right?" Zed asked.

"No, invariably they're not, Zed," I answered. "But, you can help make them feel they're part of the process if they want this. It's a lot of work and mental maneuvering, but always remember that, ultimately, you're the designer and they're the client. If you're subtle about this, they'll understand that they need to trust you with the design side of the project. However," I added, "They may have some valuable insights into your work. Don't discount what the client has to offer. As I mentioned last week," I added, "You can make those suggested changes on the sheet that covers your artwork, or on the artwork itself. These are final roughs, not the Mona Lisa. Changes are bound to happen, and it could come from the client or from yourself."

Before I offered the students a break, I asked if there were any other questions about the client evaluation.

"We're at the end of the creative problem-solving circle," Zed stated. "Does this mean that we start at the beginning again?"

Steve answered for me, "It makes sense, doesn't it? We now have a new set of problems to resolve, so we start at the top to define the problems and analyze the possible solutions."

I agreed, "You all just had a taste of the client evaluation," I said. "The most important issue related to the contract and how to present it to the client. Always have the contract on hand, but be aware of each point in the contract so you can discuss it with the client. Timing is important, as well as your business acumen. The client needs to be happy, have faith in your progress and professionalism. And," I reminded them, "Always have a pen handy that is full of ink and ready for the client to use as they sign the papers.

"Each team had problems with their presentations and with their designs. However," I added, "Every team also had solid reasons for each element in the site designs.

"Every one of you stressed the importance of Frieda's history in her business. This was a great way to appeal to the client's sense of pride." I continued, "Every team also showed continuity throughout the site designs. Some of you need to work on tweaking some of the individual elements, but the sites are well thought out. It was obvious that you all researched your subject.

"Take a break," I said, "And when you return, we'll start to think about on some of the issues and potential problems associated with designing in Flash."

The students seemed relieved they made it through this process. They all made a beeline for the door, ready to change into more comfortable clothes.

Ideas for working on the designs in Flash

In this part of the class, I wanted the class to start thinking more about where they were going to take their designs next. So, in the hope of generating some more ideas, I decided to give a little teaser of the Flash MX functionality. My plan was to work with the roughs of one of the student design groups and incorporate some dynamic or interactive Flash effects. Then, next week, we'd regroup and talk about whatever other ideas they come up with.

As the students returned from their break, and sat down, I turned to Bonnie and Zed and asked them to pull their design up on the screen. Bonnie instantly opened up the main page.

"So, now we want to start thinking about what Flash can do to enhance our designs. How do you intend to make your design work in Flash MX?" I asked.

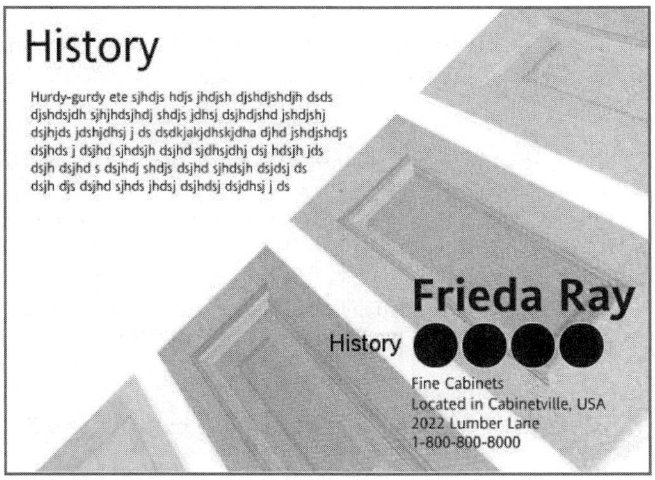

Bonnie and Zed sat scrutinizing the designs on-screen. Bonnie then sat up, clicked open their history page, and pointed towards the upper left-hand portion of the page, "Well, it might only seem like only a minor detail, but I think we need some kind of *smoothing* to make our copy-holding triangle appear on screen." Said Bonnie. "If the shape was to simply appear out of nowhere, it'd feel like I might as well be working in HTML. I suppose I want to get as much out of Flash MX as possible for this."

"You've already heard me say about not using functionality purely because it's available, but for minor details like this – of which each feature will add to the overall design, feel, and professionalism – I think it's worth exploring them. These are the details that make animated Flash sites stand out over static HTML sites."

"The cross-browser and cross-platform compatibility also gives me a lot of confidence when it comes to making decisions on things like this," said Bonnie. "With JavaScript and DHTML animation, it was usually a case of limiting certain aspects with the design because of the major rendering differences on the user's side."

"OK, so what about just animating the triangle?" said Zed. "We could use an alpha tween as a transition, like we did with text in the lesson on typography effects in Flash. The corner triangle could reveal itself when the user clicks on one of the buttons."

"This is certainly one possibility, Zed. But you could place more emphasis on the information by making this triangle move onto the screen. The dynamic of the shape moving onto the stage from off it certainly pulls the eye towards it."

Bonnie agreed, "Using animation for impact sounds like the way to go. It'll also make Frieda's site stand out over the plain old HTML sites of the other carpenters."

"I guess we could even use a different color triangle for each section," said Zed. "We could color code the triangles to coordinate with the buttons."

"Actually, I also wanted to talk to you about your buttons," I said. "The way you have them at the moment is what is known in web design as *Mystery Meet*.

"Mystery Meet refers to links or hyperlinks that don't reveal their destination or action until you click on them. The most extreme example of this is a number of identical uniform buttons, each leading to different locations."

"You mean, because all our buttons look the same, the user won't know where they are going?" asked Bonnie.

"Sure. If you don't explicitly show the user the different options, then they will be meeting with the unknown," I offered.

Bonnie pointed to the area to the left of the buttons, in particular the word *History* in this region of the history page, "But this area will change to provide the user with information about each button. Isn't this enough?"

"Although this might seem like enough, the fact is that the user will need to rollover every button to see what the available options are," I said. "If the options are on display immediately, then it saves the user the task of discovering and remembering the available sections. I'm a little surprised that this passed you by Bonnie."

"My hyperlinks are usually displayed in text," said Bonnie. "So I often don't have to think about this. I rarely place hyperlinks on anything else, unless it's for enlarging images or a visual use, in which case I'll link from the image."

"Visual clues are what we need on these buttons," said Zed. "We'll have to work on this for the final design."

"If you make the buttons individual with different graphics," I said, "Make sure that you provide some rollover text to reinforce it. Ambiguous images or icons can mean different things to different people, so it's always best practice to be straight with them. I pointed at Frieda's name on the screen. "You'll want to make Frieda's name a bit smaller. This way, it won't seem so obvious, and it will also align on the right with the buttons.

"Are there any other animated elements you intend to use?" I asked.

"Zed wanted to go crazy with animation!" said Bonnie. "Luckily, he's started on his anime cartoon outside of class and seems to have got it out of his system."

"I still think we need some form of intro or way to draw the interface," enthused Zed. "Like the triangle we talked about earlier, I don't like the idea of the website just appearing out of thin air. It should be drawn piece by piece, in front of the viewer's eyes."

"I must admit that I'm pretty keen on this idea too," said Bonnie. "For too long now, my web pages have just appeared in the browser window, and Flash websites seem to have a definite smooth flow to them."

I was hoping that Bonnie would mention the fluidity of a typical Flash site, "This is because they can optionally be displayed piece by piece through animation or masking. If you want to only display, or gradually display a portion of your image, then you'll find masks in Flash MX particularly useful."

"Masks? You mean like those in Photoshop?" asked Steve.

"Well, it's the same principle Steve, but not quite as flexible. As you probably know, in Photoshop, masks allow you to control the opacity of a layer, but Flash is limited to a mask being either on or off."

"Err, so what exactly is a mask?" Zed asked.

> *"A mask is simply a device that controls what portion of an image is displayed, making it useful for trimming or framing elements of an image. Practically speaking, they work in the opposite way that you might expect: when you create a mask in Flash, you are defining the area of the image that you want to show with your mask shape, not the area that you want to cover."*

I continued, "Masks can also be useful for creating any number of cool effects, so let's take a look at them in action as part of your design!"

Using masks to create dynamic transitions in your Flash designs

"There are a number of ways to perform masking in Flash, but the simplest way is to turn a layer into a masking layer. Let me show you all how easy it can be."

I sat at Bonnie's machine and created a new Flash movie, importing a JPEG image of their background design, `cabinet_diagonal.jpg`, into the existing layer, which I renamed image. Clicking Insert > Layer, I added a new layer, which I then labelled mask, and drew a bright green square onto it.

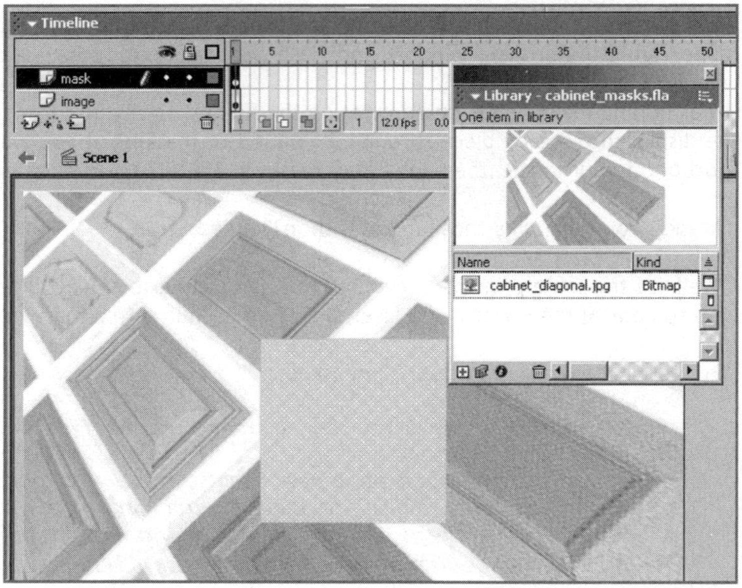

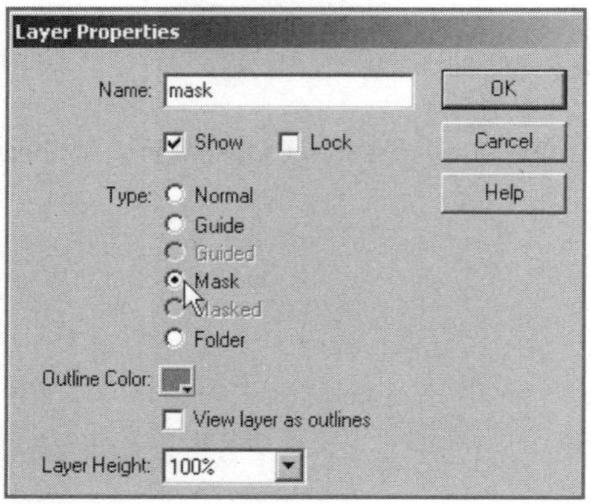

"At the moment, this is just an ugly green square in front of your image. Now, if I double click on the mask layer to bring up the Layer Properties window, I can change its Type to Mask. I'll click OK and you'll notice that the layer icon will visibly change.

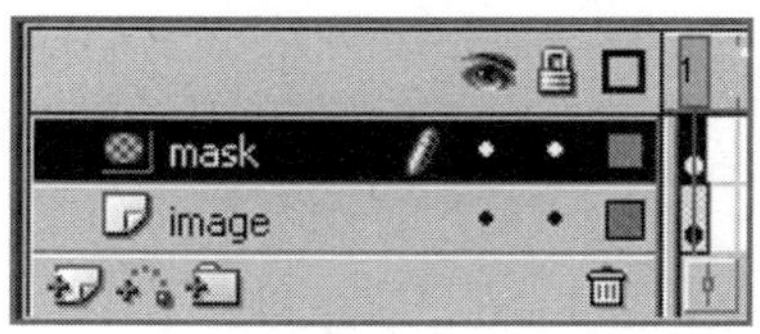

"Even though the layer is now a mask layer, it isn't actually masking anything just yet. The image layer needs to be *told* that we want it to be masked by the other layer. So, when I drag the image layer up to meet the mask layer, an indented shadow to the right of the layer icon appears."

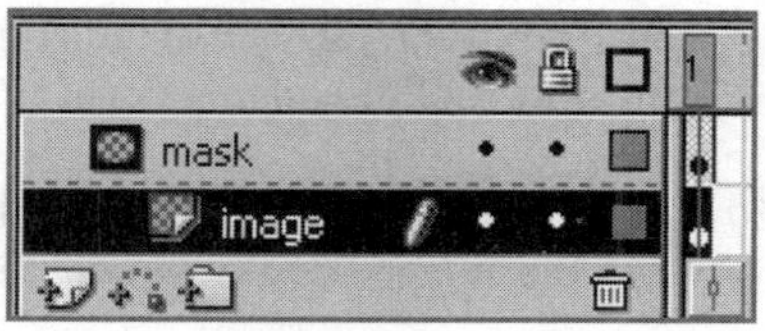

"When I release the image layer onto the mask layer, the image layer icon is indented and changed. The image is now masked by the content of the layer above it – the mask layer.

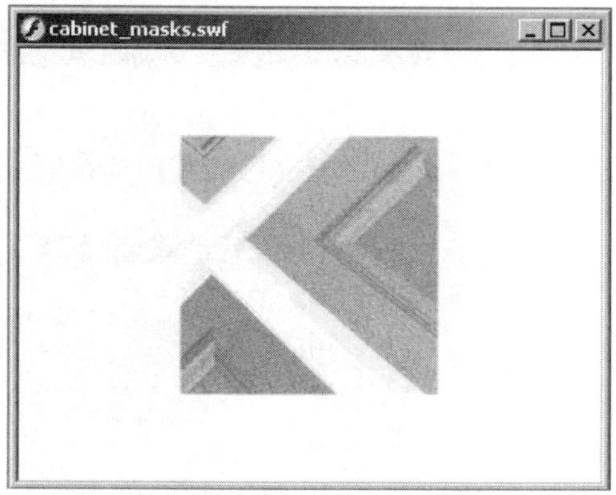

"When the movie is published or tested, Control > Test Movie, the masking is clearly seen. If you want to stop a particular layer being masked, change the layer type back to normal via the Layer Properties dialog.

"If you want to check the masking within the Flash environment without having to publish the movie, just lock all the mask and masked layers in the timeline and you can see a preview" I locked both the layers in the movie and showed them how this worked.

"It might also be useful for you to know that you can mask a number of layers with one mask."

"Let me see if I'm getting all of this," Lisa said. "Any content on the mask layer will be used as a mask right?" I nodded. "So this means that we could reveal the background image gradually with a tween on the mask layer?" she finished.

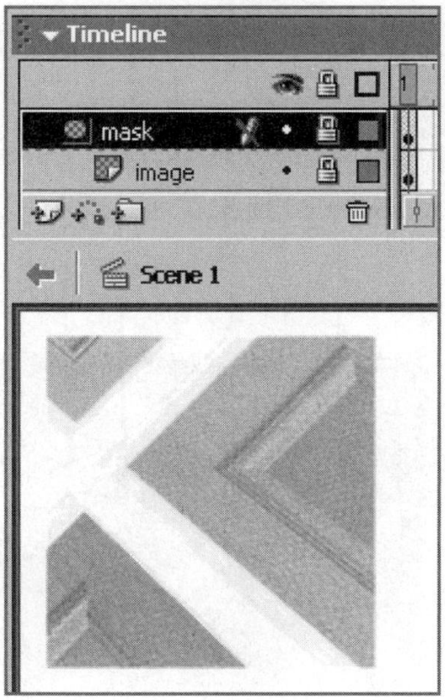

"Of course," I replied, quite proud of her shrewd deductions, "This would allow you to draw the interface when the website first loads, and you'd be able to achieve all manner of transitions. Time to put your thinking caps on, to decide which motion will work best." I added, "Think about your shapes as you do this. See how the white area on this image creates a cross that points off in four different directions?"

Bonnie and Zed nodded as I continued, "When you include the motion, it won't seem so obvious, but be aware of the shapes you create when you cut into your original image.

Deb spoke up now, "And I we should preferably keep it simple and fast. There's nothing more frustrating than having to wait ages for something to work."

"As long as it's smooth, I don't think it will be that infuriating if it only happens once." I said. "I'll make a basic transition with you for this image so that you can get a clear idea of where you want to go with it. I'll make a mask that tweens from no size at all to reveal the whole of the content of the stage."

I converted the square into a graphic symbol, and added a new keyframe at frame 50 of the mask layer. I also extended the frames of the image layer to frame 50 to ensure that it was displayed all through the tween.

"The square on the first keyframe will be tiny, and over the 50 frames, it will grow to cover the whole of the stage, showing all of the image eventually. The animation then will start by showing nothing, because the mask will be so small."

I changed the size of the square on the first keyframe to 0% using the Transform panel and changed the square on the second keyframe to cover the whole stage using the Free Transform tool to roughly cover it.

"Now that we have the two extreme sizes of the square, we just need to add the motion tween." I selected a frame inbetween the two keyframes on the mask layer and chose Motion from the Tween drop-down menu in the Property inspector.

"If I now run the movie, you'll see a simple yet effective transition."

"The content is gradually revealed in a film-like transition," I said. "This sure beats the slap-bang of something appearing on-screen all at once and without any grace."

"Yeah, I don't think it feels like it takes too long either." Bonnie said. "I thought 50 frames might feel like an overkill, but it isn't."

"Right then, I hope this has all given you something to think about and start playing with during the week," I stated. "I want you all to think about what you really want to create within your dynamic and interactive Flash sites – and we'll talk about some of your ideas next week in class.

"Next week I also want you each to give a presentation to the rest of the class about any design topic that has taken your fancy during your own investigation in the world of design. After that you'll really be used to speaking in front of others! Additionally, sharing our research will help us to learn about some of the subjects that we haven't yet covered in class. Remember, any topic that you think the rest of us might find interesting."

And with that, the students started to collect heir belongings and head for the exit.

Summary

In this chapter we've emphasized the importance of human perceptions and how to create visual and intellectual unity for the viewer:

- **Visual unity** – created with the elements of design, directed by the principles of design
- **Intellectual unity** – relating to the overall *theme* of the site, created by the client's business, or via a metaphor/analogy about the client's business, and emphasized with visual unity

We've also learned about the following attributes that can help to create unity within designs and individual web pages:

- **Proximity** – involves the use of positive and negative space, and all the elements of design to create relationships *between* and *among* the objects on the page. Proximity relates to visual unity, but it can also be used throughout a site to help create a *theme*.

- **Repetition** – related to the repeated use of symbols, signs, and the elements of design to create relationships among these objects for visual unity. The use of repetition *throughout* a site is known as continuity.

- **Continuity** – visual and intellectual unity carried throughout a site. Visual continuity comes from using all the elements and principles of design in a consistent manner, while intellectual continuity results from carrying a theme throughout the site in a consistent manner.

- **Variety** – used to develop rhythm, asymmetrical balance, direction, contrast, emphasis, and proportion. Variety used within the boundaries of proximity, repetition, and continuity, creates interest and vitality in a site.

Next, we returned to our study of the client/designer relationship to look at presentation styles and client evaluation. As part of our running project, each student design team met with the client to present their finalized roughs of their designs, encountering various problems with both presentation and their site designs. As we worked through the presentations, the importance of the contract was emphasized.

After the client evaluation, it was clear that we were back at the top of the creative problem-solving circle. It was time to define the next set of problems, and to resolve the issues as they analyzed how they could finalize their designs in the Flash MX. In order to stimulate some creative design solutions using Flash, we learned about creating dynamic effects with masks.

In the next class we'll push our creativity even further by discussing a variety of design topics, from patterns and symmetry to physics and kinetics, and then studying some examples of interactivity within Flash MX designs.

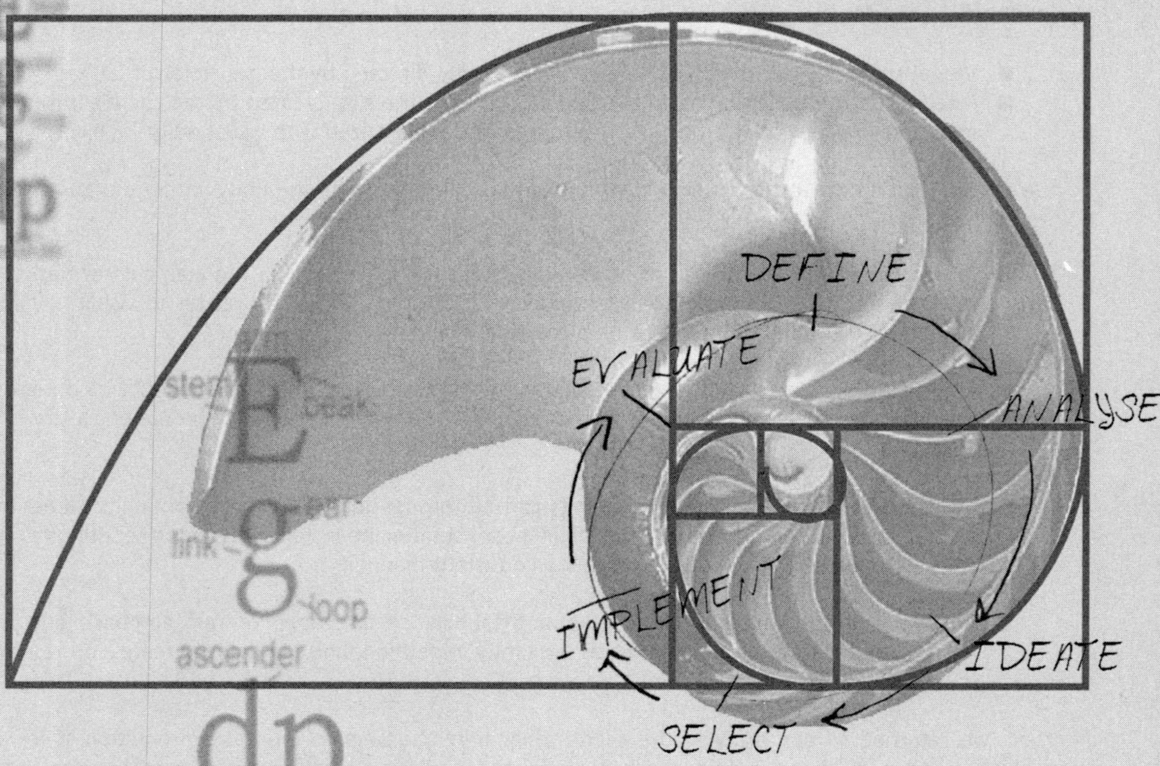
DEFINE
ANALYSE
IDEATE
SELECT
IMPLEMENT
EVALUATE

Chapter 11
Creativity Unleashed

Objectives

In today's class you will learn about:

- Creative patterns and symmetry
- The golden ratio for composition
- Using grids for drawing
- Physics in design
- Utilizing both the left-brain and the right-brain for our designs
- Some ideas for interactive Flash websites

Introduction

Last week, each team presented their projects to the client. With this exercise, they learned how to improve on their presentation skills, and they also got some critical feedback and gained more information about what the client wanted from their site. With this in mind, they began tweaking their projects in earnest.

Each team had their own problems in the presentations, and also some issues with their finalized roughs, so we briefly discussed resolutions to the problems. I also asked them to think about how they might utilize Flash to make their sites more dynamic this week. We also talked about the idea of unity in design, both visual and intellectual, and how this principle forms the capstone to the combined use of all the elements and principles of design.

Several weeks ago, I asked the students to prepare information that they could share with their fellow students. This project was designed to help them feel more comfortable presenting a project in front of others. It would also help them feel more confident, as each student would share a skill they had either learned during the course or had already known from their own experiences. So this week, each of the students would talk about their topics, sharing their own insight and understanding with the group.

Lisa - patterns and symmetry
Bonnie - drawing skills
Deb - golden ratio/rectangle

As each student entered the room and settled at the table, I asked them to tell me about their research, and I wrote their topic on the board for the rest of the class to see. Lisa wanted to talk about *patterns and symmetry*, and Bonnie was anxious to share her new *drawing skills*. Deb stated she wanted to talk about the *composition of the golden ratio*.

Zed - gravity/movement
Wes - gestalt and linear time

Zed, surprisingly, wanted to share some information about the *gravity and physics effects in design*. Wes was enigmatic at first, but finally admitted his subject related to the *left-brain/right-brain quandary*. The concepts of *gestalt and linear time* would also play an important part in his presentation.

As Steve entered the classroom and settled in at the table with the rest of the students, he suggested his topic was probably more suitable for the following week. "I want to talk about printing, and maybe it would be best to share what I know next week," he said. "If we need to prepare Frieda's name for any collateral printed material, I can expand upon some of that process."

Steve - printing

I thanked Steve, "Your topic would certainly help, and it will indeed be quite timely next week."

"Plus," Steve added as he waved his arms around to include his fellow classmates, "By the time these guys are all through expounding on their topics, I'll be ready to work on our Flash project."

"All right then, let's get started," I settled in with the rest of the students. "In this week's class you'll learn from each other about all the topics you see on the board. If we have time at the end, we'll also start to learn about incorporating simple elements of interactivity in your Flash designs to improve your users' experience – and we'll see some simple examples of how we might do this."

I looked around and said, "OK, we don't have to go in order of the list, so whoever wants to start first, just jump up and go to it."

Lisa stood, "Actually, I want to get mine over with," she said. "My research on patterns and symmetry is fairly straightforward."

Patterns and symmetry

Lisa began to set up her work, and started talking to the rest of the class, "You all know I have experience in theater lighting, but I've discovered a new interest with patterns and symmetry. I became more interested in this topic since we learned about the principle of balance. I want to share what I've learned since our class on the principles of design.

"I did a little research and ended up learning a lot about patterns and repetitive shapes." She smiled, "Actually, I ended up having a great time!"

As she arranged her work, she began to tell us more about symmetry, "I found that the term *symmetry* has many different aspects. One of them is about balance, one of the principles of design. Remember, earlier in the course we learned about asymmetrical and symmetrical placement of elements, and how it can affect our designs.

"Symmetry also concerns the repetition of patterns. This symmetry can be found in Native American basket weavings or some African pottery, for instance.

"The third facet of symmetry relates to mathematics. **Mathematical symmetry** is a property possessed by an object if it remains unchanged by certain operations. For example, a circle still looks the same, even if you rotate it, move it sideways, or mirror it. The three types of mathematical symmetry are **reflective** symmetry, **rotational** symmetry, and **translational** symmetry.

"The various math symmetries are named for how we can use each shape. For example, a polygon, as you all know, is a shape defined by its edges, and it's usually named by the number of sides it has. Ancient Greek mathematicians named these shapes, and they're the same names we use today."

"Some shapes can be used to make regular patterns, and these patterns can be used for texture, value, color combinations, or to make other shapes." Lisa looked at Bonnie, "These patterns are great for creating backgrounds for our sites, too."

Reflection

Lisa continued, "When you use any shape for a pattern, there's often a limited number of things you can do with it without altering the shape. One way you can alter a pattern is by reflecting it. If the shape stays the same, even when it's reflected, or mirrored, over some straight line, the shape is known to have *reflective symmetry*."

She showed us a picture of a pentagon, "I made this shape in Flash, and I manipulated it to show you the different forms of mathematical symmetry and pattern-making.

"Notice that this pentagon has vertical reflective symmetry, but it doesn't have horizontal reflective symmetry."

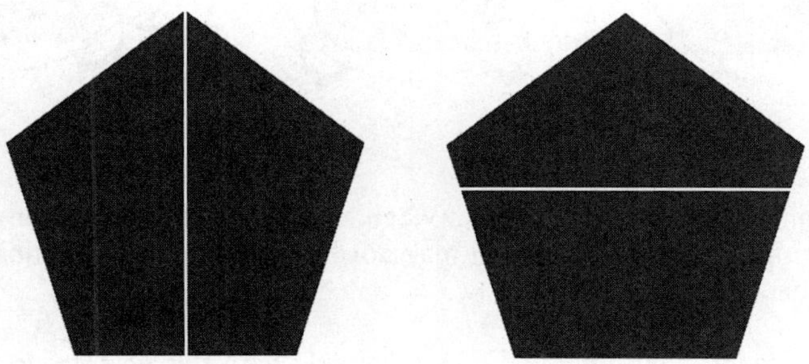

She showed us another picture to display her point. "You can divide it down the middle and each side reflects the other side. You can also slice it along its other 72° angles, and it still displays reflective symmetry. Why 72°, you ask? Well, I'll tell you..."

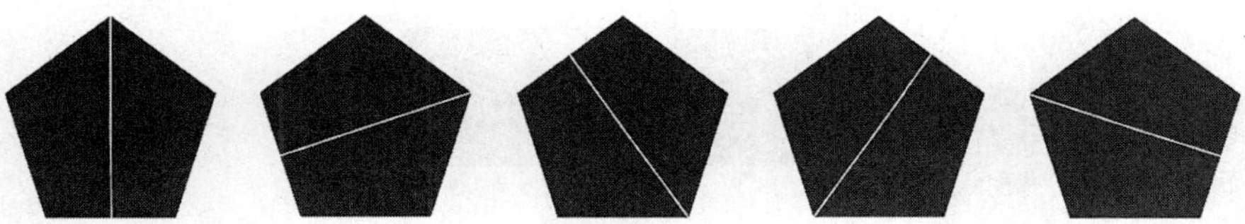

Rotation

She showed us another view of the pentagon, this time enclosed by a circle, showing five points marked at 72°, "When a shape exhibits *rotational symmetry*, it means the object remains unchanged when rotated through some angle about a point. Remember, a circle has full rotational symmetry because it is unchanged when rotated through *any* angle.

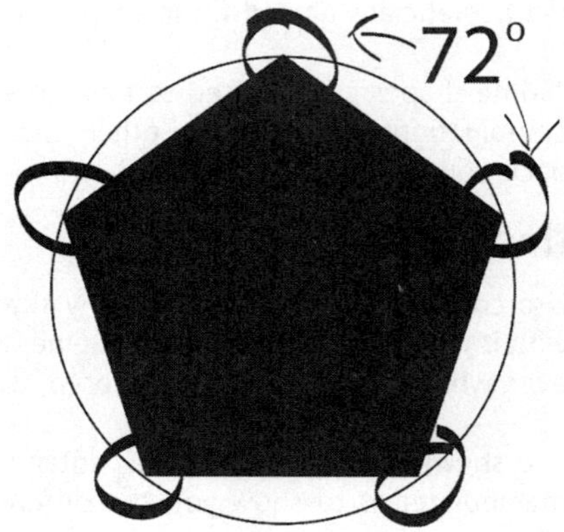

"Even though it doesn't have complete rotational symmetry, the pentagon has rotational symmetry at 72°. I can rotate the pentagon by 72° five times, and each time it will look just like the original pentagon." She showed us an example of two rotations for the pentagon, "As you can see, the pentagon shows rotational symmetry along 72°, 144°, 216°, 288°, and 360°. The last rotation puts the pentagon back to where it began."

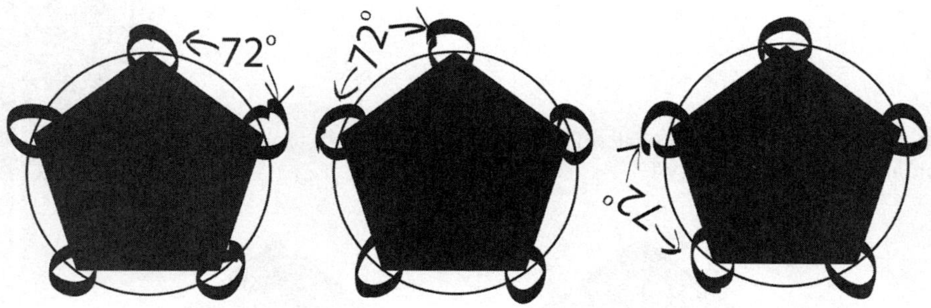

Translation

"The third kind of symmetry is *translation*; this is when a shape or pattern remains the same when shifted to the right or left, or up and down. A pattern may not have reflective or rotational symmetry, but it will usually have translational symmetry."

She looked at all the students, "I'll show you how this works with this next group of pictures." She pulled some more images from her pile on the table. "These images are created with translational symmetry in mind. Here, I've taken a polygon, duplicated it, and shifted some to the right and left and up and down. Each polygon rests right next to the other. Translational symmetry can be used to make tiling. **Tilings** are also called **tessellations**, and they're arrangements of polygons that interlock perfectly with no overlapping."

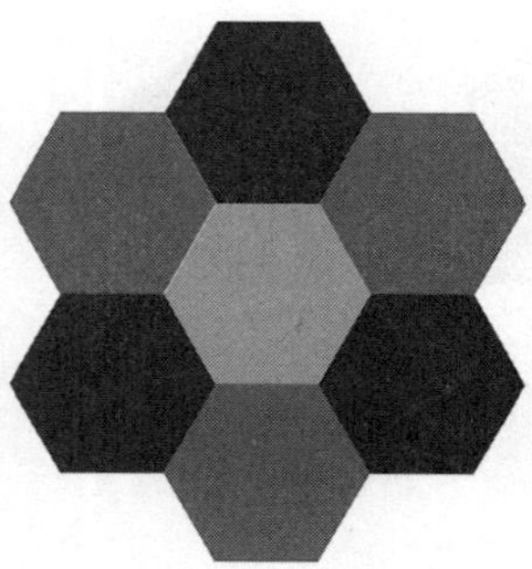

She showed us three different tiling patterns, "I discovered that there are a few different polygons that you can tile perfectly: triangles, squares, and hexagons. These shapes can create patterns when you shift them in different directions." She pointed at the images, "Although these particular shapes fit each other well, all polygons aren't so straightforward.

"Quilt makers are familiar with these shapes, and they use them often to make their quilts. I think they probably know that a pentagon won't work for a regular tiling pattern." She showed us an image where she had placed three pentagons together without overlapping.

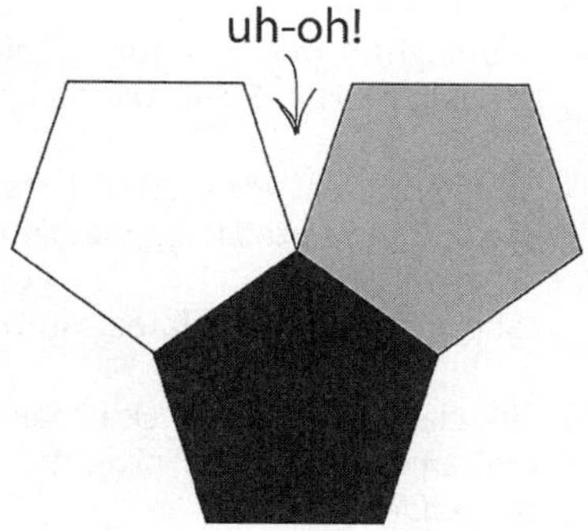

"As you can see, there's still an opening left, and it's not large enough to hold another pentagon. But," she added, "We can create more tilings if we remove the restriction of using only a single type of regular polygon."

She showed us a pattern made from pentagons and triangles. "When you combine polygons, you can come up with some interesting patterns. All these can be used for backgrounds, or even as textures on items in your sites."

She laid those pictures down, and picked up her last picture to show us. "Wes mentioned the artist M.C. Escher at the beginning of this course. Escher is famous for his complicated tessellations, all of which were developed with mathematical symmetries.

"Take a look at www.mcescher.com sometime, or Douglas R. Hofstadter's book, *Gödel, Escher, Bach: An Eternal Golden Braid,* ISBN: 0465026567.

"M.C. Escher created tilings or tessellations using irregular polygons. These are polygons that have sides of different lengths. Tilings using irregular polygons are limitless in number."

She showed us a picture of a rabbit pattern. "I created this simple pattern in a Photoshop – now I can import it into Flash and use it as a fill pattern. This isn't as complicated as the work Escher did, but I tried to emulate him by using irregular polygons in rotational, reflective, and translational symmetry."

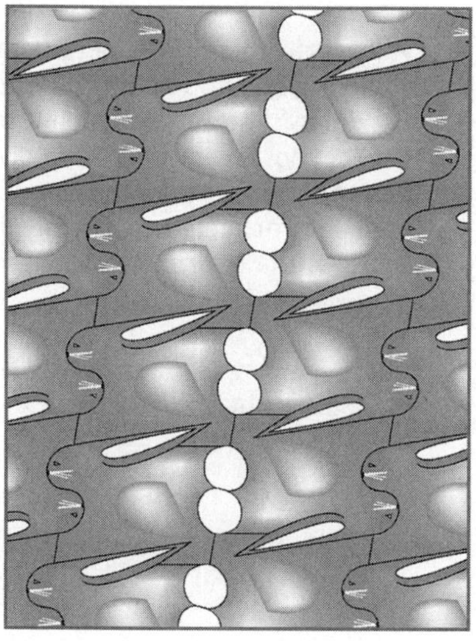

The students couldn't keep quiet, "Let me see that, Lisa!" Wes reached across the table to snag the picture. "This would make a really nice fabric pattern!"

Bonnie looked over Wes's shoulder, "Super pattern for men's boxer shorts!"

Steve laughed, "I was thinking the same thing!"

As the students passed Lisa's work around, she finished her talk. "All the patterns I showed you today are called **periodic tilings**, because they all have a pattern that is repeated throughout the tessellation.

"There are also tiling schemes that can be referred to as **aperiodic tilings**, meaning they don't have a pattern that repeats throughout the entire tiling. If you extend some of these designs in all directions, you'll find the same pattern is never repeated in most of these designs. If you want to check some of these out, try the *Aperiodic Tiling Page* of the University of Wisconsin at www.uwgb.edu/dutchs/symmetry/aperiod.htm. The information presented here provides a great introduction to the study of these tessellations."

"I thought it might be fun to talk about tilings and patterns because they're easy to create using the basic drawing tools in Flash, and tilings seem perfect for creating striking backgrounds in different websites."

"That's a great idea, Lisa," I stated. "You've done a wonderful job showing us how to use polygons for patterns, and explaining mathematical symmetry."

"She sure has!" Zed stated. He was still analyzing Lisa's drawing, "I think she deserves some applause."

The class obliged, and Lisa took her bow. Deb asked to be next up. "I think Lisa and I were thinking along the same lines for our projects," she said. "I'm sticking with math, and I want to talk about what's known as the *golden ratio*."

The golden ratio

Deb pulled her materials together, and stood in front of the class, "Earlier in this course, we all used the Rule of Thirds in our compositions, and we learned that this form of composition, like many other things, came from the ancient Greeks.

"Today, I'm going to show you how they also developed the **golden ratio**, and how we can use this tool for more interesting layout designs."

"Boy, these ancient Greeks were all over the place," Zed sighed. "Will we ever stop learning from them?"

Deb laughed, "Not until we find formulas to replace what they originally gave us. Until then, we use what we have."

She went to the board and began to write some formulas. As she wrote, she began to explain the golden mean and its impact on our lives, "In around 500 BCE, Greek scholars asked themselves how a line segment could be divided into two pieces that would have the most appeal and aesthetic balance.

"Amazingly, there seemed to be a general agreement on the answer, even though the question was based on personal aesthetics." She pointed at the board. "The Greeks claimed that the most visually pleasing division of a line segment had the property that the ratio of the length of the long piece to the length of the short piece is the same as the ratio of the length of the entire line to length of the long piece.

$$\frac{L}{S} = \frac{L+S}{L}$$

"This is the simplest way I know how to present this information," Deb stated. "The *L* here is the longest piece, and the *S* is the shortest piece."

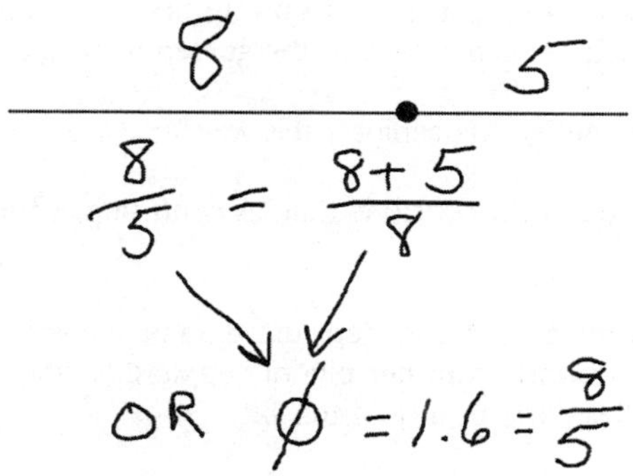

"We can represent this puzzle in the equation shown on the white board. This, ladies and gentlemen, is the formula for the golden ratio. The symbol I'm using here to represent the golden ratio is a Greek letter pronounced *phi*. For the equation to be true, *L* must be around 8 and *S* must be about 5, so the fraction 8/5, or the number 1.6, is an approximation of phi. This number is known as the golden ratio, and I'll now talk about its practical implications."

The golden rectangle

"It's just a hop, skip, and jump from the golden ratio to the golden rectangle," she stated. "This is a rectangle where the long side is phi multiplied by the length of its short side. This rectangle can be any size, but its sides must have a ratio of around 8/5."

Deb turned and noticed Bonnie's puzzled face, "I think this part will be much simpler than the theory behind the golden ration of a line segment that we've just seen," Deb stated. "You've all got notepaper with you, so just take a look at the size and proportions of a piece of that paper."

Everyone grabbed their notebooks and opened them to see the 8.5" by 11" paper, and Deb continued, "If you take the long side measurement and divide it by the short side, you'll get 1.29 for this rectangle. This is far from the golden ratio of 1.6 – so if the paper manufacturers had wanted a *perfect* ratio in the beginning, they would have taken that 8.5" width and multiplied it by 1.6 to give us paper that is 13.5" long, rounded off to the nearest half inch."

She showed us a picture that contained a drawing of a 35mm slide, a picture of one of Frieda's cabinet doors, and a photograph of a lily pond. Each image included its dimensions in inches below it, "Which one do you think comes closest to the golden ratio?" she asked. "All you have to do is divide the largest number by the smallest number."

35mm x 23mm

27" x 16"

5" x 4"

All of them took to scribbling on their notepads. Steve was the first to say something, "Wow, Deb. This is interesting; for the 35mm slide, I got 1.52. For Frieda's cabinet, I got 1.69, and for the photograph, I got 1.25. This means that Frieda's cabinets come closest to the golden rectangle than the other two images. She's far closer to the golden ratio!"

Wes and Zed nodded and looked at each other's figures, "That's what we got, too. That's pretty amazing," Wes stated. "Do you think Frieda knows about this? Maybe she designed her cabinets to fit the golden rectangle."

"I don't know about that," Deb said. She looked at me, "Did you design the cabinets this way?"

I laughed. "No – but I'm happy they're so aesthetically pleasing! You might conclude that, as confusing as the golden ratio might first seem to be, it's actually quite intuitive."

Deb nodded and continued, "If you think this is interesting, let me take it one step further, and show you how this golden ratio can be seen in nature." She pulled some artwork from her pile of supplies, "I would draw this, but I wanted to measure it accurately so you could all see the beauty of this bit."

She showed us a golden rectangle that had been divided along the golden mean. "I'm going to show you this in overlays and in a very simplified version without all the math and spreadsheets. It won't match the exact logarithmic spiral you might find on the Internet, with all the math involved," she added.

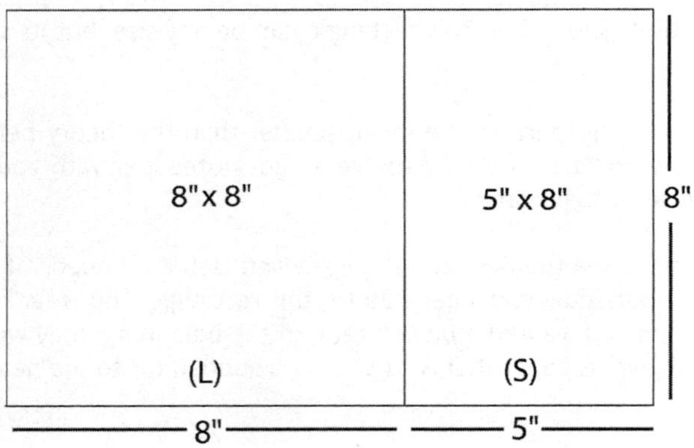

"Erm... yes, please make it as basic as possible," Bonnie sighed.

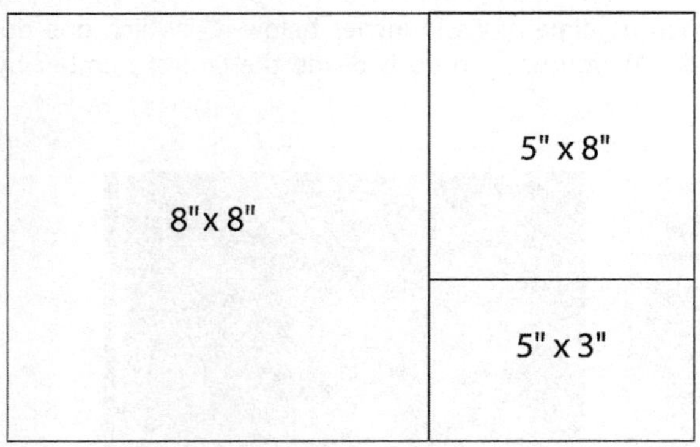

Deb began, "I divided this piece like you saw me do with the line segment earlier. This long side is *L*, and it's eight inches. The short side is *S*, and is five inches, just like the line segment I showed you earlier." she added, "And the long side forms a square."

"Oh!" Bonnie said, "I see that now."

Deb pulled a flap over the artwork, and we saw how she had divided the least wide section of the rectangle into two more sections. "Once I have this measurement, I can go through the smaller rectangles, and divide them again. As you can see, the square is now at the top, and the golden rectangle is below the square." She pointed out the square in the top right of the paper, and then pulled another flap over the artwork.

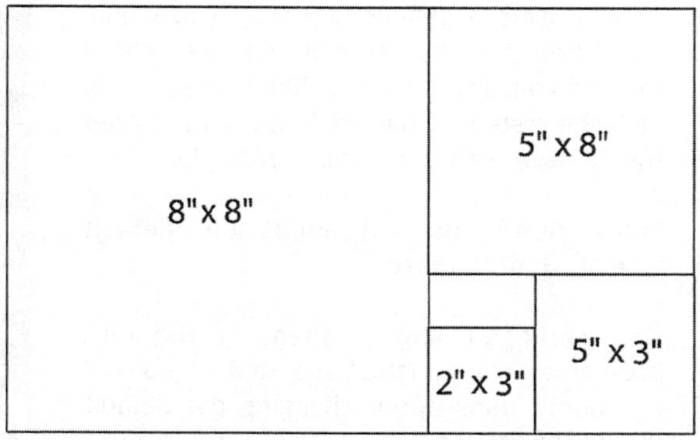

"I just repeated this step, and then, I drew what is known as a **logarithmic spiral**, although this one isn't in perfect mathematical sequence," she stated. "A logarithmic spiral might look familiar to you, because it's the same shape as a chambered nautilus."

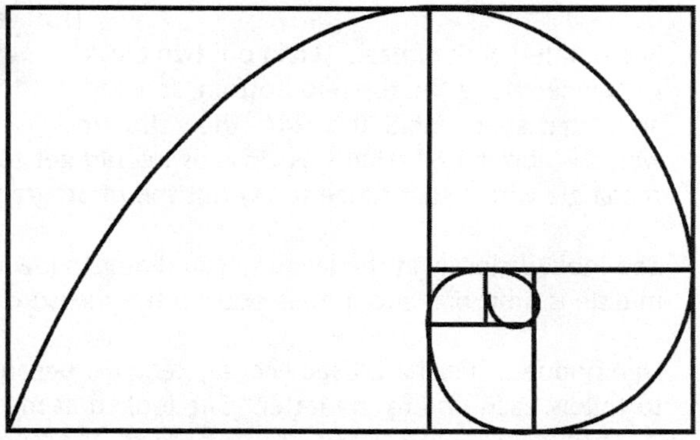

She pulled over a transparent flap that showed a photograph of a chambered nautilus.

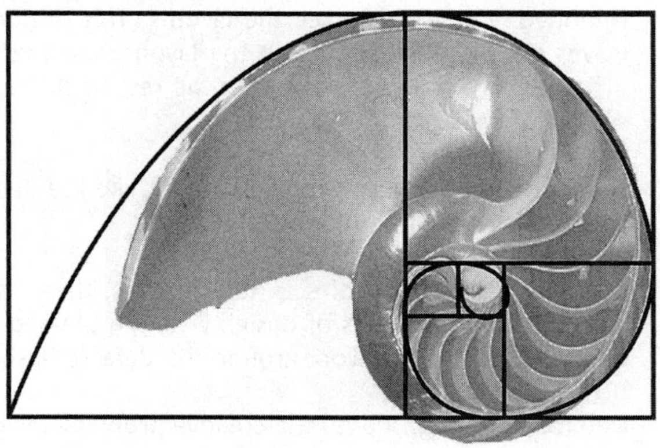

"That's awesome," Zed said. He appeared to be transfixed with the precision of the logarithmic spiral in relation to the chambered nautilus. "I never realized nature had so much to do with math. Is this something we can use in our compositions too?"

Deb answered, "Of course. I drew out a sample of what I'd do with a Flash site if I used this formula." She showed a mock-up of where she had used the golden rectangle.

"If you use the default format of 550 x 400, you'll find it isn't in accord with the golden ratio. If you divide 550 by 400, you get 1.38. So," she stated, "I had to fudge a bit to get this to align with the golden rectangle."

"Why didn't you just adjust the default format, Deb?" I asked.

Deb shrugged and grinned, "I did this presentation last night," she said. "I guess I just didn't think about changing the default size of the format."

She pointed at the image. "I laid out two black rectangles along the top and bottom, so I had an image space of 550 x 344, the ratio of which is about 1.64. That's as close as I could get to the golden ratio. Then," she added, "I used the golden rectangle within that space to lay out the photographs and text."

Zed looked closely at the layout, "You didn't follow the golden rectangle precisely," he said. "That leaf in the middle is a bit big, and it goes outside the measured space."

Deb nodded, "I call it artistic license, Zed. Just because the measurements are precise doesn't mean we need to follow each one to the letter." She looked at me for assurance, "Isn't that right?"

I nodded, and asked to see the layout, "This is indeed well balanced in many respects, Deb. You have the leaves on the left leading into the layout, and the single leaf points up into the text." I looked up at her, "That leaf is a little different than the rest of the leaves. It would have been nice to see the single leaf as a sample of that group of leaves."

Deb nodded, "I thought about that, but like I said, I did this in about ten minutes last night. I was in a rush to get this presentation done."

I laughed, "If you did this in ten minutes, then I'm really impressed. You've learned your lessons in the elements and principles of design well. I'm pleased to see you using the golden rectangle for composition, too. You managed to work around the default Flash format creatively to achieve your goal."

Deb looked smug, "I used the creative problem-solving process to arrive at my decisions. But," she admitted, "It was the fastest I've ever used that process!"

Wes added, "Now, if she could only play her drums as well as she designs."

Deb shot Wes a look. "I'm getting there. I'm determined, at any rate." She looked at the rest of the class, "Do any of you have any questions about any of my research?"

Bonnie shook her head, "I'm no math whiz, so I appreciate how you've simplified the golden rectangle for us here. I'm just a little confused over the terms – can you state them again for me?"

Deb agreed, "Very simply, the golden ratio approximates to the number 1.6. This is also known as the *golden mean* or the *golden section*, and can be calculated by the fraction 8/5 – or five sections as the short part to eight sections as the long part. The golden rectangle is a rectangle that is measured by the ratio of the golden mean. The long part of the rectangle would be eight units, and the short side is five units."

Wes looked up from some numbers he was sketching on a piece of paper. He crowed, "I've got it! If the long side is, say, eight units of measurement, then the short side should be five units of measurement!"

We all looked at Wes oddly. "That's what I just said, Wes," Deb stated.

Wes looked sheepish. "Oh... well... that nautilus was cool... ahem..."

Golden ratio in composition

Steve added, "The use of the golden mean for composition is great, but even when I use it turned upside down, backwards, or sideways, it gets to be pretty boring after a while." He added, "At least, to me it does. I like the flexibility of using various grid systems like the organic shaped grids or circular grids." He looked at Lisa and grinned. "If it wasn't for this project, I never would have known to use anything other than square grids or the Rule of Thirds."

"In the late 1800s, a German psychologist named Gustav Fechner studied whether the dimensions of this format were truly more visually pleasing than any other rectangle," I stated. "He discovered that 75% of the participants in this study chose the format that fitted the dimensions of the golden rectangle."

Steve looked at me, "Really? I'm going to start doing some measuring around the house. It would be interesting to see if things like the television screen and some of the paintings around the house fit this 1.6 golden ratio."

Wes agreed. "I'm going to start using it with my artwork again. I used this composition some years ago, but stopped for the same reasoning you gave, Steve. It started to get old."

"You don't always have to use the golden ratio for the composition," I added. "You can use it for the format, and use other grid systems, like the Rule of Thirds, to achieve your design goals."

I looked around, "OK, who wants to go next?"

Bonnie offered, "I'm ready! I'm going to talk about my experiences with learning to draw, so that will give us all a little break from math."

Everyone applauded Deb's work, and Bonnie stood up to present her project.

Drawing with grids

Bonnie prefaced her talk with a short explanation about her work, "When Linda told us we could use grids to draw, I thought it sounded like cheating. But, I was willing to give it a try, and now I'm hooked. Since I'm still a newbie at drawing, I thought it might be a good idea to work with black and white, and leave color out of the picture for now, so to speak."

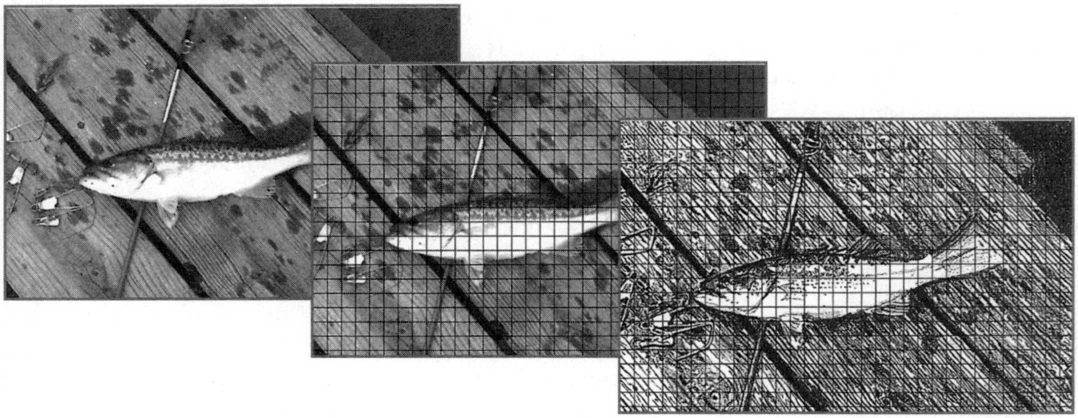

She held up a photograph of a fish, "I thought I'd start with a simple shape, too. Something that contained enough contrast to help me define the positive and negative areas."

Bonnie noticed the grimace on Deb's face. "My dad is into fishing," she explained, "And there are plenty of these pictures around his house. I figured this one would be easy, because the fish is a simple shape. I didn't realize I would get so into drawing that I'd complete the whole scene." She shrugged, "I didn't practice the principle of economy, I guess!"

Bonnie continued, "Anyway, I used a graphics application to make a grid – you can use any graphic software program like Photoshop or Flash – and I printed the grid out onto acetate. Then, I laid the picture under the grid like this." She showed us the photograph with the grid overlay.

"From that point, I used the same grid and printed it out on a regular piece of paper. By using the same grid to draw as I used for the photograph, I knew my picture would be in proportion to the original photograph. I traced the grid onto my drawing paper using a piece of graphite paper under the grid." She smiled at Wes, "Wes showed me how to do this. You just lay the graphite paper between the object you're tracing and the drawing pad, and go to town."

She held up a copy of the drawing with the grid, "This is what I ended up with, and believe me, it took a long time! Creating all that wood grain was a pretty painful process.

"Since the grid was traced with graphite paper, it was fairly easy to eliminate. I did the drawing in ink. When it was fully dry, I just erased the grid." She showed us the final picture. "This is my first attempt at drawing, and I'm really pleased with the result."

Zed peered at the drawing, "Wow, Bonnie. I'll say you should be proud. It looks like you did dots or crosshatching in all the black areas, too?"

Bonnie shook her head, "No, Zed. Wes showed me how to color those in with ink. But I had to learn about how the amount of ink affected the paper, too. If I laid down too much ink, it made glossy patches on the paper. It made the work look splotchy. Believe it or not, I did this three times before I got it right."

Bonnie sighed, "I think I probably could have drawn this in Flash with the Pen tool using the grid for reference, but I did enjoy being hands on with it."

"Actually, I'm glad you drew this by hand, Bonnie. You could extend your work into illustration if you keep this up," I said.

As the class passed her artwork around, she pulled some more work from her portfolio bag. "Even though I felt like I was cheating using a grid, it helped so much that I was encouraged to try a few other things. Wes showed me something called scratchboard, and I'm nuts about it."

Scratchboard

She showed us two shell patterns. "A **scratchboard** is a board covered with black ink. Underneath the ink is a white chalky surface made of clay – it's also sometimes called clayboard. You can use any sharp item to scratch out a pattern or drawing, but I found that some sharp objects like my designer's scalpel aren't really appropriate for scratchboard. I ended up cutting too deep at times, and the knife would tear the paper underneath.

"I ended up using a variety of tools. I used a stylus, an awl, and a wire brush. Since the scratchboard requires a delicate touch, I was able to slow down and really look at what I was drawing. I had to draw the light shapes and leave the shadows alone, so the process helped me to clearly identify the positive and negative shapes. I was able to distinguish the shapes more easily for some reason."

She grinned, "I especially like scratchboard, because when I made a mistake I could always touch it up with India ink!"

Wes laughed, "I taught her that trick, too."

As the students passed these two images around, Steve asked Bonnie, "What in the world are you doing hanging around with Wes?"

Bonnie grinned, "We had a truce. I wanted to learn more about art, so I paid Wes a visit. When you want to talk about art, Wes doesn't run out of words. He also becomes very gracious."

Wes laughed, "I don't think I have a problem running out of words on any topic, really."

We all laughed. "Bonnie, these are really good, " I said. "Did you try anything else?"

Stippling

Bonnie nodded, "I did try one more thing. I remembered Wes's talk about pointillism," Bonnie began. "This was a technique used by post-impressionist artists. They used little dots to depict light and dark values and color. I wanted to try using stippling, which is a way to show value with dots of ink, graphite, or paint. So I took this picture of a bonsai, and tried to stipple the picture. I used the same method I did with the fish, using a grid. But," she added, "By the time I was through stippling, my hand was about to fall off. I'll never try that again on a picture with so much detail!"

She showed us the stippled ink drawing, "The next thing I tried was a collage. Wes didn't help me with this one. The scratchboard projects helped me realize that I need to keep my shapes simple, and my details to a minimum. So I simplified the shapes, and cut out paper to portray an image."

She showed us her last drawing. "I limited myself to three shades of paper, and I cut out the images as I saw fit, along the value shapes. This was actually a lot more fun, and I think I did a good job reducing the detail."

Wes let out a low whistle, "I think that's a pretty good example of abstraction, Bonnie."

Bonnie shrugged, "I don't know what I did, but I do know that it was great to get away from the computer for a bit. I never knew I had this in me!"

I applauded, and the rest of the students joined me. Bonnie blushed, and bowed. Lisa said, "I'm so jealous! I didn't know you were doing all this. You've given me hope. Maybe you can show me some of these processes sometime."

Bonnie nodded as she packed up her artwork, "I'd love to help you. That way, I'll make an excuse to do more myself. I know that these exercises helped me gain more confidence. I can see depth, values, and shapes more readily now."

She sat down and smiled, "If I can keep this up, I might just design a Flash site for my artwork."

Steve laughed, "Boy, that's a far cry from your attitude when you first came to class."

Everyone agreed, and Bonnie admitted, "I didn't realize how much I was restricting myself. Even though I used boxes to create this artwork, they're helping me to see *outside of the box*."

Wes congratulated her on working so hard, "Bonnie really wanted to learn, and I think her passion for learning helped her see things quite clearly."

"Thanks, Wes!" Bonnie said. "But I do miss sparring with you."

We all laughed. "Maybe you'll get a chance again soon," Zed said. "Wes seems to ask for it."

Before Wes could respond, Zed volunteered to be next up.

Gravity and physics in design

Zed pulled up a chair, stood on it, and proceeded to climb up on the table to tower over us. As we looked up at him, he looked back down at us and said, "As you all know, I'm extremely interested in animation and movement in Flash. Steve helped me with my presentation, because I wanted to know more about how things move in real life."

He held two tennis balls, one in each hand, "Physics seemed pretty complicated at first, but it's really just a bunch of formulas that explain why things happen. What I wanted to learn was how things move with gravity. We don't have gravity inside the Flash software, so if I want to show how things move in reality I have to learn how gravity affects these objects. I'm going to show you some simple gravity problems today, and how we can use them in Flash."

"I hope you hurry," Deb said. "My neck is killing me from looking up at you."

Zed grinned, "OK, here we go." He showed us the tennis balls he held in his hand. "These balls are both the same size and the same weight. I'm going to drop one, and I'm going to toss the other one outwards. Both actions will take place at the same height, and at the same time. Which one do you think will land first?"

"Oh, the dropped ball will fall faster," Bonnie said. "Everyone knows that."

Zed smiled smugly, and I saw Steve and Deb smile, too. Zed asked Bonnie to watch the ground, since the balls would fall pretty quickly. "I want you to see for yourself if you're right or not."

He asked for complete silence, and he then threw one ball and dropped the other one.

She shook her head, "It's hard to believe, but I think they both landed at the same time."

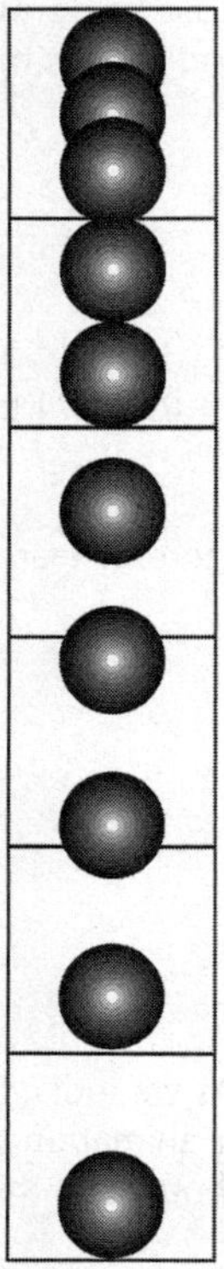

Zed climbed down, and brushed away the dirt his shoes left on the table surface, "It was hard for me to believe the first time, too. But they did land at almost the same time. I'll show you some pictures to explain why this happens."

He showed us an image of a ball falling through six different boxes, "This is a drawing based on a stroboscope image of a ball falling. The camera was timed to flash and take a picture at regular intervals – it effectively *blinked* ten times, showing ten different locations of a falling ball."

Zed went to the board to write down his explanation, "The measure of the acceleration due to gravity near the earth's surface is $g = 9.8\ m/s^2$. Here, the *m* stands for meters, and the *s* stands for seconds. It's squared, so that means that the velocity increases the longer something falls. Oh," he added, "The 9.8 is usually rounded off to ten."

He shrugged, "The easy way to remember how this works is to know that each second the ball falls, it increases speed by 10 m/s. If it starts off at 0, after one second, the ball is traveling at 10 m/s. After two seconds, it's traveling at 20 m/s. In three seconds, it's traveling at 30 m/s. I know that 30 m/s is about 70 miles per hour, so after three seconds, that ball is really moving."

$$g = 10\ m/s^2$$

Wes agreed, "It'd kill any ant unlucky enough to be directly under it!"

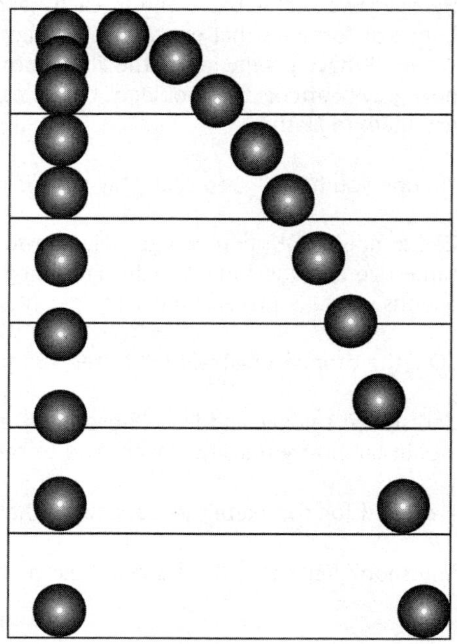

Deb rolled her eyes, "OK, now tell us about the ball that goes sideways. Tell us why it lands at the same time as the other ball."

Zed looked up like he was seeking an answer from some unknown source. He snapped his fingers, and answered, "Both balls are subject to the same gravitational acceleration, $g = 10\ m/s^2$, so the time it takes to fall down isn't affected by how far the ball travels horizontally."

Bonnie shook her head again, "This goes against nature."

Steve laughed, "I'm afraid it *is* nature, Bonnie. It's just hard to believe. Gravity is a powerful force. By looking at the position of stars, astrophysicists have observed how gravity can even affect light."

Lisa was concentrating on the balls in the drawing, "So if we drew a ball in Flash, and we wanted to show one going down and another going out and down, they would have to land at the same time to appear realistic, right?"

"If they left the same height at the same time with no air resistance, yes," Zed answered. "The first ball that is dropped is in what we call **free fall**. The second ball is in what is known as **projectile motion**. Projectile motion is determined by the time of flight and the initial speed and direction, or velocity."

Bonnie grinned, "You're starting to sound like Steve," she said. "I want to know how we can show this projectile motion movement. Does it arc or is it straight?"

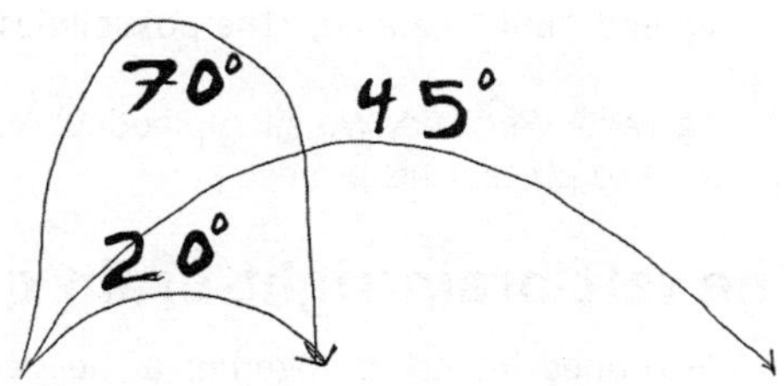

Zed drew three lines on the board, all arcing at different angles, "I wanted to know the same thing, Bonnie. Steve told me that anything traveling in projectile motion goes in an arc. This is because there's a change of the height of each projectile, due to the force of gravity."

He pointed at the arcs, "When you shoot or throw something up against gravity, it doesn't stop the force of gravity. When the ball is thrown, the force due to gravity slows it down in the vertical direction, and so depending on how fast the upwards part of the throw was, after some time it would stop moving upwards and be at its maximum height, which you can see as the top of the curve."

"Let's say this is a ball," Lisa said. "When it gets at that apex, does it hang there for any length of time?"

"Well," Zed answered, "For a brief moment it would have no upwards or downwards motion, but it would still be moving horizontally."

"So when you throw a ball, it goes faster at the beginning and end than at the apex," Lisa said. "I never knew gravity was so precise."

"It is as long as you don't have a wind affecting the ball," Zed said. He pointed at the board, "If these balls were all thrown as hard as each other, the ball thrown at a 20° angle would land nearer to the thrower than the ball thrown at 45°, because it was thrown more across than up, so doesn't go as high and it lands sooner. The ball thrown at 70° doesn't go as far as the ball thrown at 45° either. This is because most of the throw effort was used sending it up and not across. It would spend longer in the air though."

"So why does the 45° angle always go further than any other angle?" Bonnie asked.

Zed answered, "Because the horizontal and vertical motions are divided equally. The ball would stay in the air longer than with the 20° angle launch as it has more vertical speed, but it also travels with greater horizontal speed and direction than the 70° angle launch."

Wes studied the arcs on the board, "So you need to be a physics major to shoot a hoop or make a goal!"

Steve laughed, "I guess it helps! I think Zed's thoughts can help us with movement in Flash, too. Especially when we want objects to move as realistically as possible."

Bonnie sighed, "The world runs on math. How can we avoid it?"

"No more than we can avoid the ancient Greeks, I'm afraid," Wes answered. "I want to go next, because I think my topic would fit in perfect here."

I nodded and asked if anyone had any more questions for Zed.

"I don't have any questions for Zed, but I have one for Steve," Lisa said. She looked at Steve, "Do you tutor physics or something?"

We all laughed. "I will if you want, Bonnie," Steve answered. "Physics actually has a lot to do with how we move things around in Flash, and how we see things in real time. It also has a lot to do with things we don't see, but what we can imagine."

Deb moaned, "I'm not wearing my watch, but I know we don't have time for quantum physics."

I agreed. "But," I added, "The possibilities *are* fascinating. We'll have to talk about them some day."

"Agreed," Wes said. We all applauded Zed as he picked up his tennis balls and artwork. As he settled, Wes stood to present his project.

The left-brain/right-brain quandary

We rubbed his hands together as he stood to talk to the rest of the class, "I'm going to talk about the quandary that faces many designers today. This perplexing problem occurs when designers come from a variety of diverse backgrounds." He pointed at each one of the students, "For instance, in our group we have designers that come from the fields of mathematics, the arts, print, web, and even from occupations as diverse as scientists and writers."

He waved his hand at Zed and grinned, "And, then we have folks who have no earthly idea what they're doing."

"Hey!" Zed laughed, "I resent that last remark!"

Wes continued, "As we get older, we'll develop other interests, and some of these interests might seem to be far from the field of design. But, I'm going to show you today how to incorporate some of these diversities. This may help us get along with other people we don't understand, and it may help us get through any confusion about our own capabilities."

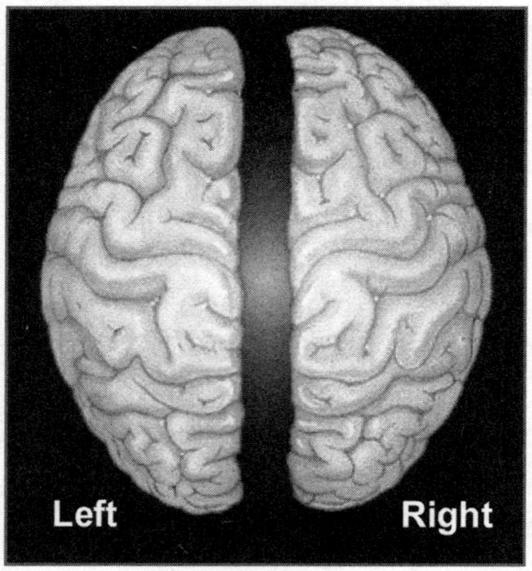

Wes showed us a picture of the human brain, "Throughout history, scholars have suspected we consist of dual personalities. It was only a little over forty years ago that scientists defined the organization of the brain and its function. Today, we're well aware that we have right-brain/left-brain functionality. This is something the ancient philosophers and scientists only mused upon.

"You may already know that the right side of the brain typically controls the left hand, and that the left side of the brain controls the right hand.

"You may also know that the left hemisphere of the brain is known as the dominant lobe. But," he added, "There are also many qualifiers to this statement. Not everyone is the same, so I'm just going to use scientific standards here to avoid getting bogged down in theoretical debates."

"As if we'd ever want argue with you, Wes," Deb said, laughing.

Wes ignored Deb and began to write a list on the board, "The right-brain is known to be the most mature part of the brain. Even though the left-brain is dominant, the right-brain develops more rapidly in the first months after we're conceived. The right-brain has also been linked to early evolutionary patterns of behavior."

He wrote the words *left* and *right* on the board, "Our *mammalian* brain, is what keeps us alive. This fairly uncivilized part of our brain developed millions of years ago, and controls our original instincts to feed, fight, and flee, among other basic needs. This brain can be quite rigid, obsessive, compulsive, and paranoid. It's also the judge of our experiences, since it seems to sense only pleasure or pain."

"Since it develops faster, the right-brain seems to be more in touch with this mammalian brain. However, since our brains have evolved beyond the simplistic need for fight or flight, our instincts are now tempered by our environment, and by our choice of free will."

Wes wrote a list of attributes under the right-brain list. "The right-brain is the keeper of *emotions*. It recognizes feelings, but it can't seem to give us the words to describe these feelings. That," he stated, "Comes from the left side of the brain."

The other words he wrote were *laughter*, *ecstasy*, *love*, *aesthetics*, and *harmony*. "The right-brain is where our feelings become authentic. Beyond this, the right-brain is also where we process *shapes*. People who have damaged the right sides of their brain through accident or stroke often have difficult times recognizing faces, including their own.

"The right-brain helps us understand the images of Lisa's polygons. It also helps us recognize and comprehend the validity of positive and negative *spaces*. This is the side of the brain that helps us see shapes as groups, and helps us understand and visualize *unity* or *gestalt*."

He wrote a list of attributes under the heading for the left-brain. "The left-brain function is totally different to right-brain function," Wes stated. "This side of the brain functions on *time*." He circled the words *time* under the left-brain heading and *space* under the right-brain heading. "Seems we have a little discrepancy between time and space here," he grinned.

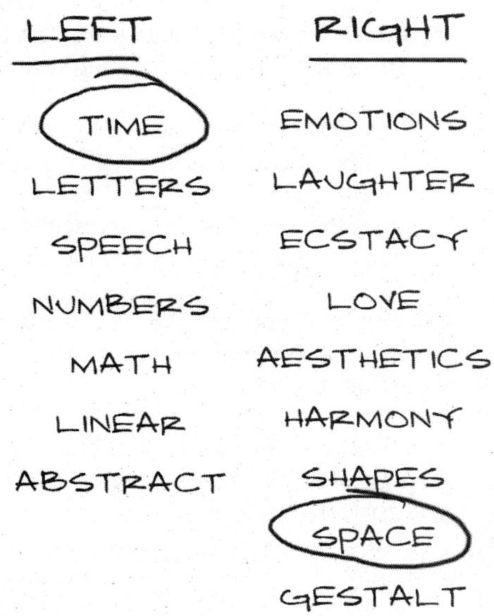

Steve grinned back at Wes, "Are we back to physics?"

"I guess you could say that, Steve," Wes said. "I circled those just for you." He turned to the rest of us, "It's interesting to consider how we've learned to use Flash during this course, in relation to the various functions of the left and right sides of the brain."

Wes addressed me, "I supported your use of manual drawing exercises throughout this course. I just couldn't put my finger on why you wanted us to draw out our ideas before we produced them in Flash. I just assumed it was because you wanted to preserve the fine art of learning to see images, and that you wanted more people to be able to draw what they see. But now," Wes mused, "I think I know why you did what you did, and it has nothing to do with preserving an art form."

I shrugged my shoulders, "So tell me why I designed the course this way, and I'll tell you if you're on the money. Sounds like you're heading in the right direction."

Wes asked the class, "Do you all remember when Deb talked about rhetorical figures in poetry and prose?" We all nodded. "Well, we wouldn't be able to use those figures of thinking if the right side of our brains didn't function." He wrote some of the rhetorical figures on the board with Deb's help.

METAPHOR

ANALOGY

IRONY

PERSONIFICATION

PUNS

SIMILE

"These figures of *metaphor*, *analogy*, *irony*, *personification*, *puns*, and *simile* can only be used and recognized by the right side of the brain. This side of our brain doesn't understand spoken language as much as it does music or song. This is the side of the brain that is creative and intuitive. This is the side of the brain devoted to myths and dreams, to the visual metaphor that defines us as designers.

"This is also the side of the brain that is nonlinear. When I remembered that the right-brain doesn't think in linear time, it occurred to me that we needed to practice thinking in shapes and the cohesiveness of gestalt before we tackled the timeline in Flash. In fact, it's the left-brain that displays similar characteristics to Flash timeline. The left side gives us the comprehension of past, present, and future."

Zed leaned forward and asked, "You mean we have a timeline in our brains?"

Wes nodded, "Yup! Or at least some clever equivalent of a timeline."

We all laughed and Wes continued, "Deb described the function of the left side of the brain when she talked about how the Greeks gave us abstract thinking along the lines of linearity and continuity with the alphabet. The left-brain is like the alphabet. It thinks with linearity, abstractness, and with continuity.

"The left-brain is where we learn to read and write, and where we comprehend mathematics. This side of the brain helps us communicate with others, and it also helps us communicate with ourselves."

"Abstract thinking sounds like a right-brain function," Bonnie said. "Isn't abstract similar to artistic license to change something from its original concrete existence?"

Wes nodded, "You said the right word, Bonnie. The left-brain is analytical; the right-brain is more concrete. It seems that the right-brain can paint a landscape, but the left-brain would have to tell the right-brain how to abstract the view."

"So if we learn how to draw, that's a right-brain function. But, to learn how to abstract, we would need left-brain capabilities," Steve mused. "That's why it's so hard for a lot of beginning artists to create convincing abstract work."

Bonnie agreed, "I know it was hard to simplify that bonsai I did for today's project."

Wes thought a moment, and then continued, "Perhaps I can explain the difference between the two brains with this analogy. When we listen to music, we can hear all the instruments at once, and they make a cohesive whole. This is the gestalt capability of the right-brain.

"But," he explained, "When a few people are talking at once, we can't decipher what's being said, because the left-brain is singular. We can only listen and hear one voice at a time, because language isn't musical or harmonic. It's a bunch of meaningless abstract noises created by speaking the sounds of abstract and meaningless alphabet shapes. The only way we can understand them is through the left-brain."

Bonnie looked interested, "So if the left side of our brain is severely damaged, we could lose the ability to speak and understand language and numbers."

Wes nodded, "Exactly! The odd thing is that a number of people with left-brain damage can still remember and sing words to songs they learned before their misfortunes."

"The two different hemispheres of our brains seem determined to do their own thing," Lisa said. "I thought both hemispheres worked together."

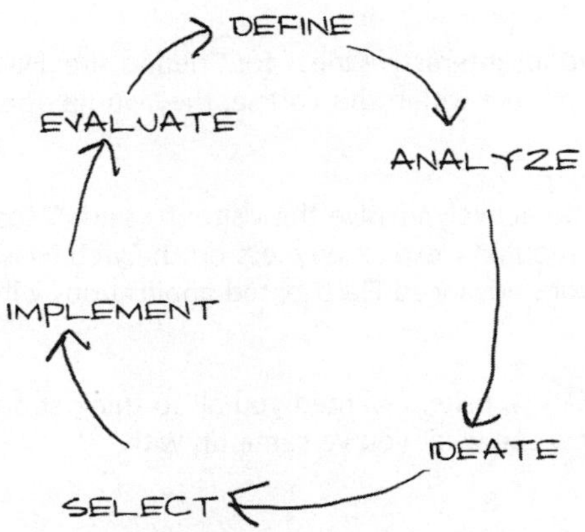

Wes agreed, "You're right about both sides working together. The right side of the brain defines dimension and space, while the left side defines time." He drew the creative problem solving process on the board, "When we define and analyze a problem, we're using the left side of the brain."

He pointed at ideation, "When we brainstorm and imagine possibilities, we're using the right side of the brain. When we select and implement our ideas, we're back to using the left side of the brain, under the instruction of the right-brain. Then again," Wes shrugged, "It's all relative to the situation."

"I guess when we evaluate, we're using both sides of our brain?" Lisa asked. "We critique along the lines of the elements and principles of design, but we also have feelings about our work or the work produced by other designers."

Wes nodded, "We're the only beings on earth that can question a subject and dispute the answer. This is abstract thinking, and it belongs to the left side of the brain. On the other hand," he added, "We also use metaphor to express our thoughts about how we feel about something. To create or critique a design, we must be able to combine the gestalt with the linear."

"Especially in Flash!" Zed stated. "This is awesome! I can see now why we had to do all that drawing. It was our right-brain telling our left-brain how to express our ideas."

Wes looked at me, "So if we immediately sat down to the timeline, our left-brain would have taken over. This is the ultimate environment for the left-brain. Instead," he said, "You took us to shapes first. You showed us a stage, and helped us create positive and negative spaces both manually and in Flash."

I replied, "It sure helps to begin with metaphors, imagery, and simple geometric shapes. Since you all had to learn so much so quickly, I had to begin with the basics. The timeline is left-brain functionality, and shapes are right-brain functionality. If you combine the two within the elements and principles of design, you have a form of unity, which is the goal of the right-brain. But," I added, "The left-brain is probably pretty pleased that you managed to put everything in the timeline the right way!" "

"I'll say!" Bonnie stated. "I remember I felt like I was constantly wading through mud. Now," she added, "I feel a little more balanced."

That seemed like a good place for Wes to finish up his presentation, so I asked the class if they were happy with what they'd learned from each other, and they all seemed very content. Wes took a bow to his applause, and the students all went off for a short break, still talking about left-brain versus right-brain issues.

When they returned, my plan was to take a glance at some advanced Flash functionality, in the hope of inspiring them to push the limits with their designs.

Interactivity in Flash MX

Wes had just spoken about how designers can use the power of both right-brain and left-brain functionality to help themselves create shapes within the framework of time. Flash MX allows for a high degree of interactivity, so users can become truly involved in the process. Interactivity is the key to exciting and dynamic websites, and is one of the main reasons Flash is so popular, replacing the static and uneventful websites of yesterday.

In this part of the class, I wanted the students to start thinking about interactive ideas for Frieda's site. Even though these interactive elements would not be created for the project within this course, they would open up the students' thinking for future Flash developments.

"The key to making interactive sites that visitors will return to is to actively involve the visitor," I said. "Most Internet users are familiar with games and applications, so they shouldn't expect any less on the web. Flash is the key to highly interactive designs, from simple games to more advanced Flash-based applications with totally user-friendly interfaces.

"Last week I asked you all to come up with some ideas for Frieda's website. I wanted you all to think about interactivity as a future direction for your Flash content. Let's now see what you've came up with."

Wes sat up, "Deb and I have something already."

"Good work." I said. "Let's take a look."

Wes opened a movie on his machine called `3D_cabinet.swf`. The cabinet rotated on screen according to where he moved his mouse cursor.

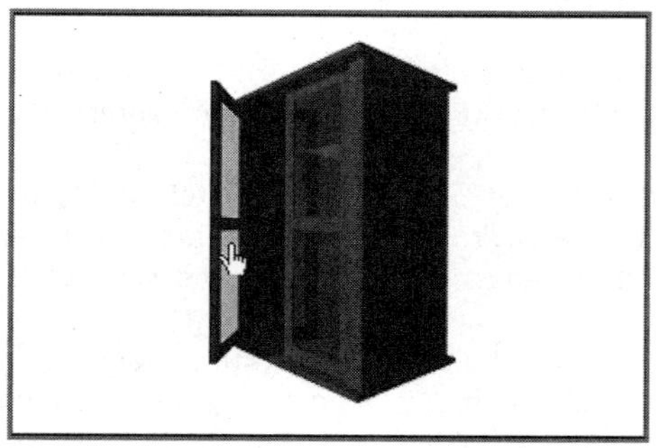

"This was inspired from watching Steve looking at the Macs on the Apple Computer website." Wes wrote the URL on the white board:

www.apple.com/hardware/gallery

"The gallery on the site lets you turn the hardware around and view it from nearly any different angle," Wes said. "I thought this might be cool in Flash, so Deb and I went to it."

"Why didn't I think of that?" Steve said.

"I think you were too wrapped up in the hardware to realize what you were doing!"

Steve laughed, "I guess I was."

"Tell us how the interaction works," I said.

"It's quite simple really," Deb said. "Maybe Wes should explain it to you though." Deb nudged Wes.

"If I must," Wes groaned. "Firstly, the rotating cabinet is an imported video, called `newcabglass.mov`, created by one of Deb's old workmates. Deb has been playing with Flash MX a little outside class, and she found that Flash can import video files."

"Wow!" Zed slobbered.

"That's precisely the reason why I didn't cover it in class," I said. "The tendency is to get excited at the thought of using video and not consider the problems associated with it – like inflated file sizes for instance."

"Yeah, that's what we found out too!" said Wes. "Anyway, we've left this SWF out of Frieda's final website, and have just created it to see what we could do really.

"OK, imported video assets consist of frames, so a video's timeline can be navigated by inputting a `gotoAndStop()` ActionScript command in the Actions panel. Because the video was 30 frames long, Deb decided to make a button for each frame, each of which would send the video timeline to a different frame. These buttons were laid along the video and each was given its own ActionScript."

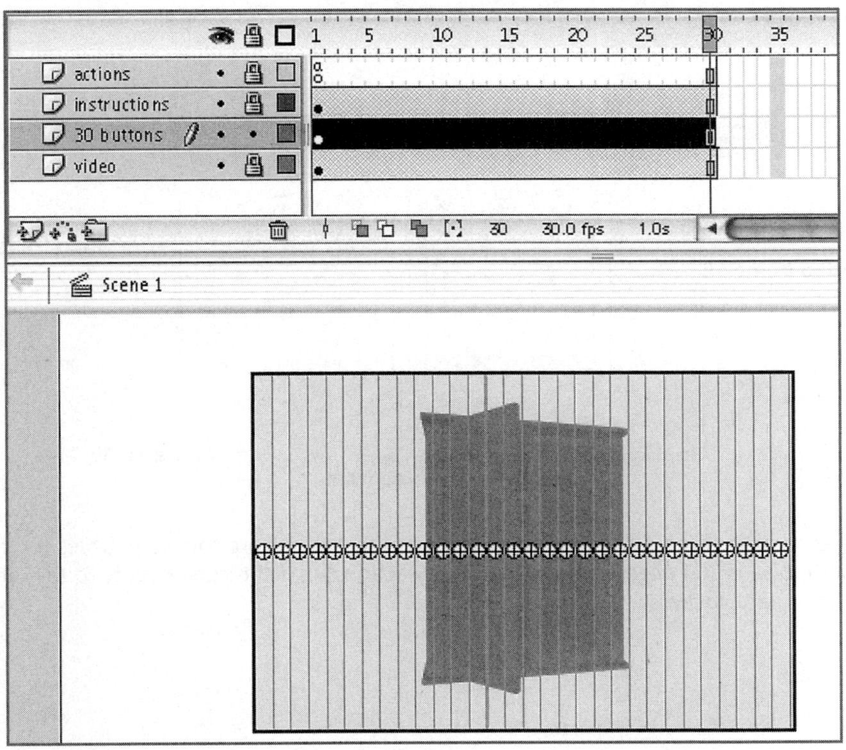

"The buttons here are invisible," Deb said. "The symbol they are all instances of only has a Hit state, so they don't show anything, but they still work like buttons.

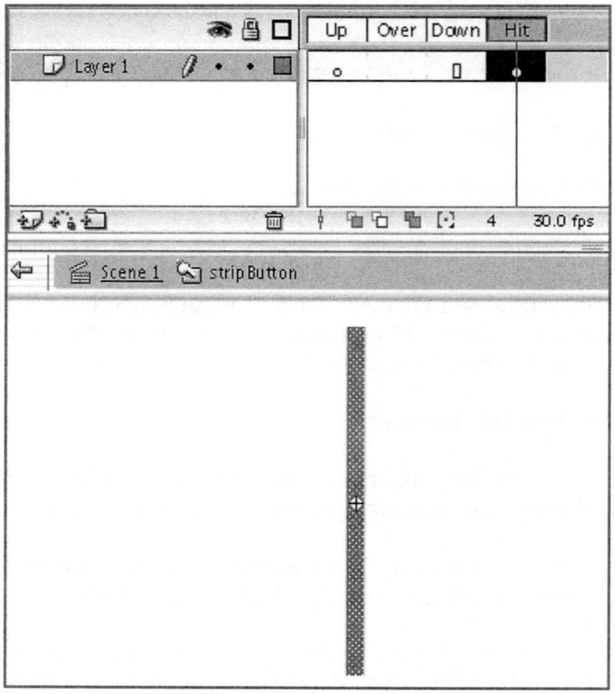

"The other special consideration is how the buttons are coded. Each has code to trigger a change when the cursor rolls over them – if you click on any of the buttons, and open up the Actions panel via Window > Actions, or by pressing F9, you'll see the required ActionScript code for each button."

```
on (rollOver) {
    gotoAndStop(28);
}
```

"When we first tried the movie, the navigation didn't seem intuitive, and the rotation was all wrong. We then changed the way that the buttons worked, so that the center button was frame 1 of the video – the cabinet straight on, and moving the cursor left or right tilted the cabinet in the chosen direction."

Deb showed everyone a schematic diagram that indicated how the interactive rotation effect was achieved in their Flash movie:

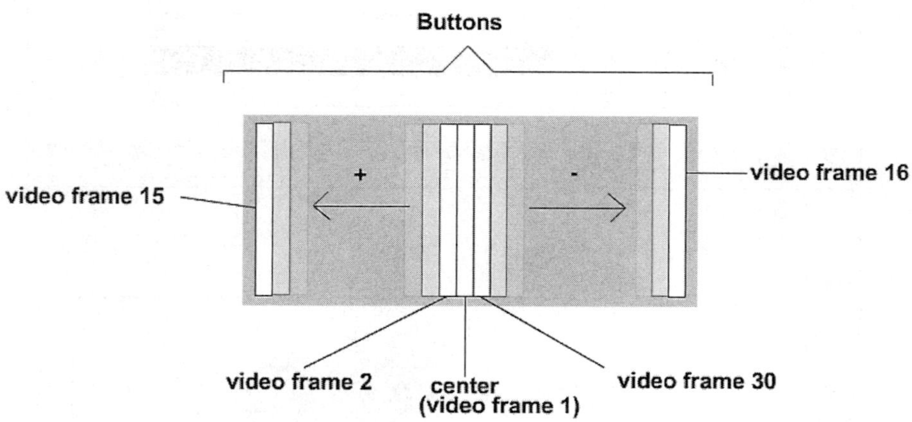

She went on to explain, "The diagram here shows how the buttons are told to behave. The normal rotation of the cabinet movie is 360 degrees in a clockwise direction. So, if the cursor veers to the left of the center, the cabinet is rotated clockwise.

"Conversely, the cabinet is rotated anti-clockwise if the cursor is to the right of the center.

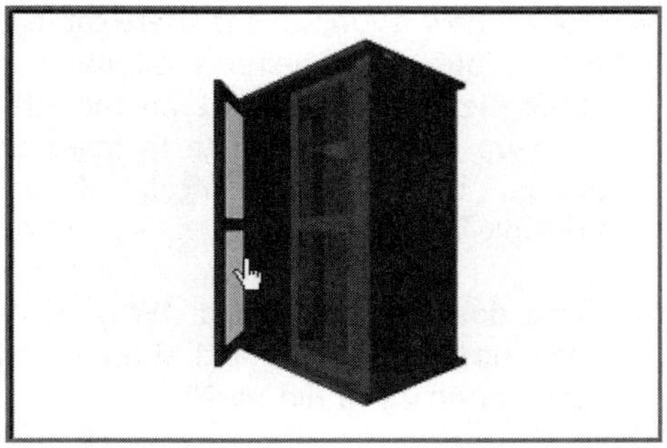

"The further in one direction the cursor is sent, the more the cabinet is rotated in that set direction.

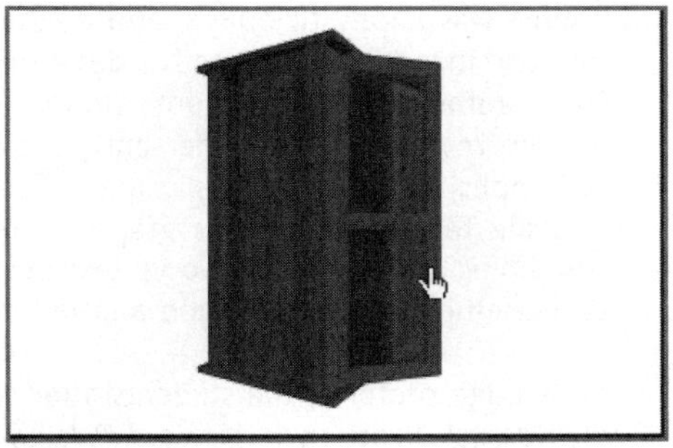

"The normal rotation of the cabinet is 360 degrees in a clockwise direction."

"That's pretty cool!" Zed said.

"Thanks Zed. If you'd all like to look at the Flash file, I'd be happy to supply it to you all – it's called `3D_cabinet.fla`," Deb said. "This way you can take a look at how it was constructed in detail. In reality, it isn't too difficult. It's just creatively utilizing some of the skills that we've all learned in previous classes, and expanding on these skills by doing our own research into using ActionScript and importing video into Flash."

"I think the end result is really effective." I said. "This is a superb use of basic `gotoAndStop()` actions, combined with buttons and an imported video asset. By the way, if any of you are particularly interested in learning more about Flash and video, it'd be worth your while checking out the book *Macromedia Flash MX Video*, available from friends of Ed, ISBN: 1-903450-85-3.

"Right, let's look at one more example of an interactive Flash design before we wrap up this session," I said. "What did you guys come up with?" I looked towards the Bonnie and Zed.

"Nothing as impressive as that revolving video!" Bonnie said. "But I suppose our idea shows some elements of interactivity.

"We thought about allowing Frieda's visitors to try viewing cabinets in different woods to decide which one they like best. We decide to do this as a persuasive device to show the visitors what Frieda could make them.

Bonnie opened up a Flash movie called `wood_textures.swf` on her computer.

"Here's how it looks – the users can click on the various wood textures on the right to apply them to the cabinet on the left. This mock-up isn't good enough to make people swoon, but it quite nicely shows the principle."

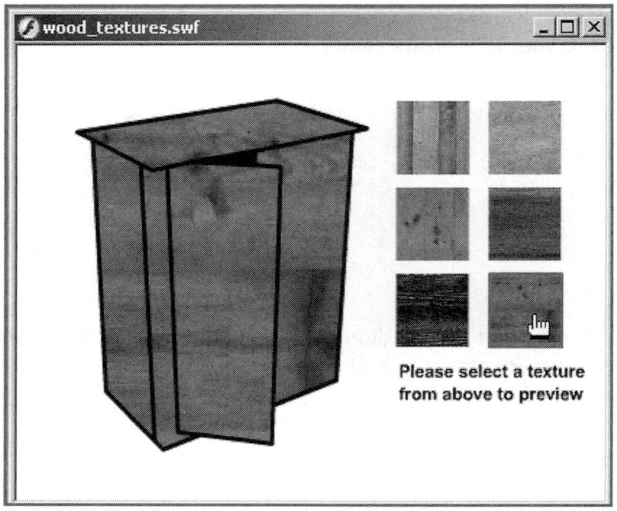

"Sure does Bonnie," I said. "Why don't you open up the FLA file and show us all the basics of how you did this?"

Bonnie was happy to oblige, and opened up the workings of her interactive design in the Flash authoring environment. Bonnie then briefly reviewed how she and Zed had accomplished the effect using a simple masking technique, various graphic symbols containing the different wood textures, the ever-useful Flash buttons, and a little bit of ActionScript.

I was quite proud of the students after seeing their designs in action in this class. "Well, you've all become Flash designers today," I said.

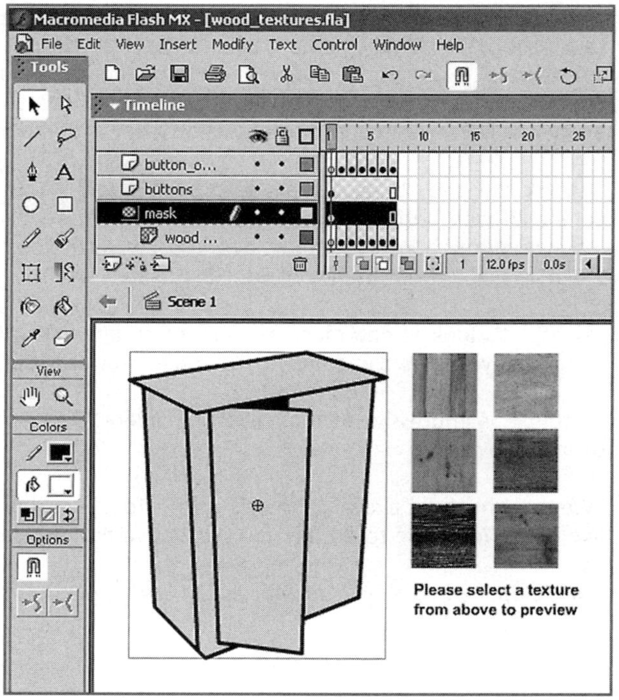

"What you've all done here is started to think interactively within the Flash MX format. If any of you were unsure or a little apprehensive about Flash MX at the start of this course, I think these designs prove that you're all fairly proficient now – and that if there's something you don't know, you've got confidence to go and find out about it. The important thing to point out is that you don't all have to be ActionScript programmers to create something effective.

"Coupling creativity with your basic skills is more than enough to get you started in the realm of Flash interactivity. Once you start experimenting with buttons and eventually ActionScript, there is no telling where you can take it.

"The important thing is to keep writing your interactive ideas down. Even if you don't have the ability to make them now, you'll eventually be able to come back to the problem with new-found skills and create it later.

"Next week, we'll finish our class projects and get them ready them for the web."

"That sounds like we can finally go home!" Zed said. I nodded, watching the majority of the students bolt for the door.

Summary

In this chapter we've studied a wide variety of diverse topics that can be very useful to a designer's creative development:

- **Patterns and symmetry** – We saw that various polygons can be used to create patterns, tilings, and tessellations. These are ideal for developing textures and backgrounds for Flash sites, and are easily created using the Flash drawing tools.

- **Golden ratio and golden rectangle** – We learned how we can use the golden ratio and the golden rectangle to achieve an aesthetic design layout.

- **Drawing techniques and tools** – We utilized a grid to replicate realistic drawings, used scratchboard to learn about creating positive and negative shapes, and showed how we could abstract images into simple two-dimensional shapes.

- **Physics and kinetics in design** – We realized how gravity can affect motion, and how we can depict realistic motion in Flash, focusing on free fall and projectile motion, two of the most common forms of the effects of gravity.

- **Right-brain/left-brain functionality for designers** – We learned how to design in Flash using all of our faculties.

We also took a look at some basic ideas on how to implement interactivity in our Flash MX designs. Next week, we'll learn about printing, and publishing our final projects in Flash. We'll also present a course summary, highlighting what each student has learned during this design course.

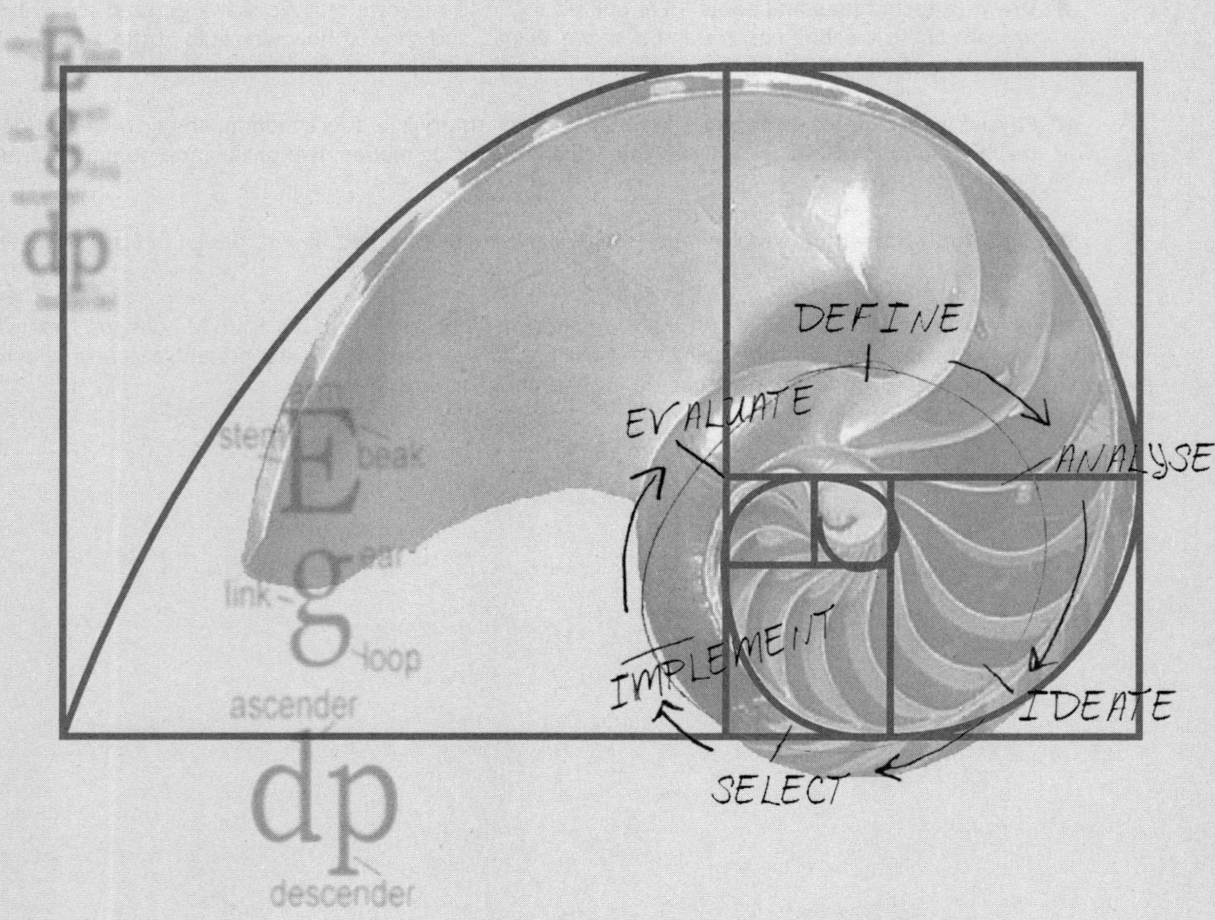

DEFINE
ANALYSE
IDEATE
SELECT
IMPLEMENT
EVALUATE
stem
beak
ear
link
loop
ascender
dp
descender

Chapter 12

Print and Publishing

Objectives

In today's class you will learn about:

- The printing process, including print size, resolution, and color
- Publishing your designs on the web

Introduction

"Well, this is it," Zed entered the classroom and laid his portfolio bag on the table. "This is the last class. I sure learned more than I bargained for with this course."

"How do you mean, Zed?" I asked.

"When I first asked for this class for my birthday, I thought I'd learn how to animate. I didn't realize I'd learn things like math, physics, art history, *and* Flash MX. I've really learned a lot."

"I agree," Bonnie stated as she entered the room. "I thought static design was all there was to life. I can see now why my clients were curious about Flash. I'm very happy I've changed my attitude about this interactive form of communication."

Steve and Lisa entered the room, and Wes and Deb followed them. "Good morning, everyone!" We greeted each other, and they settled in at the table.

"Well, this is it," Wes stated. "Hard to believe our time has passed so quickly."

Steve agreed. "Last week's class was great. I learned so much from your presentations."

I agreed, and leaned forward to address the class, "All of you have so much to bring to the design experience." I looked at Zed. "Zed, you sure surprised us with your interest in physics. Your information about gravity was interesting."

"Yeah, and that was just about stuff close to earth," Zed flung his scarf around his neck. "Wait till I get a chance to tell you about what happens in deep space!"

We all laughed. "It can wait, Zed," Bonnie stated. "You're about as close to deep space as I want to get for now." She looked at Deb, "Your information about the golden ratio was interesting, thanks for that."

Deb nodded, "You're welcome. I was impressed with Wes's project on right-brain and left-brain functions."

Zed snorted, "I think your right brain went wild lately, Deb. I don't know too many folks who would quit their job, braid their hair, and get a tattoo all within a few weeks."

Deb blushed, and the rest of us laughed. "I realize what I did," Deb admitted. "I hope I can find a middle ground from here."

Wes shook his head, "Don't get boring on us, Deb. You have a lot of entertainment factor left in you, I'm sure."

I looked around. "Well, I guess the only person left to present their research is Steve," I stated. "Today, we'll learn how to publish our sites, but first we'll learn more about the printing process. Steve will tell us what he knows, and we'll go from there."

Steve stood and went to the board, ready to give his presentation on the printing process.

Working with a printer

Steve turned to face us, and began talking about why we might want to learn more about the print process. "As designers, it helps to know about converting images from screen to print, even if we think we'll never use it," he said. "But, if we find ourselves in a situation where we're designing a mark or logo for a client in Flash MX, we may find this client may want our designs made available to a printer or a service bureau."

He waved his arms at the computers along the other wall. "We learned a lot about how to prepare our work for optimum viewing on the screen," he stated. "But this isn't what our client needs for a major print job like four-color brochures using the CMYK process, or a large number of flyers where the quality from a desktop printer is insufficient."

He continued, "I'm not going to show you how to construct a newsletter or brochure. All this takes skill sets and software other than Flash. Today, I'm going to show you how to prepare your vector-based or bitmap logo or mark for Frieda's printer from your Flash MX program." He grinned, "That should be enough for one day."

Steve turned to write a comparison between preparing art and type for screen and for print on the whiteboard. "When we prepare our work for Flash, we used RGB color, which we know stands for Red, Green, and Blue, and 72 **ppi**, or pixels per inch, for artwork, typefaces, and photographs, unless we use vector images. For print, we need to use CMYK color or grayscale and we need to prepare our work at a larger **dpi**, or dots per inch. The dpi is also measured in **lpi**, or lines per inch," Steve added. "The lpi is measured by the lines of dots in a halftone print. Let me cover the ppi and lpi first, and we'll get to lpi when I talk about converting bitmaps for printing."

Steve pointed at the terms *ppi* and *dpi* on the board. "Basically, these two terms are interchangeable when it comes to print. ppi becomes dpi when the image goes from screen to print. The main problem with printing web graphics is the transfer of 72 ppi to the print environment. Although 72 ppi is fine for screen viewing, it's a very low dpi resolution for print."

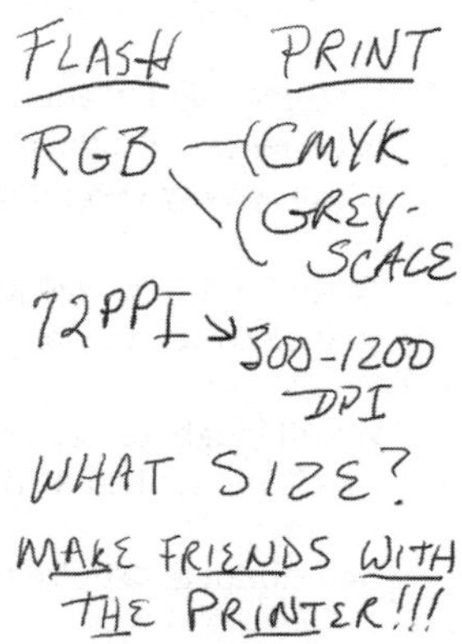

He kept writing, "For print, we need to provide various sizes for the printer, and we need to specify how these images will be used for the client. It's always best to know the exact size needed by the printer so we can do the work ourselves. This way," he added, "We have control over the quality.

"The important thing to remember is this." He wrote the next clue to print success on the board. "*Make friends with your printer.*"

WHAT KIND OF PRINTER- MAC? IBM?

WHICH SOFTWARE?

WHEN DO THEY NEED THE ART?

WHAT SIZE?

WHAT RESOLUTION?

He turned back to the class. "The printer understands how little we might know about the print process. They will help you work with price, paper, inks, color, and print resolution, if you need to know all this." He turned to write this list on the board. "If worst comes to worst, take your work to the printer and he or she will tell you what they need.

"You'll need to know what type of computer the printer uses, and try to modify your files to their software and computer make. If they use Macs, you need to find out how to convert your files if necessary. If they only use Photoshop, you need to have or find a compatible version of this software to convert your files."

He continued, "If someone needs the logo or mark for an ad for a magazine or newspaper, the production manager of the publication is similar to the printer down the road. They carry the same responsibilities of prepress work, and they'll let you know what they need for the ad."

Steve grinned, "Once you supply them with the right size logo, you can only hope and trust they'll get everything else right. Sometimes the print job will be what they call a 'rush' job, and you won't have a chance to look things over before the print run. Other times," he added, "You'll have a chance to check the prepress pages or proofs before the actual run. If you have a chance to do this, I recommended you do it. That way you can make sure the logo is the right color, size, and proportion for the job."

Print size and resolution

"In the meantime, let's learn a little bit so we don't look like lambs lost in the woods," he stated. "Let's talk about the size and resolution issues first. When it comes to Flash," he grinned, "We're in luck."

Vector images

Steve continued with his explanation of the difference between screen images and images for print. "I think it was wise that we all used type for Frieda's mark. The type within Flash is vector-based, so we have little problem with creating a file for the printer. The vector-based image is infinitely scalable without loss of resolution."

Steve reminded us, "The images I'm talking about are our vector-based image files. We can always just hand a typeface file to the printer, but the problem we have between our work and the printer's conception of our work is kerning, or any other alterations we made to the type image."

"If you have a graphic software program that allows you to save your type as 'outline' in the type pull down menu, use it. It will make your life easier," Steve said, "What this does is convert the type from type to an image. When you convert the type to an outline image, your printer's computer will see it as an image, and it won't mess up the type.

"Not all computers carry the same typefaces, and not all software programs read these typefaces either. Unless you can supply the type you use to the printer in a file, it would be to your advantage to convert the type to image if you can.

"Just don't convert the type to an outlined image before you finish with the sizing or color mode. If you do, you'll have to work with the type as an outlined image, with vector points."

He turned to us and emphasized, "Printers will tell you that the most common problem they have with artwork coming from designers is the inability to match typefaces between the designed work and what the printer has available in their computer."

"You need to supply the font with the artwork, or convert your type to outline. These are the only two options you have if you want the perfect match to what you designed."

Can we move to the computers?" Steve asked me. "I think it would be easier to see this process as I do it on the computer, with the software program."

I agreed, and we all moved to a computer. Steve sat, and we circled around him to see how we could convert our designs from screen to the print process.

"This is for those images that aren't vectors," Steve said. "Some of us might make type or images in other programs and import them to Flash. These images, if not vector images, would consist of pixels, and are called bitmaps."

Steve pulled up the Flash MX software and the site that he and Lisa designed. He began to explain the process. "When we change size or color of an image, this is called **resampling**.

"Compared to vector images, where we can resize the image without any loss, resampling a pixilated image isn't a good thing," he added. "Every time we change the size of the pixilated image, we alter the number and size of pixels. This means the pixels jump around to recreate the image, and each time we do this, the image is altered. I'll talk more about resampling in a bit – for the moment let's look at exporting vector graphics.

Exporting the mark

"There is a way to retain Flash content in vector form. This vector image can then be opened in a suitable application and the color mode changed. Flash is able to export to EPS or Adobe Illustrator format, and vector drawing applications, like Illustrator or Freehand are able to import these formats in vector form.

"There isn't much you have to do to in Flash to export in these formats. Firstly you need to separate the logo from the rest of the content. One way to do this is to copy and paste them from the main movie into a new one. Everyone looked over at Steve's Mac."

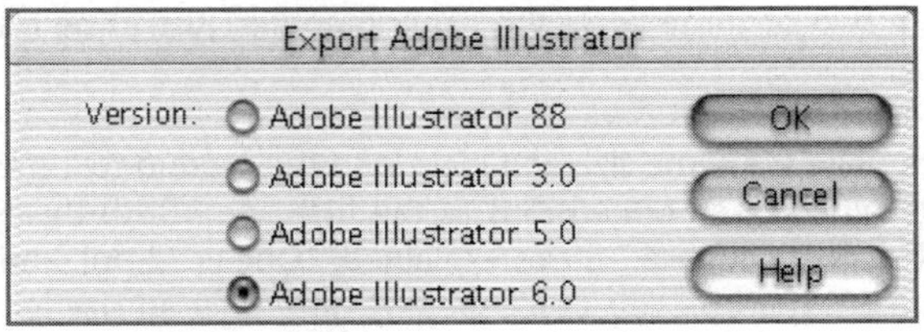

"Now we can export the logo alone as an EPS or Adobe Illustrator file by clicking File > Export Image... and selecting `.eps` or `.ai`. When you're exporting to Illustrator format, be sure to save at the highest version for maximum compatibility."

"I then need to open the file in Adobe Illustrator or another vector application. When we open the exported logo file in Illustrator, the color mode is automatically changed to CMYK mode. I can now go ahead and resize the image size without any loss of quality."

Once Steve had changed the image size, he stated, "The vector-based image was easy. The problem with bitmap images is that the transfer to print is much more complicated. Let's deal with that now."

"What if we wanted to export the logo for the web?" Bonnie interrupted

"That's easy Bonnie, Flash gives us loads of export options. Instead of selecting `.eps` or `.ai`, choose `.jpg`, `.png` or `.gif`."

Bitmap images

Steve looked a bit lost for a moment due to Bonnie's distraction, and took a moment to gather his thoughts. He continued, "So, if we want to save time and frustration, assume that your bitmap work will be used for print when you first begin your design. This way, you can make your original images large enough to compensate for the change from screen display to print production. This will use up a lot of file space, but you will reduce the size for Flash, and keep the original as a backup for later use in another program. When you make the original image, create it at 600 ppi. Save it once it's created, and keep it safe in a separate file. This way," Steve explained, "You'll have a large enough image to resize for the print process, but it won't kill the file space in your Flash project.

Resizing

"Enlarging a bitmapped image to more than 10% of its original size and intended resolution will alter the look of the artwork," Steve continued. "This is one reason why vector images are much better than bitmaps. I can't emphasize this enough," Steve reminded us. "Vector images, like the ones we can create in Flash, can be enlarged or reduced with little loss of image clarity, and it's the best type of image to pass to the printer."

"Fortunately, Frieda has photographs of her cabinets. We can have those images reproduced from her negatives and hand the second set of photographs off to the printer. If we're responsible for the final look of a printed piece, we can check the printer's proof before they actually do the print run. This way," he added, "We can make sure the print image matches the colors if printed in color, or values if printed in black and white, of the photographs."

He brought up a bitmap image in Flash. "The quality of this photograph has been altered to accommodate the 72 ppi format of Flash MX. I didn't keep a copy of the original, and the client wants this image for a printed piece. What do I do now?"

Wes answered, "Cry?"

Steve laughed, "That might be a good choice, but I have another way to handle the problem." He made two copies of the image. "I always make a copy of the image to work from, so I don't tear my hair out over losing the one image I have left," he said. "Sometimes I make two or three while I'm experimenting, just to be on the safe side."

He kept one image the same size and increased the second to 1200 ppi, with the same screen dimensions as the first one. "Both these images are 150 pixels square," Steve explained. "One is 72 ppi, and the other one is 1200 ppi. You don't see any difference in size, do you?"

Everyone agreed. "In fact, both images are about 5 kilo bytes in size. Now, look at the print sizes," he said. He brought up the image size on each one and we viewed the print size. "As you can see, the 72 ppi image size is 150 pixels square, but the print size is 2.083 inches square. The 1200 ppi image is 150 pixels square, but the print size has reduced to 0.125 inches square."

"This is a calculated size, and almost impossible to measure on the screen, due to various screen resolution sizes. The only way to see the difference is to actually print out the images."

Steve printed out the images. He them showed them to us. "Wow, what a difference in size," Lisa stated. "Let me get this straight," she added. "The larger the ppi, the smaller the print image, if you keep the pixel dimensions – the height and width – the same size."

"Yep," Steve agreed. "Although they look the same on the screen, they don't look the same when you print out the separate images from a graphics program. If you put both these images in a web page at the same dimensions, even if they're of different resolutions, they would print out the same size..."

"...because you've captured the images in the same screen resolution," Lisa stated. "But, when you print them out as separate graphic images, they really show their true print image size."

Steve nodded, "It's the only way to check your images, if you want them to be as accurate as possible in size. Don't print them from your Flash or web page, print them out from a graphic software program."

For position only

Steve asked Wes to grab his portfolio bag while he continued to explain the print images. "If you want to display how large your logo or mark will be for the printer, just bring the image up, and make it the right size at 72 dpi, and you can print it either in color or black and white. This will give the printer a working area and he'll know that it's not the correct image, because you'll write *FPO* on the image. This stands for *For Position Only*.

He showed us a sample of his and Lisa's logo ready at FPO for the printer. "Make sure you mark it clearly, but don't cover it up completely," Steve said. "Give the printer plenty of space to see the actual image."

He pulled another board from his bag, "When you deliver the FPO to the printer, make sure that it's the right size." Steve showed us a board that had different sizes of Frieda's name pasted on it. "Remember," Steve said, "This is just for bitmapped images, not for vector images."

"Each style of printing may require a different ppi," Steve said. "If the printer wants 600 ppi/dpi, since the logo will be used on a glossy magazine or other high quality print job with photos, then it's best to supply the 600 ppi. You might be tempted to supply a 300 and 1200 ppi/dpi at the same time, but don't waste your time. Each print job will be different, and each one will require a different size bit of artwork. Very seldom will you need to supply anything larger than 600 ppi," Steve added.

Halftone images

"The other measurement used in the print industry is **lpi**, or lines per inch," Steve stated. "This measurement is described as the resolution, or coarseness of a halftone, and it represents the number of rows of dots to each inch in the halftone screen."

"What's a halftone, Steve?" Zed asked.

Steve answered, "This is a method of reproducing continuous tone images on a printing press by breaking it up into a pattern of equally spaced dots of varying size. These dots produce various tones, shades, or values: the larger the dots, the darker the value. We already talked about dpi, which is dots per inch. The lpi is the number of lines per inch that carry these dots," Steve concluded.

"These lpi measurements are fairly easy to remember, as they're about half of the dpi. A 65-line screen is used to print low-budget items like coupons, or flyers. An 85-lpi is used to print newspapers. The 150-lpi is the one we're most interested in, since 150-line is a great halftone print screen. You would need 300 ppi/dpi images for a 150-line halftone screen. Anything higher than this is considered art magazine material, and would be printed on high-quality paper."

"These printouts should clear up any other questions you have," said Steve as he passed them around

- **Monochrome** – A single color. Monochrome usually refers to a black-and-white image. Also referred to as line art or bitmap mode. Need to supply at 1200 DPI/PPI for monochrome.

- **Halftone** – A method of generating an image on a press or laser printer that requires varying densities or shades to accurately render the image. This is achieved by representing the image as a pattern of dots of varying size. Larger dots represent darker areas, and smaller dots represent lighter areas. Need to supply images at 300 DPI/PPI for halftones (CMYK/Grayscale)

- **Combination Halftone (Combo)** – An image that is a combination of elements from halftone and line art. The most common occurrences are images where the labeling of the image is outside of the halftone area. The requirements for this type of image are that the text be crisp and clear, while the quality of the halftone is unchanged. The only way to do this is by combining the properties of the two image types. Need to supply 600 DPI/PPI for combination halftones.

He went back to his computer and opened Photoshop. "I'm going to show you how to use a 72 ppi image to make a suitable image for print for halftone," he stated. He pulled up an image of an animal skull. "This would be the 150 lpi, or 300 ppi/dpi. Most graphic programs will have an image size menu, and the ways you access the functionality will be pretty similar, so the principles of what I show you hold true with whatever you're using.

"When you have to use a 72 ppi JPG, it doesn't matter if the image program is vector-based or not, because you've still got the problem of pixels. I talked about resampling before, and I'm about to show you how resampling will affect your artwork."

Steve repeated the definition of resampling, and explained how it affected bitmapped images. "When you change the pixel dimensions and display size of an image, you're resampling the image. When you **downsample**, you're decreasing the number of pixels, and information is deleted from the image.

"When you **resample up**, or increase the number of pixels, new pixels are added, based on color values of existing pixels. When you resize an image, you're telling the computer how many pixels you want deleted or added to an image."

He showed us a close-up of the skull image near the antler area. "You can see the pixels here," he said. "What we want to do is resample this image to make it palatable for halftone printing. This means I need to make this image 300 ppi, or 150 lpi."

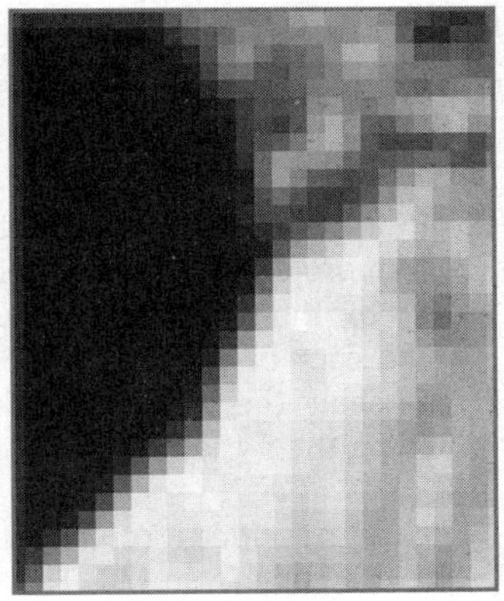

He opened up the Image Size drop-down menu in Photoshop. "To resample a file up, you find the Image > Image Size drop-down menu and select it. Tell the image sizer what print size you'll need. In this case, I'll choose five inches wide."

When Steve selected the image size, the pixel dimensions also changed. "Make sure you have the boxes for Constrain Image and Resample Image, or similar, selected," Steve stated. "Now, check to see if there's an Auto selection. If there is, go there and select 150 LPI. Then go back to the Image Size window."

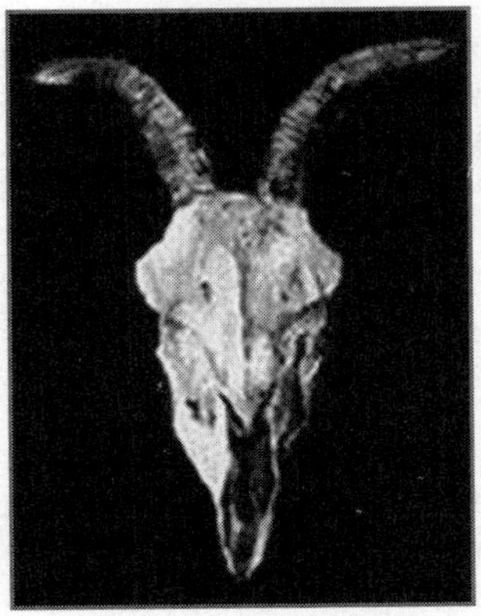

He showed us how that changed the ppi in the Image Size dialogue box. "It was 72 ppi, and now it's set at 300 ppi," he said. "We're ready to push the button to resize this baby."

"What if we don't have an Auto button in the Image Size dialogue box?" Lisa asked.

Steve answered, "Just choose your ppi of 300, and then change the print file size." He showed us the final image. "You may find you need to use an Unsharp Mask, or blur it just a touch to soften the edges and loose whatever pixilation might stand out, or what we would call *ragged edges*," Steve added. He magnified the same area on the skull that he magnified with the 72 ppi image. "The close-up shows that the image is softened, and that it can be used for print," he stated.

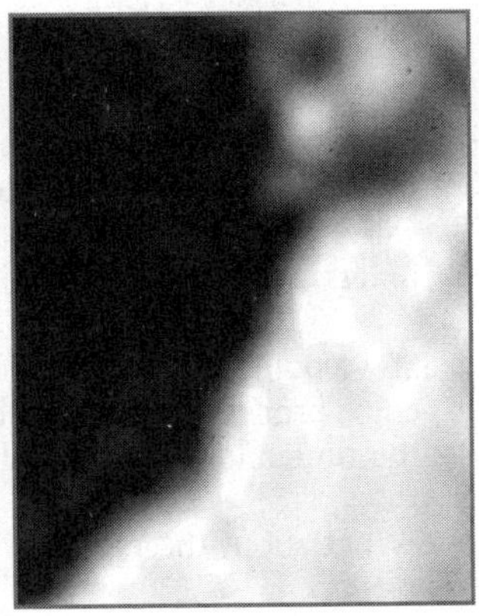

"Don't you lose some detail?" Bonnie asked. "The close-up looks so blurry."

"You do lose detail, Bonnie," Steve said, "But the final image in print will look a heck of a lot better than the 72 ppi image."

He looked around at everyone. "If no one has any questions, let's move onto changing color modes for the printer."

Zed shook his head, "I don't have questions, but I have a statement. I'm sure glad we used vector shapes for Frieda's logo!"

Print color

"We learned about CMYK color and RGB color a few classes ago, the day we went to the theater," Steve said. "CMYK color is subtractive color, and it's used for inks and other print applications.

"RGB is additive color, and it stands for Red, Green, and Blue. These are the colors used for the web and our Flash projects." He continued, "We can always take our RGB Flash images to the printer, and ask them to take care of the problem of converting the colors. If we want more control over the final product, it's best if we take care of all the conversions ourselves. In fact," Steve noted, "The largest problem with print jobs is matching the type in the design. The second largest problem is handing the printer RGB images without telling them they need to be converted to CMYK color.

"Plus," he added, "You might find that most of your friendly neighborhood printers and service bureaus won't have a copy Flash MX. This is the third biggest problem printers have with designers. If you supply files in software formats that the printer doesn't have, you won't have a print job. This could be a huge problem, if you're expecting them to open your files from your client's site or from files you have on a disc or CD."

Steve jumped up and went to the board to write a list of various print color jobs. "Your logo or the print job will define the color process used," Steve said. "If your logo is black, this is the cheapest way to go. Your color logo may be printed in black ink with a halftone screen if it's a black and white print job. In this case," he suggested, "It would be a good idea to supply a black and white copy of your logo or mark to the printer, and a logo that's also in grayscale, to show various tonal values created by the colors in the job."

"That's a good point, Steve," I interrupted. "When you design a mark or logo, try out the design as black and white and in grayscales before you finalize the design. You may find that you'll need to modify the image to accommodate black and white printing. It's not really a good idea to modify a logo design. Creating the image to carry itself across a range of printing options is the optimum choice."

Steve agreed. "Also, if your logo is two colors, it can help to define a two-color print job," Steve added. "The printer may use the two colors to print the rest of the flyer or brochure. But," he added, "Usually a printer will use black and another color, especially if there's type in the job. They like their print type to be black, unless you specify otherwise. A two-color printer is the type of printer most smaller print shops own."

Steve pointed at the four-color print job on the board. "This is a print job using four flat colors, or the four-color process. Just remember, every time the printer changes colors, he has to clean the press. This adds to the time and price of a job."

"What about three colors?" Zed asked.

Steve answered, "Three colors is an odd number, Zed. If it's run on a two-color press, the third color means that the job will take another run. If it's run on a four-color press, it will run with an empty ink well, but you're still paying for four colors. Three colors can best be obtained by using one or two colors and a screen."

"Is the screen like a transparency in most graphic software programs?" Lisa asked.

"It is," Steve agreed. "If you use two colors, and make one of them a screen to provide the third color, then you'll save your client a lot of money."

He walked back to the computer and said, "Just remember that the more complicated you get with color, the more it will cost you and your client. Fluorescent and metallic inks are harder to work with than standard inks. Four flat PMS colors will cost more than a four-color process. PMS stands for the Pantone Matching System we learned about on our 'color' day in class. If you stick with CMYK and the four-color process and avoid PMS colors, the printer may be able to go straight from your job to another job. That may save time on clean-up and set-up for the printer, and will save money for you in the long run."

Steve stated. "If we design our client's logo in Flash, like we did here in class, we can keep the design and transfer it to another software package to convert the colors and size of the file.

Steve opened one of the files he exported from Flash into Photoshop, making sure that the resolution was 300 dpi and that the color mode was RGB.

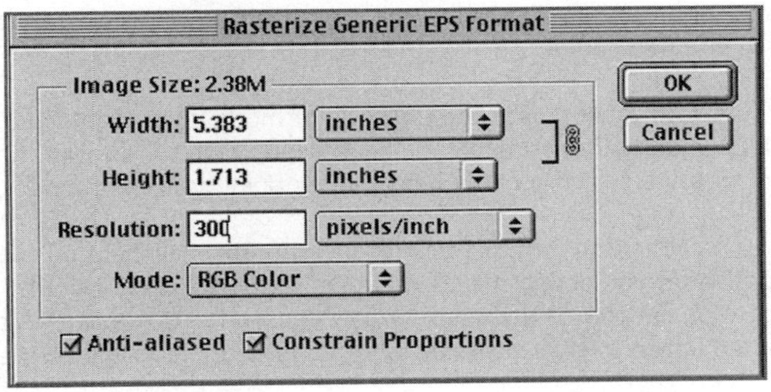

He then explained the standard color conversion process. "Most every graphic software program does RGB to CMYK conversions," Steve stated. "These conversion programs basically all work the same way. You just find the color conversion menu, which could affect the whole document, as in Illustrator, or just the image, as in Photoshop. In Photoshop the color mode is changed via Image > Mode."

"First," he cautioned, "You create another window for the image, Image > Duplicate in Photoshop, and keep the original at RGB so you can compare the changes once you've converted the second image. Then, you convert the second image from RGB to CMYK." Steve changed Frieda's name from RGB to CMYK.

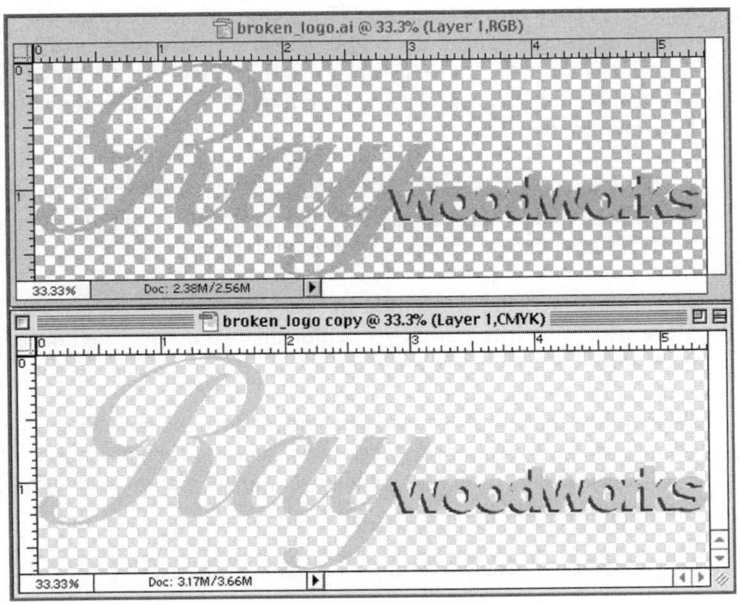

Bonnie asked, "I noticed the color in Frieda's name changed a bit when you changed the color mode, Steve. Why did that happen?"

Steve explained, "That's called **color shifting**, Bonnie. If you take an RGB image to a printer, they will do just what I did. This is called a **standard color mode change**. When you make the change yourself, you have a chance to make color corrections to make sure the CMYK image looks similar to the RGB image. Plus, you can adjust come of the contrast and value."

He turned to the class, "If you're designing for print, you design in CMYK color mode. If you design for computer applications, you design in RGB color mode. We already learned why we use RGB in computer applications when we learned about color spaces. The computer is capable of portraying images in RGB only. The CMYK color space in our computer displays CMYK colors as closely as they'll get. Frankly, it's just something everyone in the printing and design industry puts up with.

"You can print out the CMYK conversion and see if it matches the RGB image, too," Steve said. "You can always decide on your colors for either one, based on the knowledge that these colors might be used for both applications.

"One method is to use and match your colors as closely as possible to that color system. We talked about how this is done in Photoshop a few weeks ago." Of course," he waved at the screen, "You're never going to see exactly what you see on the screen in print. Once you've viewed the colors on a good monitor, print will seem dull. Plus," he added, "If you want to be kind to your client's budget, you won't use more than two colors in a logo for PMS process colors, as I mentioned earlier."

He thought a second and added, "Just make sure your artwork is in the CMYK color mode if you want color, or grayscale color mode if you want black and white halftones when you send it out. Don't have it in the Pantone color mode or anything else, unless your printer tells you they want your work in these color modes.

Steve nodded, "The printer can help you match colors, too. But, it's best to incorporate their help on the front end of the design process. If you wait until after you design the client's logo, you might be in trouble." He added, "Sometimes, printers will give you color samples of the colors you've chosen for the image. This way, you can match your own computer printed image to their own colors, or choose colors to match the colors they use on their press."

He turned back to the computer. "The color changes here aren't so horrible. I can make the color corrections I need by using various color menus in the software program." He added, "If the color changes were drastic, I would work with the RGB image, rather than the CMYK image. Then I would repeat the process of duplicating the image, and converting it to CMYK. I would repeat the process until I have a fairly close match between the two."

Once he had the CMYK image corrected to his satisfaction, he pressed the 'print' button. "I want to see if the printed image is as I imagined it from manipulating the screen image. I'll print out both the RGB and the CMYK images to see if there's anything I missed."

After we viewed the two printed images, Steve and Lisa agreed that it met with their satisfaction. "Now," Steve said, "We write down every color that we used in the image." This will need to be finished once we go back and finalize the actual artwork.

"Remember that I just showed you the way to change the color mode in a vector-based image. A bitmap change will be much more complicated, and will take much more time to remedy the color compensations. But," Steve added, "Once you have it done, keep an extra file for yourself so you don't have to go through the process again."

"Any questions?" Steve asked. "I think I'm about talked out!"

Lisa laughed, "I'm just glad I have you on my team, Steve. This makes life a lot easier."

"This sure gives me a whole new outlook on image sizes," Bonnie added. "I'm so glued to 72 ppi, and that isn't all that good if I have bitmap images I could be using for a client's print job."

"It's better to reduce, rather than, expand the size of the image, Bonnie," I stated. "Vector images are the way to go for printing, but you can always work around bitmap images, too. Just remember to keep files on your client of different images and sizes, and you're in good shape."

"Way to go, Steve, good job," Wes patted Steve on the back.

"Sure enough, Steve," Zed added. He started the applause, and Steve stood to take his bow.

"Well, everyone," I said. "You just learned how to resample bitmaps and how to save vector images for the printer. Steve also showed you how to convert your RGB images to CMYK or grayscale for the printer. He also gave you some very useful print-related information.

"I think it's time for a short break," I stated. "When you come back, we'll tackle the graphic user's manual, then we'll publish your Flash sites."

"Yes!" Zed pumped his fist in the air. "I'm ready to publish!"

The graphic user's manual

When the class returned from break, I asked them to sit at the table one more time. "We're going to learn how to hand over information to a service bureau or printer. This way," I said, "The printer won't have last minute questions about minor things, and you both can rest assured that most of your questions have been answered.

"The graphic user's manual is basically a small book or file of images and instructions for your client's images. These files consist of various views of your client's mark or logo, and instructions on typefaces used in the text of any copy for an ad or a brochure. Most designers spend months working on these manuals. The manuals you'll learn about today cover the minimum basics the printer would need to know about your client's graphic material."

"Why would we need to do this?" Zed asked. "It seems to me that all a printer needs to do is look at the client's site and take the look from what we have online."

Steve laughed. "Zed, a printer is usually a very busy person. Their work relies on how many print jobs they can shove into a day. They don't have time to cruise to a site and make mental images and notes of what we've designed."

"Thanks, Steve," I said. "Zed, Steve is right. We need to be explicit about our colors, our typefaces, and our style for the client. Often, our clients complain that their site isn't doing well. This may not be due to anything we've done. It could be that their collateral design products don't match the site. Their business cards, brochures, newsletters, or other print material may fall short of the quality they need, because every thing might look different. If this is the case, then it could affect traffic to their site."

"Is it OK if we design their business cards and stationery?" Bonnie asked. "That way, everything would have the same look."

"Of course it is, Bonnie. Just make sure you use the proper software and work with your printer on paper, prices, inks, and any other details. Also, make sure you include this in your client brief and contract."

Lisa asked, "Would it be good to ask for their print business after the site is designed?"

"That's another resounding yes, Lisa," I stated. "If the client comes to trust us and our Flash design work, there's no reason not to ask for their print business as well.

"For now, let's concern ourselves with the basics." I picked up a binder and began to show it to the class. "Steve and Lisa already made their graphic user's manual, so I'll share this with you this morning. This following information needs to be printed neatly, and compiled in a simple folder. Make sure your contact information is placed on the outside, and if you use a binder, you might want to place the client's name along the spine of the binder."

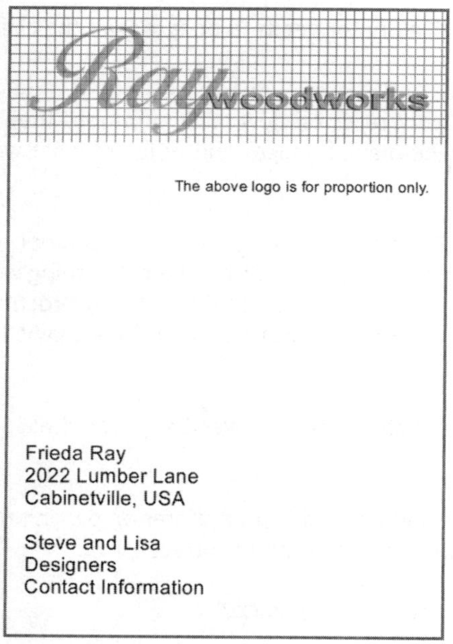

"You want to transfer the logo or mark, and the information about type to the printer." I said.

"As Steve mentioned, supply the logo to the printer in a compatible software program on disk or CD. Talk with the printer to see which they would prefer. If you supply vector-based images, you'll have less trouble in the long run. Bitmap images are fine, also – just be aware they may want different sizes for different printed products.

"Then, on this first page, print the logo or mark out so the printer can see how the subtractive colors will look. If you're not available, the printer can make his adjustments based on this image. At the bottom, away from the logo so they don't think it's part of the logo, print the contact names and the logo color information. You could even add that this logo is also on a disk enclosed with the information."

I showed them a page with Frieda's logo, as well as all contact information. "Notice that this page was laid out on a grid. You can see how the information is aligned along the left side. Since most people will flip the page from the right side, you'll have less wear on the information if it stays away from possible marks and tears along the right side."

I flipped over to the next page. "This is another page with your mark or logo, but this time, you'll place a grid over the artwork.

Most designers use registration marks," I said, "But registration marks are used when you want to place artwork or type in a specific location on a page." I set the binder on the table and drew a registration mark on the board. "In your case, you don't know how the artwork will be used, so the registration mark is moot. A grid will show the printer the exact proportions of your artwork and the exact locations of each color."

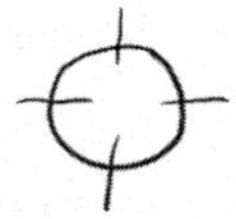

Ray woodworks

The above logo is for grayscale only.

Ray woodworks

The logo above is for B&W printing only.

Frieda Ray
2022 Lumber Lane
Cabinetville, USA

Steve and Lisa
Designers
Contact Information

I showed them another page in the binder. "The next page will show how Frieda's name would look if it were used as a grayscale or as a black and white image. If you make these specifications, the printer will have no question on how you intended the image to be used."

The next page held some type. "This page shows the typefaces Steve and Lisa used in Frieda's Flash site. They specified which typeface to use in Frieda Ray's headings, subheadings, and body copy. If you were more advanced, you would actually specify what the actual kerning between letters would be, and you would have pages that showed various samples of body copy with the headings. For now, this will suffice, since you'll be working more on Flash than you will with printing."

I pointed at the fourth page with the typestyles. "Steve and Lisa let the printer know how all portions of Frieda's type needs to be tracked, and indicated that each line of type is to be based on the *0* baseline, which is the normal line base in most computer type programs. They also indicated how much leading to place within each line of type."

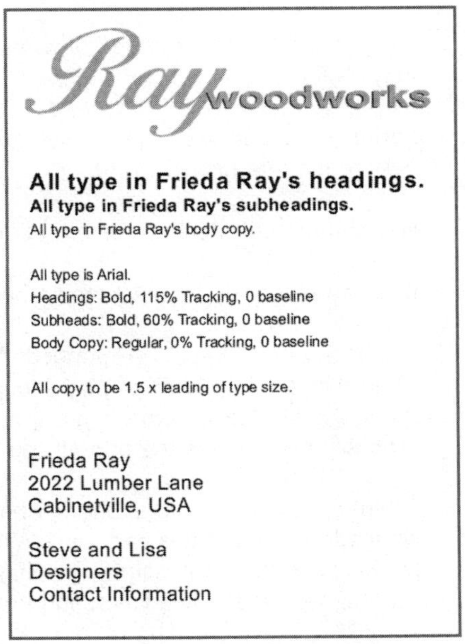

Ray woodworks

All type in Frieda Ray's headings.
All type in Frieda Ray's subheadings.
All type in Frieda Ray's body copy.

All type is Arial.
Headings: Bold, 115% Tracking, 0 baseline
Subheads: Bold, 60% Tracking, 0 baseline
Body Copy: Regular, 0% Tracking, 0 baseline

All copy to be 1.5 x leading of type size.

Frieda Ray
2022 Lumber Lane
Cabinetville, USA

Steve and Lisa
Designers
Contact Information

I drew a business card, letter-sized rectangle, and an envelope on the board. "You might want to resample your images to see how they hold up for these three items – the business card, the letterhead, and the envelope. If you find that your image loses detail or too much resolution when it's too small, then find out what the image threshold is, and make a note that the image can't go below a certain size."

Bonnie asked, "If you wanted to design the stationery, would that also go in the user's manual?"

"Yes," I answered, "But you would also indicated where and how each item would be located with measurements, and you would also include the artwork on a disk, compatible to the printers computer and software." I drew some measurements on the stationery. "You would indicate every measurement possible, so there's no misunderstanding how the stationery stands in your design. Every direction going into the placement of the logo or mark and your other information would contain a measurement."

I added, "And make sure you aligned everything within a grid. If you need extra pages to place grids over the stationery to show location, then add those pages."

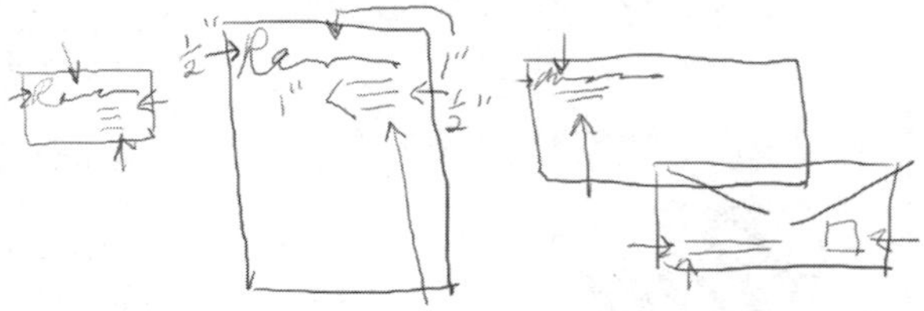

Steve agreed, He pointed to their logo in the manual, "Lisa and I designed Frieda's name with a shadow behind the word '*woodworks*'." When we supply the art for her name to the printer, he may ask us to separate the shadow and supply this on a separate file. This way," he added, "They can print the shadow in the separate color from the color of the word on top the shadow. I always assume I'm speaking a foreign language when I talk with a printer. That way I remember to over-explain my design measurements, rather than leave something out."

"As far as I'm concerned, I am speaking a different language to when this course began," Bonnie stated. "I've learned to walk, talk, and at least take a look outside that box I've created for myself."

"It seems a shame to have to think outside the box only to box it all up with grids," Wes shook his head. "But, I think we can eventually stretch those grids to include some pretty cool designs."

Zed agreed, "I never realized how much we base on grids. Everything I see these days seem to be enclosed in grids."

I grinned, "When you begin to see everything enclosed in grids, then I know you've learned to see how we design our commercial world."

Wes shuddered, "Remind me how to make a circle."

Deb patted Wes on the back, and asked, "Are there a specific number of pages to the graphic user's manual?"

"Good question, Deb," I responded. "There's no rule stating how many pages to include. I've worked with some that are hundreds of pages long, but they also include how to use logos within web sites, television spots, and how to structure radio spots." I pointed at the binder on the table. "At this time, this is all you will probably need unless the printer asks for more information."

"Helpful," Lisa muttered as she finished making her notes. She looked up. "Steve already taught me a lot as we made this book this past week. We spent time at his office doing this so we'd have something to show for his project. It was helpful just having it around for my own use, because I kept forgetting how much tracking we used in headlines, and how we used certain elements within a page."

Steve nodded, "We're working on one for the Flash site, too. That way we have a manual that specifies how we did everything, in case either one of us forgets our goals and structure for the site."

"That's a great idea, Steve and Lisa," I stated. "It's easy to forget the client's goals when we're busy playing with our designs."

"Speaking of playing with our designs," Zed said, "When are we going to publish our sites?"

I looked around. "Are there any more questions?" No one said a word. "You just learned how to make a very basic graphic user's manual for a service bureau or print shop to display how to use your client's design elements. Now," I looked at Zed, "We'll learn how to publish our clients' sites."

"Yes!" Zed literally ran for the computers, and we all followed, shaking our heads at Zed's incredible energy.

Publishing your websites

The class had reached the pinnacle of the web design process. With Frieda's sites finished, all they had left to do was to publish the content and make it live.

"For many of you, the publishing process might be a little daunting," I began. "This is because there are many things that can go wrong, and for the first few times, they usually will.

"Because of this, and as Bonnie might tell you, it is always a good idea to test your content online at a private test location, rather than going live straight away. A private test location isn't a special set-up, it is just a web address or URL that is not publicly known or linked to from anywhere. This way, the location is only accessible by those who know the full web address."

"I have my own test website which has password protected areas." Bonnie said. "Each client has their own folder on the test site, and is invited to view the finalized version before it goes live. By this point, I've rigorously tested the content for bugs, browser issues or anything else."

"Bonnie has kindly offered to allow us to upload Frieda's sites to her test server, so that we can test the content and see how it looks in all the glory of the web. Before we get to the stage where we put our content online, we need to publish our content from Flash in a browser-friendly format.

"Teams," I said. "Open your Flash movies and we'll begin."

Publishing from Flash

"A traditional HTML page consists of text and images. Each of these images is called from a folder and is displayed on the page." I said. "Even though a Flash SWF is a self-contained package, it still needs to be placed in a HTML page before it can go online."

Bonnie laughed. "So even though Flash is all powerful," she said, "It still relies on little old HTML to show it off?"

"Not really Bonnie." I replied. "SWFs don't rely on HTML, they are simply embedded in HTML pages to conform to browser standards. The HTML does nothing besides act as a container for the Flash SWF. Later in class, we'll look at different ways of presenting Flash movies, but for now let's make a HTML doc containing our Flash."

I turned on my laptop and the projector and started explaining. "There are many options when publishing from Flash, allowing you to publish in a variety of formats. These are accessible from File > Publish Settings....

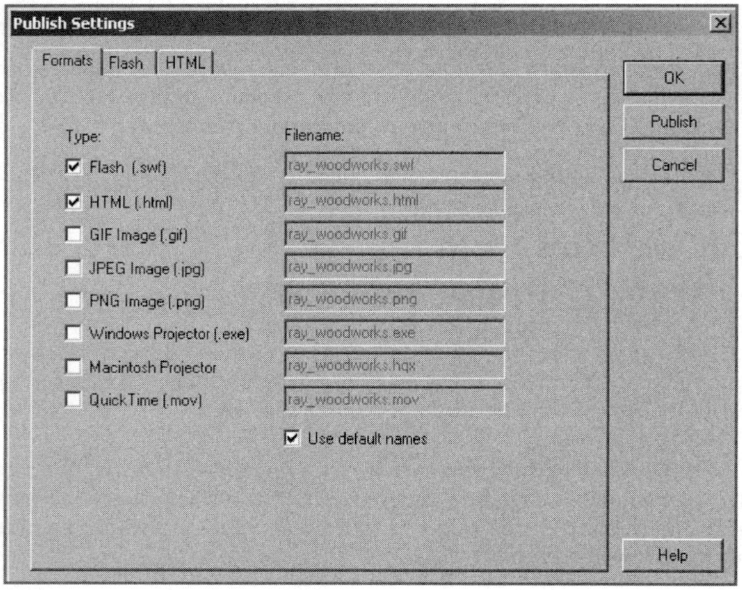

"The only formats that we need here should already be selected, these are Flash and HTML. If they aren't, check them and uncheck everything else. Most of the other formats aren't really worth discussing here as they are only useful for specific tasks, this is with the exception of the Windows and Macintosh Projector formats.

"These formats will produce executable or application files, which run independently of any browsers and don't require the Flash plugin. Projector files are totally self-contained projects so they are ideal for putting on CDs or other offline projects, and they also allow you to run the Flash movie as a full-screen presentation.

"Many of you might have already seen projector files running. They are usually found as the interactive section on music CDs."

Zed's eyes lit up. "You mean that I can put Flash movies on CD?" he said.

"When is the first Anime Zed CD available?" Wes said dryly. "You've done it now Linda! I'll forever be subjected to CDs through the mailbox."

"Sorry Wes!" I whispered. "I'm sure Zed will have forgotten about it by the end of class."

"Let's concentrate on publishing for the masses first." Deb said. "Carry on Linda."

"Sure Deb." I said. "Let's start with the Flash settings, which we get to using the Flash tab at the top of this window. This now presents us with the default settings for our Flash movie. You might recognize this from an earlier class where we covered JPEG compression; this screen has the default JPEG compression setting about half way down.

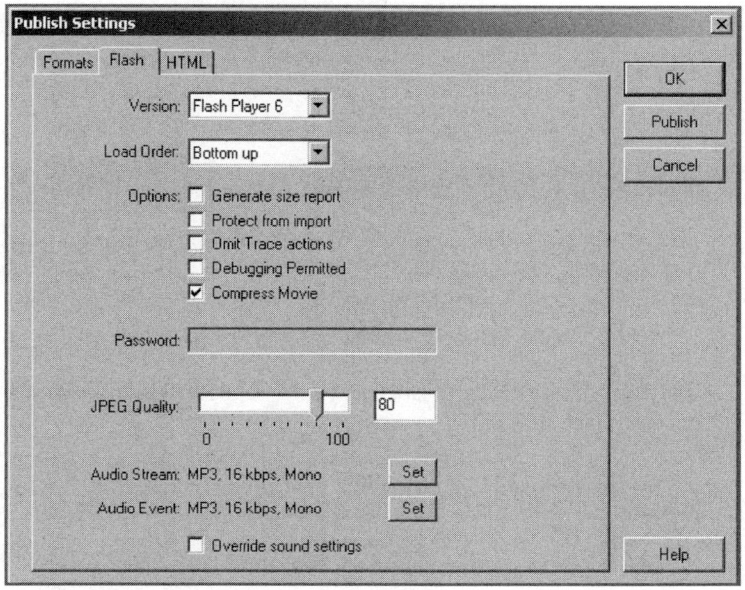

"Most of the settings here are fine as they are. We need to ensure that the version is set as Flash 6, and that Compress Movie is ticked. This will ensure that the final SWF file is extra small because Flash compresses the vector information.

"If you are afraid of others downloading your SWF file and stealing your graphics," I looked at Zed, "For instance, you might want to protect your animations Zed, make sure that Protect from import is ticked. This will prevent others importing your SWF file into Flash and stripping out your graphics."

"Nice one teach." Zed said. "Don't want plagiarists ripping me off."

"Plagiarism is the highest form of flattery." Wes said. "That's how cult figures are born."

"Don't give him any ideas Wes." I said. "Right, let's take a look at the HTML tab.

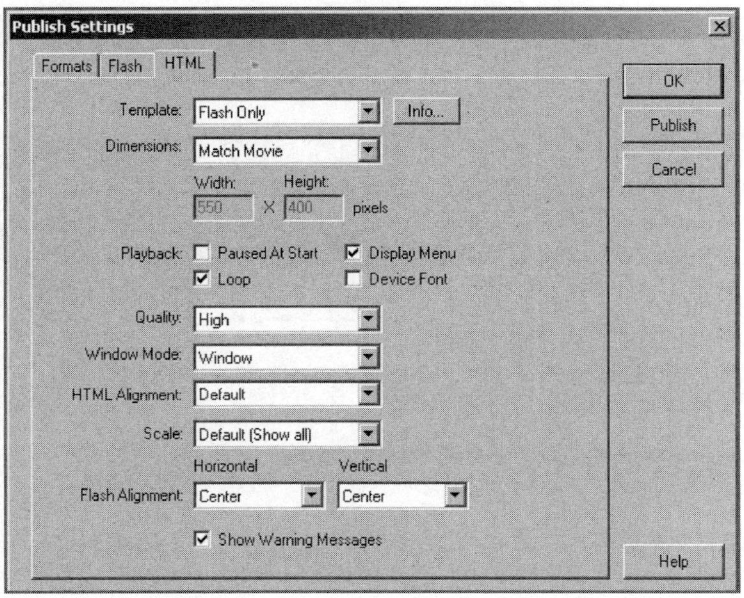

"The first thing you should know is that Flash produces all the relevant HTML code for you."

Bonnie sighed. "You mean these guys don't need to learn how to hand code HTML?" she said.

"Yes." I said. "Flash will do all the hard work for them. It might save you a little time too Bonnie."

"Don't be such a code-monkey Bonnie!" Steve joked.

"Check that your settings are like this." I said, pointing at the projection. "These will produce an adequate HTML page for our Flash movie. When your settings match this, click OK."

"Why not publish?" Bonnie asked.

"We aren't quite ready to do that yet," I replied. "Because we need to make sure that they are saved in a suitable place first.

"Firstly, you need to create a folder on your hard disk and call it *frieda ray project* for instance. If you come to work on a number of projects, you might want to number the projects suitably."

"I number all my projects." Bonnie said. "And then keep a spreadsheet of all of them, so I never get mixed up."

"For your projects, a folder called *frieda ray project* will suffice. You'll need to create one somewhere on the hard disk away from the current FLA files. This will give you a fresh area to store finalized files.

"You then need to save a copy of your FLA into this folder." I said. "Don't copy the file there, make sure you save it from Flash. Although this seems bizarre, it's good to do this because Flash retains the file size of all the symbols in the Library, even when they are deleted. For this reason, a fresh *Save As* produces a new file and rebuilds the Library, removing any file space that was retained from removed symbols and imported items.

"Although the size of the FLA doesn't impact on the size of the published SWF it's good practice to break free in this way. This also places the file in a fresh area, away from countless development files.

"Once you've saved your FLA in the *frieda ray project* folder, you can select File > Publish Preview > Default (HTML) and Flash will do its business, producing a HTML and SWF file, and opening the files in a browser. The HTML and SWF files will handily be placed in the same location as the FLA, in the *frieda ray project* folder."

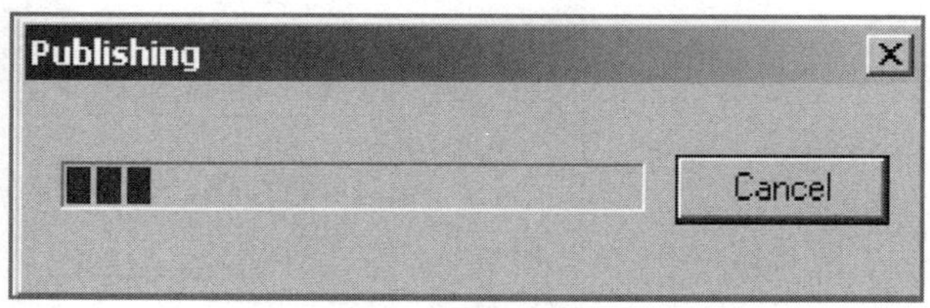

"Once the progress bar is done, your browser will open and the HTML file with the embedded SWF movie is shown. I've chosen to demonstrate this with Steve and Lisa's project as I know it's the nearest to being finished, so don't think it's favoritism!"

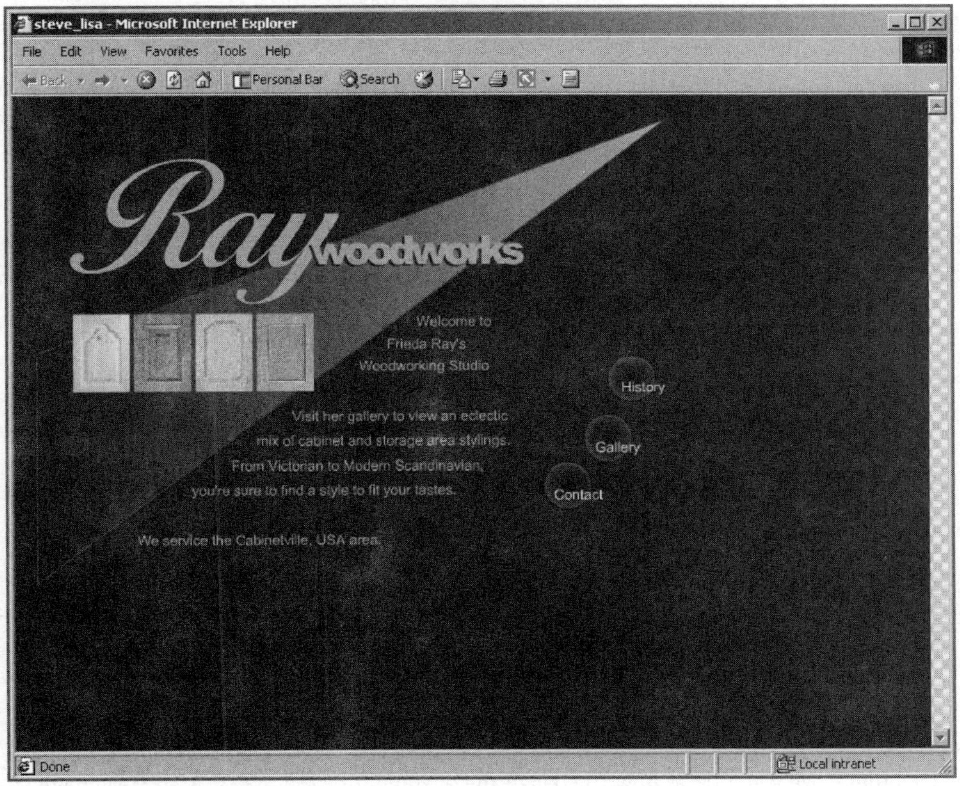

"Groovy!" Zed exclaimed. "It looks like it's finished."

"Almost," Bonnie added, "But not quite. The alignment looks wrong and it doesn't fit the window."

"These attributes can be changed Bonnie." I said. "The page looks as it looks because we told it to be that way in the Publish Settings. Flash was told to publish the movie at 550 x 400 pixels, and to position it in the default position.

"There are a number of different ways to present Flash movies, from pop-up windows sized to the Flash size, to SWFs that cover the whole browser area. We'll take a look at these in a moment, to help you decide which is the best method for your site and for the user.

"For now though, I want you all to see what Flash has produced." I opened up the *frieda ray project* folder on my laptop.

"There are three files – the original FLA, the Flash produced HTML file and the SWF file. To see how big your final SWF movie is, select it and choose File > Show Info for Mac or Right-click and select Properties on a PC.

"Now we can see what's in this HTML file if we open it in a browser and select View > Source on Internet Explorer or View > Page Source on Netscape. For most of you, this window probably contains a lot of garbled lingo. This is in fact the HTML code that Flash has produced for us, containing information to embed the flash SWF and other tidbits of data."

```
ray_woodworks.html - Notepad
File Edit Format Help
<HTML>
<HEAD>
<meta http-equiv=Content-Type content="text/html;  charset=ISO-8859-1">
<TITLE>ray_woodworks</TITLE>
</HEAD>
<BODY bgcolor="#630000">
<!-- URL's used in the movie-->
<!-- text used in the movie-->
<OBJECT classid="clsid:D27CDB6E-AE6D-11cf-96B8-444553540000"

codebase="http://download.macromedia.com/pub/shockwave/cabs/flash/swflash.cab#version=6,0,0,0
"
 WIDTH="550" HEIGHT="400" id="ray_woodworks" ALIGN="">
 <PARAM NAME=movie VALUE="ray_woodworks.swf"> <PARAM NAME=quality VALUE=high> <PARAM
NAME=bgcolor VALUE=#630000> <EMBED src="ray_woodworks.swf" quality=high bgcolor=#630000
WIDTH="550" HEIGHT="400" NAME="ray_woodworks" ALIGN=""
 TYPE="application/x-shockwave-flash"
PLUGINSPAGE="http://www.macromedia.com/go/getflashplayer"></EMBED>
</OBJECT>
</BODY>
</HTML>
```

"There's no need to worry too much about what all this means," I said. "I just wanted to show you it, so you know what's there. We will look at how to change the alignment of the SWF in the HTML page later on, but for now, though, I want to talk about the different ways Flash websites are presented."

Presenting Flash designs

"The chances are that you've all seen the main methods, but just haven't taken much notice of them." I said. "As Bonnie pointed out earlier, sometimes Flash movies can stick out unless they are properly presented.

Flash Formats

1. **In an HTML file at its original size**
2. **Scaled to the browser window**
3. **In a pop-up browser window**
4. **Integrated with HTML content**

"There are a number of ways to present Flash content." I placed a slide on the OHP.

"Each of these is very different, and deserves individual treatment. Before we do that, let's look at the capabilities of Frieda's audience."

"I guess we'll be working with a screen resolution of 800 by 600." Bonnie said. "Am I right?"

"Sure Bonnie." I said. "I think that's about right. Unless you are creating for a particularly technology-focused client, it's usually best to design for the minimum screen resolution of 800 x 600 pixels. You can virtually guarantee that all web users are running at least this resolution."

"By default, most computers start up in this resolution and most people never actually get round to changing it, or some people leave it at this setting so that the text is easier to read. The default Flash format of 550 x 400 sits in the browser quite nicely at this size, and even with the browser window filling the screen, there isn't too much blank space around the Flash movie.

"Now, let's look at the different presentation formats." I said. "The first on the list is how we already have our first page, but for the benefit of Bonnie and anyone else who found the composition missing something, the Flash movie can be aligned in the browser window.

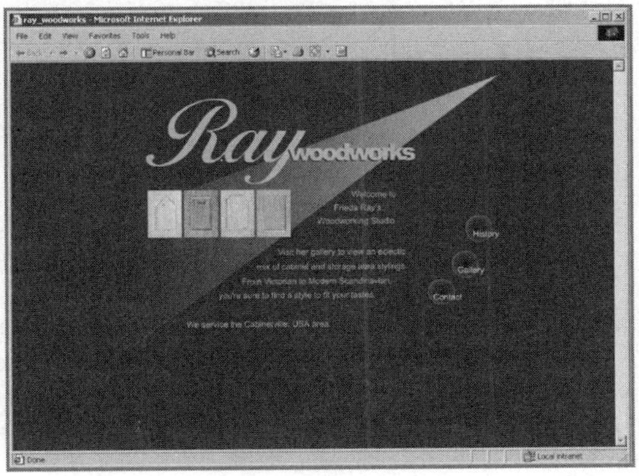

I opened an HTML document with central horizontal alignment.

"This format sees the Flash movie centered horizontally according to the size of the browser window. This is much neater than letting the Flash movie sit in the top left position."

"This is better," Wes said. "But the Flash movie might need a frame or some form of outline."

I opened the next HTML file.

"This format has the Flash movie centered vertically and horizontally, so whenever the user rescales or resizes the browser window, the Flash movie will maintain a central position."

"I like it." Bonnie said. "It sits quite comfortably there."

"I'm still feeling the space." Wes said. "I'm not diggin' it man."

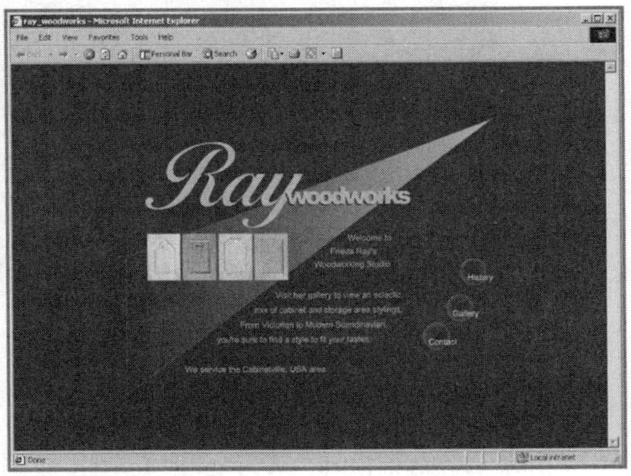

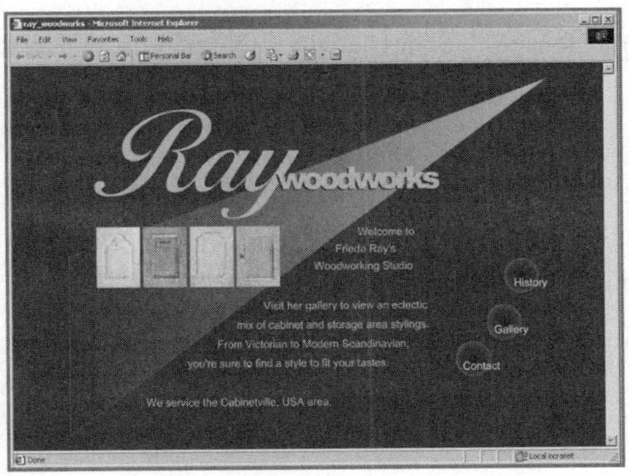

"In that case Wes, the next option, number two on the list, is for you." I said. I opened the HTML file.

"In this format, the Flash movie is scaled to the size of the browser window. Because Flash uses scalable vectors, the movie can be resized and doesn't lose any quality. This option is fine for fully vector-based sites, but the cracks start to show when you use sites that contain images. JPEG compression doesn't scale well!"

"That's it for our site then Deb." Wes groaned. "Our JPEG image is likely to look inferior if we scale it."

"I'm sure there is a suitable option for you Wes." I said. "The next option might actually be the ideal choice." I opened the HTML file.

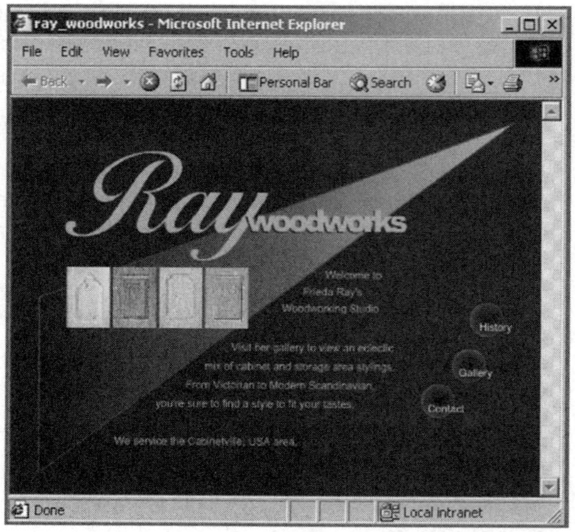

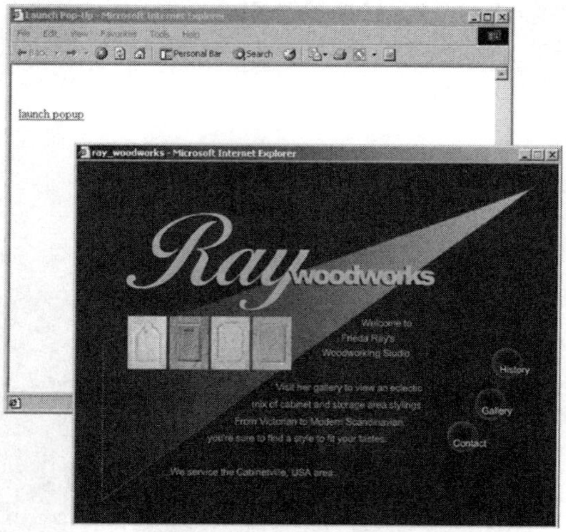

"Opinions on the third format, the pop-up window, are polarized. From a developer's point of view, the pop-up is neat and suitably framed. However, many users hate any popping windows because they are synonymous with advertisements and banners.

"The pop-up window is usually launched through a link from the splash page. The size of the pop-up can be set, so the Flash movie fits it snuggly. In this example, I've set the pop-up to be 600 x 450 pixels, but it could be tighter. You might have also noticed that the pop-up has none of the traditional browser buttons and bars, because these can be switched off, allowing better focus on the Flash movie."

"I'm not that keen on this option." Bonnie said. "I hate having too many windows on screen, especially those which I didn't even create!"

"I think it might work." Wes said. "But I'd like to inform the viewer what is going to happen on the splash screen."

"The option has really gone into overdrive since people started doing it with Flash websites." I said. "It might not be for everyone, but it presents the content in an uncluttered way, and removes the temptation to hit the back button."

"Why do we need to hide the back button?" Bonnie asked. "No website is an island."

"Because Flash movies are contained within one HTML page, hitting the back button just sends the viewer away from the site. Flash MX has a way around this in the way of anchors, so you might want to take a look at them if you'd like to tackle the problem.

"Now onto the last format, Flash integrated into HTML content."

I opened the friends of ED website at www.friendsofed.com.

"What's this?" Deb asked. "What happened to Frieda's stuff?"

"This is the friends of ED website," I replied, "I've brought this up because it shows a balance between HTML and Flash elements. The area in the top left of the website is a Flash movie, whilst the rest of it is HTML content."

"The Flash element compacts a great number of lists and information into a small space. And all the images here are randomly fetched dynamically from a large list.

"Although this option isn't suitable for Frieda's site, it's a good way of dealing with a great deal of information and a site that is updated often."

"So for Frieda's site we have a choice out of the previous options then?" Bonnie asked. "Can we have a little time to talk it over in our teams?"

"Because each format requires a little work, I think it's best if we all go with the very first option, a centered Flash movie. If you want to experiment with these different formats, I'll supply you with all the HTML files before the end of class. Take five minutes to decide which option you would have gone for?" I popped off to fetch a coffee.

When I returned to class I asked the teams which format they might have used for Frieda's site if they had an alternative option.

"Although Deb hates pop-up windows just as much as me," Wes said, "We would have gone for option three, presenting the Flash movie in a pop-up window."

"Wes says it reminds him of hanging his work," Deb said. "He likes the framing and the total immersion. I'm just after an easy life!" Deb laughed.

"How about you Bonnie and Zed?" I asked.

"I think the one that you've chosen for the class is the ideal one." Bonnie said. "I like the idea of centering the movie depending on the size of the browser window, rather than restricting the user to have to resize their window. Zed agrees with me." Bonnie grabbed Zed's head and made him nod.

"I agree." Zed said robotically. Bonnie let him go. "Although I'd most likely use the same format as Wes and Deb for my own stuff. Hiding all the browser assets and hiding the clutter would be far more of an immersive and cinematic experience. I want the viewers to suspend their disbelief, not to click on any buttons to check their e-mail half way through one of my animations."

"That's a pretty convincing argument Zed." I said. "You might want to look at projector files to enhance this experience further." I turned to Steve and Lisa. "What have you both come up with?"

"We favor the scale to browser option." Steve said. "If the monitor is a format, then this is a page-filler. I think it's great that vectors are totally scalable and Flash adheres to this, it's a definite asset to work with." Lisa nodded.

"OK class, we've just got time to have a brief look at FTP."

Uploading the files

"Before placing the content online," I said. "It's usually a good idea to check it offline. This can show you any instant errors, and save you some time.

"If your site is functional, you're ready to put it on the World Wide Web." I said. "Before you can put anything online, you need a host. As we talked about it an earlier class, a host will store your files and allow access to them via the Internet.

"Uploading is the process of taking the files on your computer, and placing them onto the host's server. Uploading is performed via **FTP**, or File Transfer Protocol. FTP is used to both send and receive files.

"To send files via FTP, you need an FTP client. Although most Internet browsers can work with FTP, it is usually best to have a dedicated FTP application like *CuteFTP* for Windows or *Fetch* for Macs, amongst others.

"We aren't going to go into detail about these programs here, as they all work slightly differently and covering all their quirks and capabilities is outside the scope of this course. Besides, each program comes with full instructions. You can download free trials of CuteFTP and Fetch from www.cuteftp.com and http://fetchsoftworks.com, if you want to investigate further."

"Once you've uploaded your sites, just remember to check them thoroughly, before you go announcing them to the world!"

Class summary

Today, we learned about the printing process, and how it pertains to logos and marks designed in Flash MX. We talked about resampling vector-based and bitmap images, and how to change Flash images from RGB color mode to CMYK color mode with a graphic software program.

The main printing points to remember are:

- Make sure the printer has the typeface file, or that the type in the design has been converted to outlines.
- Make sure the color mode or space has been changed from RGB to CMYK.
- Keep colors to a minimum.
- Make friends with your printer, especially before you begin a design job.

We also covered some new terms:

- **ppi** = pixels per inch. This is how a bitmap image is displayed on the screen.
- **dpi** = dots per inch. This is a measure of ink used in the printing process. Ppi and dpi can be interchangeable when moving from screen images to images for print.
- **lpi** = lines per inch. This is the measurement of dots per line in a halftone screen. 150 lpi would equal 300 dpi or ppi.

We then recapped on how vector images, which are produced in Flash, are the best images to use for printing, as the size of the image can be changed with no loss of quality

Next we talked about the *graphic user's manual*, which is used either by the designer or printer to reproduce a client's work online or in print. This manual includes, at the minimum:

- All specs on type
- Color matching systems for web and/or print
- Grids on artwork to show placement of images
- Placement, if needed, on printed images

Moving back to Flash, we looked at how to publish sites from Flash MX and how to present sites on the web in HTML:

- In an HTML file at its original size
- Scaled to the browser window
- In a browser pop-up window
- Integrated with HTML content

Finally we took a brief look at using FTP to place content online.

The end of the beginning

Once we had finalized our site publications, we gathered at the table to wrap up our course of instruction. As we settled in, we heard a soft knock at the classroom door. Lisa jumped up from the table and asked, "I hope you don't mind terribly that I had a special person come by to meet you."

Everyone looked up at Lisa. "I don't mind at all, Lisa," I answered.

Wes laughed, "I'm sure all of you will be interested. It's the person who worked the theater lights the day Lisa presented her additive lighting performance."

"Ah-ha!" Zed wiggled his eyebrows. "We'll meet the mystery person!"

Lisa stated, "Don't get excited. It's not that big a deal." She went to answer the door.

Wes winked at Zed. "*You* might get excited, but that's another story."

Lisa spoke a few words with the person outside the door and glanced back in at the class. She looked back out and said, "Come on in, we need to get on with the class."

Lisa held her hand out, and led a teenage girl into the room. "I want you to meet my daughter, Cora."

Cora was taller than her mother, with long hair and a contagious smile. “Great to meet you, Cora,” I said. I held out my hand and shook hers. “Your mother sure has come a long way with this class. I'm glad you're joining us today.”

“Mom's really enjoyed this class,” Cora replied. “She's got stuff all over the place at home now. She's even dragged me into some of her design work.” Cora laughed, “I hate physics, but I love art history.”

Wes grinned, “Cora's a big fan of anime, Zed.”

Zed looked at Cora with interest. “We'll have to talk about that, Cora, do you like doughnuts?”

Cora nodded and grinned, “I like your scarf, Zed. Uncle Wes told me the story about how you looked for one after you got attached to the one you borrowed from the theater.”

Zed was in the middle of flipping his scarf back over his shoulder, but froze at that last sentence. “*UNCLE* Wes?”

All of us stopped in our tracks and looked back and forth between Wes and Lisa. They grinned, and Deb smiled, “Lisa and Wes are brother and sister.”

Bonnie leaned back in her chair. “No!”

“Yes!” Cora laughed. “I was the one who worked the theater lights they day you all visited. Mom and I worked for a week on how we could best show all of you how additive lighting works. Uncle Wes knew it was me, and he had a hard time keeping it secret.”

“So it was you!” Steve laughed. “I've wondered for weeks who Lisa had stashed in her life. You guys sure do keep a good secret.” He looked at Lisa. All this time working with you, and you never said a word.”

“I had my reasons,” Lisa said. “I wanted to gain more confidence and skill with my designs, and I told Wes I didn't want him all over me or have anyone comparing the two of us during the course.”

Everyone was mesmerized with Lisa and Wes, looking back and forth between the two of them. “I keep trying to find similarities between you two, now that I know you're related,” Bonnie said. She shook her head. “I knew you two had some sort of connection, but I couldn't figure out what it was.”

“Well, this is interesting,” I stated, “Since we're about to talk about your goals from the beginning of this course. I wanted to remind you all what your goals were at that time, so you could see how close or how far you've gone in those directions.” I looked at Lisa. “I get the connection with your goal and your desire to keep Wes' relationship with you under wraps.”

Lisa nodded, “It's tough having such a talented, outgoing sibling.”

Wes nodded, “Yeah! It's tough having such a talented, shy sibling!”

“I looked at your original goals last night,” I said, “And thought it might be good to let you know how far you've come in such a short time.”

“That would be cool!” Zed rubbed his hands together. “I don't even remember what my goals were.”

“That doesn't surprise me somehow,” Bonnie said with a grin.

I gathered a piece of paper from my binder, and went to the board to write the students' goals from the first class. I began to remind them the basics of their core instruction.

"During this course, you learned about the creative problem solving process. You also learned about the elements and principles of design, and how to apply them to designs within Flash MX.

"You learned how to operate Flash MX, and how to work with a client and a printer." I turned to the class. "Some of you learned how to draw, and others learned to have more confidence in their skills."

* Bonnie - Reach a variety of people with visual information
* Deb - A better job or advance in current job
* Lisa - Learn new ways to communicate
* Steve - Feel confident with Flash MX software
* Wes - New vehicle to express creativity
* Zed - Understand the concepts of good design

I pointed at the board. "These were your goals at the beginning of the course. I would like each of you to tell us if you managed to meet this goals, or if you've fallen far short of them."

Zed

I looked at Zed. "Why don't you go first?" Everyone looked at Zed , and he scratched his chin thoughtfully. He folded his hands on the table, and began to speak. "I feel like a totally different person than I did at the beginning of the course," Zed stated. "I think my changes came with hanging out with a bunch of creative people. You all showed me there's more to life than chat rooms and cheesy special effects on websites."

He stood to shake hands with Wes, and continued on around the room to shake everyone's hand. As he did, he told that person what they taught him in the class. "Wes, you taught me that it's cool to be creative, even if you're old and frustrated." Wes choked, and everyone laughed.

"Bonnie, you taught me that life is basically structured, and it's up to the designer to maintain *some* sort of structure so we can be understood. I really enjoyed working with you on this project, because you kept me in line. Thanks!"

Steve stood to shake hands with Zed. "Steve, you taught me there's more to life than a monitor. If it weren't for you, the only print I would still be reading is anime cartoons. Thanks for all the books you mentioned, and for the tutoring in basic physics. I'll put that to use, for sure!"

Steve patted Zed on the back and sat down. Zed made his way to Lisa. "Lisa, thanks for teaching me about color and light. You're way cooler than your brother, and you've got a beautiful daughter."

Lisa laughed and pushed him away from Cora. "Move on, now, Zed."

Zed grinned and went to Deb. "Deb, thanks for teaching me that it's OK to change. Thanks, too, for all your information on the ancient Greeks. I never realized how cool those dudes were. They did all the grunt work, and all we need to do is learn it so we can go even further."

Zed sat back down. "I'll thank you in a little bit, Linda. I want to hear what everyone else says first."

I nodded my head and smiled. "You taught me a lot, Zed. I'm impressed with your enthusiasm and your willingness to learn without being shoved into a topic. You've been great!"

I looked at Wes. "What do you have to say about your goals?"

Bonnie

Wes tapped his fingers on the table. "I want to go last," he stated. He turned to Bonnie. "What do you have to say for yourself, lady?"

Bonnie grinned. "When I stated I wanted to reach a variety of people with visual information, I had no idea I would be learning how to do this with a tool that irritated me in the beginning. I'm totally hooked now," she admitted. "I realize that we can reach people with a variety of visual information, and Flash is one way to do this and have fun. It's also the best tool around to develop print applications with vector imaging. And," she added, "It's a great visual aid to show time and space."

Everyone applauded. "I think you've come a long way, Bonnie," Wes said. "You fought it all the way, but I'm glad you gave in to the idea that we have so many ways to express ourselves. Don't ever box yourself in again, please!"

Bonnie nodded, "I'm glad we're all going to stay in touch. I need my creative friends!"

Steve

Steve cleared his throat. "I've already managed to get a raise at work, since I've managed to prove my new skills with a real-time client. He was looking for someone to take over his Flash site, and I was just the person to handle the situation."

"Yay!" Lisa applauded. "I was hoping you'd get that promotion!"

Steve looked at Lisa and grinned, "It's a pretty good feeling for an old guy. I know more about Flash than anyone at the studio now. I definitely know more about design! So," he concluded, "I feel I really accomplished my goal." He looked at Lisa again and said, "I think you more than accomplished your goal, too."

Lisa

Lisa nodded, "I sure have. I want to thank my brother for keeping his mouth shut during the course. It was nice not being in your artistic shadow, Wes."

Wes smiled, and blew Lisa a kiss. "You're welcome, little sis." He grinned at Deb, and she groaned.

Deb

"I think I blew my goal." Deb leaned forward and crossed her arms on the table. "But I feel so much better about myself. I think I have a few opportunities coming my way, including designing a new Flash site for Lisa, since she'll be busy with a new project. She'll need a site to promote her new business of fabric designs."

Lisa looked confused, and Cora, Wes, and Deb began to laugh. Wes added, "We sold your rabbit tessellation to a fabric designer. You're about to have your rabbits crawling all over some person's piece of clothing."

Cora hugged her mother, "Are you surprised? I'm so proud of you, mom!"

"I don't know whether to yell at you guys or cry," Lisa stated. "This is way over my head!"

"Be happy," Wes stated. "We copied the design, thanks to Cora, while you were out shopping the day after the last class. We managed to sell it within two days, and we only contacted five fabric designers. After we sold it, two of the previous designers called back to buy it, too. But," Wes wiped away fake tears, "It was already gone..."

Lisa shook her head and looked at me. "See what I mean? If you knew Wes was my brother, this course would have been intolerable for me." She looked at Deb. "I guess I need to thank you, too. You managed to keep our secret well."

Deb laughed, "When I found out you two were related, it certainly made Wes look more palatable. I figured if he had a sister as sweet as you, there had to be something to him, somewhere..." She looked at Wes with curiosity. "If I could just find it..."

Wes

Wes threw his hands up in the air. "I give up. If you can't see my merits, then there's something wrong with you! After all, I did manage to reach my goal." He looked up at the board, just to remind himself what his goal was. "I did learn to use a new vehicle to express my creativity."

"Do you think you'll ever use it, Wes?" I asked. "You never seemed very fond of this whole commercial application to Flash. Will you use it for your artwork?"

Wes nodded. "Oh, sure," he stated. "But first, I'll have to buy another computer. Deb has taken over at least half my studio."

Bonnie leaned forward and asked, "OK, my curiosity is getting the better of me. Do you two have something going on?"

Deb looked shocked. "Bonnie! What a question to ask in front of everyone."

Bonnie blushed, "I'm sorry, I guess I'm wrong."

Wes stated, "You're not wrong, Bonnie. Deb has a huge crush on me, but I refuse to be submissive to her demands. I'm being very cool."

Deb laughed, "Uh-huh, right."

Goodbye?

I laughed, "Before we go any further, like out the door, I want to give you all some encouragement and resources. This course was just a taste of design. In fact," I added, "This course gave you the very basics you need to know to develop a good design."

As I talked, I went to the board to make some notes. "You all learned that designers are more than people who plan visual communications. Designers are also architects, mathematicians, artists...or at least art historians...and creators. You also need to know about writing, artwork, photographs, and printing processes, as well as how to use both sides of your brain!"

The class laughed. "These lists don't seem as daunting now," Bonnie stated. "If you'd told us this at the beginning of the course, I would have left!"

A few other students agreed. "I wanted to open doors for all of you," I replied. "Some doors needed to be opened slowly, and some needed to be opened and entered quickly, before they smacked you in the face."

"Seems you mentioned something about that at the beginning of the course," Steve smiled.

"I did," I agreed. "Now, it's up to you to reach for the stars. All of you have talents you can bring to the design process to make it a positive experience for yourselves. I looked at Zed, "You can put your new knowledge of gravity and motion to use to design animation, or to create realistic movement within Flash. Just remember to use movement as an element of design, not just because it's cool!" Zed grinned.

I turned to Bonnie, "You now know why some of your clients want the interactivity of Flash. A whole new avenue of revenue is now open to you. If you let Steve tutor you on printing, you'll just about be your own graphic agency.

"Wes, you will have fun with your artistic ideas, too. You don't have to use Flash just for commercial applications."

Wes nodded, "I'm thinking about doing a site on art history, and graphic design history as well. After all," he added, "The only limits are the ones I place on myself with this program."

I nodded, "Lisa, I'm excited about your new career in fabric design. Your research on polygons and symmetry really paid off. I hoped that some of you would research the material I've given you so you could take it further."

Lisa smiled, "If it wasn't for this course and Flash, I never would have known about polygons in the first place. I'm happy about my new skills."

I agreed, "I think Steve proved that the willingness to add to our knowledge can pay off in big ways." I looked at Steve. "Congratulations on that promotion. It was great to have a student my age!"

Steve laughed, "Being around younger folks sure helps me stay young. I'll never be too old to learn something new, and with computers, something new is always around the corner."

Deb agreed. "I changed a lot because of what I learned in this course. It seems we can't get away from the competitive side of design, but at least I know I can have a good time with what I know. Design is business, but it's also the most creative job in the world, in my opinion."

I agreed, "From here, I would like for all of you to pursue what interests you. Design covers so many fields, and these fields contain many positions to work within. You can build Flash sites, but you can also research and build on your own interests.

"Use the Internet to research topics. Read. Learn more about our history as designers. There's no limit to what you can do, if you make the time to do it.

"Oh, and I almost forgot, I have something for you all..." I said "This week's assignment! See if you can find the time to finish off Frieda's website, I'd love to see how your skills progress."

Deb grinned and looked at me. "Before you go any further, we all have something for *you*."

Zed ran out of the room, and Wes followed. Steve, Lisa, Bonnie, Deb, and Cora stood and gathered around me as I sat at the table with a look of surprise on my face.

"You guys have been wonderful," I said. "I've had a lot of fun with this class..."

Just then, Zed and Wes walked in with a huge box. They set it down by me, and they all begged me to open it. Inside was a basket and a huge espresso coffee machine. The basket held two tickets to the theater, coffee, a bottle of aspirin, and a white silk scarf. All of them had also drawn pictures of themselves for me to remember them by. "I used a grid!" Lisa said.

I laughed, "What great pictures! You all are too much! I'll never forget this class. Thank you all so much!"

Zed draped the scarf around my neck, and I claimed I felt instantly smarter. Everyone explained the gifts and thanked me for the course. They slowly gathered their belongings and left me with an empty room. As they left, I thought, "Nothing like a positive experience in a positive space."

Then, I gathered my own things and left for a week's vacation in Aruba. I deserved it.

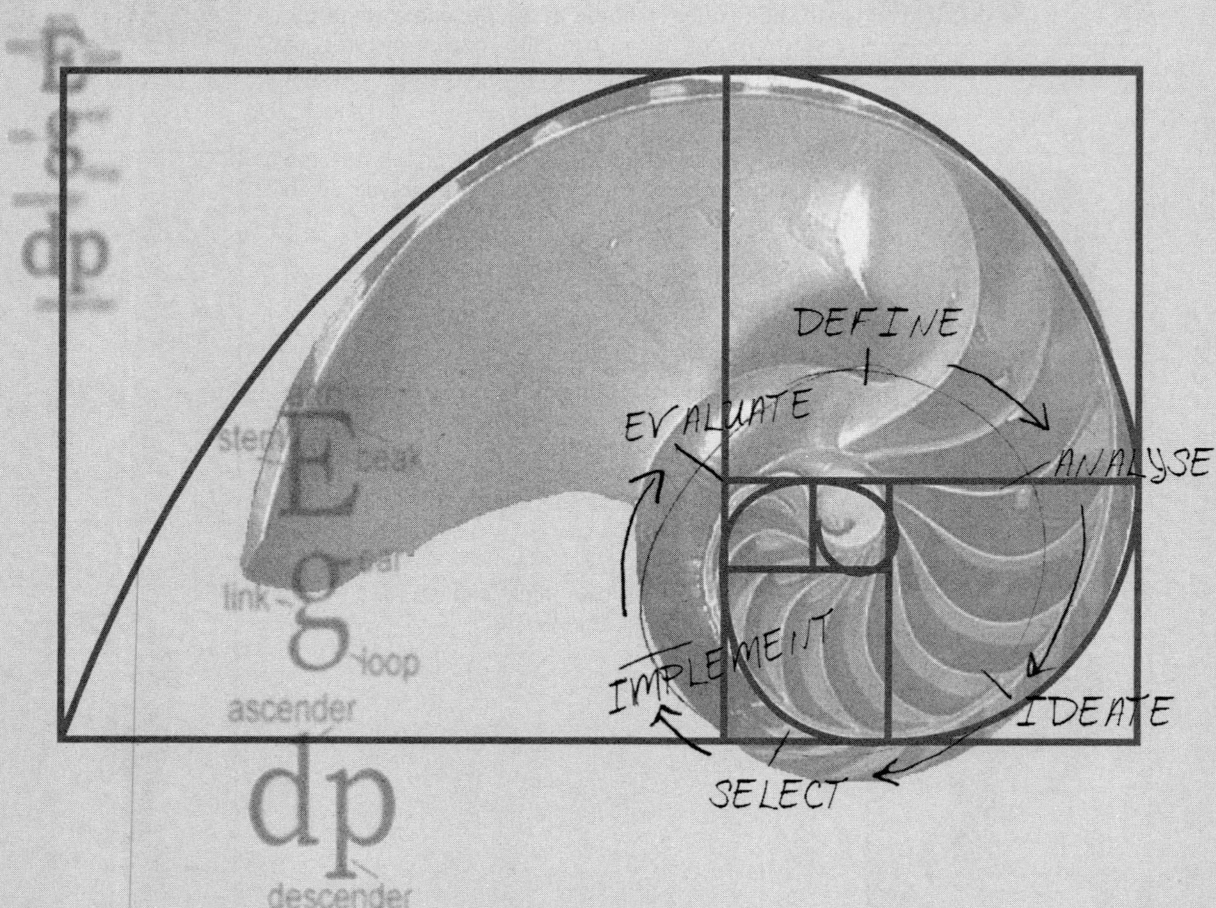
DEFINE
ANALYSE
IDEATE
SELECT
IMPLEMENT
EVALUATE
stem
beak
bar
link
loop
ascender
descender

Index

The index is arranged hierarchically, in alphabetical order. Many second-level entries also occur as first-level entries. This is to ensure that you will find the information you require however you choose to search for it.

friends of ED particularly welcomes feedback on the layout and structure of this index. If you have any comments or criticisms, please contact: feedback@friendsofED.com

A

B

C

D

R

S

T

Publication Date: April 2002

Price: $29.99

If you've never used Flash before, this is the book for you. It uses a series of structured exercises to give you the broad, solid foundation knowledge you need to start your exploration of Flash from scratch. Foundation Flash MX uses a proven sequential, detailed, and accessible tutorial style to ensure that you'll retain your learning and be able to draw on it throughout your Flash career.

Macromedia Flash MX is an exciting product, providing rich creative opportunities for Flash designers and developers at all levels of ability and experience. No single book can hope to provide adequate coverage of all aspects of Flash MX, which is why this book focuses relentlessly on the core skills that you need to get you started: understanding the interface; familiarizing yourself with the creative tools and their capabilities; grasping the relationships between the different components that make up a Flash movie; getting insight into how to put all the pieces together and hook them up with ActionScript. All these aspects (and much more) are covered in detailed tutorials and exercises, reinforced with a case study that runs throughout the book to apply everything in a real-world context.

If you're looking for a book that'll give you a rock solid grounding in Flash MX, then this is the title for you.

Publication Date: June 2002

Price: $24.99

Some Flash users like the depth, comfort and security of the linear tutorial approach. Others respond better to a more laid-back model. This book is for you if you're a denizen of the latter group; it's rich in images and examples, and restrained in its use of narrative. It gives you a fast but thorough and structured introduction that'll get you started with Flash MX quickly.

This entry-level tutorial uses a visual tutorial model to teach you the core knowledge you need to get started with Flash MX. It's rich in images and examples, and is aimed at the reader who prefers to learn by example and play rather than by following a fixed tutorial route. This book is completely modular, so you can read it in any order you like, and come back to specific modules for reference purposes later.

Publication Date: June 2002

Price: $24.99

The best, most requested effects that you've seen on the Web and elsewhere, explained by two Photoshop Experts: Al Ward and Colin Smith. In response to feedback from their popular web sites and magazine articles, Al and Colin have teamed up with friends of ED to answer your questions. They've packed in lots of useful information, not just how to create a certain effect, but other tips too, like how to improve your workflow, variations on effects, and creative suggestions to help you express yourself further.

This book is for both the enthusiastic amateur and experienced pro alike - it's full of techniques and advice that will help Photoshop users from intermediate to advanced. This book will help you to stock up your armoury; you'll have a range of weapons for all occasions and be able to deploy them faster and more effectively.

The book is divided into three main sections; the first two are Al and Colin working individually to create the most wanted effects, and in the third section, Al and Colin combine their skills in three different design projects. These projects were selected to demonstrate how designers tackle a variety of tasks when working with others; the questions and issues that may arise, and how the final product is achieved.

The focus is on tutorials and how to create effects rather than lengthy descriptions of individual tools. The majority of requests that Al and Colin receive are about producing stunning images, not explaining the tools, so that's what they've concentrated on. We've kept one thing in mind during the making of this book: what do our readers really want?

Al and Colin found they didn't have the space or time on their sites (actionfx.com and PhotoshopCafe.com) to pass on all their knowledge to visitors - people kept asking them for more, more, more... so here it is: more information, more effects, more tips... and lots more!

Photoshop has helped to create an army of devoted followers, not by being relatively easy to pick up, but by having a huge range of creative options available to you once you have learned the basics. You can then let your imagination run wild...

With Foreword by Scott Kelby:

"One of the most powerful features of Photoshop, may be the effect it has on the people who use it. People who use Photoshop are hungry for information, they're hungry to learn the latest tricks, the hot new techniques, and that common interest has an amazing way of bringing like-minded people together."

As with all Friends of ED books, we offer efficient, comprehensive email support absolutely free.

Notes

Notes

friendsof ED

DESIGNER TO DESIGNER™

friends of ED writes books for you. Any suggestions, or ideas about how you want information given in your ideal book will be studied by our team.

Your comments are valued by friends of ED.

For technical support please contact support@friendsofed.com.

Freephone in USA 800.873.9769
Fax 312.893.8001

UK contact: Tel: 0121.258.8858
Fax: 0121.258.8868

Registration Code: 40033251LU041901

Learn Design with Flash MX - Registration Card

Name ....

Address ....

City ....State/Region ....

Country ....Postcode/Zip ....

E-mail ....

Profession: design student ☐ freelance designer ☐
part of an agency ☐ inhouse designer ☐
other (please specify) ....

Age: Under 20 ☐ 20-24 ☐ 25-29 ☐ 30-40 ☐ over 40 ☐

Do you use: mac ☐ pc ☐ both ☐

How did you hear about this book?..........

Book review (name)..........

Advertisement (name) ....

Recommendation ....

Catalog ....

Other ....

Where did you buy this book? ....

Bookstore (name) ....City..........

Computer Store (name)..........

Mail Order..........

Other..........

How did you rate the overall content of this book?
Excellent ☐ Good ☐
Average ☐ Poor ☐

What applications/technologies do you intend to learn in the near future?..........

....

What did you find most useful about this book? ....

....

What did you find the least useful about this book? ....

....

Please add any additional comments ....

....

What other subjects will you buy a computer book on soon?

....

....

What is the best computer book you have used this year?

....

....

Note: This information will only be used to keep you updated about new friends of ED titles and will not be used for any other purpose or passed to any other third party.

ISBN: 1904344003

friendsof ED

DESIGNER TO DESIGNER™

NB. If you post the bounce back card below in the UK, please send it to:

friends of ED Ltd.,
30 Lincoln Road,
Olton,
Birmingham.
B27 6PA

NO POSTAGE
NECESSARY
IF MAILED
IN THE
UNITED STATES

BUSINESS REPLY MAIL

FIRST CLASS *PERMIT #64* *CHICAGO, IL*

POSTAGE WILL BE PAID BY ADDRESSEE

friends of ED,
29 S. La Salle St.
Suite 520
Chicago Il 60603-USA